IRONWORK IN MEDIEVAL
An archaeological study

by
Ian H Goodall

THE SOCIETY FOR MEDIEVAL ARCHAEOLOGY
MONOGRAPH 31

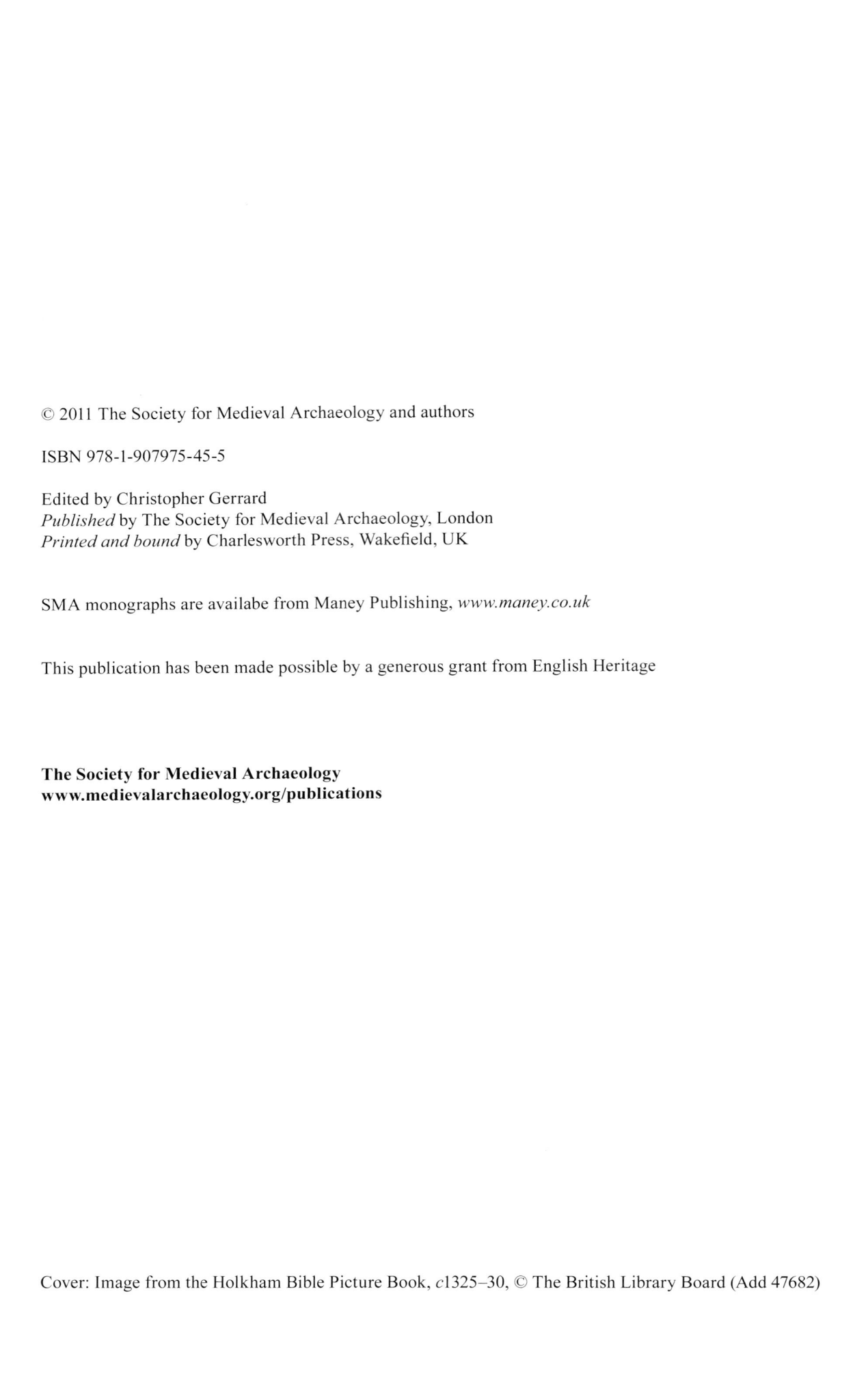

© 2011 The Society for Medieval Archaeology and authors

ISBN 978-1-907975-45-5

Edited by Christopher Gerrard
Published by The Society for Medieval Archaeology, London
Printed and bound by Charlesworth Press, Wakefield, UK

SMA monographs are availabe from Maney Publishing, *www.maney.co.uk*

This publication has been made possible by a generous grant from English Heritage

The Society for Medieval Archaeology
www.medievalarchaeology.org/publications

Cover: Image from the Holkham Bible Picture Book, *c*1325–30, © The British Library Board (Add 47682)

CONTENTS

List of figures		v
Foreword		vii
Preface		viii
Summaries		x
Acknowledgements		xi
Abbreviations		xi
I H Goodall's major published works on metalwork		xii

1 Iron smelting and smithing
1.1 Iron smelting — 1
1.2 Iron smithing — 1
1.3 Bar iron and incomplete forgings — 3

2 Metalworking tools
2.1 Anvils — 7
2.2 Tongs — 7
2.3 Pincers — 8
2.4 Hammers — 8
2.5 Flatters and set hammers — 9
2.6 Chisels and sets — 9
2.7 Punches and drifts — 10
2.8 Fullers — 10
2.9 Mandrels — 10
2.10 Nail-heading tool — 11
2.11 Files — 11
2.12 Fire tools — 11

3 Woodworking tools
3.1 Axes — 21
3.2 Adzes — 22
3.3 Slices — 22
3.4 Chisels — 23
3.5 Gouges — 23
3.6 Auger bits — 23
3.7 Saws — 25
3.8 Drawknives — 26
3.9 Shaves and spokeshaves — 26
3.10 Planes — 26
3.11 Files, rasps and floats — 26
3.12 Reamers — 26
3.13 Claw hammers — 26
3.14 Claws — 27
3.15 Punches — 27
3.16 Pincers — 27
3.17 Wedges — 27
3.18 Compasses — 27

4 Stoneworking and plastering tools
4.1 Quarrying and the working of stone — 43
4.2 Wedges — 43
4.3 Hammers and mauls — 44
4.4 Crows — 44
4.5 Picks, pickaxes and mattocks — 44
4.6 Hammer-axes — 45
4.7 Axes — 45
4.8 Punches — 45
4.9 Chisels — 45
4.10 Saws — 46
4.11 Stone augers — 46
4.12 Setting out tools — 46
4.13 Hoisting equipment — 46
4.14 Trowels — 46
4.15 Slaters' tools — 47
4.16 Millstone dressing tools — 47
4.17 Steeling and repairing tools — 47

5 Textile manufacturing tools
5.1 Fibre preparation — 59
5.2 Heckles — 59
5.3 Carding combs — 60
5.4 Weaving combs — 60
5.5 Forceps — 60
5.6 Tenter hooks — 60
5.7 Harbicks and cloth shears — 60
5.8 Needleworking tools — 61

6 Tanning and leatherworking tools
6.1 Tanning — 67
6.2 Currying — 67
6.3 Leatherworking tools — 67

7 Agricultural tools
7.1 Ploughs — 77
7.2 Spades — 77
7.3 Shovels with iron blades — 79
7.4 Forks — 79
7.5 Turf cutters — 79
7.6 Hoes — 79
7.7 Rakes and harrows — 80
7.8 Billhooks — 80
7.9 Weedhooks — 80
7.10 Reaping hooks — 81
7.11 Sickles — 81
7.12 Scythes — 82
7.13 Pitchforks — 82
7.14 Spuds — 82
7.15 Ox goads — 82
7.16 Bells — 82

8 Knives, shears and scissors
8.1 Knives — 105
8.2 Shears — 111
8.3 Scissors — 113

9 Building ironwork and furniture fittings
9.1 Structural ironwork — 161
9.2 Door, window and furniture fittings — 164

10 Locks and keys
10.1 Box and barrel padlocks — 231
10.2 Padlocks operated by revolving keys — 234
10.3 Locks — 235

10.4	Padlock keys	237
10.5	Keys	240
10.6	Miscellaneous keys	243

11 Household ironwork

11.1	The hearth	297
11.2	The kitchen	297
11.3	Lighting	299
11.4	Fire-steels	300
11.5	Buckets	301
11.6	Hooks	301
11.7	Balances	301
11.8	Chains, links and related fittings	301
11.9	Rings	302
11.10	Washers	302
11.11	Collars	302

12 Buckles and personal equipment

12.1	Buckles	339
12.2	Strap-ends	342
12.3	Belt slides	342
12.4	Belt hooks	342
12.5	Purse-frames	342
12.6	Scabbard fittings	343
12.7	Jew's harps	343

13 Horse equipment

13.1	Horseshoes	363
13.2	Oxshoes	363
13.3	Horseshoe and oxshoe nails	363
13.4	Curry-combs	364
13.5	Bridle bits	364
13.6	Bridle bosses	366
13.7	Harness fittings	366
13.8	Stirrups	366

Bibliography 383

Index 391

LIST OF FIGURES

1.1	Forge at Walthan Abbey, Essex	1
1.2	Smithies at Alsted, Surrey, and Goltho, Lincolnshire	2
1.3	Iron smelting and smithing: Bar iron and partly forged objects (A1–A17)	5
2.1	Anvils: representations in medieval manuscripts	7
2.2	Blacksmiths in a forge, Franco-Flemish, 14th-century manuscript	8
2.3	Hammers: terminology	9
2.4	Tongs and pincers (A18–27)	13
2.5	Hammers, cold chisels and hot chisels (A28–49)	15
2.6	Hot chisels, cold and hot sets, and punches (A50–75)	17
2.7	Drifts, fuller, mandrels, nail-heading tool, file, and poker (A76–93)	19
3.1	Types of medieval axe	22
3.2	Axes: terminology	23
3.3	Axes (B1–13)	29
3.4	Axes (B14–23)	31
3.5	Axes, adzes, slices, and chisels (B24–39)	33
3.6	Spoon bits (B40–65)	35
3.7	Spoon bits, gouge bits, and twist bits (B66–92)	37
3.8	Saws, drawknife, spokeshave irons, float, reamer, claw hammers (B93–119)	39
3.9	Claw hammers, claws, punch, wedges, and dividers (B120–151)	41
4.1	Wedges and pickaxes (C1–13)	49
4.2	Pickaxes and hammer-axe (C14–18)	51
4.3	Hammer-axe, axe, punches, and chisels (C19–38)	53
4.4	Saw, scriber, plumb-bob, lewis, and trowels (C39–49)	55
4.5	Hammer, picks, and mill-pick (C50–63)	57
5.1	Heckle teeth (D2–D43)	63
5.2	Weaving-combs, forceps, tenter hooks, and shearboard hooks (D44–73)	64
6.1	Slickers and leatherworking knives (E1–19)	71
6.2	Creasers, awls, needles, and stilettos (E20–47)	73
6.3	Awls and needles (E48–71)	75
6.4	Needles and stilettos (E72–83)	76
7.1	Spades: terminology	78
7.2	Coulters, ploughshares (F1–5)	85
7.3	Spade-irons (F6–12)	89
7.4	Spade-irons, shovel, and forks (F13–20)	91
7.5	Turf cutters, hoes, rake and harrow teeth, and billhook (F21–39)	93
7.6	Weedhooks and reaping hooks (F40–69)	95
7.7	Sickles (F70–82)	97
7.8	Sickles (F83–90)	99
7.9	Scythes (F91–112)	101
7.10	Scythes and pitchforks (F113–124)	103
7.11	Pitchforks, spuds, ox goads, bells, and bell clappers (F125–145)	105
8.1	Knives: terminology	107
8.2	Types of medieval whittle tang knife	108
8.3	Types of medieval scale tang knife	110
8.4	Frequency of types of medieval knife	111
8.5	Chronological range of types of medieval knife	111
8.6	Types of medieval shears	114
8.7	Knives (G1–26)	117
8.8	Knives (G27–47)	119
8.9	Knives (G48–71)	121
8.10	Knives (G72–96)	123
8.11	Knives (G97–120)	125
8.12	Knives (G121–143)	127
8.13	Knives (G144–165)	129
8.14	Knives (G166–188)	131
8.15	Knives (G189–210)	133
8.16	Knives (G211–231)	135
8.17	Knives (G232–254)	137
8.18	Knives (G255–269)	139
8.19	Knives (G270–290)	141
8.20	Knives (G291–310)	143
8.21	Knives (G311–330)	145
8.22	Knives (G331–354)	147
8.23	Knives (G355–376)	149
8.24	Knives (G377–397)	151
8.25	Shears (G398–427)	153
8.26	Shears (G428–438)	155
8.27	Shears (G439–467)	157
8.28	Shears (G468–488)	159
8.29	Shears and scissors (G489–521)	161
9.1	Types of medieval nail	166
9.2	Cramps, timber dogs, beam stirrup, hooked bracket, angle tie, and ties (H1–28)	173
9.3	Staples (H29–55)	175
9.4	Staples (H56–71)	177
9.5	Staples (H72–97)	179
9.6	Staples (H98–126)	181
9.7	Staples (H127–150)	183
9.8	Staples (H151–171)	185
9.9	Wallhooks (H172–200)	187
9.10	Wallhooks and hooks (H201–224)	189
9.11	Hooks, eyed spike and ring, looped straps, wall anchors, holdfast, S-hooks, clench bolts, and roves (H225–253)	191
9.12	Hinge pivots (H254–287)	193
9.13	Hinge pivots (H288–316)	195
9.14	Hinge pivots (H317–342)	197
9.15	Hinge pivots (H343–375)	199
9.16	Hinge pivots and hinges (H376–400)	201
9.17	Well cover (H404)	202
9.18	Hinges (H401–403, H405–412)	203
9.19	Hinges (H413–419)	205
9.20	Hinges (H420–437)	207
9.21	Hinges (H438–471)	209
9.22	Hinges (H472–501)	211
9.23	Hinges, straps, corner binding, strip, and binding strip (H502–528)	213
9.24	Strip and binding strips (H529–549)	215
9.25	Binding strips and stapled hasps (H550–577)	217
9.26	Stapled hasps (H578–582)	219
9.27	Stapled hasps and hasps (H583–606)	221
9.28	Hasps (H607–620)	223
9.29	Hasps, keyhole plates, and handles (H621–646)	225
9.30	Handles (H647–662)	227
9.31	Latch rests, door flail, door bolts, U-shaped bracket, and hooks (H663–685)	229
9.32	Window grille (H686)	231
9.33	Window bars (H687–705)	231
9.34	Window bar (H706)	235
10.1	Types of medieval barrel padlock	238
10.2	Diagram showing operation of lock I146	242
10.3	Types of medieval padlock key	243
10.4	Types of medieval key	244
10.5	Chronological range of types of medieval key	247
10.6	Box padlocks, barrel padlocks, and pivoting fins (I1–19)	251
10.7	Barrel padlocks and padlock bolts (I20–46)	253
10.8	Padlock bolts and barrel padlocks (I47–68)	254
10.9	Barrel, padlocks and padlock bolts (I69–80)	257
10.10	Barrel padlocks (I82–89)	259
10.11	Barrel padlocks and padlock bolts (I90–110)	261
10.12	Padlock bolts, barrel padlocks, box padlocks, padlock shackles, embossed padlocks, and stapled padlock hasps (I111–137)	263
10.13	Embossed padlocks, stapled padlock hasps, locks, key tip mount, lock bolts, and tumbler (I138–153)	265
10.14	Lock bolts, tumblers, wards, and padlock keys (I154–185)	267
10.15	Padlock keys (I186–211)	269
10.16	Padlock keys (I212–220)	271
10.17	Padlock keys (I221–248)	273

10.18 Padlock keys (I249–269)	275
10.19 Padlock keys and keys (I270–303)	277
10.20 Keys (I304–329)	279
10.21 Keys (I330–340)	281
10.22 Keys (I341–372)	283
10.23 Keys (I373–389)	285
10.24 Keys (I390–421)	287
10.25 Keys (I422–445)	289
10.26 Keys (I446–475)	291
10.27 Keys (I476–486)	293
10.28 Keys (I487–516)	295
10.29 Keys (I517–523)	297
10.30 Keys (I524–552)	299
10.31 Keys (I553–585)	301
11.1 Fire-fork, poker, hook, skillet or colander handle, and trivets (J2–10)	311
11.2 Trivets and griddle plate (J11–14)	313
11.3 Flesh-hooks (J15–32)	315
11.4 Ladles, spoon, and cleavers (J33–42)	317
11.5 Cleavers and fish hooks (J43–71)	319
11.6 Candlesticks (J72–95)	321
11.7 Candlesticks (J96–120)	323
11.8 Candlesticks and fire-steels (J121–134)	325
11.9 Buckets (J135–137)	327
11.10 Bucket, bucket hoops and handle loops (J139–147)	331
11.11 Handle straps and handles (J148–161)	333
11.12 Hooks (J163–173)	335
11.13 Hooks and balances (J175–184)	337
11.14 Chains, rings, and links (J185–221)	339
11.15 Chains, links, and chain fittings (J222–247)	341
11.16 Chain fittings and hooks (J248–276)	343
11.17 Rings, washers, and collars (J277–311)	345
12.1 Main types of buckle	348
12.2 Frequency of types of medieval buckle	349
12.3 Buckles (K1–56)	353
12.4 Buckles (K35–56)	355
12.5 Buckles (K57–97)	357
12.6 Buckles (K98–138)	359
12.7 Buckles (K139–175)	361
12.8 Buckles (K176–208)	363
12.9 Buckles (K209–260)	365
12.10 Buckles, pins and plates (K261–282)	367
12.11 Strap-ends, belt slides, belt hooks, purse frames, scabbard mount, scabbard chape, and jew's harps (K283–304)	369
13.1 Types of medieval horseshoe nail	371
13.2 Types of medieval bridle bit cheek-piece	373
13.3 Horseshoes (L1–15)	377
13.4 Horseshoes (L16–32)	379
13.5 Curry-combs (L33–46)	381
13.6 Bridle bits (L47–56)	383
13.7 Bridle bits (L57–79)	385
13.8 Bridle bosses and harness fittings (L80–111)	387
13.9 Bridle bosses, harness fittings, and stirrups (L112–124)	389

FOREWORD

This monograph is the publication of the late Ian Goodall's doctoral thesis on medieval ironwork in Britain which was submitted to the Department of Archaeology, University College, Cardiff, in 1980. Thirty years on, it remains the definitive survey of iron tools and other fittings in use during the period *c*1066 to 1540 AD. Exceptional in a north-western European context for its range and coverage of artefacts from both rural and urban excavations, much of the material described here was recovered during 'rescue' projects in the 1960s and 1970s funded by the State through the Ministry of Public Works and Buildings and their successors. It immediately established Ian as one of Britain's leading authorities on all things ferrous and later medieval.

Only a month before Ian's unexpected death in 2006, I met with him to discuss a report he had been preparing on the metalwork finds from Clarendon Palace in Wiltshire. As he worked his way through fragments of medieval arrowheads and knives, modern bicycle bells and lawn-mower blades, I asked why he had never published his thesis. Ian explained to me then that, after leaving Cardiff, his career with Royal Commission on the Historical Monuments of England and latterly English Heritage had been as an architectural historian rather than any strictly academic or archaeological enterprise and, although he had continued to compile reports on assemblages all the while, he had just never had the time to sit down and update his original work. By the time we had time to think more seriously about how his thesis might be brought to a wider audience, Ian had gone.

Certainly there is neither academic nor professional reason why his thesis should not now be published, indeed it is a work ideally suited to wider dissemination because it is relevant, useful, and difficult to access. The text contains almost everything necessary to identify, date and understand medieval iron objects. In scope and detail there is still no published parallel and, as such, it will be essential for almost any archaeologist working in later medieval archaeology, particularly in the fields of excavation, finds study, museums and research.

That said, a thesis serves a very different purpose to a published text and, although this monograph is faithful to the original as far as is possible, some changes have been necessary. In the first place the whole typescript was re-typed, and I am grateful for a small grant from the Society for Medieval Archaeology who paid for this task. Thereafter, English Heritage sponsored the editing, re-setting and final publication and, without their intervention, this project could not have been completed. The task of preparing the monograph for publication has been undertaken by Alejandra Gutiérrez. The main challenge has been to update as many of the bibliographical references as possible because, of course, most references in the original thesis refer to then unpublished reports which have since appeared as articles and monographs. The dating of the Winchester finds has also been updated here in those few cases where the published reports (Goodall 1990) offer a different date to that thought correct at the time of writing the thesis in 1980. A list of Ian Goodall's major publications on metalwork is also provided arranged by date. This new bibliography should be of tremendous value to all those researching medieval metalwork and in search of further bibliography and parallels.

Finally, there have also been changes to the format. Ian's original thesis comprised three volumes: text, catalogue and figures, which were arranged into chapters according to object type, covering all types of iron artefacts and tools except weapons, armour, arrowheads and spurs. For this publication, the three original volumes have been re-combined by theme, rather than keeping the catalogue as an appendix at the end of the text. This will allow the reader to check illustrated examples and read descriptions more comfortably within each chapter and theme rather than constantly shuffling pages. Some re-drawing of the finds has also been undertaken where the quality of the originals has faded. I would like to thank Norfolk Museums and Archaeology Service for their permission to use the drawing for D1 (Figure 5.1). I am grateful too to John Clark, formerly of the Museum of London, for adding the preface.

Christopher Gerrard
October 2010

PREFACE

Ian Goodall and the study of medieval ironwork

The name of Ian Goodall is surely known to anyone who has consulted archaeological reports on medieval sites in Britain published in the last 30 years or so. It will be even more familiar – even if they never met him or benefited from his advice – to those who have themselves faced the task of contributing the small finds section to such a report. For it is impracticable, or at least unwise, to write a report on excavated medieval iron artefacts without referring to at least one and probably several of the many such reports Ian himself wrote between 1970 and his early and unexpected death in 2006. I see, for example, that I and the other contributors to a volume on medieval horse equipment from London, published in 1995, listed in our joint bibliography some seventeen of his articles; the introduction to the second edition added another. Moreover, it may be revealed, Ian was the referee asked by English Heritage to assess the merits of that publication at typescript stage. His extensive and detailed comments were of immense value to the authors.

Most of Ian's published contributions to the subject were simply titled 'Iron objects', or a variation of that misleadingly simple designation; many ran to less than a dozen pages. But their small scale belies the wealth of knowledge and experience that lay behind the author's ability to identify and to diagnose the significance of sometimes heavily corroded and not immediately recognizable 'iron objects', and to set them in their historical context.

Ian Goodall was born in York in 1948, and in 1966 went to University College Cardiff to study archaeology. After graduation, he went on to begin the research that was to culminate in the award of a PhD for his thesis *Ironwork in Medieval Britain: an Archaeological Study*. However, Ian was still engaged on this work when in 1972 he returned to York to take up a post with the then Royal Commission on the Historical Monuments of England (later to be amalgamated with English Heritage). While contributing to major and productive research and publication projects on the buildings of York and of North Yorkshire for the Commission, he made time not only to travel extensively to study groups of medieval ironwork from excavations and in museum collections, but to begin the writing of the series of specialist reports on iron finds for which he remains so well known – the first to be published (I think) comprising the material from excavations carried out between 1970 and 1972 at Waltham Abbey, Essex.

I first met Ian when he came to London to look at ironwork in the medieval collections of the Guildhall Museum, later the Museum of London. We were agreed in our admiration of the work of John Ward Perkins, who had pioneered a new approach to the study of medieval artefacts in the *London Museum Medieval Catalogue*, published in 1940. We commiserated over the fact that the typologies and chronologies that Ward Perkins had proposed, useful though they were, were based upon so little in the way of well-dated material. Medieval ironwork in museum collections, although sometimes of high quality and individual interest, then comprised largely stray finds from building sites or from rivers, lacking any trustworthy external evidence for date or for context of use.

Major campaigns of excavation on large and productive medieval urban sites, such as those in Winchester, York and London, were to change that picture. But in the meantime there were many excavations of smaller sites, both urban and rural, which, although they individually might produce little medieval ironwork, could provide the dating and context information lacking in the old museum collections. Ian Goodall set himself the task of bringing that information together, of identifying and recording the similarities between find 1 from site A and find 2 from site B, and their relationship to find 3 from site C. Although his work on the iron artefacts from Martin Biddle's excavations in Winchester was a major contribution to the publication *Artefacts from Medieval Winchester: Object and Economy in Medieval Winchester* that appeared in 1990, the extraordinary range of artefacts from smaller sites was essential to the corpus of material that Ian assembled for his thesis. Although in many cases, alongside work on his thesis, he contributed a specialist report for the site publication, in other cases he incorporated in his thesis material from sites that remained unpublished, or published in not readily accessible form: the finds from Weoley Castle, Birmingham, perhaps, or the extraordinary 'hoard' of 13th-century sickles in Scarborough Museum from Ayton Castle, North Yorkshire.

By the time Ian submitted his thesis in September 1980 he had already built up an intensive knowledge of medieval iron finds from sites throughout Britain and an unparalleled expertise in their identification. In the Foreword to the thesis, Ian noted that 'Books, periodicals and unpublished objects have been examined to a terminal date of early 1980'. Some of the unpublished material was indeed to reach publication (in his Foreword Ian mentioned the Winchester material, publication then forthcoming), while he went on to study and publish other groups of iron finds himself, as his reputation spread and excavators recognized his expertise.

But his many individual publications, constrained as they were by the limits of a single site report and the specific requirements of 'relevance', allowed little scope for a discursive approach; finds must be interpreted in the context of the site, not in the wider context of similar objects from elsewhere. Larger publications of finds from multiple sites, such as the two volumes of the Winchester finds report, allowed more space for discussion – the presence of a large number of a particular type of artefact would warrant an introductory discussion, even the proposal of a typological and chronological classification, not feasible in the case of reports on individual sites where there might be only one or two examples. And there was always the need for reference to comparanda; sometimes a most valuable aspect of one of Ian's smaller reports is an extensive list of comparable material (with reference often to others of his own publications). Ian also contributed a short but valuable chapter on 'The medieval blacksmith and his products' to the CBA Research Report *Medieval Industry* in 1981, including within its brief compass illustrations of an extraordinary range of medieval iron objects, from blacksmith's tongs to currycombs – his own drawings, originally produced for his thesis.

It was always Ian's hope – a hope shared by anyone who was privileged to see and make use of a copy of his thesis – that it would one day be published. Sadly, this was not to be in his lifetime. Yet here it is at last.

Ian's original Foreword set out the scope of his work, limiting 'the medieval period' to c1066 to 1540, and excluding weaponry and spurs from his coverage. The contents list defines the overall approach: objects are dealt with under clear functional headings such as 'woodworking tools'. Introductory paragraphs set the particular tool, household object or fitting in its historical context. Ian often defines, with drawings, the terminology he uses for parts of an object – useful for any report writer wishing to describe an unfamiliar artefact, and uncertain perhaps of the difference between the 'butt' and the 'poll' of an axe. For many objects he establishes a typological classification based upon form, to which he then applies a chronology drawn from stratified examples. This was of course the time-honoured approach that had been adopted by John Ward Perkins in the *London Museum Medieval Catalogue*, though Ward Perkins lacked the strong foundation of stratified examples that Ian was able to call on to support his conclusions about dating. And indeed in some cases – keys, for example, and shears – one can make a direct comparison between the typologies established by the two authors; Ian sometimes provides a useful list of correlations between the two. No doubt if he himself were preparing this volume for the press he would have refined his typologies on the basis of more recent finds, perhaps refined his dating – but others may now do that.

Terminologies and typologies make this volume a resource for any finds specialist needing to describe iron artefacts; there is, in spite of the existence of some thesauri, still a great lack of agreed standards. But it is the catalogue and illustrations that define this work as essentially a corpus: a brief catalogue entry for each item, including a date or date range derived from its archaeological context, and in nearly every case an outline drawing. An archaeological corpus of this type is an old idea, but time and time again such bodies of material prove their usefulness. The search for parallels for a particular object, whether it is a site find or in a museum collection, can be a tedious one, often dependent upon happenstance even if the researcher has access to a library containing all the county and local journals and monographs in which so many relevant finds reports have appeared – note the extent and range of the Bibliography of the present work. With this volume as a tool, the finds specialist will find comparative examples to hand – even that 'unidentified object' may suddenly yield its identity as a result of a search through the pages of Ian's drawings.

Much has changed in medieval archaeology since Ian submitted his thesis in September 1980. Major finds have been made and published; research into such relevant subjects as metallurgy has advanced. Yet there is nothing else that brings together such a wealth of everyday ironwork from such a range of medieval sites, from towns, villages, castles, manors and farmsteads.

It is a tool ready to be used.

John Clark
Curator Emeritus, Museum of London
April 2010

SUMMARY

This monograph is a survey of iron tools and other fittings in use during the medieval period, defined here as *c*1066 to 1540 AD. It is designed to help identify, date and understand medieval iron objects from archaeological excavation. The major categories of finds covered are tools from metalworking, woodworking, stoneworking, plastering, textile manufacture, tanning and leatherworking and agriculture. There are also sections on knives, shears and scissors, building ironwork, locks and keys, household ironwork, buckles and dress accessories and horse equipment. Weapons, armour, arrowheads and spurs are excluded. Both text and drawings derive from a doctoral thesis completed in 1980.

RÉSUMÉ

Le présent livre est une étude d'objets et ustensiles en fer en usage durant la période du haut Moyen Age (*c*1066 to 1540 apr JC). Il a pour objectif d'aider l'indentification, la dation et la compréhension des objets en fer trouvés lors de fouilles archéologiques. Les principales catégories d'objets couvert sont les outils utilisés pour travailler le métal, le bois, la pierre, le travail du plâtre, la production de textile, le tannage et le travail du cuir en général ainsi que des outils utilisés pour les travaux agricoles. Il y a aussi des parties dédiées aux couteaux, cisailles et ciseaux, des objets utilisés dans le domaine du bâtiment, des serrures ainsi que des clefs, des ustensiles de cuisine, des boucles et autre accessoires vestimentaires ainsi que du matériel équestre. Les armes ainsi que les armures, les pointes de flèche et les éperons sont en revanche exclus de cette étude. Le texte comme les dessins et autres croquis proviennent tout deux d'une thèse de doctorat terminée en 1980.

RESUMEN

El presente libro es un estudio de los objetos y utensilios de hierro en uso durante la Edad Media (*c*1066 to 1540 dC). Tiene como fin el ayudar a identificar, fechar y comprender los objetos férreos procedentes de excavaciones arqueológicas. Las principales categorías de objetos que se consideran son las herramientas para trabajar el metal, la madera, la piedra, para enyesar, tejer, teñir, trabajar el cuero y aquéllas utilizadas en las tareas agrícolas. Hay además apartados sobre cuchillos, tijeras, cerraduras y llaves, objetos empleados en la construcción de edificios, aquéllos utilizados en la casa, hebillas, adornos para el vestido y elementos para el aderezo de la caballería. Se han excluído armas, puntas de fechas y estribos. Tanto el texto como los dibujos derivan de una tesis doctoral concluída en 1980.

ORIGINAL ACKNOWLEDGEMENTS (1980)

The work on which the thesis was based was undertaken with the aid of a Major State Studentship between 1969 and 1972, and continued during the author's appointment to the Royal Commission on Historical Monuments (England). Unpublished objects have been examined to a terminal date of early 1980.

Many people gave assistance during the preparation of the original thesis, and I should particularly like to thank Dr G C Dunning and J G Hurst for allowing me to examine their collections of books and offprints. J W G Musty, L Biek and the staff of the Ancient Monuments Laboratory, as well as the staff of the Drawing Office of the Inspectorate of Ancient Monuments, have been of considerable help. Many excavators kindly gave access to their unpublished material, which has been incorporated here and is appropriately acknowledged in the catalogue. The finds from medieval Winchester undoubtedly include the most significant unpublished objects. Museum collections have in general only been examined for objects from stratified contexts, and I should particularly like to thank B W Spencer and J Clark (formerly Museum of London), J M Lewis (National Museum of Wales, Cardiff), D A Hinton (formerly Ashmolean Museum, Oxford) and Mrs R Taylor (Birmingham City Museum and Art Gallery) for their help.

The compilation of the original thesis on which this monograph is based was greatly assisted by the patient supervision and helpful advice of Dr W H Manning. Mrs E M Goodall typed the text and the reductions of the line drawings are by A D Perry. My wife, Alison, deserves my final and greatest thanks, however, for without her considerable assistance in reading the text and preparing the illustrations, the original thesis could never have been completed in time.

ABBREVIATIONS

The following abbreviations have been used in the catalogues:

L: length
W: width
H: height
D: diameter
DAMHB: Department of Ancient Monuments and Historic Buildings
Sf: small find.

I H GOODALL'S MAJOR PUBLISHED WORKS ON METALWORK

Goodall, I H, 1970 'Metal', in M G Jarrett, 'The deserted village of West Whelpington, Northumberland: second report', *Archaeologia Aeliana* 4th series 48, 280–292 (183–302)

Goodall, I H, 1971 'Iron objects', in C F Tebbutt, G T Rudd, and S Moorhouse, 'Excavation of a moated site at Ellington, Huntingdonshire', *Proceedings of the Cambridge Antiquarian Society* 63, 67–68 (31–73)

Moorhouse, S and Goodall, I H, 1971 'Iron', in S Moorhouse, 'Finds from Basing House, Hampshire (c.1540–1645): Part two', *Post-Medieval Archaeology* 5, 36–57

Goodall, I H, 1972 'Iron', in S Moorhouse, 'Finds from excavations in the refectory at the Dominican Friary, Boston', *Lincolnshire History and Archaeology* 1, 21–53 (21–53)

Goodall, I H, 1972 'Industrial evidence from the villa at Langton, East Yorkshire', *Yorkshire Archaeological Journal* 44, 32–37

Goodall, I H, 1973 'Iron objects', in P J Huggins and R M Huggins, 'Excavation of monastic forge and Saxo-Norman enclosure, Waltham Abbey, Essex, 1972–73', *Essex Archaeology and History* 5, 168–175 (127–184)

Goodall, I H, 1973 'Metalwork', in H E J Le Patourel, *The moated sites of Yorkshire*, The Society for Medieval Archaeology Monograph 5, 91–95

Goodall, I H, 1974 'Appendix VI: Metalwork', in G Beresford, 'The medieval manor of Penhallam, Jacobstow, Cornwall', *Medieval Archaeology* 18, 139–140 (90–145)

Goodall, I H, 1974 'Barrel padlock', in S Moorhouse, 'A late medieval domestic rubbish deposit from Broughton, Lincolnshire', *Lincolnshire History and Archaeology* 9, 40–41 (21–53)

Goodall, I H, 1974 'Iron objects', in E Russell, 'Excavations on the site of the deserted medieval village of Kettleby Thorpe, Lincolnshire', *Journal of the Scunthorpe Museum Society* Series 3 (Archaeology) 2, 30–36

Goodall, I H, 1974 'Iron objects', in E C Klingelhöfer, *Broadfield deserted medieval village*, British Archaeological Report 2, Oxford, 56–58

Harvey, Y, with I H Goodall and L Biek, 1975 'Catalogue', in C Platt and R Coleman-Smith (eds), *Excavations in medieval Southampton 1953–1969, Volume 2: the finds*, Leicester University Press, 254–293

Goodall, I H, 1975 'Metalwork from Goltho', in G Beresford, *The medieval clay land village: excavations at Goltho and Barton Blount*, The Society for Medieval Archaeology Monograph 6, 79–96

Goodall, I H, 1975 'Metalwork from Barton Blount', in G Beresford, *The medieval clay land village: excavations at Goltho and Barton Blount*, The Society for Medieval Archaeology Monograph 6, 96–98

Goodall, I H, 1975 'Metalwork', in P L Drewett, 'Excavations at Hadleigh Castle, Essex, 1971–1972', *Journal of the British Archaeological Association* 3rd series 38, 138–146 (89–154)

Goodall, I H, and Tylecote, R F, 1975 'Chingley Forge metalwork', in D Crossley, *The Bewl Valley ironworks, Kent, c1300–1730*, Royal Archaeological Institute Monograph, 59–84

Goodall, I H, 1976 'Iron objects', in L Ketteringham, *Alsted: excavations of a thirteenth–fourteenth century sub-manor house with its ironworks in Netherne Wood, Merstham, Surrey*, Research Volume of Surrey Archaeological Society 2, 55–60

Goodall, I H, 1976 'Copper alloy objects', in L Ketteringham, *Alsted: excavations of a thirteenth–fourteenth century sub-manor house with its ironworks in Netherne Wood, Merstham, Surrey*, Research Volume of Surrey Archaeological Society 2, 61

Goodall, I H, 1976 'Metalwork', in T G Hassall, 'Excavations at Oxford Castle, 1965–73', *Oxoniensia* 41, 298–303 (232–308)

Goodall, I H, 1976 'The metalwork', in O Bedwin, 'The excavation of Ardingly fulling mill and forge, 1975–76', *Post-Medieval Archaeology* 10, 60–64

Goodall, I H, 1976 'Iron', in J Woodhouse, *Barrow Mead, Bath, 1964 excavation*, British Archaeological Report 28, Oxford, 33–35

Goodall, I H, 1977 'Iron objects', in P Everson, 'Excavations in the Vicarage Garden at Brixworth, 1972', *Journal of the British Archaeological Association* 130, 94 (55–122)

Goodall, I H, 1977 'Iron objects', in F Williams, *Pleshey Castle, Essex (XII–XIV century): excavations in the bailey, 1959–1963*, British Archaeological Reports 42, 174–183

Goodall, I H, 1977 'Metalwork', in G Beresford, 'Excavation of a moated house at Wintringham in Huntingdonshire', *Archaeological Journal* 134, 257–279 (194–286)

Goodall, I H, 1977 'The metalwork', in P Charlton, J Roberts, and V Vale, *Llantrithyd. A ringwork in South Glamorgan*, Cardiff, 46–51

Goodall, I H, 1977 'Iron objects', in B Durham, 'Archaeological investigations in St Aldates, Oxford', *Oxoniensia* 42, 142–148 (82–203)

Goodall, I H, 1977 'Iron', in P Armstrong, *Excavations in Sewer Lane, Hull 1974*, East Riding Archaeologist 3, Hull Old Town Report Series 1, 63–67

Goodall, I H, 1977 'Medieval iron objects', in R Hanworth and D J Tomalin, *Brooklands, Weybridge: the excavation of an Iron Age and medieval site 1964–5 and 1970–71*, Surrey Archaeological Society Research Volume 4, 73–75

Goodall, I H, and Carter, A, 1977 'Iron objects', in H Clarke and A Carter, *Excavations in King's Lynn 1963–70*, Society for Medieval Archaeology Monograph 7, 291–298

Goodall, I H, 1978 'The iron objects' and 'Medieval iron objects', in J Collis, *Winchester Excavations. Volume II. 1949-1960. Excavations in the suburbs and the western part of the town*, Winchester, 28 and 139

Goodall, I H, 1978 'Iron objects', in G Coppack, 'An excavation at Chapel Garth, Bolton, Fangfoss, Humberside', *Yorkshire Archaeological Journal* 50, 140–145 (93–150)

Goodall, I H, 1978 'The iron-work', in J H Williams, 'Excavations at Greyfriars, Northampton 1972', *Northamptonshire Archaeology* 13, 152 (96–160)

Goodall, I H, 1978 'Iron objects', in A E S Musty, 'Exploratory excavation within the monastic precinct, Waltham Abbey, 1972', *Essex Archaeology and History* 10, 157–160 (127–173)

Goodall, I H, 1979 'Iron objects', in D D Andrews and G Milne, *Wharram. A Study of Settlement on the Yorkshire Wolds 1, Domestic Settlement, Areas 10 and 6*, The Society for Medieval Archaeology Monograph 8, 115–123

Goodall, I H, 1979 'Iron objects', in G H Smith, 'The excavation of the hospital of St Mary of Ospringe, commonly called Maison Dieu', *Archaeologia Cantiana* 95, 129–137 (81–184)

Goodall, I H, 1979 'Iron objects', in P A Rahtz, *The Saxon and Medieval Palaces at Cheddar*, British Archaeological Reports British Series 65, 263–274

Goodall, I H, 1979 'The iron objects', in F Williams, 'Excavations on Marefair, Northampton, 1977', *Northamptonshire Archaeology* 14, 70–71 (38–79)

Goodall, I H, Ellis, B and Oakley, G E, 1979 'The iron objects', in J H Williams, *St Peter's Street, Northampton, Excavations 1973–6*, Northampton, 268–277

Addyman, P V, Goodall, I H, Carver, M O H, Gee, E A, Geddes, J, Morgan, R, 1979 'The Norman church and door at Stillingfleet, North Yorkshire', *Archaeologia* 106, 75–105

Goodall, I H, 1980 'Objects of iron', in P Wade-Martins (ed), *Fieldwork and excavations on village sites in Launditch Hundred, Norfolk*, East Anglian Archaeology Monograph 10, 129–141

Goodall, I H, 1980 'Iron objects', in A D Saunders, 'Lydford Castle, Devon', *Medieval Archaeology* 24, 165–167 (123–186)

Goodall, I H, 1980 'Iron objects', in C Halpin, 'Late Saxon evidence and excavation of Hinxey Hall, Queen Street, Oxford', *Oxoniensia* 48, 64–65 (41–69)

Goodall, I H, 1980 'Iron objects', in N Palmer, 'A beaker burial and medieval tenements in The Hamel, Oxford', *Oxoniensia* 45, 189–191 (124–225)

Goodall, I H, 1980 'Objects of copper alloy', in P Wade-Martins, 'North Elmham Park', *East Anglian Archaeology* 9, 499–505

Goodall, I H, 1980 'The iron objects', in P Wade-Martins, 'North Elmham Park', *East Anglian Archaeology* 9, 509–516

Goodall, I H, 1980 *Ironwork in Medieval Britain: an archaeological study*, unpublished PhD thesis, Department of Archaeology, University College, Cardiff

Goodall, I H, Rigold, S E and Christie, P M, 1980 'Metalwork and bone objects', in P M Christie and J G Coad, 'Excavations at Denny Abbey', *Archaeological Journal* 138, 253–263 (138–279)

Goodall, I H, 1981 'Ironwork', in C Woodfield, 'Finds from the Free Grammar School at the White Friars, Coventry', *Post-Medieval Archaeology* 15, 86–87

Goodall, I H, 1981 'The medieval blacksmith and his products', in D W Crossley (ed), *Medieval Industry*, Council for British Archaeology Research Report 40, 51–60

Goodall, I H, 1982 'Iron objects', in J C Murray (ed), *Excavations in the medieval burgh of Aberdeen 1973–81*, Society of Antiquaries of Scotland Monograph 2, Edinburgh, 188–189

Goodall, I H, 1982 'Iron objects', in J G Coad and A D F Streeten, 'Excavations at Castle Acre Castle, Norfolk, 1972–77, County House and Castle of the Norman Earls of Surrey', *Archaeological Journal* 139, 227–235 (138–301)

Goodall, I H and Goodall, A R, 1982 'Metal objects', in R A Higham, J P Allan and S R Blaylock, 'Excavations at Okehampton Castle, Devon. Part 2, The Bailey', *Proceedings of the Devon Archaeological Society* 40, 103–106 (20–151)

Goodall, I H, 1983 'Iron objects', in A Streeten, *Bayham Abbey: Recent research, including a report on excavations (1973–76) directed by the late Helen Sutermeister*, Sussex Archaeological Society Monograph 2, 105–109

Goodall, I H, 1983 'The small finds', in K Jarvis, *Excavations in Christchurch 1969 to 1980,* 76–7, Dorset Natural History and Archaeological Society Monograph 5, 76–77

Goodall, I H, 1983 'Iron objects', in P Mayes and L Butler, *Sandal Castle Excavations 1964–73*, Wakefield Historical Publications, Wakefield, 240–251

Goodall, I H, 1984 'Iron objects', in A Rogerson and C Dallas, *Excavations in Thetford 1948–59 and 1973–80*, East Anglian Archaeological Report 22, 77–105

Goodall, I H, 1984 'Iron objects', in J P Allan, *Medieval and post-medieval finds from Exeter 1971–1980*, Exeter Archaeological Report 3, 337–338

Goodall, I H, 1984 *'The barrel padlock'*, in P J Woodward, '*Wimborne Minster, Dorset, excavations in the town centre, 1975–80*', Dorset Natural History and Archaeological Society 105, 71 (57–74)

Goodall, I H, 1985 'Iron objects', in M Atkin, A Carter and D H Evans, 'Excavations in Norwich 1971–1978 Part II', *East Anglian Archaeology* 26, 201–213

Goodall, I H, 1985 'Ironwork', in C M Cunningham and P J Drury, *Post-medieval sites and their pottery: Moulsham Street, Chelmsford*, Council for British Archaeology Research Report 54, 51–57

Goodall, I H, 1985 'The iron objects', in A Saville, 'Salvage recording of Romano-British, Saxon, medieval, and post-medieval remains at North Street, Winchcombe, Gloucestershire', *Transactions of the Bristol and Gloucestershire Archaeological Society* 103, 125–126 (101–139)

Goodall, I H, 1986 'Four medieval iron objects from Rathmullan, County Down', *Ulster Journal of Archaeology* 48, 132–133

Goodall, I H, 1987 'Iron objects', in R D Bell and M W Beresford (eds), *Wharram. A study of settlement on the Yorkshire Wolds. Volume III: the Church of St Martin*, The Society for Medieval Archaeology Monograph 11, 171

Goodall, I H, 1987 'Padlock', in P Armstrong and D Tomlinson, *Excavations at the Dominican Priory, Beverley,1960–83*, Humberside Heritage Publication 13, 37–38

Goodall, I H, 1987 'Objects of iron', in G Beresford, *Goltho: the development of an early medieval manor c850–1150*, English Heritage Archaeological Report 4, 177–187

Goodall, I H, 1987 'Objects of iron', in P Armstrong and B Ayers, 'Excavations in High Street and Blackfriargate', *East Riding Archaeology* 8 / Hull Old Town Report 5, 197–201

Goodall, I H, 1987 'Iron objects', in J G Coad, A D F Streeten and R Warmington, 'Excavations at Castle Acre Castle, Norfolk, 1975–87, the bridges, lime kilns, and eastern gatehouse', *Archaeological Journal* 144, 293–295 (256–307)

Goodall, I H, 1988 'Iron objects', in T J James and A M Robinson, *Clarendon Palace*, Society of Antiquaries of London Research Report 45, 208–223

Goodall, I H, 1989 'Iron objects', in T G Hassall, C E Halpin and M Mellor, 'Excavations in St Ebbe's, Oxford, 1967–1976. Part I: Late Saxon and medieval domestic occupation and tenements, and the medieval Greyfriars', *Oxoniensia* 54, 224–229 (153–277)

Goodall, I H, 1989 'Iron objects', in D Austin, *The deserted medieval village of Thrislington, County Durham, excavations 1973–1974*, The Society for Medieval Archaeology Monograph 12, 126–134

Goodall, I H, 1990 'The medieval iron objects from Winchester', in M Biddle (ed), *Winchester Studies. Artefacts from Medieval Winchester. Part i. Object and Economy in Medieval Winchester*, Clarendon Press, Oxford, 36–41

Goodall, I H, 1990 'Tools', in M Biddle (ed), *Winchester Studies. Artefacts from Medieval Winchester. Part i. Object and Economy in Medieval Winchester*, Clarendon Press, Oxford, 130

Goodall, I H, 1990 'Metal-working tools', in M Biddle (ed), *Winchester Studies. Artefacts from Medieval Winchester. Part i. Object and Economy in Medieval Winchester*, Clarendon Press, Oxford, 198–199

Goodall, I H, 1990 'Heckle or woolcomb teeth', in M Biddle (ed), *Winchester Studies. Artefacts from Medieval Winchester. Part i. Object and Economy in Medieval Winchester*, Clarendon Press, Oxford, 214–216

Goodall, I H, 1990 'Weaving comb', in M Biddle (ed), *Winchester Studies. Artefacts from Medieval Winchester. Part i. Object and Economy in Medieval Winchester*, Clarendon Press, Oxford, 234

Goodall, I H, 1990 'Tenter-hooks', in M Biddle (ed), *Winchester Studies. Artefacts from Medieval Winchester. Part i. Object and Economy in Medieval Winchester*, Clarendon Press, Oxford, 234–239

Goodall, I H and Keene, D, 1990 'Harbicks (shear-board hooks)', in M Biddle (ed), *Winchester Studies. Artefacts from Medieval Winchester. Part i. Object and Economy in Medieval Winchester*, Clarendon Press, Oxford, 239–240

Goodall, I H, 1990 'Tanning, currying and leather-working tools', in M Biddle (ed), *Winchester Studies. Artefacts from Medieval Winchester. Part i. Object and Economy in Medieval Winchester*, Clarendon Press, Oxford, 247–250

Goodall, I H, 1990 'Wood-working tools', in M Biddle (ed), *Winchester Studies. Artefacts from Medieval Winchester. Part i. Object and Economy in Medieval Winchester*, Clarendon Press, Oxford, 273–277

Goodall, I H, 1990 'Stone-working tools', in M Biddle (ed), *Winchester Studies. Artefacts from Medieval Winchester. Part i. Object and Economy in Medieval Winchester*, Clarendon Press, Oxford, 299–302

Goodall, I H, 1990 'Building ironwork', in M Biddle (ed), *Winchester Studies. Artefacts from Medieval Winchester. Part i. Object and Economy in Medieval Winchester*, Clarendon Press, Oxford, 328–349

Goodall, I H, 1990 'Horticultural tools', in M Biddle (ed), *Winchester Studies. Artefacts from Medieval Winchester. Part i. Object and Economy in Medieval Winchester*, Clarendon Press, Oxford, 450–452

Goodall, I H, 1990 'Iron buckles and belt-fittings', in M Biddle (ed), *Winchester Studies. Artefacts from Medieval Winchester. Part ii. Object and Economy in Medieval Winchester*, Clarendon Press, Oxford, 526–528

Goodall, I H, 1990 'Iron binding strips and mounts', in M Biddle (ed), *Winchester Studies. Artefacts from Medieval Winchester. Part ii. Object and Economy in Medieval Winchester*, Clarendon Press, Oxford, 787–788

Goodall, I H, 1990 'Iron domestic implements', in M Biddle (ed), *Winchester Studies. Artefacts from Medieval Winchester. Part ii. Object and Economy in Medieval Winchester*, Clarendon Press, Oxford, 818–820

Goodall, I H, 1990 'Chains, links, chain fittings, rings, and washers', in M Biddle (ed), *Winchester Studies. Artefacts from Medieval Winchester. Part ii. Object and Economy in Medieval Winchester*, Clarendon Press, Oxford, 821–827

Goodall, I H, 1990 'Knives', in M Biddle (ed), *Winchester Studies. Artefacts from Medieval Winchester. Part ii. Object and Economy in Medieval Winchester*, Clarendon Press, Oxford, 835–860

Goodall, I H, 1990 'Shears and scissors', in M Biddle (ed), *Winchester Studies. Artefacts from Medieval Winchester. Part ii. Object and Economy in Medieval Winchester*, Clarendon Press, Oxford, 861–863

Goodall, I H, 1990 'Iron fittings from vessels', in M Biddle (ed), *Winchester Studies. Artefacts from Medieval Winchester. Part ii. Object and Economy in Medieval Winchester*, Clarendon Press, Oxford, 967–968

Goodall, I H, 1990 'Iron fittings from furniture', in M Biddle (ed), *Winchester Studies. Artefacts from Medieval Winchester. Part ii. Object and Economy in Medieval Winchester*, Clarendon Press, Oxford, 971–979

Goodall, I H, 1990 'Iron fittings for lights', in M Biddle (ed), *Winchester Studies. Artefacts from Medieval Winchester. Part ii. Object and Economy in Medieval Winchester*, Clarendon Press, Oxford, 981–982

Goodall, I H, 1990 'Locks and keys', in M Biddle (ed), *Winchester Studies. Artefacts from Medieval Winchester. Part ii. Object and Economy in Medieval Winchester*, Clarendon Press, Oxford, 984–1036

Goodall, I H, 1990 'Stirrups', in M Biddle (ed), *Winchester Studies. Artefacts from Medieval Winchester. Part ii. Object and Economy in Medieval Winchester*, Clarendon Press, Oxford, 1042

Goodall, I H, 1990 'Bridle bits and associated strap-fittings', in M Biddle (ed), *Winchester Studies. Artefacts from Medieval Winchester. Part ii. Object and Economy in Medieval Winchester*, Clarendon Press, Oxford, 1043–1046

Goodall, I H, 1990 'Curry-combs', in M Biddle (ed), *Winchester Studies. Artefacts from Medieval Winchester. Part ii. Object and Economy in Medieval Winchester*, Clarendon Press, Oxford, 1053–1054

Goodall, I H, 1990 'Horseshoes', in M Biddle (ed), *Winchester Studies. Artefacts from Medieval Winchester. Part ii. Object and Economy in Medieval Winchester*, Clarendon Press, Oxford, 1054–1067

Goodall, I H, 1990 'Arrowheads', in M Biddle (ed), *Winchester Studies. Artefacts from Medieval Winchester. Part ii. Object and Economy in Medieval Winchester*, Clarendon Press, Oxford, 1070–1074

Goodall, I H, 1990 'Iron sheet-binding', in M Biddle (ed), *Object and Economy in Medieval Winchester*, Clarendon Press, Oxford, 1102

Goodall, I H, 1990 'Iron objects', in J R Fairbrother, *Faccombe Netherton. Excavations of a Saxon and medieval manorial complex*, British Museum Occasional Paper 74, 403–425

Goodall, I H, 1990 'Iron objects', in J Blair (ed), *St Frideswide's monastery at Oxford, archaeological and architectural studies*, Gloucester, 43–44

Goodall, I H, 1991 'The ironwork', in P Armstrong, D Tomlinson and D H Evans, *Excavations at Lurk Lane, Beverley, 1979–82*, Sheffield Excavation Report 1, 132–146

Goodall, I H, 1992 'Iron objects', in G Milne and J D Richards (eds), *Wharran: a study of settlement on the Yorkshire Wolds 7*, York University Archaeological Publications 9, 49–52

Goodall, H I, and Ottaway, P, 1993 'Iron objects', in C Dallas, *Excavations in Thetford by B K Davison between 1964 and 1970*, East Anglian Archaeology 62, 96–116

Goodall, I H, 1993 'Belt-fittings and accessories', in S Margeson, *Norwich households: the medieval and post-medieval finds from Norwich survey excavations 1971–1978*, East Anglian Archaeology 58, 24–40

Goodall, I H, 1993 'Shoes accessories', in S Margeson, *Norwich households: the medieval and post-medieval finds from Norwich survey excavations 1971–1978*, East Anglian Archaeology 58, 60–63

Goodall, I H, 1993 'Furniture and coffin fittings', in S Margeson, *Norwich households: the medieval and post-medieval finds from Norwich survey excavations 1971–1978*, East Anglian Archaeology 58, 74–83

Goodall, I H, 1993 'Lighting', in S Margeson, *Norwich households: the medieval and post-medieval finds from Norwich survey excavations 1971–1978*, East Anglian Archaeology 58, 83–86

Goodall, I H, 1993 'Iron hearth equipment', in S Margeson, *Norwich households: the medieval and post-medieval finds from Norwich survey excavations 1971–1978*, East Anglian Archaeology 58, 86–89

Goodall, I H, 1993 'Iron vessels', in S Margeson, *Norwich households: the medieval and post-medieval finds from Norwich survey excavations 1971–1978*, East Anglian Archaeology 58, 94–95

Goodall, I H, 1993 'Implements', in S Margeson, *Norwich households: the medieval and post-medieval finds from Norwich survey excavations 1971–1978*, East Anglian Archaeology 58, 118–136

Goodall, I H, 1993 'Miscellaneous fittings', in S Margeson, *Norwich households: the medieval and post-medieval finds from Norwich survey excavations 1971–1978*, East Anglian Archaeology 58, 139–142

Goodall, I H, 1993 'Structural ironwork', in S Margeson, *Norwich households: the medieval and post-medieval finds from Norwich survey excavations 1971–1978*, East Anglian Archaeology 58, 143–148

Goodall, I H, 1993 'Iron door, window and furniture fittings', in S Margeson, *Norwich households: the medieval and post-medieval finds from Norwich survey excavations 1971–1978*, East Anglian Archaeology 58, 148–155

Goodall, I H, 1993 'Lock furniture, hasps and keys', in S Margeson, *Norwich households: the medieval and post-medieval finds from Norwich survey excavations 1971–1978*, East Anglian Archaeology 58, 155–163

Margeson, S with Goodall, I H, 1993 'Metalworking', in S Margeson, *Norwich households: the medieval and post-medieval finds from Norwich survey excavations 1971–1978*, East Anglian Archaeology 58, 174–177

Goodall, I H, 1993 'Iron woodworking tools', in S Margeson, *Norwich households: the medieval and post-medieval finds from Norwich survey excavations 1971–1978*, East Anglian Archaeology 58, 177–181

Goodall, I H, 1993 'Iron stone-working and plastering tools', in S Margeson, *Norwich households: the medieval and post-medieval finds from Norwich survey excavations 1971–1978*, East Anglian Archaeology 58, 181

Goodall, I H, 1993 'Textile manufacture and needlework', in S Margeson, *Norwich households: the medieval and post-medieval finds from Norwich survey excavations 1971–1978*, East Anglian Archaeology 58, 182–189

Goodall, I H, 1993 'Iron currying and leather-working tools', in S Margeson, *Norwich households: the medieval and post-medieval finds from Norwich survey excavations 1971–1978*, East Anglian Archaeology 58, 189–190

Goodall, I H, 1993 'Iron horticultural and agricultural tools', in S Margeson, *Norwich households: the medieval and post-medieval finds from Norwich survey excavations 1971–1978*, East Anglian Archaeology 58, 193–195

Goodall, I H, 1993 'Iron horseshoes', in S Margeson, *Norwich Households. Medieval and Post–medieval Finds from Norwich Survey Excavations 1971–78,* East Anglian Archaeology 58, 225–227

Goodall, I H, 1993 'Weapons and armour', in S Margeson, *Norwich households: the medieval and post-medieval finds from Norwich survey excavations 1971–1978*, East Anglian Archaeology 58, 227–229

Goodall, I H, 1993 'Iron objects', in H K Murray and J C Murray, 'Excavations at Rattray, Aberdeenshire. A Scottish deserted burgh', *Medieval Archaeology* 37, 175–179 (109–218)

Goodall, I H, 1993 'Iron', in G G Astill, *A medieval industrial complex and its landscape: the metalworking watermills and workshops of Bordesley Abbey*, Council for British Archaeology Research Report 92, 165–180

Goodall, I H, 1994 Ironwork report in 'The finds', in D C Mynard, *Excavations on medieval and later sites in Milton Keynes, 1972–80*, Buckingham Archaeological Society Monograph 6, 69–83

Goodall, I H, 1994 'Iron objects', in H Quinnell and M R Blockley with P Berridge, *Excavations at Rhuddlan, Clwyd 1969–73, Mesolithic to Medieval*, Council for British Archaeology Research Report 95, 178–190

Goodall, H I, 1995 'Iron objects', in D Phillips and B Heywood, *Excavations at York Minster volume I: from Roman fortress to Norman cathedral*, 484–488

Goodall, I H, and Wright, N, 1996 'Iron objects', in A Schlesinger and C Walls, 'An early church and medieval farmstead site: excavations at Llanelen, Gower', *Archaeological Journal* 153, 135–136 (104–147)

Goodall, I H, 1996 'Iron objects', in D H Evans, 'Excavations at the Skipwith Manor, Habrough, South Humberside', *Post-Medieval Archaeology* 29, 106 (63–127)

Goodall, I H, 1997 'Iron objects', in A G Vince, S J Lobb, J C Richards and L Mepham, *Excavations in Newbury, Berkshire, 1979–1990*, Wessex Archaeology Report 13, 36–42

Goodall, I H, 1997 'Lock', in A G Vince, S J Lobb, J C Richards and L Mepham, *Excavations in Newbury, Berkshire, 1979–1990*, Wessex Archaeology Report 13, 103

Goodall, I H and Montague, R, 1997 'Iron objects', in A G Vince, S J Lobb, J C Richards and L Mepham, *Excavations in Newbury, Berkshire, 1979–1990*, Wessex Archaeology Report 13, 105–110

Goodall, I H, 1997 'Iron objects', in M Shaw, 'The excavation of a late 15th- to 17th-century tanning complex at The Green, *Post-Medieval Archaeology* 30, 33–35 (1–60)

Goodall, H I, 1998 'Arrowheads', in T B James and A Robinson, *Clarendon Palace*, Society of Antiquaries of London Research Report 45, 222–223

Goodall, H I, 2000 'Iron objects', in P Ellis (ed), *Ludgershall Castle, Wiltshire, a report on the excavations by Peter Addyman, 1964–1972*, Wiltshire Archaeological and Natural History Society Monograph 2, 143–156

Goodall, H I, with A Goodall, 2000 'Metalwork from the Motte', in R Higham and P Barker, *Hen Domen, Montgomery: a timber castle on the English-Welsh border: a final report*, University of Exeter Press, 94–98

Goodall, I H, 2002 'The metalwork', in P Mayes, *Excavations at a Templar preceptory. South Witham, Lincolnshire 1965–67*, The Society for Medieval Archaeology Monograph 19, 96–110

Goodall, I H, 2002 'Iron objects', in P Page, K Atherton and A Hardy, *Excavations of the moated manor at Hardings Field, Chalgrove, Oxfordshire 1976–9*, Thames Valley Landscapes Monograph 24, 92–106

Goodall, I H, 2002 'Iron objects', in B D Mynard and R Ivens, 'The excavation of Gorefields: a medieval nunnery and grange at Stoke Goldington', *Records of Buckinghamshire* 42, 43–51 (19–101)

Goodall, I H, 2002 'Iron', in C Dallas and D Sherlock, *Baconthorpe Castle, excavations and finds, 1951–1972*, East Anglian Archaeological Report 102, 63–65

Goodall, I H, 2005 'Iron objects', in M Biddle, *Nonsuch Palace. The material culture of a noble Restoration household*, Oxbow Books, Oxford, 373–411

Goodall, I H, 2007 'Iron artefacts', in C Caple, *Excavations at Dryslwyn Castle 1980–95*, The Society for Medieval Archaeology Monograph 26, 247–257

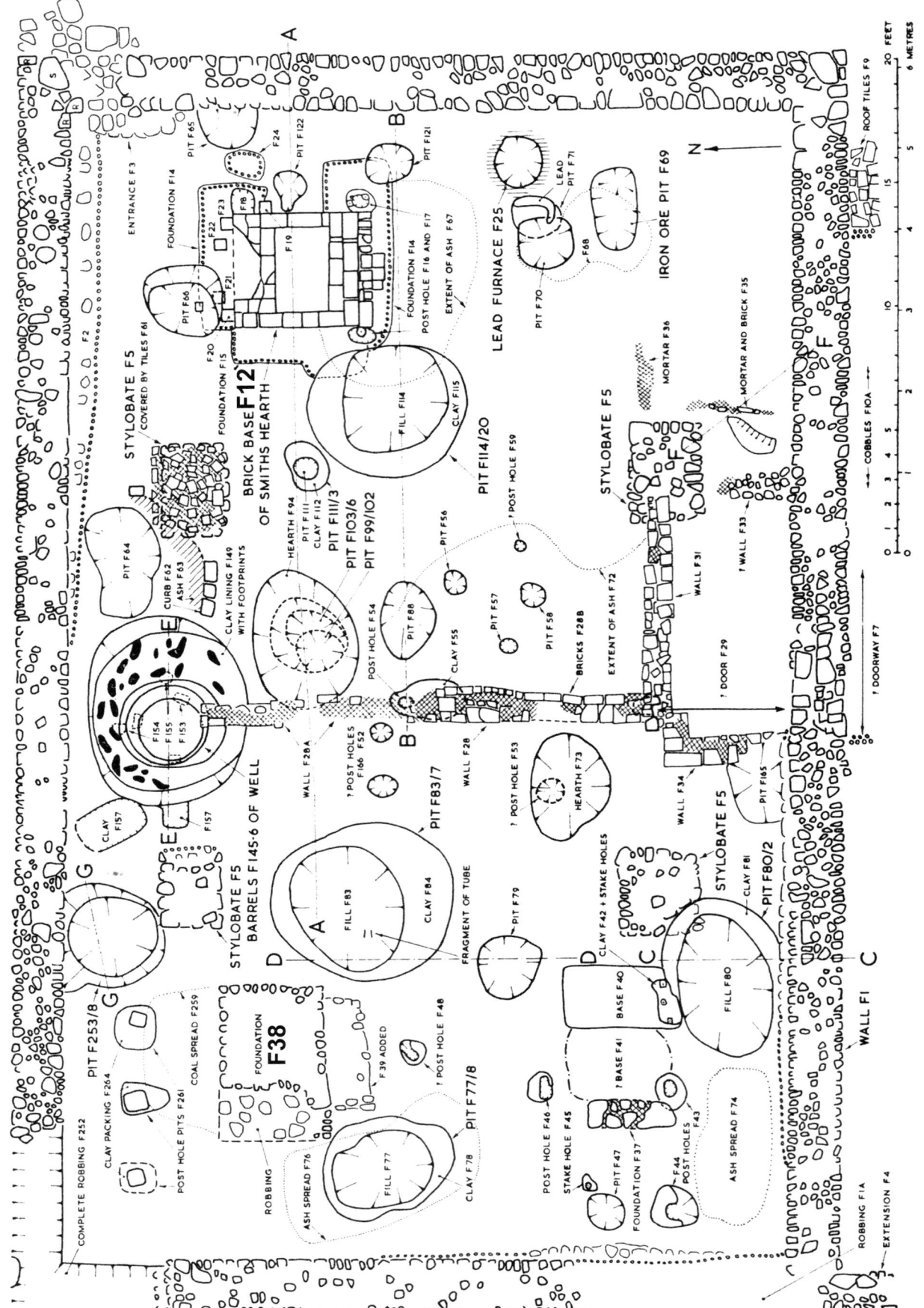

FIGURE 1.1
Forge at Waltham Abbey, Essex (after Huggins and Huggins 1973, fig 2)

1

IRON SMELTING AND SMITHING

Iron ore deposits are widespread in Britain, the main types being carbonate, haematite and limonite whose incidence is discussed by Tylecote (1962, 175–179). Quarrying with trenches as well as tunnelling is known from the Forest of Dean (Schubert 1957, 123, pls XIII–XIV) but widely occurring bell-pits are more frequent evidence of medieval deep mining of iron ore (Tylecote 1962, 284–285; Beresford and St Joseph 1979, 256, fig 107). Bell-pits near Sedgeley, West Midlands, had 1.5m diameter openings, a depth of 4.6m to 6.1m, and a maximum diameter of 3.6m.

1.1 IRON SMELTING

Archaeological evidence for iron smelting is considerable and is discussed elsewhere (Tylecote 1962; 1976; Schubert 1957; Crossley 1981). A brief outline of the process is given here.

Iron ore was frequently roasted before smelting in a bloomery or blast furnace to make it more porous and more easily reduced. Medieval bloomery furnaces are of two basic types, the horizontally developed and the vertically developed bowl furnace, each with slag-tapping facilities. In use a charge of ore and charcoal was placed in the furnace and during smelting some of the lighter impurities were tapped off as slag until at the end cinders, slag and a bloom of iron were left at the bottom. The extracted bloom was consolidated on a string hearth by repeated hammering and with intermittent re-heating, the attached cinders being removed and the entrapped slag driven out to produce a bloom of wrought iron. This was then cut into pieces and if necessary rendered into bar iron for the blacksmith. Towards the close of the medieval period the blast furnace, which produced liquid iron in addition to slag, was developed. The first blast furnace definitely known to be in existence in Britain was at Newbridge, Sussex, in 1496 (Tylecote 1962, 301).

Iron smelting and smithing produce many waste products, not all unique to a single stage, and interpretations drawn from them, particularly where they are found without structural association, should be based on scientific examination. The products of smelting include the raw bloom with its entrapped slag and attached cinders, furnace bottoms, slag and tap slag, whilst smithing of the raw bloom produces slag hammered out of the bloom and hammer scale formed on its outer surface. The final forging also produces hammer scale and fine, almost microscopic, drops of slag.

1.2 IRON SMITHING

Blacksmith's forges or smithies are known from a number of excavated sites, and include the 13th-century bloomery and adjacent smithy at Godmanchester in Cambridgeshire (Webster and Cherry 1975, 260, fig 96), where one room of a two-room building was used as a smithy and remains of four contemporary iron-smelting furnaces were found in a building to the rear. Medieval documents indicate that string hearths were sometimes attached to bloomeries (Salzman 1967, 31; Tylecote 1962, 287–289) and were sometimes separate (Schubert 1957, 126–127), and it is at present unclear whether this smithy housed a string hearth or was a conventional smithy.

At Waltham Abbey, Essex, a forge built about 1200 on the home farm of the Augustinian Abbey survived the Dissolution and stood, not necessarily in use, into the 17th century (Huggins and Huggins 1973). Iron ore and bloomery products indicate that the site, if not the building, was used for iron smelting. The forge (Figure 1.1), built as a three-bay aisled building 15.7m by 10.1m, was certainly used for making complete objects since bar iron, incomplete forgings and a series of tools (catalogued below) were found, as well as two smith's hearths surrounded by concentrations of hammer scale. One

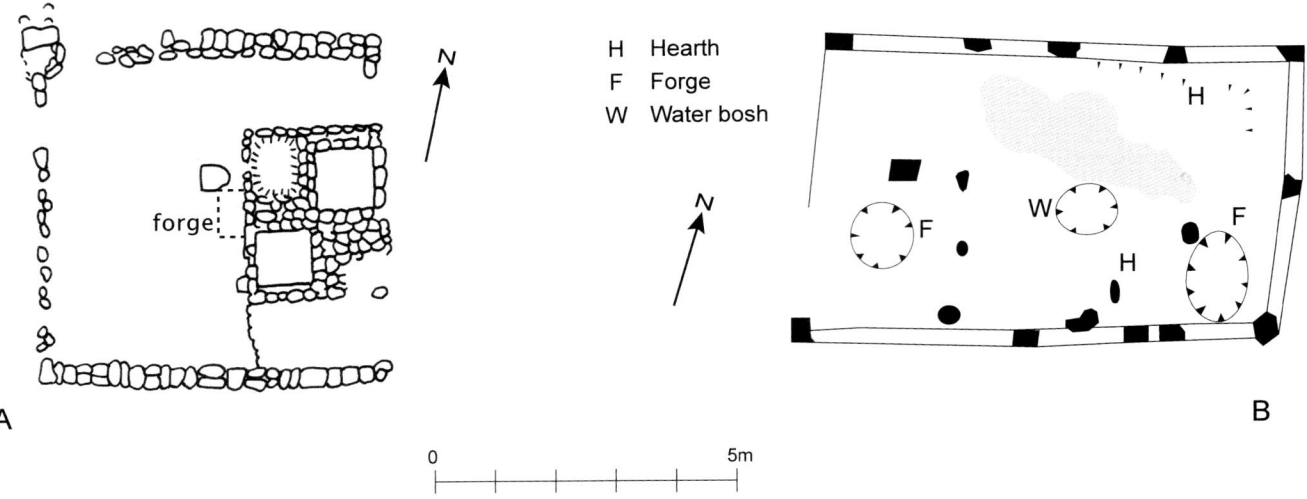

FIGURE 1.2
A: Smithy at Alsted, Surrey (after Ketteringham 1976, fig 19). B: Smithy at Goltho, Lincolnshire (after Beresford 1975, fig 22)

hearth (F12) consists of a rectangular brick base, 1.67m by 1.42m surviving five courses high and set on a wider foundation; the other hearth (F38) survives only as a flint and chalk foundation, 1.9m by 1.4m. Both have separate foundations which could have supported a water bosh. The more complete hearth is very similar to that in a smithy of c1395–1405 at Alsted, Surrey (Ketteringham 1976, 25–29, figs 19–21), where the 6.0m by 5.5m building (Figure 1.2A) had a rectangular stone hearth with fire-pit, working surface and space for bellows, as well as a large sandstone block immediately in front to support the anvil block. Hammer scale was found on the floor surrounding the stone and along the front of the hearth, and the site produced a number of tools which may be related either to the smithy or to earlier iron smelting.

The late 14th to early 15th-century smithy at Goltho, Lincolnshire (Beresford 1975, 46, figs 21–22), a timber building 8.0m by 5.0m (Figure 1.2B) surrounded by a yard surfaced with smithing slag, had two pits which produced smithing furnace bottoms (Tylecote 1975). The later pit, to the SE, was used until the time of desertion. A clay-lined pit in the floor may have been a water bosh or cooling water-basin, but no blacksmith's hearth similar to those at Waltham Abbey or Alsted was found. A small quantity of bar iron, and a few tools and other objects do, however, indicate the forging of objects.

Blacksmiths frequently also acted as farriers, and the late 14th to mid 15th-century smithy at Huish, Wiltshire, was evidently used by a farrier (Thompson 1972, 115, fig 1). The building, which was destroyed by fire, was 3.0m by 2.4m and had two hearths, in one of which were two horseshoes, a claw hammer, a poker and other indeterminate objects. The forge at Waltham Abbey produced evidence connected with farriery in the form of four horseshoes, two oxshoes and 160 horseshoe nails (Huggins and Huggins 1973).

The smithies already noted are mainly on monastic, manorial or village sites, but excavation in Southampton, Hampshire, located part of the floor of a late 12th or early 13th-century urban smithy floor (Platt and Coleman-Smith 1975, I, 238, 267, 349, pl 74).

The smithy must have been an important building during the construction and occupation of castles, and several have produced relevant finds. Iron slag, bar iron, tongs, a sledgehammer, chisel and axe from Deganwy Castle, Gwynedd, are probably from a smithy. They were found together at a depth of 61mm in an isolated hole in the bailey of Henry III's castle, begun 1245 and destroyed 1263, but could be of earlier date since the site had been in intermittent occupation for many centuries (Alcock 1967). Ironworking, probably initially including the smelting of ore, was the main activity in a workshop on the motte at Lismahon, Co. Down (Waterman 1959a, 152, 155–156) during the 13th and 14th centuries, and hammer scale and forging hearth slag were found with scrap iron and bronze on the site of a 14th-century workshop at Bramber Castle, West Sussex (Barton and Holden 1977, 38, 66–67). West of the gatehouse-keep sundry nails, horseshoes, etc, were found in a probable 14th-century context with very little slag and may imply a second smithing area (Barton and Holden 1977, 67; ex inf E W Holden).

Less certain evidence comes from Lyveden, Northamptonshire, where a roughly rectangular paved area 6.5m by 4.2m with areas of burnt clay and stone, charcoal, iron slag and coal has been interpreted as a probable smithy in use c1200–1350 (Steane and Bryant 1975, 4–9, 21–22, figs 7–8).

At Walsall, West Midlands, a 4.0m by 11.0m building of 13th or 14th century date may have served as a forge and later as a fuel store (Wrathmell and Wrathmell 1974–75, 27–29, 51, figs 2–4, pl II).

1.3 BAR IRON AND INCOMPLETE FORGINGS

The blacksmith's raw material, other than scrap iron collected for reuse, comprised pieces of iron cut from blooms and lengths of bar iron of varying size and cross section. Purchases of iron for use in medieval building-work are often mentioned in accounts (Salzman 1967, 286–288), and the iron was both native and foreign, the former including specifically named Weardale, Gloucester and Wealden iron, and the latter particularly Spanish iron. The iron is often priced and bought by the stone or hundredweight, or in sizes called gad, seam and hes. It was sometimes just held in store, but was also bought for particular use, such as Spanish iron for window bars bought at Corfe in 1292, or for hooks and bands at Dover in 1363. Steel, often from Sweden, was also bought for tool and knife edges (Salzman 1967, 288).

A shaped, rectangular sectioned bar from Winchester (**A1**) proved on examination to be a dense, well-worked piece of wrought iron with few slag inclusions. A bar fragment (**A2**) from Deganwy Castle found with other blacksmith's equipment and iron slag, has a chisel-cut end, indicating that it is part of a once larger piece. The shape of the chisel-cut shows the characteristic way the blacksmith cut metal, since it was important not to cut entirely through the iron and dull the edge of the chisel on the hard face of the anvil. In practice the smith reduced the force of the hammer blows on the chisel just before the cut was complete, and then often broke it by hand.

Two pieces of iron (**A3**–**A4**) are known from a site with ironworking evidence at Newbury, Berkshire, but over 100 pieces of sheet iron, bar iron of square, rectangular and round section, and lengths of iron wire come from the forge at Waltham Abbey. **A5**–**A10** are a representative selection, whilst **A11**–**A15** are shaped pieces, some perhaps scrap iron or partly forged objects. Definitely identified incompletely forged objects from the site, catalogued below, include those of six auger bits and a key, but it is impossible to be certain whether other objects such as a padlock bolt head and lock wards belong to incomplete objects, are scrap, or were in actual use. Other incomplete forgings include keys from Gloucester and Goltho, the latter from the croft with the late 14th to early 15th century smithy which produced a little bar iron (**A16**). Chingley and Tattershall College produced knife moods, and **A17**, a shaped, partly forged piece of iron comes from Lyveden.

A1 BAR
Winchester, Hampshire.
Late 11th to early 12th century.
Rectangular section bar shown by metallurgical examination to be dense, well-worked wrought iron with few slag inclusions. Weight 1.28kg (2.81 lb). L 280mm.
Biddle 1990, fig 38, no. 37.

A2 BAR
Deganwy Castle, Gwynedd.
Unstratified in bailey of castle of 1245–63, on site with earlier occupation. Found with blacksmith's equipment and iron slag. Rectangular section bar, chisel-cut across one end. L 108mm.
Excavated by W Greenhalgh. For site see Alcock 1967.

A3 BAR IRON?
Newbury, Berkshire.
12th to 13th century.
Rectangular section bar. L 31mm
Ford 1979, 25, fig 3.2.

A4 BAR IRON
Newbury, Berkshire.
Unstratified. ?13th century.
Rectangular section piece of iron. Weight 1.1kg (2 lb 9 oz). L 113mm.
Ford 1979, 25, fig 3.3.

A5 BAR IRON
Waltham Abbey, Essex.
16th/17th century destruction debris plus derived pottery from forge built c1200. Rectangular section bar, one end probably chisel cut. L 104mm.
Goodall 1973a, 170, fig 11.1.

A6 BAR IRON
Waltham Abbey, Essex.
13th and 16th century.
Rectangular section bar. L 133mm.
Goodall 1973a, 170, fig 11.2.

A7 BAR IRON
Waltham Abbey, Essex.
12th/13th century.
Rectangular section bar. L 70mm.
Goodall 1973a, 170, fig 11.3.

A8 BAR IRON
Waltham Abbey, Essex.
15th/16th century.
Square section bar fragment. L 161mm.
Goodall 1973a, 170, fig 11.4.

A9 ROD
Waltham Abbey, Essex.
16th century.
Rod fragment, circular section. L 127mm.
Goodall 1973a, 170, fig 11.5.

A10 WIRE
Waltham Abbey, Essex.
15th/16th century.
Wire fragment, 3mm diameter. L 123mm.
Goodall 1973a, 170, fig 11.6.

A11 BAR IRON
Waltham Abbey, Essex.
16th century.
Octagonal section bar fragment. L 94mm.
Goodall 1973a, 170, fig 11.7.

A12 BAR IRON
Waltham Abbey, Essex.
16th/17th century destruction debris plus derived pottery from forge built c1200. Tapered bar fragment, rectangular section. L 71mm.
Goodall 1973a, 170, fig 11.8.

A13 BAR IRON
Waltham Abbey, Essex.
Possibly 13th century.
Tapered bar fragment, rectangular section. L 62mm.
Goodall 1973a, 170, fig 11.9.

A14 BAR IRON
Waltham Abbey, Essex.
16th/17th century destruction debris plus derived pottery from forge built c1200. Curved, rectangular section bar thickened at one end. L 210mm.
Goodall 1973a, 170, fig 11.10.

A15 BAR IRON
Waltham Abbey, Essex.
12th/13th century.
Bar fragment, chamfered sides. L 58mm.
Goodall 1973a, 26, fig 11.11.

A16 BAR IRON (not illustrated)
Goltho, Lincolnshire.
Late 14th to early 15th century.
A few pieces of generally rectangular section iron, found near smithy and representing metal used in it.
Goodall 1975a, 87.

A17 INCOMPLETE FORGING
Lyveden, Northamptonshire.
Second quarter 13th century.
Shaped piece of rectangular section bar. L 78mm.
Bryant and Steane 1971, 55, fig 13f.

SMELTING AND SMITHING

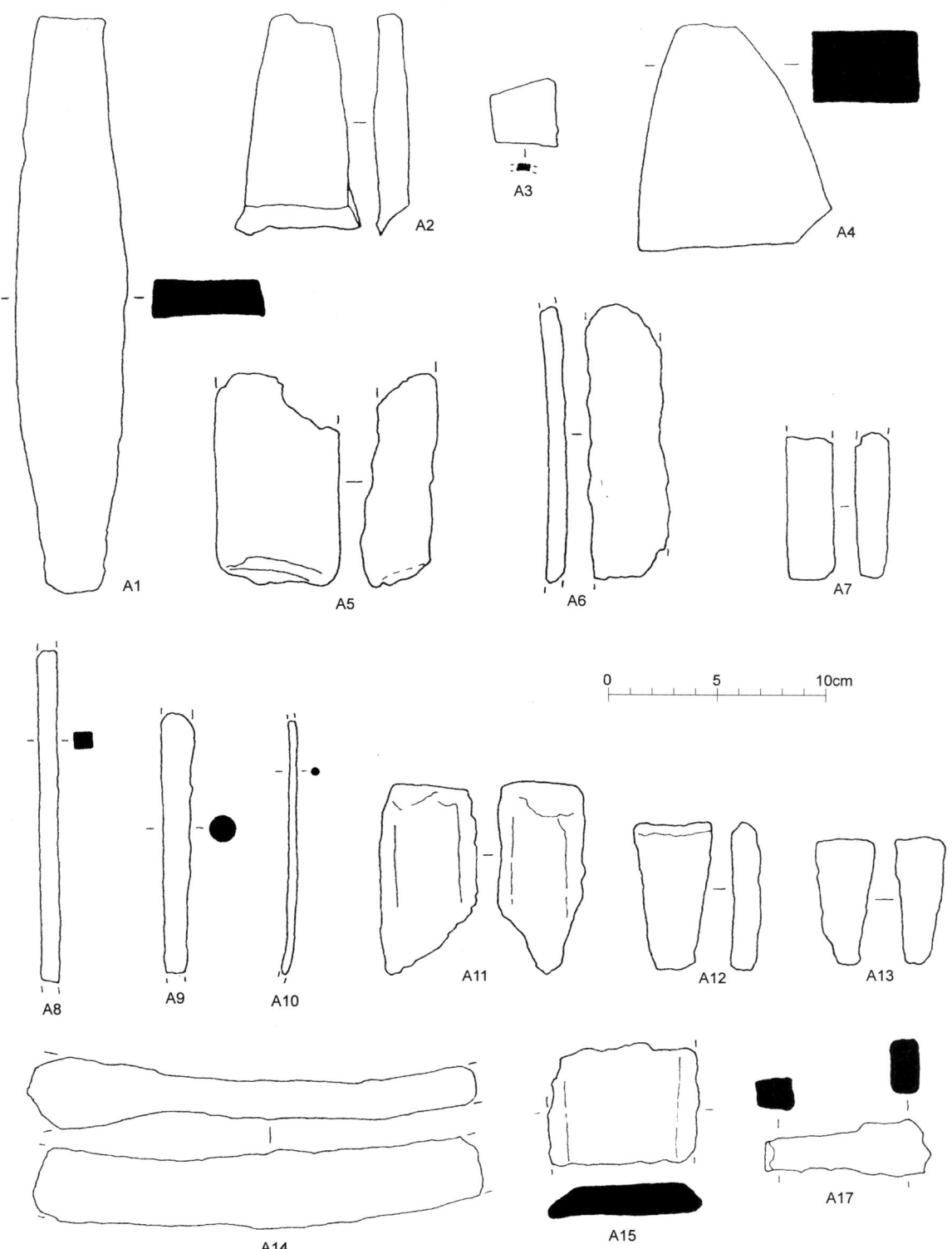

FIGURE 1.3
Iron smelting and smithing: Bar iron and partly forged objects

2
METALWORKING TOOLS

The blacksmith probably required the widest range of tools of the medieval craftsmen in metal, and this is reflected in the surviving tools which include tongs, pincers, hammers, chisels and punches. The following account draws much of its practical information about smithcraft and tools from COSIRA 1955 and Smith 1966.

2.1 ANVILS

Representations of blacksmiths are not infrequent in medieval illuminated manuscripts, where they sometimes appear symbolically as St Eloi and sometimes as craftsmen at work in a forge. No anvils have yet been found, but illuminations indicate that they were set into the flat tops of wooden blocks which served both to raise them to the required height and to absorb some of the shock of the impact of hammer on anvil. Accounts for Dover Castle (Salzman 1967, 347) record that an anvil was bought in 1265 as well as 'a wooden block on which to put an anvil in the smithy'. The anvil was placed close to the smith's hearth for practical purposes, and a stone base surrounded by hammer scale in front of the hearth in the forge at Alsted, Surrey, (Ketteringham 1976, 25, 28, figs 20–21) probably supported such a block.

Anvils were of several types, but they are frequently depicted as simple blocks of iron, as in the 11th-century Caedmon manuscript (Figure 2.1A) or the Holkham Bible of c1325–30 (Figure 2.1B; and see cover illustration). Other illustrations (Figures 2.1C–D) clearly show beaked anvils with one or two conical end projections for shaping forgings, and an inventory of smith's tools at Rochester in 1363 (Salzman 1967, 347) includes both an 'anuell' and a 'bicorne', the latter evidently an anvil with two horns or cones.

2.2 TONGS

Tongs were used by craftsmen in non-ferrous metals for moving and pouring crucibles, and the down-turned jaws of A18 are ideally shaped for gripping the rim of a small crucible.

Tongs are one of the blacksmith's basic tools, used to hold the work at all stages of forging, and the range in size and shape reflects the differing uses. Any one smith might have several pairs of tongs, and an inventory of smith's tools at Rochester in 1363 (Salzman 1967, 347) includes '8 tonges' and a 'spentonge' or gripping tongs.

Medieval tongs A19–25 have hinged jaws with gripping faces held by rivets, which, when complete,

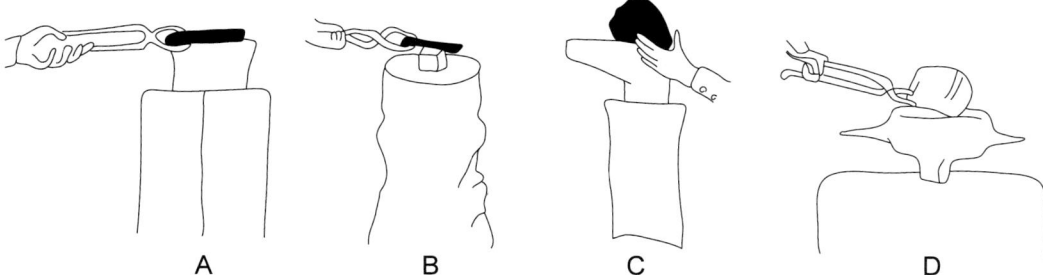

FIGURE 2.1
Anvils: representation in medieval manuscripts. A: English, 11th century. B: English, c1325–30. C: Franco-Flemish, c1340. D: English, c1250 (A: Wilson 1976, 264, pl XIII. B: See cover; C–D: Harvey 1975a, pls 120–121)

often have domed heads. The straight handles, called reins by modern smiths, are almost parallel when the tongs are in use, enabling the smith to grip and manoeuvre them conveniently. Most handles are now incomplete, but the one complete handle of **A23**, and both of **A24**, have knobbed terminals whose purpose was to prevent a loop slipped over the ends from sliding off. The loop saved the blacksmith effort when undertaking a sustained or repetitive job, since it held the handles in tension and allowed the tongs to be put down without the forging dropping from the jaws. The flattened ends of **A19** may have acted similarly, the loop being slipped over them whilst they were held together, and being prevented from sliding off by their springing apart when released.

The jaws vary in form, those of the larger pairs of tongs **A19–21** being broad and straight or gently curved with flat gripping faces suitable for holding heavy pieces of iron. The long handles, only complete on **A19**, will have enabled them to be used in forging at great heat. Smaller tongs were used when a firmer grip was required and when the iron did not require strong heat for forging, as well as for delicate, small work. The jaws of **A22–24** are either straight or gently curved, and all have flat faces; those of **A22–23** taper towards the tip and are not unlike armourers' hammers. The small pair of tongs **A25** are most appropriate for small-scale work.

2.3 PINCERS

The blacksmith frequently acted as a farrier shoeing horses, as finds from the smithies at Huish, Wiltshire, and Waltham Abbey, Essex, demonstrate. At Huish (Thompson 1972, 115) one of the hearths contained two horseshoes, a claw hammer and a poker, whilst at Waltham Abbey four horseshoes, two oxshoes and 160 horseshoe nails were recovered (Huggins and Huggins 1973).

Tongs were used during the forging of horseshoes and nails, but the shoe was removed from the hoof with pincers with curved jaws and a broad, sharp gripping edge capable of gripping a nail and levering it out. Pincers **A26** have such jaws as well as shaped handles identical to a pair held by St Eloi, patron saint of blacksmiths, as depicted in the 14th-century Luttrell Psalter (Millar 1932, 27–28, f 52, reproduced in Webber 1971, 25). The hooked end may have held a loop which closed over the knobbed end of the opposing handle. **A27**, which are slightly larger, have straight handles. Carpenters as well as blacksmiths used pincers, and these examples could have been used by either craftsman.

2.4 HAMMERS

An inventory of blacksmith's tools at Rochester in 1363 (Salzman 1967, 347) includes four sledgehammers, two large hammers and four small hammers. The sledgehammer was used during the dividing and working of blooms of iron into bars, in heavier forging such as drawing down and cutting bar iron, and for striking top anvil tools such as set hammers. The other hammers were used during later stages of forging.

Sledgehammers can be divided by use into the heavier swing sledge (today 3.63–9.07kg, 8–20 lb) set on a long handle and swung with two hands, and the lighter hand sledge (2.72–3.63kg, 6–8 lb) set on a shorter handle and swung from shoulder height. During the initial forging, as a 14th-century illuminated manuscript depicts exactly (Figure 2.2), the swing sledge was wielded by the striker, who was the smith's apprentice or labourer, while the

FIGURE 2.2
Blacksmiths in a forge, Franco-Flemish 14th-century manuscript (Harvey 1975a, pl 119)

smith held a hand sledge and gripped the hot iron on the anvil with tongs.

Medieval sledgehammers are of two types: **A28** a double-faced sledge, **A29–31** cross-pane sledges. **A28**, found with other items of blacksmith's equipment and iron slag, has an octagonal-sectioned head and gently rounded faces designed to spread the force of the blow without cutting the iron. The cross-pane sledges **A29–31**, with their panes set at right angles to the handles, were used to draw down the iron. **A29–30** have heads with flat undersides and cheeks which rise either side of the eye, probably to ensure more secure hafting, whilst **A31** has instead an expansion around the eye and a more centrally set cross-pane arm. Wooden handles must often have been secured in the eye by wedges or nails, either from the start or after they worked loose, and a nail survives in **A31**.

Hand hammers used for general work at the anvil are of two types: with a face and either a cross-pane or straight pane. The cross-pane is set at right angles to the handle, the straight pane in the same plane. The face of either might be used for striking tools such as punches and chisels, but the pane was used to concentrate blows on a small area during forging and spread the iron crosswise or lengthways. **A32–34** are all cross-pane hammers with flat undersides, **A32–33** having cheeks which rise either side of the eye, **A34** an expansion around the eye. The fiddle-key horseshoe nail used to secure the haft in the eye of **A32** perhaps implies that it was used by a farrier. **A35** is the down-turned pane from a cross-pane hammer. No straight-pane hammer is yet known, but the type is present on both pre- and post-medieval sites, and will have been used by the medieval blacksmiths.

The blacksmith is unlikely to have had sole use of these hammers since the sledgehammer was also used by the stonemason and the hand hammer by the carpenter, the cross-pane starting nails, the head driving them in. Claw hammers, although used by farriers shoeing horses, are discussed below under woodworking tools (Chapter 3).

Bronzesmiths and craftsmen in other fine metals must at times have used hammers similar to the lighter blacksmiths' hammers, but some of the more delicate work might have required a hammer such as **A36** with its two differing arms.

2.5 FLATTERS AND SET HAMMERS

Flatters and set hammers, smoothing tools whose function is to smooth out flaws and crude forgings, are placed on the iron and struck with a sledge or a heavy hand hammer. Modern set hammers are generally uniform in size from top to bottom, whilst the bottom of flatters spreads outwards. They may have flat or convex faces with sharp or rounded edges, according to the purpose for which they are required. The set hammer **A37** is burred by striking and has an oval convex face and rectangular eye for hafting.

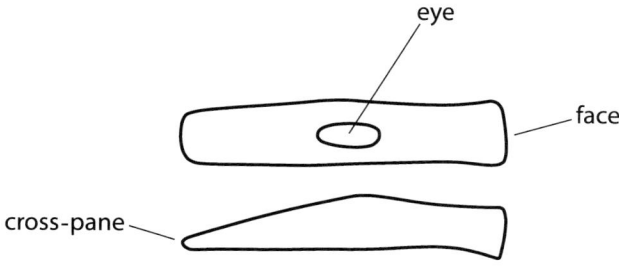

FIGURE 2.3
Hammers: terminology

2.6 CHISELS AND SETS

Chisels and sets are principally blacksmiths' tools for cutting iron, the chisel struck with a hand hammer and generally hand held, the set struck with a sledgehammer and either hafted or rodded. Cold and hot chisels and sets cut cold and hot iron respectively, although certain differentiation between them is not always possible and is unlikely to have applied in practice. Modern chisels for cutting cold iron are made from steel containing about 0.875 per cent carbon, those for cutting hot iron of steel containing 0.75 per cent carbon, the difference being accounted for by the softness of hot iron which can be cut by a correspondingly softer metal. An awareness of the property of steel is demonstrated by chisels **A50–51**, both of which have been shown to have steeled tips and wrought iron bodies. **A43** is completely wrought iron, although it may have been intended to weld on a steel edge.

The blacksmith did not have sole call on these tools, and some of the smaller chisels may have been used by craftsmen in other metals, particularly by bronze-founders for trimming risers and flashes off castings. Cold chisels are also used by masons, but on the whole their chisels tend to be longer and stouter than the smiths' and have flaring blades.

Cold chisels

The cold chisel is today short and thick, often just long enough to be held in a clenched hand and having a relatively sharp edge to enable it to cut cold metal. **A38–42** are all incomplete, **A38** and **A40** having burred heads but lacking cutting edges, and the remainder vice versa.

Hot chisels

Hot chisels, unless held with a wire loop, must be long enough to keep the hand away from the heat of the job and slender enough to be driven into the soft, hot metal. The blade may be sharp or slightly rounded in section.

A43–51 vary considerably in size, a variation which reflects both the range of bar iron to be cut and objects to be forged. Most of the hot chisels are complete and retain expanded and sometimes burred heads, and metallurgical examination has shown **A50–51** to have steeled blade edges and wrought iron stems. **A43**, which is of wrought iron without a steel edge, may be a hot chisel at an intermediate stage of forging. Precision was needed when forging items such as locks and purse frames, and some of the smaller chisels may have been used in their manufacture.

Cold sets

Cold sets resemble cold chisels but are stouter. **A52–54**, all from the forge at Waltham Abbey, Essex, are variously incomplete, **A53** having a burred head and, like the others, no indication of an eye for a haft. All may have been rodded, namely held by an iron rod wrapped round the body a couple of times with enough left over to form a handle. Cold sets are today sometimes hafted, but the defect of the haft lies in its rigidity which, although giving better control, can severely jar the holder's arm or break when the tool is struck by a sledgehammer.

Hot sets

Hot sets, the equivalent of a hot chisel but with a face for striking and an axe-like blade, are capable of more precise work than cold sets and are now usually hafted. The hot set from the smithy floor at Goltho, Lincolnshire, **A55**, has a burred face and the asymmetrical blade shape suggests that it may be a reused axe blade fragment.

2.7 PUNCHES AND DRIFTS

Punches are used to make holes in hot iron and drifts to enlarge, open out or smooth the hole. Certain identification of punches and drifts is impossible, since a headless stout punch may resemble a slender drift. Punches are also used in woodworking to sink nail heads, and these cannot easily be distinguished from blacksmiths' punches and drifts.

Punches

Punches used by the blacksmith to make holes in hot iron can be round, rectangular or any other required shape, and unless rodded or hafted must be long enough to keep the hand away from the forging.

The majority of surviving punches, where sufficiently complete, have heads burred by hammering and stems tapering either to a flattened tip or to a point. **A56–69** are all of rectangular section with flattened tips while **A60–65** taper to points and are of rectangular or square section. **A61–62** are unusual in having a circular section to the upper, hand-held part of their stems. **A66–67** also taper to points but are of octagonal and circular section respectively. **A68** is also octagonal but lacks any taper to its rounded, flat tip, whilst **A69** resembles it but is incomplete.

Punches **A56–69** could have been hand-held, but **A70–73** must have been held by iron rods looped round their thickened stems. All have burred heads and none of their stems has any indication of an eye for a haft.

Particular jobs often required their own tool, and punches **A74–75** may both have punched nail-holes in horseshoes. Horseshoes contemporary with them all had countersunk nail-holes, that is nail-holes set within a rectangular recess, and they may have punched the actual hole through the countersinking, itself produced by a tool such as **A57**. **A74–75** may also, however, have been used to make holes in strap hinges and similar objects.

Drifts

Drifts are normally shorter and stouter than the punches used to make the holes that they are smoothing or enlarging, and they characteristically have a short taper to the head and a longer one to the tip, a shaping which allowed them to be driven right through the hole. **A76–85** are of square, rectangular and circular section at the tip, and vary considerably in size. The larger drifts **A76–77** may have been used on such objects as hammer heads and picks.

2.8 FULLERS

Fullers are used by the blacksmith for making shoulders before drawing down, and for drawing iron in a particular direction. Small hand-held fullers resemble chisels and sets but have rounded noses; larger fullers are rodded. **A86** may be a fuller, which would today be used in conjunction with a bottom fuller set in the anvil.

2.9 MANDRELS

Two Shene inventories, for 1444 and 1473, mention mandrels (Salzman 1967, 348). The earlier records '5 mandrels, 6 iron bolsters specially made for 6 mandrels, ... 4 mandrels for hinges', and the later 'a round iron mandrel, 4 square iron mandrels for making hinges'.

Modern floor mandrels take the form of cones which can stand up to 1.37m (4½ ft) high and are used for forming hub bands, rings, hoops, etc. Hand mandrels are essentially small bars of iron, sometimes tapering and of round or rectangular section, which in use either rested on the face or edge of the anvil and were used for forging small rings and collars and for bending iron. The size and shape of the hand mandrel is determined by that of the object being forged, and the circular section mandrels may substitute for or complement the beak of an anvil. **A87–90** are possible hand mandrels, two with whittle tangs for insertion in a handle, two with riveted tangs. **A87–88** have tapering, circular-sectioned arms, suitable, amongst other objects, for forging small circular hose and shoe buckles. **A89–90** have straight, rectangular-sectioned arms. It must be emphasized that the identification of **A87–90** as mandrels is not certain.

2.10 NAIL-HEADING TOOL

The bolsters mentioned in connection with the mandrels in the Shene inventory were iron plates with holes in them which were placed under the iron being punched. **A91** is probably too slight to be a bolster, but it may be a nail-heading tool equivalent to the '3 nailtol' of the 1363 Rochester inventory or '2 iron naile tooles' of the 1473 Shene inventory (Salzman 1967, 347–348). In use the tapered shank of the nail was dropped into the appropriate hole in the tool, with the smaller opening uppermost, and the head formed by hammering.

2.11 FILES

Metalworkers, farriers and carpenters all used files, but the difference between them lies in the form of the teeth, the woodworkers' file having coarser teeth than the metalworkers' to prevent it becoming clogged with dust. The file was an important finishing tool for the metalworker, who used it to remove rough edges, smooth out casting marks and give the final shaping to an object. It was especially useful for the delicate work of such craftsmen as the locksmith, but it must have been universally used, farriers employing it for example to sharpen their knives and smooth newly forged horseshoes. Such a variety of tasks will have required files of varying size and cross section, as modern examples testify, but few medieval examples survive. **A92** is flat with diagonally cut teeth.

2.12 FIRE TOOLS

The medieval smithies at Waltham Abbey and Goltho both produced coal used to fuel the blacksmith's hearth, but neither produced the poker, rake or shovel used to manage it.

Pokers are used to loosen the fire and stir the fuel, letting out gases and allowing the bellows to operate more efficiently. Modern pokers take the form of a long iron rod, tapering to the tip from a simple loop handle but **A93**, from one of the two hearths in the smithy at Huish, has a socket evidently for a wooden handle.

Modern rakes with L-shaped ends and loop handles may double as pokers, but more characteristically they have a split end and down-turned arms. They are used to loosen the fuel, gather it together and separate out clinker. No medieval example is known.

Some of the medieval spades and shovels with iron-shod blades (**F6–17**) may have been used by blacksmiths to replenish fuel or remove ashes, since they resemble one shown in a 14th-century illumination (Figure 2.2) resting against the opening of a coal store serving a blacksmith's hearth. Shovels with entirely iron blades will have been more appropriate for some uses, but they are infrequent medieval finds. **F18** was probably used to fuel a glass kiln.

A18 TONGS
South Witham, Lincolnshire.
1137–85 to c1220.
Incomplete arm from small pair of tongs with down-turned jaws. L 64mm.
Goodall 2002, 100, fig 7.3, no. 28.

A19 TONGS
Criccieth Castle, Gwynedd.
Site c1230–1404.
Tongs with flat, straight jaws and long handles with flattened ends. L 269mm.
O'Neil 1944–45, 42. National Museum of Wales, Cardiff 41.246.1.

A20 TONGS
Deganwy Castle, Gwynedd.
Unstratified in bailey of castle of 1245–63, on site with earlier occupation. Found with blacksmith's equipment and iron slag. Gently curved jaws, handles broken. L 251mm.
Excavated by W Greenhalgh. For site see Alcock 1967.

A21 TONGS
Gloucester, Gloucestershire.
Late 12th/13th century.
Narrow, straight jaws, handles broken.
L 212mm.
Excavated by H Hurst.

A22 TONGS
Weoley Castle, West Midlands.
Around 1270–1600.
Tapering, straight jaws, broken handles.
L 240mm.
Taylor 1974. For site see Oswald 1962. Birmingham City Museum, WC366.

A23 TONGS
Old Sarum, Wiltshire.
Principally medieval, to 14th century.
Gently curved jaws, knobbed end to one handle, other broken. L 198mm.
Salisbury and South Wiltshire Museum, O.S.D2.

A24 TONGS
Netherton, Hampshire.
Mid 14th century.
Gently curved jaws, handles with knobbed ends. L 146mm.
Goodall 1990-27.

A25 TONGS
Winchester, Hampshire.
12th, ?13th century.
Both arms broken. L 78mm.
Goodall 1990-3, fig 41, no. 40.

A26 PINCERS
Denny Abbey, Cambridgeshire.
On floor of period 1169–1308, ? in use to 1539.
Pincers with broad jaws. Longer handle, has knobbed terminal, other hooked and broken.
L 254mm.
Goodall et al 1980, no. 9.

A27 PINCERS
Norwich, Norfolk.
In 1507 fire deposit.
Pincers with broad, curved jaws and plain straight handles.
L 290mm.
Carter et al 1974–47, 47, pl 1.4.

METALWORKING TOOLS

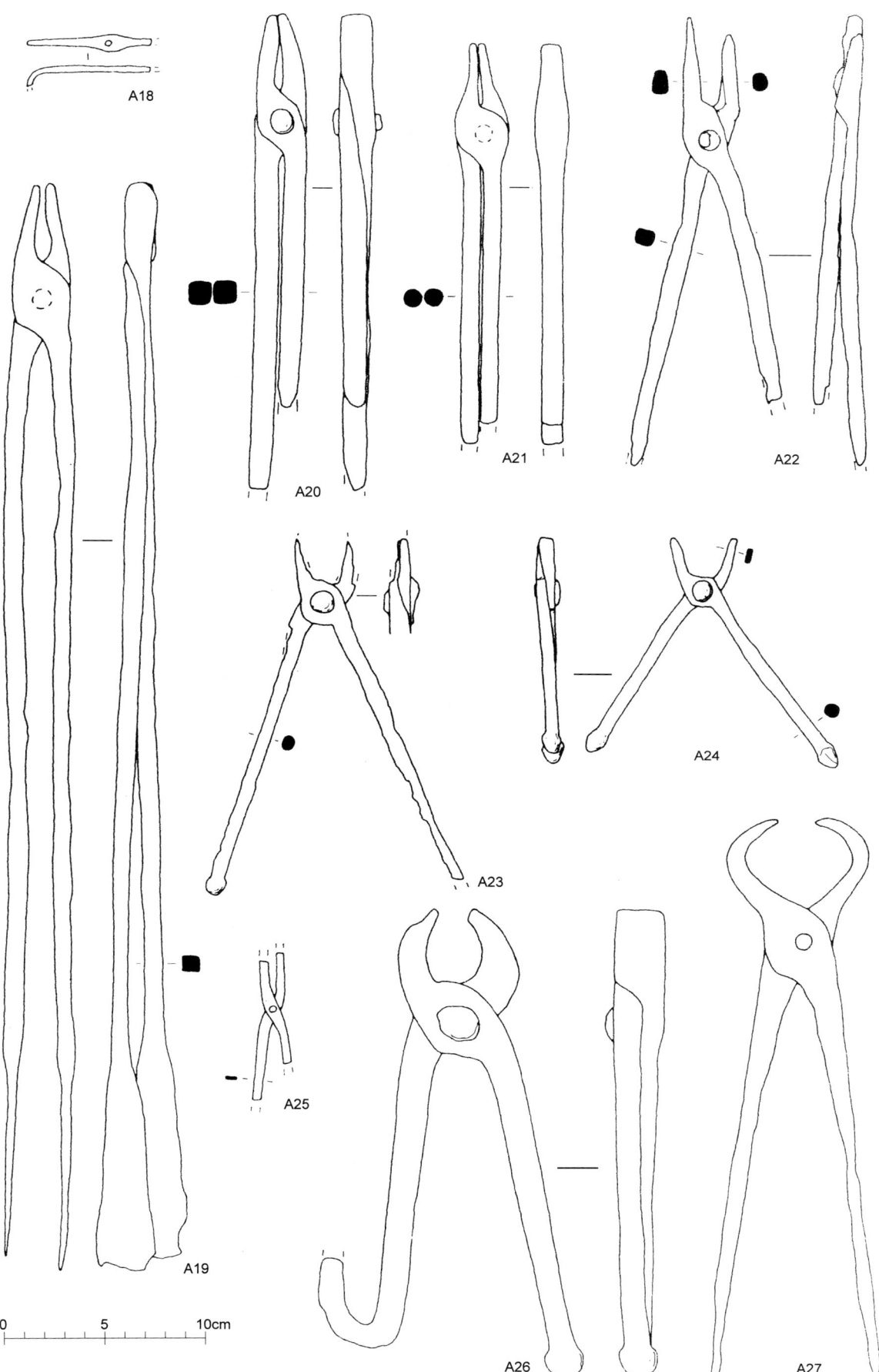

FIGURE 2.4
Metalworking tools: Tongs and pincers

A28 SLEDGEHAMMER
Deganwy Castle, Gwynedd.
Unstratified in bailey of castle of 1245–63, on site with earlier occupation. Found with blacksmith's equipment and iron slag. Double-faced hammer of octagonal section, expanded around the rectangular eye. L 157mm.
Excavated by W Greenhalgh. For site see Alcock 1967.

A29 SLEDGEHAMMER
Thetford, Norfolk.
11th century.
Cross-pane hammer of rectangular section with flat underside.
Cheek rises beside eye. L 121mm.
Goodall 1984.

A30 SLEDGEHAMMER
Castell-y-Bere, Gwynedd.
Site c1221–95.
Cross-pane hammer of rectangular section with flat underside. Cheek rises beside eye. L 221mm.
Butler 1974, 97, fig 9.15.

A31 SLEDGEHAMMER
Weoley Castle, West Midlands.
Around 1270–c1380.
Cross-pane hammer with rounded face and expansion round eye which retains part of wooden handle and securing nail. L 175mm.
Taylor 1974. For site see Oswald 1962.
Birmingham City Museum, WC361A.

A32 HAMMER
Old Sarum, Wiltshire.
Second half of the 11th century.
Cross-pane hammer of rounded section towards face, rectangular to pane. Fiddle-key horseshoe nail in eye. Cheek rises beside eye, flat underside. L 85mm.
Stone and Charlton 1935, 184, fig 3.1.

A33 HAMMER
Wintringham, Cambridgeshire.
Early 14th century.
Cross-pane hammer of octagonal section towards face, rectangular to pane.
Cheek rises beside eye, flat underside.
L 104mm.
Goodall 1977a, 257, fig 46.62.

A34 HAMMER
West Hartburn, Durham.
Site 13th to 16th century.
Cross-pane hammer, pane broken.
Expansion around square eye. L 105mm.
For site see Still and Pallister 1964; 1967.

A35 HAMMER
Winchester, Hampshire.
13th century.
Down-turned pane from cross-pane hammer. L 30mm.
Goodall 1990-8, fig 60, no. 401.

A36 HAMMER
Ellington, Cambridgeshire.
Second half 12th to second half 13th century.
Slender hammer of rectangular section with slight expansion around eye.
One long pointed arm, other short and blunt. L 48mm.
Goodall 1971, 68, fig 12.19

A37 SET HAMMER
Ospringe, Kent.
Around 1483–1550.
Burred head, rectangular eye for haft, oval convex face. L 111mm.
Goodall 1979c, 129, fig 130.1

A38 COLD CHISEL
Waltham Abbey, Essex.
Lowest silt in well dug c1300, filled in late 15th or early 16th century.
Burred head, broken rectangular-sectioned stem. L 204mm.
Goodall 1973, 170, fig 11.16.

A39 COLD CHISEL
Waltham Abbey, Essex.
16th century.
Broken rectangular-sectioned stem. L 201mm.
Goodall 1973a, 170, fig 11.17.

A40 COLD CHISEL
Deganwy Castle, Gwynedd.
Unstratified in bailey of castle of 1245–63, on site with earlier occupation. Found with blacksmith's equipment and iron slag.
Burred head, broken rounded rectangular stem. L 55mm.
Excavated by W Greenhalgh. For site see Alcock 1967.

A41 COLD CHISEL
Theodoric's Hermitage, West Glamorgan.
Site 13th–15th century.
Broken stem with blade. L 86mm.
National Museum of Wales, Cardiff, 49.140.23.

A42 COLD CHISEL
Theodoric's Hermitage, West Glamorgan.
Site 13th–15th century.
Broken stem with blade. L 103mm.
National Museum of Wales, Cardiff, 49.140.23.

A43 HOT CHISEL
Winchester, Hampshire.
Mid to late ?13th century.
Enlarged head, waisted rectangular-sectioned stem. Broadening to blade.
Blade found to consist of ferrite and slag.
L 176mm.
Goodall 1990-3, fig 41, no. 41.

A44 HOT CHISEL
Stonar, Kent.
Around 1275–1330.
Expanded head, rectangular-sectioned stem.
L 166mm.
Excavated by N Macpherson-Grant.

A45 HOT CHISEL
Thetford, Norfolk.
?11th century.
Expanded head, rectangular-sectioned stem.
L 104mm.
Goodall 1984.

A46 HOT CHISEL
Northampton.
Later 15th century.
Burred head, rectangular-sectioned stem.
L 82mm.
Goodall et al 1979, 273, fig 119.63.

A47 HOT CHISEL
Goltho, Lincolnshire.
Unstratified on croft occupied from late Saxon period to late 14th or early 15th century.
Burred head, octagonal-sectioned stem.
L 80mm.
Goodall 1975a, 87, fig 41.89.

A48 HOT CHISEL
South Cadbury, Somerset.
11th–12th century.
Burred head, rectangular-sectioned stem.
L 72mm.
Alcock 1995.

A49 HOT CHISEL
Southampton, Hampshire.
11th–12th century.
Burred head, rectangular-sectioned stem.
L 73mm.
Harvey 1975b, 276, fig 250.1971.

METALWORKING TOOLS

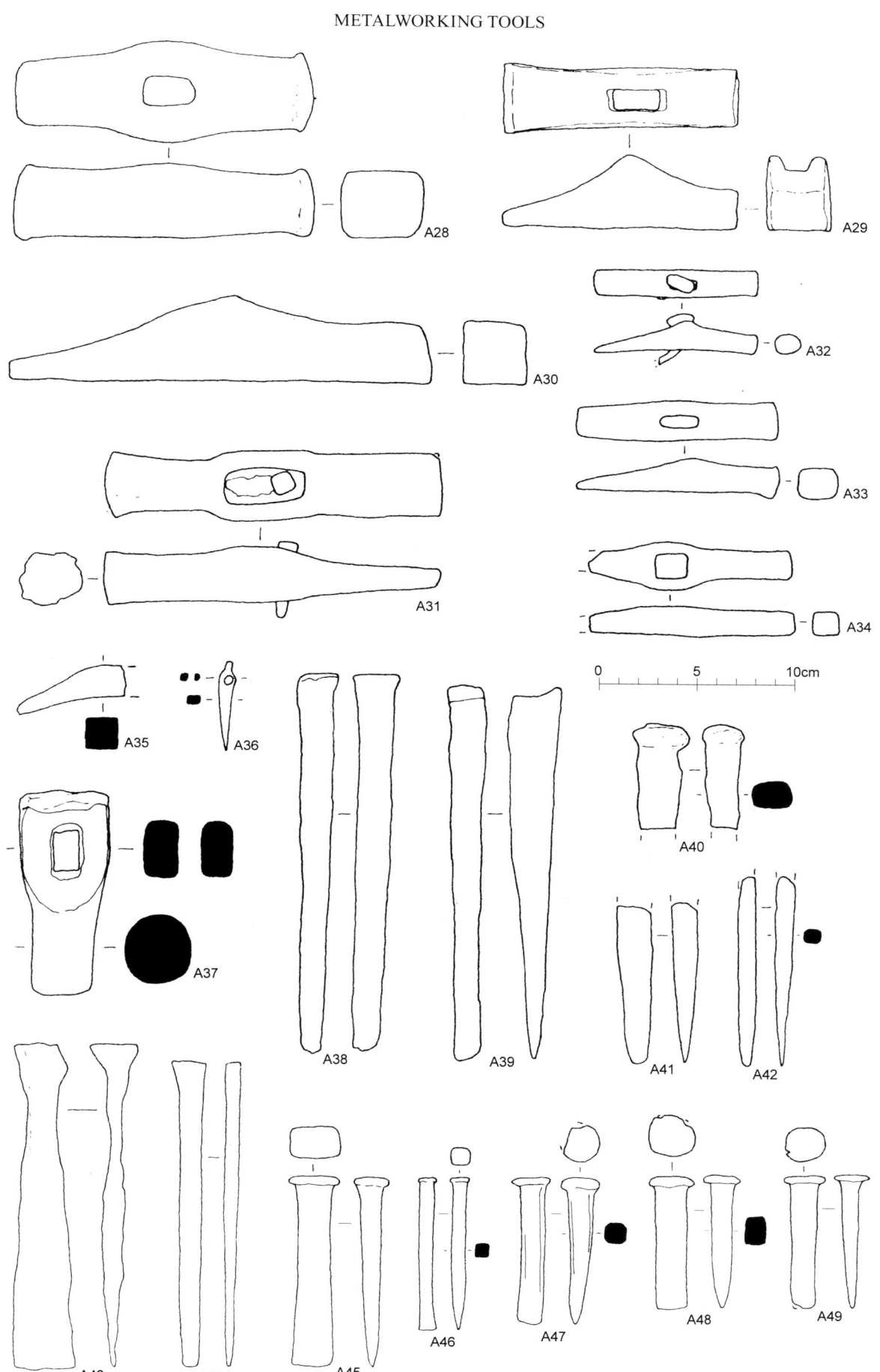

FIGURE 2.5
Metalworking tools: Hammers, cold chisels and hot chisels

A50 HOT CHISEL
Winchester, Hampshire.
16th to 17th century.
Burred head, rectangular-sectioned wrought iron stem, steel edge. L 62mm.
Goodall 1990-3, fig 41, no. 43.

A51 HOT CHISEL
Winchester, Hampshire.
Early 12th century.
Burred head, rectangular-sectioned wrought iron stem, steel edge. L 45mm.
Goodall 1990-3, fig 41, no. 42.

A52 COLD SET
Waltham Abbey, Essex.
12th–13th century.
Broken, octagonal-sectioned stem. L 156mm.
Goodall 1973a, 170, fig 11.14.

A53 COLD SET
Waltham Abbey, Essex.
With derived 12th, 13th century pottery.
Burred head, broken rounded-sectioned stem. L 116mm.
Goodall 1973a, 170, fig 11.17.

A54 COLD SET
Waltham Abbey, Essex.
Late 13th, early 14th century.
Broken, octagonal-sectioned stem.
L 111mm.
Goodall 1973a, 170, fig 11.13.

A55 HOT SET
Goltho, Lincolnshire.
Late 14th to early 15th century. From floor of smithy.
Burred head, asymmetrically shaped blade of rectangular section. L 77mm.
Goodall 1975a, 87, fig 41.90.

A56 PUNCH
Hen Blas, Clwyd.
Probably 13th century.
Rectangular section, tip damaged. L 148mm.
Leach 1960, 23, fig 13.13.

A57 PUNCH
Kettleby Thorpe, Lincolnshire.
14th to early 15th century.
Burred head, rectangular-sectioned stem.
L 104mm.
Goodall 1974a, 33, fig 18.12.

A58 PUNCH
Winchester, Hampshire.
Late 13th century.
Rectangular section. L 102mm.
Goodall 1990-3, fig 41, no. 45.

A59 PUNCH
Hen Caerwys, Clwyd.
Around 1450–1520.
Broken, rectangular-sectioned stem. L 88mm.
Excavated by G B Leach.

A60 PUNCH
Loughor Castle, West Glamorgan.
Site c1106 to late 13th century.
Burred head, rectangular-sectioned stem. L 204mm.
Excavated by J M Lewis.

A61 PUNCH
Hen Blas, Clwyd.
12th–14th century.
Circular-sectioned stem becoming rect-angular. L 132mm.
Leach 1960, 23, fig 13.15.

A62 PUNCH
Hen Blas, Clwyd.
12th–14th century.
Circular-sectioned stem becoming rect-angular. L 112mm.
Leach 1960, 23, fig 13.16.

A63 PUNCH
Dyserth Castle, Clwyd.
Site 1241–63.
Broken, rectangular-sectioned stem. L 61mm.
Glenn 1915.

A64 PUNCH
Winchester, Hampshire.
12th century.
Rectangular-sectioned stem. Mostly ferrite and slag. L 58mm.
Goodall 1990-3, fig 41, no. 44.

A65 PUNCH
Dyserth Castle, Clwyd.
Site 1241–63.
Rectangular-sectioned stem. L 57mm.
Glenn 1915.

A66 PUNCH
Waltham Abbey, Essex.
Lowest silt in well dug c1300, filled in late 15th, early 16th century.
Burred head, octagonal-sectioned stem tapering to oval tip. L 102mm.
Goodall 1973a, 170, fig 11.19.

A67 PUNCH
Gomeldon, Wiltshire.
13th–14th century.
Burred head, circular-sectioned stem.
L 73mm.
Musty and Algar 1986.

A68 PUNCH
Northolt Manor, Greater London.
1300–1350 with 13th-century residual material.
Burred head, octagonal-sectioned stem, rounded tip. L 199mm.
Excavated by J G Hurst.

A69 PUNCH
Gomeldon, Wiltshire.
13th–14th century.
Burred head, square-sectioned stem.
L 101mm.
Musty and Algar 1986.

A70 PUNCH
Dyserth Castle, Clwyd.
Site 1241–63.
Burred head, octagonal-sectioned stem becoming rectangular. L 83mm.
Glenn 1915.

A71 PUNCH
Goltho, Lincolnshire.
Croft A: late Saxon to late 14th or early 15th century.
Burred head, rectangular-sectioned stem slightly waisted below head. L 92mm.
Goodall 1975a, 87, fig 41.88.

A72 PUNCH
Northampton.
Later 14th–15th century.
Burred head, rectangular-sectioned stem.
L 89mm.
Goodall 1979b, 71, fig 17.18.

A73 PUNCH
Waltham Abbey, Essex.
12th–16th century.
Burred head, rectangular-sectioned stem.
L 108mm.
Goodall 1973a, 170, fig 11.20.

A74 PUNCH
Glastonbury Tor, Somerset.
Probably 10th–11th century.
Rectangular-sectioned stem, shaped tip.
L 141mm.
Rahtz 1970, 53, fig 23.8.

A75 PUNCH
Thetford, Norfolk.
11th century.
Rectangular-sectioned stem, tapering to head and shaped tip. L 98mm.
Goodall 1984.

METALWORKING TOOLS

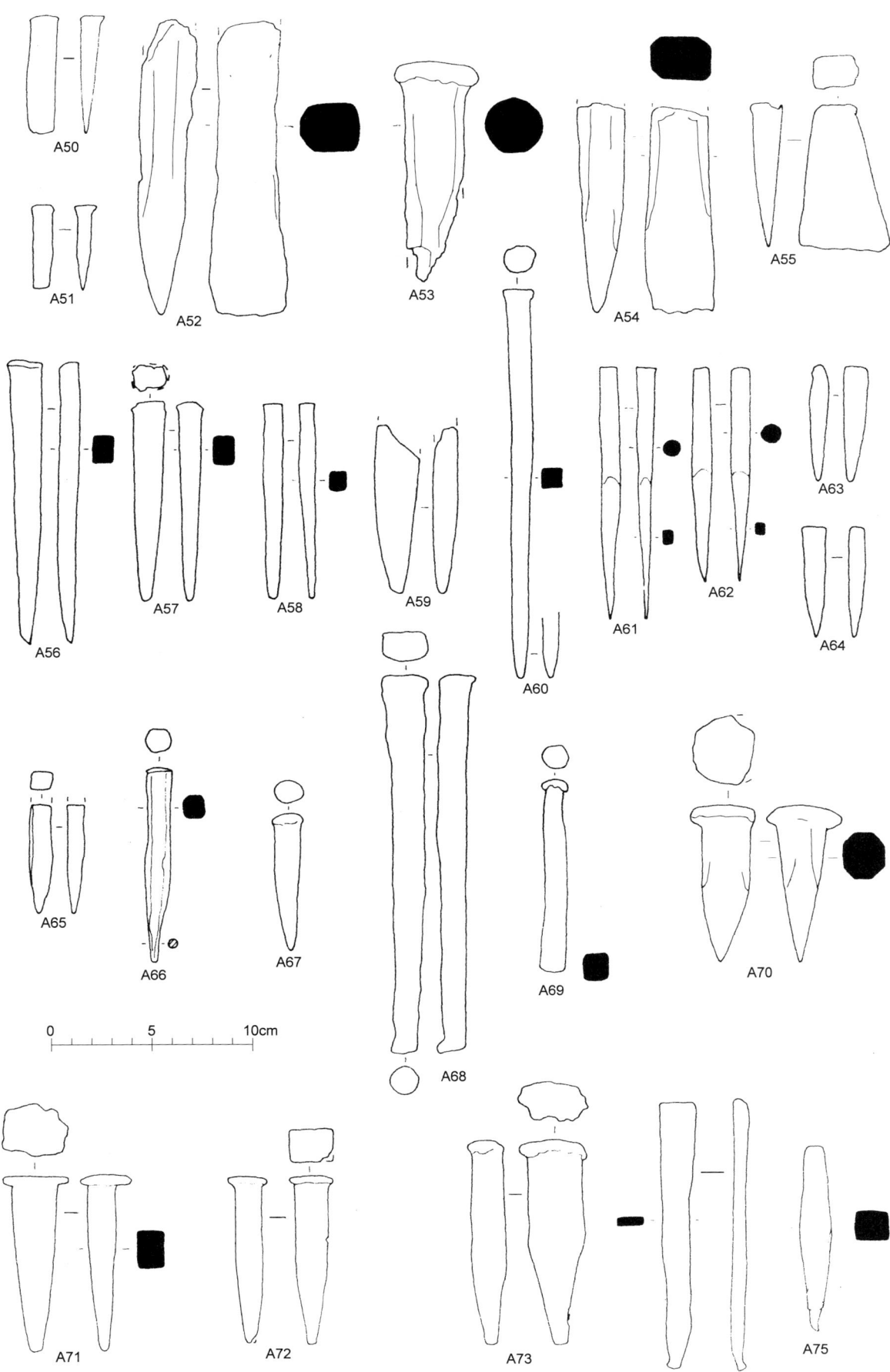

FIGURE 2.6
Metalworking tools: Hot chisels, cold and hot sets, and punches

A76 DRIFT
Castell-y-Bere, Gwynedd.
Site c1221–95.
Damaged rounded-sectioned head becoming rectangular. L 182mm.
Butler 1974, 97, fig 8.12.

A77 DRIFT
Weoley Castle, West Midlands.
Around 1270–c1380.
Rounded-sectioned head becoming square. L 163mm.
Taylor 1974; Oswald 1962, 25.

A78 DRIFT
Waltham Abbey, Essex.
16th century.
Circular-sectioned stem becoming square. L 103mm.
Goodall 1973a, 170, fig 11.18.

A79 DRIFT
Alsted, Surrey.
Around 1270–1400. From ironworking site.
Rounded-sectioned stem becoming rect-angular at blade. L 85mm.
Goodall 1976a, 56, fig 35.38.

A80 DRIFT
Cambokeels, Durham.
Later 14th to early 16th century.
Rectangular-sectioned stem. L 84mm.
Bowes Museum, Barnard Castle. For site see Hildyard and Charlton 1947; Hildyard 1949.

A81 DRIFT
Hen Caerwys, Clwyd.
Around 1450–1520.
Rectangular-sectioned stem. L 81mm.
Excavated by G B Leach.

A82 DRIFT
Southampton, Hampshire.
12th century.
Rectangular-sectioned stem. L 75mm.
Harvey 1975b, 277, fig 250.1974.

A83 DRIFT
Seacourt, Oxfordshire.
Pre-1400.
Broken, rectangular-sectioned stem. L 62mm.
Biddle 1961–62, 177, fig 30.2, scale 1:4, not 1:3.

A84 DRIFT
Bramber Castle, West Sussex.
14th century. From workshop area in M1.
Rectangular-sectioned stem, circular at tip. L 70mm.
Barton and Holden 1977, 64, fig 20.2.

A85 DRIFT
Bayham Abbey, East Sussex.
Late 15th, early 16th century.
Rectangular-sectioned stem. L 68mm.
For site see Streeten 1983.

A86 FULLER (?)
Kilton Castle, Cleveland.
15th century.
Burred head, shaped rectangular-sectioned body. L 100mm.
Excavated by F A Aberg.

A87 MANDREL (?)
Dyserth Castle, Clwyd.
Site 1241–63.
Tapering circular-sectioned body, whittle tang. L 126mm.
Glenn 1915. Natural Museum, Wales, Cardiff, 15-248/14.

A88 MANDREL (?)
Dyserth Castle, Clwyd.
Site 1241–63.
Tapering circular-sectioned body, whittle tang. L 71mm.
Glenn 1915. Natural Museum, Wales, Cardiff, 15-248/21

A89 MANDREL (?)
Writtle, Essex.
Around 1306–c1425.
Rectangular-sectioned arm with double-riveted tang. L 166mm.
Rahtz 1969b, 87, fig 48.71.

A90 MANDREL (?)
Weoley Castle, West Midlands.
Site c1270–1600.
Rectangular-sectioned arm with double-riveted tang. L 124mm.
Birmingham City Museum, 18341. For site see Oswald 1962.

A91 NAIL-HEADING TOOL (?)
Cambokeels, Durham.
Later 14th to early 15th century.
Broken strip with three differently sized countersunk holes. L 82mm.
Hildyard 1949, 199, fig 3.18.

A92 FILE
Manor of the More, Rickmansworth, Hertfordshire.
1520–30.
Flat file with diagonally cut teeth and whittle tang, incomplete. L 136mm.
Biddle *et al* 1959, 184, fig 19.36.

A93 POKER
Huish, Wiltshire.
From hearth in 14th to mid 15th century smithy.
Roughly circular-sectioned poker, tip lost, socket damaged. L 290mm.
Shortt 1972, 120, fig 4.

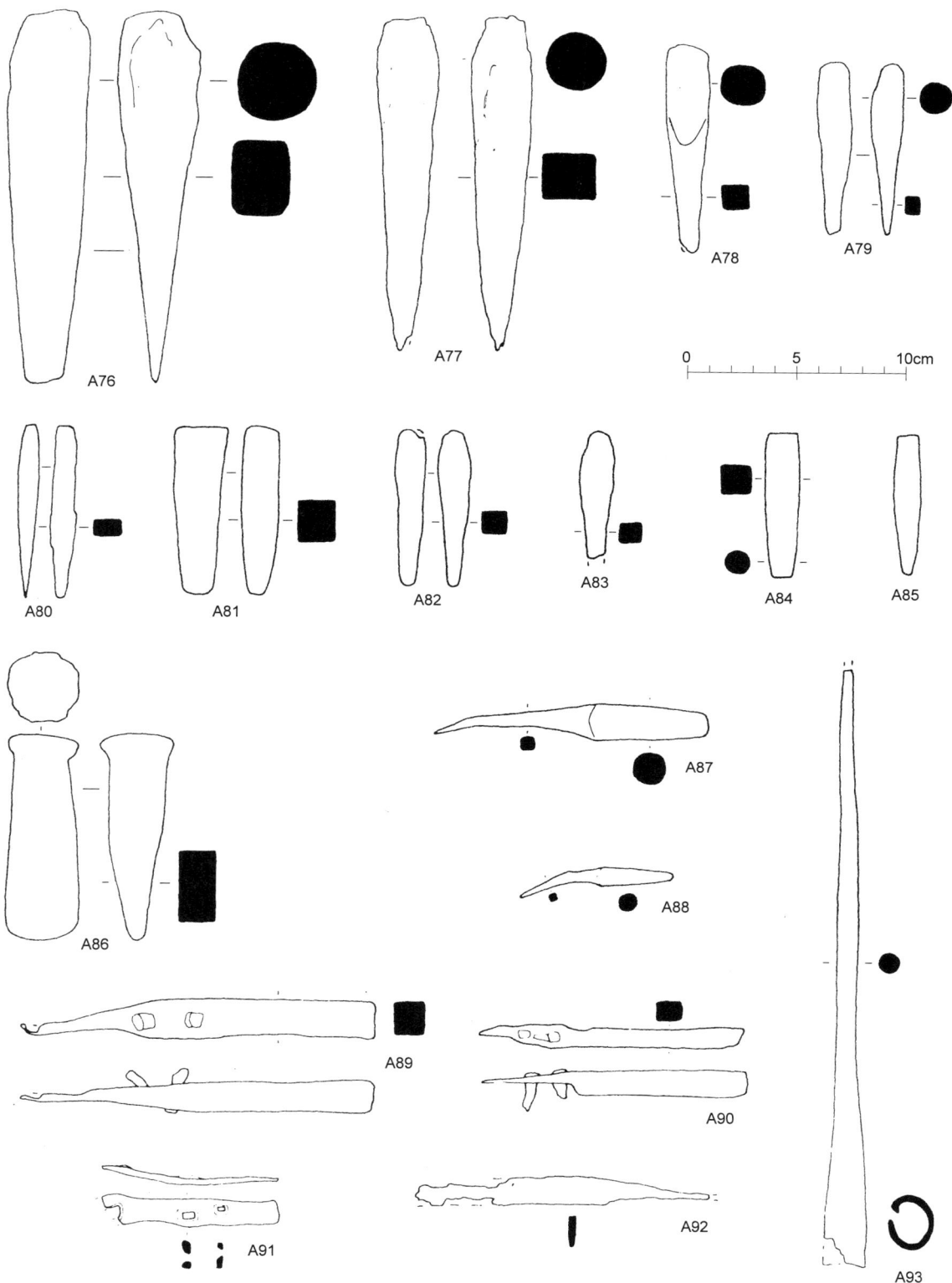

FIGURE 2.7
Metalworking tools: Drifts, fuller, mandrels, nail-heading tool, file, and poker

3
WOODWORKING TOOLS

Woodworking was one of the most important crafts of the medieval period, embracing such trades as those of the carpenter, wheelright, millwright, and shipwright. Wooden building remained the rule during the medieval period, just as it had before, and it is of interest that even in the royal establishment as late as 1344 there were 138 carpenters against only 24 masons (Harvey 1975a, 123).

Tools used in the woodworking and allied trades range from those used for felling, splitting and sawing timber to those used for shaping, fitting and even dismantling it.

3.1 AXES

The axe, the woodworker's basic tool, was used for felling trees, splitting and trimming trunks and branches, and smoothing and dressing a range of timbers from posts and planks to spokes. Modern crafts have, or had, specialised axes which feature in trade catalogues (Salaman 1975, 46–66), but the diversity of forms which these demonstrate must be comparatively modern. Medieval axes, which must have been used for as many purposes, are not as infinitely varied and can be divided into six main types, excluding battle-axes. Types 1–6 (Figure 3.1) may be correlated with Ward Perkins' classification (1967, M55–63) as follows:

1, 2 = I
3 = III
4 = II
5 = IVB
6 = IVA

The named parts of the axe are shown in Figure 3.2. Medieval woodworking axes, including those used for dressing planks, generally have blades with a sharpening bevel on both sides of the cutting edge, and few have fully developed sockets. Stamped marks are found on only one axe, and that is from a late Saxon to 17th-century context, and no axe has any decoration on the blade. The illustrated axes in the *London Museum Medieval Catalogue* undoubtedly incorporate a significant number of post-medieval axes (Ward Perkins 1967).

Type 1

The woodman's axe (Type 1), a sturdy tool with a thick, heavy blade, was mounted in a long handle and used for felling trees and cutting and splitting trunks in the manner shown in the Bayeux Tapestry (Stenton 1957, 16, pl 38). The known medieval examples **B1–10** have flaring symmetrical blades and lugs, which are generally rounded, above and below the eye, to enable the handle to be securely hafted. Most of these axes, when sufficiently complete, have polls or thickened butts which make them steadier to handle and easier to direct, and also allowed them to be used as hammers or be hammered themselves. A Bible of *c*1100 (Ward Perkins 1967, 56) shows such an axe being used with a heavy mallet to split a log. Felling axes seem also to have been used for trimming logs, the carpenter cutting such notches in the log as a guideline for trimming and then chopping out larger V-shaped cuts before working along the side of the plank, cutting deeply and splitting off wood close to the line. Two 16th-century illustrations by Rodler (Salzman 1967, 196) and Jost Amman (Rifkin 1973, 95; Goodman 1964, 30) show this method in use, and each also shows a bearded axe lying in wait for subsequent close trimming and smoothing.

Type 2

Axes of Type 2 have asymmetrically flaring blades with

down-turned rear edges, the larger examples of which may have been used as felling axes in the manner of Type 1 axes. In general, however, they are slighter in construction and lack the poll of the other axes, and are likely to have been used as hatchets for lopping and chopping wood. The larger axes **B13–14** have lugs below the eyes, but the smaller axes **B11–12** are plain.

Axes **B12–14** show the usual method of forging axes by wrapping the iron around the eye and hammer-welding it against the back of the blade.

Type 3

Type 3 axes have long, narrow rectangular blades attached to sockets by slender shanks, and the Bayeux Tapestry (Stenton 1957, 169, pls 38, VII) shows such axes being used by carpenters dressing planks and shipwrights trimming them. This type of axe, known from a number of pre-Conquest sites, is one of the most common types of axe shown in medieval representations of carpentry, appearing as late as the 14th century (Ward Perkins 1967, 58). The incomplete blade and shank fragment **B15** is, however, the only firmly dated medieval example.

Type 4

Axes with triangular-shaped blades constitute Type 4, and were probably used for trimming and dressing timber. The fore-edges of **B16** and **B18** are straight and rise in line with the eye, but that of **B17** is slightly curved.

Type 5

Type 5 axes have bearded blades with pointed heels set below the base of the eye or socket. These axes were probably used for trimming, a job for which their broad blades are well suited. The complete axes **B19–21** all have polls and lugged eyes, the poll being particularly suitable for heavy hammering, including the pounding together of joints in timber-framed buildings. **B22** is an incomplete blade fragment.

Type 6

Type 6 axes have bearded blades with flat heels set below the base of the eye or socket. **B23–25** conform to the type of side-dressing axe shown in the 16th-century illustrations noted above. The axes were lying around waiting to be used for trimming once the main waste wood had been removed by stouter axes. **B23–24** have sockets, and although **B25** has the more usual medieval lugged eye, it may nevertheless be of post-medieval date. It is unusual in having its blade set to one side, viewed from above.

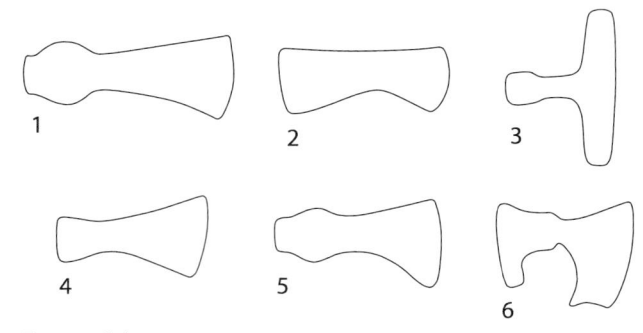

FIGURE 3.1
Types of medieval axe

Axe fragments

B26–27 are blade fragments retaining part of the cutting edge, each however too incomplete to classify.

3.2 ADZES

Adzes, which differ from axes by having their blades set at right angles to the handle, are used for removing heavy waste, levelling, shaping or trimming the surfaces of timber. There are few actual medieval examples, but variation in blade forms amongst those that survive reflects the range of jobs they had to perform. The broad blade of **B28** is suitable for adzing planks, but more specialised adzing will have been carried out by **B29–30** which have narrow, slightly flaring blades. The slender poll of these latter adzes was used to drive in nails which could not be removed from timber but which had to be driven in sufficiently to be cleared by the adze blade. Salzman (1967, 342) notes that during work at Restormel Castle in 1343 6d was spent on 'an ades for smoothing old timber, because the timber is so full of nails that the carpenters would not set their own tools to it', and more recently Mercer (1968, 92–93) records that early 20th-century shipbuilders also used the peg-shaped hammer polls of their adzes to sink the nails below adze level. It is of interest that the shipwright in the Bayeux Tapestry (Stenton 1957, 169, pls 38, VII) appears to be using a short-handled adze with broad blade and poll.

Adzes **B29–30** may just be narrow enough to have been used for cutting mortices, which is what **B31** with its simple eye and narrow, parallel-sided blade must have been used for. Mortices were often started with augers and chisels, but adzes are likely to have been used for those in the major posts of timber-framed buildings, and for long chase mortices.

3.3 SLICES

The slice is a long, broad chisel with a socketed handle which was driven by hand pressure rather than by a mallet. The tool is used with a planing and pushing action

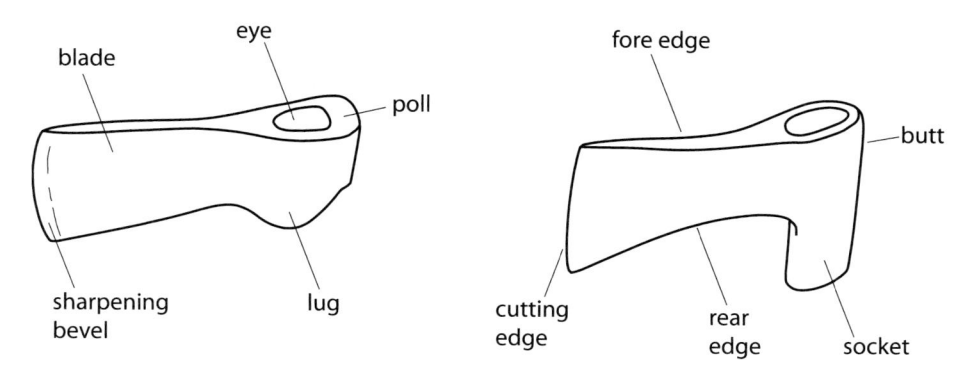

FIGURE 3.2
Axes: Terminology

to pare-off shavings, and is employed by the shipwright for fairing and removing waste from the deck and elsewhere, and especially from places where the adze cannot reach. It also has a more general application for cleaning up the sides of large mortices in construction work and for levelling surfaces.

The modern slice (Salaman 1975, 143–144; McGrail 1977, 62–63) has a blade 50–100mm in breadth and up to 760mm in overall length. The deep socket, frequently flanged on the older tools, has a flat lower face set in line with the back of the blade in order to keep the hand clear when paring a flat surface. **B32–33** have blades which are characteristically bevelled only on the upper face, **B33** having a worn blade and retaining part of its wooden handle. Both these slices come from contexts more appropriate to general carpenters' tools than those of shipwrights.

3.4 CHISELS

Woodworking chisels with narrow rectangular blades sharpened at one end and hafted at the other are used for edging, notching, hollowing and morticing wood, and for carving it. They are subdivided according to the shape and thickness of the blade, which determined the type of work undertaken, and the main groups are firmer, paring, morticing, and carving chisels.

Firmer chisels are general purpose tools with a flat blade with parallel sides strong enough to be struck with a mallet. They are used to roughly side-cut wood along a scribed line prior to finer paring as well as to cut out mortices already begun with an auger. Modern firmer chisels often have a single bevel to the cutting edge combined with bevelled edges for better clearance when working in corners (Salaman 1975, 139) but **B34**, probably a firmer chisel, has a plain blade with a double bevelled cutting edge.

Paring chisels, which cannot always be distinguished from firmer chisels, generally have long, thin, lighter blades and are used with shoulder or hand pressure rather than with mallets. In woodworking they followed the firmer chisel, smoothing its rough cuts and being used for fine paring and trimming. **B35**, probably a paring chisel, has a plain blade with a double bevelled cutting edge.

Morticing chisels used with mallets have stout blades with a sharp bevel to the cutting edge. These chisels, as their name implies, were used to cut mortices and the like direct from the wood without the preliminary augering associated with the use of firmer chisels on the larger mortices. **B36** is an incomplete morticing chisel with a single bevelled cutting edge, and **B37–38** are similar incomplete blades.

B39, apparently with a blade at either end, may be a carver's tool. The flaring blade resembles the modern spade chisel used in carving during lighter finishing operations (Salaman 1975, 126, fig 205m).

3.5 GOUGES

Gouges are similar to chisels but have hollow cross-sectioned blades for cutting curved surfaces. No medieval gouge is yet known.

3.6 AUGER BITS

Augers with iron bits set in transverse wooden handles were used to bore holes in wood. Timber-framed buildings, roof trusses, and other timber constructions including smaller items such as furniture and panelling required holes for wooden pegs, and augers were also used to start cutting mortices which were then finished with firmer chisels. Small bits were used for such purposes as boring holes in knife and tool handles for the insertion of whittle tangs. Medieval documents (Salzman 1967, 345) record 'an iron augur for making holes in bemes' at Westminster in 1443, and a 'waternawger' in 1404 and a 'wateravger' in 1419, both needed for work at London Bridge. Representations of augers show straight and winged handles being worked with two hands, as well as breast augers which were given additional force by pressing the chest on a pad set on top of the shank. Salzman (1967, 345) notes that breast augers are mentioned in ship-building accounts but apparently not in ordinary building accounts, and the Bayeux Tapestry (Stenton 1957, 169, pls 38, VIII) clearly shows one in use during the construction of a ship, as does a medieval manuscript illustrated by Mercer (1968, fig 162). Larger augers with tapering blades were used by wheelwrights to hollow the inside of the felloes of wheels, as an illustration by Jost Amman shows (Rifkin 1973, 97). In common with many other medieval tools, the blades of auger bits must often have been steeled. The London Bridge accounts record the payment of 4d in 1382 'for steeling a nauegore' (Salzman 1967, 345).

Auger bits are of three main types: spoon bit, gouge bit and twist bit, each with a shank and terminal which fitted into a wooden handle. The terminals are lanceolate, tapered or eyed, the latter as yet only represented in manuscript illuminations. The lanceolate and tapered terminals seem to have fitted loosely into rectangular holes in the wooden handles, since none shows signs of having been pinned or riveted in position, or having had a clenched tip. The lanceolate terminal, tapering in side view from a broadened base, is the most common as well as the most practical form since it gave plenty of leverage to the handle. The tapering terminal, rather like that of an auger would cause the edges of the head to rub the socket in the handle, eventually rounding it and preventing the bit turning fully and cutting efficiently.

Blanks for auger bits

The forge at Waltham Abbey in Essex produced six blanks for auger bits, a typical example **B40** having a lanceolate terminal yet to be drawn out and a shank awaiting the blade. The blank is probably of wrought iron to which a steeled blade would have been forged.

Spoon bits

Spoon bits are the most common type of auger bit to be found, surviving in greater numbers and with a wider size range than either gouge or twist bits. The blades have a gouge-shaped body with a spoon-like nose, both the edges and nose being sharpened. The spoon bit cut chiefly downwards, ceasing to cut sideways as soon as the maximum width of the blade was reached. Most blades have parallel edges, although a number have a slight taper. The spoon bit is efficient since the sharpened edges enabled it to cut when rotated in either direction, and the sharpened nose cut the centre of the hole, leaving no core.

Medieval spoon bits have been classified according to terminal form and catalogued in increasing order of size.

Type 1

Spoon bits with lanceolate terminals **B41–68** range in length from 77mm to 415mm, and their blades in width from 4mm to 27mm. The terminals are generally an elongated lozenge shape in front view, the elongation sometimes being extreme, and the shanks are generally rectangular or octagonal in section. The smaller bits have blades which are proportionately longer in relation to the length of the shank than the larger bits partly as a consequence of their size and partly because the upper part of the blade held the shavings during use, the nose allowing them to be withdrawn from the whole which was thus kept clean. The narrowest blades, particularly those of **B41**, **B44**, **B48–49**, **B51–52** and **B57**, are suitable for boring holes in knife handles whereas the widest, **B62**, **B64**, **B67–68**, are better suited for starting mortices and drilling peg-holes for major structural timbers.

Type 2

B69–71, the few spoon bits with tapering terminals, grade in size from 95mm to 247mm in length, their blades from 6mm to 14mm in width. The shanks are again rectangular or octagonal.

Type 3

Representations of augers not infrequently show wooden handles set through the eyed terminal of a spoon bit. Rodler's illustration of 1531 (Salzman 1967, 196) shows just such a spoon bit in the foreground. No actual medieval example is yet known, but earlier and later examples of the type all seem to be larger bits used for building or boat construction. The eye would allow considerable pressure to be exerted on the bit.

Incomplete spoon bits

B72–73 are spoon bits with broken shanks lacking their terminals.

Gouge bits

Gouge bits have hollowed blades sharpened along the edges and a sharpened nose which is either cross-cut or rounded downwards but never spoon-shaped. In contrast to the spoon bit, the gouge bit produces a cylindrical cut in the wood, leaving a plug-like core which has to be removed, and in consequence gouge bits are smaller in length and blade width than spoon bits, ranging from 90mm to 170mm in length and from 6mm to 13mm in width.

Type 1

Gouge bits **B74–79** have lanceolate terminals. The blades vary considerably in depth and have cross-cut and rounded noses.

Type 2

B80 has a tapering rectangular terminal and a cross-cut nose.

Incomplete gouge bits

B81–82 have broken shanks and lack their terminals, but both have rounded noses, the former more acutely shaped.

Twist bits

Twist bits have solid shanks, rounded or rectangular in section, with a short spiral groove at the tip, and are suitable for cutting small round holes in timber, particularly for boring pilot holes for nails, etc, where the cleanness of the hole is not of great importance. Doors of ledge and batten construction may have the ledges pegged to the battens, but nails driven through strap hinges to fix them to this double thickness of wood would not have gone in straight and holes were probably bored for them, as was done on the 12th-century church door at Stillingfleet, North Yorkshire (Addyman and Goodall 1979, 90, fig 9).

The twist bit is today called a gimlet bit and is, like the gimlet, in effect a miniature auger (Salaman 1975, 82, 208). Salzman (1967, 345) quotes a 15th-century poem which mentions a 'wymbylle', that is, a wimble or gimlet, but otherwise the only reference he records is mention of a 'gemelot' at Nottingham in 1416. **B83–86** are twist bits, although **B84** is not certainly medieval, and its shank with its thickened, parallel-sided section immediately below the head differentiates it from **B83** and **B85**. Three of the bits, however, are certainly late medieval.

Type 1

B83–85 are twist bits with tapering rectangular heads, the most practical type for these small bits which range from 130mm to 140mm in length and from 4 to 8mm in blade width. Such bits would not require the pressure needed to justify a lanceolate head.

Type 2

Twist bits with eyed heads are known amongst modern tools as shipwrights gimlets (Salaman 1975, 208, fig 209, nos 1955–56), but no medieval example is known.

Incomplete twist bits

B86 is an incomplete bit lacking its head.

Incomplete auger bits

B87–92 are auger bits with heads and incomplete shanks or blades, the latter unclassifiable. All have lanceolate heads.

3.7 SAWS

Saws were used in woodworking to convert trees into planks, to make joints, and for general bench work, and the range of types available reflects these diverse uses. Few actual medieval saw blades survive but according to Goodman (1964, 125) pictorial representations indicate that four main types were in use, namely the large frame or pit-saws used for ripping timber into boards, the small frame saw for bench work, the hand-saw, and the two-man cross-cut saw.

Saw teeth are cut in differing ways (Salaman 1975, 405), with rip teeth, for cutting along the grain, filed straight across at right angles and presenting a series of chisel-like edges which cut away the wood. Cross-cut teeth, for cutting across the grain, are filed at an angle of about 60 degrees in alternative directions. The tips of these teeth, known as points, sever the wood fibres, and most modern saws have them bent or set sideways, alternately right and left, in order to cut a kerf or saw-cut slightly wider than the thickness of the blade to prevent it binding in the wood.

Large frame saws

Axes are shown in use in the Bayeux Tapestry (Stenton 1957, 169, pls 37–38) felling trees needed for building the invasion fleet, and the axe and wedge appear to have been usual tools used in medieval tree felling. Tree trunks, if not split with an axe and wedge, were sawn with pit-saws. The term pit-saw is to some degree a misnomer, since in addition to being sawn over a pit, timber was also mounted on a sawing horse or on trestles for the same purpose. Salzman (1967, 343) notes that there are occasional references to the digging of saw-pits. In 1535, when Hengrave Hall was being built, 10s 8d was paid 'for makyng xvj sawye pitts at Sowe wood', and in the same year, after timber had been sawn for use at Hampton Court, 20 saw-pits were filled up. The saw-pit was in fact a trench in which the bottom sawyer stood, with the timber supported over the pit and the top sawyer standing on top guiding the saw. Excavations at Barton Blount, Derbyshire, revealed an early 15th-century saw-pit 3.20m long, 0.91m wide, 1.83m deep, with oak and ash sawdust at the bottom (Beresford 1975, 45, fig 20, pl VB). Goodman (1964, 132) notes that medieval representations often show the timber mounted on a trestle, as in a 15th-century illustration reproduced by Salzman (1967, pl 19), or on a trestle and crutches. Salzman (1967, 343) notes only a single reference to trestles, in the account for building 'The Bell' at Andover in 1534, where there is mention of 'grett naylis to make sawyng trestilles'. No pit-saw blade fragment is yet known.

Cross-cut saws

The cross-cut saw with a straight blade of the same width throughout and two large handles at each end (Goodman 1964, 143) is thought by Salzman (1967, 342–343) to be the equivalent of the whip-saw of medieval documents. It was used for sawing up planks into smaller sections, but no specimen survives.

Small frame saws

Pictures of joiners' and cabinet makers' workshops show small frame saws with the blade set in the lower part of a wooden frame (Goodman 1964, 126–127, fig 134). The frame, following modern terminology (Salaman 1975, 409, figs 598, 617) has straight or curved side-pieces or cheeks with a central bar or stretcher between and a blade kept in tension by a cord between the tops of the side-pieces. A toggle stick is used to adjust the cord. **B93–94** are probably from such saws the latter retaining a hole which may have been used to hold it in the frame.

Hand-saws

Hand-saws were used for cutting up timber, and modern examples (Salaman 1975, 421) have their teeth sharpened either for ripping along the grain or for cross-cutting. Smaller hand-saws with thinner blades were used for making joints and for general bench work.

An inventory of York Minster in 1399 mentions a 'handsagh', two 'handsawes' are also listed at Durham in 1404, and the London Bridge accounts mention a 'tenonsawe' in 1423 (Salzman 1967, 343). The modern tenon-saw or back-saw has a thin rectangular blade stiffened on the back by a strip or iron, but it is improbable that the medieval tenon-saw was so formed.

B95 is a medieval hand-saw which, like modern examples, has a blade which tapers towards the tip and in cross-section tapers from the cutting edge to the back in order to minimise friction in the kerf and reduce binding. The points of the teeth slope away from the handle, and **B95** is therefore a push-saw which acted when pushed away from the user. The teeth are slightly cross-cut, that is set alternatively to opposite sides, in order to enlarge the kerf.

3.8 DRAWKNIVES

Drawknives, used for removing surplus wood and for rounding and chamfering, are capable of removing much wood quickly. The common form of modern drawknife (Salaman 1975, 175) consists of a flat or curved blade some 203–457mm in length and up to about 75mm in width, bevel-ground on the front edge, with tapering tangs for wooden handles at each end bent round to point in the direction of the cutting edge. **B96** is part of the curved blade of a medieval drawknife whose incomplete tang would originally have been clenched over the end of the wooden handle to prevent the two parting, since the tool was drawn towards the user.

3.9 SHAVES AND SPOKESHAVES

Shaves and spokeshaves are used to shave and smooth wood, especially circular work such as handles, spokes, casks, etc, and both have cutting irons mounted in wooden stocks shaped to form handles at each end (Salaman 1975, 455–463).

The modern wooden spokeshave has a straight stock from 101 to 406mm overall length, the ends cut away to form handles either side of a middle section which has a shaped triangular recess for the iron, itself 38–127mm long and 6–25mm wide. Modern irons have tangs turned up at right angles and inserted into holes in the stock, but **B97–98**, neither necessarily medieval, have straight tangs in line with the blade. Both appear complete, **B97** having shaped tangs, but the method of securing them in the stock is uncertain. **B99**, with a hole suggesting the use of rivets, may be a spokeshave iron.

3.10 PLANES

Planes used for levelling, smoothing and shaping the surface of wood have wooden stocks housing a plane-iron or blade which medieval illustrations (Goodman 1964, 56–65) frequently show secured by a wedge. No medieval plane-iron has yet been recognised.

3.11 FILES, RASPS AND FLOATS

Files, rasps and floats are all available to the present-day woodworker for smoothing and shaping wood. Woodworkers' files are likely to be more coarsely cut than the metalworkers' to prevent the face blocking with dust. The rasp is like the file, but unlike it has teeth formed separately with a punch rather than the straight grooves cut with a chisel. **B100** is probably a float, a very coarsely cut file or rasp with parallel teeth. Modern floats (Salaman 1975, 197) have teeth spaced 4–5 to the inch (25mm) and are occasionally used for cleaning and mortices. They are also used by plane makers for shaping the bed and throat of a plane.

3.12 REAMERS

Reamers are used for enlarging previously bored holes, and modern examples include the hand-reamer as well as taper bits and auger bits used as part of an auger (Salaman 1975, 83, 86, 40–42, 390–391). **B101–112** are hand-reamers with tapering square shanks 8–19mm in width with tangs inserted into wooden handles. No handles survive, but they were no doubt cross handles.

3.13 CLAW HAMMERS

The claw hammer is a general purpose hammer used for driving and extracting nails both by woodworkers and by other craftsmen including blacksmiths and farriers. It is generally impossible to attribute a hammer to a particular craft, and all are therefore considered together, although **B123**, found with a poker and two horseshoes in a smithy hearth at Huish, Wiltshire, must be a farrier's tool.

Medieval claw hammers **B113–126** have flat or gently curved claws, and the strongly down-curved claws of many modern claw hammers are not represented. The flat, straight claws are well adapted for ripping, that is, tearing down partitions and buildings and similar rough work, whilst the greater curvature of the other claws gives more leverage for the extraction of nails. A disadvantage of the claw hammer must have been the tendency of its handle to loosen in the eye or break as a result of leverage applied to the head, and this inherent weakness was counteracted by deepening the eye and sometimes creating a socket, or by extending the sides of the eye down as lugs or as straps. **B113** is plain, but **B114–116** all have deepened eyes, **B116** having a fully developed socket open to one side. **B117–118** have lugs below the eye, **B119–125** side straps which are nailed whenever they are both sufficiently complete and clear. Side straps forged in one with the head can be seen to occur most frequently, and they seem to have been effective in securing the handles. Certainly none of the claw hammers with straps retains any nail or wedge in its eye, as do all those with deepened eyes or sockets. The nails in **B114** and **B116** and wedges in **B115** may be original features, or have been inserted to secure loose heads.

The hammer heads have rounded, polygonal and rectangular faces opposite the claw, and a few (**B113**, **B120**, **B123** and **B125**) are burred from use. **B126** is the claw from a hammer.

A claw hammer from Alsted in Surrey (Goodall 1976a, 56, fig 34.11) with a rounded cheek, the stubs of a strongly down-curved claw, hexagonal face and wooden handle, is certainly a modern intrusion into a medieval level.

3.14 CLAWS

Claw hammers were able to extract nails, and the stouter ones could have withstood considerable leverage, but claws are specifically intended for levering open boxes and cases. Claw **B127** has a cranked shank with upturned claw, **B128** a straight shank with the claw in line, and both were originally hafted in wooden handles. They are both lighter examples particularly suitable for opening boxes, **B128** resembling the modern so-called 'Gents' Opener', a strip of steel about 200mm long and 25mm wide with a claw at one end and a turned handle at the other (Salaman 1975, 90).

3.15 PUNCHES

The nail punch, a short blunt tapering tool, was used to sink nail heads below the surface of wood either for aesthetic reasons or to prevent them catching. B129 is of rounded section and tapers towards both ends.

3.16 PINCERS

Pincers were used by carpenters and coopers for pulling nails, as well as by blacksmiths and farriers shoeing horses. They are considered above under metalworking tools (**A26–27**).

3.17 WEDGES

Wedges of differing sizes are used for tree-felling and wood-splitting as well as for securing wooden handles in the eyes of various craft tools.

Tree-felling and wood-splitting wedges

Tree-felling with axes (Salaman 1975, 488) involved chopping a 'sink' or 'birdsmouth' on the side of the trunk on which the tree was to fall and then enlarging this at the same time as driving large wedges into a cut in the back of the trunk to ease it over and topple it. The large wedges used for this purpose are similar to those used for splitting trunks, the modern cleaving wedge being 100–230mm long and often fluted on both faces (Salaman 1975, 503). **B130–132** are all plain and rectangular in section, and could have been used for either purpose. **B131–132** are both incomplete, although the former retains a strongly burred head, absent on the only complete wedge, **B130**.

Tool handle wedges

The heads of hafted tools such as axes, picks and hammers must often have been secured on their wooden handles by iron nails and wedges driven into the wood through the top of the eye either at the initial hafting or when they worked loose. Hammers **A31–32** and **B114** and **B116** retain nails, axe **B21**, hammer **B115** and picks, pickaxes and hammer-axes **C14**, **C15** and **C19** retain wedges, and the small wedges **B133–147** may have been used similarly. Some might equally have had structural uses in buildings.

3.18 COMPASSES

Compasses, small examples of which are sometimes called dividers, have straight, equal-length legs connected by a moveable joint, and were used by carpenters and stonemasons to take measurements and describe circles. **B148–151** vary in size and completeness, but all have interleaved joints.

B1 AXE
York.
Construction deposit of Baile Hill, raised 1068/9.
Poll, lugs above and below eye, flaring symmetrical blade.
Weight 1.375kg. L 212mm, cutting edge W 72mm (restored).
Addyman and Priestley 1977, 139, 143, fig 10.5

B2 AXE
Rhuddlan, Clwyd.
Probably 12th century.
Poll, lugs above and below eye, flaring symmetrical blade.
Weight 1.2kg. L 171mm, cutting edge W 88mm (restored).
Goodall 1994, fig 17.1, no. 1.

B3 AXE
Hen Domen, Powys.
First half 13th century.
Flaring symmetrical blade broken across eye. Start of lugs above and below eye. L 215mm, cutting edge W 101mm (restored).
Higham and Rouillard 2000, no. 74.

B4 AXE
Ayton Castle, North Yorkshire.
13th century.
Flaring near symmetrical blade broken across eye with lugs above and below. L 159mm, cutting edge W 97mm (restored).
Rimington and Rutter 1967, 60, fig 11.37/18.

B5 AXE
Weoley Castle, Birmingham, West Midlands.
c1270–1600.
Burred poll, lugs above and below eye, flaring symmetrical blade. L 176mm. Cutting edge W 70mm.
Taylor 1974. For site see Oswald 1962.

B6 AXE
Weoley Castle, Birmingham, West Midlands.
c1270–1600.
Poll, lugs above and below eye which retains ferrified wood from handle, flaring symmetrical blade. L 231mm, cutting edge W 92mm (restored).
Taylor 1974. For site see Oswald 1962.

B7 AXE (not illustrated)
Norwich, Norfolk.
In 1507 fire deposit.
Lugs above and below eye, flaring symmetrical blade. L 225mm, cutting edge W 90mm.
Goodall 1993e, fig 130.1385. For site see Carter et al 1974–77, 47.

B8 AXE
Rhuddlan, Clywd.
?14th century.
Tip from flaring symmetrical blade. L 43mm, cutting edge W 76mm.
Goodall 1994, fig 17.1, no. 2.

B9 AXE
Hangleton, West Sussex.
Around early 14th century.
Tip from flaring symmetrical blade. L 73mm, cutting edge W 47mm.
Holden 1963, 171, fig 37.10.

B10 AXE
Hull, Humberside, East Riding of Yorkshire.
15th century.
Tip from flaring symmetrical blade. L 78mm, cutting edge W 41mm.
Goodall 1977b, 65, fig 27.76.

B11 AXE
North Elmham Park, Norfolk.
c1050–c1150.
Plain eye, flaring asymmetrical blade with down-turned rear edge. L 145mm, cutting edge W 56mm.
Goodall 1980a, 513, fig 166.49.

B12 AXE
East Hill Farm, Houghton Regis, Bedfordshire.
c1000–1400.
Plain eye, flaring asymmetrical blade with down-turned rear edge. L 166mm, cutting edge W 57mm (restored).
Luton Museum and Art Gallery, L/5/338/38.

B13 AXE
Baconsthorpe Castle, Norfolk.
c1440–1560.
Lug below eye, flaring asymmetrical blade with down-turned rear edge. L 197mm, cutting edge W 88mm.
DAMHB Reserve Collection.

WOODWORKING TOOLS

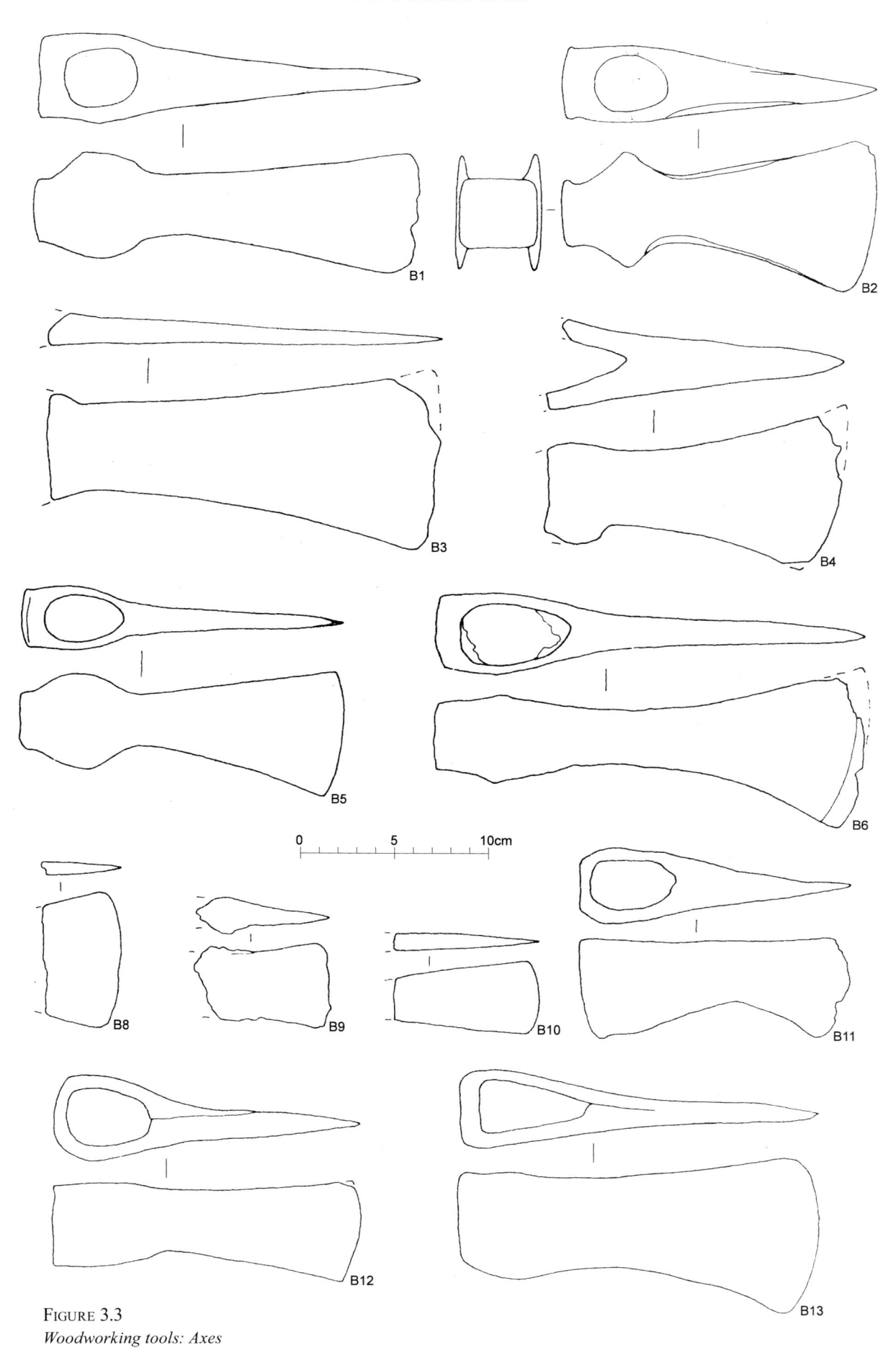

FIGURE 3.3
Woodworking tools: Axes

B14 AXE
West Whelpington, Northumberland.
Topsoil in croft with medieval and
post-medieval occupation.
Lugs below eye, flaring asymmetrical blade
with down-turned rear edge.
L 192mm, cutting edge W 93mm.
For site see Jarrett 1962; 1970.

B15 AXE
Winchester, Hampshire.
Probably mid 12th century.
Incomplete blade and shank. L 141mm.
Cunliffe 1964, 157, fig 54.4.

B16 AXE
Northampton.
From Northampton Castle. Site: late Saxon
to 17th century.
Poll, lug below eye, triangular blade with
struck mark. L 209mm, cutting edge
W 116mm.
Northampton Central Museum D194/1960.

B17 AXE
Burton-in-Lonsdale, North Yorkshire.
Later 13th–mid 14th century.
Plain eye, triangular blade. Residues of
beech (*Fagus sylvatica*) handle. L 126mm,
cutting edge W 72mm.
Moorhouse 1971a, 93, fig 3.2.

B18 AXE
East Hill Farm, Houghton Regis,
Bedfordshire.
*c*1000–1400.
Plain eye, triangular blade. L 163mm,
cutting edge W 88mm (restored).
Luton Museum and Art Gallery, L/6/338/38.

B19 AXE
Deganwy Castle, Gwynedd.
Unstratified in bailey of castle of 1245–63,
on site with earlier occupation. Found with
blacksmith's equipment and iron slag.
Poll, lugs above and below eye, bearded
blade. L 146mm, cutting edge W 75mm.
Excavated by W Greenhalgh. For site see
Alcock 1967.

B20 AXE
Montgomery Castle, Powys.
Unstratified from site occupied 1223–1649.
Poll, lugs above and below eye, bearded
blade. L 138mm, cutting edge W 76mm.
Knight 1994.

B21 AXE
Weoley Castle, Birmingham, West Midlands.
*c*1080–1600.
Poll, lugs above and below eye which has
wedge with adhering wood, bearded blade.
L 170mm, cutting edge W 109mm
(restored).
Birmingham City Museum, WC362. For site
see Oswald 1962.

B22 AXE
Waltham Abbey, Essex,
Late 14th–15th century.
Fragment including cutting edge of bearded
axe. L 50mm, cutting edge W 150mm
(restored).
Huggins 1972, 124.

B23 AXE
Wroughton Copse, Fyfield Down, Wiltshire.
Probably 12th century.
Shaped socket with extended lower lugs,
shaped and chamfered bearded blade.
L 115mm, cutting edge W 95mm.
Excavated by P J Fowler.

WOODWORKING TOOLS

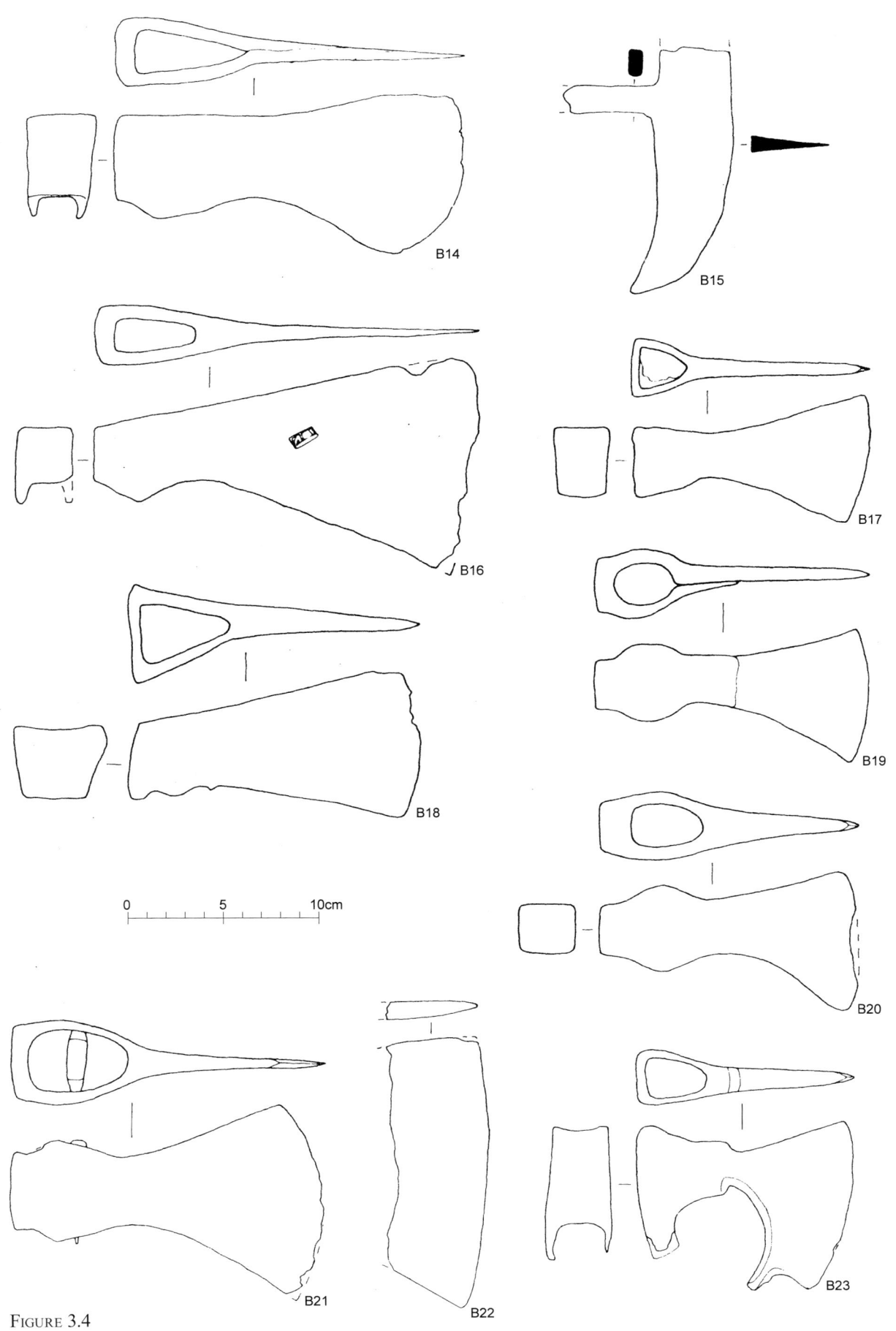

FIGURE 3.4
Woodworking tools: Axes

B24 AXE
Portsmouth, Hampshire.
1475–1500.
Strengthened butt, shaped socket, stamped mark on bearded blade. L 214mm, cutting edge W 143mm.
Fox and Barton 1986, fig 157.2.

B25 AXE
Crane Godrevy, Cornwall.
Unstratified from 15th to early 17th century site.
Poll, lugs below eye, bearded blade set to one side. L 167mm, cutting edge W 166mm.
Excavated by C Thomas.

B26 AXE
Winchester, Hampshire.
1250–1320.
Axe blade fragment, L 34mm, cutting edge W 69mm incomplete.
Goodall 1990-8, fig 58.392.

B27 AXE
Winchester, Hampshire.
14th century.
Axe blade fragment. Metallurgy: steel-cored blade. L 30mm, cutting edge W 78mm.
Goodall 1990-8, fig 58.393.

B28 ADZE
Thetford, Norfolk.
Late 11th century.
Flat blade broadening out to cutting edge with single-sided sharpening bevel. Blade set at an angle to, and broken across base of eye. L 141mm, cutting edge W 94mm.
Goodall 1984.

B29 ADZE
Goltho Manor, Lincolnshire.
c1100–c1150.
Poll, lugs above and below eye, curved blade widening slightly to cutting edge. L 208mm, cutting edge W 43mm.
Goodall 1987, fig 156.2.

B30 ADZE
Castle Acre Castle, Norfolk.
c1175–c1200.
Poll, lugs above and below eye, curved blade widening slightly to cutting edge. Eye blocked with iron-impregnated wood.
L 196mm, cutting edge W 45mm.
Goodall 1982, fig 38, no. 1.

B31 ADZE
Rochester, Kent.
Last quarter 12th century.
Plain eye, narrow, near flat, parallel-sided blade. L 219mm, cutting edge W 25mm approximately.
Harrison 1970, 112, fig 6.

B32 SLICE
Clough Castle, Co. Down.
c1225–50.
Damaged open socket, flat blade broadening out to damaged cutting edge bevelled on upper face only. L 174mm, blade W 59mm (restored).
Waterman 1954, 137, fig 11.4.

B33 SLICE
Winchester, Hampshire.
13th century.
Flanged socket with stub of wooden handle, flat blade broadening out to worn cutting edge bevelled on upper face only. L 120mm excluding handle, cutting edge W 43mm.
Goodall 1990-8, fig 59.394.

B34 CHISEL
Glastonbury Tor, Somerset.
12th–16th century.
Plain blade with double bevel cutting edge and whittle tong for insertion in handle.
L 266mm, cutting edge W 21mm.
Rahtz 1970, 53, fig 23.11.

B35 CHISEL
Weoley Castle, Birmingham, West Midlands.
Site: c1080–c1600.
Plain blade with double bevel cutting edge, whittle tong for handle. L 273mm, cutting edge W 17mm.
Birmingham City Museum, WC433. For site see Oswald 1962.

B36 CHISEL
Winchester, Hampshire.
Late 12th to mid 13th century.
Blade fragment with single bevel cutting edge. L 76mm, cutting edge W 8mm.
Goodall 1990-8, fig 59.395.

B37 CHISEL
Staines, Surrey.
1300–1500.
Blade fragment, single bevel cutting edge.
L 83mm, cutting edge W 18mm.
Excavated by K R Crouch.

B38 CHISEL
Badby, Northamptonshire.
15th–16th century or later.
Blade fragment, single bevel cutting ege.
L 73mm, cutting edge W 15mm.
Excavated by Mrs M Gray.

B39 CHISEL
Cheddar, Somerset.
Late 10th–12th century.
Rectangular stem, double bevel cutting edge(s). L 163mm, cutting edge W 14mm.
Goodall 1979d, 267, fig 90.6.

WOODWORKING TOOLS

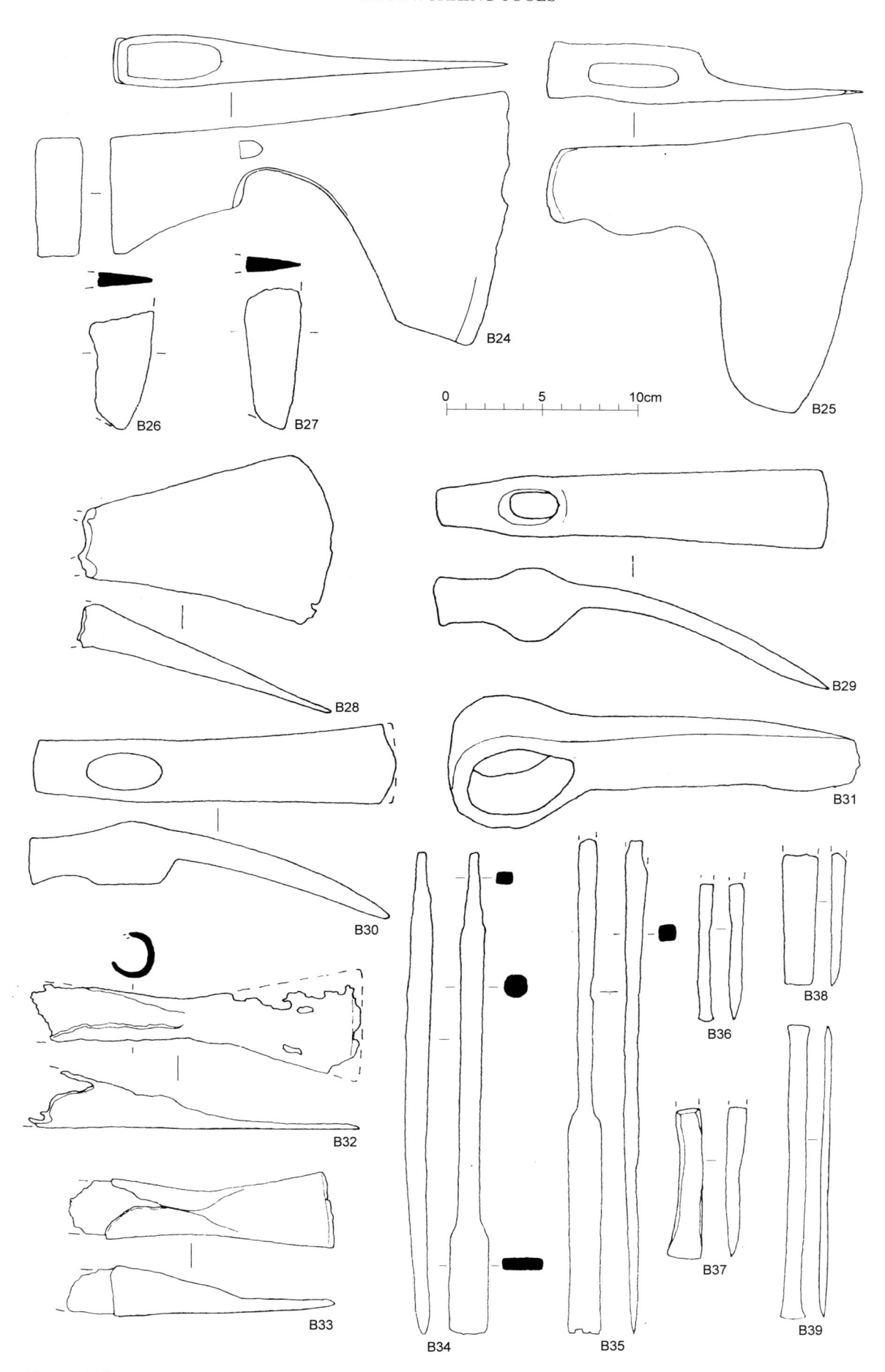

FIGURE 3.5
Woodworking tools: Axes, adzes, slices, and chisels

33

B40 BIT
Waltham Abbey, Essex.
12th/13th and 16th century.
Incomplete forging for bit comprising lanceolate terminal yet to be drawn down and shank awaiting blade. L 66mm. One of six.
Goodall 1973a, 170, fig 11.12.

B41 SPOON BIT
Goltho, Lincolnshire.
Late 14th–early 15th century. From smithy floor.
Broken lanceolate bit. L 77mm, blade W 7mm.
Goodall 1975a, 87, fig 41.92.

B42 SPOON BIT
Grenstein, Norfolk.
Late 14th or possibly early 15th century.
Lanceolate terminal. L 84mm, blade W 8mm.
Goodall 1980c, fig 77, no. 17.

B43 SPOON BIT
North Elmham Park, Norfolk.
c1150–c1600.
Lanceolate terminal. L 92mm, blade W 7mm.
Goodall 1980a, 513, fig 266.52.

B44 SPOON BIT
Waltham Abbey, Essex.
Lower topsoil and debris over building of c1200–c1540.
Incomplete lanceolate bit. L 93mm, blade W 7mm.
Huggins 1972, 124.

B45 SPOON BIT
London.
Around later 14th century.
Broken lanceolate bit. L 93mm, blade W 8mm.
Henig 1974, 191, fig 38.56.

B46 SPOON BIT
South Witham, Lincolnshire.
c1229 to c1308–13.
Lanceolate terminal. L 102mm, blade W 7mm.
Goodall 2002, fig 7.2, no. 24.

B47 SPOON BIT
Wharram Percy, North Yorkshire.
Late 15th to early 16th century.
Lanceolate terminal. L 107mm, blade W 11mm.
Goodall *et al* 1979, 118, fig 62.55.

B48 SPOON BIT
Grenstein, Norfolk.
Late 14th or possibly early 15th century.
Lanceolate terminal. L 117mm, blade W 7mm.
Goodall 1980c, fig 77, no. 16.

B49 SPOON BIT (?)
Pleshey Castle, Essex.
Early/mid 10th century to modern.
Lanceolate terminal, blade damaged but possibly near complete. L 117mm, blade W 8mm.
Goodall 1977c, 177, fig 38.16.

B50 SPOON BIT
Somerby, Lincolnshire.
15th–mid 16th century.
Lanceolate terminal. L 130mm, blade W 11mm.
Mynard 1969, 84, fig 13.IW88.

B51 SPOON BIT
St Catharine's Hill, Winchester, Hampshire.
Chapel: 12th century to 1538–40.
Lanceolate terminal, damaged blade. L 131mm, blade W 4mm.
Hawkes *et al* 1930, 246, fig 29.13.

B52 SPOON BIT
South Witham, Lincolnshire.
c1220–late 13th century.
Lanceolate terminal. L 132mm, blade W 9mm.
Goodall 2002, fig 7.2, no. 23.

B53 SPOON BIT
Baginton Castle, Warwickshire.
Site: 14th–15th century.
Lanceolate terminal. L 137mm, blade W 12mm.
Herbert Art Gallery and Museum, Coventry.

B54 SPOON BIT
London.
Late 15th, early 16th century.
Lanceolate terminal, ?incomplete. L 138mm, blade W 17mm.
Excavated by F C Willmot. Site at 66 Foyle Road.

B55 SPOON BIT
South Witham, Lincolnshire.
c1220–late 13th century.
Incomplete lanceolate terminal. L 153mm, blade W 16mm.
Goodall 2002, fig 7.2, no. 22.

B56 SPOON BIT
Thetford, Norfolk.
11th century.
Tip broken. L 157mm.
Goodall 1984.

B57 SPOON BIT
Lyveden, Northamptonshire.
1475–1500.
Lanceolate terminal. L 159mm, blade W 11mm.
Steane and Bryant 1975, 139, fig 52.252.

B58 SPOON BIT
Somerby, Lincolnshire.
15th–mid 16th century.
Incomplete lanceolate terminal. L 158mm, blade W 14mm.
Mynard 1969, 84, fig 13.IW87.

B59 SPOON BIT
Gloucester.
14th–15th century.
Incomplete lanceolate terminal, damaged blade. L 177mm, blade W 10mm.
Excavated by H Hurst.

B60 SPOON BIT
Glottenham, East Sussex.
Mid to late 12th century.
Lanceolate terminal. L 250mm, blade W 18mm.
Excavated by D Roberts.

B61 SPOON BIT
Brooklands, Weybridge, Surrey.
1200–1325.
Lanceolate tapering terminal. L 294mm, blade W 18mm.
Goodall 1977d, 73, fig 45.14.

B62 SPOON BIT
Cheddar, Somerset.
Early 13th century.
Lanceolate terminal. L 301mm, blade W 24mm.
Goodall 1979d, 267, fig 90.146.

B63 SPOON BIT
Clough Castle, Co. Down.
c1200–c1225.
Damaged lanceolate terminal. L 321mm, blade W 16mm.
Waterman 1954, 135–137, fig 11.2.

B64 SPOON BIT
Goltho Manor, Lincolnshire.
Topsoil, early to mid 12th century.
Broken lanceolate bit. L 314mm, blade W 27mm.
Goodall 1987, fig 156.4.

B65 SPOON BIT
Bramber Castle, West Sussex.
1075–1180.
Possibly lanceolate terminal. L 327mm, blade W 21mm.
Barton and Holden 1977, 64, fig 20.1.

WOODWORKING TOOLS

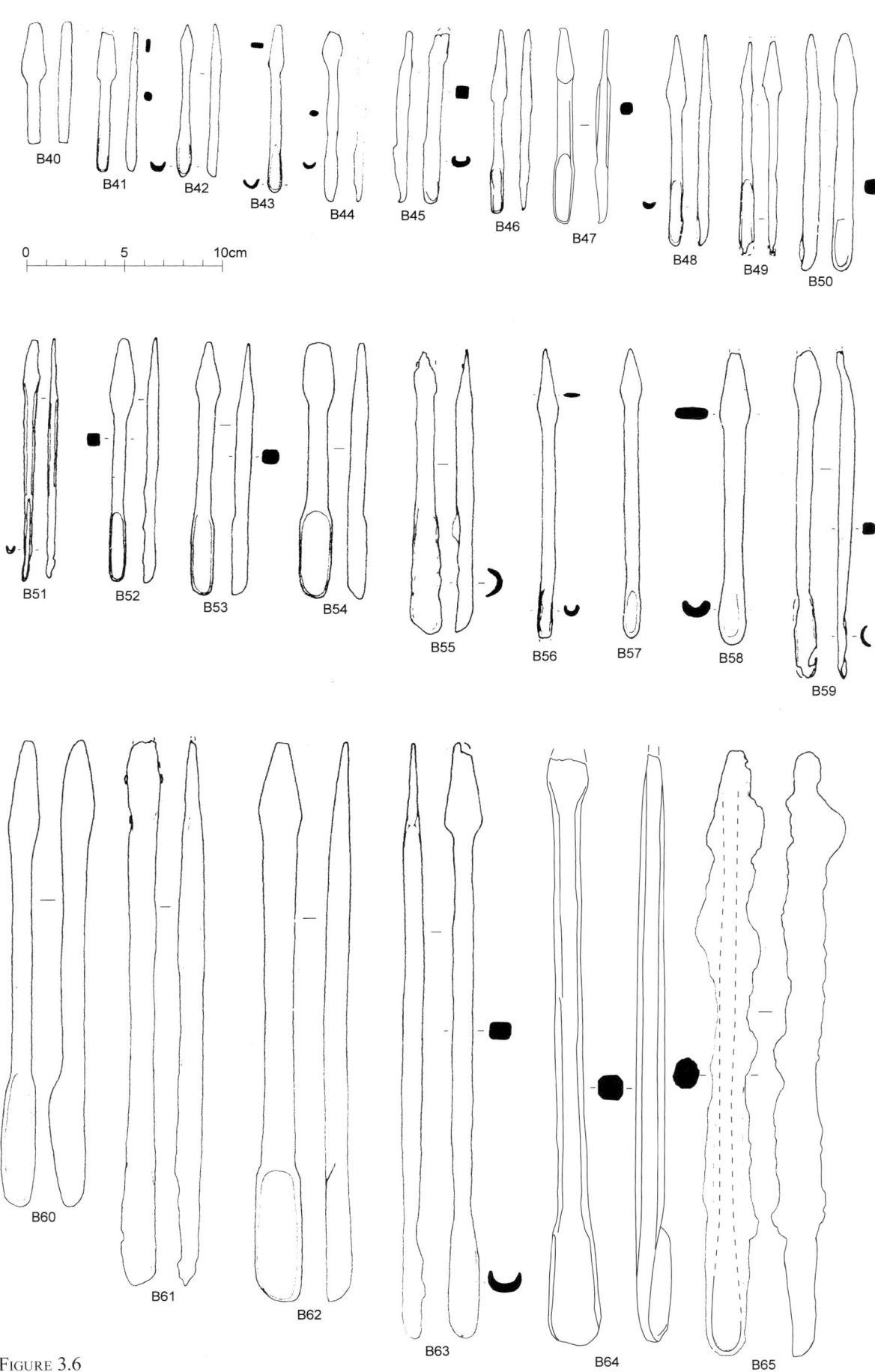

FIGURE 3.6
Woodworking tools: Spoon bits

B66 SPOON BIT
Castle Neroche, Somerset.
c1067–early 12th century.
Lanceolate terminal, damaged blade.
L 340mm, blade
W 18mm.
Davison 1972, 41, fig 18.1.

B67 SPOON BIT
Mileham, Norfolk.
13th–14th century.
Lanceolate terminal. L 364mm, blade
W 24mm.
Waterman 1945, 135.

B68 SPOON BIT
Clough Castle, Co. Down.
c1225–50.
Damaged lanceolate terminal, blade tip broken. L 415mm, blade W 27mm.
Waterman 1954, 135–137, fig 11.1.

B69 SPOON BIT
Waltham Abbey, Essex.
12th/13th and 16th century.
Blade and ?incomplete shank. L 95mm, blade W 6mm.
Goodall 1973a, 170, fig 11.21.

B70 SPOON BIT
Alsted, Surrey.
c1270–1350.
Tapering terminal, tip lost. L 178mm, blade W 13mm.
Goodall 1976a, 56, fig 34.12.

B71 SPOON BIT
Wallingstones, Hereford and Worcester.
First half 12th century.
Tapering terminal. L 247mm, blade W 14mm.
Bridgewater 1970–72, 100, fig 16.31.

B72 SPOON BIT
Alsted, Surrey.
c1250–1405.
Shank broken, terminal lost. L 135mm, blade W 12mm.
Goodall 1976a, 56, fig 35.39.

B73 SPOON BIT
Waltham Abbey, Essex.
16th/17th century plus derived medieval material.
Blade and broken shank. L 158mm, blade W 20mm.
Goodall 1973a, 170, fig 11.22.

B74 GOUGE BIT
Pleshey Castle, Essex.
Early/mid 16th century to modern.
Lanceolate terminal, blade possibly near complete.
L 90mm, blade W 8mm.
Goodall 1977c, 177, fig 38.15.

B75 GOUGE BIT
Thelsford Priory, Warwickshire.
Site: 1200/1212–1536.
Incomplete lanceolate terminal, blade incomplete.
L 97mm, blade W 7mm.
Excavated by Mrs M Gray.

B76 GOUGE BIT
Northampton.
Middle Saxon–15th century.
Lanceolate terminal. L 104mm, blade W 7mm.
Goodall et al 1979, 273, fig 119.64.

B77 GOUGE BIT
Rayleigh Castle, Essex.
Site c1070–c1350.
Lanceolate terminal. L 114mm, blade W 6mm.
Prittlewell Priory Museum, Southend. For site see Helliwell and Macleod 1965.

B78 GOUGE BIT
Christchurch, Hampshire.
Possibly 13th century.
Incomplete lanceolate terminal. L 147mm, blade W 12mm.
Goodall 1983b, fig 34.48.

B79 GOUGE BIT
Writtle, Essex.
c1229–32.
Lanceolate terminal. L 179mm, blade W 11mm.
Rahtz 1969b, 87, fig 48.79.

B80 GOUGE BIT
Winchester, Hampshire.
1093–94.
Tapering terminal, slightly swollen at base. Wood attached to tip. L 150mm overall, blade W 12mm.
Goodall 1990-8, fig 59.397.

B81 GOUGE BIT
Wharram Percy, North Yorkshire.
Mid 15th to early 16th century.
Shank broken. L 65mm, blade W 10mm.
Goodall 1979a, 123, fig 64.103.

B82 GOUGE BIT
Seacourt, Oxfordshire.
Mid to late 12th to late 14th century.
Shank broken. L 93mm, blade W 13mm.
Biddle 1961–62, 177, fig 30.3, scale 1:4, not 1:3.

B83 TWIST BIT (?)
Oxford.
c1325–c1400.
Tapering terminal. L 135mm, blade W 8mm.
Goodall 1977e, 142, fig 26.21.

B84 TWIST BIT
Montgomery Castle, Powys.
Unstratified; site 1223–1649.
Broken tapering terminal. L 140mm, blade W 7mm.
Excavated by J K Knight.

B85 TWIST BIT
Clarendon Palace, Wiltshire.
Site: c1072 to later 15th century.
Distorted tapering terminal. L 130mm, blade W 4mm.
Goodall 1988, fig 73.1. For site see Borenius and Charlton 1936.

B86 TWIST BIT
London.
Late 13th–14th century.
Broken shank. L 72mm, blade W 5mm.
Henig 1974, 191, fig 38.57.

B87 BIT
Clough Castle, Co. Down.
c1200–c1225.
Broken lanceolate terminal and blade.
L 90mm.
Waterman 1954, 141, fig 13.4.

B88 BIT
Walton, Buckinghamshire.
12th–13th century.
Lanceolate terminal. L 40mm.
Farley 1976, 267, fig 49.3.

B89 BIT
Pleshey Castle, Essex.
Mid 13th–early/mid 16th century.
Lanceolate terminal, blade broken. L 81mm, blade W 7mm.
Goodall 1977c, 177, fig 38.17.

B90 BIT
Bramber Castle, West Sussex.
13th century.
Lanceolate terminal broken shank. L 166m.
Barton and Holden 1977, 64, fig 19.9.

B91 BIT
Winchester, Hampshire.
14th century.
Lanceolate terminal, shank broken.
L 82mm.
Goodall 1990-8, fig 59.398.

B92 BIT
Weoley Castle, Birmingham, West Midlands.
Site: c1080–c1600.
Shank broken. Lanceolate terminal retains part of iron-impregnated wooden handle.
L 85mm.
Birmingham City Museum, WC429A. For site see Oswald 1962.

WOODWORKING TOOLS

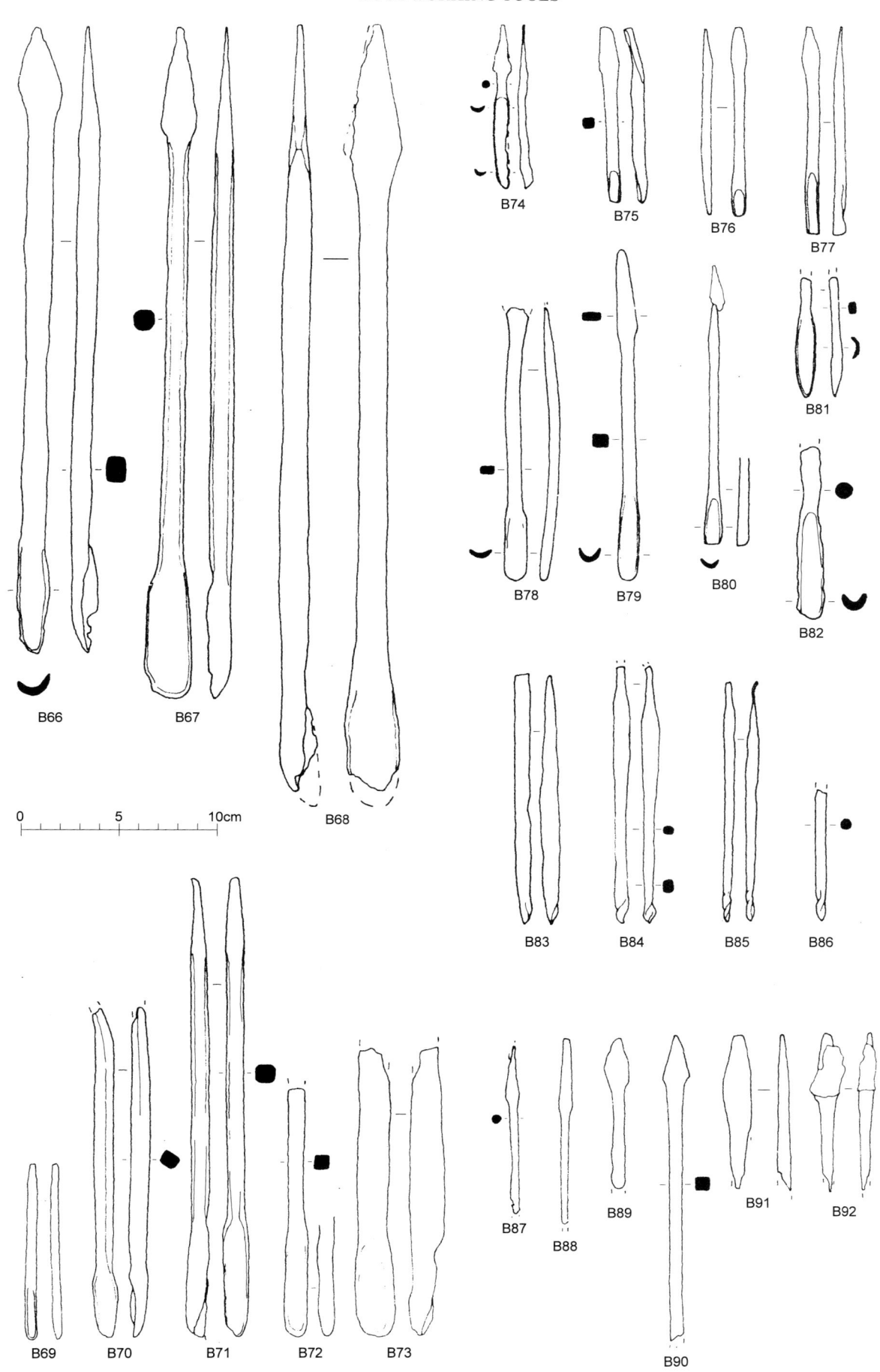

FIGURE 3.7
Woodworking tools: Spoon bits, gouge bits, and twist bits

B93 SAW
Pinsley, Southwick, Hampshire.
11th century.
Saw blade, straight back, slender cross section. Teeth damaged, approximately 8½ points per inch (25.5mm).
Portsmouth City Museums. From site of motte and bailey castle, in top of pit.

B94 SAW
Goltho, Lincolnshire.
Unstratified on croft with Late Saxon to late 14th- or early 15th-century occupation.
Saw blade, broken across hole at one end. Teeth corroded, 3½ points per inch (25.5mm).
Goodall 1975a, 87, fig 41.93.

B95 SAW
Windcliff, Isle of Wight.
13th century.
Push-saw, blade incomplete, tang bent slightly out of plane of blade. Teeth set 4½ points per inch (25.5mm).
Dunning 1939, 135–137, fig 3; reproduced in Mercer 1968, fig 205.

B96 DRAWKNIFE
Hangleton, West Sussex.
Around early 14th century.
Curved blade, bevel ground on front edge, with tang for insertion in wooden handle. Incomplete. L 55mm.
Holden 1963, 171, fig 37.9.

B97 SPOKESHAVE IRON
Waltham Abbey, Essex.
16th/17th century and derived medieval pottery.
Blade with distorted, shaped side arms in line with back of blade. W 137mm.
Goodall 1973a, 170, fig 11.23.

B98 SPOKESHAVE IRON
Wharram Percy, North Yorkshire.
Early 16th–20th century.
Blade with horizontal side arms. W 122mm.
Area 6, SF11245, Pd VII; Andrews and Milne 1979, 44, 54.

B99 SPOKESHAVE IRON (?)
Northolt Manor, Greater London.
1300–1350.
Flat curved blade with perforated projection to one side, broken, the other object in poor condition, but 'there may be a slight thinning from concave to convex edge'.
L 10mm.
Hurst 1961, 289, fig 76.18.

B100 FLOAT
Wroughton Copse, Fyfield Down, Wiltshire.
12th–13th century.
Rectangular-sectioned rasp with coarse teeth and curved back. L 106mm.
Excavated by P J Fowler.

B101 REAMER
Lyveden, Northamptonshire.
Second quarter 13th century.
Tapering square shank. L 78mm.
Bryant and Steane 1971, 55, fig 13c2.

B102 REAMER
Weoley Castle, Birmingham, West Midlands.
Site: c1080–1600.
Tapering square shank. L 98mm.
Birmingham City Museum and Art Gallery, S32. For site see Oswald 1962.

B103 REAMER
Lyveden, Northamptonshire.
Second half 13th century.
Tapering square shank. L 108mm.
Bryant and Steane 1971, 55, fig 13c1.

B104 REAMER
West Hartburn, Durham.
13th–16th century.
Tang broken. L 76mm.
Still and Pallister 1964, 200, fig 5.39.

B105 REAMER
Goltho, Lincolnshire.
Late 14th to early 15th century smithy floor.
Tapering square shank. L 84mm.
Goodall 1975a, 87, fig 41.91.

B106 REAMER
Dyserth Castle, Clwyd.
Castle occupied 1241–63.
Tapering square shank. L 105mm.
Glenn 1915.

B107 REAMER
Alsted, Surrey.
c1250–1405.
Tapering square shank. L 131mm.
Goodall 1976a, 56, fig 35.41.

B108 REAMER
Bramber Castle, West Sussex.
14th century.
Tapering square shank. L 110mm.
Barton and Holden 1977, 64, fig 20.3.

B109 REAMER
Northampton.
c1410–20 to c1500.
Tapering lozenge section shank. L 124mm.
Goodall et al 1979, 273, fig 11g.62.

B110 REAMER
Northolt Manor, Greater London.
1300–1370.
Tapering square shank. L 132mm.
Excavated by J G Hurst.

B111 REAMER
Stonar, Kent.
c1275–1385.
Broken tang and tapering rectangular section shank. L 114mm.
Excavated by N Macpherson-Grant.

B112 REAMER
Hangleton, West Sussex.
13th or 14th century.
Complete. L 124mm.
Hurst and Hurst 1964, 137, fig 13.11.

B113 CLAW HAMMER
Winchester, Hampshire.
Late 11th–12th century.
Flat claw, slight swelling around eye, rectangular face. L 106mm.
Goodall 1990-8, fig 60.400.

B114 CLAW HAMMER
Alvechurch, Hereford and Worcester.
c1500.
Broken, gently curved claw, expansion round eye with three nails which formerly secured wooden handle, rounded face. L 152mm.
Oswald 1954, 9, pl 5.9.

B115 CLAW HAMMER
Hen Domen, Powys.
c1200.
Gently curved claw, expansion round socket with cross-shaped wedges to seams former wooden handle. L 150mm.
Higham and Rouillard 2000, no. 72.

B116 CLAW HAMMER
Rhuddlan, Clwyd.
Mid to late 13th century.
Flat claw, partly open socket, expansion round eye with nail to secure handle, rounded face. L 75mm.
Goodall 1994, fig 17.1, no. 4.

B117 CLAW HAMMER
Clough Castle, Co. Down.
c1250.
Flat broken claw, lugs below eye, neck, rectangular face. L 127mm.
Waterman 1954, 140, fig 12.9.

B118 CLAW HAMMER
South Witham, Lincolnshire.
Late 13th century to 1308–13.
Flat claw, lugs below eye, rectangular face. L 109mm.
Goodall 2002, fig 7.2, no. 26.

B119 CLAW HAMMER
Guildford.
13th century.
Flat claw, side straps, expansion round eye, remains of wooden handle, rounded face. L 113mm.
Excavated by F W Holling. From Tunsgate, Guildford.

WOODWORKING TOOLS

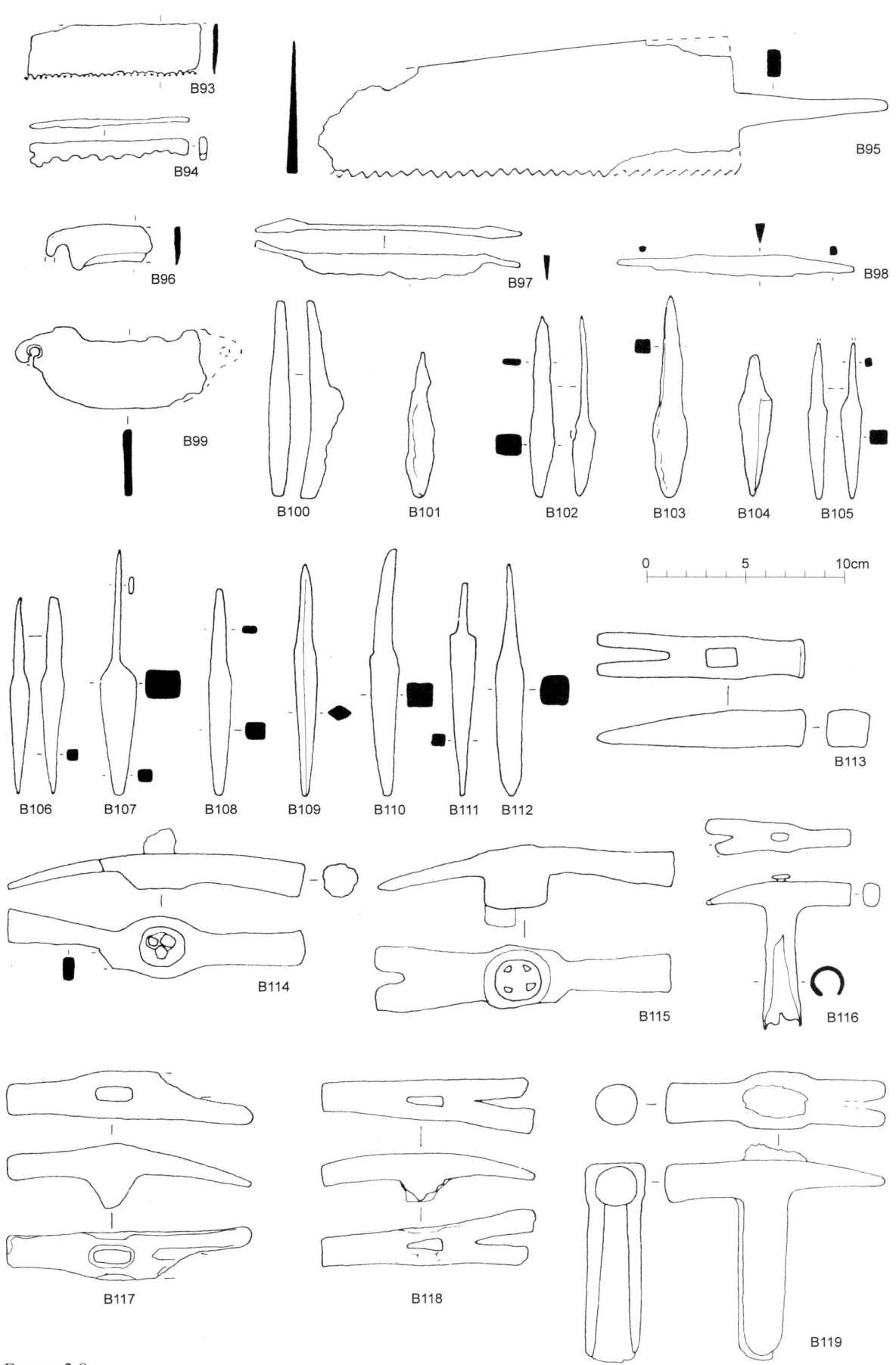

FIGURE 3.8
Woodworking tools: Saws, drawknife, spokeshave irons, float, reamer, and claw hammers

B120 CLAW HAMMER
South Witham, Lincolnshire.
Late 13th century to 1308–13.
Gently curved claw, broken straps, burred rounded face. L 111mm.
Goodall 2002, fig 7.2, no. 25.

B121 CLAW HAMMER
Hen Blas, Clwyd.
13th–14th century.
Flat claw, broken straps, rounded face.
L 96mm.
Leach 1960, 23, fig 13.5.

B122 CLAW HAMMER
Stonar, Kent.
13th–14th century.
Flat claw, broken nailed side straps.
L 165mm.
Excavated by N Macpherson-Grant.

B123 CLAW HAMMER
Huish, Wiltshire.
14th–mid 15th century.
Flat claw, broken straps, slight expansion round eye, octagonal-sectioned neck, rounded face. L 65mm.
Shortt 1972, 120, fig 4.27.

B124 CLAW HAMMER
Northampton.
Later 15th century.
Curved claw, nailed straps, rectangular face.
L 126mm.
Goodall et al 1979, 272, fig 119.61.

B125 CLAW HAMMER
North Elmham Park, Norfolk.
c1150–c1600.
Flat claw, nailed straps, slight expansion round eye, rounded face. L 95mm.
Goodall 1980a, 513, fig 266.54.

B126 CLAW HAMMER
Rhuddlan, Clwyd.
(Later?) 13th century.
Single broken claw. L 50mm.
Goodall 1994, fig 17.1, no. 5.

B127 CLAW
Castle Acre Castle, Norfolk.
Pre-1085.
Broken, cranked shank with upturned claw.
L 163mm.
Goodall 1982, fig 38, no. 2.

B128 CLAW
London.
Late 15th to early 16th century.
Rectangular shank, broken tang. L 270mm.
Excavated by F C Willmot. Site at 66 Foyle Road.

B129 PUNCH
Northampton.
Late Saxon–15th century.
Circular-sectioned stem tapering to head and blunt point. L 84mm.
Goodall 1979b, 71, fig 17.8.

B130 WEDGE
Stretham, East Sussex.
Over building destroyed in 14th century or earlier.
L 217mm.
Excavated by A Barr-Hamilton.

B131 WEDGE
Winchester, Hampshire.
13th century.
Blade tip broken, head burred. L 178mm.
Goodall 1990-8, fig 60.409.

B132 WEDGE
Alsted, Surrey.
c1250–1405.
Head lost. L 143mm.
Goodall 1976a, 56, fig 35.37.

B133 WEDGE
Llantrithyd, South Glamorgan.
Early to mid 12th century.
Slightly burred head. L 43mm.
Goodall 1977f, 47, fig iron 2.24.

B134 WEDGE
Hen Gaerwys, Clwyd.
c1450–1520.
Burred head. L 45mm.
Excavated by G B Leach.

B135 WEDGE
Winchester, Hampshire.
14th–?15th century.
Slightly burred head. L 46mm.
Goodall 1990-8, fig 60.406.

B136 WEDGE
Dyserth Castle, Clwyd.
Site occupied 1241–63.
L 48mm.
Glenn 1915.

B137 WEDGE
Burnham Church, Humberside.
c1300–1320.
L 48mm.
Excavated by G Coppack.

B138 WEDGE
Grenstein, Norfolk.
12th to late 14th or early 15th century.
Burred head. L 49mm.
Goodall 1980c, fig 77, no. 19.

B139 WEDGE
Wharram Percy, North Yorkshire.
Late 15th to early 16th century.
Slightly burred head. L 56mm.
Goodall 1979a, 118–120, no. 57.

B140 WEDGE
Criccieth Castle, Gwynedd.
Site: c1230–1404.
Slightly burred head. L 56mm.
O'Neil 1944–45, 42, pl X.30.

B141 WEDGE
Hen Domen, Powys.
Site: c1070–14th century
Slightly burred head. L 57mm
Higham and Rouillard 2000, no. 76.

B142 WEDGE
London.
Late 15th to 16th century.
L 59mm.
Excavated by F C Willmot. Site at 66 Foyle Road.

B143 WEDGE
Llantrithyd, South Glamorgan.
Early to mid 12th century.
Slightly burred head. L 63mm.
Goodall 1977f, 47, fig iron 2.23.

B144 WEDGE
Chingley, Kent.
Second half 13th century.
Slightly burred head. L 66mm.
Goodall 1975d, 60, fig 27.6.

B145 WEDGE
Chingley, Kent.
Second half 13th to mid 14th century.
Slightly burred head. L 65mm.
Goodall 1975d, 60, fig 27.7.

B146 WEDGE (not illustrated)
Winchester, Hampshire.
1090–93.
L 68mm, W 13mm tapering to 10mm.
Goodall 1990-8, 277, no. 405.

B147 WEDGE
Winchester, Hampshire.
Mid 15th century.
Broken blade. L 74mm.
Goodall 1990-8, fig 60.407.

B148 COMPASS
Hampton Wafer, Hereford and Worcester.
11th to early 14th century.
Heavily corroded; hint of rivet at top and possible slot for interlinked arms. L 170mm.
Stanford 1967, 87, fig 7.14.

B149 COMPASS
Grenstein, Norfolk.
Late 14th or early 15th century.
Lugs intersect at top. L 94mm.
Goodall 1980c, fig 77, no. 18.

B150 COMPASS
Low Caythorpe, Humberside.
First half 14th century.
One of two lugs from pair of dividers.
L 60mm.
Coppack 1974, 41, fig 5.3.

B151 COMPASS
The Hamel, Oxford.
Mid 16th century.
Both arms broken. L 92mm.
Goodall 1980d, fig 29, no. 14.

WOODWORKING TOOLS

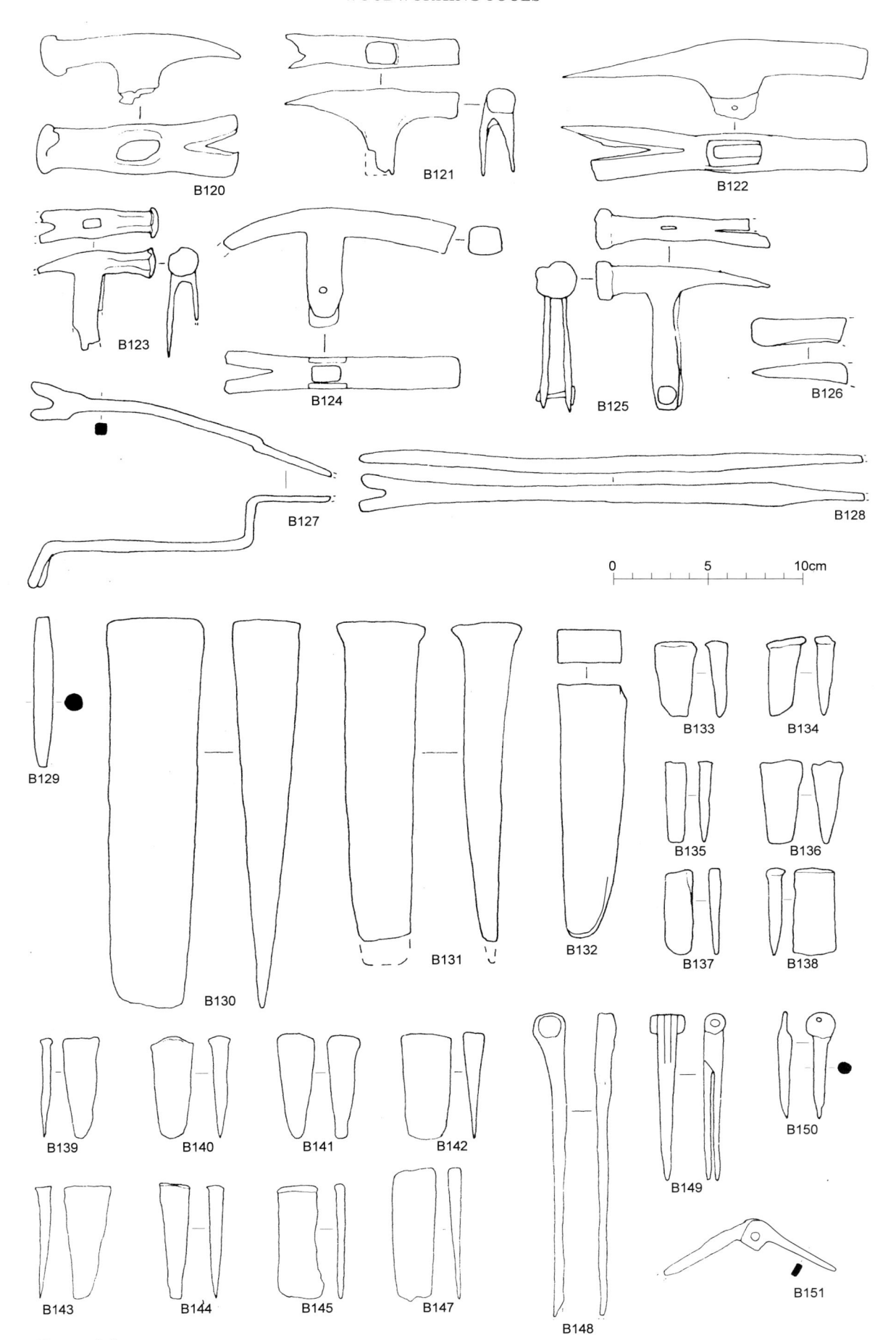

FIGURE 3.9
Woodworking tools: Claw hammers, claws, punch, wedges, and dividers

4

STONEWORKING AND PLASTERING TOOLS

Churches, castles and manor houses were already being built of stone during the early medieval period, but it was not until the late 12th and 13th centuries that the timber walls of peasant houses in almost all stone-producing areas were replaced by walls built of stone (Beresford and Hurst 1971, 93–95). Comparatively few medieval mason's tools survive, but they are frequently mentioned in building accounts (Salzman 1967, 123–124, 330–340), and representations of building work most frequently depict work on stone buildings.

4.1 QUARRYING AND THE WORKING OF STONE

Medieval stone quarries such as those at Barnack, Northamptonshire (Beresford and St Joseph 1979, 254–255), survive as earthworks, but information about tools and the implications this has for techniques of extraction comes from documentary sources. Tools specifically mentioned in relation to quarrying stone (Salzman 1967, 331–332) are wedges, mauls, heavy hammer-axes, smaller broach axes, and crows, as well as spades, shovels, hoes, picks and pickaxes which were no doubt principally used to remove the overburden and waste.

The first stage in opening a quarry involved removing the overlying earth down to the top layer of stone which, although generally of inferior quality, and fissured and unsuitable for cutting into blocks, was useful as rubble. After this rag had been removed, the freestone proper was quarried with wedges, mauls and crows, and the blocks then reduced by further splitting and sawing before being broached and scappled to the required dimensions.

Some of the tools used in quarrying were also used in building work, particularly for demolition for which picks, pickaxes and mattocks were also used. Stone, including ornamental stonework such as plinths, string courses and voussoirs, was supplied ready worked and cut to measure directly from the quarry or was worked up in a lodge on the building site. Moulds and templates were used to guide the mason, who scribed their design onto the stone, and other setting out work was done with squares and compasses. The finished work was produced with axes, punches and chisels, the saws and borers referred to in documents being used to cut up and pierce blocks of stone. Large blocks of stone were moved with lewises, and actual building construction involved using trowels and plumb-lines and levels.

Roofing required the quarrying of stone slates and their preparation with hammers and picks, and the mason might also produce and maintain millstones with mill-picks and bills.

4.2 WEDGES

Wedges were used for quarrying stone for heavy work in actual building operations. At Scarborough in 1425, for instance, 'gavelocks [crows], mattokes, and wegges' were supplied not only for the quarry but for 'takyng downe of the Constable Toure ... whilk was in point to fall' (Salzman 1967, 332). Wedges were also used for stone robbing, and two of large size from possible early 16th-century robbing were found *in situ* in the wall at Rest Park, North Yorkshire (Le Patourel 1973, 42, 95).

In quarrying, after clearing the overburden, the lines chosen for splitting the stone into blocks were marked and wedges driven home along them until it split as desired. Picks, pickaxes or hammer-axes are likely to have been used to cut the slots into which the wedges were placed before being driven in with a sledgehammer or maul. The large iron wedge **C1** with its large burred head may have been used alone to split stone. It weighs 2.422kg (5 lb 5½ oz) and may be similar to the wedges implied by an entry for 'wedges weighing 16 lb' used for getting stone for Magdalen College in 1474 (Salzman

1967, 331). Heavier wedges are implied by the '10 iron wegges, weighing 100 lb' mentioned at Stapleton in 1399.

Arkell (1947) describes two methods of splitting stone in recent use, the older using a jad or race, a double-edged axe, and wedges and slats, and the more recent plug and feathers. Both involved placing a central 'wedge' between iron side pieces in a prepared hole or slot and driving it into the stone. **C2–5** may have been used in the manner of modern plug and feathers, **C2** as the central wedge driven between the outer wedges **C3–5**. The smaller wedges **C3–5** are turned over at the top, as are feathers to prevent them slipping too far into the stone (Arkell 1947, 60, fig 9; Purcell 1967, 45, pls 15–16), and they have keeled or ridged sections which would have exerted considerable pressure on the stone as the central wedge was tapped down until the stone split. They are small, however, and it is possible that they had a structural use and are not tools. The curvature and burring of **C2** suggests that it is a mason's tool subjected to heavier blows than if used as a blacksmith's cold chisel, but certainty is impossible. **C6–7** are not unlike the wedge and slat described by Arkell (1947, 121, fig 18), a slender wedge similar to **C6** being placed in an axe-cut slot between iron plates not unlike **C7** and driven into the stone.

Wedges **C8–9**, as their shape and find-spots indicate, were probably intended for use in actual building operations, although neither shows severe signs of wear. Both have a mason's mark struck on one face, and Salzman (1967, 127) records a recent mason stating that he only used his mason's or banker's mark on the hafts of his tools.

Wedges **C10–11** may have been used in quarrying stone or slate or in building work.

4.3 HAMMERS AND MAULS

Hammers were used in the quarry and during building work, and iron mauls are frequently listed alongside wedges and crows in lists of tools supplied to quarries. These lists sometimes call them simply 'mauls' or 'great mauls', but some used for obtaining stone for Magdalen College in 1474 are described a '3 great mauls of iron and steel, weighing 70 lb', and at Oxford in 1514 there is mention of 'a male of yryn' weighing 21 lb (Salzman 1967, 331–332). Heavy double-headed sledgehammers shown in modern use during the splitting of stone (Purcell 1967, pls 10a, 15b, 16a) are probably equivalent to the medieval maul, but no certain example is yet known unless some of the sledgehammers ascribed to blacksmiths are instead quarriers' tools. **A28** is certainly a blacksmith's tool since it was found with other metalworking equipment, but there must be more doubt about **A29–31**.

Sledgehammers were also used for breaking, rather than working, stone. At Warblington in 1518, 4d was 'payd for ye making of a scleyg for [to] brek ye grytt stonys', and the 1532 Westminster accounts note 'a great stone, poz. xvj lb qr'. There is also mention of '2 stonhamers called bateryngaxes' in 1444, '12 skabelinghambers for the roughleyers' in 1532, and 'setting hambers' (Salzman 1967, 335). Some of the hammers described above, **A32–36**, may have been used by masons.

4.4 CROWS

Crows and gavelocks, the latter large crows, appear in lists of tools used in quarries and for building operations (Salzman 1967, 331–332). During the building of Vale Royal Abbey in 1278, 3s was paid 'pro ij cornailis [crows] ferries pro lapibus levandis de quarrera', and in 1334 at Knaresborough Castle there is mention of 'an iron gavelock for breaking stones in the quarry'. Tools used in getting stone for Magdalen College in 1474 included 'a tool called a crowe or iron, weighing 72 lb', and at Oxford in 1514 'a crawe of yrne' weighing 91 lb is mentioned. Crows were not reserved for quarry use, however, for at Scarborough in 1425 'gavelockes, mattokes, and wegges' were supplied for the quarry and for taking down the Constable Tower. At Winchester Castle in 1222 payment was made 'for 2 crows to break the walls and 3 wedges' (Colvin 1971, 130–131).

No crows survive from archaeological contexts, but some appreciation of their use in levering stone from the bed can be gained from photographs of them in use at Weldon quarry (Purcell 1967, 36, pls 10 and 11). The size of crow in use there would clearly have been of little use in building work, but it explains the considerable size implied by the documentary references.

4.5 PICKS, PICKAXES AND MATTOCKS

Medieval documents include references to picks, pickaxes and mattocks in combination which imply that they were used in various stages of quarrying stone as well as in building work. Picks and pickaxes must have been used in the removal of the overburden and ragstone prior to the start of quarrying, as well as for digging foundations and breaking down walls. Such work must have been harsh, and it is not surprising that picks are sometimes mentioned in documents because they required repair. At Durham in 1533, 2d was paid 'for sharpening the pykke' at the quarry, and at Woodstock in 1256 there is a charge 'for sharpening and mending picas' and crawes' (Salzman 1967, 332–333). **C12–14** are single-bladed picks, all retaining traces of their handles. That of **C13** has been identified as birch, and that of **C14** is secured in the eye by an iron wedge. These picks are suitable for general purpose use, and are occasionally shown in illuminations being wielded by one of the besieged garrison evidently as a weapon and not a tool.

Picks are first mentioned in documents as 'picas', or more usually as 'picois' or 'pykoys', but in time the term becomes corrupted to the modern form 'pickaxe'. At Woodstock in 1494 a smith received payment 'for stelyng of ij pykax...' and at Westminster in 1532 there is mention of 24 'pykaxis' weighing 1½ cwt 10 lb, and 'iij pyckaxis with hamber heedis provided for brekyng downe of the greate Toure in the palesse' (Salzman 1967, 330, 333). The qualification 'with hamber heedis' added to the term pickaxe in this last document may be no more than pedantry, but it certainly refers to such medieval pickaxes as **C15–17**. These all retain their hammer arms complete, but the pick arm of **C16** is broken. **C15** has a wedge which formerly secured the handle in the eye, while **C16–17** have lugs descending below the eye to increase the security of the handle. No pickaxe resembling the Roman dolabra (Manning 1976, 27–28, figs 17, 76, 18.77) is known, and it is possible that the surviving pickaxes represent the only medieval type.

Mattocks, tools with a pick arm combined with an adze-like blade, are mentioned in documents although less frequently than picks. The adze-like blade was ideal both for breaking up soil and loose rock and for taking down masonry, in the latter case breaking up mortar and levering apart blocks of stone. During the pulling down of Abingdon Abbey in 1539 there was 'paied to Richard Smythe for the making of viij Ies to viij mattokes at iiijd the I – ijs vii d' (Salzman 1967, 333). Such work required a good edge, and in 1538 a smith was paid 'for new transposyng of x mattocks wᵗ stelyng of the same' in connection with the demolition of Chertsey Abbey (Salzman 1967, 331). No mattock is yet known from a medieval context.

4.6 HAMMER-AXES

After extraction, blocks of stone were sometimes further split to create more manageable pieces, and the next process involved reducing or roughly dressing the stone and removing waste before fine tooling was undertaken. In recent times the rough surface was reduced with sledgehammers and picks (Arkell 1947, 115; Purcell 1967, 46, 88, pl 45a), and medieval documents confirm that similar tools were in use before.

Sledgehammers have been noted above, but other tools listed are the 'pulyng ax' or 'polax' and the 'kevel', both forms of heavy hammer-axe, and the smaller 'brocheax' (Salzman 1967, 331). These hammer-axes must have been for the preliminary reducing and scappling of stone blocks and for roughly shaping the blocks during final working either in the quarry or the mason's lodge. **C18–19** are hammer-axes, both with expansions around their eyes but neither with lugs. **C18** retains part of an ash handle, of interest because ash is frequently mentioned in documents as the wood used for handles (Salzman 1967, 251, 335). **C19** has an iron nail and wedge through its eye to secure the handle.

4.7 AXES

The axe was used by the mason for surface dressing, as masonry testifies and many illustrations show, including a drawing of about 1250 by Matthew Paris (Salzman 1967, pl 4; Harvey 1975a, pl 18). Documents refer to these axes as 'hachiis' or as stoneaxes (Salzman 1967, 334–335), and they were used either to give the final finish to a stone, as the diagonal and vertical tooling of Romanesque architecture indicates (Clapham 1934, 116), or as a preliminary to final dressing with claw chisels. The axes used had two vertical cutting edges, as has **C20** with its two equally sized blades and slender lugs below the eye.

4.8 PUNCHES

Arkell (1947, 123–124, figs 19–20) illustrates a range of modern tools, but no medieval equivalent of the pitching tool used to remove the rough on the stone prior to the use of the punch is known.

The mason's punch was used for rough dressing stone during its final working into shape, and the range in size of the surviving punches **C21–27** today, also known as points, reflects the scale of work on which they were used. The burred heads of such punches as **C24** and **C26** imply their use with hammers, but mallets must have been used with some of the others.

4.9 CHISELS

The mason's chisel, used for dressing, shaping and carving stone, differs from the carpenter's chisel in its stoutness and in having a striking face and stem in one with the blade. The blade itself is often flared and bevelled on both faces.

Chisels **C28–38**, all mason's chisels, range widely in size but less so in blade form. All have expanded heads, few with marked burring, and it is possible that all were struck with wooden mallets which give a smoother and more controlled operation. If modern practice is a guide (J Duffield pers comm), the narrow-bladed chisel **C28** could have been used on the edge of a block of stone for working down almost to the marked line. The central area of the stone, hitherto only worked by the pitching tool and punch, would probably have been worked with a claw chisel or its equivalent before a smooth finish was produced with a chisel of the type represented by **C29–34**. No equivalent is yet known of the modern bolster with a blade of 50–130mm wide and used to produce a fine finish, nor of the sheet iron drag used to remove chisel marks on the soft stone. Salzman (1967, 334) notes that no implement named in the building accounts can be identified as the drag, and suggests that in the medieval period the blade of the mason's hammer was used with a drawing motion to perform the same function.

Carving mouldings and decorative details required specialised tools, and **C35–37** may have been used to carve grooves. They are slender and have narrow blades, and could be the equivalent of the modern quirking tool (Arkell 1947, 123, fig 20.6). They may also have been used for more detailed carving, a possible use for the flared, single-edged bevelled blade **C38**.

4.10 SAWS

Stone was split with wedges and cut with saws. Documents imply at least two sizes of saw, since there are references to 'a saw for sawing stone, 4 ft long' at Westminster in 1329, and a further reference in 1532 to 'stone sawis for masons' bought at 8d (Salzman 1967, 336). **C39**, an incomplete saw with a long narrow blade, was probably used for cutting stone.

4.11 STONE AUGERS

Stone was pierced with borers or augers, but no surviving example is known. Documents refer to 'a great borer, 3½ ft long' at Westminster in 1329, to the purchase of 'an instrument called a stoon naugor' at Salisbury in 1479, and to purchases of 'ston persers for the masons' at Hampton Court in 1533 (Salzman 1967, 336). An auger might have been used in quarrying for drilling holes for the insertion of wedges, as was practiced before the advent of pneumatic drills (Purcell 1967, 46).

4.12 SETTING OUT TOOLS

Quarrying, working stone and building all required some degree of setting out. The lines along which stone had to be split and subsequently reduced required marking, and the carving of ornamental stonework such as plinths, strings, tracery and hood moulds involved the use of squares and templates.

Squares were generally made of wood, and are usually depicted as such in illuminated manuscripts, but there are documentary references to squares made up of iron which are not yet supported by any actual example. There were '2 irons made in the shape of sqwiers' in the lodge at Westminster in 1387, and in the lodge at Portchester in 1430 '3 squaryngirnes' (Salzman 1967, 339). The 'moldes' or templates which were used as a guide for masons had to have the required shape transferred to the stone by a scriber such as **C40**, found in a masons' working area. No doubt any object with a pointed tip might have been used.

Dividers or compasses are tools common to masons and carpenters, and those described above (**B148–151**) are all probably small enough to be carpenters' tools. Masons used them for setting out mouldings and arranging arches and window tracery.

Plumb-levels and plumb-lines were used to maintain horizontal joints and vertical faces in masonry during construction, and representations show both using a plumb or lead weight as a guide (Harvey 1975a, pls 14 and 18). In 1444 '19 plomettes of lead' are mentioned at Shene (Salzman 1967, 339), and several plumb-bobs survive, amongst them **C41** with an iron staple, and **C42** with rust encrustation implying a lost staple.

4.13 HOISTING EQUIPMENT

The movement of large blocks of stone, including keystones and bosses from vaults, was often done by means of a lewis. Salzman (1967, 322–333) identifies two types, one an arrangement of three iron wedges side by side on a bar, the other and earlier two crescent-shaped irons hung from a common ring. **C43** is probably the centre wedge from one of the multiple lewises, its centre bar now appearing to be integral. It was used with two outer wedges which were forged with an outer bevel, and all three were inserted in a specially cut hole and hoisted with a loop and hook. The crescent-shaped irons hung from a common ring with their convexities facing inwards and their lower ends inserted in holes cut diagonally in the stone.

Representations often show large grips or scissors bolted together and acting as giant pincers (Harvey 1975a, pl 22), and Salzman (1967, 323) identifies these with the 'robenettes' of documents. No medieval example is known.

Hooks are often shown lifting materials via hoists or cranes (Harvey 1975a, pls 18–19), and some discussed below under 'Household ironwork' (Chapter 11) may be from building works.

4.14 TROWELS

Masons, bricklayers and plasterers made constant use of trowels, which therefore occur frequently in documents, although references are normally restricted to statements such as 'ij trowell in the logge' at Scarborough in 1425, payment 'for 15 trowellis at 6d each' at Westminster in 1532, or payment at Cambridge Castle in 1295 'for working 3 pieces of iron to make 12 truell for the masons' (Salzman 1967, 335–336).

Entries can be more detailed, as in the spending of 3d on 'a trulle or iron for smoothing the walls' at Southampton in 1301 (Salzman 1967, 336).

All the medieval trowels (**C44–49**) have cranked tangs which were originally set in a wooden handle, and most have the large blades needed for spreading mortar, cement and plaster. **C44** is roughly triangular in shape, as **C45** may have been, but **C46–48** have diamond-shaped blades. **C48** is smaller than the others and may have been used for pointing or for plastering in small or restricted areas. **C49** has an oval blade whose rounded edges are probably more appropriate for a plasterer than a mason or bricklayer.

4.15 SLATERS' TOOLS

Medieval roofs were thatched, tiled or covered with stone slates, and stone for slates is likely to have been quarried or mined with tools similar to those employed in quarrying stone. Tools in recent use are described by Aston (1974, 41–42, fig 17) and Purcell (1967, 60, pls 27b and 28).

Splitting slates from large blocks of stone by frost action may be a post-medieval technique (Arkell 1947, 132), in which case the medieval slatter is likely to have used a hammer with two cutting edges such as **C50** for this purpose. This type of hammer is still used for removing waste from blocks and for splitting them, as well as for trimming the edges of the slate to their final shape (Arkell 1947, 133–135, fig 22; Purcell 1967, 60–61, pl 30; Aston 1974, 50, fig 27.212, 386, 4802). No example of the heavier hammer combining hammer head and cutting edge, and used recently for trimming slates to shape, is known (Arkell 1974, 148, fig 25; Purcell 1967, 61, pl 31; Aston 1974, 50, fig 28).

Two types of pick used to make the hole in a slate are known, one with an eye for a handle, the other used a separate, independent wooden handle. **C51**, too small to have been used in quarrying, has two pick blades and a lugged eye for a wooden handle. Picks **C52–62** taper more or less equally towards each end and in use were inserted into wooden handles with tapering holes cut close to the top (Arkell 1947, 133–135, 148, figs 22, 25; Purcell 1967, 61, pl 31; Aston 1974, 50, fig 27.2145, 2149, 4796–99, fig 29). The pick was turned round when one head became blunt and the fresh end was used, and when this in turn became blunt a new pick was inserted. Slatters, like millstone dressers, would have had a supply of picks which were sharpened and reworked by the smith as required. Some of the larger picks, such as **C62**, may in fact be mill-picks.

The hole in a slate was probably made with numerous light taps of the pick, the blows being directed towards the centre and from one side of the slate only (Arkell 1947, 135). Salzman (1967, 234) quotes a number of payments for piercing slates, including that at Woodstock in 1285 'pro j perforatore sclate per ij dies', but also suggests that a drill was sometimes used. In 1313 Simon de Norton, tiler, was paid 1d 'for a hide bought whereof to make a spyndelthoung for boring slates'.

4.16 MILLSTONE DRESSING TOOLS

Mill-picks and mill-bills used to level and dress millstones are hafted in the manner of slatters' picks in wooden handles called thrifts (Freese 1957, 102–107, pl 28b, c). Mill-pick **C63**, found in a mill-sluice, is similar to a slatter's pick but larger, and was used for the preliminary levelling of millstones and sometimes for chipping away unworn high spots on stones in use. The mill-bill, with wide cutting edges at each end rather like those of the slatter's hammer, levelled the surface and dressed the furrows of the millstone. These tools were rapidly blunted, and a dozen mill-bills might be blunted in dressing the furrows and have to be reground and eventually reworked if the steeled edge was worn away.

4.17 STEELING AND REPAIRING TOOLS

Medieval tools, particularly those of masons, were often made with a steel cutting or working edge, but despite this they lost their edges and there are many documentary references to the purchase of steel for shutting or welding onto the edges of tools. Salzman (1967, 288) records '6 sheaves of steel for putting on the iron tools of the masons' at Ely in 1323, and the use of 94 lb of Spanish steel at Portchester in 1397 'for the hardening of the axes and other tools of the masons'. In 1538, when Chertsey Abbey was being pulled down, the smith was paid 6d 'for new shuttyng poyntyng and stelyng of vj crowes of irne' and 10d 'for new transposing of x mattocks w^t stelyng of the same'.

In addition to re-steeling tools, blacksmiths also had to rework or 'batter' tools when they were worn by use. At Sheppey in 1365 the smith was paid 'for battering of 1,594 masons' axes, at ¼d each, and for battering 5,720 masons' tools at 1d for 20', and in 1348 at Westminster there are payments 'to Katherine the smith-wife for steeling and battering of the masons' tools' (Salzman 1967, 336–337).

C1 WEDGE
Castell-y-Bere, Gwynedd.
Site: c1221–1295.
Burred head. Weight 2.422 kg (5 lb 5½ oz).
L 164mm.
Butler 1974, 97, fig 8.12.

C2 WEDGE
Seacourt, Oxfordshire.
Mid to late 12th to late 14th century.
Burred head, curved distorted shank.
L 138mm.
Biddle 1961–62, 177, fig 30.5, scale 1:4, not 1:3.

C3 WEDGE
Wharram Percy, North Yorkshire.
Late 15th to early 16th century.
Down-turned head set to one side, ridge shank. L 82mm.
Area 6, SF12137, Pd VI; Andrews and Milne 1979.

C4 WEDGE
Bayham Abbey, East Sussex.
Probably derived from late 15th to early 16th century material.
Down-turned head set to one side. L 74mm.
Goodall 1983a, fig 45.15.

C5 WEDGE
Wharram Percy, North Yorkshire.
Early 10th to 20th century.
Head set to one side, ridged shank. L 65mm.
Goodall 1979a, 118–120, fig 62.58.

C6 WEDGE
Copt Hay, Tetsworth, Oxfordshire.
Late 12th, 13th century.
Broken rectangular stem, slightly flaring blade. L 110mm.
Robinson 1973, 101, fig 23.9.

C7 WEDGE
Winchester, Hampshire.
15th–16th century.
Broken blade, slightly burred head.
L 82mm.
Goodall 1990-8, fig 60.408.

C8 WEDGE
Castle Acre Priory, Norfolk.
From water channel under reredorter.
Reredorter built in mid 12th century; site late 11th century to 1537 with later use of some buildings.
Tapering rectangular section, slightly burred head, mason's mark on one face.
Weight 2.112 kg (4 lb 10½ oz), L 202mm.
DAMHB Collection, London. For site see Raby and Reynolds 1952.

C9 WEDGE
Castle Acre Priory, Norfolk.
From water channel under reredorter.
Reredorter built in mid 12th century; site late 11th century to 1537 with later use of some buildings.
Tapering rectangular section with mason's mark on one face. Weight 1.913 kg (4 lb 3½ oz), L 219mm.
DAMHB Collection, London. For site see Raby and Reynolds 1952.

C10 WEDGE
Clough Castle, Co. Down.
c1250 to early 14th century.
Burred head. L 64mm.
Waterman 1954, 137, fig 11.5.

C11 WEDGE
Burton-in-Lonsdale, North Yorkshire.
Later 13th century–mid 14th century.
L 90mm.
Moorhouse 1971a, 95, fig 3.20.

C12 PICK
Lydney Castle, Gloucestershire.
12th century, possibly into 13th century.
Single-ended pick with remains of wooden handle. L 231mm.
Casey 1931, 252, pl XXV.7.

C13 PICK
Weoley Castle, Birmingham, West Midlands.
c1200–1230.
Single-ended pick, socket formed by wrapping iron round against left face of blade which has traces of welds from initial forging. Found with birch handle, not preserved. L 235mm.
Oswald 1962–63, 130, fig 51.5.

STONEWORKING AND PLASTERING TOOLS

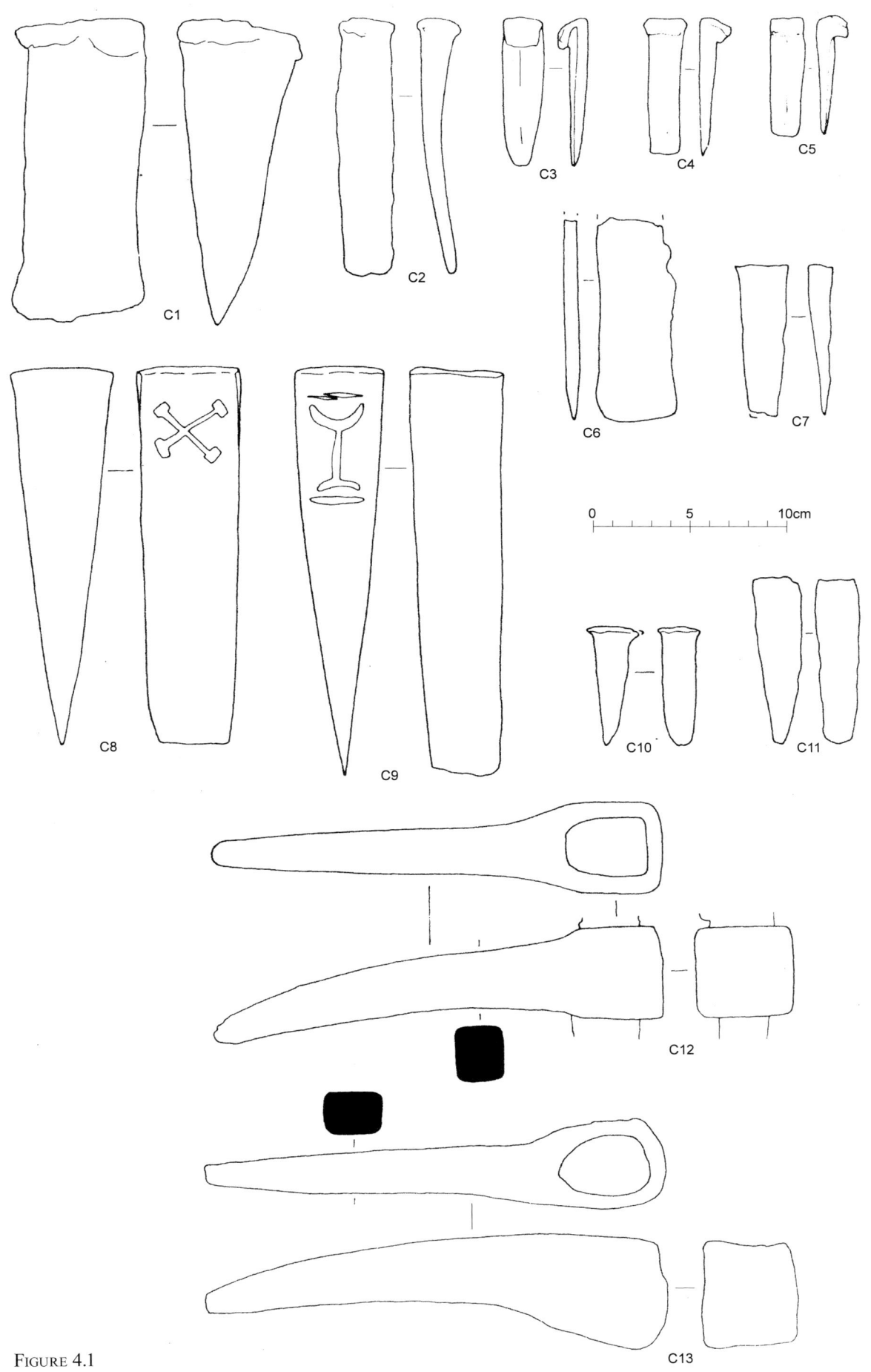

FIGURE 4.1
Stoneworking tools: Wedges and pickaxes

C14 PICK
Lydford Castle, Devon.
*c*1250–1300.
Single-ended pick with part of wooden handle of oval section secured in eye by iron wedge. L 457mm.
Goodall 1980b, fig 18.2.

C15 PICKAXE
Llanstephan Castle, Dyfed.
Site: 12th to 15th century.
Rectangular-sectioned arms with expansion round eye which retains wedge which formerly secured handle. L 287mm.
Excavated by Mrs L Murray-Thriepland and G Guilbert. For site see King 1963.

C16 PICKAXE
Castle Acre Priory, Norfolk.
From narrow sewer drain under reredorter. Reredorter built in mid 12th century; site late 11th century to 1537 with later use of some buildings.
Pick arm broken, swelling round eye. Lugs below eye. L 305mm.
DAMHB Collection, London. For site see Raby and Reynolds 1952.

C17 PICKAXE
Coventry, Warwickshire.
From tower of city wall built 1404, taken down 1461.
Lugs below eye. L 334mm.
Herbert Art Gallery and Museums, Coventry. Shelton Collection.

C18 HAMMER-AXE
White Castle, Gwent.
Site: 12th century onwards, roofless and derelict by 16th century.
Axe blade with vertical cutting edge, hammer head burred. Expansion around eye which retained fossilized remains of ash (*Fraxinus*) handle. L 249mm.
DAMHB Collection, London. For site see Radford 1962.

STONEWORKING AND PLASTERING TOOLS

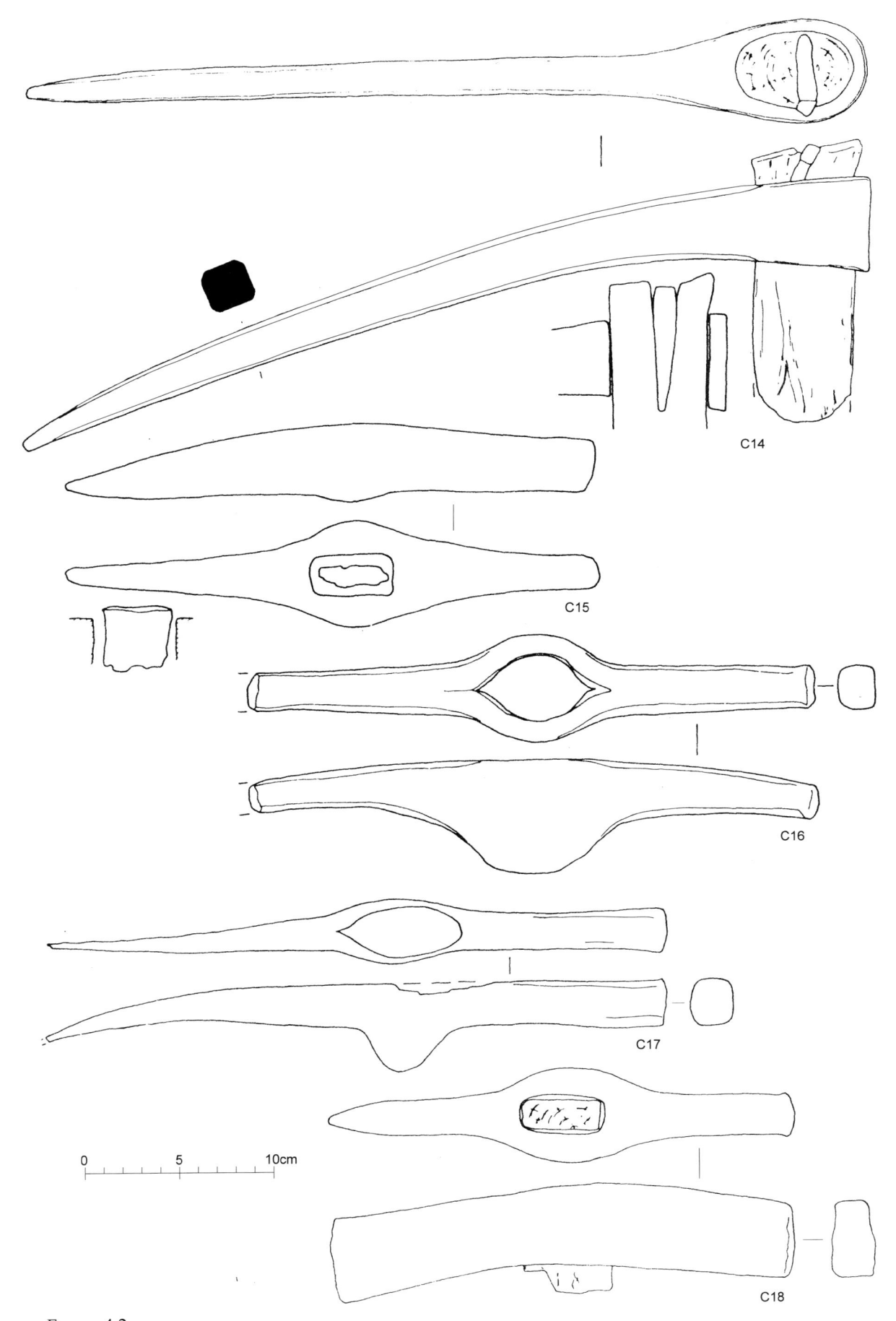

FIGURE 4.2
Stoneworking tools: Pickaxes and hammer-axe

C19 HAMMER-AXE
Fountains Abbey, North Yorkshire.
Site: 1132–1539 with later robbing.
Axe blade with vertical cutting edge, hammer plain. Slight expansion around eye which retains nail and wedge which secured former handle. L 223mm.
DAMHB Collection, London.

C20 AXE
Fountains Abbey, North Yorkshire.
Site: 1132–1539 with later robbing.
Expansion around eye, two vertical cutting edges. Lugs below eye. L 181mm.
DAMHB Collection, London.

C21 PUNCH
King's Lynn, Norfolk.
c1250–1300.
Burred head and octagonal-sectioned stem. L 257mm.
Goodall and Carter 1977, 295, fig 134.38.

C22 PUNCH
Winchester, Hampshire.
Late 10th–11th century.
Expanded head and broken, circular-sectioned stem. L 236mm.
Goodall 1990-9, fig 67.412.

C23 PUNCH
Winchester, Hampshire.
Late medieval.
Broken rounded stem becoming rectangular towards tip. L 205mm.
Goodall 1978a, 139, fig 56, scale 1:2, not 1:1.

C24 PUNCH
Southampton, Hampshire.
1250–1300.
Burred head to circular-sectioned stem becoming rectangular towards tip. L 199mm.
Harvey 1975b, 279, fig 251.2019.

C25 PUNCH
Weoley Castle, Birmingham, West Midlands.
c1270–1600.
Expanded head and octagonal-sectioned stem becoming rectangular towards tip. L 170mm.
Taylor 1974. For site see Oswald 1962.

C26 PUNCH
Winchester, Hampshire.
1250–1320.
Burred head and octagonal-sectioned stem becoming rectangular towards tip.
L 120mm.
Goodall 1990-9, fig 67.413.

C27 PUNCH
Folkestone, Kent.
Mid 12th century.
Rectangular-sectioned punch, incomplete.
L 82mm.
Pitt-Rivers 1883, 463, pl XVIII.20.

C28 CHISEL
Criccieth Castle, Gwynedd.
Site: c1230–1404.
Expanded head, octagonal-sectioned stem.
L 279mm.
O'Neil 1944–45, 42, pl X.25.

C29 CHISEL
Wharram Percy, North Yorkshire.
Late 15th to early 16th century.
Expanded head, octagonal-sectioned stem becoming rectangular towards broken, flaring blade. L 334mm.
Goodall 1979a, 118, fig 62.56.

C30 CHISEL
Weoley Castle, Birmingham, West Midlands.
Site: c1080–1600.
Slightly expanded head, octagonal-sectioned stem becoming rectangular towards flaring blade. L 271mm.
Birmingham City Museum, WC 432. For site see Oswald 1962.

C31 CHISEL
Barton Blount, Derbyshire.
15th century.
Expanded head, octagonal-sectioned stem, flaring blade. L 160mm.
Goodall 1975b, 97, fig 46.6.

C32 CHISEL
Winchester, Hampshire.
Mid 12th–early 13th century.
Expanded head, octagonal-sectioned stem.
L 156mm.
Goodall 1990-9, fig 67.414.

C33 CHISEL
Upton, Gloucestershire.
Late 13th to late 14th century.
Expanded head, rectangular-sectioned stem, flaring blade. L 123mm.
Hilton and Rahtz 1966, 120, fig 14.31.

C34 CHISEL
Kennington, Greater London.
From foundations of building built 1353–55.
Expanded head, rectangular-sectioned stem.
L 71mm.
Dawson 1976, 87, fig 13.13.

C35 CHISEL
Dyserth Castle, Clwyd.
Site: 1241–63.
Expanded head, rectangular-sectioned stem.
L 292mm.
Glenn 1915.

C36 CHISEL
Weoley Castle, Birmingham, West Midlands.
Site: c1080–1600.
Slightly expanded head, rectangular-sectioned stem. L 249mm.
Birmingham City Museum, lab. no. 833. For site see Oswald 1962.

C37 CHISEL
Weoley Castle, Birmingham, West Midlands.
c1270–1600.
Damaged expanded head, octagonal-sectioned stem becoming rectangular towards blade. L 217mm.
Taylor 1974. For site see Oswald 1962.

C38 CHISEL
Winchester, Hampshire.
Late 13th century.
Broken rectangular stem with flaring blade with single-sided bevel. L 91mm.
Goodall 1990-9, fig 67.415.

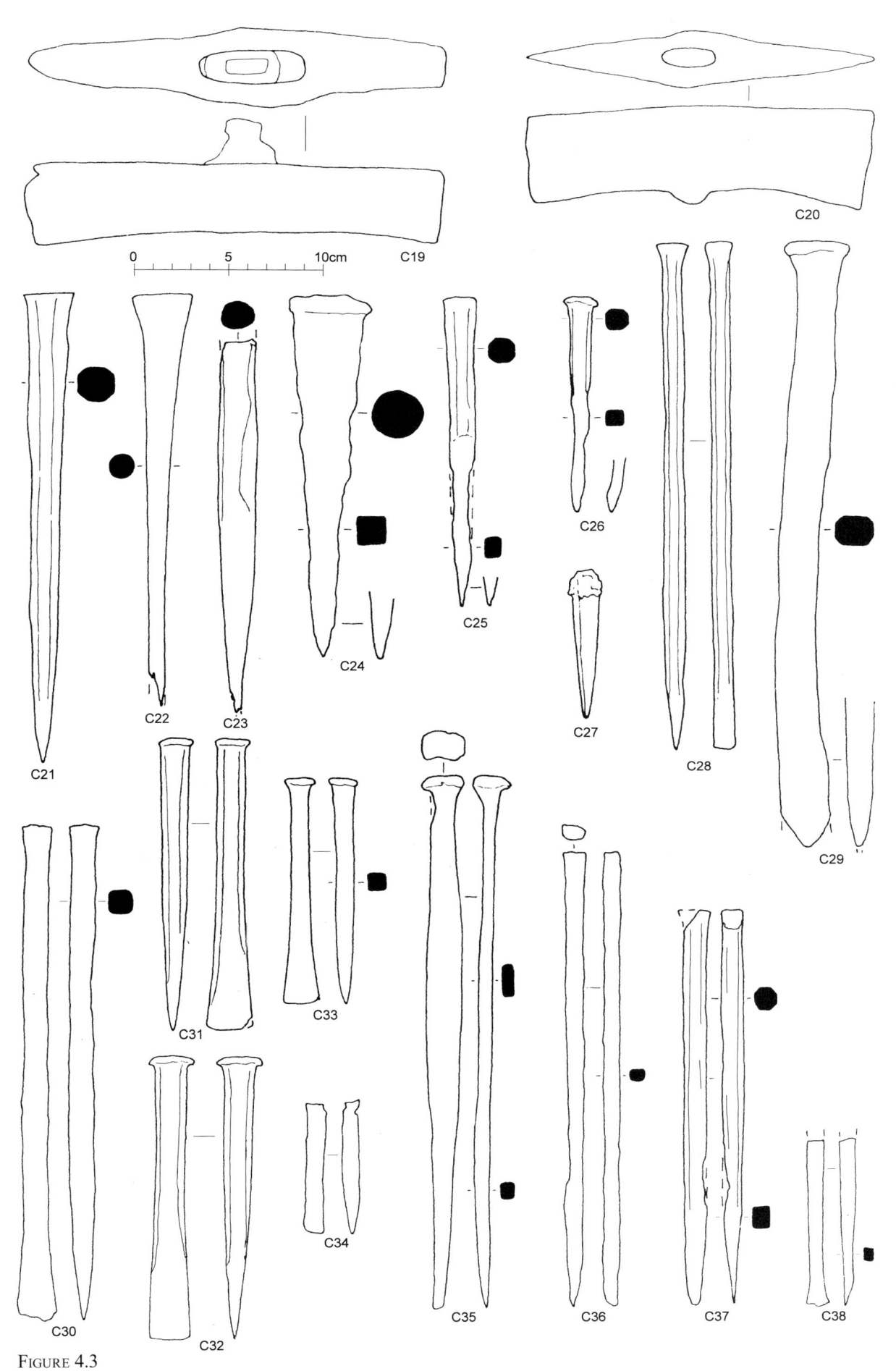

FIGURE 4.3
Stoneworking tools: Hammer-axe, axe, punches, and chisels

C39 SAW
Skenfrith Castle, Gwent.
Site: probably late 11th to 15th/16th century.
Push saw with broken blade and tang. Teeth, three to one inch (26mm), not set. Collar from former wooden handle at junction of blade and tang. L 345mm.
DAMHB Collection, London. For site see Craster 1970.

C40 SCRIBER
Conway, Gwynedd.
c1280 to 1400.
Tapering blade with whittle tang. L 141mm.
Excavated by L A S Butler. From the Old Vicarage.

C41 PLUMB-BOB
Lydney Castle, Gloucestershire.
12th century, possibly into 13th century.
Lead plumb-bob with iron staple. D 45mm.
Casey 1931, 254, pl XXXVI.20.

C42 PLUMB-BOB
Norwich.
15th–17th century.
Lead plumb-bob of irregular elongated shape. Slight encrustation of rust suggests former attachment to iron fitting. L 74mm.
Hurst and Golson 1955, 101, fig 24.11.

C43 LEWIS
Rievaulx Abbey, North Yorkshire.
Site: 1131–1538 with later robbing.
Central wedge from lewis with broken bar, ?originally separate, close to top. L 152mm.
DAMHB Collection, London.

C44 TROWEL
Castell-y-Bere, Gwynedd.
Site: c1221–1295.
Cranked tang, triangular blade. L 224mm.
Butler 1974, 97, fig 8.14.

C45 TROWEL
Castell-y-Bere, Gwynedd.
Site: c1221–1295.
Cranked tang, broken ?triangular blade. L 141mm.
Butler 1974, 97 (14-H).

C46 TROWEL
Winchester, Hampshire.
c1110.
Cranked tang with clenched tip, diamond-shaped blade. Blade ferrite with a hardness of 127 HV. L 264mm.
Goodall 1990-9, fig 68.421.

C47 TROWEL
Winchester, Hampshire.
Late 13th–early 14th century.
Cranked tang with clenched tip, diamond-shaped blade. Tip lost. L 237mm.
Goodall 1990-9, fig 68.422.

C48 TROWEL
Winchester, Hampshire.
?Early 14th century.
Cranked tang, damaged diamond-shaped blade. L 168mm.
Goodall 1990-9, fig 68.423.

C49 TROWEL
Winchester, Hampshire.
Perhaps pre-12th century.
Broken cranked tang, damaged oval blade. L 194mm.
Goodall 1990-9.

STONEWORKING AND PLASTERING TOOLS

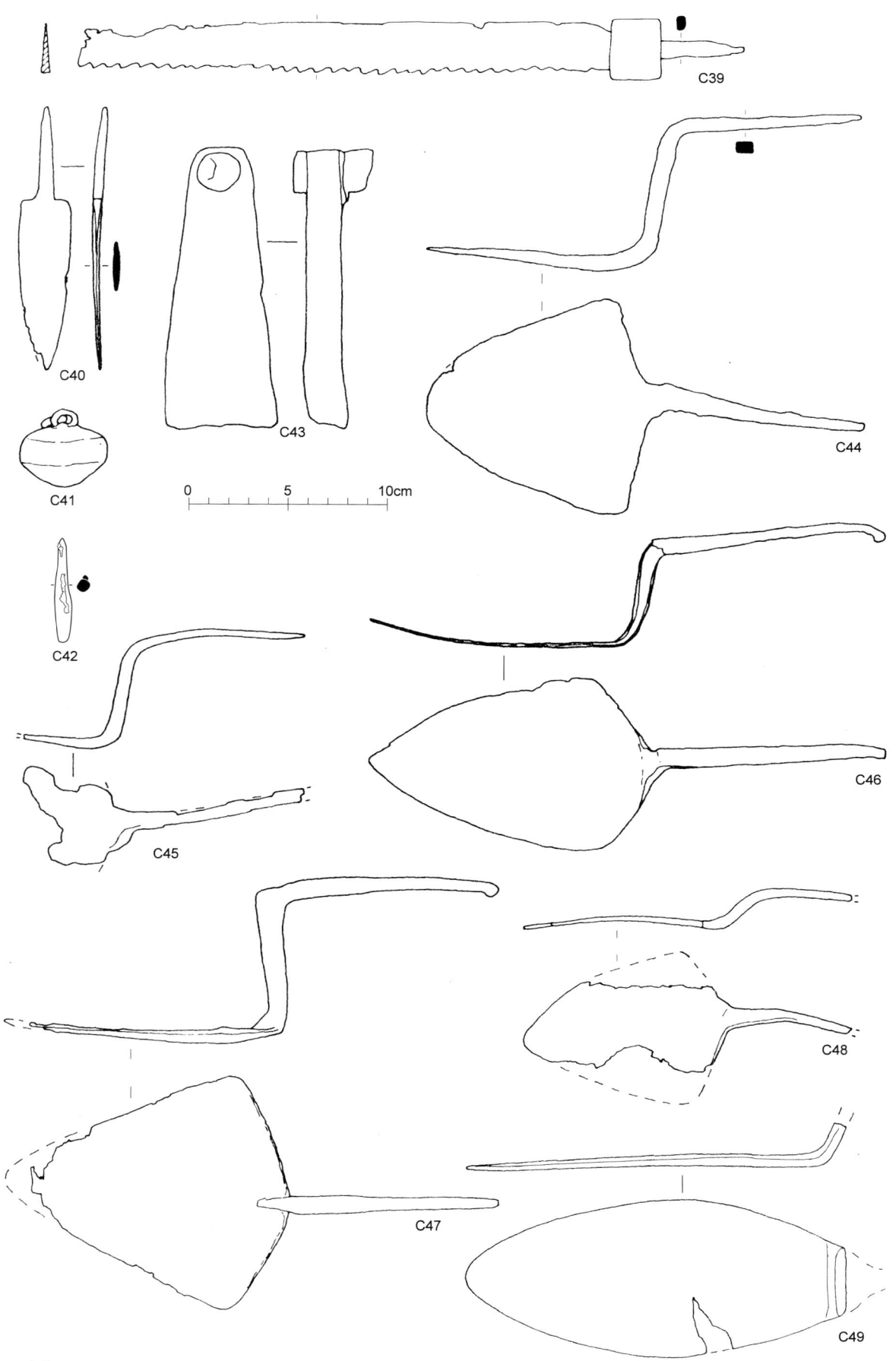

FIGURE 4.4
Stoneworking and plastering tools: Saw, scriber, plumb-bob, lewis, and trowels

C50 HAMMER
Goldsborough, North Yorkshire.
Site: 13th–15th century.
Two cutting edges, expansion round and below circular eye. L 163mm.
Excavated by P V Addyman.

C51 PICK
Kirkcudbright Castle, Dumfries and Galloway.
c1288–1308.
Double-ended pick of rectangular section with lugs below eye. L 155mm.
Dunning et al 1957–58, 137–138, fig 7.1.

C52 PICK
Hen Domen, Powys.
First half 13th century.
Tapering rectangular section. L 96mm.
Barker and Higham 2000.

C53 PICK
Winchester, Hampshire.
Late 13th–early 14th century.
Tapering rectangular section. Tip consists of ferrite with some partly spheroidised pearlite. Carbon content in the range of 0.1–0.2%, but on one side it rises to 0.6%. Hardness of low carbon areas is 95 HVI.
L 102mm.
Goodall 1990-9, fig 67.419.

C54 PICK
Winchester, Hampshire.
c1400–c1450.
Tapering rectangular section. L 103mm.
Goodall 1990-9, fig 67.420.

C55 PICK
Wroughton Copse, Fyfield Down, Wiltshire.
12th–13th century.
Tapering circular section. L 111mm.
Excavated by P J Fowler.

C56 PICK
Winchester, Hampshire.
c1138–41.
Tapering rectangular and circular sections.
L 118mm.
Goodall 1990-9, fig 67.418.

C57 PICK
Winchester, Hampshire.
10th century.
Tapering rectangular section, one end damaged. L 121mm.
Goodall 1990-9, fig 67.417.

C58 PICK
Bramber Castle, West Sussex.
14th century.
Tapering rounded rectangular section.
L 125mm.
Barton and Holden 1977, 66, fig 20.14.

C59 PICK
Woodperry, Oxfordshire.
12th to 14th century pottery.
Tapering rectangular section. L 130mm.
Ashmolean Museum, Oxford, 1873. 54.
Wilson 1846.

C60 PICK
Weoley Castle, Birmingham, West Midlands.
c1270–1600.
Tapering rectangular section. L 129mm.
Taylor 1974; Oswald 1962.

C61 PICK
Beckery Chapel, Glastonbury, Somerset.
12th–13th century, ?earlier.
Tapering square shank. L 152mm.
Rahtz and Hirst 1974, 61, fig 22.14.

C62 PICK
King's Lynn, Norfolk.
c1250–1350.
Tapering rectangular section. L 176mm.
Goodall and Carter 1977, 295, fig 134.39.

C63 MILL-PICK
South Witham, Lincolnshire.
c1220 to late 13th century. From mill sluice.
Tapering rectangular section. L 212mm.
Goodall 2002, fig 7.3, no. 29.

STONEWORKING AND PLASTERING TOOLS

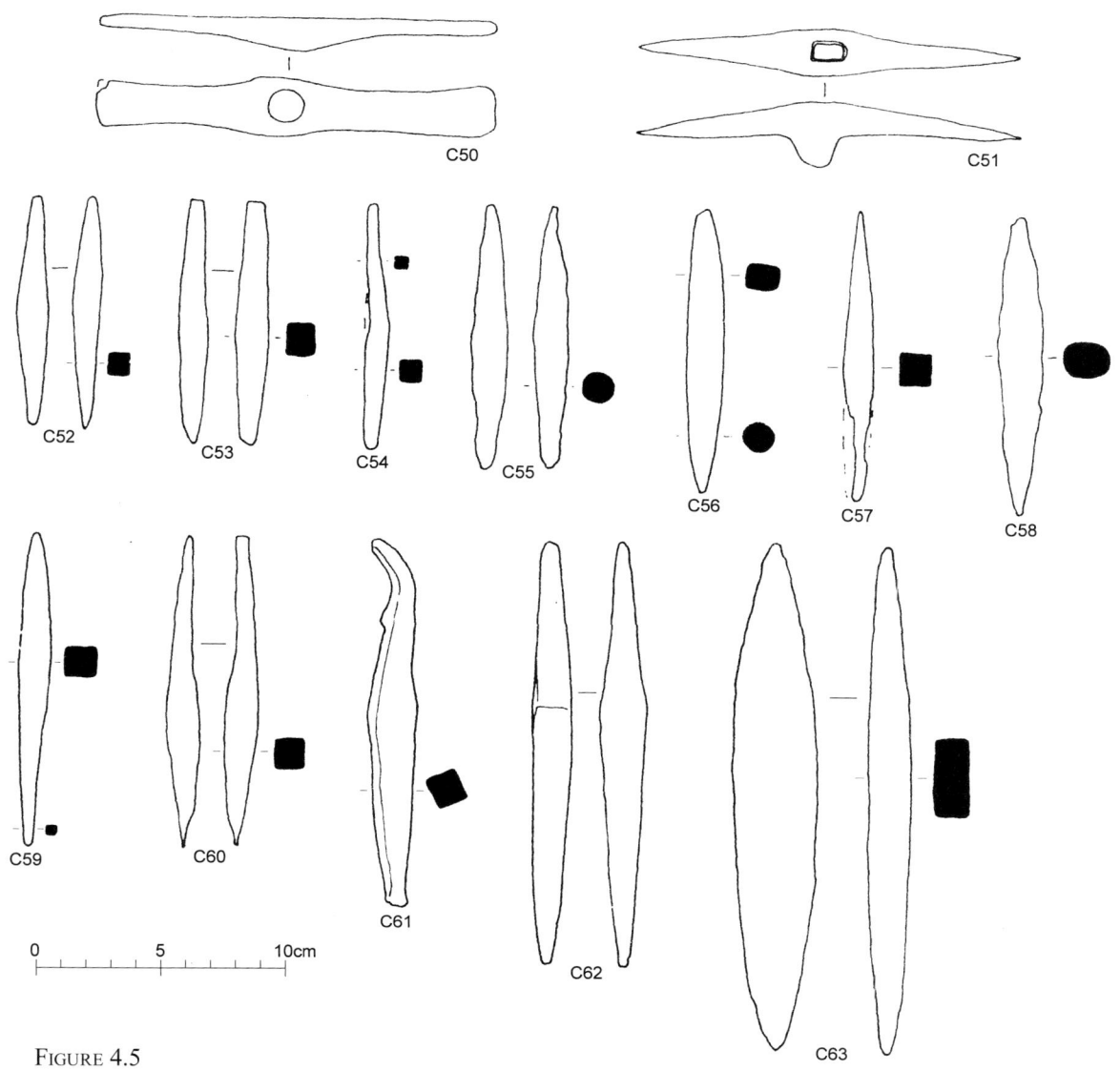

FIGURE 4.5
Stoneworking tools: Hammer, picks, and mill-pick

5

TEXTILE MANUFACTURING TOOLS

The wool trade was for centuries the main source of England's wealth, and the production of the raw materials for weaving cloth involved the use of such tools as heckles, carding combs and weaving combs. Forceps, tenter hooks, harbicks and cloth shears were used in the finishing of the cloth (for general works relevant to textile manufacture see Jenkins 1965, 176–184; Barker 1957; Patterson 1957; Rose 1957; Woodhouse 1957).

5.1 FIBRE PREPARATION

Wool and flax fibres were prepared for spinning with heckles and carding combs. Wool was sorted after shearing, that of better quality being used for ordinary cloths, the worst for coarse cloth, and it was then washed or scoured to remove grease, perspiration salts and foreign matter such as dust and burrs. After drying it was disentangled and the fibres separated by combing or carding. Long stapled wools generally used for making worsted and fine cloths were prepared for spinning with heckles which brought their fibres as near as possible parallel. The short stapled wools, together with the shorted fibres left on the combs which were unsuitable for worsted cloth, were processed with carding combs which thoroughly mixed all the fibres.

Linen was woven from the best fibres in the stems of flax. After pulling, the flax stalks were dried, deseeded and then retted to enable the bark to be peeled from the woody core. The fibres were separated from the core by crushing and beating or scutching, and the scutched fibre was then combed to split up the flax and separate the fibres, often with a heckle similar to that used in wool preparation. The fibres were then twisted into yarn, the fine yarns used for weaving high quality linen, the coarse for rope, etc.

5.2 HECKLES

To avoid confusion with earlier woolcombs made entirely of iron, and in order not to imply their use solely with wool, the combs used in preparing both wool and flax fibres for spinning are termed heckles.

Medieval heckles most commonly survive as individual iron teeth, since few complete or partially complete examples are known. Earlier examples and medieval representations provide evidence of their form, however, and of alternative methods of mounting the iron teeth. The most common medieval and earlier type of heckle had two or more rows of iron teeth set in a rectangular wooden block with a handle. The block sometimes had an iron binding on the underside and along the front and sides, as have heckles of middle Saxon to medieval date from Wicken Bonhunt in Essex (Wade 1980), Thetford in Norfolk (Goodall 1984) and Århus in Denmark (Andersen *et al* 1971, 138–139). A heckle from a Viking grave at Harrold, Bedfordshire, however, evidently had no such binding (Evison 1970, 39, 42, fig 12 i–k). Heckle tooth **D12** retains a small fragment from the underside of such a sheet binding, but its absence from the other teeth is in no way significant since teeth and binding were separate elements. **D1** is an alternative form of heckle with its teeth set in a semicircular-sectioned, iron-bound head which may have fronted a deeper wooden block and handle.

Medieval illustrations imply that the teeth may sometimes have been fitted into fixed 'stock-cards'. A 15th-century illustration (Salzman 1964, 213) shows a woman drawing handfuls of wool through a group of upright iron teeth set into the top of a circular stand, whilst another of 14th-century date, although of Italian origin (Patterson 1957, fig 159) shows bundles of flat fibres being drawn through a group of teeth set in a bench top. It is possible that the longer teeth are from such fittings.

Surviving heckle teeth **D1–43** vary considerably in length, the complete ones (**D1–19**) from 88mm to 177mm, and the incomplete ones, of which **D20–43** are a selection, are up to 203mm. Insufficient complete heckle teeth survive for the lengths to be particularly significant, although there is a concentration between 93 and 109mm in length. Modern techniques of 'hand-hackling' flax fibre (Woodhouse 1957, 159) may offer some explanation of the differing lengths of heckle teeth since they involve drawing heckles with 178mm long teeth through the flax, then others with more closely spaced, 128mm long teeth, and if necessary others with increasingly fine and more closely set teeth to produce finer yarns. Heckle teeth are both circular and rectangular in section, and all taper to a point. The heads are plain, flattened or have a side expansion, the shaping perhaps intended to secure them more firmly in the wooden block.

Heckles were generally used in pairs and their teeth warmed before use. A mass of wool was transferred from one comb to another and back until only long parallel fibres remained. A 14th-century illustration (Patterson 1957, fig 156) shows a pair in use in conjunction with a propped upright stand.

5.3 CARDING COMBS

Carding combs, wooden boards with handles and rows of inclined iron wire teeth, were used in pairs to disentangle wool and bind the fibres together, a small quantity of wool placed on one cad being teased out until a perfect mixture of fibres resulted. A 15th-century illustration shows a pair of combs in use (Salzman 1964, 213), but no medieval example is yet known. A fragment of a comb from a later 16th to 17th-century context comes from Northampton (Goodall *et al* 1979, 273, fig 119.65).

5.4 WEAVING COMBS

Spun thread was woven on looms and iron weaving combs such as **D44–45** were used to beat in the weft, particularly in tapestry-work and rug weaving. **D44** is incomplete and a band of tinning along the toothed edge may have been intended to counter corrosion which would have discoloured the cloth. **D45** is almost complete and holes in the side edges and along the top show that it was set in a handle, probably of wood. Both weaving combs have worn teeth, and both probably had handles which were set at an angle to the blade.

5.5 FORCEPS

After weaving, the first stage of 'finishing' cloth involved hanging it over a rail or spreading it on a table and removing extraneous matter with forceps. **D46** has the fine, precise tips needed in forceps used to remove particles before cloth was sent to be fulled.

5.6 TENTER HOOKS

Woollen and linen cloth was fulled, the former in order to felt and thicken the cloth and so cause the fibres to adhere to each other and obliterate in the weave, the latter to separate the stiff groups of fibres into smaller and softer ones. After fulling, scouring and rinsing, the wet cloth was stretched on tenters to dry.

References to the leasing of tenter grounds are common in medieval town records (Salzman 1964, 224), and a tenter ground is depicted in the Moorfields area of London on a map of 1559–60 (Holmes 1966, 113, pls XXXVIII and XLb). The medieval tenter or tenter frame comprised two horizontal wooden rails supported by vertical posts. The pairs of rails each had a row of tenter hooks set along them, the hooks pointing upwards in the upper rail and downwards in the lower. Cloth was attached to the hooks and tension adjusted by utilising housings in the posts. Some stretching of cloth was legitimate and necessary, but there was a temptation to stretch cloth excessively and weaken it, and in the 16th century ordinances were issued against the use of powerful racks with levers, winches and ropes (Salzman 1964, 224).

Iron tenter hooks **D47–71** are slender and have tapering shanks and hooks, the latter commonly straight and either perpendicular (**D68**), inturned (**D52**) or out-turned (**D49**). Some of the less common hook shapes, such as the hooked tip of **D55**, the curved hook of **D58**, and the strongly out-turned hook of **D47** may be the result of distortion during use. Complete hooks range in length from 18 to 39mm, and shanks from 20 to 54mm. Some 55 more medieval tenter hooks from Winchester, not catalogued, have hooks between 18 and 32mm in length (Goodall 1990-6). This range in tenter hook size reflects the differing types of cloth stretched, and the spacing of hooks in the tenter frames will have varied accordingly. Tenter hooks with 25mm long hooks on a tenter frame in the Tolson Memorial Museum in Huddersfield (West Yorkshire) are some 70mm apart.

5.7 HARBICKS AND CLOTH SHEARS

After tentering, a softer finish was given to woollen cloth by shearing. The cloth was stretched over a bar and the nap raised by brushing with teasels mounted in a wooden frame, as depicted in the cloth-workers' window of *c*1460–65 at Notre Dame, Semur-en-Anxois, France (Carus-Wilson 1957, 110, pl XVIb; Harvey 1975a, pl 111). The cloth was then transferred to a cropping board or horse for shearing, and a misericord at Brampton, Cambridgeshire (Carus-Wilson 1957, 106, pl XVc) shows this process under way with the cloth secured to the board by a pair of harbicks or shearboard hooks of the type represented by **D72–73**. Harbicks are double-ended hooks, and the misericord shows that one hook was fixed in the selvedge of the cloth and the other in the padded surface of the board. **D72–73** are of iron and have straight arms; two other examples from Winchester are of copper alloy and have curved arms (Goodall and Keene 1990). All four are decorated or shaped in some way.

No large pairs of cloth shears similar to those depicted on the Lane Chapel in Cullompton, Devon, and elsewhere are yet known (Carus-Wilson 1957, 104–109, pls XIII, XVe, XVIa, c–d). They have large bows and broad, flat-ended blades, and modern examples can be over 1m long with blades about 46cm long. **G474** may be a blade and handle fragment.

5.8 NEEDLEWORKING TOOLS

Iron tools suitable for use in needleworking could also all have been used by other craftsmen. Some of the shears and scissors discussed below (**G418–421**) may have been used to cut cloth and thread, just as some of the needles **E60–80** will have been used for sewing cloth rather than leather. **E81–83** may also have been used in needleworking.

D1 HECKLE
Norwich.
In 1507 fire deposit.
Part of heckle with teeth set in semicircular iron-bound top. L 147mm.
Goodall 1993f, fig 134, no. 1420.

D2 HECKLE TOOTH
Winchester, Hampshire.
13th century.
Complete. L 88mm.
Goodall 1990-4, 216, no. 59.

D3 HECKLE TOOTH
Llanstephan Castle, Dyfed.
Site: 12th to 15th century.
Shaped head, tip lost. L 93mm.
Excavated by G Guilbert.

D4 HECKEL TOOTH
Llantrithyd, South Glamorgan.
Early to mid 12th century.
Complete. Shaped head. L 95mm.
Goodall 1977f, 47, iron object fig 2.34.

D5 HECKLE TOOTH
Goltho Manor, Lincolnshire.
11th century.
Complete. L 96mm.
Goodall 1987, fig 156.13.

D6 HECKLE TOOTH
Winchester, Hampshire.
Mid to late 13th century.
Shaped head, distorted but complete shank. L 97mm.
Goodall 1990-4, fig 44.56.

D7 HECKLE TOOTH
Rhuddlan, Clwyd.
?Mid 13th century.
Complete but distorted. Shaped head. L 98mm.
Goodall 1994, fig 17.1, no. 9.

D8 HECKLE TOOTH
Winchester, Hampshire.
13th century.
Shaped head, tip lost. L 99mm.
Goodall 1990-4, 216, no. 58.

D9 HECKLE TOOTH
Eaton Socon, Cambridgeshire.
In medieval ditch fill but probably derived from settlement with floruit in 11th century.
Complete. Shaped head. L 102mm.
Addyman 1965, 65, fig 11.3.

D10 HECKLE TOOTH
Upton, Gloucestershire.
Mid to later 13th century.
Complete. L 104mm.
Rahtz 1969a, 108, fig 12.95.

D11 HECKLE TOOTH
Winchester, Hampshire.
Mid to ?late 13th century.
Complete. L 105mm.
Goodall 1990-4, fig 44.55.

D12 HECKLE TOOTH
Winchester, Hampshire.
Late 13th–early 14th century.
Complete. Fragment of binding plate from handle 16mm below head. L 106mm.
Goodall 1990-4, fig 44.61.

D13 HECKLE TOOTH
Winchester, Hampshire.
Mid to late 13th century.
Complete. Metallurgy: ferrite with some grain; boundary carbide and slag; very heterogeneous; hardness 109 HVI. L 109mm.
Goodall 1990-4, fig 44.57.

D14 HECKLE TOOTH
Stonar, Kent.
c1225–1275.
Complete. L 118mm.
Excavated by N Macpherson-Grant.

D15 HECKLE TOOTH
Lyveden, Northamptonshire.
1475–1500.
?Complete. L 125mm.
Steane and Bryant 1975, 134, fig 50.192.

D16 HECKLE TOOTH
Thuxton, Norfolk.
Site: 12th to end 14th century.
Complete. Shaped head. L 136mm.
Excavated by L A S Butler.

D17 HECKLE TOOTH
London.
Late 13th to 14th century.
Complete. Shaped head. L 151mm.
Henig 1974, 195, fig 39.93.

D18 HECKLE TOOTH
Gloucester.
14th/15th century.
Complete. L 173mm.
Excavated by H Hurst.

D19 HECKLE TOOTH
Oxford.
c1325 to c1400.
Complete but distorted. L 177mm.
Goodall 1977e, 142, fig 26.20.

D20 HECKLE TOOTH
Northampton.
Late Saxon to ?later 14th century.
Shaped head, shank broken. L 60mm.
Goodall 1979b, 71, fig 17.14.

D21 HECKLE TOOTH
Brixworth, Northamptonshire.
12th to 14th century.
Broken shank. L 67mm.
Goodall 1977g, 94, fig 9.13.

D22 HECKLE TOOTH
Walton, Aylesbury, Buckinghamshire.
12th–13th century.
Circular section, tip lost, shaped head. L 69mm.
Farley 1976, 267 fig 49.1.

D23 HECKLE TOOTH
Northampton.
11th–14th century.
Shaped head, shank broken. L 72mm.
Goodall 1979b, 71, fig 17.12.

D24 HECKLE TOOTH
Walton, Aylesbury, Buckinghamshire.
12th–13th century.
Head broken. L 72mm.
Farley 1976, 267, fig 49.2.

D25 HECKLE TOOTH
Winchester, Hampshire.
Late 11th–12th century.
Tip broken. L 74mm.
Goodall 1990-4, fig 44.53.

D26 HECKLE TOOTH
Oxford.
First half 12th century.
Shank broken. L 82mm.
Goodall 1977e, 142, fig 26.19.

TEXTILE MANUFACTURING TOOLS

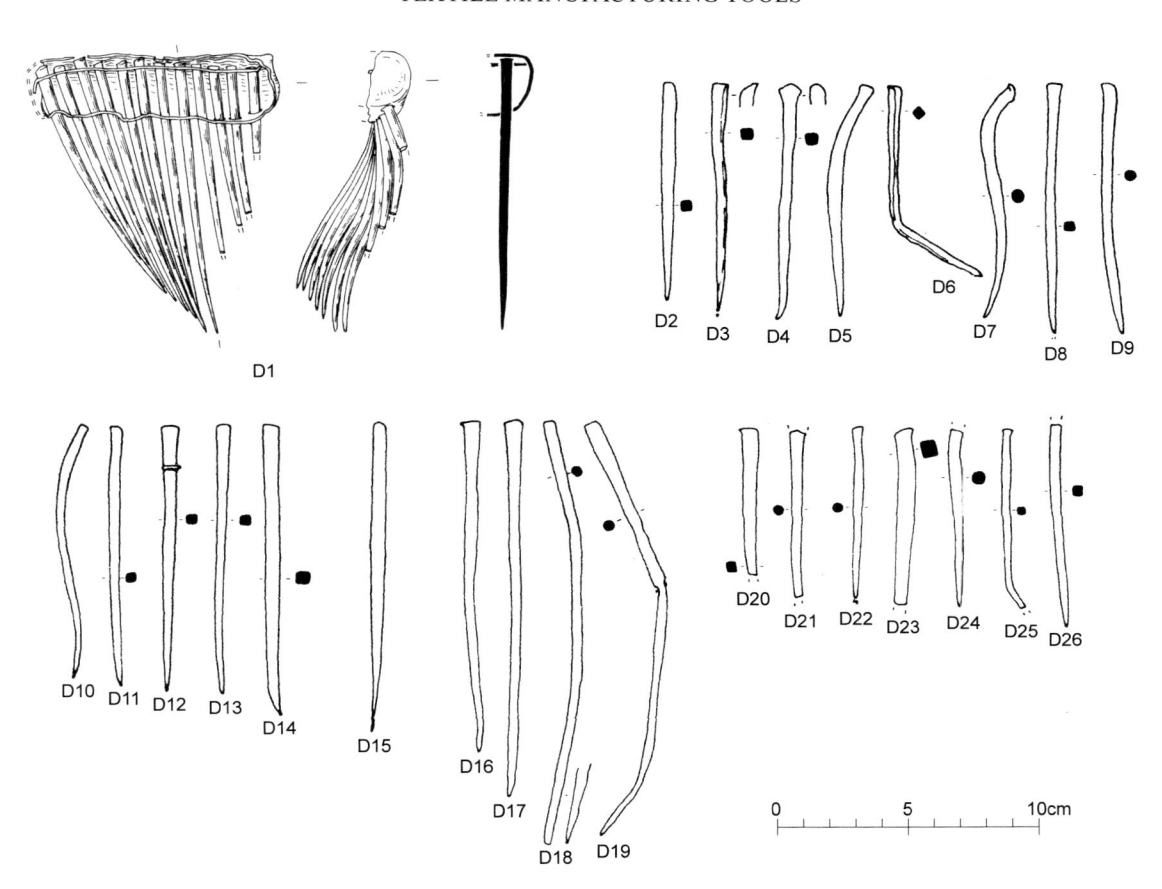

FIGURE 5.1
Textile manufacturing tools: Heckle teeth

D27 HECKLE TOOTH
Brixworth, Northamptonshire.
Saxon to mid 15th century.
Shank broken. L 82mm.
Goodall 1977g, 94, no. 14.

D28 HECKLE TOOTH
Winchester, Hampshire.
13th century.
Shaped head, tip lost. L 88mm.
Goodall 1990-4, 216, no. 60.

D29 HECKLE TOOTH
Wroughton Copse, Fyfield Down, Wiltshire.
Site: c1150–1315.
Shank broken. L 93mm. Five others of similar length.
Excavated by P J Fowler.

D30 HECKLE TOOTH
Goltho Manor, Lincolnshire.
c1100–1150.
Shank broken. L 94mm.
Goodall 1987, 178, no. 12.

D31 HECKLE TOOTH
Llantrithyd, South Glamorgan.
Early to mid 12th century.
Shank broken. L 98mm.
Goodall 1977f, 43, iron object fig 2.32.

D32 HECKLE TOOTH
Llantrithyd, South Glamorgan.
Early to mid 12th century.
Shank broken. L 99mm.
Goodall 1977f, 47, iron object fig 2.33.

D33 HECKLE TOOTH
London.
Late 13th to mid 14th century.
Shaped head, broken shank. L 102mm.
Henig 1974, 195, no. 97.

D34 HECKLE TOOTH
Wallingstones, Hereford and Worcester.
1300/25 to 1500.
Head broken. L 102mm.
Bridgewater 1970–72, 104, no. 75.

D35 HECKLE TOOTH
Wharram Percy, North Yorkshire.
Early 15th century.
Head and tip lost. L 102mm.
Goodall 1979a, 118, fig 62.53.

D36 HECKLE TOOTH
Wharram Percy, North Yorkshire.
Late 15th to early 16th century.
Tip lost. L 106mm.
Goodall 1979a, 118, fig 62.54.

D37 HECKLE TOOTH
Winchester, Hampshire.
Late 11th–12th century.
Shaped head, tip lost. L 107mm.
Goodall 1990-4, fig 44.52.

D38 HECKLE TOOTH
London.
Late 13th to mid 14th century.
Shaped head, tip lost. L 108mm.
Henig 1974, 195, no. 129.

D39 HECKLE TOOTH
Northampton.
11th to 14th century.
Shank broken. L 124mm.
Goodall 1979b, 71, fig 17.11.

D40 HECKLE TOOTH
Thuxton, Norfolk.
Site: 12th to end 14th century.
Tip broken. L 128mm.
Excavated by L A S Butler.

D41 HECKLE TOOTH
Wharram Percy, North Yorkshire.
Late 15th to early 16th century.
Shaped head, broken shank. L 142mm.
Area 6, SF 20898, Pd VI; Andrews and Milne 1979.

D42 HECKLE TOOTH
Stonar, Kent.
c1275–1385.
Tip broken. L 184mm.
Excavated by N Macpherson-Grant.

D43 HECKLE TOOTH
Stonar, Kent.
c1275–1385.
Tip broken. L 203mm.
Excavated by N Macpherson-Grant.

D44 WEAVING COMB
Winchester, Hampshire.
12th century.
1.5mm thick, broken, sheet iron comb with straight, toothed blade and sloping side. 10mm band of tinning immediately above teeth. W 68mm.
Goodall 1990-5, fig 49.224.

D45 WEAVING COMB
Newbury, Berkshire.
c1350–90.
1.5mm thick sheet iron comb with straight, toothed blade and shaped back. Teeth, lost in centre, 6mm deep, with 14 in a 30mm length. 15 holes along back, two groups of four at lower corners. W 243mm.
Goodall 1997, fig 19, no. 3.

D46 FORCEPS
London.
Late 13th to 14th century.
Looped bow and spatulate arms terminating in pointed tips with simple, decorative edge filing. L 123mm.
Henig 1974, 191, fig 38.55.

D47–68 TENTER HOOKS
Winchester, Hampshire.
Goodall 1990-6, fig 44.55.
D47 Late 13th–early 14th century. H 19mm. BS 2123. Goodall 1990-6, fig 50.288.
D48 Mid to ?late 13th century. H 17mm. Goodall 1990-6, fig 50.251.
D49 Mid to ?late 13th century. H 18mm. Goodall 1990-6, 236, no. 252.
D50 Mid to late 10th century. H 21mm. BS 4244. Goodall 1990-6, 235, no. 225.
D51 14th to ?15th century. H 14mm (broken). Goodall 1990-6, fig 50.296.
D52 Mid to ?late 13th century. H 18mm (broken). Goodall 1990-6, 237, no. 254.
D53 13th century. H 24mm. Goodall 1990-6, fig 50.279.
D54 Mid to late 13th century. H 21mm. Goodall 1990-6, 237, no. 257.
D55 Early 13th century. H 21mm. Goodall 1990-6, fig 50.238.
D56 14th–?15 century. H 28mm. Goodall 1990-6, fig 50.299.
D57 13th century. H 30mm. Goodall 1990-6, fig 50.266.
D58 Mid 12th–mid 13th century. H 26mm. Goodall 1990-6, 236, no. 244.
D59 Early to mid 13th century. H 31mm. Goodall 1990-6, fig 50.247.
D60 Early to mid 13th century. H 38mm. Goodall 1990-6, fig 50.248.
D61 Mid 13th century. H 24mm. Goodall 1990-6, 236, no. 249.
D62 Late 14th–15th century. H 18mm (broken). Goodall 1990-6, fig 50.300.
D63 13th century. H 26mm. Goodall 1990-6, fig 50.265.
D64 13th century. H 32mm. Goodall 1990-6, fig 50.269.
D65 13th century. H 31mm. Goodall 1990-6, fig 50.268.
D66 Late 11th–early 12th century. H 33mm. Goodall 1990-6, fig 50.230.
D67 c1250/60–c1310/20. H 37mm. Goodall 1990-6, fig 50.285.
D68 11th century. H 39mm. Goodall 1990-6, fig 50.229.

D69 TENTER HOOK
Rhuddlan, Clwyd.
Later(?) 13th century.
Shank and hook broken. H 9mm.
Goodall 1994, fig 17.1, no. 12.

D70 TENTER HOOK
Brixworth, Northamptonshire.
Saxon to mid 15th century.
Hook broken. H 8mm.
Goodall 1977g, 94, no. 16.

D71 TENTER HOOK
Brixworth, Northamptonshire.
Medieval.
Complete. H 18mm.
Goodall 1977g, 94, fig 9.15.

D72 SHEARBOARD HOOK
Winchester, Hampshire.
Medieval.
Straight arms with hooked ends, spirally twisted centre. L 108mm.
Goodall and Keene 1990, fig 51.309.

D73 SHEARBOARD HOOK
Winchester, Hampshire.
15th century.
Straight arms, central moulding with decorative grooves formed by wound-round lengths of wire. L 64mm.
Goodall and Keene 1990, fig 51.308.

TEXTILE MANUFACTURING TOOLS

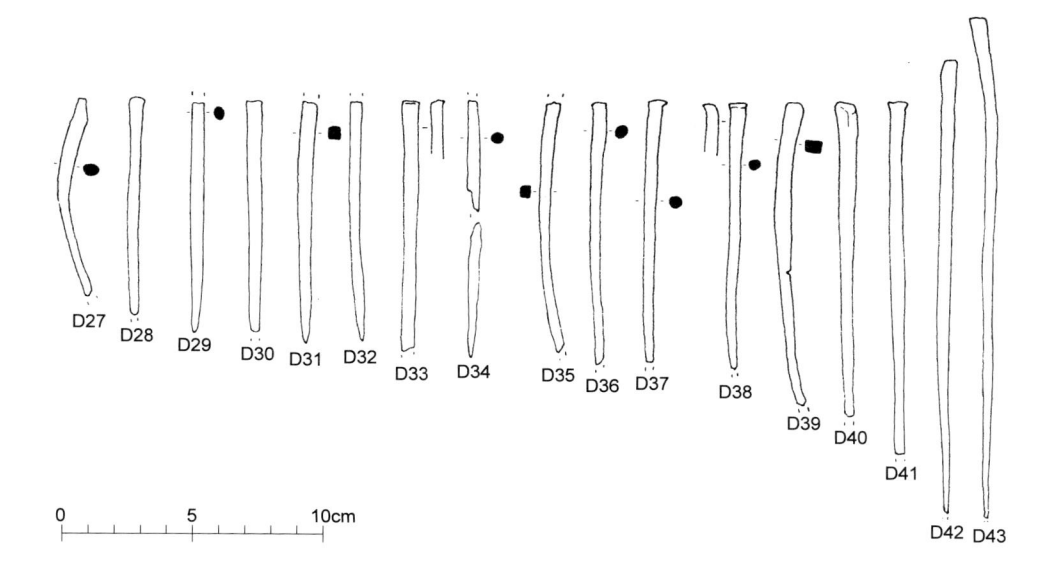

FIGURE 5.2
Textile manufacturing tools: Heckle teeth

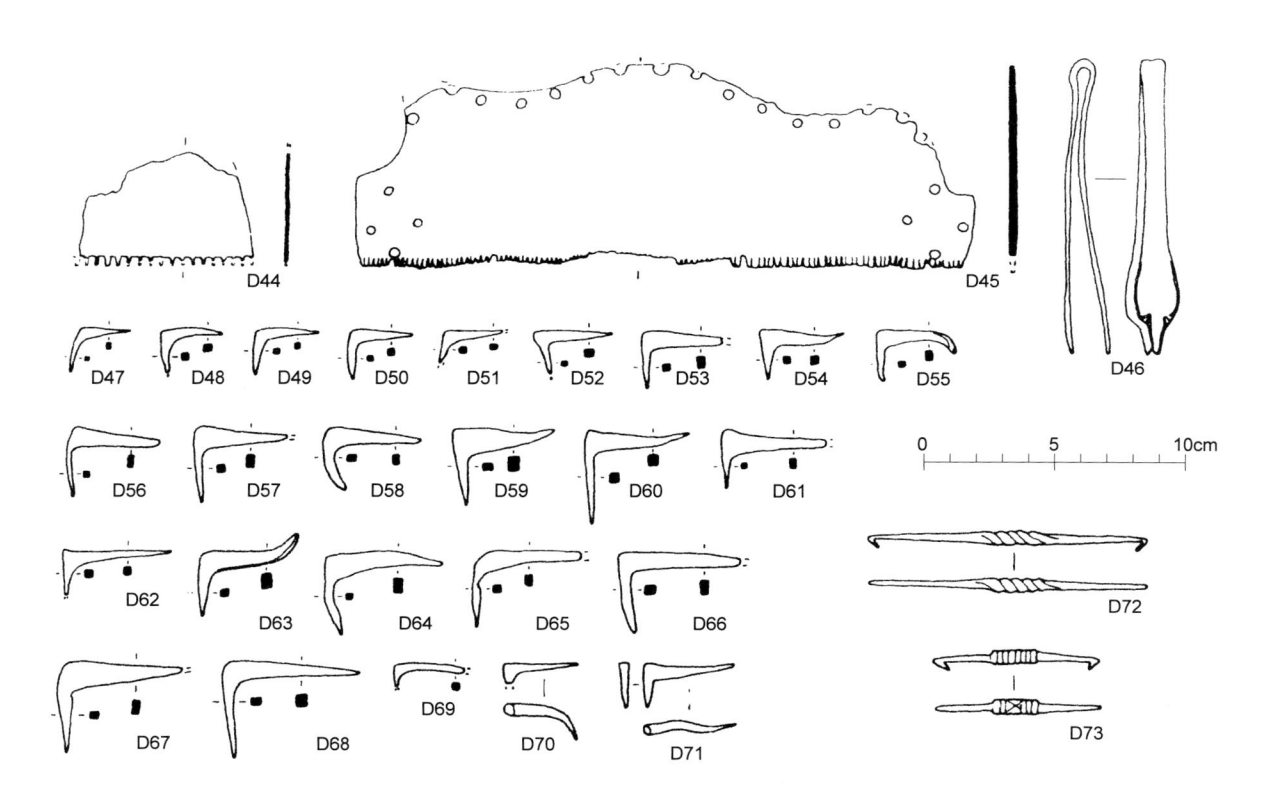

FIGURE 5.3
Textile manufacturing tools: Weaving combs, forceps, tenter hooks and shearboard hooks

6
TANNING AND LEATHERWORKING TOOLS

Practically all processes of leather production and finishing have been mechanised, and details of the older, long-established procedures described below are taken from Waterer 1957 and 1968, Attwater 1961, Jenkins 1965 and Thomson 1978.

6.1 TANNING

Various preparatory processes had to be undertaken before tanning was begun, the first involving trimming away the ragged edges of hides and skins with shears or a knife before they were washed to remove blood and dung, and to re-hydrate them if necessary. The hides were next immersed in lime liquors to loosen the hair roots and lower layers of the epidermis which were scraped off over a wooden beam with a wide, blunt-edged curved knife which today has handles projecting horizontally from each end. A similar but sharp knife removed flesh from the underside, and a blunt-edged scudding knife was then used to remove short or broken hairs, dirt, and lime compounds. After this preparation the hides or the skins were immersed in a series of tanning liquors.

No medieval unhairing, fleshing or scudding knife similar to the modern examples illustrated by Waterer (1968, pl 4) and Jenkins (1965, fig 44, pl 164) is yet known, but it is not improbable that some of the knives and shears catalogued below (Chapter 8) were used to trim hide edges.

6.2 CURRYING

Tanned leather is stiff and badly coloured, and has to be dressed by the currier to acquire the pliancy, smoothness, grain and colour necessary for use. The currier's first task was to remove the 'bloom' and dried tanning liquor clogging up the grain by soaking and softening the hide in water and then scouring it with a hard brush. A knife called a slicker (or sleaker) was used to force out the dirt retained under the hair roots or just below the grain layer, and the flesh side was then shaved until the surface was smooth and the leather of even substance all over. The currier's shaving knife (Waterer 1957, fig 115; 1968, pl 4) has a double-edged rectangular blade 250mm to 300mm long, 150mm deep, with one handle in the same plane and the other at right angles to it. The edges are turned at a right angle to the blade with a steel. After shaving, leather was impregnated on one or both sides with grease, which was rubbed in with a slicker; surplus grease was removed and the surface smoothed with a slicker with a slightly turned edge.

No medieval currier's shaving knife is yet known, but **E1–10** are all probably slickers. Modern slickers (Jenkins 1965, 198) have a flat steel blade some 150mm wide and 100mm deep set in a wooden handle, and **E1**, **E4** and **E7** all retain traces of such handles. Few of the medieval slickers are as wide as these modern ones, however, since complete blades range in width from 97mm to 148mm, and in depth from 17mm to 39mm. They were secured in their handles by tapering and generally pointed side arms set in the same plane but at right angles to the blade. The slicker resembles such carpenter's tools as the shave, spokeshave and drawing knife, and **E9** was published as a spokeshave, but it can be distinguished from these by size, by its distinctive method of hafting, and by the position of its sharp edge along the bottom of the blade.

6.3 LEATHERWORKING TOOLS

Knives, which may be divided into cutting knives and paring knives, are probably the most important tool of the craftsmen in leather. Other tools to survive are creasers used for edge finishing, awls for piercing, and needles for sewing and stitching. No punch is yet known.

Cutting knives

Harness makers, saddlers, shoemakers and glovers all used leather of differing thicknesses, and there is some variation in the types of knife used to cut it.

The round or half-moon knife, so-called from the shape of its blade, was used to cut heavy material such as harness leather, but no medieval example is yet known.

E11–14 will have been used to cut thinner leather, and various post-medieval illustrations show similar knives being used by shoemakers. The knives have waisted blades with cutting edges curving out to the tip and a spike in line with the back of the blade. The spike, although sometimes exaggerated as on **E14**, is generally unlikely to have been conveniently usable as an awl although it may have been used for piercing holes for thongs. On **E12** the spike is in fact little more than one end of a second cutting edge which could have been used for trimming. These knives resemble the modern butt knife, used to cut sole leather (Waterer 1968, pl 5.24), and combine the functions of the modern ranging knife and welt knife.

E15 resembles a modern clicking knife used for cutting thinner leather. The type characteristically has a narrow, thin blade which may today be straight, curved, or curved only at the tip (Waterer 1968, pl 5, 18–20).

Paring knives

E16–19 are paring or skiving knives with broad, triangular blades which flare out towards the cutting edge. They were used to shave away thin pieces from the flesh side of a hide to level its surface or reduce its substance, particularly at edges where there could be excessive thickness. Another use was in bevelling or scarfing, that is cutting through a piece of leather at a continuous angle so that it could be joined invisibly to a second piece. **E16–18** have slender blades, but the more substantial blade of **E19** has a ground cutting edge and from its shaping was intended for use by a left-handed worker. Modern paring knives can be similarly shaped (Attwater 1961, 26, fig 7).

Creasers

Today most flat work is given a crease line, single or double, fairly close to the outer edge in order to finish it. The crease compresses the leather and gives it a slightly darker and shiny line which, although decorative, is primarily functional since the compression hardens the leather, makes it more resistant to wear, and seals any joint. Lines are also creased in other places away from the edge to give embellishment.

E20–21 are single line creasers of similar form, both with incomplete tangs originally hafted in wooden handles. In use, to make the crease line permanent, the creaser was heated, the amount of heat varying according to the nature of the leather.

Awls

Medieval awls **E22–59** are of many different kinds, from fine to coarse, and of round, square and diamond-shaped section according to the hole to be pierced and stitch to be used. Most (**E22–58**) are straight, although a few of the incomplete ones may have lost curved tips similar to **E59**, itself a curved awl used for corner sewing or closing. The majority of awls (**E22–49**) taper evenly and often almost imperceptibly towards each end, but the expanded shoulders of **E50–55** and reduced shoulders of **E56–58** allowed greater pressure to be exerted on the handle of the awl during use. The expanded shoulders are found on a modern saddler's seat awl, and the reduced shoulders on a pegging awl (Waterer 1968, pl 7 D–E).

All the awls have square or diamond-sectioned tangs, so shaped to prevent the tool turning in the handle, but the blades vary in cross section. **E22–29**, **E50–51**, **E53–54** and **E58–59** are square, **E30–38** diamond-shaped, **E39–43** diamond-shaped but rounded at the tip, and **E44–49**, **E52** and **E55–56** round. **E48** retains a bone handle, whilst traces of wooden handles remain on **E44** and **E47**.

Some of the larger tools such as **E52** and **E54** may not be awls, and might have been used as steels to sharpen and turn the edges of slickers used during the last stages of currying.

Needles

Medieval needles were made in both iron and copper alloy, iron being used for both large and small needles. The iron needles are of two main types: Type 1 generally with circular-sectioned shanks; Type 2 with similar shanks which become triangular towards the point. Needles of each type can be either straight or curved.

— Type 1: Needles **E60–74** generally have circular-sectioned shanks, and complete examples range in length from 46mm to 171mm. The eyes of **E60–64** are punched within the thickness of the shank, whilst **E65–72** have expanded eyes. **E73–74** are shank fragments.

— Type 2: **E75–80** are needles with circular-sectioned shanks which become triangular towards the point. **E75** is an unfinished needle requiring only the punching of the eye, but **E76–78** have expanded eyes of differing shapes. **E79–80** are shank fragments.

Iron needles such as **E60–64** are likely to have been used for sewing either textiles or leather since their plain form and eye would have offered no resistance to either material. They will have had many uses with textiles, or they could be saddlers' tools. The curvature of **E63** resembles that of a modern horse collar maker's needle. The larger needles with expanded eyes, **E71–72**, may have been used for netting, and some of the others for thonging. Needles with triangular-sectioned points are used by glovers, but **E75–78** have the wrong type of eye and are too large. Similar needles between 102mm and 456mm in length in a 1959 catalogue are termed 'packing needles' (ex inf V Wynne).

Stilettos

E81–83 are probably stilettos used to make the eyelet holes through which cords or laces were threatened (Groves 1966, 94–95, pls 9 and 157). All have, or had, small riveted handles with shaped caps or terminals and long, tapering shanks. **E81** has a rectangular perforation through the shank which would have allowed it to be used in the manner of a bodkin for re-threading cords or laces.

E1 SLICKER
Netherton, Hampshire.
Medieval.
Blade with remains of wooden handle and broken upright side arms. W 97mm.
Goodall 1990-28, fig 9.1 no. 43.

E2 SLICKER
Netherton, Hampshire.
Medieval.
Blade with upright side arms, both broken. W 34mm.
Goodall 1990-28, fig 9.1 no. 44.

E3 SLICKER
Newbury, Berkshire.
c1200–1230.
Upright side arms broken. W 97mm.
Goodall 1997, fig 19, no. 4.

E4 SLICKER
King's Lynn, Norfolk.
c1250–1300.
Blade with remains of wooden handle along back and upright side arms, one broken. W 105mm.
Goodall and Carter 1977, 295, fig 133.37.

E5 SLICKER
Wroughton Copse, Fyfield Down, Wiltshire.
12th–13th century.
Blade with broken upright side arms. W 105mm.
Excavated by P J Fowler.

E6 SLICKER
Wroughton Copse, Fyfield Down, Wiltshire.
12th–13th century.
Blade with upright side arms, both broken. W 26mm.
Excavated by P J Fowler.

E7 SLICKER
Wintringham, Cambridgeshire.
Late 13th century.
Broken blade with traces of wooden handle and upright side arm. W 78mm.
Goodall 1977a, 257, fig 46.61.

E8 SLICKER
North Elmham Park, Norfolk.
c1150–c1600.
Blade with upright side arms, one broken. W 115mm.
Goodall 1980a, 513, fig 266.55.

E9 SLICKER
Knaresborough Castle, North Yorkshire.
12th century.
Blade with upright side arms, one broken. W 131mm.
Waterman 1953, 213, fig 1.22.

E10 SLICKER
Winchester, Hampshire.
Early to mid 11th century.
Blade with broken upright side arms. W 148mm.
Goodall 1990-7, fig 53b.325.

E11 KNIFE
King's Lynn, Norfolk.
c1150 to 1250.
Blade and tang broken. L 157mm.
Goodall and Carter 1977, 295, fig 133.36.

E12 KNIFE
Oakham Castle, Leicestershire.
13th to 14th century. Leather offcuts and shoes also found in moat.
Tang complete, damaged blade with cutler's mark. L 132mm.
Gathercole 1958, 33, fig 10.2.

E13 KNIFE
Waltham Abbey, Essex.
1530–70.
Blade and tang broken. L 132mm.
Excavated by P J Huggins. From Sun Street.

E14 KNIFE
Goltho, Lincolnshire.
Croft A: late Saxon to late 14th or early 15th century.
Blade fragment. L 43mm.
Goodall 1975a, 87, fig 41.94.

E15 KNIFE
Criccieth Castle, Gwynedd.
Site: c1230–1404.
Whittle tang broken, curving blade. L 88mm.
O'Neil 1944–45, 42, pl X.39.

E16 KNIFE
Wallingstones, Hereford and Worcester.
First half 13th century.
Tang broken, curved cutting edge. L 72mm.
Bridgewater 1970–72, 100, fig 16.12.

E17 KNIFE
Wallingstones, Hereford and Worcester.
First half 13th century.
Tang broken, straight cutting edge. L 76mm.
Bridgewater 1970–72, 100, fig 16.11.

E18 KNIFE
Hampton Wafer, Hereford and Worcester.
Site: probably 11th to early 14th century.
Tang broken, curved cutting edge. L 97mm.
Stanford 1967, 87, fig 7.7.

E19 KNIFE
Kidwelly Castle, Dyfed.
Medieval.
Tang complete, cutting edge straight and ground. L 222mm.
For site see Fox and Radford 1933.

TANNING AND LEATHERWORKING TOOLS

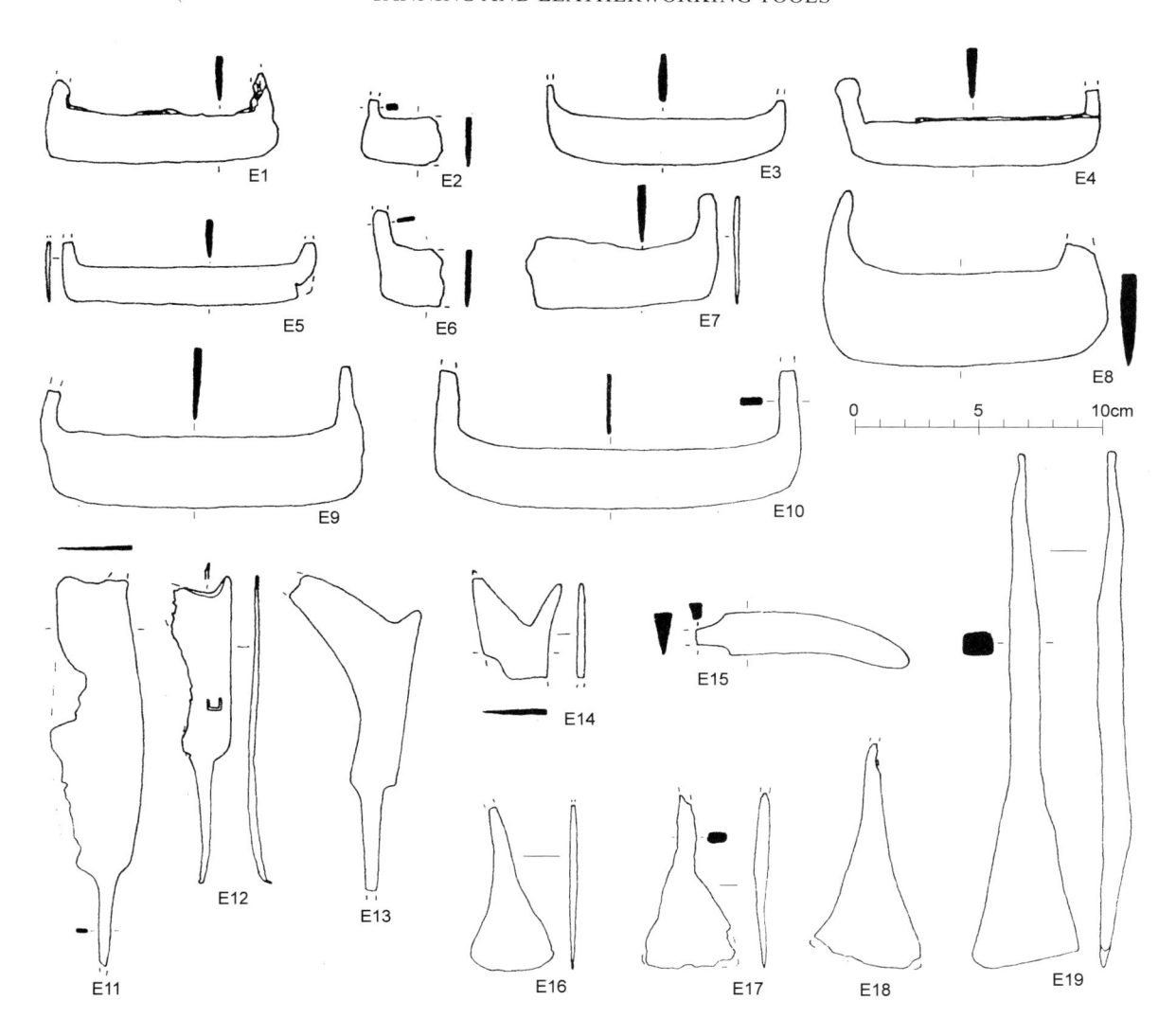

FIGURE 6.1
Tanning and leatherworking tools: Slickers and leatherworking knives

E20 CREASER
Netherton, Hampshire.
Late 13th to early 14th century.
Tong broken. L 99mm.
Goodall 1990-28, fig 9.1 no. 46.

E21 CREASER
Winchester, Hampshire.
Mid 15th century.
Tong broken. L 129mm.
Goodall 1990-7, fig 54.335.

E22 AWL
Wroughton Copse, Fyfield Down, Wiltshire.
12th century.
Rectangular-sectioned awl. L 60mm.
Excavated by P J Fowler.

E23 AWL
Winchester, Hampshire.
Late 11th–12th century.
Rectangular-sectioned awl, tip broken.
L 74mm.
Goodall 1990-7, 249. no. 327.

E24 AWL
Wroughton Copse, Fyfield Down, Wiltshire.
Site: 12th–13th century.
Rectangular-sectioned awl, broken.
L 83mm.
Excavated by P J Fowler.

E25 AWL
Winchester, Hampshire.
Mid 12th–early 13th century.
Rectangular-sectioned awl, tips lost.
L 98mm.
Goodall 1990-7, fig 53b.330.

E26 AWL
Lochmaben Castle, Dumfries and Galloway.
Late 14th century.
Rectangular-sectioned awl, one end broken.
L 108mm.
Macdonald and Laing 1974–75, 148, fig 11.19.

E27 AWL
Portchester Castle, Hampshire.
11th or 12th century.
Rectangular-sectioned awl. L 112mm.
Hinton 1977, 204, fig 109.64, scale 2:3, not 1:3.

E28 AWL
Burnham Chapel, Humberside.
c1300–1320.
Rectangular-sectioned awl. L 114mm.
Excavated by G Coppack.

E29 AWL
Faxton, Northamptonshire.
Site: 12th to 15th century.
Rectangular-sectioned awl. L 114mm.
Excavated by L A S Butler.

E30 AWL
Wroughton Copse, Fyfield Down, Wiltshire.
13th century (? mid) to early 14th century.
Diamond-sectioned awl, tip broken.
L 67mm.
Excavated by P J Fowler.

E31 AWL
London.
Late 13th to mid 14th century.
Broken, diamond-sectioned awl. L 67mm.
Henig 1974, 195, fig 39.96.

E32 AWL
Ospringe, Kent.
Demolition c1550–70 on site founded c1230.
Diamond-sectioned awl. L 91mm.
Goodall 1979c.

E33 AWL
Wroughton Cose, Fyfield Down, Wiltshire.
13th century (? mid) to early 14th century.
Diamond-sectioned awl, broken. L 92mm.
Excavated by P J Fowler.

E34 AWL
Winchester, Hampshire.
Early 14th century.
Diamond-sectioned awl. L 97mm.
Goodall 1990-7, fig 53b.332.

E35 AWL
Cambokeels, Durham.
Later 14th to early 15th century.
Diamond-sectioned awl, broken one end.
L 108mm.
Hildyard 1949, 199, fig 3.20.

E36 AWL
St Catharine's Hill, Winchester, Hampshire.
Chapel 12th century to 1538–40.
Diamond-sectioned awl, broken. L 113mm.
Hawkes et al 1930, 246, fig 29.12.

E37 AWL
Upton, Gloucestershire.
Late 13th to late 14th century.
Rectangular-sectioned shank. L 117mm.
Hilton and Rahtz 1966, 121, fig 14.21.

E38 AWL
Cambokeels, Durham.
Late 14th to early 16th century.
Diamond-sectioned awl, damaged at centre, broken both ends. L 132mm.
Hildyard 1949, 199, fig 3.19.

E39 AWL
Tullwick, Berkshire.
Site: medieval and early post-medieval.
Diamond-sectioned awl, rounded at point.
L 77mm.
Excavated by Mrs J Naish.

E40 AWL
Wroughton Copse, Fyfield Down, Wiltshire.
12th–13th century.
Diamond-sectioned awl, becoming rounded near to broken tip. L 81mm.
Excavated by P J Fowler.

E41 AWL
Badby, Northamptonshire.
15th to 16th century and later.
Diamond-sectioned awl, rounded near tip.
L 95mm.
Excavated by Mrs M Gray.

E42 AWL
West Hartburn, Durham.
Site: 13th to 16th century.
Diamond-sectioned awl becoming rect-angular at broken end, rounded at other.
L 95mm.
Excavated by L Still.

E43 AWL
St Peter's Street, Northampton.
Later 15th century.
Diamond-sectioned awl, one tip broken.
L 104mm.
Goodall et al 1979, 273, fig 119.57.

E44 AWL
Newbury, Berkshire.
c1170–1200.
Rectangular-sectioned tang with wood graining from former handle. Rest of circular section. L 67mm.
Goodall 1997, fig 19, no. 5.

E45 AWL
Wroughton Copse, Fyfield Down, Wiltshire.
12th–13th century.
Rectangular-sectioned tang, circular section blade. L 67mm.
Excavated by P J Fowler.

E46 AWL
Winchester, Hampshire.
Late 14th century.
Circular-sectioned awl, tip broken. L 73mm.
Goodall 1990-7, fig 53b.333.

E47 AWL
Goltho Manor, Lincolnshire.
Around late 11th century.
Ferrified wood on rectangular section tang.
Awl of rounded section outside handle.
L 90mm.
Goodall 1987, fig 156.28.

TANNING AND LEATHERWORKING TOOLS

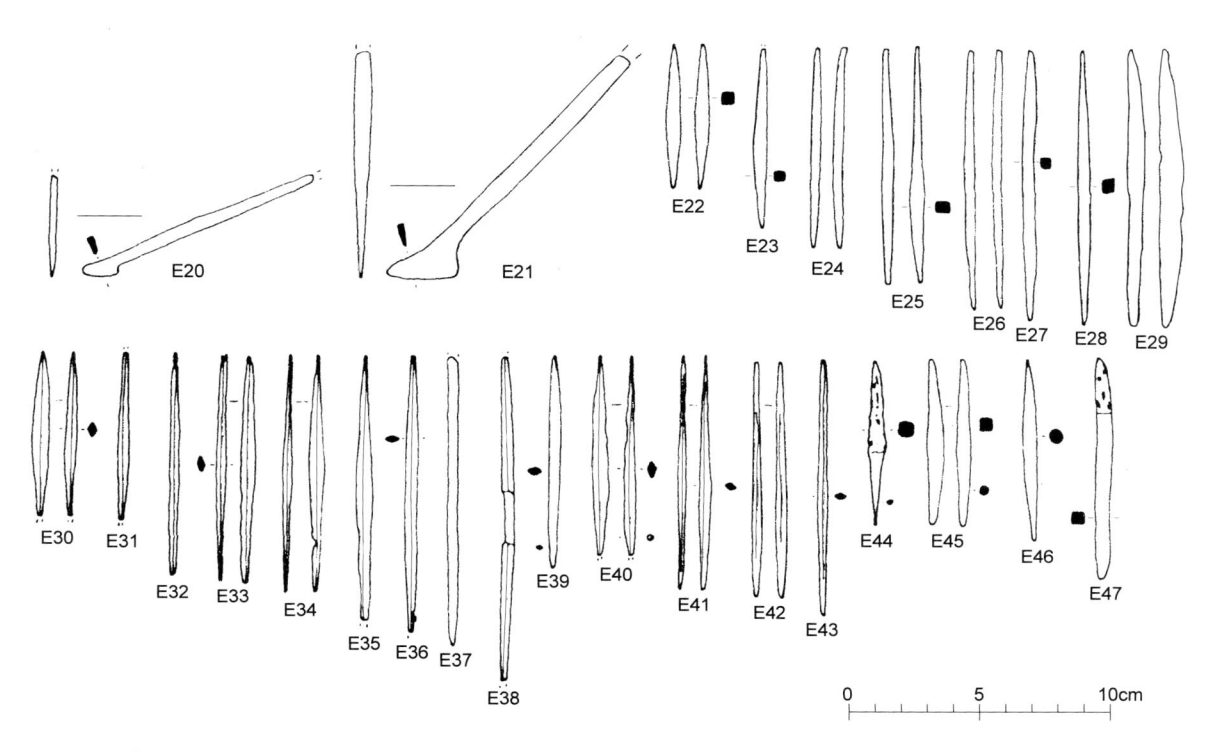

FIGURE 6.2
Tanning and leatherworking tools: Creasers and awls

E48 AWL
Waltham Abbey, Essex.
c1540, with a little later material.
Rounded-sectioned awl in bone handle.
L 121mm.
Huggins 1972, 117, fig 28.2.

E49 AWL
Winchester, Hampshire.
Late 13th–early 14th century.
Awl with rectangular-sectioned tang, round blade. L 115mm.
Goodall 1990-7, fig 53b.331.

E50 AWL
Lismahon, Co. Down.
Later 13th or 14th century.
Rectangular-sectioned tang, expanded shoulder, circular-sectioned blade. L 102mm.
Waterman 1959a, 162, fig 61.1.

E51 AWL
Wharram Percy, North Yorkshire.
Early 16th to 20th century.
Rectangular-sectioned awl, expanded shoulder, tips broken. L 102mm.
Goodall 1979a, 118, fig 62.52.

E52 AWL
Waltham Abbey, Essex.
c1540, with a little later material.
Circular-sectioned awl, tang broken.
L 10mm.
Huggins 1972, 124. From f65.

E53 AWL
Durham.
Later 11th to mid 12th century.
Broken rectangular-sectioned awl with expanded central shoulder. L 120mm.
Carver 1979, 17, fig 13.15/1574.

E54 AWL
South Witham, Lincolnshire.
Late 13th century to 1308–13.
Tanged, circular-sectioned awl. L 115mm.
Goodall 2002, fig 7.3, no. 27.

E55 AWL
Netherton, Hampshire.
Medieval.
Rectangular-sectioned tang, expanded shoulder, round blade. L 117mm.
Goodall 1990-28, fig 9.1, no. 49.

E56 AWL
London.
?Late 13th to mid 14th century.
Tanged, circular-sectioned awl. L 68mm.
Henig 1974, 191, fig 38.59.

E57 AWL
Waltham Abbey, Essex.
c1540.
Tanged, circular-sectioned awl. L 94mm.
Huggins 1972, 124. From F64, Building I.

E58 AWL
Winchester, Hampshire.
Late 11th–12th century.
Rectangular-sectioned awl. L 104mm.
Goodall 1990-7, 249, no. 329.

E59 AWL
Winchester, Hampshire.
14th–15th century.
Rectangular-sectioned awl, curved blade.
L 83mm.
Goodall 1990-7, fig 53b.334.

E60 NEEDLE
St Peter's Street, Northampton.
11th century to c1410–20.
Circular-sectioned needle. L 46mm.
Goodall *et al* 1979, 273, fig 119.59.

E61 NEEDLE
London.
Late 13th to 14th century.
Circular-sectioned shank. L 58mm.
Henig 1974, 195, fig 39.87.

E62 NEEDLE
Upton, Gloucestershire.
Late 13th to late 14th century.
Rectangular-sectioned shank, broken across eye. L 57mm.
Hilton and Rahtz 1966, 102, fig 14.34.

E63 NEEDLE
St Catharine's Hill, Winchester, Hampshire.
Chapel site: 12th century to 1538–40.
Circular-sectioned shank, eye and point broken. L 108mm.
Hawkes *et al* 1930, 246, fig 29.127.

E64 NEEDLE
London.
Late 13th to mid 14th century.
Circular-sectioned shank, eye broken.
L 132mm.
Henig 1974, 195, no. 88.

E65 NEEDLE
Lyveden, Northamptonshire.
15th century.
Eye and circular-sectioned shank broken.
L 50mm.
SF 252, J. For site see Steane and Bryant 1975.

E66 NEEDLE
London.
Late 13th to mid 14th century.
Circular-sectioned shank, eye and point broken. L 54mm.
Henig 1974, 195, no. 89.

E67 NEEDLE
Llantrithyd, South Glamorgan.
Early to mid 12th century.
Circular-sectioned shank, tip lost. L 57mm.
Goodall 1977f, iron object fig 2.28.

E68 NEEDLE
London.
Late 13th to mid 14th century.
Circular-sectioned shank. L 73mm.
Henig 1974, 195, no. 91.

E69 NEEDLE
Grenstein, Norfolk.
Late 14th or possibly early 15th century.
Circular-sectioned shank, eye and tip broken. L 63mm.
Goodall 1980c, fig 77, no. 21.

E70 NEEDLE
London.
Late 13th to mid 14th century.
Circular-sectioned shank. L 86mm.
Henig 1974, 195, fig 39.86.

E71 NEEDLE
Maison Dieu, Ospringe, Kent.
c1270 to 1483.
Rectangular-sectioned shank, eye and tip broken. L 94mm.
Goodall 1979c.

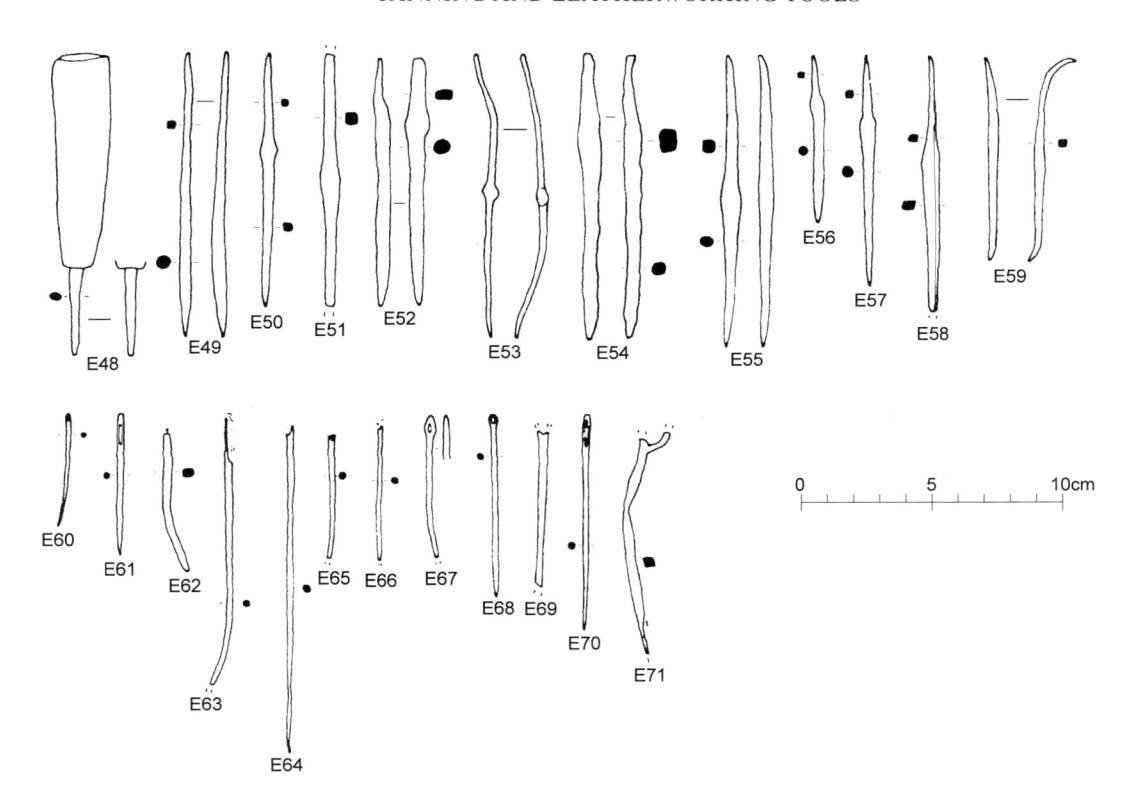

FIGURE 6.3
Tanning and leatherworking tools: Awls and needles

E72 NEEDLE
King's Lynn, Norfolk.
c1250–1350.
Circular-sectioned shank. L 171mm.
Goodall and Carter 1977, 295, fig 134.40.

E73 NEEDLE
Llantrithyd, South Glamorgan.
Early to mid 12th century.
Broken, circular-sectioned shank. L 61mm.
Goodall 1977f, 47, iron object fig 2.29.

E74 NEEDLE
St Peter's Street, Northampton.
15th century.
Diamond-sectioned shank becoming circular. L 85mm.
Goodall *et al* 1979, 273, fig 119.58.

E75 NEEDLE
London.
?Late 13th to mid 14th century.
Part-forged needle. Shank of circular section becoming triangular towards point. Head flattened but eye not yet punched. L 139mm.
Henig 1974, 195, fig 39.92.

E76 NEEDLE
London.
Late 13th to mid 14th century.
Circular-sectioned shank becoming tri-angular towards tip. L 128mm.
Henig 1974, 195, fig 39.85.

E77 NEEDLE
London.
Around later 14th century.
Circular-sectioned shank becoming tri-angular, point broken. L 114mm.
Henig 1974, 195, fig 39.84.

E78 NEEDLE
London.
?Late 13th to mid 14th century.
Circular-sectioned shank, triangular towards point, L 159mm.
Henig 1974, 195, fig 39.90.

E79 NEEDLE
London.
Late 13th to mid 14th century.
Circular-sectioned shank, triangular at point. Eye lost. L 72mm.
Henig 1974, 195, no. 94.

E80 NEEDLE
Brooklands, Weybridge, Surrey.
c1150 to 1325.
Broken shank, partly triangular in section, rest corroded. L 51mm.
Goodall 1977d, 73, fig 45.16.

E81 STILETTO
Grenstein, Norfolk.
Late 14th or possibly early 15th century.
Circular-sectioned shank with rectangular hole, iron riveted handle and end cap.
L 134mm.
Goodall 1980c, fig 77, no. 20.

E82 STILETTO
Pleshey Castle, Essex.
Early to mid 16th century destruction.
Circular-sectioned shank with shaped terminal and wooden handle with three copper-alloy rivets. L 126mm.
Williams 1977, 176, fig 38.14.

E83 STILETTO
Wharram Percy, North Yorkshire.
Early 16th to 20th century.
Rounded rectangular-sectioned shank with moulded cap and former riveted handle.
L 171mm.
Goodall 1979a, 123, fig 64.104.

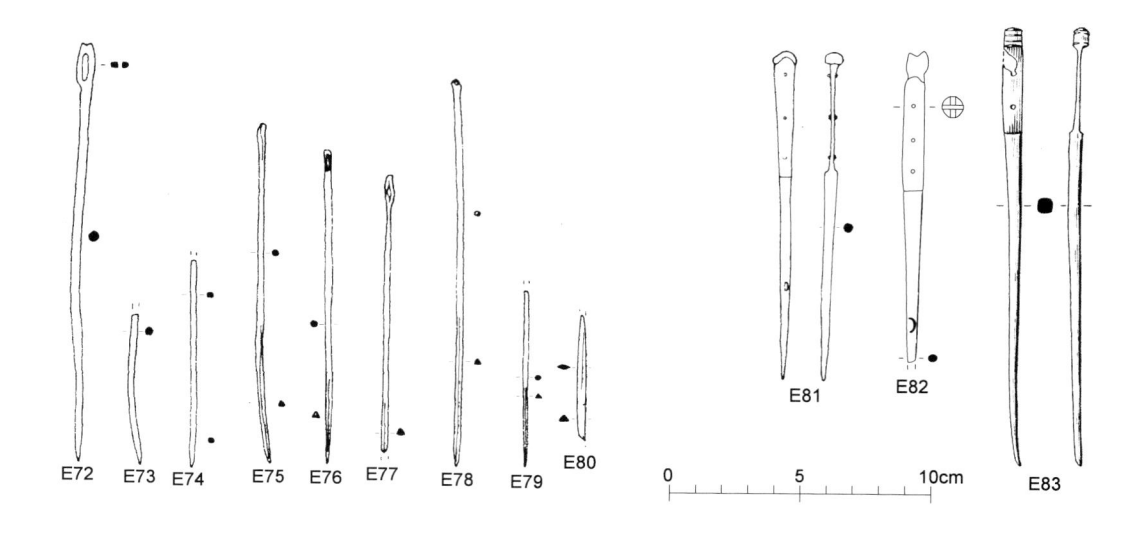

FIGURE 6.4
Tanning and leatherworking tools: Needles and stilettos

7
AGRICULTURAL TOOLS

7.1 PLOUGHS

Ploughs are illustrated in a number of medieval manuscripts and mentioned in agricultural treatises and manorial accounts, but they are less well represented as archaeological finds. Illustrations, which show them in differing degrees of detail, include that in the 11th-century Caedmon manuscript (Higgs 1965, 7, pl 11a), and one in a mid 12th-century manuscript (Hartley and Elliott 1931, pl 7c). A late 13th-century diagram in the cartulary of the Cistercian nunnery of Nun Cotham in Humberside (Lincolnshire) has the individual parts named (Colvin 1953; original reproduced in Higgs 1965, 7, pl 11b). Two early 14th-century representations occur in the Holkham Bible (Hassall 1954, 68–69, f 6) and the Luttrell Psalter (Hartley and Elliott 1928, pl 24d).

The medieval plough was of wood, with iron restricted to the coulter, ploughshare, and chains and associated fittings used to attach it to the plough team. The share beam and stilt of an oak plough are known from Waltham Abbey, Essex, where they were deposited in a ditch between about 1450 and 1500 (Huggins 1972, 116–117, fig 27, pl 3D). The plough evidently differed in some details from those shown in earlier medieval representations, although it closely resembles one in a 15th-century Danish mural (Huggins 1972, 116–117).

Coulters

The coulter, a heavy knife-like blade fixed vertically in the beam of a plough, cut a furrow slice in front of the ploughshare. Illustrations show long iron coulters with deep blades and thick shanks projecting through the beam and often wedged in place. No firmly dated medieval coulters are known, although **F1–2** from London are possibly of this date.

Ploughshares

The tip of the share beam was protected from wear by an iron ploughshare which undercut the slice made in the ground by the coulter and created a furrow. Late Saxon flanged ploughshares with triangular blades are known from St Neots, Cambridgeshire (Addyman 1973, 94, fig 19.30) and other sites. **F3–5** are incomplete medieval ploughshares, all flanged.

7.2 SPADES

Medieval spades were commonly of wood with an iron edging to the blade to prevent wear, although examples with blades entirely of wood or iron are known. The spade-iron is sometimes specified in documents, as at Canterbury in 1277 when 3 'spadetres' and 9 'soueltrowes' (shovel trees) were bought as well as 2 'spadhisenes' and 4 'souelhisenes' (Salzman 1967, 330). Spades also frequently appear in medieval illuminated manuscripts (Hassall 1970), where they are generally shown with an iron edging on a symmetrical or asymmetrical blade. The symmetrical blade has two shoulders of equal width cut straight across or sloping, whereas the asymmetrical blade has a single shoulder which is normally cut straight across. Straight-shouldered spades are well adapted for digging, but those with rounded or sloping shoulders should perhaps be regarded as shovels used with arm rather than foot pressure (Figure 7.1).

Archaeological excavations have produced a number of wooden spades, some with blade and shaft made in on piece, others with the two separate. A spade and shovel from a probable late 11th-century pit at Pevensey Castle, East Sussex (Dunning 1958, 215–216, fig 6), a shovel from the packing of a 13th-century timber-lined well at Loppington, Shropshire (Rowleys House Museum,

Shrewsbury), and a spade from the edge of a medieval ditch at Chester (Anon 1953), all have shaft and blade in one, the Chester spade having a T-shaped handle and the others, probably incomplete, no hand-grip at all. Wooden shovel blades with holes and pegs to secure separate, lost shafts come from a 12th to 13th-century well at Duffield Castle, Derbyshire (Cox 1887, 161) and from mid 12th to mid 14th-century levels at King's Lynn, Norfolk (Carter 1977, 373, fig 173, 81–82). All these spades and shovels have asymmetrical blades, the Pevensey Castle and Chester spades straight shoulders and rectangular and triangular blades respectively. None of the blades bears any trace of a spade-iron, although this does not exclude their former existence since some appear to have been shrunk rather than nailed into place. Wooden-bladed spades and shovels were, however, used for handling grain for malting and for mixing mortar. Six 'bare shofelles for the playsterers to make morter with' were bought at Windsor in 1533, and similar entries occur in many earlier accounts (Salzman 1967, 338). Illustrations showing plain wooden shovels being used to mix mortar are also not uncommon (Salzman 1967, pls 6b, 19).

Spade-irons are known from a number of sites, and **F6–17** are classified according to their form, shape, and means of attachment to the wooden blade. They fall into three types: with triangular mouths (Type 1), round mouths (Type 2) and straight mouths (Type 3).

Type 1: Triangular-mouthed spade-irons

The spade-iron is grooved throughout to receive the sides of the wooden blade and is of the same width throughout, thereby creating a triangular blade edge. **F6** is of this type and is apparently complete. No nail-holes are recorded, and it was probably shrunk into place on the wooden blade.

Type 2: Round-mouthed spade-irons

These may be sub-divided into three groups (A–C):
— Type 2A: The spade-iron is grooved throughout to receive the sides of the wooden blade. **F7** is of a similar width throughout, although the rounded blade edge is worn.
— Type 2B: The spade-iron is grooved throughout to receive the sides of the wooden blade, but the base is deepened to produce a triangular-shaped blade edge. The tip of **F8** is shallow in comparison with those of **F9–10**, and it also has a comparatively shallow groove which was evidently insufficient to keep the blade and spade-iron securely together since a clip has been inserted through the spade-iron to bind it to the blade. None of the examples has any nail-holes, and they were evidently shrunk into position.

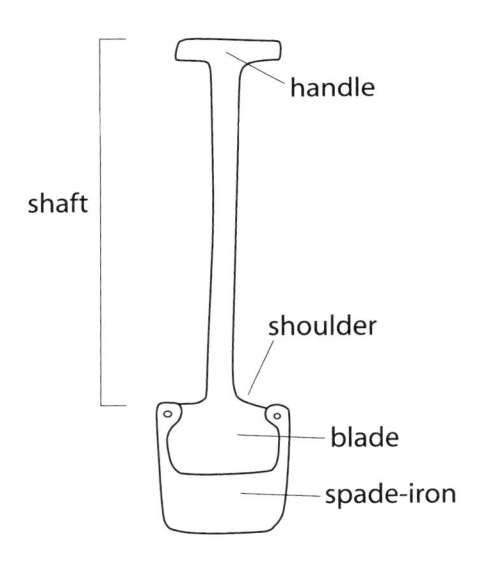

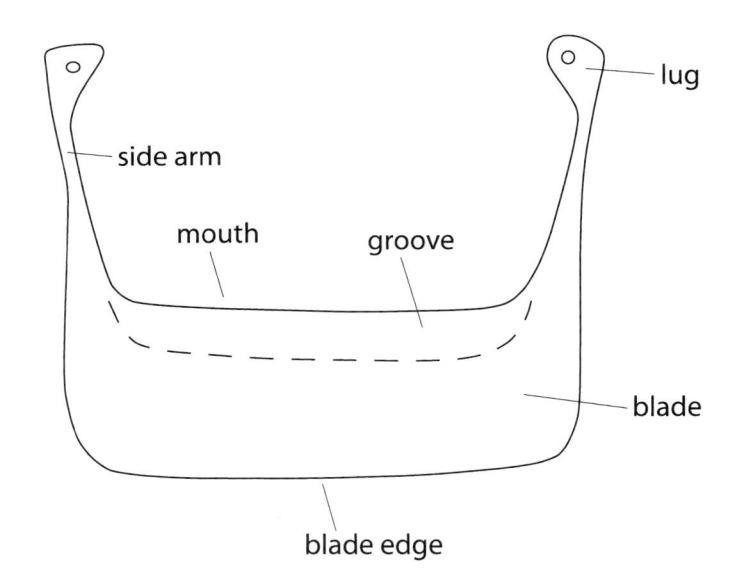

FIGURE 7.1
Spades: terminology

— Type 2C: The spade-iron has a rounded mouth with a groove which only runs a short distance up the side which then becomes a flat, straight side arm. **F11** is of this type, but it is insufficiently complete for the precise method of attachment to be known.

Type 3: Straight-mouthed spade-irons

The base of the mouth is grooved and the spade-iron has flat, straight side arms and a rectangular blade. **F12–15** are examples of the type, but only **F15** has complete side arms terminating in lugs which gripped the blade and were nailed through it from front to back. The corners of all the blades are rounded, probably in large part through wear. **F16–17** are fragmentary straight-mouthed spade-irons.

Discussion

Spade-irons **F6–17** and the wooden spades and shovels are too few in number for many conclusions to be drawn, although it is of interest that the chronological range of the various forms represented in manuscripts (Hassall 1970) coincides well with that of the actual objects. Triangular or roughly triangular spade blades are depicted throughout the medieval period, as the spade-irons confirm, but rectangular-shaped blades, shown less commonly in early medieval manuscripts, occur mainly in 14th-century and later contexts. The more complete spade-irons come from flat-bladed spades with blades between 160 and 260mm in width.

The triangular and round-mouthed spade-irons seem to have been shrunk onto the wooden blades, since none has any sign of a nail-hole. A weakness in this method is indicated by the need to repair the Lydford Castle spade, **F8**. Representations do, however, clearly indicate that some were nailed in place, and not necessarily through specially formed lugs (Hassall 1970, fig 1e–f). Straight-mouthed spade-irons with only a grooved base cannot have been shrunk into position, and this type must normally have had nailed lugs terminating the side arms. An alternative method of attachment would have been for the side arms to turn over and run along the top or shoulder of the blade, but illustrations do not seem to show such a method.

Spades and shovels were used for a variety of purposes, including cultivation, clearing overburden and waste from quarries, digging pits, ditches and building foundations, and moving fuel and ashes. The find-spots of the medieval spades and spade-irons are therefore of some interest. The Pevensey Castle objects seem to have been used in connection with storage in the pit in which they were found, and the Chester spade may have been used to dig or maintain a ditch. The Loppington spade and four spade-irons **F8**, **F10**, **F12** and **F16**, however, come from wells or their construction pits.

7.3 SHOVELS WITH IRON BLADES

Shovels with iron-edged wooden blades have been discussed above, but some with entirely iron blades also existed. The two types must at times have been used alongside each other, but those with metal blades will have been used for work which involved great heat. **F18** was found on the hearth of a glass kiln, and on such a site it may have been used for such purposes as lifting vessels when hot, filling crucibles, and shovelling out the ashes of kilns. Similar shovels might have found a use in other trades, including those of the potter and tiler.

7.4 FORKS

F19–20 are socketed garden forks with three prongs. Such tools are rarely shown in illustrations or mentioned in documents, and they were clearly in much less common use than spades and shovels. They are most likely to have been used in gardens, although **F19** was apparently lost while cleaning out a garderobe.

A three-pronged fork with a perforated tang from The Mounts, Pachesham (Surrey) is probably of recent date (Lowther 1948, 7, pl A; ex inf A W G Lowther).

7.5 TURF CUTTERS

Turf cutters were used during excavation and earth-moving as well as in gardening. The moat at Weoley Castle was dug between about 1270 and 1280 and the material spread over the interior, raising its level by 0.9 to 1.2m. **F21**, from the bottom puddled clay layer of the moat, must have been used during its excavation to cut blocks of turf before they were lifted with a shovel or spade. It is anchor-shaped with a crescentic blade and central socket which retains part of the original wooden handle. **F22–23** may be less complete turf cutters, the former in particular perhaps a gardener's tool.

7.6 HOES

Medieval hoes **F24–29** are both socketed and tanged, those with tangs having them set at right angles to the blade. All have triangular blades except **F29**, which is rectangular with curved shoulders, and all but **F26**, which is gently curved, have straight blade edges.

Socketed hoes **F24–25** were probably used in gardening for weeding and breaking up the surface of the soil, whereas the tanged hoes **F26–28** and **F29** are more likely to have been used for other purposes. At Vale Royal in 1278 'labourers with spades and hoes clearing [the earth] in various quarries' are mentioned, and an illustration of about 1450 shows a workman mixing mortar with a triangular hoe, perhaps socketed, set at an angle on the end of a long handle (Salzman 1967, 126, pl 1). **F26**, from its find-spot, was clearly used for clearing out a garderobe.

One or other of the socketed hoes **F24–25** may have fitted onto the end of a shepherd's stave. Illuminated manuscripts show shepherds carrying houlettes, long straight staffs with an iron spud at one end used to pick up a clod of earth and throw it close to a sheep to drive it back to the flock (Salzman 1957, 92–93).

7.7 RAKES AND HARROWS

Illustrations in medieval manuscripts show hand rakes in use during threshing and gathering corn together in the field (Hartley and Elliot 1931, pl 1, 86), and also the harrowing of fields with horse-drawn harrows (Hartley and Elliot 1928, pl 23b). These rakes and harrows, like those used in gardening to level dug ground, must often have been made entirely of wood, but **F30–35** are rake and harrow teeth with the characteristic long taper to the base and short taper to a clenched tang tip. The length of the tang indicates the thickness of the back of the rake or frame of the harrow. It is impossible to distinguish large rake from small harrow teeth, but perhaps **F35** is the only near certain harrow tooth.

7.8 BILLHOOKS

The billhook is a tool used for forearm chopping with short cutting actions, unlike the swinging movement used with an axe, and it was employed for coppicing, lopping the stems and branches of young trees, and for laying hedges. Many regional varieties exist today (Salaman 1975, 75, fig 108), but the range was probably not as wide during the medieval period.

F36 is a type of billhook known as a hedge-bill or a slasher which is today set on a long handle and used to clear brambles. The bevelled back of **F36** must have effectively given it two cutting edges, one stouter than the other and capable of heavier work. **F37**, which has a flanged and nailed socket and straight-ended blade, may also be a slasher. **F38–39** are much larger, however, and both have nailed, flanged sockets with closed bases which allowed handles to be very firmly attached. The hooked blade backs were probably used to spike and gather the next pieces of wood required for chopping, and the bevelling of the blade end of **F39** imply that is was also used with a pushing action. These longer billhooks were probably used to trim the posts and rails of wattle and gate hurdles and to split hazel rods (Jenkins 1965, 22–23, fig 5, pls 29 and 71). Thin branches were probably trimmed with billhooks with more strongly curved blades (Jenkins 1965, pl 31).

Billhooks are shown in use for coppicing in a manuscript of about 1500 (Higgs 1965, 8, pl 13b), and all have short wooden handles and curved blades without hooked backs. The axe-like projection from the backs of some billhooks in illuminated manuscripts (Higgs 1965, 8, pl 17b; Hartley and Elliot 1928, pl 21b) is unmatched on any extant blade.

7.9 WEEDHOOKS

Weeds were a continuing hazard to medieval crops, particularly in the open field where strips in the hands of a careless husbandman could spread weeds to those of others. Weeding was undertaken with a weedhook and crotch, the latter a long wooden stick forked at one end and used to hold the weed in place while its stalk was being cut. Labours of the Month frequently depict weeding, and that for June in a late 14th-century calendar (Higgs 1965, 8, pl 15a) shows a man cutting a thistle with these two tools, the weedhook hafted on a long plain wooden handle. The scene is repeated in countless manuscripts.

The major weeds to be removed were 'thystles', 'dockes', 'cockledrake' or corn-cockle which was poisonous to stock, and 'gouldes', presumably marigolds (Hellier and Moorhouse 1978, 10). Weeding of the cereal crop began in late May or early June, but thistles were not cut until July since, if cut earlier, each root would throw up three or four plants, and if cut later their seed would already have disappeared (Anstee 1970–72, 114–115).

Medieval weedhooks **F40–63** have been classified according to method of hafting and blade form. The letters signify the same blade shape, irrespective of haft.

Type 1: Tanged weedhooks

These may be sub-divided into four groups (A–D):
— Type 1A: Weedhooks **F40–50** have crescent-shaped blades which are commonly evenly curved, as are **F43** and **F46**, but which can be more strongly recurved, as are **F40** and **F45**. The cutting edge runs round the inner side of the blade, often extending some ways towards the tang as on **F42** and **F50**, and more extremely on **F45**, thereby producing a longer and more efficient cutting edge. The tangs, where complete, are generally clenched, a necessary safeguard on a tool which was pulled.
— Type 1B: **F51** has a half-moon blade with curved outer edge and straight cutting edge. The tang is broken.
— Type 1C: **F52–53** are weedhooks with wedge-shaped blades which have almost straight cutting edges and

partly straight backs. Both have plain tangs, one probably incomplete.
— Type 1D: Weedhooks **F54–55** have triangular blades with straight or near straight cutting edges. **F55** has a clenched tang tip, and the handle was further secured by a coiled iron collar which bound it and the tang tightly together.

F56 is too incomplete a fragment to classify with certainty beyond suggesting it could be Type 1B, C or D.

Type 2: Tanged and flanged weedhooks

These may be sub-divided into four groups (A–D):
— Type 2A: **F57** has a strongly recurved crescent-shaped blade and a near complete tang with flanges which gripped the shaft of the wooden handle.
— Type 2B: The half-moon blade of **F58** is complete, that of **F59** less so, but both have flanged and clenched tangs.
— Type 2C: Weedhooks **F60–61** have wedge-shaped blades with straight cutting edges and a partly straight back. The tang of **F60** is flanged and clenched, that of **F61** broken but nailed through the flanged section.
— Type 2D: **F62** has a triangular blade and incomplete nailed and flanged tang.

Type 3: Socketed weedhooks

Few examples of this type are known.
— Type 3D. **F63** has a wedge-shaped blade and broken, nailed socket.

Discussion

The most numerous type of weedhook (**F40–56**) has a simple tang, although some (**F57–62**) have additional flanges to secure them more firmly to the wooden handle. **F63** is the only socketed weedhook. The weedhook was used with a vigorous pulling action, and it is not surprising that many of the more complete tangs have clenched tips, including some of those with flanged tangs. **F61** and **F63** had nailed handles. The majority of weedhooks are from 12th to 14th-century contexts, and it would seem that during the late medieval period the tanged handle lost ground to that with additional flanges.

Anstee (1970–72, 114) comments that in the Queen Mary Psalter the weedhooks are shown cutting the weeds above the ground, and suggests that it is reasonably certain that, as in later times, they were cut just below the surface. Such representations are usual, however, and may be no more than an artistic convention which enabled the iron blade to be shown. It is also possible that in certain cases the ground was too hard for the blade to penetrate.

Blade shapes are of some significance in relation to their method of use and to what they could cut. Some of the crescent-shaped blades, which are the most numerous type, are probably too slender to push into the ground, and they may have been used for surface cutting of weeds. The other blade forms are stouter and will have entered the ground easily. The broad backs of the half-moon blades, and near straight backs of the wedge-shaped blades, may have been used occasionally with a pushing action like a spud to cut the stems of certain weeds. The shape and width of the cutting edges determined which weeds were cut, some of the recurved crescent-shaped blades being too narrow for the thick stems of thistles.

A number of the weedhooks may also have been used as pruning hooks, especially for removing buds or suckers from plants not easily reached with a knife. It is better, however, to classify **F40–63** as weedhooks rather than pruning hooks.

7.10 REAPING HOOKS

Reaping hooks, used with a forearm swing in a similar way to the billhook, have curved blades with their edges lying entirely to one side of the handle, unlike the sickle with its curved back blade.

Medieval reaping hooks are either tanged or socketed, and **F64–66** have the stubs of narrow, concave blades developing without shoulders from the tang. The cutting edge of **F64** broadens out as it leaves the tang, whereas on **F65–66** blade and tang continue in a smooth curve. **F67–69** are socketed reaping hooks, **F67** the most complete with a strong concave blade. **F68–69** retain little more than the short socket and stub of a blade.

7.11 SICKLES

Sickles were used for harvesting cereal crops, and medieval illustrations frequently show them in use, but they rarely survive in anything like complete form and are mainly represented by blade or blade and tang fragments. Two main types, classified according to the shape of the blade and its relation to the tang, can nevertheless be isolated. All have balanced blades, several of which are filled to form fine teeth.
— Type 1: The blade, generally comparatively narrow for the size of the sickle, curves fairly sharply away from the end of the tang before straightening out. **F70–82** are variously incomplete blade and tang fragments. None of the few complete tangs has a clenched tip, and the blades are commonly triangular in section. The only sickle with a thickened back rib, **F76**, is not certainly medieval. **F71** has a stamped mark on the front of the blade close to the

tang, and is filed on the underside to form fine teeth. No filling has been observed on the other blades, although corrosion may in some case obscure or have removed it. The cutting edge on most blades begins at or close to the angle between tang and blade, and few have a rectangular sectioned length at the base of the blade.
— Type 2: The blade, which is broad and rises from a short rectangular sectioned stem set next to the angle with the tang, is at first gently curved and almost in line with the handle before its curvature increases. **F83–95** were found bundled together in the same context as an axe, spearhead, shears, pitchfork and three sickle blade fragments **F105–107**. **F96** is another example of the type of sickle, but from a different site.

Sickle blades

F97–104 are sickle blade fragments which include the tip, and all are fairly narrow and may come from Type 1 sickles. **F97–99** and **F102** all have flattened tips of rectangular section which were presumably intended to be stronger and less liable to distortion than the more slender, tapering tips of the other examples. **F100–101** have cutting edges with filed undersides. **F105–112** are curved sickle blade fragments, **F105–107** found with Type 2 sickles **F83–95** and presumably of that type. The others are more slender and maybe from Type 1 sickles.

Discussion

Medieval sickles all have balanced blades almost invariably of simple triangular section with tapering or flattened tips. The cutting edge is sometimes filed on the underside to produce a sharp and sometimes toothed edge which would have sawn the stalks being cut as the sickle was pulled towards the user. Illustrations most frequently show the reaper cutting the stalks quite low down, where they were firmer (Higgs 1965, 9, pl 18 b–c).

7.12 SCYTHES

Medieval illustrations often show scythes in use in haymaking, but they were also used for mowing grass, and documents mention their use for mowing barley, oats, rye, peas and beans. The scythes are depicted with long handles with pairs of handgrips and long, gently curved iron blades (Higgs 1965, 8–9, pls 17a–b, 18a and 19a).

F113–118 are scythes, **F115** perhaps post-medieval. **F113**, complete but for the centre of the blade lost in modern disturbance, has a straight parallel-sided blade with a back which curved gently to the tip and a short clenched tang at right angles to it. The blade is of triangular section, but on **F113** and **F115** it has a thickened back rib. **F114** is a blade fragment with parallel sides and then a curved back, and **F115** is gently curved throughout. **F116–118** are blade tips, **F116** certainly from a scythe, the others possibly from large pairs of shears.

7.13 PITCHFORKS

Medieval pitchforks **F119–127** are tanged and have pairs of tines which are either straight or curved in side view. No socketed pitchfork, as depicted in a 12th-century chronicle, is known (Higgs 1965, 8, pl 17a). Pitchforks were used to move bound sheaves of corn and bundles of hay, thatching straw, reeds, etc about, and their size varies according to use. The tines are of circular, rectangular and diamond section, and complete tangs taper to a point and are never clenched. **F126–127**, which are of large size, may be hayforks.

7.14 SPUDS

Spuds are hafted iron blades of varying shapes and sizes which were used to clean earth from ploughs and digging tools and in weeding. **F128–130** are tanged spuds with flat, rectangular blades and rounded shoulders.

7.15 OX GOADS

Ploughing scenes in medieval manuscripts often show the ploughman or his assistant encouraging the team along with a whip or a long stick (Hartley and Elliot 1931, pl 7c; 1928, pl 24d). The stick was sometimes made more useful by the addition of an iron goad similar to **F131–133**.

7.16 BELLS

Bells **F134–138** are probably sheep or cow bells, all made of sheet iron with their handles and clapper supports either combined (**F134–135**) or separate (**F138**). The latter is a sophisticated arrangement since both the clapper and its swivel loop support must have moved independently. None of these bells retains its clapper, but **F139–145** are examples of these, all with hooked suspension loops. **F139–140** are small enough to have been used with bells such as **F134**, **F136** and **F138**, but the others must have come from larger bells. **F143–145** are all of identical length, 135mm, and may be from portable ecclesiastical bells of a type known in Ireland (Coffey 1909, 47–48, 65–67, figs 51, 64–65).

The sheet iron bells were probably made from single pieces of iron forged into shape and brazed together down the side seams. The overall copper-alloy plating noted on **F134**, **F136** and **F138** probably derives from lavishly used brazing metal, and it would have protected the bells from rusting and thus prevented them staining the wool of the sheep. A late 13th-century bestiary shows a small flock of sheep led by a bell-wether (Higgs 1965, 7, pl 9b).

F1 COULTER
London.
Medieval (?).
Gently curved rectangular shank, triangular section blade. L 650mm.
Ward Perkins 1967, 124, pl XXII.1.

F2 COULTER
London.
Medieval (?).
Gently curved rectangular shank, triangular section blade. L 690mm.
Ward Perkins 1967, 124, pl XXII.2.

F3 PLOUGHSHARE
Wroughton Copse, Fyfield Down, Wiltshire.
12th century (?).
Incomplete flanged ploughshare with thickened base. L 161mm.
Excavated by P J Fowler.

F4 PLOUGHSHARE
Huish, Wiltshire.
12th to mid 15th century.
Incomplete flanged ploughshare. L 105mm.
Shortt 1972, 124, fig 6.48.

F5 PLOUGHSHARE (?)
South Witham, Lincolnshire.
1137–85 to c1220.
Incomplete flanged ploughshare. L 72mm.
Goodall 2002, fig 7.3, no. 30.

AGRICULTURAL TOOLS

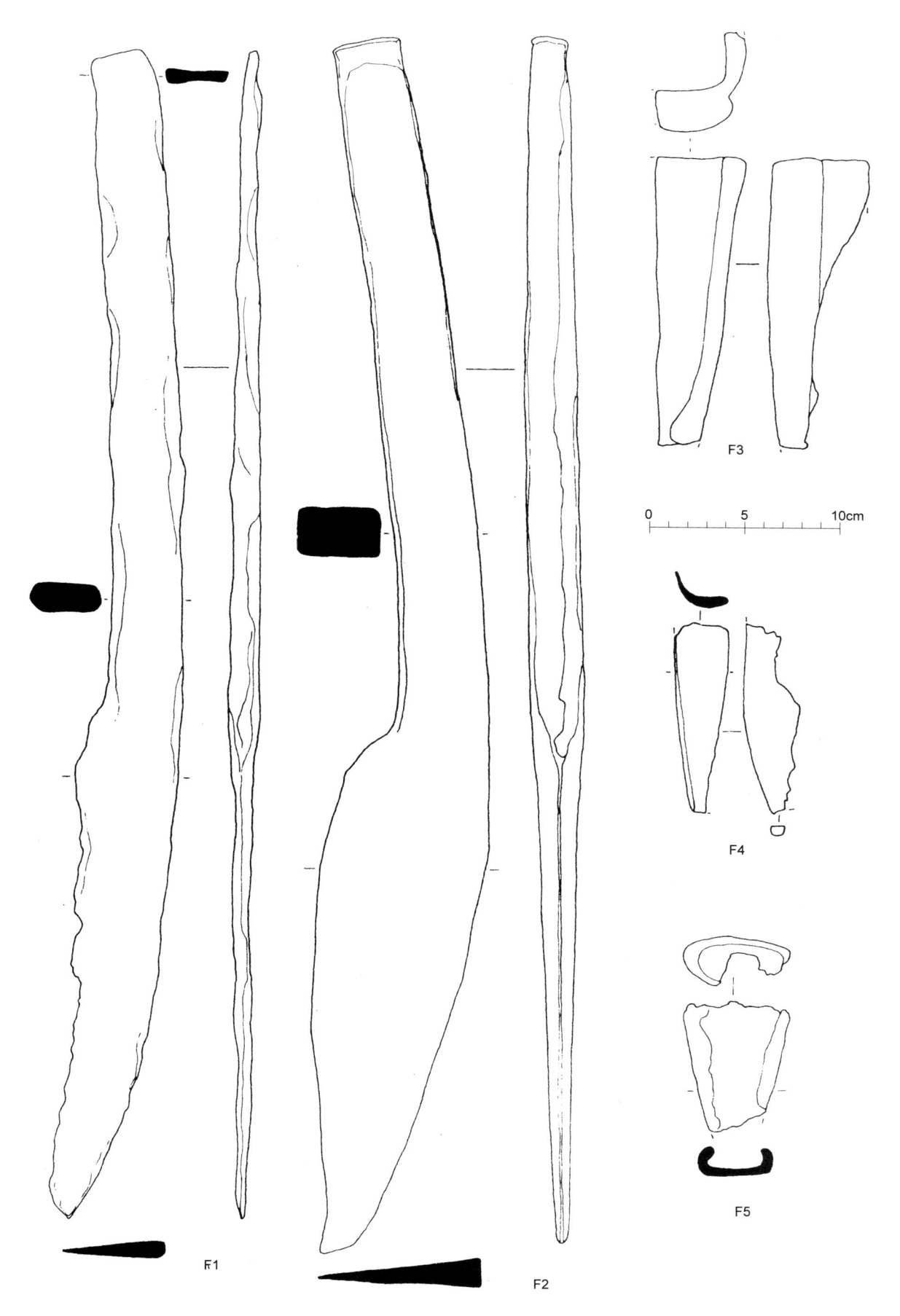

FIGURE 7.2
Agricultural tools: Coulters and ploughshares

F6 SPADE-IRON
Chew Valley Lake, Somerset.
13th century or later.
Triangular mouth and blade edge, grooved throughout. W 208mm.
Rahtz and Greenfield 1977, 326, fig 121.9.

F7 SPADE-IRON
Thetford, Norfolk.
11th century (?medieval or post-medieval disturbance).
Round mouth and blade edge with straight sides grooved throughout. W 143mm.
Goodall 1984.

F8 SPADE-IRON
Lydford Castle, Devon.
Mid 13th century, from infill of well.
Round mouth, grooved throughout. Triangular blade. Iron clip through blade represents a repair intended to secure wooden blade and spade-iron more firmly. W 240mm.
Goodall 1980b, fig 18.3.

F9 SPADE-IRON
Netherton, Hampshire.
Mid 13th century.
Round mouth, grooved throughout. Deep triangular blade. W 221mm.
Goodall 1990-28, fig 9.2 no. 72.

F10 SPADE-IRON
Steyning, West Sussex.
c1450 to 1500. From tipping infilling well 1.
Round mouth, grooved throughout. Deep triangular blade. W 191mm.
Excavated by Miss J Evans.

F11 SPADE-IRON
Bishops Waltham, Hampshire.
1450 to 1500.
Rectangular mouth with groove along edge and in lower part of side arms. Upper part of most complete side arm flat and straight. W 162mm.
Lewis 1985, fig 23.8.

F12 SPADE-IRON
Lyveden, Northamptonshire.
From construction pit of well dug and in use c1200 to 1350.
Incomplete rectangular mouth with grooved edge and broken straight, flat side arm. Rectangular blade, slightly rounded corner. W 104mm.
Steane and Bryant 1975, 139, fig 52.251.

AGRICULTURAL TOOLS

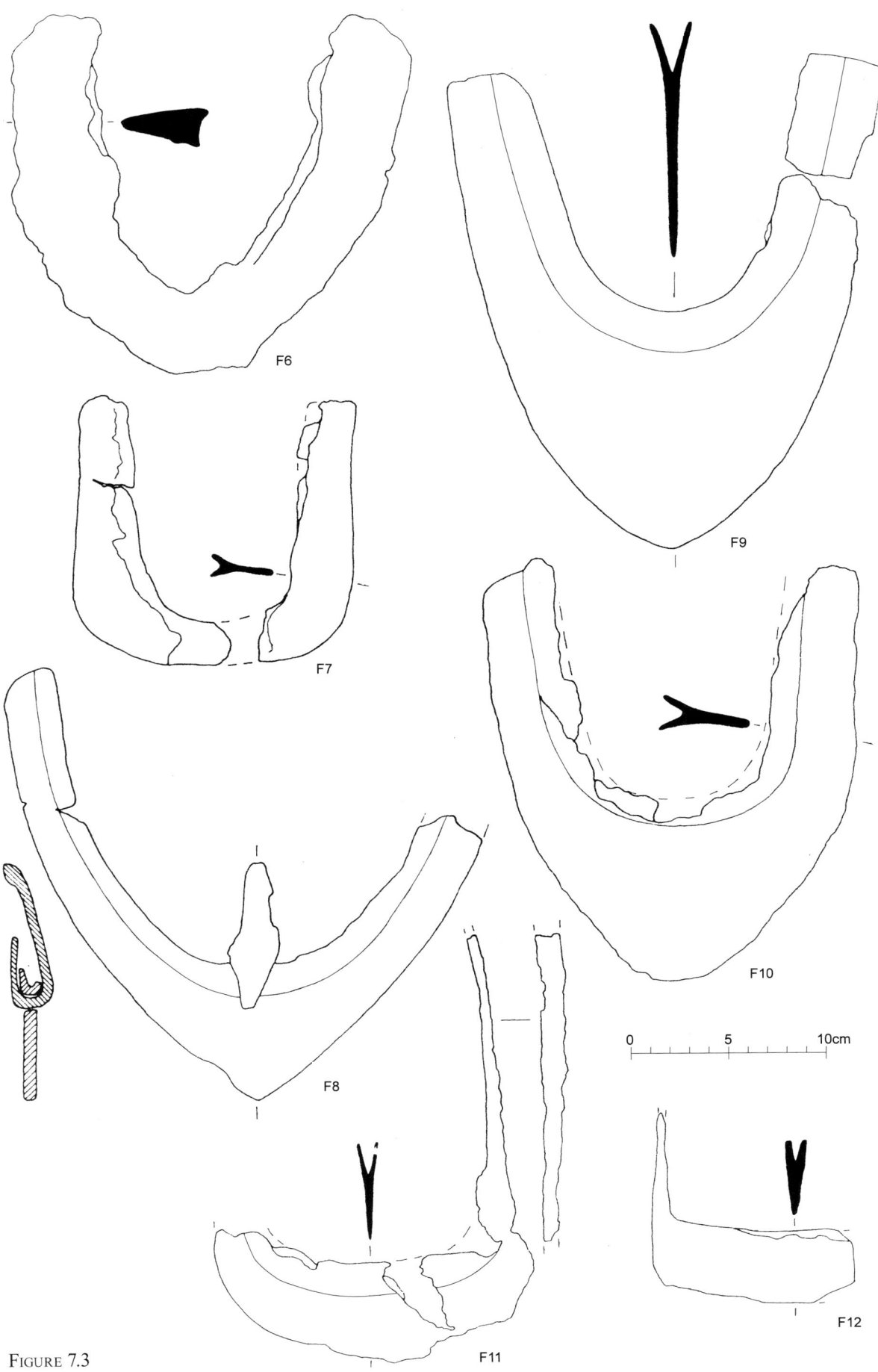

FIGURE 7.3
Agricultural tools: Spade-irons

F13 SPADE-IRON
Northolt Manor, Greater London.
First half 14th century.
Rectangular mouth with grooved edge and incomplete straight, flat side arms. Rectangular blade with rounded corners. Blade W 202mm.
Excavated by J G Hurst.

F14 SPADE-IRON
Badby, Northamptonshire.
15th to 16th century and later.
Incomplete rectangular mouth with grooved edge and base of flat side arm. Rectangular blade with worn corner. W 127mm.
Excavated by Mrs M Gray.

F15 SPADE-IRON
Tattershall College, Lincolnshire.
1540–c1560.
Rectangular mouth with grooved edge and flat side arms, originally straight but now distorted, ending in nailed lugs. Rectangular blade with rounded corners. Blade W 180mm.
Excavated by L J Keen.

F16 SPADE-IRON
Lyveden, Northamptonshire.
From construction pit of well dug and in use c1200 to 1350.
Fragment with grooved edge from spade-iron with rectangular mouth and blade.
W 114mm.
Steane and Bryant 1975, 139, fig 52.250.

F17 SPADE-IRON
Grenstein, Norfolk.
Late 14th or possible early 15th century.
Fragment with grooved edge from spade-iron with rectangular mouth and blade.
W 86mm.
Goodall 1980c.

F18 SHOVEL
Blunden's Wood, Hambledon, Surrey.
Later 13th, early 14th century. Found on eastern hearth of glass kiln A.
Incomplete and distorted iron shovel blade. 25mm length close to broken end of one edge is rolled over and apparently once projected up or away from main blade.
W 136mm.
Wood 1965, 72–74, fig 10.

F19 FORK
The Old Manor, Askett, Buckinghamshire.
1475 to 1515. From garderobe.
Socketed fork with three prongs. L 323mm.
Beresford 1971, 366, fig 22.

F20 FORK
Badby, Northamptonshire.
15th to 16th century and later.
Socketed fork with three prongs. L 360mm.
Excavated by Mrs M Gray.

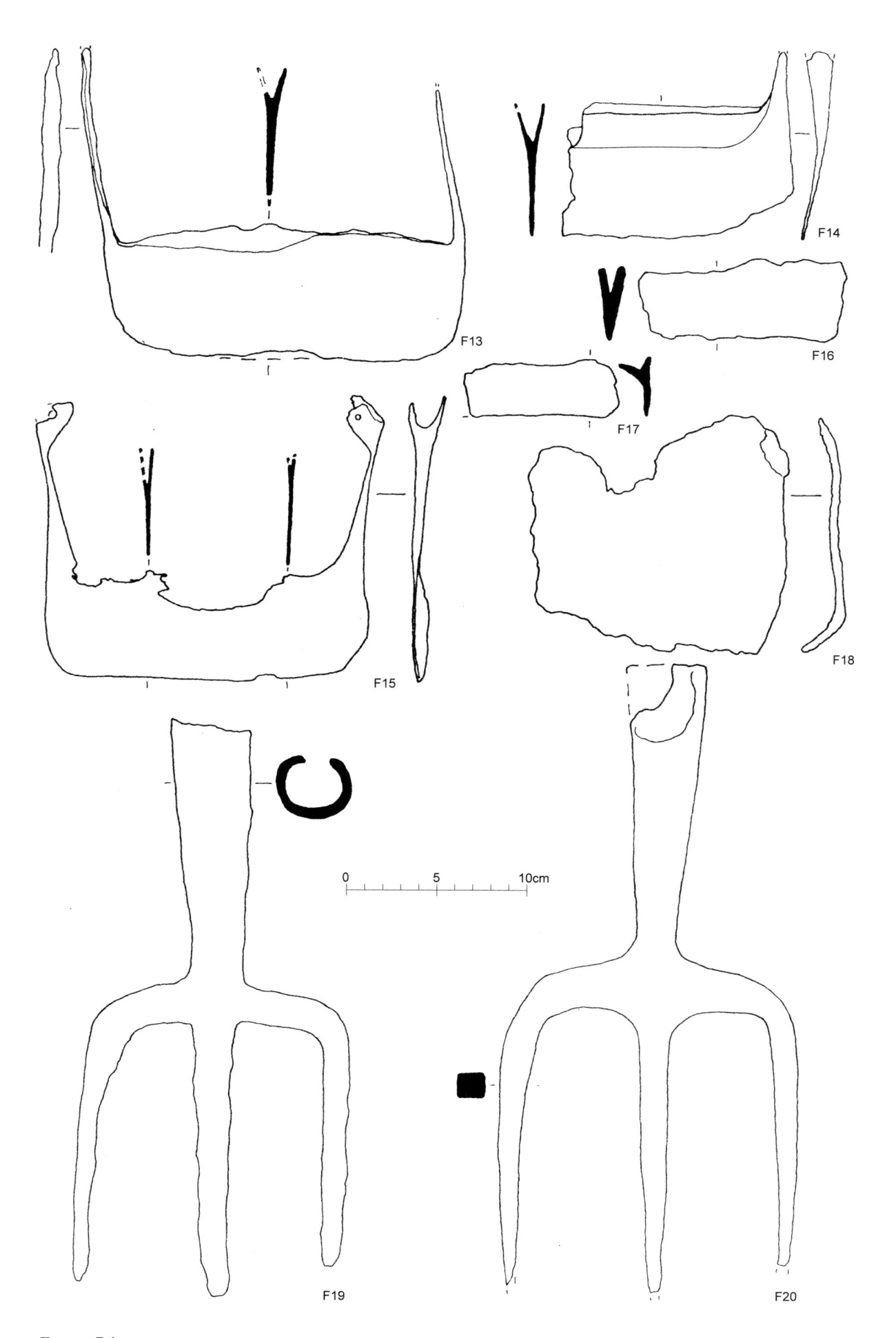

FIGURE 7.4
Agricultural tools: Spade-irons, shovel and forks

F21 TURF CUTTER
Weoley Castle, Birmingham, West Midlands.
From bottom puddled-clay layer of moat, dug c1270–80.
Crescent-shaped blade with central socket retaining traces of wooden handle.
W 132mm.
Taylor 1974. For site see Oswald 1962.

F22 TURF CUTTER
Huish, Wiltshire.
12th to mid 15th century.
Crescent-shaped blade, broken shank which may have developed into socket. W 69mm.
Shortt 1972, 120, fig 5.35.

F23 TURF CUTTER (?)
Hen Caerwys, Clwyd.
c1450 to 1520.
Flanged socket, incomplete blade. L 107mm.
Excavated by G B Leach.

F24 HOE
Upton, Gloucestershire.
Mid to later 13th century.
Triangular blade, long socket with hole for nail. L 188mm.
Rahtz 1969a, 108, fig 12.87.

F25 HOE
Hampton Wafer, Hereford and Worcester.
Site: probably 11th to early 14th century.
Triangular blade, curved edge, damaged socket. L 116mm.
Stanford 1967, 87, fig 7.6.

F26 HOE
Brandon Castle, Warwickshire.
From garderobe of keep of 1226–66.
Damaged triangular blade set at right angles to broken tang. W 109mm.
Chatwin 1955, 81, fig 11.17.

F27 HOE
Lochmaben Castle, Dumfries and Galloway.
Late 14th century.
Incomplete triangular blade set at right angle to broken broad tang. W 63mm.
Macdonald and Laing 1974–75, 148, fig 11.16.

F28 HOE
Winchester, Hampshire.
?Mid 15th century.
Incomplete triangular blade at right angles to broken tang. W 145mm.
Goodall 1990-11, fig 108.907.

F29 HOE (not illustrated)
Norwich, Norfolk.
In 1507 fire deposit.
Rectangular blade with curved shoulders set at right angles to tang which broadens out near tip. L 190mm, blade W 200mm.
Goodall 1993g.

F30 RAKE TOOTH
Broadfield, Hertfordshire.
c1220 to c1450.
Tapering rectangular-sectioned tooth, clenched tang tip. L 115mm.
Goodall 1974b, 56, fig 22.6.

F31 RAKE TOOTH
Copt Hay, Tetsworth, Oxfordshire.
13th century.
Tapering rectangular-sectioned tooth, tang broken. L 116mm.
Robinson 1973, 101, fig 23.10.

F32 RAKE TOOTH
Brixworth, Northamptonshire.
Saxon to mid 15th century.
Curved, tapering rectangular section, probably broken across blade of tang.
L 98mm.
Goodall 1977g, 94, fig 9.9.

F33 RAKE TOOTH
Lyveden, Northamptonshire.
First half 15th century.
Tapering rectangular-sectioned tooth with clenched tip to tang. L 114mm.
Steane and Bryant 1975, 121, fig 46.33.

F34 RAKE TOOTH
Winchester, Hampshire.
15th–?16th century.
Tapering rectangular-sectioned tooth, tang broken. L 115mm.
Goodall 1990-11, fig 108.908 [Goodall 1980 says WP3008].

F35 HARROW TOOTH
Portchester Castle, Hampshire.
Immediately prior to construction of building between 1521 and 1527.
Rectangular-sectioned tooth, tang broken.
L 178mm.
Hinton 1977, 204, fig 109.65.

F36 BILLHOOK
North Elmham Park, Norfolk.
c1050–c1150.
Flattened, partly closed socket and blade with bevelled back edge curving gently to hooked tip. L 268mm.
Goodall 1980a, 513, fig 266.50.

F37 BILLHOOK
Netherton, Hampshire.
Mid 13th century.
Open socket with two holes for securing nails. Parallel-sided blade, hooked tip to cutting edge. L 206mm.
Goodall 1990-28, fig 9.2 no. 75.

F38 BILLHOOK
Weoley Castle, Birmingham, West Midlands.
c1270 to 1600.
Partly open socket, closed at base, with hole for securing nail. Parallel-sided blade with hooked end to cutting edge and rear point.
L 360mm.
Taylor 1974. For site see Oswald 1962.

F39 BILLHOOK
Norwich, Norfolk.
In 1507 fire deposit.
Nailed, partly open socket, closed at base. Parallel-sided blade with rear point.
L 296mm.
Goodall 1993g, fig 145.1518.

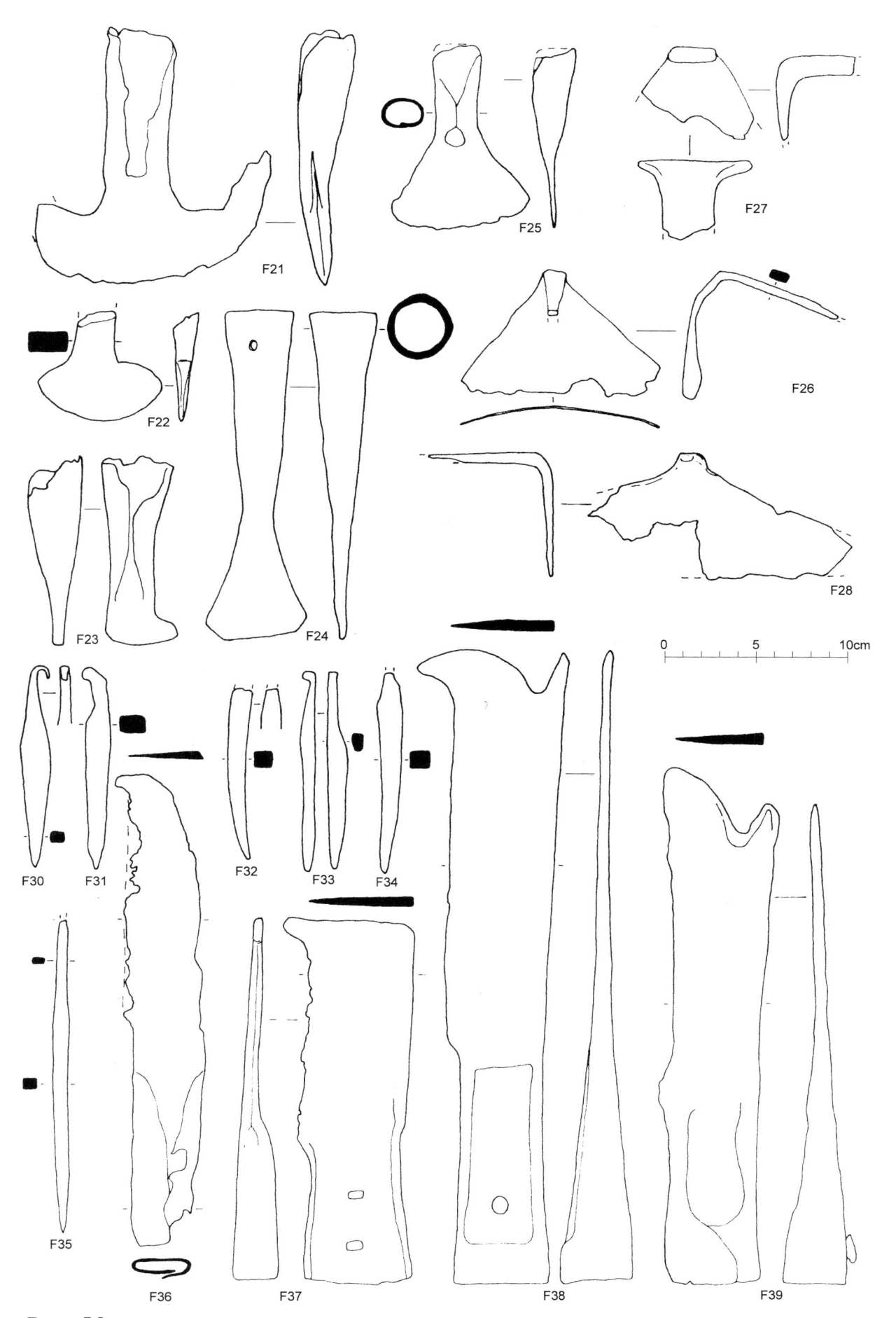

FIGURE 7.5
Agricultural tools: Turf cutters, hoes, rake and harrow teeth, and billhooks

F40 WEEDHOOK
Goltho Manor, Lincolnshire.
c1100–1150.
Broken, strongly recurved crescent-shaped blade with tip of clenched tang missing.
L 94mm.
Goodall 1987, fig 156.30.

F41 WEEDHOOK
Thetford, Norfolk.
12th century.
Crescent-shaped blade, tang broken. L 62mm.
Goodall 1984.

F42 WEEDHOOK
Woodperry, Oxfordshire.
12th to 14th century.
Crescent-shaped blade and plain tang, tip reduced in length since first published.
L 99mm.
Wilson 1846, 122 and figure.

F43 WEEDHOOK
Abingdon, Oxfordshire.
12th or 13th century.
Crescent-shaped blade, broken tang. L 88mm.
Parrington 1976, 47, fig 37.13.

F44 WEEDHOOK
Clough Castle, Co. Down.
c1200 to c1225.
Crescent-shaped blade with clenched tang tip. L 91mm.
Waterman 1954, 137, fig 11.13.

F45 WEEDHOOK
Dyserth Castle, Clwyd.
Site: 1241–63.
Sharply recurved crescent-shaped blade extending towards tang which has broken clenched tip. L 134mm.
Glenn 1915.

F46 WEEDHOOK
Upton, Gloucestershire.
Mid to later 13th century.
Crescent-shaped blade with tang. Blade tip lost, tong tip distorted. L 78mm.
Rahtz 1969a, 108, fig 12.130.

F47 WEEDHOOK
Newbury, Berkshire.
c1260–90.
Crescent-shaped blade, tang broken. L 58mm.
Goodall 1997, fig 19, no. 6.

F48 WEEDHOOK
Lyveden, Northamptonshire.
Late 13th, very early 14th century.
Broken crescent-shaped blade, complete tang. L 104mm.
Bryant and Steane 1971, 55, fig 13e.

F49 WEEDHOOK
Netherton, Hampshire.
Mid 14th century.
Broken crescent-shaped blade and tang.
L 87mm.
Goodall 1990-28, fig 9.2, no. 80.

F50 WEEDHOOK
Clough Castle, Co. Down.
Site: c1200 to early 14th century, re-occupied in 15th or early 16th century.
Broken crescent-shaped blade, tang tip clenched. L 91mm.
Waterman 1954, 137, fig 11.14.

F51 WEEDHOOK
Lyveden, Northamptonshire.
Second quarter 13th to very early 14th century.
Half-moon shaped blade, tang broken.
L 49mm.
Steane and Bryant 1975, 119, fig 45.14.

F52 WEEDHOOK
Woodperry, Oxfordshire.
12th to 14th century.
Wedge-shaped blade and plain tang, tip reduced in length since first published.
L 130mm.
Wilson 1846, 122 and figure.

F53 WEEDHOOK
Copt Hay, Tetsworth, Oxfordshire.
13th century.
Broken wedge-shaped blade, tang complete.
L 79mm.
Robinson 1973, 101, fig 23.8.

F54 WEEDHOOK
Woodperry, Oxfordshire.
12th to 14th century.
Triangular-shaped blade, plain tang. L 91mm.
Ashmolean Museum, Oxford, 1873.57. For site see Wilson 1846.

F55 WEEDHOOK
Goltho, Lincolnshire.
Late 13th to early 14th century.
Triangular-shaped blade, clenched round tang tip. Former wooden handle further secured by small iron collar. L 115mm.
Goodall 1975a, 86–87, fig 41.86.

F56 WEEDHOOK
Winchester, Hampshire.
Late 15th–early 16th century.
Tang and blade broken. L 65mm.
Goodall 1990-11, fig 108.906.

F57 WEEDHOOK
Rhuddlan, Clwyd.
14th century, ?earlier part, or conceivable 1290–1300.
Strongly recurved crescent-shaped blade with pair of flanges at base of broken tang.
L 124mm.
Goodall 1994, fig 17.1, no. 13.

F58 WEEDHOOK
Wallingstones, Hereford and Worcester. c1250.
Half-moon shaped blade, flanged tang with clenched tip. L 108mm.
Bridgewater 1970–72, 100, fig 16.32.

F59 WEEDHOOK
Wallingstones, Hereford and Worcester.
Post-1500 destruction layer with residual objects; site occupied from c1200.
Incomplete half-moon shaped blade, flanged tang with clenched tip. L 107mm.
Bridgewater 1970–72, 104, fig 16.86.

F60 WEEDHOOK
Goltho, Lincolnshire.
Croft A: late Saxon to late 14th or early 15th century.
Wedge-shaped blade, flanged tang with clenched tip. L 112mm.
Goodall 1975a, 86–87, fig 41.87.

F61 WEEDHOOK
Kettleby Thorpe, Lincolnshire.
14th to early 15th century.
Wedge-shaped blade with broken flanged and nailed tang. Iron-impregnated wood from former handle survives. L 97mm.
Goodall 1974a, 33, fig 18.10.

F62 WEEDHOOK
Low Caythorpe, Humberside.
15th to early 16th century.
Triangular blade, incomplete flanged and nailed tang. L 101mm.
Coppack 1974, 41, fig 5.1.

F63 WEEDHOOK
Somerby, Lincolnshire.
11th to 15th century.
Wedge-shaped blade with nailed socket.
L 98mm.
Mynard 1969, 85, fig 13.IW94.

F64 REAPING HOOK
Hen Domen, Powys.
After 1200, probably before 1250.
Blade and tang fragment. L 106mm.
Barker and Higham 2000.

F65 REAPING HOOK
Portchester Castle, Hampshire.
13th century.
Tang and broken blade. L 89mm.
Hinton 1977, 204, fig 109.69, scale 2:3, not 1:3.

F66 REAPING HOOK
Goltho, Lincolnshire.
Croft A: late Saxon to late 14th or early 15th century.
Broken curved blade, complete tang.
L 114mm.
For site see Beresford 1975.

F67 REAPING HOOK
Staines, Surrey.
1300–1500.
Broken curved blade with socket. L 106mm.
Excavated by K Crouch.

F68 REAPING HOOK
Lyveden, Northamptonshire.
Site: 11th to very early 14th century.
Flanged socket and base of curved blade.
L 59mm.
Bryant and Steane 1971, 57, fig 14b.

F69 REAPING HOOK
Lyveden, Northamptonshire.
Early 13th to first half 14th century.
Flanged socket, base of curved blade.
L 102mm.
Steane 1967, 29, fig 10d.

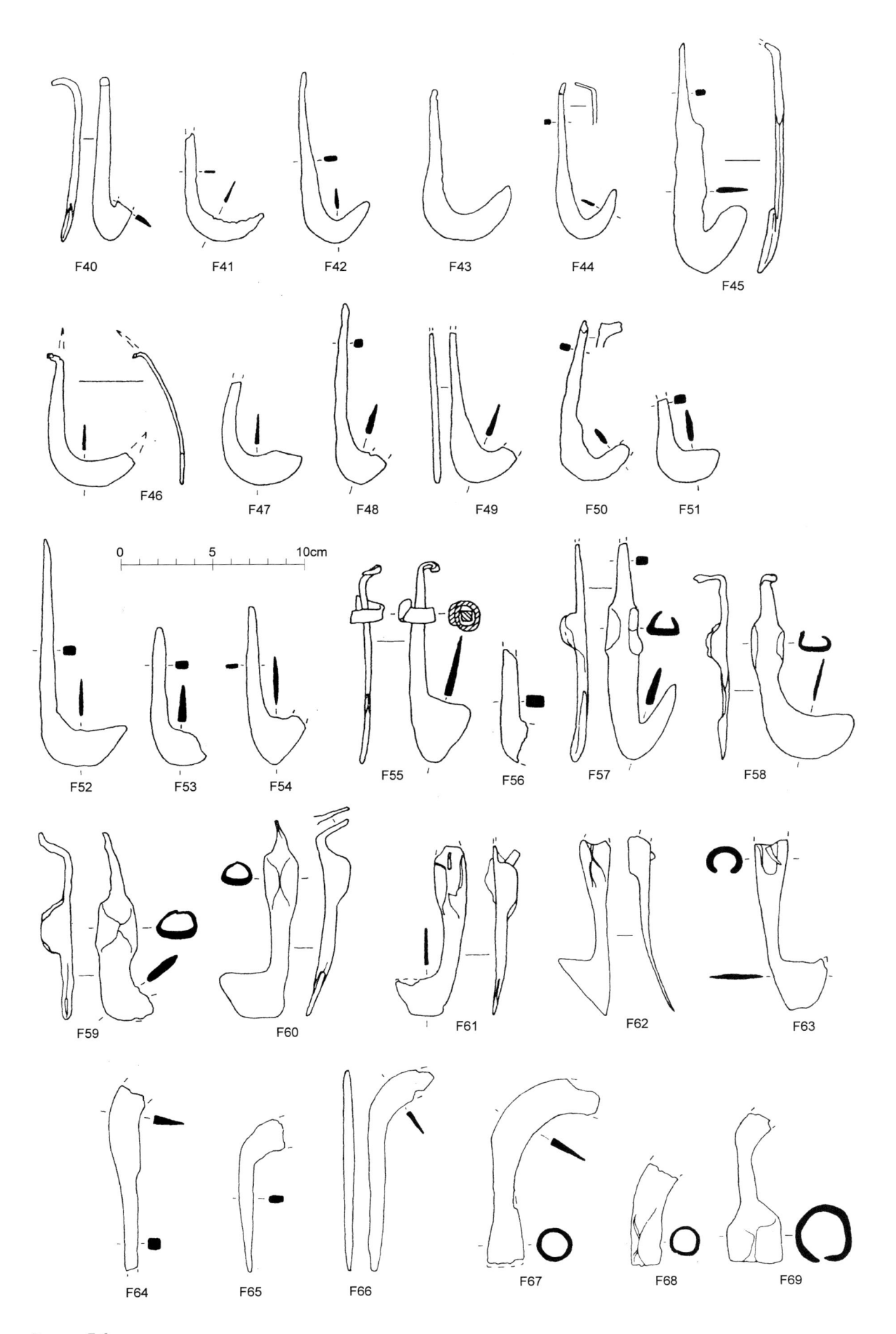

FIGURE 7.6
Agricultural tools: Weedhooks and reaping hooks

93

F70 SICKLE
Northolt Manor, Greater London.
Late Saxon to 13th century.
Blade and tang broken. L 322mm.
Excavated by J G Hurst.

F71 SICKLE
Stonar, Kent.
13th to 14th century.
Blade and tang broken. Saw-toothed cutting edge with mark on opposing face. L 489mm.
Excavated by N Macpherson-Grant.

F72 SICKLE
Thuxton, Norfolk.
Ploughsoil over site of 12th to end 14h century.
Blade and tang broken. L 237mm.
Excavated by L A S Butler and P Wade-Martins.

F73 SICKLE
Thuxton, Norfolk.
12th to end 14th century.
Tang and broken blade. L 172mm.
Excavated by L A S Butler and P Wade-Martins.

F74 SICKLE
Winchester, Hampshire.
Mid to ?late 13th century.
Blade and tang broken. Wrought iron. L 185mm.
Goodall 1990-11, fig 108.904.

F75 SICKLE
Alsted, Surrey.
c1250–1350.
Blade and tang broken. L 172mm.
Goodall 1976a, 56, fig 34.12.

F76 SICKLE
Conway, Gwynedd.
Site: 1283–?1404.
Tang complete, broken blade with thickened back rib. L 150mm.
Butler 1964, 126, fig 8.7.

F77 SICKLE
Writtle, Essex.
c1306 to c1425.
Blade and tang broken. L 176mm.
Rahtz 1969b, 87, fig 48.82.

F78 SICKLE
Writtle, Essex.
c1425 to 1521, mixed with later material.
Blade and tang broken. L 186mm.
Rahtz 1969b, 87, fig 48.81.

F79 SICKLE
London.
Late 15th, early 16th century.
Blade and tang broken. L 247mm.
Excavated by F C Willmot. Site at 66 Foyle Road.

F80 SICKLE
West Hartburn, Durham.
13th to 16th century.
Tang complete, blade broken. L 239mm.
Still and Pallister 1964, 200, fig 6.31.

F81 SICKLE
Clarendon Palace, Wiltshire.
Site: c1072 to later 15th century.
Blade and tang broken. L 312mm.
Goodall 1988, fig 73.3; Borenius and Charlton 1936.

F82 SICKLE
North Elmham Park, Norfolk.
c1150 to c1600.
Tang complete, blade broken. L 167mm.
Goodall 1980a, 513, fig 266.57.

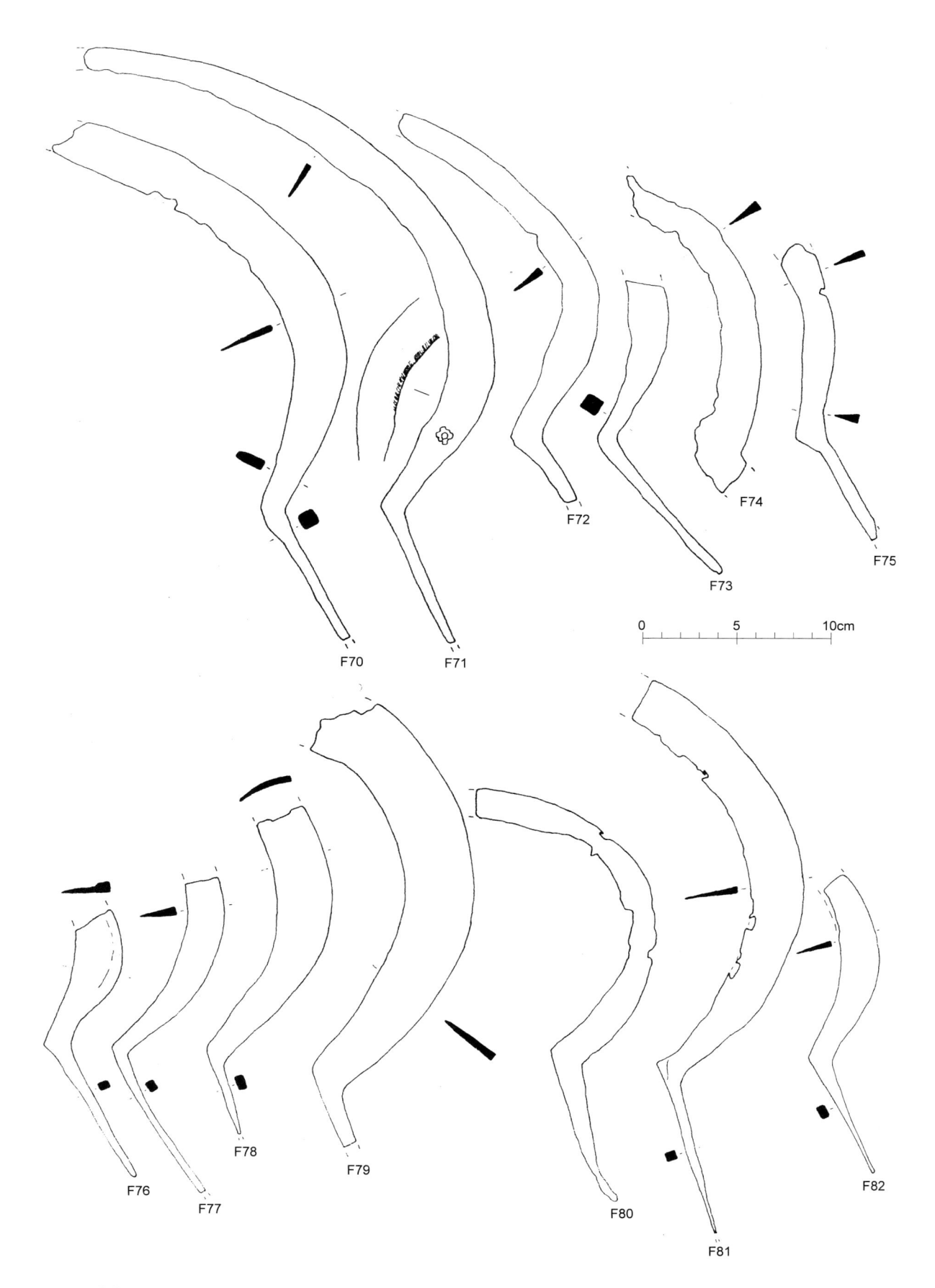

AGRICULTURAL TOOLS

FIGURE 7.7
Agricultural tools: Sickles

F83–90 SICKLES
Ayton Castle, North Yorkshire.
13th century. Found together with other sickle blades, spearhead, axe, shears and pitchfork.
Blades and tangs broken except **F83**, **F84**(?) and **F87** (blades complete), **F93** (tang complete).
(See also **F105–107**).

F83 L 312mm (Rimington and Rutter 1967, fig 11.37/4).
F84 L 280mm (Rimington and Rutter 1967, fig 11.37/5).
F85 L 314mm (Rimington and Rutter 1967, fig 11.37/7).
F86 L 325mm (Rimington and Rutter 1967, fig 11.37/1).
F87 L 307mm. Acc No 276.61.
F88 L 281mm (Rimington and Rutter 1967, fig 11.37/2).
F89 L 252mm (Rimington and Rutter 1967, fig 11.37/3).
F90 L 244mm (Rimington and Rutter 1967, fig 11.37/6).

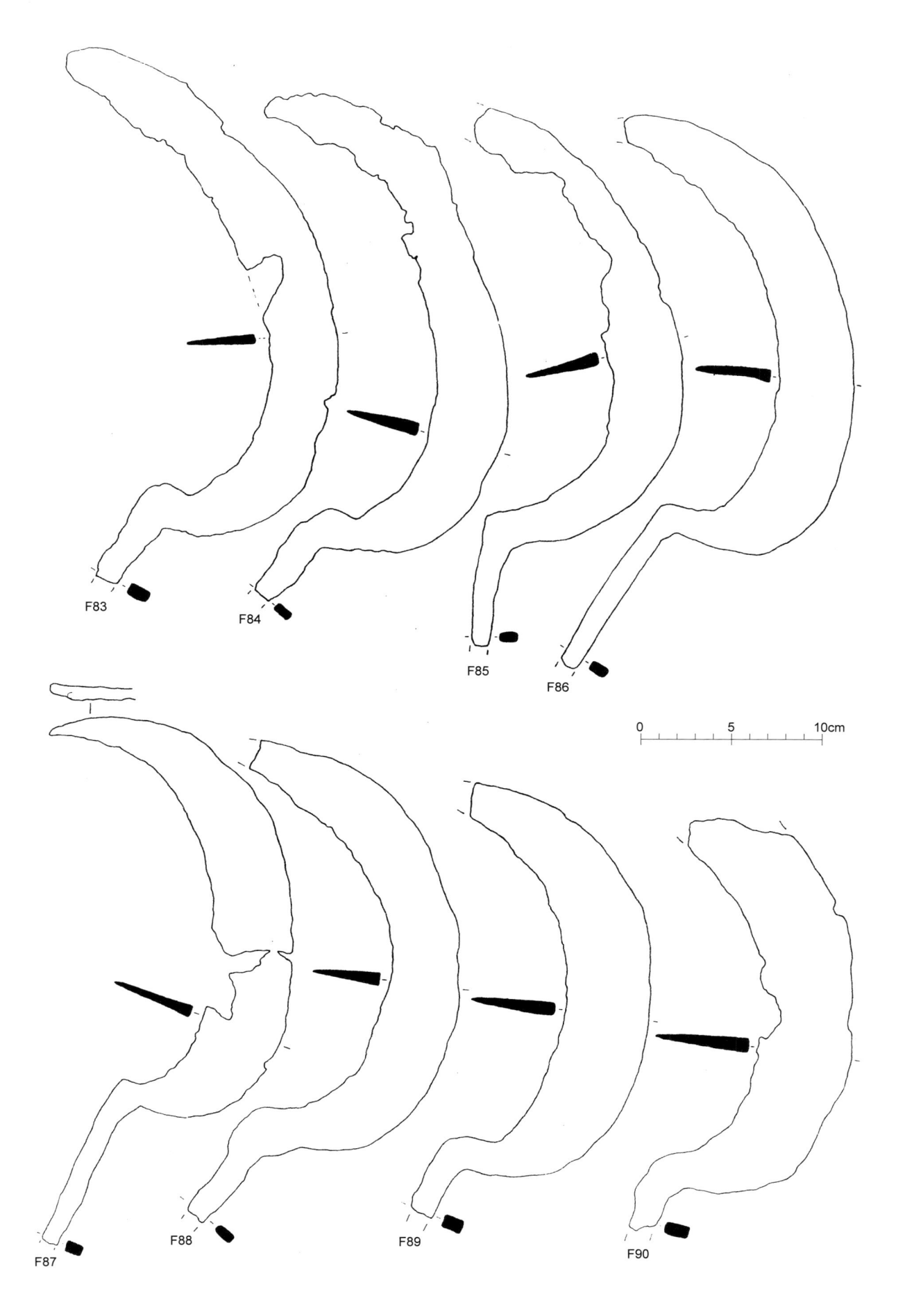

FIGURE 7.8
Agricultural tools: Sickles

F91–95 SICKLES
Ayton Castle, North Yorkshire.
13th century (see **F83**).
F91 L 271mm (Rimington and Rutter 1967, fig 11.37/8).
F92 L 216mm (Rimington and Rutter 1967, fig 11.37/9).
F93 L 122mm. Acc No 281.61.
F94 L 89mm. Acc No 280.61.
F95 L 73mm. Acc No 282.61.

F96 SICKLE
Cambokeels, Durham.
Later 14th to early 16th century.
Blade and tang broken. L 265mm.
Hildyard 1949, 199, fig 3.22. Bowes Museum, Barnard Castle.

F97 SICKLE
Old Sarum, Wiltshire.
Principally medieval, to 14th century.
Blade tip. L 151mm.
For site see Stone and Charlton 1935.

F98 SICKLE
Lyveden, Northamptonshire.
Second quarter 13th century to very early 14th century.
Blade and tang fragment. L 149mm.
Steane and Bryant 1975, 130, fig 48.142.

F99 SICKLE
Dyserth Castle, Clwyd.
Site: 1241–63.
Blade tip fragment. L 125mm.
Glenn 1915.

F100 SICKLE
Brandon Castle, Warwickshire.
13th century, ?post-1226.
Sickle blade fragment with tip, toothed cutting edge. L 269mm.
Chatwin 1955, 81, fig 11.15.

F101 SICKLE
Hangleton, East Sussex.
13th to 14th century.
Blade fragment with tip. L 226mm.
Holden 1963, 171, fig 37.7.

F102 SICKLE
Copt Hay, Tetsworth, Oxfordshire.
Late 13th to 14th century.
Blade fragment with tip. L 154mm.
Robinson 1973, 101, fig 23.7.

F103 SICKLE
Keighton, Nottinghamshire.
Early 14th century.
Blade and tip fragment. L 162mm.
Coppack 1971, 58, fig 8.6.

F104 SICKLE
Lyveden, Northamptonshire.
c1350 to 1450.
Blade tip fragment. L 146mm.
Steane and Bryant 1975, 130, fig 48.141.

F105–F107 SICKLES
Ayton Castle, North Yorkshire.
13th century. Found together with other sickles, spearhead, axe, shears and pitchfork.
Blade fragments.
Rimington and Rutter 1967, 59. (See also **F83–95**.)
F105 L 239mm. Acc. No. 279.61.
F106 L 231mm. Acc. No. 278.61.
F107 L 229mm. Acc. No. 277.61.

F108 SICKLE
Durrance Moat, Hereford and Worcester.
c1200 to 1250.
Blade fragment. L 201mm.
Oswald and Taylor 1964, 73, fig 4.22.

F109 SICKLE
Hangleton, East Sussex.
13th to 14th century.
Blade fragment. L 164mm.
Holden 1963, 171, fig 37.8.

F110 SICKLE
Stonar, Kent.
c1275–1385.
Blade fragment. L 210mm.
Excavated by N Macpherson-Grant.

F111 SICKLE
Winchester, Hampshire.
14th century.
Blade fragment. L 125mm.
Goodall 1990-11, fig 108.905.

F112 SICKLE
Wharram Percy, North Yorkshire.
Late 15th to early 16th century.
Blade fragment. L 207mm.
Goodall 1979a, 121, fig 62.59.

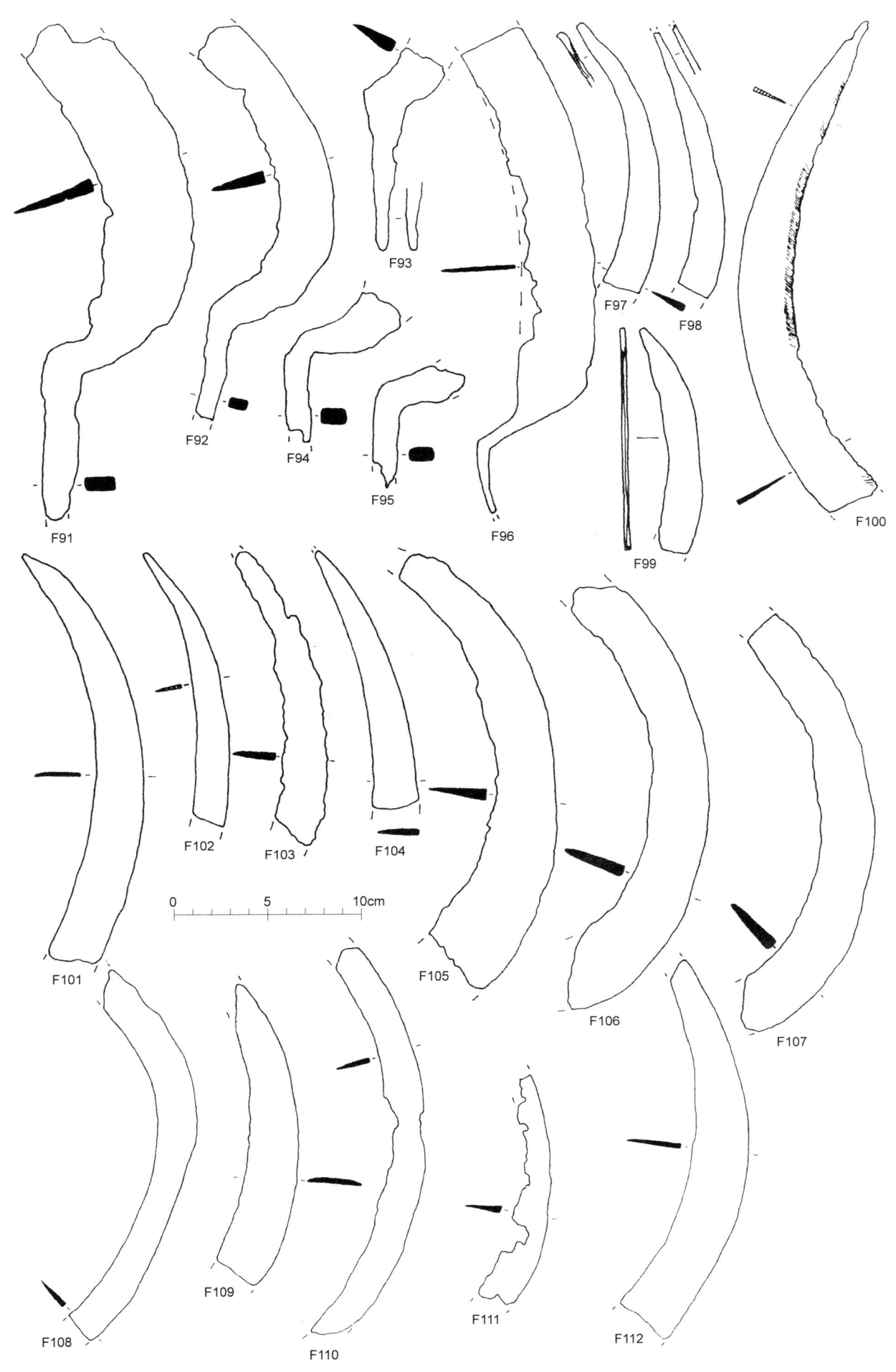

FIGURE 7.9
Agricultural tools: Scythes

F113 SCYTHE
King's Lynn, Norfolk.
c1250–1300.
Centre of blade lost in modern disturbances, rest drawn as found.
Parallel-sided blade, back curving in to tip. Clenched tang. L 530mm.
Goodall and Carter 1977, 295, fig 133.35.

F114 SCYTHE
Cheddar, Somerset.
Later 13th century to c1600.
Blade fragments with back rib. L 218mm.
Goodall 1979d, 266, fig 90.172.

F115 SCYTHE
Upton, Gloucestershire.
Possibly post-medieval, site 13th century or earlier to late 14th century.
Blade fragment, thickened back rib.
L 279mm.
Hilton and Rahtz 1966, 120, fig 13.17.

F116 SCYTHE
Thetford, Norfolk.
11th century.
Blade tip. L 164mm.
Goodall 1984.

F117 SCYTHE
Bolton, Fangfoss, Humberside.
Early 14th century.
Blade tip. L 98mm.
Goodall 1978b, 143, fig 30.23.

F118 SCYTHE
Barrow Mead, Bath, Somerset.
14th century.
Blade tip. L 107mm.
Goodall 1976b, 35, fig 11.25.

F119 PITCHFORK
Ayton Castle, North Yorkshire.
13th century. Found with sickles, spearhead, axe and shears.
Tang and near complete tines, gently curved in side view. L 193mm.
Rimington and Rutter 1967, 60, fig 11.37/20.

F120 PITCHFORK
Somerby, Lincolnshire.
11th to 15th century.
Complete, broken tines. L 129mm.
Mynard 1969, 84, fig 13.IW84.

F121 PITCHFORK
Badby, Northamptonshire.
15th to 16th century and later.
Tang broken, short curved tines straight in side view. L 143mm.
Excavated by Mrs M Gray.

F122 PITCHFORK
Thelsford Priory, Warwickshire.
In 16th century destruction deposit.
Broken tang, short tines, one broken.
L 133mm.
Excavated by Mrs M Gray.

F123 PITCHFORK
Somerby, Lincolnshire.
Site: 11th to mid 16th century.
Complete tang. Broken tines. Tip of more complete tine upturned. L 206mm.
Mynard 1969, 84, fig 13.IW85.

F124 PITCHFORK
Cambokeels, Durham.
Later 14th to early 15th century.
Complete tang, one tine broken, other gently curved. L 292mm.
Hildyard 1949, 197, fig 5.1.

AGRICULTURAL TOOLS

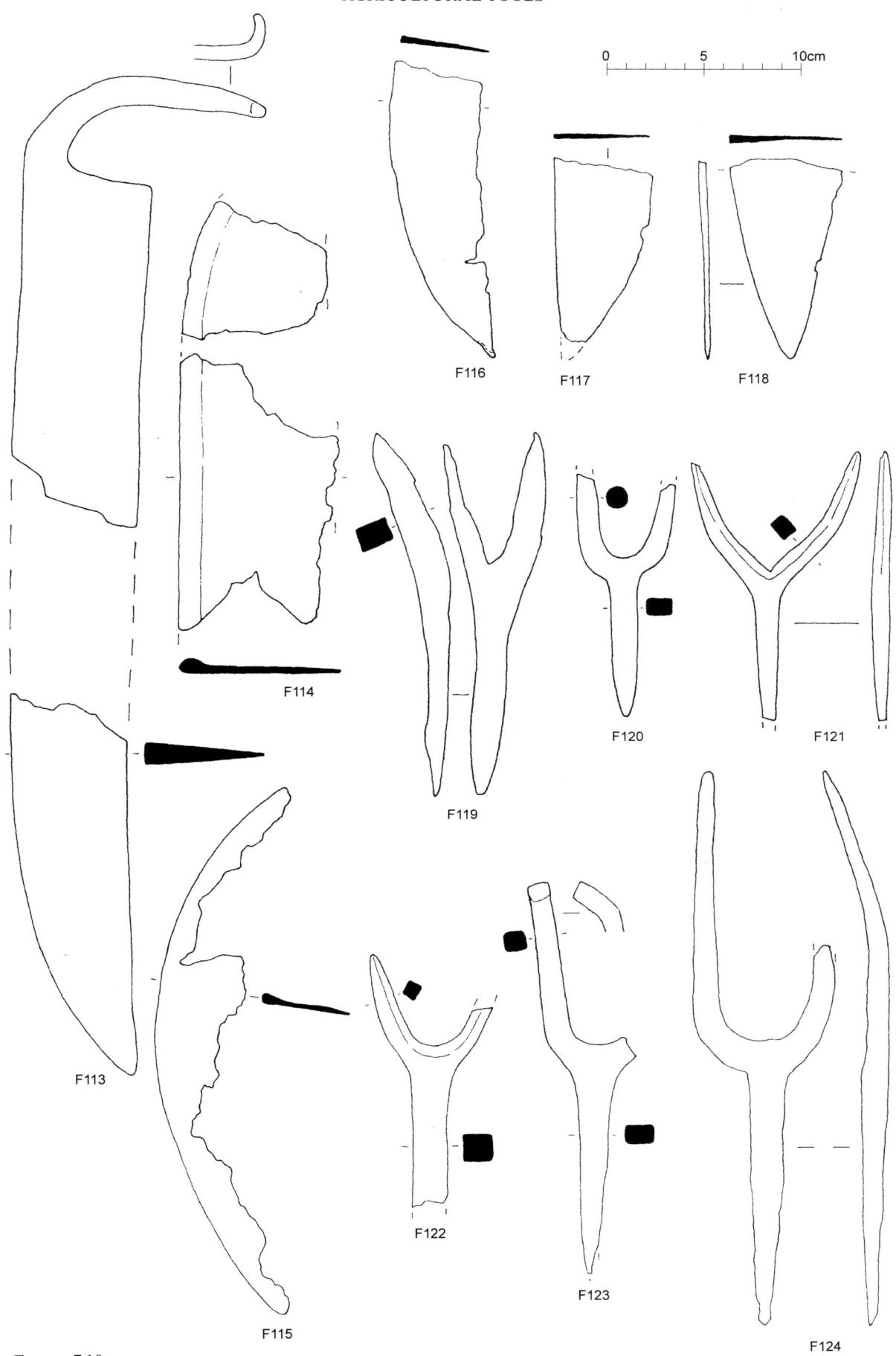

FIGURE 7.10
Agricultural tools: Scythes and pitchforks

F125 PITCHFORK
Somerby, Lincolnshire.
11th to 15th century.
Tang and tines broken. L 345mm.
Mynard 1969, 84, fig 13.IW83.

F126 PITCHFORK
West Hartburn, Durham.
Medieval to 16th century.
Tang broken, tines damaged but almost complete. L 231mm.
Still and Pallister 1967, 146, fig 4.2.

F127 PITCHFORK
Badby, Northamptonshire.
15th to 16th century and later.
Tang and tines broken, tines curved in side view. L 183mm.
Excavated by Mrs M Gray.

F128 SPUD
Shifnal, Shropshire.
13th to earlier 14th century.
Rectangular blade with curved shoulders, broken tang. L 110mm.
Barker 1964, 204, fig 44.SHI.M81.

F129 SPUD
Seacourt, Oxfordshire.
14th century.
Rectangular blade, complete tang. L 82mm.
Biddle 1961–62, 177, fig 30.4, scale 1:4, not 1:3.

F130 SPUD
Barton Blount, Derbyshire.
Croft E: late Saxon to late 15th century.
Rectangular blade, curved shoulders, broken tang. L 86mm.
Goodall 1975b, 98, fig 46.7.

F131 OX GOAD
Winchester, Hampshire.
Late 10th–?11th century.
Broken loop and point. H 19mm.
Goodall 1990-11, fig 108.912.

F132 OX GOAD (not illustrated)
Weaverthorpe Manor, North Yorkshire.
13th and 14th century.
Fragmentary ox goad.
Brewster 1972, 132.

F133 OX GOAD (?)
Sawtry, Cambridgeshire.
15th to early 16th century.
Loop with curved and pointed square-sectioned stem. L 68mm.
Moorhouse 1971b, 86, fig 4.11.

F134 BELL
Wallingstones, Hereford and Worcester.
Post-1500 destruction layer with objects from 13th century onwards.
Damaged bell retaining suspension loop for clapper. Traces of overall copper-alloy plating. W 56mm.
Bridgewater 1970–72, 104, fig 16.85.

F135 BELL
Upton, Gloucestershire.
Late 13th–late 14th century.
Damaged body and handle. W 51mm.
Hilton and Rahtz 1966, 120, fig 14.29.

F136 BELL
Wharram Percy, North Yorkshire.
Late 15th to early 16th century.
Fragment of bell and handle. Copper-alloy plating. W 37mm.
Goodall 1979a, 121, fig 63.74.

F137 BELL
Burton-in-Lonsdale, North Yorkshire.
Later 13th–mid 14th century.
Body fragment. W 34mm.
Moorhouse 1971a, 95, fig 3.21.

F138 BELL
Winchester, Hampshire.
15th century.
Damaged bell with D-shaped handle and swivelling clapper loop. Overall copper-alloy plating. W 50mm.
Luff 1990, fig 209.2278.

F139 BELL CLAPPER
Cheddar, Somerset.
Early 13th century.
Suspension hook broken. L 52mm.
Goodall 1979d, 271, fig 91.160.

F140 BELL CLAPPER
Wharram Percy, North Yorkshire.
Late 15th to early 16th century.
Hooked top. L 74mm.
Goodall 1979a, 121, fig 63.73.

F141 BELL CLAPPER
Castle Acre Castle, Norfolk.
1140s–50s deposit with derived material.
Site founded soon after 1066.
Hooked top. L 95mm.
Goodall 1982, fig 40, no.113.

F142 BELL CLAPPER
South Witham, Lincolnshire.
c1220 to 1308–13.
Hooked top. L 95mm.
Goodall 2002, fig 7.5, no. 142.

F143 BELL CLAPPER
Dyserth Castle, Clwyd.
Site: 1241–63.
Hooked top. L 135mm.
Glenn 1915.

F144 BELL CLAPPER
London.
Late 15th–early 16th century.
Hooked top. L 135mm.
Excavated by F C Willmot. Site at 66 Foyle Road.

F145 BELL CLAPPER
Burnham Church, Humberside.
Demolition c1550.
Hooked top. L 135mm.
Excavated by G Coppack.

AGRICULTURAL TOOLS

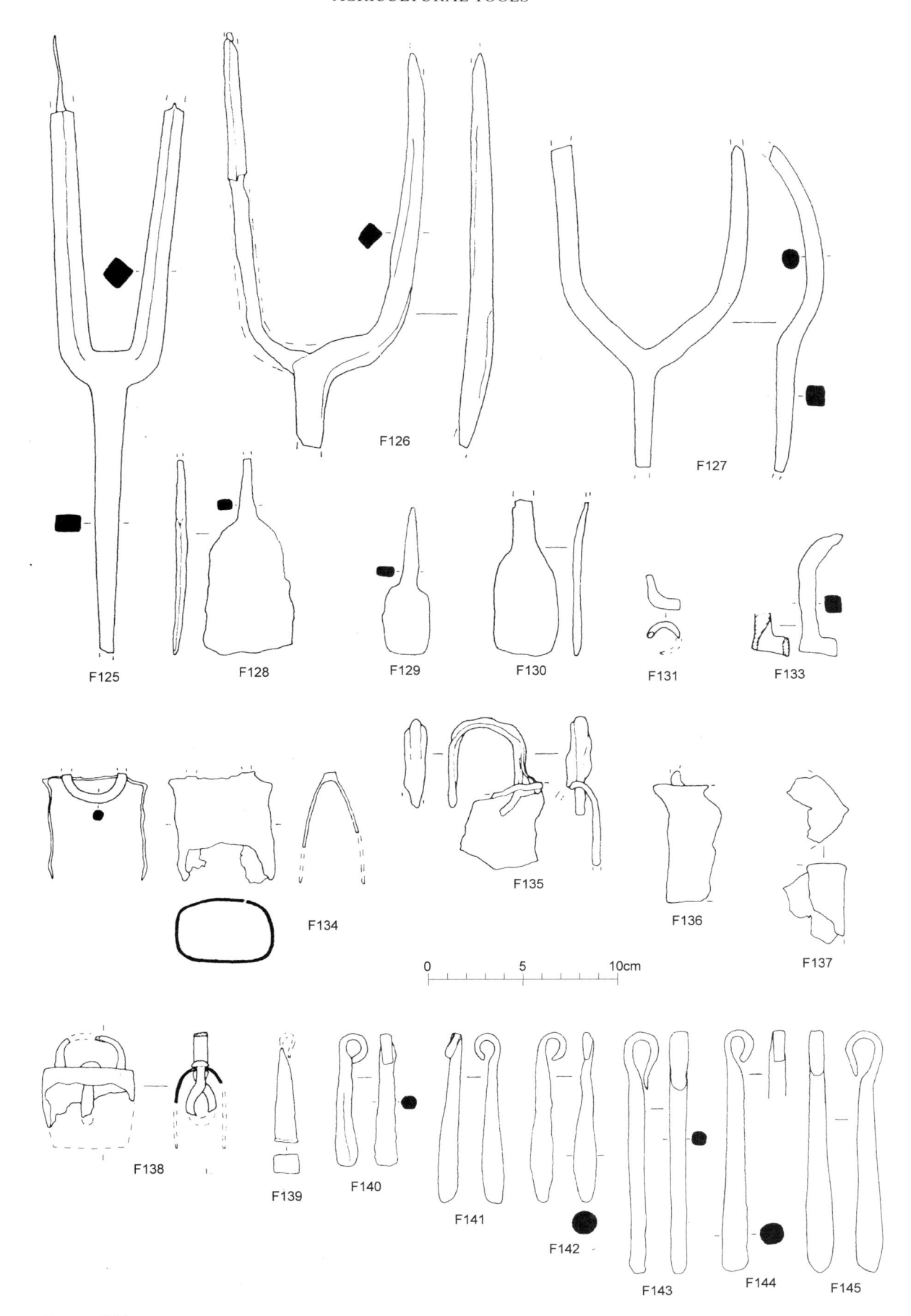

FIGURE 7.11
Agricultural tools: Pitchforks, spuds, ox goads, bells and bell clappers

8

KNIVES, SHEARS AND SCISSORS

8.1 KNIVES

The two basic types of medieval knife have whittle tangs inserted into handles and scale tangs with riveted handles. The terms used to describe their parts (Figure 8.1) are based, with a few amendments, on those in use in the Sheffield cutlery trade as recorded by Dyson (1936).

Medieval knives sometimes have a shoulder between the back of the blade and tang, and always a choil or indentation between the cutting edge and tang. Their blades can be decorated in various ways, most commonly with grooves or inlay, but occasionally with a swage, a long ornamental bevel along the back. Cutler's marks, generally inlaid with non-ferrous metal in the medieval period, are struck on the mark side of some blades; the other side is today called the pile or reverse side. Whittle tang knives may have single or multiple hilt plates at the junction between blade and tang, and many scale tang knives have riveted or soldered shoulder plates at this point. End caps occur on both types of tang handle. Rivets of iron or copper allow pass through scale tangs to hold the individual scales in place, but decorative pins are inset separately in each side.

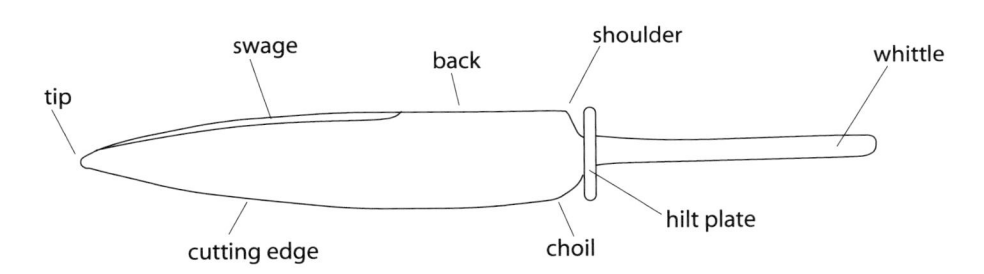

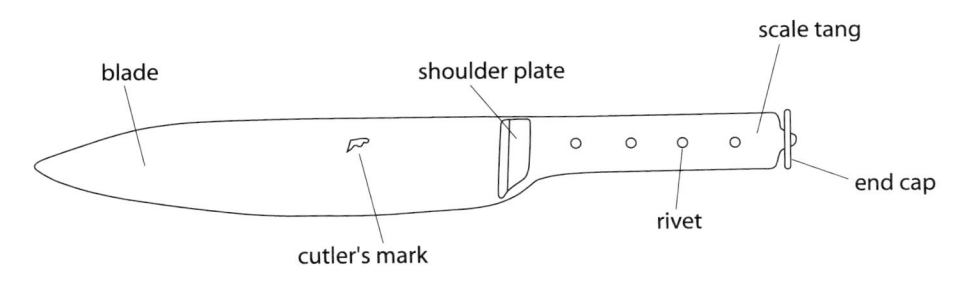

FIGURE 8.1
Knives: terminology

Knife moods

Knives were forged from strips or bars of iron generally with steel incorporated in some way or another (see Metallurgy below). **G1–3** are partly forged knives, which are called moods in the cutlery trade today to distinguish them from machine-cut blanks. All have whittle tangs.

Whittle tang knives

Whittle tang knives have pointed tangs which were inserted into wood or bone handles, and they have been classified according to blade form. Some of the catalogued knives lack tangs, but their date implies that these can only have been of whittle tang type. Ten types (A–J) may be isolated. (Figure 8.2).

Type A whittle tang knife

Blade back rises before angling down to tip. Cutting edge straight or curved.

The knife with a rising angled back is one of the more characteristic types of pre-Conquest knife, and the medieval examples **G4–17** tend to have fairly long blades which are not particularly deep, and the angling is consequently not always very marked. The angling down to the tip is generally straight, although on **G8** it is curved. Type A knives are found in contexts of 11th to 13th-century date.

Type B whittle tang knife

Blade back flat and straight before angling down to tip. Cutting edge straight or curved.

Knives **G18–39** have more or less parallel backs and cutting edges, some of which have been altered by sharpening. The angling down to the tip is frequently gentle, but it can be more marked, as on **G34**, or curved, as on **G29** and **G31**. Knives of this type occur throughout the medieval period, but they are more common in the earlier part.

Type C whittle tang knife

Blade with flat straight back parallel to cutting edge which rises close to tip to meet back.

The curvature of the cutting edges of knives **G40–47** varies from the stub end of **G40** to the gentle curve of **G42** or **G46**. The blades are all plain, with the notable exception of **G40** which has some decorative shaping close to the tip. The few known examples of the type occur throughout the medieval period.

Type D whittle tang knife

Blade black and cutting edge parallel before both taper to tip.

Knives **G48–121** represent the second most common type of medieval knife, and their size varies from small knives such as **G89–90** to long ones such as **G76** and

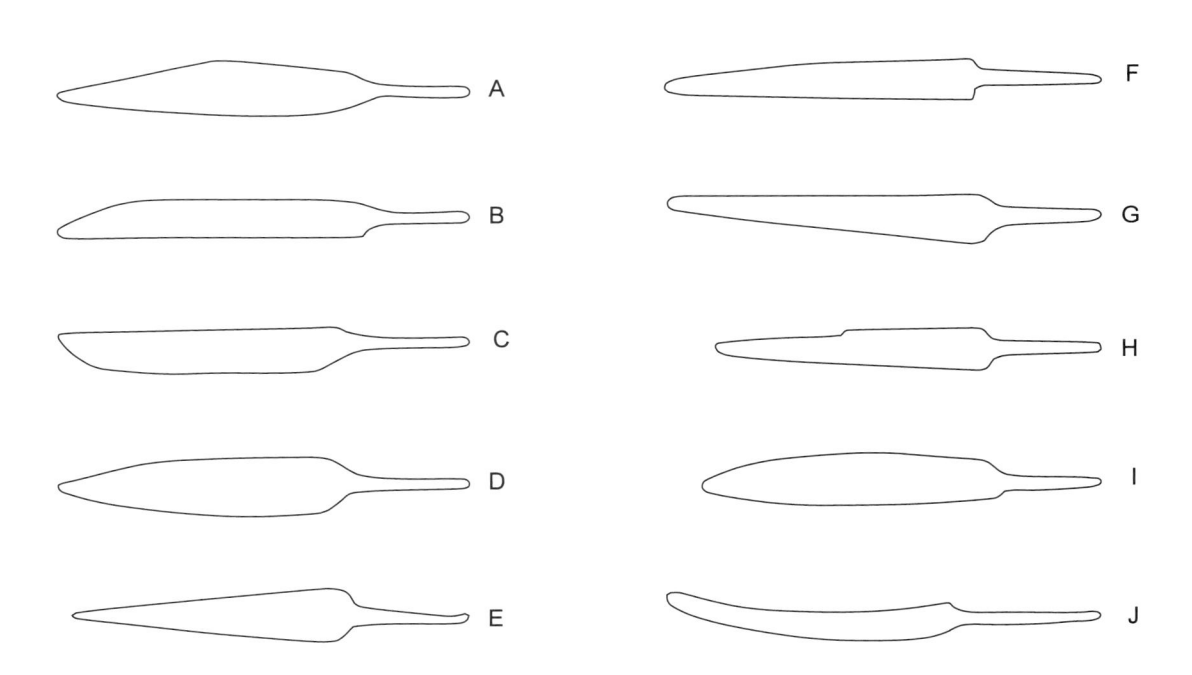

FIGURE 8.2
Types of medieval whittle tang knife

G119. The blades have no constant proportion, and although **G57–58**, for example, are of similar length, their depths are considerably different. A number of the longer, more slender blades such as **G107** and **G119** may be from single-edged knife daggers. Type D knives are found throughout the medieval period, but are particularly common in 12th and 13th-century contexts.

Type E whittle tang knife

Blade back and cutting edge taper more or less equally to tip.

G122–205 are examples of the most common type of medieval knife, and their size range is as wide, if not wider, than those of Type D. The blades range in size from small examples such as **G122–G123**, **G128** or **G151**, to **G153**, **G169**, **G197** and **G204**. Many of these larger examples are probably single-edged knife-daggers. The majority of blades taper evenly to the tip, but on **G127**, **G130**, **G135**, **G142**, **G163** and a few others it steepens and is more marked close to the end. More of these knives than of any other type with a whittle tang have cutler's marks stamped on the blade. Type E knives are found throughout the medieval period, but they occur in greatest numbers in 13th and 14th-century contexts.

Type F whittle tang knife

Blade back tapers from shoulder down to cutting edge.

The six knives of this type **G206–211** are from contexts of the 12th to 15th centuries. None of the examples has any distinctive feature.

Type G whittle tang knife

Cutting edge of blade rises to meet the tip of straight back.

The two knives **G212–213**, both with broken tangs, come from late medieval contexts, and are related to scale tang knife Type Q.

Type H whittle tang knife

Blade with stepped back.

Knives **G214–217** all lack complete blades, and the shape of the tip is consequently uncertain, but in general form they seem related to Types D and E. The closely dated examples come from contexts of the 13th to 14th century.

Type I whittle tang knife

Blade with convex curve to back.

The curvature of the back of knives **G218–257** ranges from slight to marked, and the cutting edge, although generally convex or bellied, is occasionally straight. The concave or elongated S-shaped cutting edges of some knives is the result of repeated sharpening. A number of these knives are too well finished to have been used for day-to-day practical work, and they are probably domestic. **G221**, **G228**, **G232** and **G248** have single or multiple hilt plates, **G239** a copper-alloy backing strip, while **G246** has inlaid decoration on the blade. The Southwark knife (Cowen 1971), itself probably of 12th to 13th-century date and an import from the East Baltic, is of this type and has a formidably inlaid blade. Knives of Type I are of 11th to 14th-century date, and are related to scale tang knives of Type R.

Type J whittle tang knife

Blade with concave back.

G258–260 are knives of this type, none complete, and none particularly closely dated.

Scale tang knives

Scale tang knives have flat tangs onto which separate, organic scales were riveted to form a handle. They were probably introduced during the 13th century, and in the following discussion the pre 13th-century element of any context date has been ignored. Six types (M–R) may be isolated (Figure 8.3).

Type M scale tang knife

Shoulder and choil between blade and tang. Blade back and cutting edge parallel before both taper to tip.

G261–262 are knives of this type, both from the 13th to 14th-century contexts. The blade form is identical to that of whittle tang knife Type D, and another type of scale tang knife, Type O.

Type N scale tang knife

Shoulder and choil between blade and tang. Blade back and cutting edge taper more or less equally to tip.

G263–269 are knives of this type, from 13th to 16th-century contexts, although they are most common in the 14th century. The blades are similar in size, but for the slender form of **G266**. The blade form is identical to that of whittle tang knife Type E, and another scale tang knife, Type P.

Type O scale tang knife

Back of blade and tang in line. Blade back and cutting edge parallel before both taper to tip.

Knives **G270–297** are of this type, and most have long slender blades. A significant number retain shoulder plates or evidence for them, implying that they were for personal use, whilst more robust examples such as **G280** and **G288**, the latter worn by repeated sharpening, are likely to have had more practical uses. Type O knives are known from 13th to 16th-century contexts, but are commonest in the late medieval period. They are related to knife Types D and M.

Type P scale tang knife

Back of blade and scale tang in line. Blade back and cutting edge taper more or less equally to tip.

Knives **G298–318** generally have long and slender blades with an elegant taper, and the bellied blade of **G316** is an unusual feature. Many of these knives were probably used for eating, and a number have, or had, shoulder plates fronting the handle. Type P is found almost equally commonly in contexts from the 13th to 16th centuries, and is related to knife Types E and N.

Type Q scale tang knife

Back of blade and scale tang in line. Cutting edge of blade rises to meet tip of straight back.

Knives **G319–332** mostly have long, slender blades with an even taper up to the tip, although a few blades have a more bellied form. The majority have, or had, shoulder plates, and the handle of **G321** was decorated with a row of pins linking rivet heads down the side of each scale. Type Q knives, found in contexts of 13th to 16th-century date, are related to whittle tang knives of Type G.

Type R scale tang knife

Convex curved back of blade in line with tang.

Knives **G335–335** have curved backs similar to those of whittle tang knives of Type I and come from contexts spanning the 13th to 15th centuries.

Knife uses

Knives had many uses, and as the catalogued examples indicate, there is a wide range of types and of sizes within types. Cleavers are discussed below (Chapter 11), but a number of the other knives must have had uses connected with eating or food preparation. Forks were only occasionally used during the medieval period, since the practice of eating with a knife and fork was only introduced from Italy in the 16th century.

Cutlery for the table falls into one of two categories, according to whether it was used for the carving and service of the food or for assistance in eating it. Carving in a great medieval household was a formal ritual, and the broad knife blade **G336**, of Type I or R, is probably from a carving knife. It resembles the pair of carving knives in a set apparently made for the Duke of Burgundy between 1385 and 1404 (Dalton 1907), one of which was used to cut and the other to support and carry the meat and transfer it to the plate or trencher. The smaller knives in the set, 212mm and 242mm long, of Types Q and O respectively, were probably used to cut meat and bread.

Carving knives are unlikely to have been used very far down the social scale, but many of the smaller knives must have been used widely for cutting bread and meat

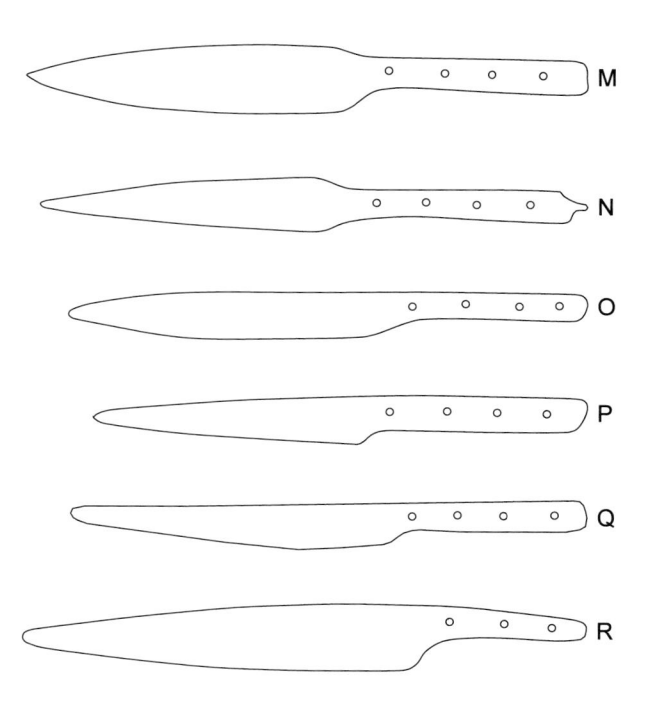

FIGURE 8.3
Types of medieval scale tang knife

and carrying it to the mouth. Various crafts will also have used some of the knives, and certain specialised leatherworkers' knives have already been noted (**E11–15**). However, leatherworking also required knives for trimming off waste from hides, and for other purposes, and these must be included amongst those classified here. A number of woodworking crafts also used different types of knife, and yet others, particularly of large size, are probably knife-daggers.

Dating of knives

Whittle tang knives were in use throughout the medieval period, their simple and practical method of hafting making them ideal for many purposes. Scale tang knives, more time consuming and costly to produce, and not all as practical, were probably introduced during the 13th century, although few of the early examples come from contexts of the 13th or 14th century alone; most are of 13th century to 14th-century date. The earliest dateable example is no longer that from Rayleigh Castle, Essex (Ward Perkins 1967, 51), since the site was occupied until c1350, not c1270.

The popularity and chronological range of the various types of medieval knife are shown in Figures 8.4 and 8.5. Many of the whittle tang knife blade forms are in fact merely continuations of pre-Conquest forms, but use of the term 'scramasax-knife' should be avoided. The

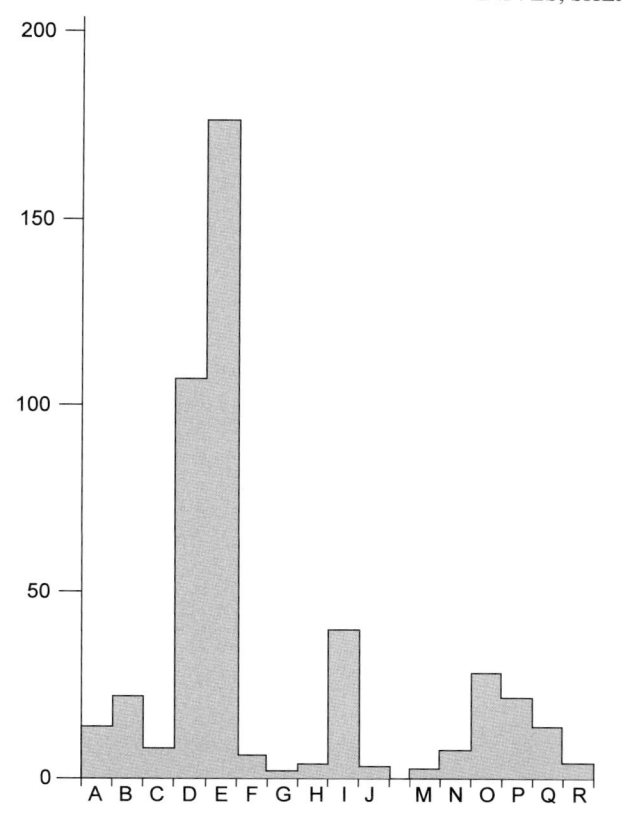

KNIVES, SHEARS AND SCISSORS

passage in Gregory of Tours about the murder of Sigibert reveals no more than that this name was applied to strong knives used by the Franks in the 6th century. No further details are given, and it should be remembered that the common word in use in Anglo-Saxon for knife was 'seax' (Evison 1961, 227). The scale tang knives repeat some of the most common whittle tang knife forms, although their blades are generally more slender.

The bolster, an expansion set between blade and tang and forged in one with them, was introduced as a method of hafting in the 16th century (Hayward 1957, 4). None of the 16th-century knives with bolsters, however, need come from a context before about 1540. A knife from Waltham Abbey, Essex (Huggins 1972, 124, from F64) comes from the destruction level inside a building of c1200–c1540, three from Hull (Goodall 1977b, 65, 70, figs 27.80–81, 29.145) are from early to mid 16th-century contexts, and one from Tattershall College, Lincolnshire (excavated by L J Keen) from a context of 1540 to c1560. A knife from Pleshey Castle, Essex (Goodall 1977c, 176, fig 38.6) is from a context of mid 13th to mid 16th century and later, and one from West Hartburn, Durham (excavated by L Still and A Pallister) is from a 13th to late 16th-century site.

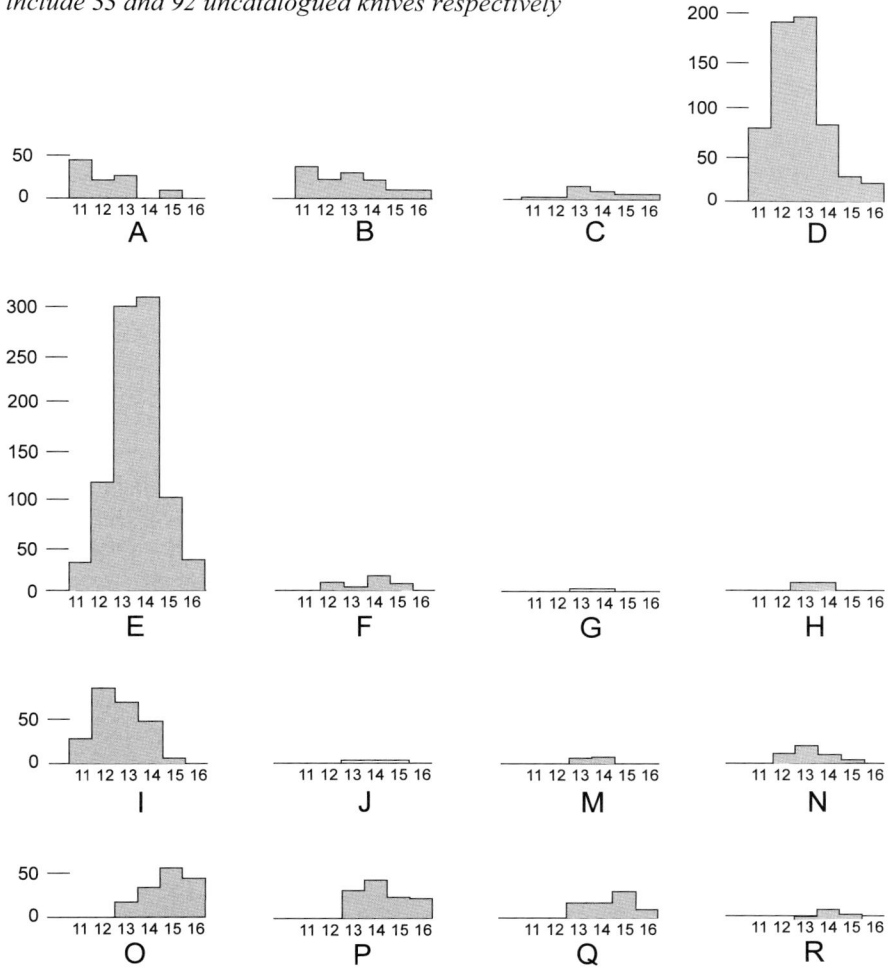

FIGURE 8.4
Frequency of types of medieval knife. Types D and E include 33 and 92 uncatalogued knives respectively

FIGURE 8.5
Chronological range of types of medieval knife. Types D and E include 33 and 92 uncatalogued knives respectively

109

Knife blade decoration

Knives sometimes have finely finished blades or handles, and a number of blades, all from whittle tang knives where the tang survives, are pattern-welded, inlaid with non-ferrous metal, or decoratively shaped in some way.

The technique of pattern-welding, described by Anstee and Biek (1961), is principally one of pre-Conquest date and applied to the forging of weapon blades, **G6**, **G15**, **G22**, **G68**, **G91**, **G131** and **G134**; and **G377–339**, are medieval knives with pattern-welded blades, several combined with steel edges.

All the knives with inlaid patterns of non-ferrous wire are fragmentary, and a number are residual in their contexts, but as a whole they are probably of 12th to 13th-century date. **G246** and **G340** have similar patterns, both including a running spiral, alternating scrolls and bar stops, and they may be compared with some of the inlay on the Southwark knife, which has been attributed to a 12th or 13th-century source in the East Baltic (Cowen 1971). **G341** has a more geometrical inlay comprising a lattice pattern between plain borders, and **G342** has simple intersecting spirals. The wire inlay on **G340** has been analysed and shown to be a silver-gold alloy, the silver predominating but with enough gold to give a 'gold' colour.

Knives **G29** and **G56** have single shallow grooves along each side of the blade, **G68** triple grooves, all serving simply as decoration in themselves and incapable of taking inlay. The deeper rectangular grooves of **G178**, **G190** and **G343–345** are more likely to have been intended to be inlaid, and some copper-alloy strip remains in **G190** and **G343**, **G178**, **G190**, **G343** and **G345** have single grooves, **G344** a pair, in all cases on only one side of the blade. The shallow grooved blades are from 11th to 13th-century contexts, the others are late medieval.

Knife **G239**, of 12th-13th century date, is unique in having a solid copper-alloy strip with incised geometrical decoration along the back of the blade, as is **G154** with three solid copper-alloy rivets set close to the back. The rivets are all roughly stamped, and the knife is of late 13th to 14th century date.

Type J knives have stepped backs, but a number of other types have decorated blade backs. **G40** has a cut out shaping close to the tip, and **G345–348** have swages or bevels along the back. The swage is a decorative feature, and is single sided on all but **G347**.

Knife handles

Knife handles of wood or bone, or their traces, are sometimes found on knives, but metal fittings from them survive more frequently. The handles of whittle tang knives were generally plain, but a few hilt plates and shoulder plates, as well as an end cap, are known. Scale tang knife handles were much more commonly embellished, and shoulder plates and end caps are found fairly frequently. Some handles are also decorated.

Whittle tang knife handles

The front end of the handles of several whittle tang knives have single or multiple hilt plates. **G107**, **G164**, **G193**, **G228** and **G349** have single hilt plates fronting the lost handle, that of **G107** of iron, the others of copper alloy or non-ferrous metal and circular or oval in shape. These knives are from contexts with dates scattered throughout the medieval period, but those with multiple hilt plates seem more closely restricted to earlier, 11th to 13th-century contexts. **G75**, **G76**, **G221**, **G232** and **G248** and **G350–351** have multiple hilt plates which consist of a series of metal plates, regularly or irregularly spaced, with gaps which were originally filled by plates of organic material. The plates of **G75**, **G76** and **G232** are of copper alloy and, like **G351**, are heater shaped. **G248** has trapezoidal-shaped plates.

Shoulder plates are normally found on scale tang knives, but they occur exceptionally on two whittle tang knives, **G203** and **G352**. The non-ferrous plates survive on **G203**, but **G352** retains only the brazing fluid. Both knives are from Pleshey Castle, Essex, but neither is certainly medieval.

Whittle tangs either terminated within handles or projected beyond their ends. **G133**, **G192** and **G242** have clenched tang tips and evidently projected beyond the handle, as did **G355–354** which have circular end caps. The clenched tip and cap both served the same function of stopping handle and tang parting company, which was also the function of collars such as those on **G96** and **G355**.

Scale tang knife handles

The individual scales from these knives are often missing, but the shape of the tang reflects that of the handle. The most common shape, found from the 13th-century onwards, has a straight back and drooping underside. **G262**, **G274**, **G299–300**, **G356–360** have straight-cut ends, **G278**, **G303–305**, **G309**, **G315**, **G325**, **G330** and **G361–366** rounded ends sometimes with a based point, and **G296** and **G367–379** an indented end. **G369** is exceptional in having a serrated underside. The next most common tang has parallel sides and either a straight-cut end (**G281**, **G321**, **G331**, **G370–373** and **G378**) or a rounded end (**G288**, **G374–377**). Three of the latter have large holes close to the end of the tang, perhaps to aid suspension. The straight-cut end, although most common in the 15th and 16th centuries, is found at an earlier date, but the rounded end seems to be restricted to the 15th and 16th centuries. The remaining scale tangs expand equally towards the end and are found from the 13th century onwards. **G263**, **G265**, **G269**, **G289**, **G291** and **G321** have straight-cut ends, **G314** a rounded end, and **G264** a pointed end.

Shoulder plates were frequently riveted or brazed in front of the handles of scale tang knives to finish them off. The plates are riveted on knives **G272**, **G277**, **G281**, **G294**, **G312**, **G321**, **G328**, **G363** and **G388**, and brazed on **G275**, **G291**, **G296**, **G308**, **G315**, **G325**, **G327**, **G331**, **G358**, **G367** and **G371**. X-radiographs have revealed the brazing fluid which held former shoulder plates on **G279**, **G287**, **G295**, **G309**, **G318**, **G323**, **G329** and **G268**. Some riveted shoulder plates may have been lost as well, and a rivet hole close to the choil might imply this. The shoulder plates are variously of copper alloy, silver and leaded pewter, and some are decorated.

End caps are varied in form, some merely being thin sheets of copper alloy, others more substantial cast fittings. End caps survive on **G263**, **G274**, **G309**, **G321**, **G356**, **G365**, **G370**, **G372–376** and **G378**, while nibs on **G265**, **G269**, **G291** and **G358** imply lost caps.

The handles were held in place by rivets, but brazing fluid along the edges of the tangs of **G308** and **G368** may be intentional. It is known on some post-medieval knives and may have held scale and tang together during riveting.

In addition to being shaped, handles were sometimes decorated with pins which did not penetrate the tang. **G321** retains some of these, set in a line between rivets, and **G366** has groups of four small pins randomly ornamenting its bone scales. **G379** has bone scales with an incomplete black letter inscription suggesting that it may be a love-knife.

The cutler

The medieval cutler made and sold any artefact having a cutter edge, including swords, daggers and other edged weapons, as well as domestic knives. The cutlery trade, in its most organised form, was divided into distinct branches comprising the blacksmith or knifesmith who made the blade and employed the grinder to sharpen it, the hafter who made the handle, the sheather who made the sheath, and the cutler who put the parts together and sold the complete article (Welch 1916, 19; Hayward 1957, 5). Cutlers' marks were regulated by the appropriate Cutlers' Company, and a writ of Edward III of 1365 ordered that every maker of swords, knives or other weapons in the city of London should place his mark on his work (Welch 1916, 35, 248–249).

Cutlers' marks are generally only recognisable on X-radiographs, unless a knife has been conserved, in which case any inlay may have been lost. Forty six medieval knives have cutlers' marks, and of these 34 are inlaid, 10 not inlaid, and 2 (**G163** and **G174**) have pairs of marks, only one of which now retains inlay. Hayward (1957) notes that the cutler inlaid his mark with copper until the mid 16th century, and it is probable that some if not all the plain marks have lost the hammer-welded mark, as must be the case with the two pairs of marks. Four marks have been analysed: **G187** is silver, **G390** copper, **G381** and **G89** probably copper, and **G343** appeared without analysis to be copper or copper alloy. Cutlers' marks start to appear in significant numbers in the 13th century, and continue on uninterrupted.

Metallurgy

Medieval knife blades were forged in several ways, and because of the high price of steel compared with iron they were usually made by combining the minimum of steel with the maximum of iron consistent with a good cutting edge. Professor R F Tylecote has undertaken much work on the metallurgy of knife blades, and the types of blade structure noted below follow his definitions. Steel can be combined with iron in four ways:

— A: By having a layer of steel covered with two plates of iron in such a way that the steel projects at the cutting edge. Sharpening such a knife will always give a steel edge to the blade.

— B: By welding on a steel strip to the edge of a piece of iron, sometimes made by piling. The steel edge will wear away with sharpening until eventually there is none left.

— C: By using a piece of piled material which consists of alternate layers of iron and steel. Given sufficient heat after welding these layers may be homogenised so that the blade consists of a piece of homogeneous steel.

— D: By having an iron core around which a piece of steel has been wrapped.

Seventy one knives have had their blades examined, and 31 have steel-edged blades, 15 steel cores, 14 piled blades, 7 iron cores, and 4 were wrought iron. The majority of steel-cored blades are from 11th to 13th-century contexts, and the steel-edged type has a general medieval date range but with greater numbers in the 13th to 15th centuries. Piled blades have a similar date range, although they are fewer in number, and the iron-cored blades are mainly 13th to 16th century. Most of the knives examined have whittle tangs but of the 6 scale tang knives examined, 4 had piled blades, 1 a steel edge, and the other was wrought iron.

8.2 SHEARS

Shears, in more common use during the medieval period than scissors, were used to cut hair and cloth, etc, to shear sheep, and in finishing cloth. The shears have been classified according to bow and blade form (Figure 8.6).

Type 1 shears

Type 1 shears have a plain bow which is no wider than the handle. No medieval example is known, but the type is a well-established pre-Conquest type.

Type 2 shears

Type 2 shears have a looped bow and a blade with a plain top at the junction between blade and handle. The blade top is curved or slanted on Type 2A and straight-cut more or less at right angles to the handle on Type 2B. The more complete Type 2A shears, **G418–442**, vary in length from 95 to 328mm and the blades generally taper to the tip, although those of **G418**, **G423**, **G426** and **G440**, and **G449–451** barely taper and instead the back angles or curves sharply to the tip. **G443–460** are mainly blade and handle fragments, although **G443** retains part of a moulded bow which is otherwise only found on a **G424**. All other bows are entirely plain, with the exception of the internally nibbed base of **G438**. **G431** has blades inlaid with figure-eight shapes which are claimed to be silver but which may be tin. The handles are round or square in section, but **G458** has a hollowed section of a type of found on sheep shears.

G461–475 are Type 2B shears, the more complete examples between 107 and 285mm in length, although some of the fragmentary blades are for shears of larger size. The smaller shears **G461–463** have sharply angled tips, but the other blades taper more or less evenly. The broad-handled shears **G466** and **G469** are probably sheep shears, as probably were the fragments **G473** and **G475**, whilst **G474** may be from cloth shears since it has a broad, parallel-sided blade of appropriate width.

Type 3 shears

Type 3 shears have a looped bow and a moulding at the junction of handle and blade. Type 3A and 3B have single cusps which are combined with a curved or sloping blade top on Type 3A and a straight-cut top on Type 3B. Type 3C has multiple cusps.

G476–492 are shears of Type 3A, none of which have the large wide blades of the preceding type. Complete pairs range from 92 to 258mm in length, and a significant number have nibbed and sometimes moulded bows. The blades either taper or have sharply angled tips, and **G491** has and inlaid cutler's mark.

The Type 3B shears **G493–499** are all small pairs with blades with angled tips. Complete examples range from 94 to 149mm in length, and several have nibbed or moulded bows.

The Type 3C shears **G500–502** are also small and have restrained multiple cusps. **G500–501** have angled blade tips, **G500** a ground edge.

Shears **G503–544** are too corroded to classify with certainty, although both have looped bows.

Discussion

Shears of Types 2 and 3 are the normal medieval type, their wide size range reflecting the diverse uses to which they were put. The smaller pairs of shears with cusped blades and moulded bows were probably for personal use, but the plain ones could have had either personal or domestic use cutting hair, thread etc. Some of the larger bladed shears may have been used for cutting cloth, and one fragment may be from a pair of cloth shears, whose use is discussed in Chapter 5. A number of shears with broad handles, frequently of U-shaped section, are probably sheep shears.

Shears of Type 2, as may be expected of the more basic and practical type, were used in greater numbers throughout the medieval period than those of Type 3. Shears of Type 3 are most common in the 13th and 14th centuries, although Type 3C seems to be a late medieval type.

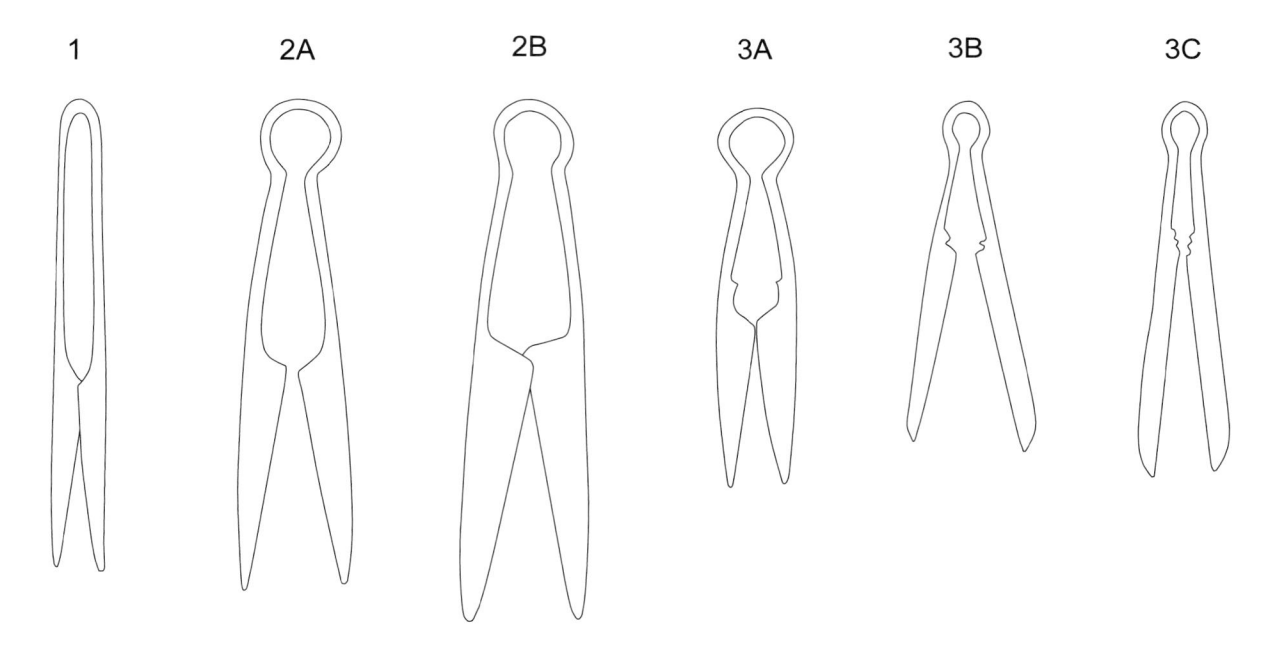

FIGURE 8.6
Types of medieval shears

8.3 SCISSORS

Scissors, comprising a pair of blades acting on a central pivot, were less commonly used in the medieval period than shears. Most of the representations noted by Ward Perkins (1967, 151) are associated with craftsmen, particularly glovers, woolmen and tailors, but none of the medieval scissors **G505–521** has the broad blade that might be associated with some of these crafts, although several have suitably long and slender blades. The scissors, the closely dated examples of which come from 13th-century and later contexts, may be classified according to the position of the finger loop.

Type 1 scissors

Scissors **G505–516** have finger loops set centrally to the handle, and most have slender blades of some length. **G505** and **G516** are the smallest, 81 and 113mm long respectively, but other more or less complete pairs are between 141 and 182mm in length.

Type 2 scissors

G517–520 are scissors with asymmetrically set finger loops, and all but **G519** are comparatively small and probably intended for personal or domestic use. **G521** is a blade fragment.

G1 KNIFE
Tattershall College, Lincolnshire.
11th century to 1440.
Complete knife mood with whittle tang.
L 147mm.
Excavated by L J Keen.

G2 KNIFE
Chingley, Kent.
Second half 13th century.
Knife mood, 'blade' incomplete, whittle tang corroded. L 185mm.
Goodall 1975d, 60, fig 27.3.

G3 KNIFE
Cambokeels, Durham.
Late 14th to early 16th century.
'Blade' and whittle tang broken. L 124mm.
Hildyard 1949, 199, fig 3.21.

G4 KNIFE
Great Yarmouth, Norfolk.
Mid to late 11th century.
Complete. L 108mm.
Rogerson 1976, 162, fig 52.5.

G5 KNIFE
Winchester, Hampshire.
Mid to late 11th century.
Complete. L 128mm.
Goodall 1990-16, 842, no. 2660.

G6 KNIFE
Winchester, Hampshire.
Mid to late 11th century.
Pattern-welded blade, broken whittle tang.
L 117mm.
Goodall 1990-16, 842, no. 2658.

G7 KNIFE
Winchester, Hampshire.
Mid to late 11th century.
Blade and whittle tang broken. L 122mm.
Goodall 1990-16, 842, no. 2659.

G8 KNIFE
Winchester, Hampshire.
1067–71.
Whittle tang broken. L 116mm.
Goodall 1990-16, fig 253.2661.

G9 KNIFE
King's Lynn, Norfolk.
Late 11th century.
Blade and whittle tang broken. L 111mm.
Goodall and Carter 1977, 293, fig 133.17.

G10 KNIFE
Great Yarmouth, Norfolk.
Late 11th or early 12th century.
Whittle tang broken. L 149mm.
Rogerson 1976, 162, fig 52.1.

G11 KNIFE
King's Lynn, Norfolk.
c1150–1200.
Complete. L 161mm.
Goodall and Carter 1977, 293, fig 133.18.

G12 KNIFE
Winchester, Hampshire.
12th century.
Complete. L 105mm.
Goodall 1990-16, 842, no. 2662.

G13 KNIFE
Winchester, Hampshire.
Early 13th century.
Blade and whittle tang broken. L 120mm.
Goodall 1990-16, fig 253.2663.

G14 KNIFE
Winchester, Hampshire.
Early 13th century.
Blade and whittle tang broken. L 122mm.
Goodall 1990-16, fig 253.2664

G15 KNIFE
Winchester, Hampshire.
13th century.
Whittle tang and pattern-welded blade broken. Metallurgy: steel-edged blade.
L 112mm.
Goodall 1990-16, 842, no. 2665.

G16 KNIFE
Winchester, Hampshire.
Mid to late 13th century.
Blade, incomplete. Metallurgy: piled blade.
L 126mm.
Goodall 1990-16, fig 253.2666.

G17 KNIFE
Goltho, Lincolnshire.
Croft A: late Saxon to late 14th or early 15th century.
Whittle tang broken. L 97mm.
Goodall 1975a, 79–81, fig 37.1.

G18 KNIFE
Winchester, Hampshire.
1050–75.
Blade and whittle tang broken. L 71mm.
Goodall 1990-16, 842, no. 2674.

G19 KNIFE
Winchester, Hampshire.
c1066–67.
Complete. Metallurgy: steel-cored blade.
L 190mm.
Goodall 1990-16, fig 253.2675.

G20 KNIFE
Winchester, Hampshire.
Late 11th–early 12th century.
Whittle tang broken. L 109mm.
Goodall 1990-16, fig 253.2677.

G21 KNIFE
Winchester, Hampshire.
Late 11th–12th century.
Blade and whittle tang broken. Metallurgy: steel-edged blade. L 106mm.
Goodall 1990-16, fig 253.2679.

G22 KNIFE
Winchester, Hampshire.
Late 11th–early 12th century.
Blade fragment. Metallurgy: pattern-welded blade. L 93mm.
Goodall 1990-16, 842, no. 2678.

G23 KNIFE
Winchester, Hampshire.
11th–?12th century.
Whittle tang broken. L 70mm.
Goodall 1990-16, 842, no. 2676.

G24 KNIFE
Winchester, Hampshire.
Late 11th–12th century.
Whittle tang broken. Metallurgy: steel-edged blade. L 80mm.
Goodall 1990-16, fig 253.2681.

G25 KNIFE
Winchester, Hampshire.
12th–early 13th century.
Blade and whittle tang broken. L 99mm.
Goodall 1990-16, 842, no. 2682.

G26 KNIFE
Winchester, Hampshire.
Late 11th–12th century.
Whittle tang broken, cutting edge worn by sharpening. Metallurgy: steel-cored blade.
L 136mm.
Goodall 1990-16, fig 253.2680.

KNIVES, SHEARS AND SCISSORS

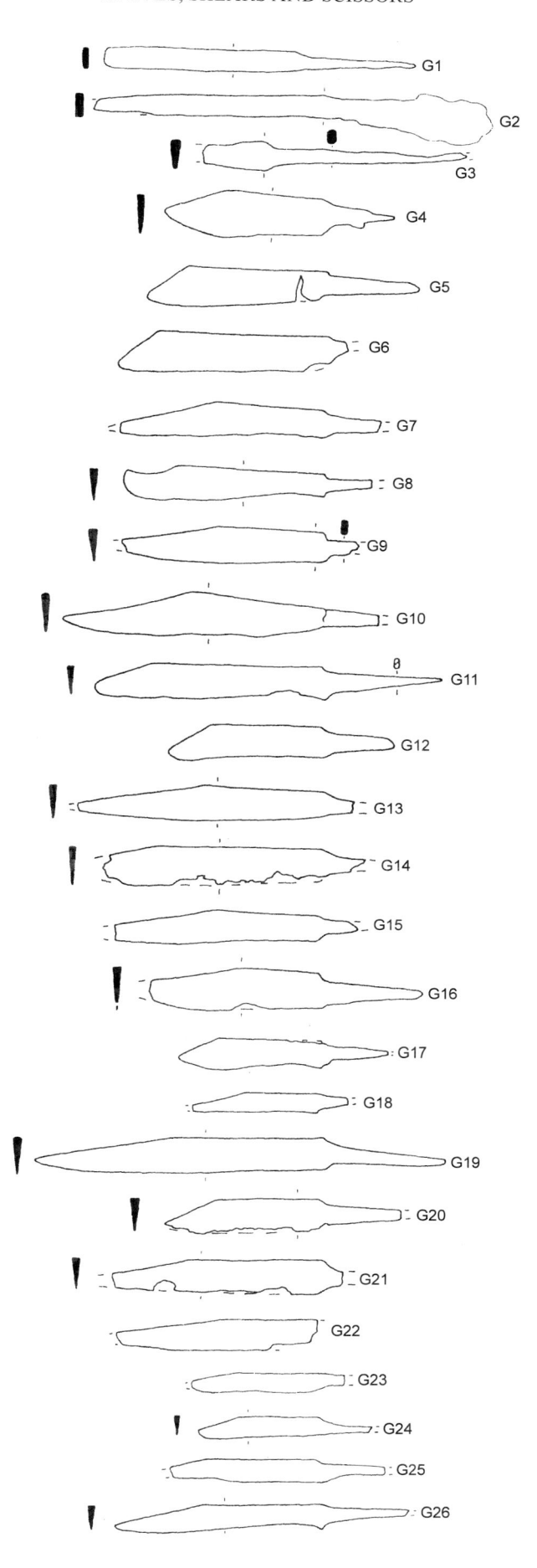

FIGURE 8.7
Knives

G27 KNIFE
Winchester, Hampshire.
Early to mid 13th century.
Whittle tang broken? Metallurgy: steel-edge blade. L 78mm.
Goodall 1990-16, 842, no. 2683.

G28 KNIFE
Winchester, Hampshire.
13th–early 14th century.
Blade and whittle tang broken. L 131mm.
Goodall 1990-16, 842, no. 2685.

G29 KNIFE
Winchester, Hampshire.
Mid–late 13th century.
Whittle tang broken. Shallow groove along blade. L 186mm.
Goodall 1990-16, fig 253.2684.

G30 KNIFE
Brooklands, Weybridge, Surrey.
*c*1150–1325.
Blade and whittle tang broken. L 145mm.
Goodall 1977d, 73, fig 45.3.

G31 KNIFE
Stonar, Kent.
*c*1275–1385.
Blade and whittle tang broken. L 100mm.
Excavated by N Macpherson-Grant.

G32 KNIFE
Stonar, Kent.
Derived from 13th-, 14th-century layers.
Blade and whittle tang broken. L 95mm.
Excavated by N Macpherson-Grant.

G33 KNIFE
Winchester, Hampshire.
14th century.
Whittle tang broken. L 84mm.
Goodall 1990-16, 842, no. 2686.

G34 KNIFE
Seacourt, Oxfordshire.
14th century.
Complete. L 153mm.
Biddle 1961–62, 175, fig 29.10, scale 1:4, not 1:3.

G35 KNIFE
Wharram Percy, North Yorkshire.
Late 15th to early 16th century.
Complete. L 111mm.
Goodall 1979a, 118, fig 61.40.

G36 KNIFE
London.
Late 15th–early 16th century.
Complete. L 109mm.
Excavated by F C Willmot. Site at 66 Foyle Road.

G37 KNIFE
Wharram Percy, North Yorkshire.
Late 15th to early 16th century.
Whittle tang broken. L 117mm.
Goodall 1979a, 118, fig 61.38.

G38 KNIFE
North Elmham Park, Norfolk.
*c*1150–*c*1600.
Blade and whittle tang broken. L 124mm.
Goodall 1980a, 510, fig 265.23.

G39 KNIFE
Greencastle, Co. Down.
Site: end 13th to mid 16th century.
Blade tip broken. Metallurgy: steel-edged blade. L 155mm.
Scott 1976, 45, figs.1.e, 6.39b.

G40 KNIFE
Castle Acre Castle, Norfolk.
1140s/1150s with derived material. Site founded soon after 1066.
Complete. Back shaped near tip. L 169mm.
Goodall 1982, fig 38, no.25.

G41 KNIFE
Lyveden, Northamptonshire.
Second quarter 13th century.
Complete. L 123mm.
Bryant and Steane 1971, 53, fig 13a9.

G42 KNIFE
Stonar, Kent.
*c*1225–1275.
Broken whittle tang retains traces of wooden handle. L 184mm.
Excavated by N Macpherson-Grant.

G43 KNIFE
Stonar, Kent.
*c*1275–1385.
Whittle tang and blade tip broken. Cutler's mark, not inlaid, on blade. L 128mm.
Excavated by N Macpherson-Grant.

G44 KNIFE
Southampton, Hampshire.
1300–1350.
Blade and whittle tang broken. L 164mm.
Harvey 1975b, 282, fig 254.2051.

G45 KNIFE
London.
Late 15th–early 16th century.
Complete, whittle tang tip clenched.
L 161mm.
Excavated by F C Willmot. Site at 66 Foyle Road.

G46 KNIFE
Somerby, Lincolnshire.
15th to mid 16th century.
Complete. L 223mm.
Mynard 1969, 83, fig 12.IW.60.

G47 KNIFE
North Elmham Park, Norfolk.
*c*1150–*c*1600.
Complete. L 158mm.
Goodall 1980a, 510, fig 265.24.

KNIVES, SHEARS AND SCISSORS

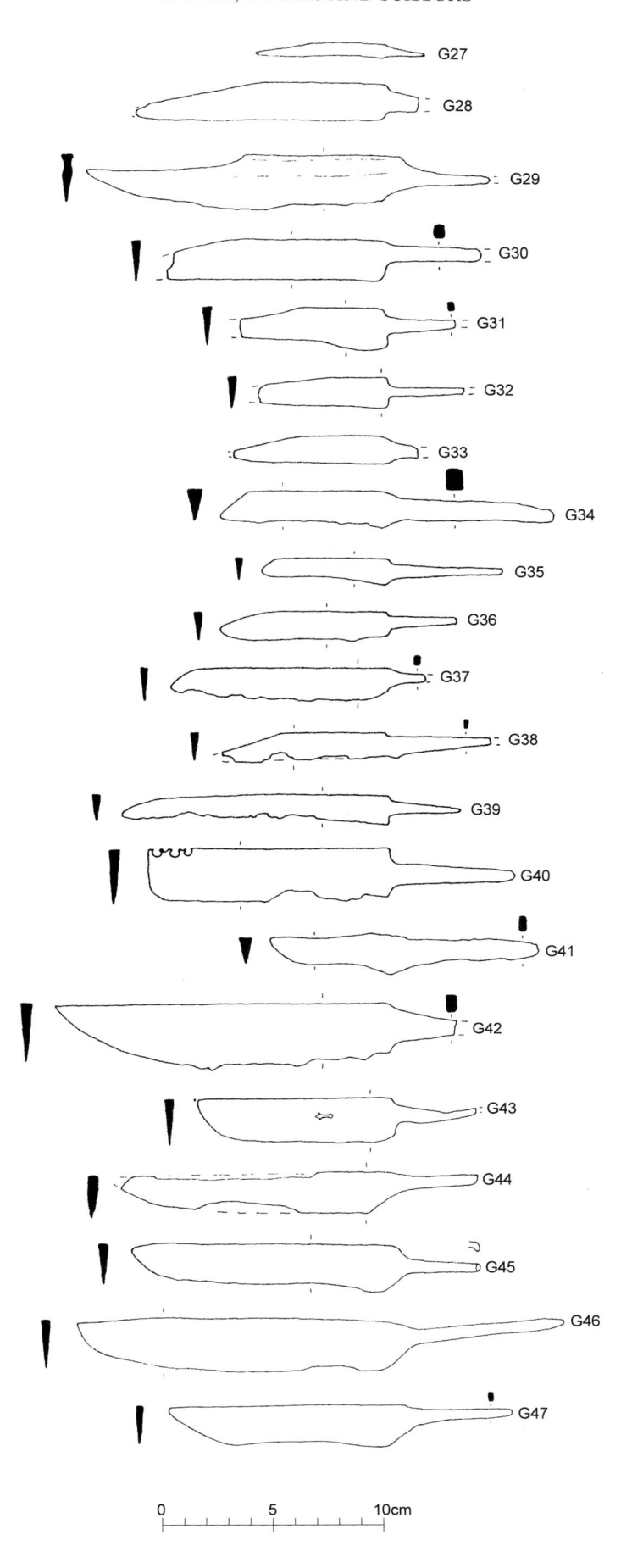

FIGURE 8.8
Knives

G48 KNIFE
Winchester, Hampshire.
1050–75.
Whittle tang broken. L 78mm.
Goodall 1990-16, fig 254.2703.

G49 KNIFE
Sulgrave, Northamptonshire.
Second half 11th century, possibly just post-Conquest.
Whittle tang broken. L 96mm.
Excavated by B K Davison.

G50 KNIFE
Sulgrave, Northamptonshire.
Second half 11th century, possibly just post-Conquest.
Whittle tang broken. L 95mm.
Excavated by B K Davison.

G51 KNIFE
Winchester, Hampshire.
Late 11th–early 12th century.
Complete. L 132mm.
Goodall 1990-16, fig 254.2713.

G52 KNIFE
Winchester, Hampshire.
Late 11th century.
Whittle tang broken. Metallurgy: steel-cored blade. L 65mm.
Goodall 1990-16, 846, no. 2705.

G53 KNIFE
Gloucester.
Roman or late 11th, early 12th century.
Whittle tang broken. L 118mm.
Excavated by H Hurst.

G54 KNIFE
Oxford.
11th–12th century.
Whittle tang broken. L 76mm.
Jope 1958, 73, fig 24a.

G55 KNIFE
Winchester, Hampshire.
11th–?12th century.
Blade fragment, worn by sharpening.
Metallurgy: piled blade. L 73mm.
Goodall 1990-16, fig 254.2708

G56 KNIFE
Winchester, Hampshire.
11th–?12th century.
Blade with shallow grooves, broken.
Metallurgy: piled blade. L 126mm.
Goodall 1990-16, fig 254.2707.

G57 KNIFE
Goltho Manor, Lincolnshire.
c1100–1150.
Whittle tang broken. L 134mm.
Goodall 1987, fig 157.50.

G58 KNIFE
Goltho Manor, Lincolnshire.
c1100–1150.
Whittle tang broken. L 106mm.
Goodall 1987, fig 156.51.

G59 KNIFE
Llantrithyd, South Glamorgan.
Early to mid 12th century.
Complete. L 112mm.
Goodall 1977f, 47, iron object fig 1.13.

G60 KNIFE
Llantrithyd, South Glamorgan.
Early to mid 12th century.
Blade and whittle tang broken. L 112mm.
Goodall 1977f, 47, iron object fig 1.14.

G61 KNIFE
Folkestone, Kent.
Mid 12th century.
Whittle tang broken. L 190mm.
Pitt-Rivers 1883, 463, pl XVIII.7.

G62 KNIFE
Castle Acre Castle, Norfolk.
Second half 12th century.
Complete. L 110mm.
Goodall 1982, fig 38, no.28.

G63 KNIFE
Winchester, Hampshire.
Early 13th century.
Complete. L 70mm.
Goodall 1990-16, fig 254.2720.

G64 KNIFE
Winchester, Hampshire.
Late 11th–early 12th century.
Whittle tang broken. Metallurgy: piled blade. L 84mm.
Goodall 1990-16, 846, no. 2710.

G65 KNIFE
Winchester, Hampshire.
Late 11th–early 12th century.
Complete. L 86mm.
Goodall 1990-16, 846, no. 2712.

G66 KNIFE
Wroughton Copse, Fyfield Down, Wiltshire.
12th century.
Whittle tang broken. L 96mm.
Excavated by P J Fowler.

G67 KNIFE
Winchester, Hampshire.
Late 11th–?mid 12th century.
Whittle tang broken. L 127mm.
Goodall 1990-16, fig 254.2714.

G68 KNIFE
Winchester, Hampshire.
Late 11th–early 12th century.
Blade fragment with grooved sides.
Metallurgy: blade pattern-welded and steel-edged. L 121mm.
Goodall 1990-16, fig 254.2709.

G69 KNIFE
Old Sarum, Wiltshire.
12th century.
Broken whittle tang retains traces of wooden handle. L 156mm.
Musty and Rahtz 1964, 143, fig 5.4.

G70 KNIFE
Eynsford Castle, Kent.
12th century.
Whittle tang broken. L 155mm.
Rigold and Fleming 1973, 105, fig 9.9.

G71 KNIFE
Long Buckby, Northamptonshire.
Site: mid 12th to early 13th century.
Complete. L 119mm.
Thompson 1956, 60, fig 3.5.

KNIVES, SHEARS AND SCISSORS

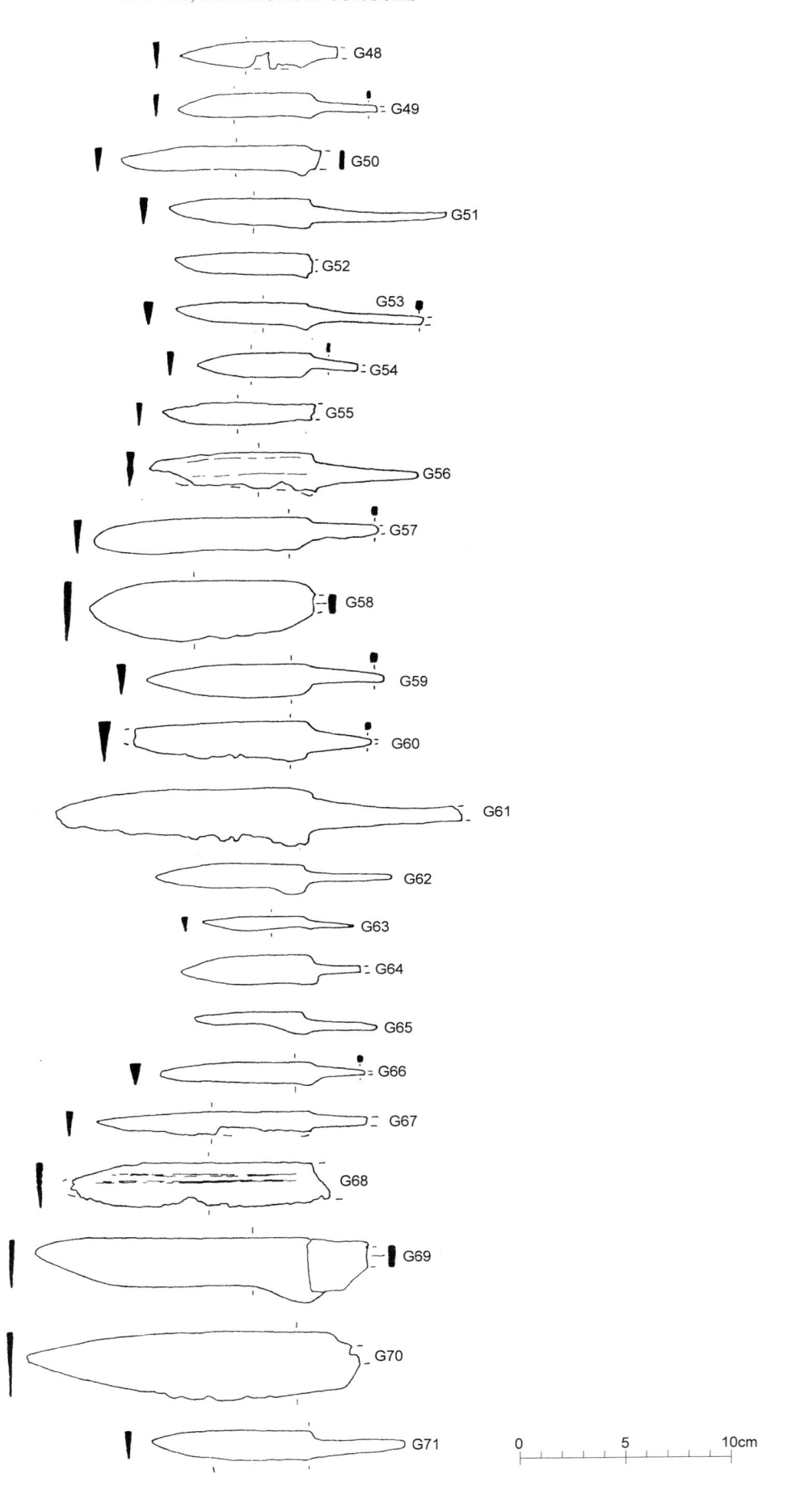

FIGURE 8.9
Knives

G72 KNIFE
Totnes Castle, Devon.
Late 12th to early 13th century.
Whittle tang broken. L 130mm.
Rigold 1954, 254, fig 9.8a.

G73 KNIFE
King's Lynn, Norfolk.
c1150–1250.
Complete knife in turned and decorated wooden handle. Whittle tang occupies under half the length of the socket in the handle, which is closed with wooden plugs. L 170mm overall, knife 125mm.
Goodall and Carter 1977, 293, fig 133.20.

G74 KNIFE
Oxford.
Late 12th century to c1250.
Whittle tang broken. L 103mm.
Goodall 1977e, 142, fig 25.9.

G75 KNIFE
Duffield Castle, Derbyshire.
Found with masonry of keep built 1177–90, demolished 1266.
Blade broken. Six copper-alloy heater-shaped plates set at junction between blade and tang. Gaps originally filled by organic plates. L 137mm.
Cox 1887, 173 and figure.For site see Manby 1959; Renn 1973, 174–176.

G76 KNIFE
Duffield Castle, Derbyshire.
Found with masonry of keep built 1177–90, demolished 1266.
Blade and whittle tang broken. Series of heater-shaped copper-alloy plates of differing thicknesses between blade and tang. L 194mm.
Cox 1886, 173 and figure. For site see Manby 1959; Renn 1973, 174–176.

G77 KNIFE
Winchester, Hampshire.
13th century.
Whittle tang broken. Mettallurgy: steel-cored blade. L 78mm.
Goodall 1990-16, 847, 2729.

G78 KNIFE
Winchester, Hampshire.
Mid 12th–early 13th century.
Blade and whittle tang broken. Metallurgy: piled blade. L 87mm.
Goodall 1990-16, 846, no. 2716.

G79 KNIFE
Winchester, Hampshire.
12th–early 13th century.
Complete. L 123mm.
Goodall 1990-16, 846, no. 2717.

G80 KNIFE
King's Lynn, Norfolk.
11th(?) to 13th century.
Blade and whittle tang broken. L 83mm.
Goodall and Carter 1977, 293, fig 133.26.

G81 KNIFE
Southampton, Hampshire.
1200–1225.
Complete. L 150mm.
Harvey 1975b, 277, fig 250.1990.

G82 KNIFE
Netherton, Hampshire.
Early 13th century.
Blade and whittle tang broken. L 81mm.
Goodall 1990-28, fig 9.2, no. 97.

G83 KNIFE
Lyveden, Northamptonshire.
Second quarter 13th century.
Blade and whittle tang broken. L 93mm.
Bryant and Steane 1971, 53, fig 13a10.

G84 KNIFE
Winchester, Hampshire.
Early to mid 13th century.
Complete. L 119mm.
Goodall 1990-16, 846, no. 2721.

G85 KNIFE
Winchester, Hampshire.
13th century.
Whittle tang broken. Metallurgy: steel-cored blade. L 91mm.
Goodall 1990-16, 846, no. 2728.

G86 KNIFE
Winchester, Hampshire.
Early to mid 13th century.
Complete. Metallurgy: steel-edged blade. L 126mm.
Goodall 1990-16, 846, no. 2722.

G87 KNIFE
Winchester, Hampshire.
13th century.
Whittle tang broken? Metallurgy: steel-cored blade. L 98mm.
Goodall 1990-16, 846, no. 2727.

G88 KNIFE
Winchester, Hampshire.
Mid 13th century.
Blade broken. Metallurgy: blade iron only. L 72mm.
Goodall 1990-16, 846, no. 2723.

G89 KNIFE
Winchester, Hampshire.
13th–early 14th century.
Complete. L 68mm.
Goodall 1990-16, 847, no. 2732.

G90 KNIFE
Winchester, Hampshire.
13th century (in 19th–20th century phase).
Complete. L 63mm.
Goodall 1990-16, 847, no. 2739.

G91 KNIFE
Winchester, Hampshire.
13th century.
Whittle tang broken. Metallurgy: blade pattern-welded and steel-edged. L 94mm.
Goodall 1990-16, 847, no. 2730.

G92 KNIFE
Hampton Wafer, Hereford and Worcester.
Site: probably 11th–early 14th century.
Blade and whittle tang broken. L 88mm.
Stanford 1967, 87, fig 7.5.

G93 KNIFE
South Witham, Lincolnshire.
c1220 to 1308–13.
Blade and whittle tang broken. L 136mm.
Goodall 2002, fig 7.1, no. 4.

G94 KNIFE
South Witham, Lincolnshire.
Late 13th century to 1308–13.
Whittle tang broken. L 88mm.
Goodall 2002, fig 7.1, no. 7.

G95 KNIFE
Lyveden, Northamptonshire.
End 13th century to very early 14th century.
Blade tip broken. L 145mm.
Bryant and Steane 1969, 38, fig 17c; 1971.

G96 KNIFE
Copt Hay, Tetsworth, Oxfordshire.
Late 13th, 14th century.
Broken whittle tang retains collar from former wooden handle, traces of which survive. L 182mm.
Robinson 1973, 101, fig 23.6.

KNIVES, SHEARS AND SCISSORS

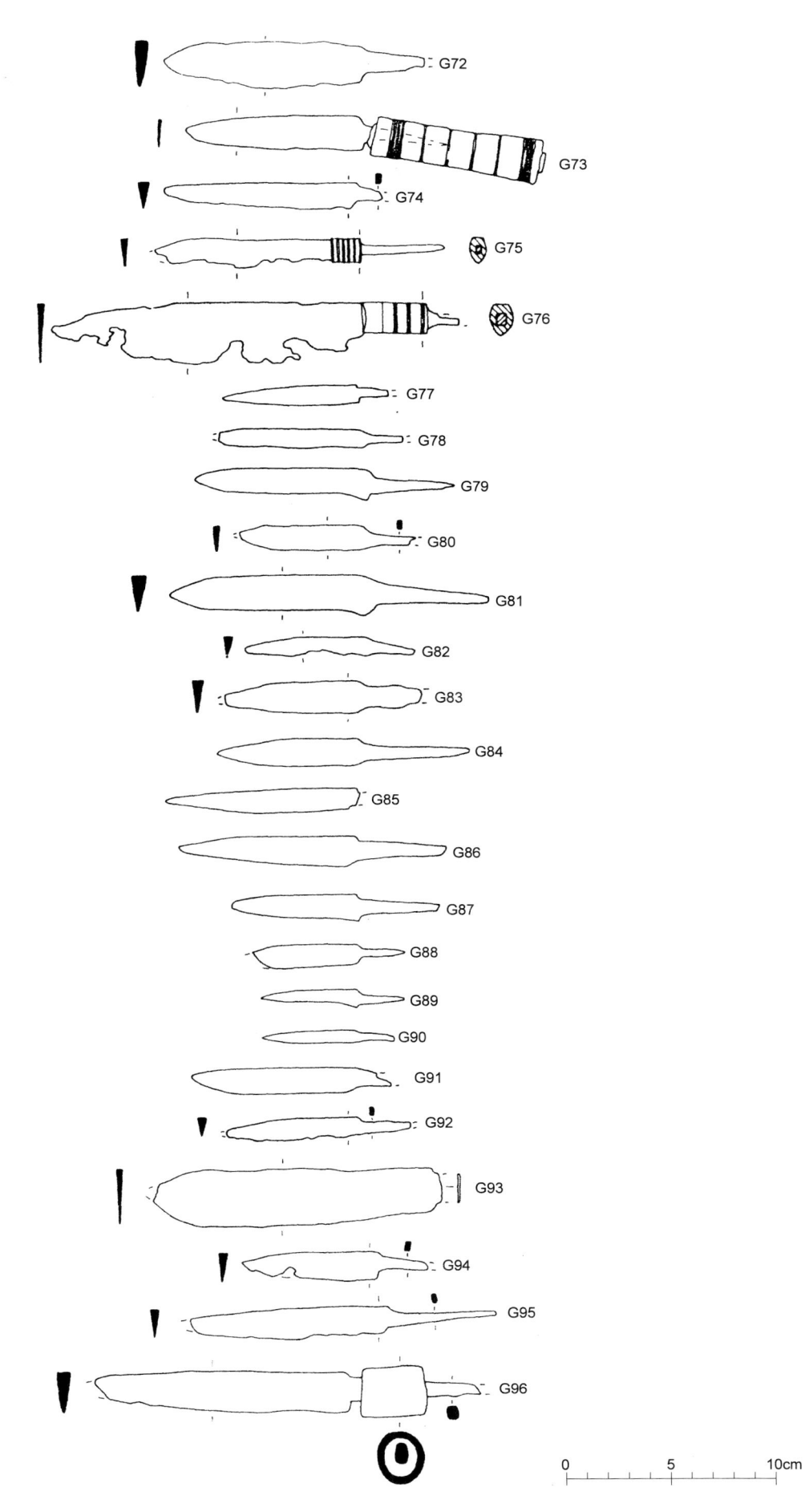

FIGURE 8.10
Knives

G97 KNIFE
Great Yarmouth, Norfolk.
13th/14th century.
Whittle tang broken. L 111mm.
Rogerson 1976, 162, fig 52.11.

G98 KNIFE
Brooklands, Weybridge, Surrey.
1200–1325.
Whittle tang broken. L 78mm.
Goodall 1977d, 73, fig 45.1.

G99 KNIFE
Wroughton Copse, Fyfield Down, Wiltshire.
13th century (mid?) to early 14th century.
Blade and whittle tang broken. L 108mm.
Excavated by P J Fowler.

G100 KNIFE
Bramber Castle, West Sussex.
Late 13th to 14th century.
Complete. L 91mm.
Barton and Holden 1977, 66, fig 20.7.

G101 KNIFE
Stonar, Kent.
c1275–1385.
Blade and whittle tag broken. Inlaid cutler's mark on blade. L 165mm.
Excavated by N Macpherson-Grant.

G102 KNIFE
Stonar, Kent.
c1275–1385.
Whittle tang broken. L 116mm.
Excavated by N Macpherson-Grant.

G103 KNIFE
Stoke Orchard, Gloucestershire.
Site: 12th–14th century.
Whittle tang broken. L 100mm.
Spry 1971, 41, fig 6.A.

G104 KNIFE
Goltho, Lincolnshire.
Croft A: late Saxon to late 14th or early 15th century.
Blade and whittle tang broken. Cutler's mark, not inlaid. L 134mm.
Goodall 1975a, 79–81, fig 37, 27, pl VII.D.

G105 KNIFE
Wintringham, Cambridgeshire.
Around early 14th century.
Blade and whittle tang broken. Inlaid cutler's marks on blade. L 90mm.
Goodall 1977a, 257, fig 43.3.

G106 KNIFE
Oxford.
c1325–c1400.
Complete. L 111mm.
Goodall 1977e, 142, fig 25.10.

G107 KNIFE
Oxford.
c1325–c1400.
Blade and whittle tang broken. Iron hilt plate. Inlaid cutler's mark. L 164mm.
Goodall 1977e, 142, fig 25.12.

G108 KNIFE
Winchester, Hampshire.
Late 14th–early 15th century.
Blade and whittle tang broken. Metallurgy: steel-edged blade. L 111mm.
Goodall 1990-16, 947, no. 2735.

G109 KNIFE
Winchester, Hampshire.
Late 14th–early 15th century.
Whittle tang broken. L 101mm.
Goodall 1990-16, 847, no. 2736.

G110 KNIFE
Criccieth Castle, Gwynedd.
Site: c1230–1404.
Complete. L 108mm.
O'Neil 1944–45, 42, pl X.37.

G111 KNIFE
Criccieth Castle, Gwynedd.
Site: c1230–1404.
Blade and whittle tang broken. L 123mm.
O'Neil 1944–45.

G112 KNIFE
King's Lynn, Norfolk.
c1350–1500.
Whittle tang broken. L 145mm.
Goodall and Carter 1977, 293, fig 133.32.

G113 KNIFE
Northampton.
15th century, from c1410–20.
Complete. L 82mm.
Goodall *et al* 1979, 268, fig 118.39.

G114 KNIFE
Barton Blount, Derbyshire.
Site: late Saxon to late 15th century.
Blade and whittle tang broken. Metallurgy: steel-edged blade. L 171mm.
Goodall 1975b, fig 46.2, pl VI.C.

G115 KNIFE
Sawtry, Cambridgeshire.
15th to early 16th century.
Blade and whittle tang broken. L 118mm.
Moorhouse 1971b, 85, fig 4.5.

G116 KNIFE
Wharram Percy, North Yorkshire.
Late 15th to early 16th century.
Cutting edge of blade shaped near tip.
L 140mm.
Goodall 1979a, 118, fig 61.39.

G117 KNIFE
Wharram Percy, North Yorkshire.
Late 15th to early 16th century.
Blade and whittle tang broken. L 148mm.
Goodall 1979a, 118, fig 62.42.

G118 KNIFE
Hen Caerwys, Clwyd.
c1450–1520.
Whittle tang broken. L 115mm.
Excavated by G B Leach.

G119 KNIFE
Ospringe, Kent.
c1483–1550.
Blade and whittle tang broken. L 180mm.
Goodall 1979c, 129, fig 19.7.

G120 KNIFE
Winchester, Hampshire.
Late 16th to ?17th century.
Whittle tang broken. L 113mm.
Goodall 1990-16, fig 254.2737.

KNIVES, SHEARS AND SCISSORS

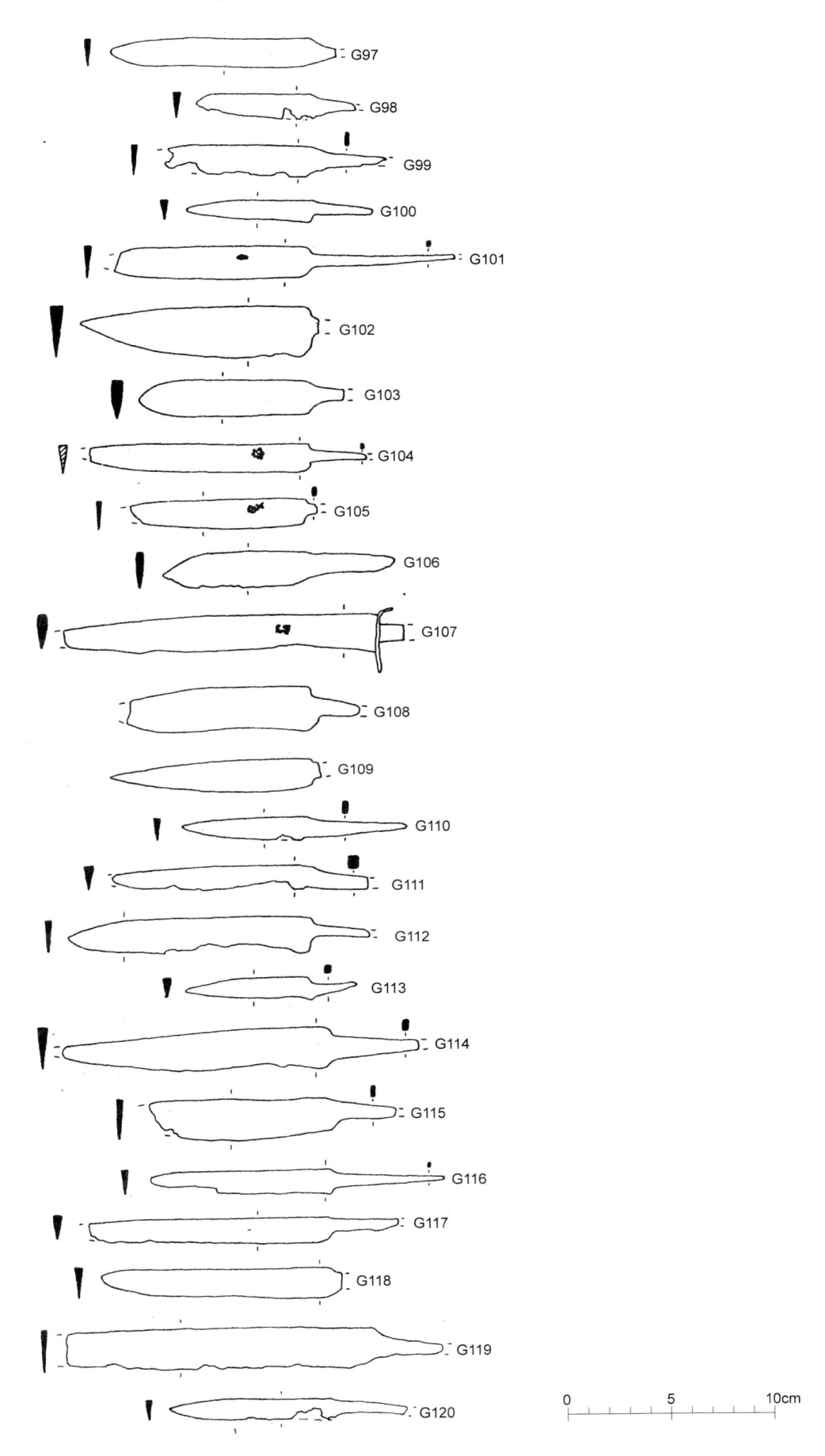

FIGURE 8.11
Knives

G121 KNIFE
Glastonbury Tor, Somerset.
12th to 16th century (presumably to the Dissolution).
Tang incomplete, cutting edge shaped by sharpening. L 96mm.
Rahtz 1970, 53, fig 23.9.

G122 KNIFE
Winchester, Hampshire.
1040–75.
Complete. L 74mm.
Goodall 1990-16, 847, no. 2747.

G123 KNIFE
Northolt Manor, Greater London.
1050–1150.
Complete. L 60mm.
Hurst 1961, 288, fig 76.1.

G124 KNIFE
Goltho Manor, Lincolnshire.
c1100–1125.
Blade broken. L 146mm.
Goodall 1987, fig 157.63.

G125 KNIFE
Goltho Manor, Lincolnshire.
c1100–1150.
Whittle tang broken. L 102mm.
Goodall 1987, fig 157.57.

G126 KNIFE
Goltho Manor, Lincolnshire.
c1100–1150.
Blade broken. L 113mm.
Goodall 1987, fig 157.48.

G127 KNIFE
Gloucester.
Disturbed late 12th-century layer.
Complete. L 115mm.
Excavated by H Hurst.

G128 KNIFE
Winchester, Hampshire.
Late 11th–12th century.
Whittle tang retains part of wooden handle. L 84mm.
Goodall 1990-16, fig 255.2751.

G129 KNIFE
Kidwelly Castle, Dyfed.
Probably 12th century.
Blade and whittle tang broken. L 212mm.
Fox and Radford 1933, 122, fig 11.4.

G130 KNIFE
Clough Castle, Co. Down.
c1225–50.
Blade tip broken. Conifer wood handle retained on whittle tang. L 186mm.
Waterman 1954, 137, fig 11.9.

G131 KNIFE
Winchester, Hampshire.
Early 13th century.
Blade and whittle tang broken. Metallurgy: pattern-welded blade. L 128mm.
Goodall 1990-16, fig 255.2757.

G132 KNIFE
King's Lynn, Norfolk.
c1050–1250.
Blade and whittle tang broken. Tang forged by folding over iron and drawing out. L 117mm.
Goodall and Carter 1977, 293, fig 133.27.

G133 KNIFE
Northolt Manor, Greater London.
1225–1300.
Whittle tang tip clenched over. L 110mm.
Hurst 1961, 288, fig 76.3.

G134 KNIFE
King's Lynn, Norfolk.
c1250–1300.
Whittle tang broken. Metallurgy: pattern-welded blade. L 120mm.
Goodall and Carter 1977, 293, fig 133.23. pl V.C.

G135 KNIFE
King's Lynn, Norfolk.
c1250–1300.
Blade and whittle tang broken. L 130mm.
Goodall and Carter 1977, 293, fig 133.22.

G136 KNIFE
Netherton, Hampshire.
Late 13th century.
Blade tip broken. L 143mm.
Goodall 1990-28, fig 9.2, no. 119.

G137 KNIFE
Castell-y-Bere, Gwynedd.
Site: c1221–95.
Complete. L 190mm.
Butler 1974, 97, fig 8.16.

G138 KNIFE
Winchester, Hampshire.
Late 13th century.
Blade and whittle tang broken. Metallurgy: steel-edged blade. L 102mm.
Goodall 1990-16, 847, no. 2764.

G139 KNIFE
Winchester, Hampshire.
Mid 13th century.
Blade broken. Metallurgy: steel-edged blade. L 110mm.
Goodall 1990-16, 847, no. 2759.

G140 KNIFE
Winchester, Hampshire.
13th century.
Blade and whittle tang broken. Metallurgy: wrought iron blade. L 131mm.
Goodall 1990-16, fig 255.2765.

G141 KNIFE
Wroughton Copse, Fyfield Down, Wiltshire.
13th century (mid?) to early 14th century.
Complete. L 155mm.
Excavated by P J Fowler.

G142 KNIFE
Writtle, Essex.
1229–32 to 1277 or 1305.
Complete. L 229mm.
Rahtz 1969b, 87, fig 47.65.

G143 KNIFE
South Witham, Lincolnshire.
Late 13th century to 1308–13 or later.
Blade tip broken. L 263mm.
Goodall 2002, fig 7.1, no. 8.

KNIVES, SHEARS AND SCISSORS

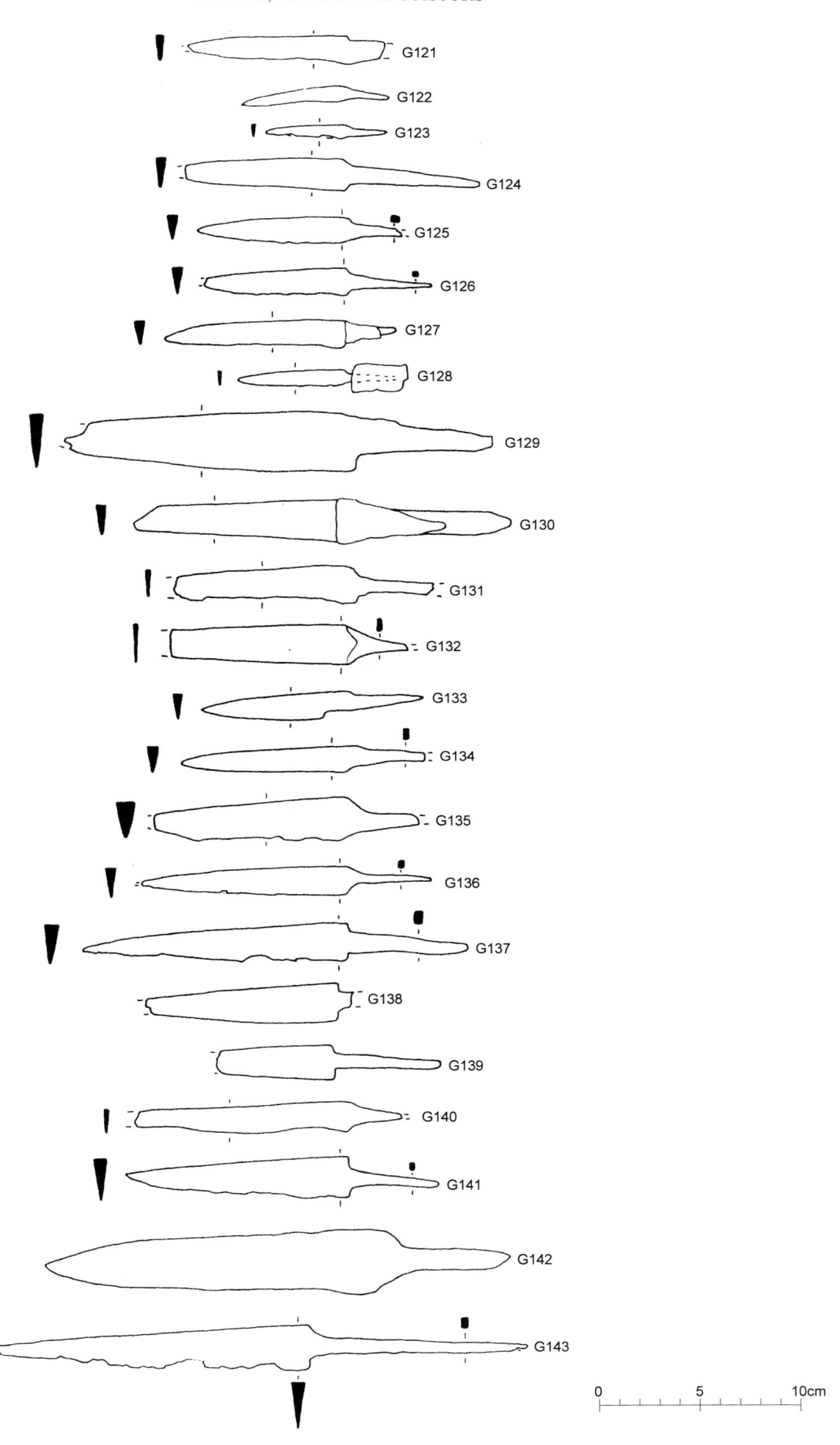

FIGURE 8.12
Knives

G144 KNIFE
Lyveden, Northamptonshire.
Late 13th century to very early 14th century.
Complete. L 165mm.
Bryant and Steane 1969, 38, fig 17e; 1971.

G145 KNIFE
Netherton, Hampshire.
Late 13th, early 14th century.
Blade and whittle tang broken. L 107mm.
Goodall 1990-28, fig 9.2, no. 115.

G146 KNIFE
Kidwelly Castle, Dyfed.
Probably 1275–1320.
Whittle tang broken. L 82mm.
Fox and Radford 1933, 122, fig 11.M.3.

G147 KNIFE
Chingley, Kent.
Second half 13th century to mid 14th century.
Whittle tang broken. Metallurgy: steel-edged blade. L 183mm.
Goodall 1975d, 60, 90, fig 27.1.

G148 KNIFE
Burton-in-Lonsdale, North Yorkshire.
Later 13th to mid 14th century.
Complete. L 101mm.
Moorhouse 1971a, 95, fig 3.4.

G149 KNIFE
London.
?Late 13th to mid 14th century.
Blade, whittle tang and wooden handle broken. L 87mm.
Henig 1974, 189, fig 37.37.

G150 KNIFE
London.
Late 13th–mid 14th century.
Blade broken. L 136mm.
Henig 1974, 189, no. 38.

G151 KNIFE
Stonar, Kent.
c1275–1385.
Whittle tang broken. L 84mm.
Excavated by N Macpherson-Grant.

G152 KNIFE
Stonar, Kent.
c1275–1385.
Complete. L 168mm.
Excavated by N Macpherson-Grant.

G153 KNIFE
Hambleton Moat, Lincolnshire.
1250–1400.
Blade broken. L 202mm.
Butler 1963, 67, fig 14.9.

G154 KNIFE
London.
Late 13th–14th century.
Broken blade with three solid copper-alloy rivets set in line close to back and roughly stamped on each face. L 105mm.
Henig 1974, 189, fig 37.35.

G155 KNIFE
Copt Hay, Tetsworth, Oxfordshire.
Late 13th, 14th century.
Complete. L 137mm.
Robinson 1973, 101, fig 23.5.

G156 KNIFE
Lismahon, Co. Down.
Later 13th or 14th century.
Whittle tang retains part of wooden handle. L 99mm.
Waterman 1959a, 162, fig 61.3.

G157 KNIFE
Lismahon, Co. Down.
Later 13th or 14th century.
Whittle tang broken. L 103mm.
Waterman 1959a, 162, fig 61.2.

G158 KNIFE
Barrow Mead, Avon.
Site: 13th–14th century.
Whittle tang broken. L 92mm.
Goodall 1976b, 34, fig 11.15.

G159 KNIFE
Winchester, Hampshire.
Mid 13th century.
Whittle tang possibly broken. Metallurgy: blade steel edged. L 135mm.
Goodall 1990-16, fig 255.2761.

G160 KNIFE
Lyveden, Northamptonshire.
Site: c1200–1500.
Whittle tang broken. L 127mm.
Steane and Bryant 1975, 122, fig 46.49.

G161 KNIFE
Rhuddlan, Clwyd.
14th century (?earlier part) or conceivably 1290–1300.
Complete. L 130mm.
Goodall 1994, fig 17.2, no. 27.

G162 KNIFE
Wintringham, Cambridgeshire.
Early 14th century.
Blade and whittle tang broken. Inlaid cutler's mark. L 120mm.
Goodall 1977a, 257, fig 43.7.

G163 KNIFE
Wintringham, Cambridgeshire.
Around early 14th century.
Whittle tang broken. Cutler's marks, one retaining inlay. L 126mm.
Goodall 1977a, 257, fig 43.6.

G164 KNIFE
Wythemail, Northamptonshire.
First half 14th century.
Blade broken. Circular copper-alloy hilt plate with two punched depressions. Handle almost certainly removed before burial, and tang 'cemented' into bone rather than driven into wood. L 200mm.
Hurst and Hurst 1969, 200, fig 60.15.

G165 KNIFE
Wintringham, Cambridgeshire.
Early 14th century.
Blade and whittle tang broken. L 150mm.
Goodall 1977a, 257, fig 43.8.

KNIVES, SHEARS AND SCISSORS

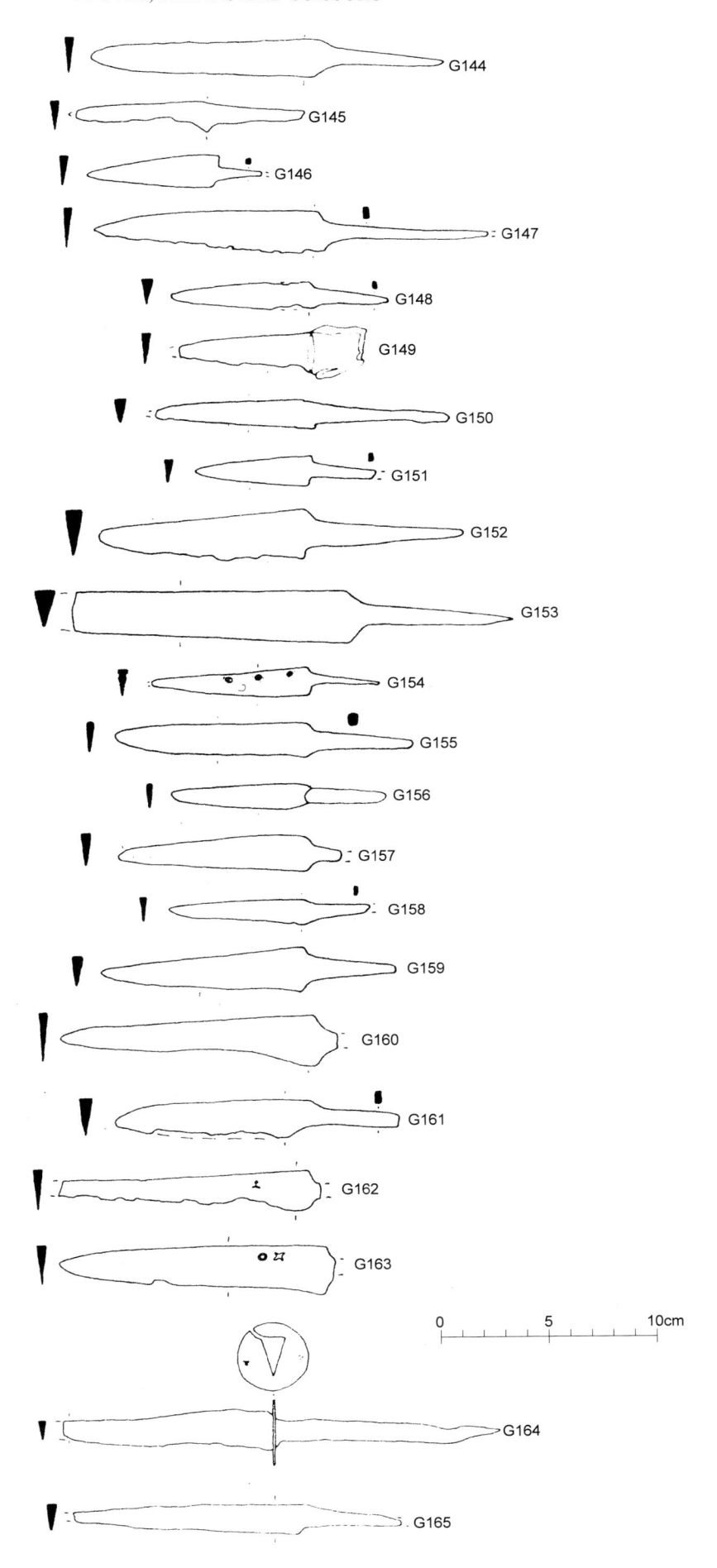

FIGURE 8.13
Knives

G166 KNIFE
Newbury, Berkshire.
c1350–90.
Complete. L 45mm.
Goodall 1997, fig 19, no. 10.

G167 KNIFE
Winchester, Hampshire.
14th century.
Complete. L 90mm.
Goodall 1990-16, 848, no. 2768.

G168 KNIFE
Winchester, Hampshire.
14th century.
Complete. L 171mm.
Goodall 1990-16, 848, no. 2771.

G169 KNIFE
Northampton.
14th century.
Whittle tang broken. End of decorated wooden handle. Cutler's mark on blade with traces of white metal. L 291mm.
Central Museum, Northampton. Found between Bearwood Street and Silver Street.

G170 KNIFE
Southampton, Hampshire.
Probably 14th century.
Whittle tang broken. Inlaid cutler's mark. L 86mm.
Harvey 1975b, 285, fig 255.2068.

G171 KNIFE
Brome, Suffolk.
Late 12th to mid 14th century.
Blade broken. L 82mm.
West 1970, 110, fig 12.5.

G172 KNIFE
Wintringham, Cambridgeshire.
Site: c1175–1340.
Complete. Cutler's mark, not inlaid. L 143mm.
Goodall 1977a, 257, fig 43.9.

G173 KNIFE
Goltho, Lincolnshire.
Croft B: late Saxon to late 14th century.
Blade and whittle tang broken. Metallurgy: steel-cored blade. L 172mm.
Goodall 1975a, 79–82, fig 37.29.

G174 KNIFE
Goltho, Lincolnshire.
Croft A: late Saxon to late 14th or early 15th century.
Whittle tang broken. Cutler's marks on blade, one inlaid. L 99mm.
Goodall 1975a, 79–81, fig 37.25.

G175 KNIFE
Goltho, Lincolnshire.
Croft A: late Saxon to late 14th or early 15th century.
Blade broken. Metallurgy: steel-edged blade. L 120mm.
Goodall 1975a, 79–82, fig 37.15.

G176 KNIFE
Goltho, Lincolnshire.
Croft A: late Saxon to late 14th or early 15th century.
Blade and whittle tang broken. Metallurgy: iron-cored blade. L 123mm.
Goodall 1975a, 79–82, fig 37.22.

G177 KNIFE
Goltho, Lincolnshire.
Croft A: late Saxon to late 14th or early 15th century.
Whittle tang broken. Metallurgy: steel-cored blade. L 150mm.
Goodall 1975a, 79–82, fig 37.14.

G178 KNIFE
Goltho, Lincolnshire.
Croft A: late Saxon to late 14th to early 15th century.
Complete. Groove close to back of one side of blade. Metallurgy: piled blade. L 151mm.
Goodall 1975a, 79–82, fig 37.16.

G179 KNIFE
Goltho, Lincolnshire.
Croft A: late Saxon to late 14th or early 15th century.
Blade and whittle tang broken. Metallurgy: iron-cored blade. L 162mm.
Goodall 1975a, 79–82, fig 37.18.

G180 KNIFE
Goltho, Lincolnshire.
Croft A: late Saxon to late 14th or early 15th century.
Blade broken. Metallurgy: iron-cored blade. L 180mm.
Goodall 1975a, 79–82, fig 37.19.

G181 KNIFE
Goltho, Lincolnshire.
Croft A: late Saxon to late 14th or early 15th century.
Blade and whittle tang broken. Metallurgy: steel-cored blade. L 176mm.
Goodall 1975a, 79–82, fig 37.28.

G182 KNIFE
Winchester, Hampshire.
14th century.
Blade and whittle tang broken. Metallurgy: steel-edged blade. L 71mm.
Goodall 1990-16, 848, no. 2769.

G183 KNIFE
Grenstein, Norfolk.
Late 14th, 15th century.
Blade and whittle tang broken. L 180mm.
Goodall 1980c, fig 76, no. 1.

G184 KNIFE
Grenstein, Norfolk.
Late 14th, 15th century.
Blade broken. L 96mm.
Goodall 1980c, fig 76, no. 3.

G185 KNIFE
Oxford.
Late 14th to mid 15th century.
Whittle tang broken. L 181mm.
Goodall 1976c, 298, fig 26.2.

G186 KNIFE
Lyveden, Northamptonshire.
1350–1450.
Blade broken. Cutler's mark, not inlaid. L 111mm.
Steane and Bryant 1975, 121, fig 46.20.

G187 KNIFE
Goltho, Lincolnshire.
Late 14th, early 15th century.
Blade and whittle tang broken. Cutler's mark inlaid with silver. Metallurgy: iron-cored blade. L 126mm.
Goodall 1975a, 79–82, fig 37.20, pl VII.A.

G188 KNIFE
Wallingstones, Hereford and Worcester.
1300–1325 to 1500.
Whittle tang broken. L 141mm.
Bridgewater 1970–72, 104, no. 68.

KNIVES, SHEARS AND SCISSORS

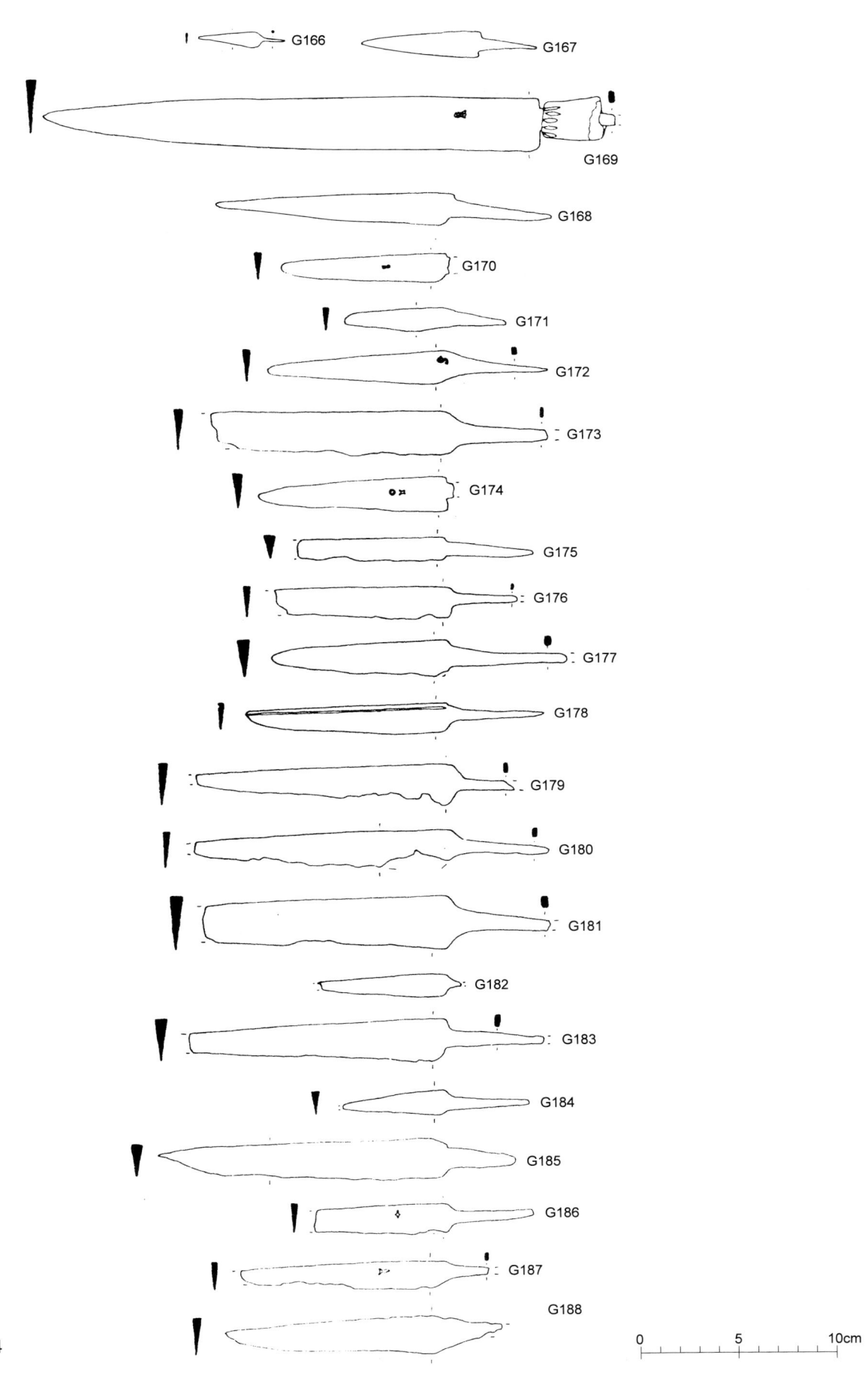

FIGURE 8.14
Knives

G189 KNIFE
Baginton, Warwickshire.
14th–15th century.
Complete. L 212mm.
Wilkins 1975, 126, fig 8.13.

G190 KNIFE
Newbury, Berkshire.
Mid 15th century.
Blade and whittle tang broken. Inlaid groove and cutler's mark on one side of blade.
L 153mm.
Goodall 1997, fig 19, no. 11.

G191 KNIFE
Winchester, Hampshire.
15th century.
Blade and whittle tang broken. Metallurgy: steel-cored blade. L 100mm.
Goodall 1990-16, 850, no. 2774.

G192 KNIFE
Lyveden, Northamptonshire.
15th century.
Blade broken, whittle tang tip clenched.
L 136mm.
Steane and Bryant 1975, 121, fig 46.35.

G193 KNIFE
Lyveden, Northamptonshire.
15th century.
Blade and whittle tang broken. Damaged, oval, copper-alloy hilt plate.
Inlaid cutler's mark. L 125mm.
Steane and Bryant 1975, 122, fig 46.51.

G194 KNIFE
Barton Blount, Derbyshire.
15th century.
Blade and whittle tang broken. Metallurgy: steel-edged blade. L 164mm.
Goodall 1975b, 96–97, fig 46.1.

G195 KNIFE
Winchester, Hampshire.
16th century.
Blade broken. Metallurgy: steel-edged blade. L 171mm.
Goodall 1990-16, 850, no. 2779.

G196 KNIFE
Theodoric's Hermitage, Margam, West Glamorgan.
Site: 13th–15th century.
Whittle tang broken. L 172mm.
National Museum of Wales, Cardiff, 49.140. 15–18.

G197 KNIFE
Somerby, Lincolnshire.
11th to 15th century.
Blade and whittle tang incomplete.
L 298mm.
Mynard 1969, 83, fig 12.IW70.

G198 KNIFE
London.
Late 15th–early 16th century.
Blade and whittle tang broken. L 130mm.
Excavated by F C Willmot. Site at 66 Foyle Road.

G199 KNIFE
Ospringe, Kent.
c1483–1550.
Blade and whittle tang broken. L 97mm.
Goodall 1979c, 129, fig 19.6.

G200 KNIFE
Ospringe, Kent.
c1483–1550.
Blade broken. L 194mm.
Goodall 1979c, 129, fig 19.8.

G201 KNIFE
Somerby, Lincolnshire.
Derived from 15th to mid 16th-century occupation.
Blade and whittle tang broken. L 293mm.
Mynard 1969, 83, fig 12.IW63.

G202 KNIFE
Winchester, Hampshire.
Late 15th to early 16th century.
Blade and whittle tang broken. Metallurgy: piled blade. L 70mm.
Goodall 1990-16, 850, no. 2775.

G203 KNIFE
Pleshey Castle, Essex.
Mid 13th/early 14th century to early/mid 16th century or later.
Blade and whittle tang broken. Non-ferrous shoulder plates. L 122mm.
Goodall 1977c, 175–176, fig 38.4.

G204 KNIFE
West Hartburn, Durham.
Site: 13th–16th century.
Blade and whittle tang broken. L 140mm.
Excavated by L Still and A Pallister.

G205 KNIFE
North Elmham Park, Norfolk.
c1150–c1600.
Complete. L 232mm.
Goodall 1980a, 510, fig 265.25.

G206 KNIFE
Llantrithyd, South Glamorgan.
Early to mid 12th century.
Blade and whittle tang broken. L 106mm.
Goodall 1977f, 47, iron object fig 1.15.

G207 KNIFE
Wintringham, Cambridgeshire.
Site: c1175–1340.
Blade broken. L 113mm.
Goodall 1977a, 257, fig 43.10.

G208 KNIFE
London.
Around later 14th century.
Blade and whittle tang broken. L 115mm.
Henig 1974, 189, fig 37.40.

G209 KNIFE
London.
Around later 14th century.
Blade and whittle tang broken. L 92mm.
Henig 1974, 189, fig 37.36.

G210 KNIFE
Northampton.
Later 15th century.
Blade and whittle tang broken. L 137mm.
Goodall *et al* 1979, 268, fig 118.40.

KNIVES, SHEARS AND SCISSORS

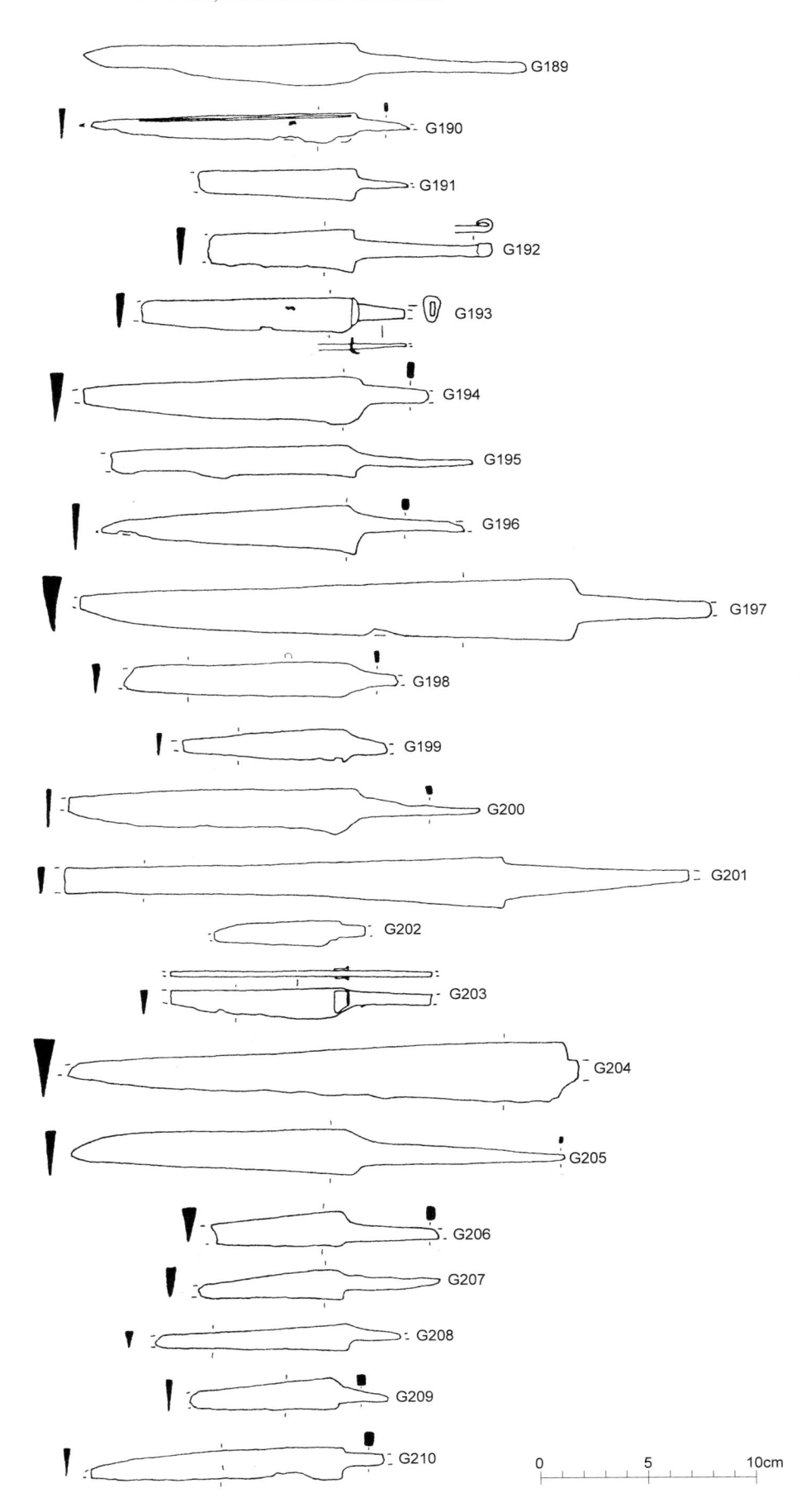

FIGURE 8.15
Knives

G211 KNIFE
Theodoric's Hermitage, Margam, West Glamorgan.
Site: 13th–15th century.
Complete. L 145mm.
National Museum of Wales, Cardiff, 49.140. 15–18.

G212 KNIFE
Stonar, Kent.
c1275–1385.
Blade and whittle tang broken. L 89mm.
Excavated by N Macpherson-Grant.

G213 KNIFE
Cheddar, Somerset.
Later 13th century to c1600.
Broken whittle tang retains traces of wooden handle. L 149mm.
Goodall 1979d, 266, fig 90.199.

G214 KNIFE
Lyveden, Northamptonshire.
c1200–1350.
Blade and whittle tang broken. L 155mm.
Steane and Bryant 1975, 121, fig 46.23.

G215 KNIFE
Stonar, Kent.
c1275–1385.
Blade and tang broken. L 83mm.
Excavated by N Macpherson-Grant.

G216 KNIFE
Stonar, Kent.
c1275–1385.
Blade and whittle tang broken. Inlaid cutler's marks on blade. L 144mm.
Excavated by N Macpherson-Grant.

G217 KNIFE
Kiln Combe, Bullock Down, East Sussex.
Site: 12th–15th century.
Blade and whittle tang broken. L 94mm.
Excavated by D J Freke.

G218 KNIFE
Gloucester.
Mid 11th century.
Blade broken. L 61mm.
Excavated by H Hurst.

G219 KNIFE
Gloucester.
Probably mid 11th century.
Blade and whittle tang broken. L 99mm.
Excavated by H Hurst.

G220 KNIFE
Winchester, Hampshire.
Late 11th–early 12th century.
Blade and tang broken. L 55mm.
Goodall 1990-16, 850, no. 2787.

G221 KNIFE
Winchester, Hampshire.
11th century.
Whittle tang broken. Butting against the shoulder, and originally fronting the handle, are a number of sheet metal plates formerly separated by organic plates. L 154mm.
Goodall 1990-16, fig 255.2748.

G222 KNIFE
Newbury, Berkshire.
c1080–1110.
Whittle tang broken. L 142mm.
Goodall 1997, fig 19, no. 9.

G223 KNIFE
Gloucester.
Probably mid 12th century.
Complete. L 97mm.
Excavated by H Hurst.

G224 KNIFE
Netherton, Hampshire.
Mid to late 12th century.
Blade and whittle tang incomplete. L 180mm.
Goodall 1990-28, fig 9.1, no. 96.

G225 KNIFE
Winchester, Hampshire.
11th–?mid 12th century.
Whittle tang broken. L 72mm.
Goodall 1990-16, 850, no. 2788.

G226 KNIFE
Winchester, Hampshire.
Late 11th–12th century.
Whittle tang broken. Metallurgy: blade steel edged. L 135mm.
Goodall 1990-16, fig 255.2790.

G227 KNIFE
Winchester, Hampshire.
Late 11th–12th century.
Blade and whittle tang broken. L 161mm.
Goodall 1990-16, fig 255.2789.

G228 KNIFE
Wroughton Copse, Fyfield Down, Wiltshire.
12th century (?).
Blade and whittle tang broken. Non-ferrous pointed oval hilt plate. L 66mm.
Excavated by P J Fowler.

G229 KNIFE
Winchester, Hampshire.
Early 13th century.
Blade broken. L 86mm.
Goodall 1990-16, 850, no. 2794.

G230 KNIFE
King's Lynn, Norfolk.
c1150–1250.
Whittle tang broken. L 105mm.
Goodall and Carter 1977, 293, fig 133.21.

G231 KNIFE
Duffield Castle, Derbyshire.
Found with masonry of keep built 1177–90, demolished 1266.
Complete. L 185mm.
Cox 1887, 173 and figure. For site see Manby 1959; Renn 1973, 174–176.

KNIVES, SHEARS AND SCISSORS

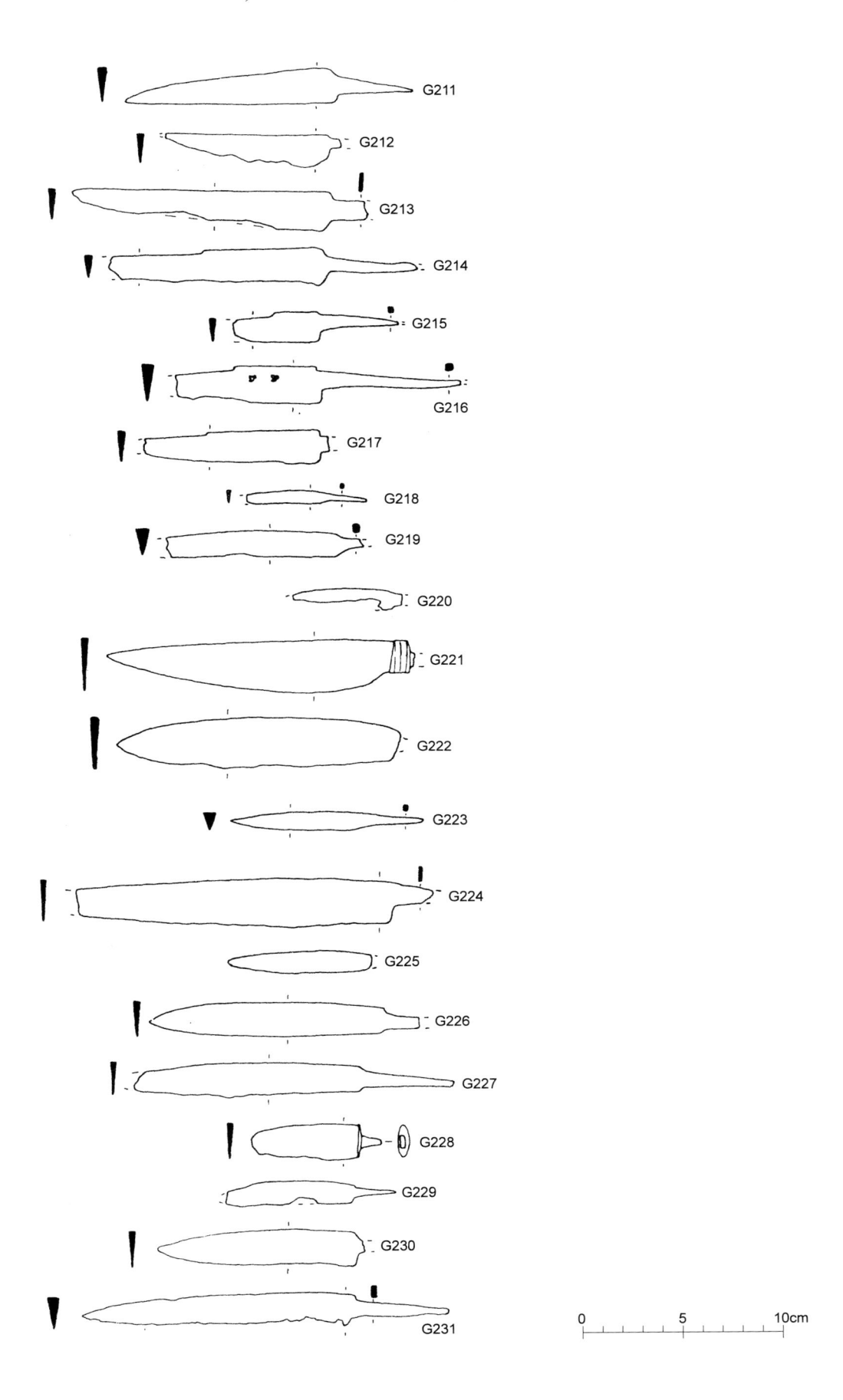

FIGURE 8.16
Knives

G232 KNIFE
Duffield Castle, Derbyshire.
Found with masonry of keep built 1177–90, demolished 1266.
Blade and whittle tang broken. Series of heater-shaped copper-alloy plates at junction of blade and tang, two 7.5 and 7mm thick, the others sheet metal. Gaps originally filled by organic plates. L 137mm.
Cox 1887, 173 and figure. For site see Manby 1959; Renn 1973, 174–176.

G233 KNIFE
Waltham Abbey, Essex.
Late 12th, early 13th century.
Complete. L 153mm.
Excavated by P J Huggins. From Romeland.

G234 KNIFE
Netherton, Hampshire.
Late 12th to mid 13th century.
Complete. L 117mm.
Goodall 1990-28, fig 9.1, no. 98.

G235 KNIFE
Netherton, Hampshire.
Late 12th–mid 13th century.
Blade and whittle tang broken. L 88mm.
Goodall 1990-28, fig 9.1, no. 99.

G236 KNIFE
Winchester, Hampshire.
Late 12th–early 13th century.
Complete. L 93mm.
Goodall 1990-16, fig 255.2792.

G237 KNIFE
Winchester, Hampshire.
Early 13th century.
Whittle tang broken. L 84mm.
Goodall 1990-16, fig 255.2793.

G238 KNIFE
Wroughton Copse, Fyfield Down, Wiltshire.
12th–13th century.
Whittle tang broken. L 113mm.
Excavated by P J Fowler.

G239 KNIFE
Winchester, Hampshire.
Late 12th–early 13th century.
Blade broken across base of whittle tang. Decorated copper-alloy strip along back of blade. L 118mm.
Goodall 1990-16, fig 255.2791.

G240 KNIFE
Wroughton Copse, Fyfield Down, Wiltshire.
12th–13th century.
Complete. L 172mm.
Excavated by P J Fowler.

G241 KNIFE
King's Lynn, Norfolk.
1200–1250.
Blade and whittle tang broken. L 119mm
Goodall and Carter 1977, 293, fig 133.19

G242 KNIFE
London.
Late 13th–mid 14th century.
Blade broken whittle tang retains traces of wooden handle and is clenched and broken. L 116mm.
Henig 1974, 189, no. 41.

G243 KNIFE
Wharram Percy, North Yorkshire.
Late 13th to late 14th century.
Blade broken. L 71mm.
Goodall 1979a, 118, fig 61.35.

G244 KNIFE
Bramber Castle, West Sussex.
Late 13th, 14th century.
Blade and whittle tang broken. L 116mm.
Barton and Holden 1977, 66, fig 20.5.

G245 KNIFE
Stonar, Kent.
Derived from deposits of c1275–1385.
Blade and whittle tang broken. L 167mm.
Excavated by N Macpherson-Grant.

G246 KNIFE
King's Lynn, Norfolk.
13th–14th century.
Whittle tang broken. Inlaid non-ferrous wire decoration along back and each side of blade (not drawn) takes form of wavy line with alternating scrolls within each curve. Along the back there are additionally bar stops between the curves. L 105mm.
Goodall and Carter 1977, 293, fig 133.29.

G247 KNIFE
Griff (Sudeley Castle), Warwickshire.
Site: 13th to 14th century.
Blade and whittle tang broken. L 113mm.
West 1968, 87, fig 4.6.

G248 KNIFE
Brooklands, Weybridge, Surrey.
c1150–1325.
Blade and whittle tang broken. Two trapezoidal plates, the front of iron, the rear of copper alloy, survive at the junction of blade and tang. L 90mm.
Goodall 1977d, 73, fig 45.4.

G249 KNIFE
Winchester, Hampshire.
13th–14th century.
Blade and whittle tang broken. L 65mm.
Goodall 1990-16, 851, no. 2795.

G250 KNIFE
Woodperry, Oxfordshire.
Site: 12th to 14th century.
Cutting edge damaged. L 117mm.
Wilson 1846.

G251 KNIFE
Badby, Northamptonshire.
Mid to late 14th century.
Whittle tang broken. L 76mm.
Excavated by Mrs M Gray.

G252 KNIFE
London.
Around later 14th century.
Blade and whittle tang broken. L 151mm.
Henig 1974, 189, fig 37.42.

G253 KNIFE
Bramber Castle, West Sussex.
14th century.
Complete. L 223mm.
Barton and Holden 1977, 66, fig 20.4.

G254 KNIFE
Goltho, Lincolnshire.
Croft A: late Saxon to late 14th or early 15th century.
Blade broken. Metallurgy: steel-cored blade. L 137mm.
Goodall 1975a, 79–82, fig 37.11.

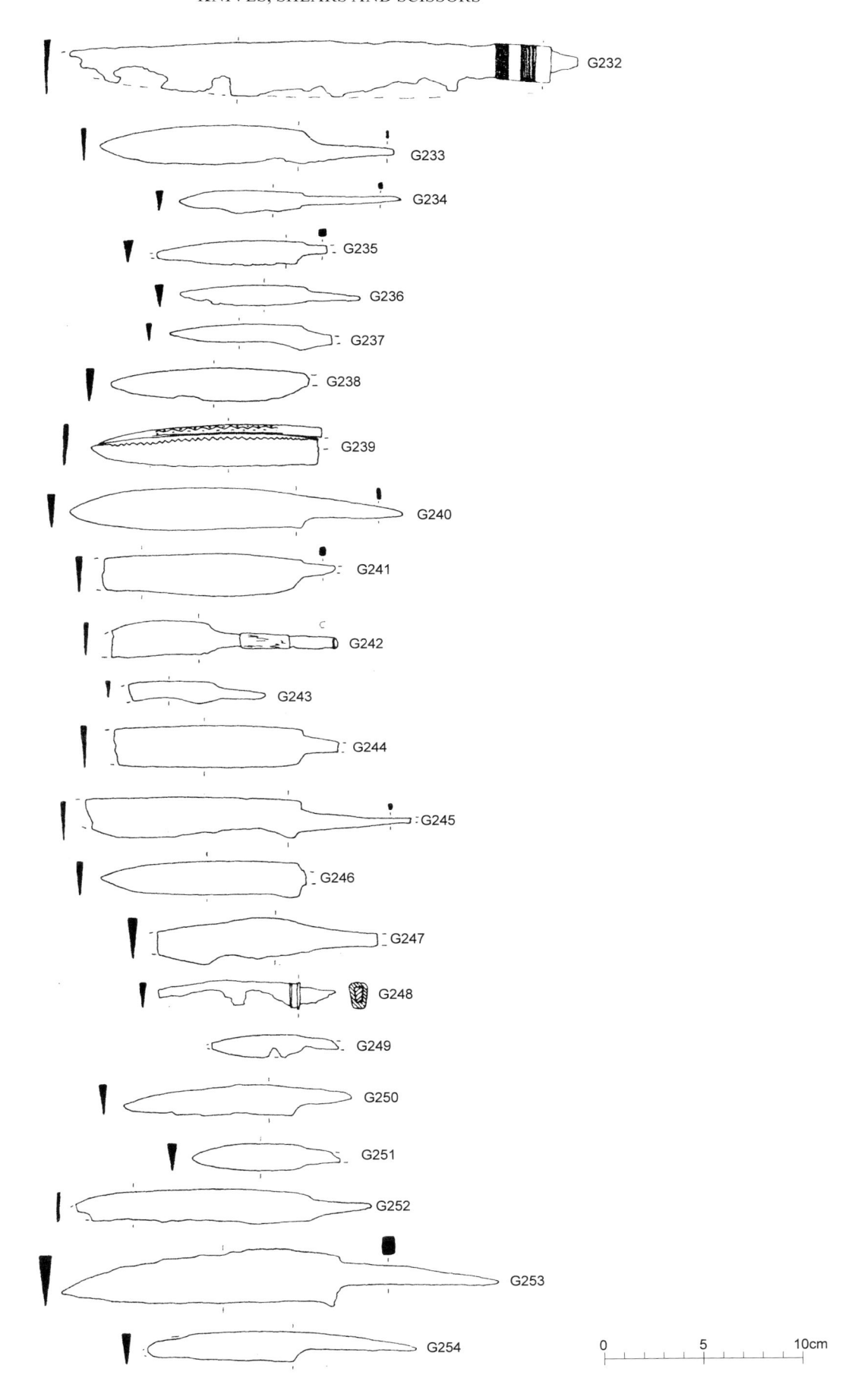

FIGURE 8.17
Knives

G255 KNIFE
Winchester, Hampshire.
15th century.
Whittle tang broken, blade damaged.
L 179mm.
Goodall 1990-16, fig 255.2797.

G256 KNIFE
Faxton, Northamptonshire.
Site: 12th–15th century.
Whittle tang broken. L 84mm.
Excavated by L A S Butler.

G257 KNIFE
Faxton, Northamptonshire.
Site: 12th–15th century.
Blade broken. L 122mm.
Excavated by L A S Butler.

G258 KNIFE
Goltho, Lincolnshire.
Croft A: late Saxon to late 14th or early 15th century.
Blade broken. Metallurgy: steel-edged blade. L 90mm.
Goodall 1975a, 79–82, fig 37.6.

G259 KNIFE
Criccieth Castle, Gwynedd.
Site: c1230–1404.
Blade broken. L 141mm.
O'Neil 1944–45, 42, pl X.35.

G260 KNIFE
St Catharine's Hill, Winchester, Hampshire.
Site: early 12th century to 1538–40.
Blade and whittle tang broken. L 152mm.
Hawkes et al 1930, 246, fig 29.I 24.

G261 KNIFE
Winchester, Hampshire.
Mid 13th–?14th century.
Blade and scale tang broken. L 109mm.
Goodall 1990-16, fig 257.2816.

G262 KNIFE
Rayleigh Castle, Essex.
c1070–c1350.
Complete. L 222mm.
Reader 1913, 169, fig 4.1; Browne 1913. For site see also Helliwell and Macleod 1965.

G263 KNIFE
Barrow Mead, Avon.
13th–14th century.
Blade broken. Iron rivets in scale tang and nib with copper-alloy cap. L 236mm.
Goodall 1976b, 34, fig 11.16.

G264 KNIFE
Stonar, Kent.
c1275–1385.
Blade broken, four rivets in tang. L 188mm.
Excavated by N Macpherson-Grant.

G265 KNIFE
Barrow Mead, Avon.
14th century.
Blade broken. Iron rivets in scale tang with nib for lost cap. L 209mm.
Goodall 1976b, 34, fig 11.14.

G266 KNIFE
Winchester, Hampshire.
Late 14th–early 15th century.
Scale tang broken. Inlaid cutler's mark.
L 203mm.
Goodall 1990-16, fig 257.2819.

G267 KNIFE
Huish, Wiltshire.
Site: 12th–15th century.
Scale tang broken. L 185mm.
Shortt 1972, 118, fig 3.14.

G268 KNIFE
Barton Blount, Derbyshire.
Site: late Saxon to late 15th century.
Blade and scale tang broken. Iron rivets. Metallurgy: steel-edged blade. L 159mm.
Goodall 1975b, 96–97, fig 46.3.

G269 KNIFE
The Hamel, Oxford.
Late 15th/early 16th century.
Blade broken. Nib for cap on end of scale tang. L 233mm.
Goodall 1980d, fig 29, no.3.

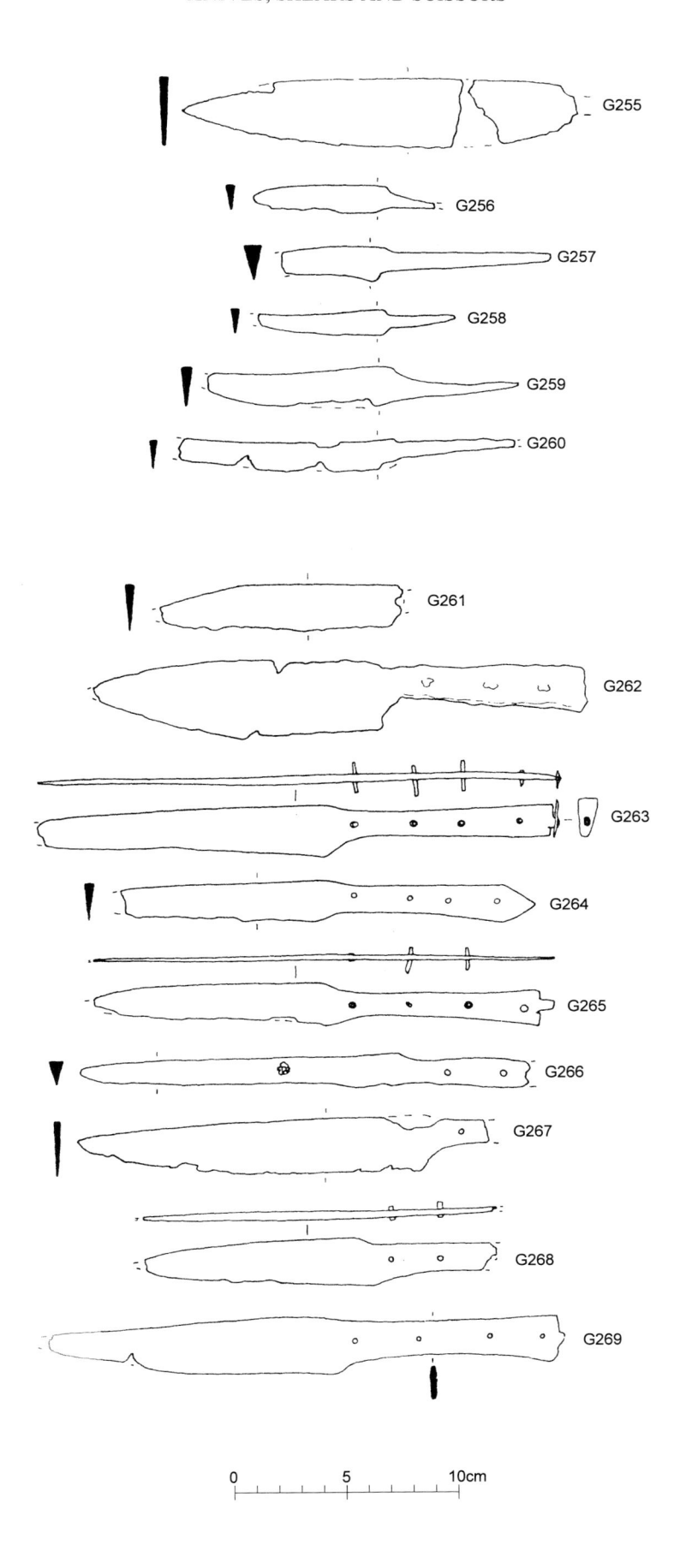

FIGURE 8.18
Knives

G270 KNIFE
Gomeldon, Wiltshire.
Late 13th to 14th century.
Blade and scale tang broken. L 114mm.
Musty and Algar 1986.

G271 KNIFE
Wintringham, Cambridgeshire.
Site: c1175–1340.
Blade and scale tang broken. Iron rivets.
L 146mm.
Goodall 1977a, 257, fig 43.14.

G272 KNIFE
Woodperry, Oxfordshire.
12th–14th century.
Blade and scale tang broken. Non-ferrous shoulder plate. L 144mm.
Wilson 1846.

G273 KNIFE
Seacourt, Oxfordshire.
14th century.
Blade tip and scale tang broken. L 138mm.
Biddle 1961–62, 175, fig 29.7.

G274 KNIFE
Grenstein, Norfolk.
Late 14th, 15th century.
Blade broken. Broken iron cap on end of scale tang. L 184mm.
Goodall 1980c, fig 76, no. 9.

G275 KNIFE
Grenstein, Norfolk.
Late 14th, 15th century.
Blade and scale tang broken. Non-ferrous shoulder plates. L 176mm.
Goodall 1980c, fig 76, no. 8.

G276 KNIFE
Huish, Wiltshire.
Site: 12th to mid 15th century.
Blade and scale tang broken. L 139mm.
Shortt 1972, 118, fig 3.16.

G277 KNIFE
Clarendon Palace, Wiltshire.
Site: c1072 to later 15th century.
Blade and scale tang broken. Copper-alloy riveted shoulder plates, one with wood graining from former handle. L 109mm.
Goodall 1988, fig 74.19; Borenius and Charlton 1936.

G278 KNIFE
Clarendon Palace, Wiltshire.
Site: c1072 to later 15th century.
Blade and scale tang broken. Three tubular copper-alloy rivets. L 192mm.
Goodall 1988, fig 74.16; Borenius and Charlton 1936.

G279 KNIFE
Northampton.
Site: Middle Saxon to c1500.
Blade and scale tang broken. Inlaid cutler's mark and brazing fluid from former shoulder plates on blade. L 104mm.
Goodall *et al* 1979, 268, fig 118.51.

G280 KNIFE
Wharram Percy, North Yorkshire.
Early 15th century.
Broken scale tang. L 107mm.
Goodall 1979a, 118, fig 62.44.

G281 KNIFE
Lyveden, Northamptonshire.
15th century, ?late.
Blade broken. Copper-alloy rivets, non-ferrous shoulder plates. L 205mm.
Steane and Bryant 1975, 122, fig 46.47.

G282 KNIFE
Waltham Abbey, Essex.
Probably 15th century.
Blade and scale tang broken. Riveted non-ferrous shoulder plates.
Inlaid cutler's mark. L 188mm.
Excavated by P J Huggins.

G283 KNIFE
Wharram Percy, North Yorkshire.
Late 15th to early 16th century.
Scale tang broken. L 106mm.
Goodall 1979a, 118, fig 62.48.

G284 KNIFE
London.
Late 15th to early 16th century.
Broken scale tang, rivet holes obscured.
L 190mm.
Excavated by F C Willmot. Site at 66 Foyle Road.

G285 KNIFE
Hen Caerwys, Clwyd.
Site: c1450–1520.
Blade and scale tang broken. L 144mm.
Excavated by G B Leach.

G286 KNIFE
Ospringe, Kent.
c1483–1550.
Blade and scale tang broken. L 133mm.
Goodall 1979c, 129, fig 19.12.

G287 KNIFE
Ospringe, Kent.
c1483–1550.
Scale tang broken. Brazing fluid from former shoulder plates. L 163mm.
Goodall 1979c, 129, fig 19.13.

G288 KNIFE
Ospringe, Kent.
c1483–1550.
Complete. L 249mm.
Goodall 1979c, 129, fig 19.11.

G289 KNIFE
Cambokeels, Durham.
Site: later 14th to early 16th century.
Blade and scale tang broken. Iron rivets.
L 153mm.
For site see Hildyard and Charlton 1947; Hildyard 1949.

G290 KNIFE
Cambokeels, Durham.
Site: later 14th to early 16th century.
Blade and scale tang broken. L 127mm.
For site see Hildyard and Charlton 1947; Hildyard 1949.

KNIVES, SHEARS AND SCISSORS

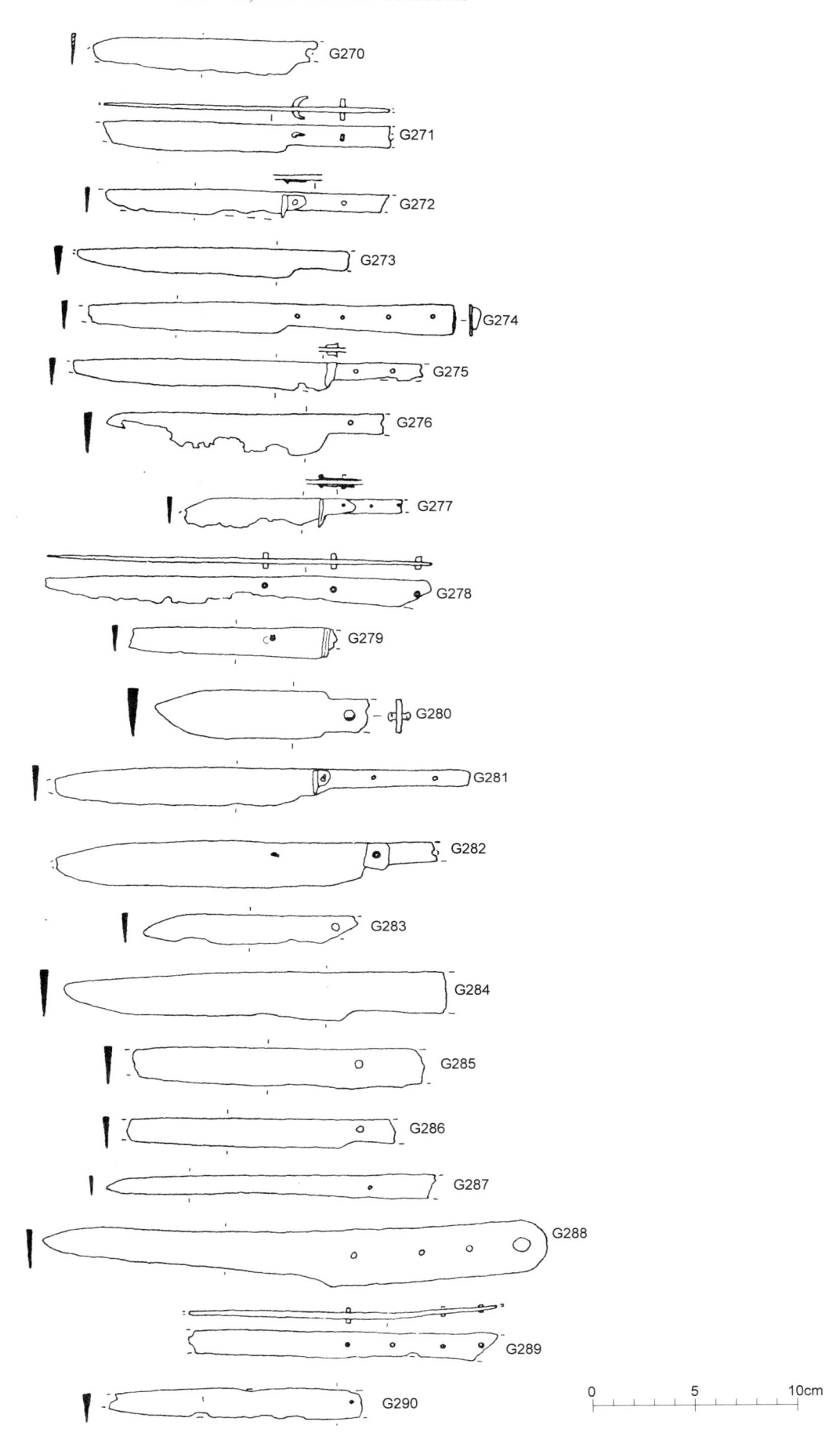

FIGURE 8.19
Knives

G291 KNIFE
Waltham Abbey, Essex.
First half 16th century.
Blade broken. Shoulder plates. Nib on end of tang for lost cap. L 195mm.
Excavated by P J Huggins. From Romeland.

G292 KNIFE
Brome, Suffolk.
16th century.
Scale tang broken. Copper-alloy rivet.
L 123mm.
West 1970, 110, fig 12.1.

G293 KNIFE
Hadleigh Castle, Essex.
16th century.
Blade and scale tang broken. Cutler's mark, not inlaid, on blade. L 107mm.
Goodall 1975c, 138, fig 28.336.

G294 KNIVES
Ospringe, Kent.
Demolition c1550–70 on site founded c1230.
Blade and scale tang broken. ?Leaded copper-alloy shoulder plates, bronze rivets with disc-shaped heads. L 155mm.
Goodall 1979c, 129, fig 19.17.

G295 KNIFE
Ospringe, Kent.
Demolition c1550–70 on site founded c1230.
Scale tang broken. Brazing fluid from former shoulder plates. L 141mm.
Goodall 1979c, 129, fig 19.15.

G296 KNIFE
Ospringe, Kent.
Demolition c1550–70 on site founded c1230.
Blade broken. Pewter shoulder plates, copper-alloy rivets. L 157mm.
Goodall 1979c, 129, fig 19.16.

G297 KNIFE
North Elmham Park, Norfolk.
c1150–c1600.
Blade and scale tang broken. Inlaid cutler's marks. L 122mm.
Goodall 1980a, 510, fig 265.29.

G298 KNIFE
Winchester, Hampshire.
13th–14th century.
Blade and scale tang broken. Metallurgy: wrought iron blade. L 113mm.
Goodall 1990-16, fig 257.2817.

G299 KNIFE
London.
Late 13th to mid 14th century.
Complete but distorted. Copper-alloy rivets.
L 152mm.
Henig 1974, 189, fig 37.44.

G300 KNIFE
Wintringham, Cambridgeshire.
Site: c1175–1340.
Complete. Inlaid cutler's mark. Tubular copper-alloy rivets. L 188mm.
Goodall 1977a, 257, fig 43.15.

G301 KNIFE
Old Sarum, Wiltshire.
13th or 14th century.
Blade and scale tang broken. L 175mm.
Musty and Rahtz 1964, 143, fig 5.3.

G302 KNIFE
Seacourt, Oxfordshire.
Site: mid to late 12th century to late 14th century.
Scale tang broken. L 181mm.
Biddle 1961–62, 174, fig 29.5, scale 1:4, not 1:3.

G303 KNIFE
Old Sarum, Wiltshire.
Principally medieval, to 14th century.
Blade and scale tang broken. Iron rivet.
L 139mm.
Salisbury and South Wiltshire Museum, Salisbury, O.S.E1.

G304 KNIFE
Old Sarum, Wiltshire.
Principally medieval, to 14th century.
Blade broken, scale tang damaged. Iron rivets, fragment of mottled grey bone handle, and cutler's mark, not inlaid, on blade.
L 140mm.
Salisbury and South Wiltshire Museum, Salisbury, O.S.C142, 30/1920–21.

G305 KNIFE
Old Sarum, Wiltshire.
Principally medieval, to 14th century.
Scale tang broken. L 182mm.
Salisbury and South Wiltshire Museum, Salisbury, O.S.C141, 30/1920–21.

G306 KNIFE
Northampton.
14th century.
Blade and scale tang broken. L 96mm.
Central Museum, Northampton. From between Bearwood Street and Silver Street.

G307 KNIFE
Seacourt, Oxfordshire.
14th century.
Blade and scale tang broken. L 166mm.
Biddle 1961–62, 175, fig 29.6, scale 1:4, not 1:3.

G308 KNIFE
Oxford.
Late 14th to mid 15th century.
Blade and scale tang broken. Non-ferrous shoulder plates. Non-ferrous metal along part of top and bottom edges of tang, which has no rivet holes. L 108mm.
Goodall 1976c, 298, fig 26.4.

G309 KNIFE
Northampton.
15th century, from c1410–20.
Broken blade with brazing fluid from former shoulder plates. Bone handle with copper-alloy cap, collar and tubular rivets.
L 145mm.
Goodall *et al* 1979, 268, fig 118.44.

G310 KNIFE
Goltho, Lincolnshire.
Croft A: late Saxon to late 14th or early 15th century.
Scale tang broken. Metallurgy: piled blade.
L 155mm.
Goodall 1975a, 79–82, fig 37.37.

KNIVES, SHEARS AND SCISSORS

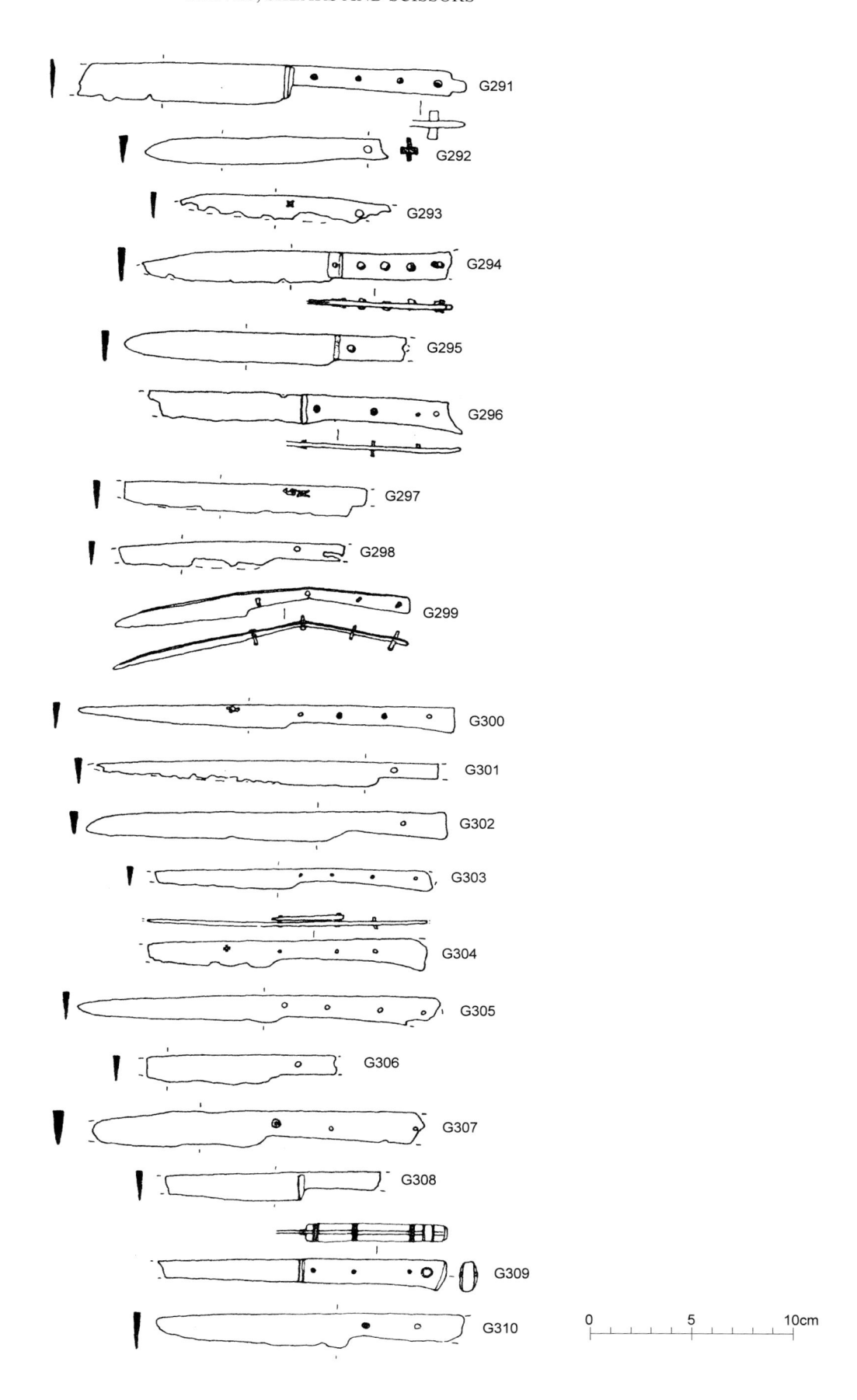

FIGURE 8.20
Knives

G311 KNIFE
Huish, Wiltshire.
Site: 12th to mid 15th century.
Blade and scale tang broken. Iron rivets.
L 226mm.
Shortt 1972, 118, fig 3.13.

G312 KNIFE
Somerby, Lincolnshire.
15th to mid 16th century.
Broken scale tang. Copper-alloy shoulder plates, one distorted, held by iron rivet.
L 130mm.
Mynard 1969, 82, fig 12.IW55.

G313 KNIFE
Somerby, Lincolnshire.
15th to mid 16th century.
Blade and scale tang broken. L 145mm.
Mynard 1969, 82, fig 12.IW54.

G314 KNIFE
Somerby, Lincolnshire.
15th to mid 16th century.
Blade broken. L 190mm.
Mynard 1969, 83, fig 12.IW61.

G315 KNIFE
Northampton.
Early 16th century.
Complete. Non-ferrous shoulder plates, wooden handle, iron rivets. L 280mm.
Goodall *et al* 1979, 268, fig 118.49.

G316 KNIFE
Waltham Abbey, Essex.
*c*1540.
Blade and scale tang broken. Rivet holes obscured. L 145mm.
Huggins 1972, 124, From F63.

G317 KNIFE
St Catharine's Hill, Winchester, Hampshire.
Site: early 12th century to 1538–40.
Blade and scale tang incomplete. L 93mm.
Hawkes *et al* 1930, 246, fig 29.I21.

G318 KNIFE
Ospringe, Kent.
Demolition *c*1550–70 on site founded *c*1230.
Blade and scale tang broken. Iron rivet, brazing fluid from former shoulder plates.
L 139mm.
Goodall 1979c, 129, fig 19.

G319 KNIFE
Rhuddlan, Clwyd.
1241/61.
Blade and scale tang broken. L 114mm.
Goodall 1994, fig 17.2, no. 31.

G320 KNIFE
Brome, Suffolk.
Later 13th to mid 14th century.
Blade and scale tang broken. L 154mm.
West 1970, 110, fig 12.3.

G321 KNIFE
Northolt Manor, Greater London.
14th century.
Broken blade with inlaid cutler's mark. Scale tang with copper-alloy shoulder plates, rivets, pins and cap. One of four rivets holds shoulder plates, and wooden handle is decorated by eleven pins in line down each side (not all surviving). Cap fitted over nib on tang end. L 156mm.
Excavated by J G Hurst.

G322 KNIFE
Goltho, Lincolnshire.
Croft A: late Saxon to late 14th or early 15th century.
Scale tang incomplete. L 109mm.
Goodall 1975a, 79–81, fig 37.38.

G323 KNIFE
Broadfield, Hertfordshire.
*c*1220–*c*1450.
Blade and scale tang broken. Cutler's mark, not inlaid, on blade. Brazing fluid from former shoulder plates. Iron rivets with fragment of bone scale with ring-and-dot decoration. L 140mm.
Goodall 1974b, 56, fig 22.4.

G324 KNIFE
Northampton.
15th century, from *c*1410–20.
Blade and scale tang broken. Iron rivet.
L 204mm.
Goodall *et al* 1979, 268, fig 118.45.

G325 KNIFE
Northampton.
Later 15th century.
Blade broken. Non-ferrous shoulder plates, iron rivets. L 181mm.
Goodall *et al* 1979, 268, fig 118.46.

G326 KNIFE
Wallingstones, Hereford and Worcester.
Post-1500 destruction layer with residual objects; site occupied from *c*1200.
Blade and scale tang broken. L 180mm.
Bridgewater 1970–72, 104, no. 90.

G327 KNIFE
Somerby, Lincolnshire.
11th to 15th century.
Broken scale tang with iron rivet. Non-ferrous shoulder plate. L 113mm.
Mynard 1969, 82, fig 12.IW51.

G328 KNIFE
Hen Caerwys, Clwyd.
Site: *c*1450–1520.
Blade and scale tang broken. Non-ferrous shoulder plates, iron rivets. L 191mm.
Excavated by G B Leach.

G329 KNIFE
Somerby, Lincolnshire.
15th to mid 16th century.
Scale tang broken. Brazing fluid from lost shoulder plates. L 172mm.
Mynard 1969, 82, fig 12.IW57.

G330 KNIFE
Somerby, Lincolnshire.
Over 15th to mid 16th-century house.
Complete. Rivet holes obscured, possible cutler's mark, not inlaid, on blade.
L 214mm.
Mynard 1969, 83, fig 12.IW64.

KNIVES, SHEARS AND SCISSORS

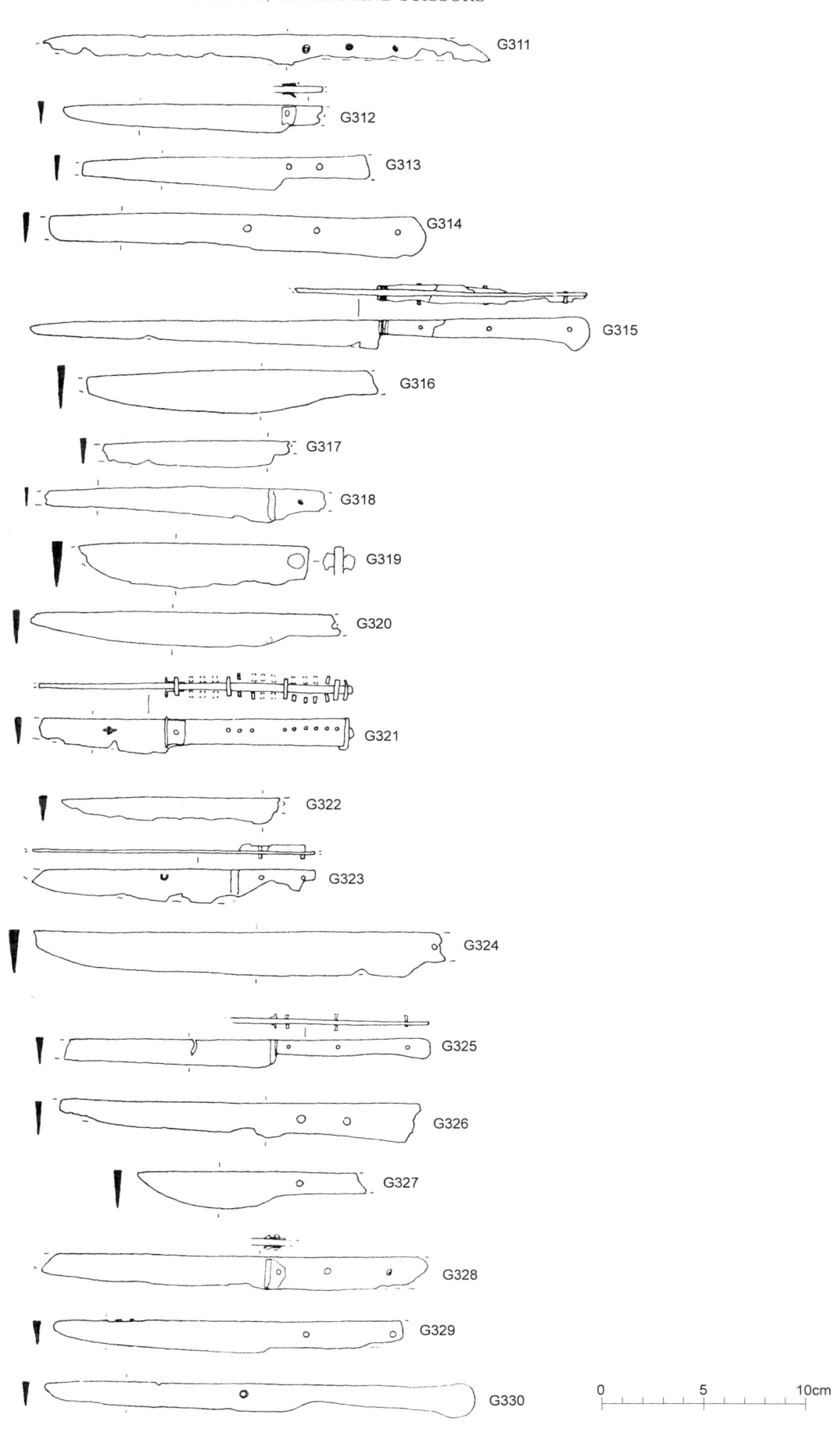

FIGURE 8.21
Knives

G331 KNIFE
West Hartburn, Durham.
Site: 13th to 16th century.
Blade broken, rivet holes in tang obscured. Shoulder plates. L 240mm.
Still and Pallister 1967, 146, fig 4.4.

G332 KNIFE
North Elmham Park, Norfolk.
c1150–c1600.
Blade and scale tang broken. Shoulder plates. L 142mm.
Goodall 1980a, 510, fig 265.26.

G333 KNIFE
Writtle, Essex.
Early 14th century.
Blade and scale tang broken. Inlaid cutler's mark. L 79mm.
Rahtz 1969b, 87, fig 47.62.

G334 KNIFE
Northolt Manor, Greater London.
1370–1475.
Blade and tang broken. L 212mm.
Hurst 1961, 291, fig 76.20.

G335 KNIFE
Huish, Wiltshire.
Site: 12th to mid 15th century.
Scale tang broken. L 187mm.
Shortt 1972, 118, fig 3.14.

G336 KNIFE
King's Lynn, Norfolk.
c1250–1300.
Blade, tang lost. L 226mm.
Goodall and Carter 1977, 293, fig 133.24.

G337 KNIFE (not illustrated)
Seacourt, Oxfordshire.
Mid 13th century.
Blade broken. Metallurgy: pattern-welded blade. L 105mm.
Biddle 1961–62, 175, fig 29.9, pl XIA, scale 1:4, not 1:3.

G338 KNIFE (not illustrated)
Winchester, Hampshire.
14th–?15th century.
Blade fragment. Metallurgy: pattern-welded and ?steel-edged. L 36mm.
Goodall 1990-16, fig 258.2845.

G339 KNIFE (not illustrated)
Winchester, Hampshire.
14th century.
Blade fragment. Metallurgy: pattern-welded blade, steel-edged. L 158mm.
Goodall 1990-16, fig 256.2809.

G340 KNIFE
Oxford.
c1400–c1550 (typologically probably 11th or early 12th century).
Blade fragment with inlaid wire decoration along each side, the wire a silver and gold alloy with silver predominating but with sufficient gold to give a 'gold' colour. Decoration on side 'a' is a running spiral with sprouting leaves (or branching plant scroll), on site 'b' a chain of linked S-curves alternately or intermittently bisected by a short bar. L 56mm.
Goodall and Hinton 1979, 142, fig 25.5.

G341 KNIFE
Stonar, Kent.
c1100–c1225.
Blade and whittle tang broken. Inlaid non-ferrous wire decoration along blade side(s).
L 102mm.
Excavated by N Macpherson-Grant.

G342 KNIFE
Winchester, Hampshire.
11th–?12th century.
Blade and whittle tang broken. Back and both sided of blade inlaid with decorative non-ferrous wire. L 43mm.
Goodall 1990-16, fig 258.2851.

G343 KNIFE
Lullington, East Sussex.
c1350.
Blade and whittle tang incomplete. Two cutler's marks inlaid with copper alloy on blade; part of copper-alloy strip inlaid in single groove near back of blade. L 119mm.
Barr-Hamilton 1970, 20, fig 4.46.

G344 KNIFE
Weoley Castle, Birmingham, West Midlands.
c1270–1600.
Blade and whittle tang broken. Two parallel grooves without inlay along one side. L 126mm.
Birmingham City Museum. For site see Oswald 1962.

G345 KNIFE
Newbury, Berkshire.
Mid 15th century.
Blade with swage and groove along one side. L 107mm.
Goodall 1997, fig 19, no. 13.

G346 KNIFE
London.
?Late 13th to mid 14th century.
Blade fragment with swage. L 57mm.
Henig 1974, 189, no. 47.

G347 KNIFE
Clarendon Palace, Wiltshire.
Site: c1072 to later 15th century.
Blade and tang incomplete. Swage to each side of blade. Inlaid cutler's mark.
L 125mm.
Goodall 1988, fig 74.14; Borenius and Charlton 1936.

G348 KNIFE
Clarendon Palace, Wiltshire.
Site: c1072 to later 15th century.
Blade and whittle tang incomplete. Swage to part of blade back. L 160mm.
Goodall 1988, fig 74.13; Borenius and Charlton 1936.

G349 KNIFE
Winchester, Hampshire.
Early 13th century.
Blade and whittle tang broken. Oval, copper-alloy hilt plate. L 110mm.
Goodall 1990-16, fig 256.2803.

G350 KNIFE (not illustrated)
Goltho Manor, Lincolnshire.
c1000–1100.
Blade and whittle tang broken. Multiple series of heater-shaped metal plates at junction between blade and tang. L 68mm.
Goodall 1987, 181.

G351 KNIFE (not illustrated)
Goltho Manor, Lincolnshire.
c1000–1100.
Blade and whittle tang broken. Multiple series of metal plates at junction of blade and tang. L 135mm.
Goodall 1987, 181.

G352 KNIFE
Pleshey Castle, Essex.
Part-destruction find probably derived from 12th to early/mid 16th-century occupation.
Blade and whittle tang broken. Brazing fluid, stippled on drawing, from former shoulder plates. L 128mm.
Goodall 1977c, 175, fig 38.9.

G353 KNIFE
Stonar, Kent.
c1275–1385.
Blade incomplete. Domed end cap end if tang, inlaid cutler's mark on blade.
L 169mm.
Excavated by N Macpherson-Grant.

G354 KNIFE
Winchester, Hampshire.
15th century.
Whittle tang fragment with circular end cap.
L 26mm.
Goodall 1990-16, fig 256.2810.

KNIVES, SHEARS AND SCISSORS

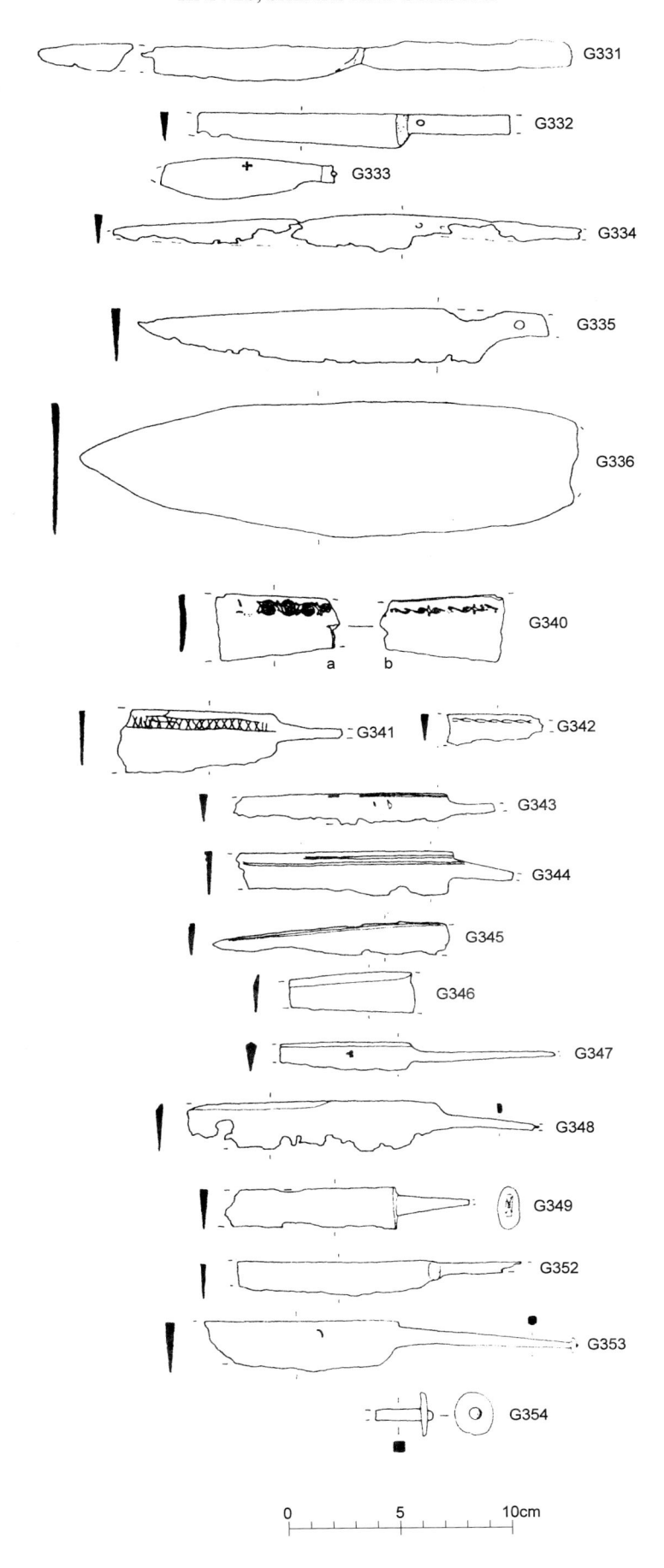

FIGURE 8.22
Knives

G355 KNIFE (not illustrated)
London.
Late 13th to mid 14th century.
Blade and whittle tang broken. Collar survives from former handle.
L 181, collar diameter 24mm.
Henig 1974, 189, fig 37.43.

G356 KNIFE
Hadleigh Castle, Essex.
13th to 14th century.
Blade and scale tang broken. Inlaid cutler's mark on blade, copper-alloy shoulder plates, hollow rivets and end-plate. Ferrified wood on tang. L 142mm.
Goodall 1975c, 138, fig 28.333.

G357 KNIFE
Southampton, Hampshire.
1300–1350.
Blade broken. Bone handle, copper-alloy rivets. L 209mm.
Harvey 1975b, 282, fig 254.2060.

G358 KNIFE
Goltho, Lincolnshire.
Croft A: late Saxon to late 14th or early 15th century.
Blade broken. Silver shoulder plate, brazed in position. Nib for end cap on end of scale tang, which retains traces of wooden handle. Metallurgy: piled blade. L 145mm.
Goodall 1975a, 79–82, fig 37.36.

G359 KNIFE
Writtle, Essex.
Destruction levels of period c1425–1521.
Blade broken. Iron rivets, remains of wooden handle. L 160mm.
Rahtz 1969b, 87, fig 47.63.

G360 KNIFE
Cambridge.
Early 16th century.
Scale tang knife, blade incomplete. Bone scales held by three rivets, and decorated with three ring-and-dot motifs. L 86mm.
Addyman and Biddle 1965, 124, fig 20.6.

G361 KNIFE
Clarendon Palace, Wiltshire.
Site: c1072 to later 15th century.
Scale tang, incomplete blade. L 140mm.
Goodall 1988, fig 74.17; Borenius and Charlton 1936.

G362 KNIFE
Old Sarum, Wiltshire.
13th or 14th century.
Blade broken. Bone scales held by iron rivets. L 136mm.
Musty and Rahtz 1964, 143, fig 5.2.

G363 KNIFE
The Mount, Princes Risborough, Buckinghamshire.
14th to early 15th century.
Blade broken. Bone handle, iron rivets, copper-alloy shoulder plates. L 128mm.
Pavry and Knocker 1953–60, 161, fig 12.6.

G364 KNIFE
Writtle, Essex.
c1306–1425.
Blade broken. L 168mm.
Rahtz 1969b, 87, fig 48.69.

G365 KNIFE
Writtle, Essex.
c1306–c1425.
Scale tang fragment with tubular copper-alloy rivets and cap. L 89mm.
Rahtz 1969b, 87, fig 48.74.

G366 KNIFE
Pivington, Kent.
Early or mid 14th century to early 16th century.
Blade incomplete, scale tang complete. Bone handle held together by three rivets, and decorated with groups of four copper-alloy pins. L 99mm.
Rigold 1962, 46, fig 8.iv.

G367 KNIFE
Northampton.
Later 15th century.
Broken blade with inlaid cutler's mark and non-ferrous shoulder plate. Riveted bone handle. L 178mm.
Goodall et al 1979, 268, fig 118.47.

G368 KNIFE
Ospringe, Kent.
Demolition c1550–70 on site founded c1230.
Blade broken. Brazing fluid from former shoulder plates. Non-ferrous metal shows on X-radiograph along edges of tang. L 99mm.
Goodall 1979c.

G369 KNIFE
Ospringe, Kent.
Demolition c1550–70 on site founded c1230.
Broken scale tang. L 85mm.
Goodall 1979c,

G370 KNIFE
Goltho, Lincolnshire.
Croft A: late Saxon to late 14th or early 15th century.
Broken scale tang with probable brass rivets and end plate. L 83mm.
Goodall 1975a, 79–81, fig 37.40.

G371 KNIFE
Winchester, Hampshire.
16th century.
Broken blade with decorated copper-alloy shoulder plates. Incomplete bone handle with copper-alloy rivets. L 91mm.
Goodall 1990-16, fig 257.2831.

G372 KNIFE
Writtle, Essex.
c1425–1521.
Scale tang with non-ferrous rivets and cap. L 98mm.
Rahtz 1969b, 87, fig 47.64.

G373 KNIFE
Wharram Percy, North Yorkshire.
Early 15th century.
Broken scale tang, rivet holes obscured, with copper-alloy cap. L 54mm.
Goodall 1979a, 119, fig 62.46.

G374 KNIFE
Bolton, Fangfoss, Humberside.
End 14th to mid 15th century.
Scale tang tip with copper-alloy end cap and collar. L 21mm.
Goodall 1978b, 143, fig 30.37.

G375 KNIFE
Northampton.
c1410–1420?
Scale tang fragment with copper-alloy cap. L 41mm.
Goodall et al 1979, 268, fig 118.52.

G376 KNIFE
Wharram Percy, North Yorkshire.
Early 15th century.
Broken scale tang with copper-alloy rivets and cap. L 80mm.
Goodall 1979a, 118, fig 62.45.

KNIVES, SHEARS AND SCISSORS

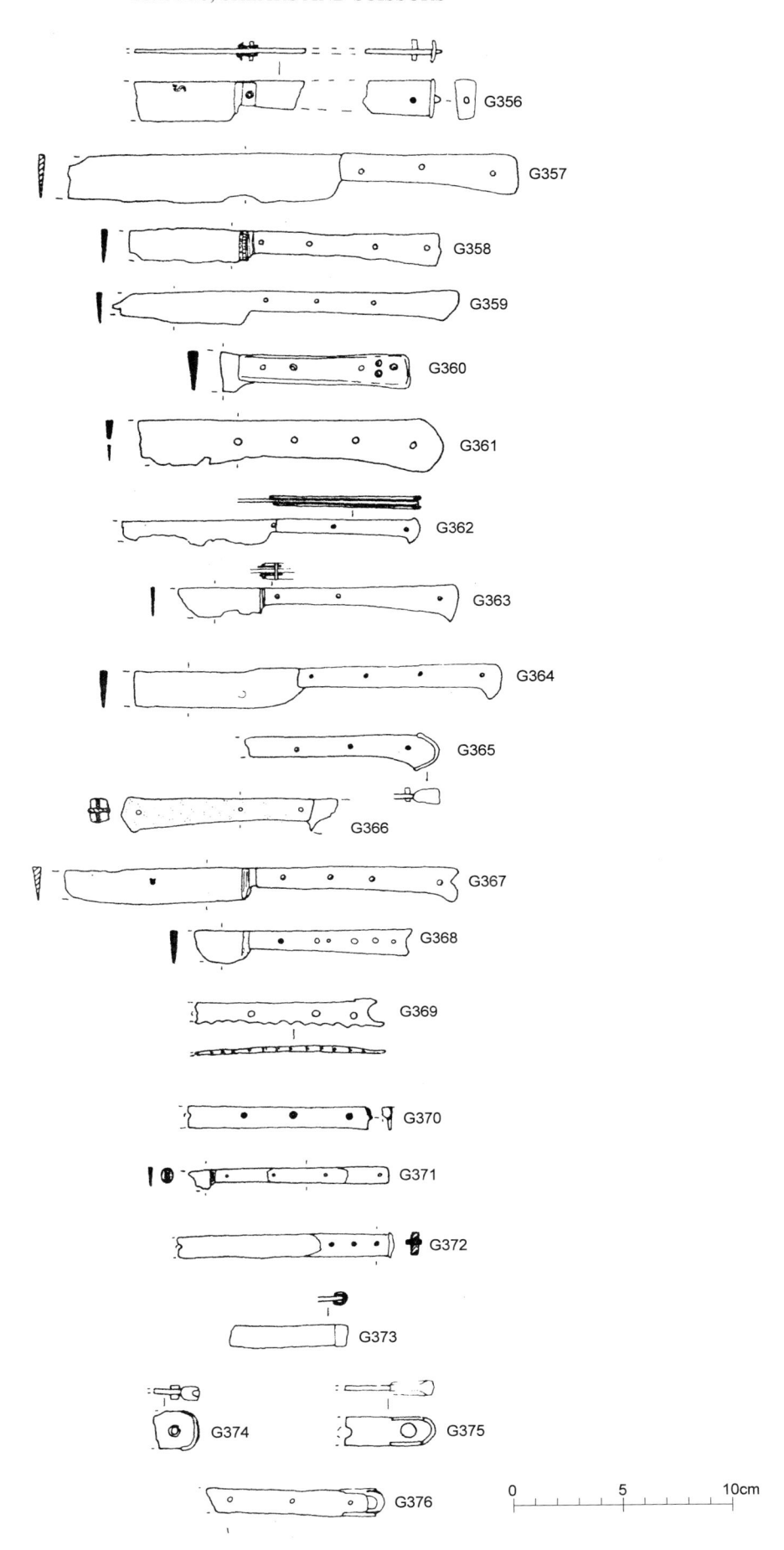

FIGURE 8.23
Knives

G377 KNIFE
London.
Late 15th–early 16th century.
Blade broken, rivet holes in scale tang obscured. L 166mm.
Excavated by F C Willmot. Site at 66 Foyle Road.

G378 KNIFE
Woodperry, Oxfordshire.
12th–14th century.
Broken scale tang with copper-alloy rivets and cap. Traces of wooden handle. L 61mm.
Wilson 1846. Ashmolean Museum, Oxford, 1873.61e.

G379 KNIFE (not illustrated)
Seacourt, Oxfordshire.
Mid to late 12th to late 14th century.
Scale tang knife handle with copper-alloy end cap and bone scales retaining part of black letter inscription ...DE BO TE.
Biddle 1961–62, 172–174, fig 29.4.

G380 KNIFE
Winchester, Hampshire.
13th century.
Blade and whittle tang broken. Inlaid cutler's mark. L 58mm.
Goodall 1990-16, fig 256.2805.

G381 KNIFE
Southampton, Hampshire.
Late 13th or early 14th century.
Blade and whittle tang broken. Inlaid cutler's marks. L 110mm.
Harvey 1975b, 279, fig 251.2013.

G382 KNIFE
Hangleton, West Sussex.
13th–14th century.
Blade fragment with inlaid cutler's mark. L 80mm.
Holden 1963, 169, fig 36.22.

G383 KNIFE
Winchester, Hampshire.
14th century.
Blade and whittle tang broken. Inlaid cutler's mark. L 52mm.
Goodall 1990-16, fig 256.2807.

G384 KNIFE
Lyveden, Northamptonshire.
1350–1500.
Blade fragment with inlaid cutler's mark. L 72mm.
Steane and Bryant 1975, 121, fig 46.38.

G385 KNIFE
Grenstein, Norfolk.
Late 14th, 15th century.
Blade and whittle tang broken. Inlaid cutler's mark. L 63mm.
Goodall 1980c, fig 76, no. 7.

G386 KNIFE
Broadfield, Hertfordshire.
c1220–c1450.
Blade and whittle tang broken. Inlaid cutler's mark on blade. L 109mm.
Goodall 1974b, 56, fig 22.1.

G387 KNIFE
Goltho, Lincolnshire.
Croft A: late Saxon to late 14th or early 15th century.
Blade and whittle tang broken. Cutler's mark inlaid probably with copper. L 57mm.
Goodall 1975a, 79–81, fig 37.26, pl VII.C.

G388 KNIFE
Goltho, Lincolnshire.
Croft A: late Saxon to late 14th or early 15th century.
Blade and scale tang broken. Shoulder plates and revets of brass. Inlaid cutler's mark. L 84mm.
Goodall 1975a, 79–81, fig 37.39.

G389 KNIFE
Goltho, Lincolnshire.
Croft A: late Saxon to late 14th or early 15th century.
Blade fragment with cutler's mark inlaid probably with copper. L 95mm.
Goodall 1975a, 79–81, fig 37.24, pl VII.B.

G390 KNIFE
Goltho, Lincolnshire.
Croft B: late Saxon to late 14th century.
Blade and scale tang broken. Cutler's mark inlaid with copper. Brazing fluid from former shoulder plates and along tang, which retains traces of wooden handle.
Metallurgy: piled blade. L 122mm.
Goodall 1975a, 79–82, fig 37.35, pl VII.E.

G391 KNIFE
Hull, Humberside.
15th century.
Blade and whittle tang broken. Inlaid cutler's mark. L 54mm.
Goodall 1997b, 65, fig 27.77.

G392 KNIFE
Winchester, Hampshire.
Late 15th–early 16th century.
Blade fragment with inlaid cutler's mark. L 36mm.
Goodall 1990-16, fig 258.2850.

G393 KNIFE
Winchester, Hampshire.
Late 14th–?15th century.
Blade fragment with inlaid cutler's mark. L 80mm.
Goodall 1990-16, fig 258.2846.

G394 KNIFE
Greencastle, Co. Down.
Site: end 13th to mid 16th century.
Blade fragment. Cutler's mark, inlaid.
Metallurgy: iron core. L 58mm.
Scott 1976, 46, figs 1.j and 6.70

G395 KNIFE
Greencastle, Co. Down.
Site: end 13th to mid 16th century.
Blade fragment with inlaid cutler's mark. L 87mm.
Scott 1976, 46, fig 1.i.

G396 KNIFE
Oakham Castle, Leicestershire.
13th to 14th century.
Broken blade with cutler's mark, not inlaid. L 180mm.
Gathercole 1958, 33, fig 10.1.

G397 KNIFE
Hull, Humberside.
15th century.
Blade and whittle tang broken. Cutler's mark, not inlaid. L 163mm.
Goodall 1997b, 65, fig 27.75.

KNIVES, SHEARS AND SCISSORS

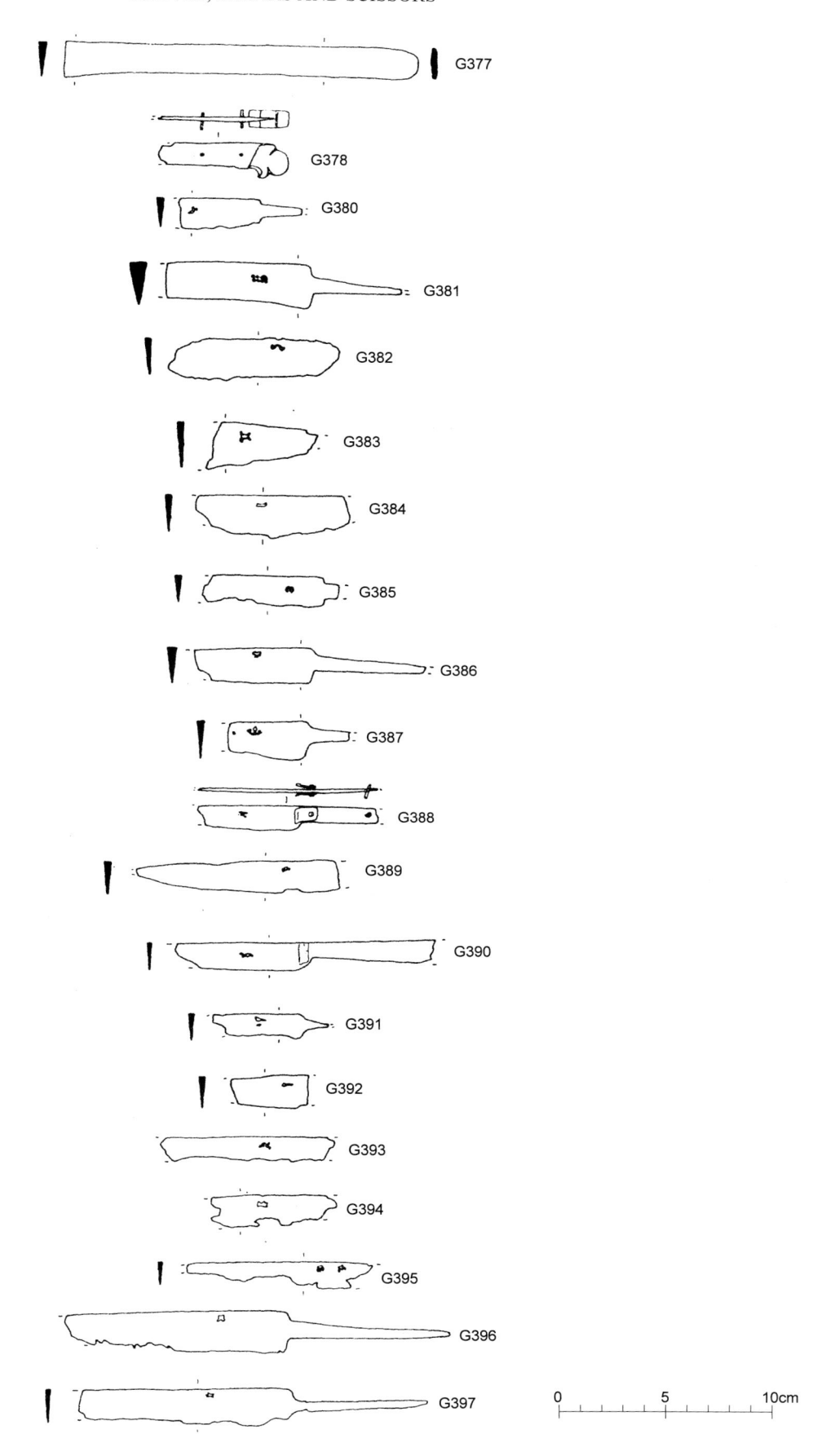

FIGURE 8.24
Knives

G398 KNIFE (not illustrated)
Winchester, Hampshire.
?Early 11th century.
Blade broken. Metallurgy: steel-cored blade.
L 113mm.
Goodall 1990-16, fig 256.2801.

G399 KNIFE (not illustrated)
Winchester, Hampshire.
Second half 13th century.
Blade and whittle tang broken. Metallurgy: blade probably steel-edged. L 72mm.
Goodall 1990-16, BS 457.

G400 KNIFE (not illustrated)
Chingley, Kent.
Second half 13th century to mid 14th century.
Blade broken. Metallurgy: blade steel-edged. L 93mm.
Goodall 1975d, 60, 90, fig 27.2.

G401 KNIFE (not illustrated)
Goltho, Lincolnshire.
Croft A: late Saxon to late 14th or early 15th century.
Blade and whittle tang broken. Metallurgy: steel-edged blade. L 69mm.
Goodall 1975a, 79–82, fig 37.8.

G402 KNIFE (not illustrated)
Greencastle, Co. Down.
Site: end 13th to mid 16th century.
Blade and whittle tang broken. Metallurgy: steel-edged blade. L 144mm.
Scott 1976, 45, figs 1.h and 6.c5.

G403 KNIFE (not illustrated)
Greencastle, Co. Down.
Site: end 13th to mid 16th century.
Blade broken. Metallurgy: steel-edged blade. L 151mm.
Scott 1976, 45, figs 1.b and 6.13.

G404 KNIFE (not illustrated)
Winchester, Hampshire.
Late 14th century.
Blade and whittle tang broken. Metallurgy: piled blade. L 62mm.
Goodall 1990-16, fig 258.2842.

G405 KNIFE (not illustrated)
Greencastle, Co. Down.
Site: end 13th to mid 16th century.
Blade and whittle tang broken. Metallurgy: piled blade. L 92mm.
Scott 1976, 46, figs 1.g and 6.E44/67.

G406 KNIFE (not illustrated)
Greencastle, Co. Down.
Sire: end 13th to mid 16th century.
Blade broken. Metallurgy: piled blade.
L 123mm.
Scott 1976, 46, figs 1.f and 6.57/42.

G407 KNIFE (not illustrated)
Winchester, Hampshire.
Mid 16th century.
Blade and whittle tang broken. Metallurgy: iron-cored blade. L 99mm.
Goodall 1990-16, fig 256.2811.

G408–415 KNIVES (not illustrated)
Winchester, Hampshire.
Knife blade fragments, examined metallurgically (Goodall and Tylecote 1990).
G408 13th–14th century. Steel-cored blade. L 79mm. Goodall 1990-16, fig 258.2847.
G409 14th century. Steel-cored blade. L 69mm. Goodall 1990-16, fig 258.2844.
G410 16th century. Steel-cored blade. L 80mm. Goodall 1990-16, fig 258.2852.
G411 14th century. Steel-edged and pattern-welded blade. L 126mm. Goodall 1990-16, fig 258.2843.
G412 15th century. Steel-edged blade. L 108mm. Goodall 1990-16, fig 258.2848.
G413 15th–?16th century. Steel-edged blade. L 72mm. Goodall 1990-16, fig 258.2849.
G414 Early to mid 13th century. Iron-cored blade. L 71mm. Goodall 1990-16, fig 258.2840.
G415 Mid 13th century. Wrought iron blade. L 86mm. Goodall 1990-16, fig 258.2841.

G416 KNIFE (not illustrated)
Greencastle, Co. Down.
Site: end 13th to mid 16th century.
Blade fragment. Metallurgy: steel-edged.
L 75mm.
Scott 1976, 45, figs 1.d and 6.39a.

G417 KNIFE (not illustrated)
Goltho, Lincolnshire.
Croft A: late Saxon to late 14th or early 15th century.
Blade and scale tang broken. Probable brass rivet and traces of wooden handle on scale tang. Metallurgy: piled blade. L 142mm.
Goodall 1975a, 79–82, fig 37.34.

G418 SHEARS
Ospringe, Kent.
c1483 to 1550.
Arm with broken bow. L 82mm.
Goodall 1979c, 129, fig 20.24.

G419 SHEARS
Criccieth Castle, Gwynedd.
Site: c1220 to 1404.
One blade broken. L 95mm.
O'Neil 1944–45, 42, no. 40.

G420 SHEARS
Water Newton, Cambridgeshire.
Site: 12th to 13th century.
Blades and bow broken. L 98mm.
Green 1962–63, 78, fig 4.2.

G421 SHEARS
Castle Acre Castle, Norfolk.
1140s deposit with derived material. Site founded soon after 1066.
Blade tips lost. L 123mm.
Goodall 1982, fig 38, no. 30.

G422 SHEARS
Kings Langley, Hertfordshire.
15th century.
Arm, bow and blade broken. L 120mm.
Neal 1973, 56, fig XV.75.

G423 SHEARS
Ospringe, Kent.
c1483 to 1550.
Arm with broken bow. L 143mm.
Goodall 1979c, 129, fig 20.23.

G424 SHEARS
Clarendon Palace, Wiltshire.
Site: c1072 to later 15th century.
One arm broken. L 151mm.
Goodall 1988, fig 75.25; Borenius and Charlton 1936.

G425 SHEARS
Dyserth Castle, Clwyd.
Site: 1241–63.
Complete. L 159mm.
Glenn 1915.

G426 SHEARS
Waltham Abbey, Essex.
12th to 13th century.
Blade and bow broken. L 168mm.
Excavated by P J Huggins. From Pentecostal Chapel.

G427 SHEARS
East Hill Farm, Houghton Regis, Bedfordshire.
c1000 to 1400.
Blades damaged. L 176mm.
Luton Museum, L/338/38.

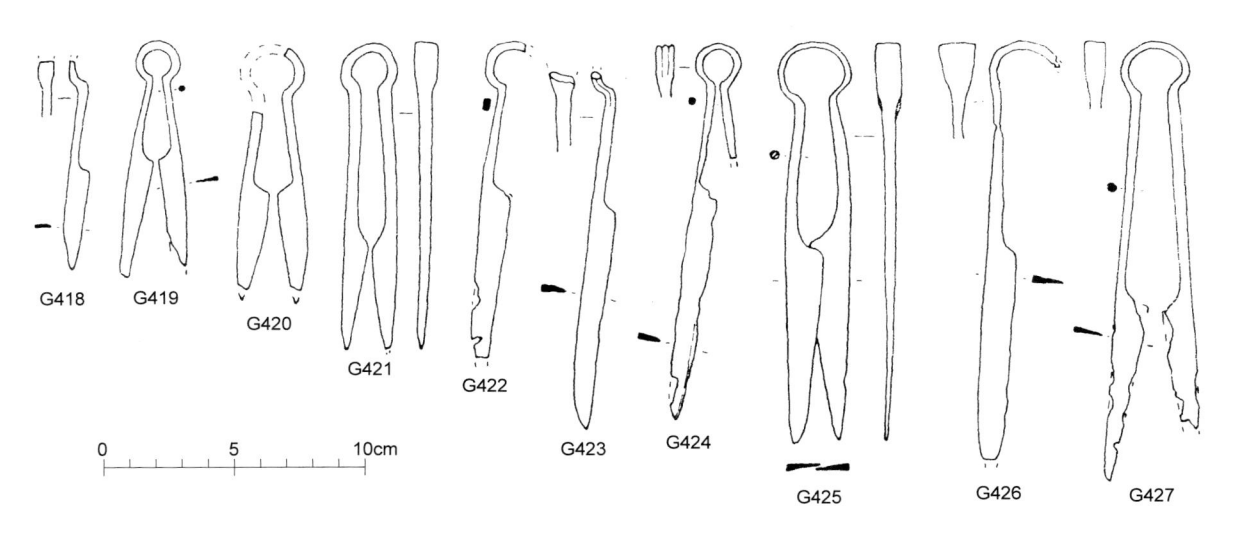

FIGURE 8.25
Shears

G428 SHEARS
Winchester, Hampshire.
Early 13th century.
Complete. L 183mm.
Goodall 1990-17, fig 260.2875.

G429 SHEARS
Goltho Manor, Lincolnshire.
11th century.
Complete. L 188mm.
Goodall 1987, fig 157.69.

G430 SHEARS
Castle Acre Castle, Norfolk.
1140s deposit with derived material. Site founded soon after 1066.
Complete. L 198mm.
Goodall 1982, fig 38, no.31.

G431 SHEARS (not illustrated)
Weoley Castle, Birmingham, West Midlands.
c1200 to 1230.
Bow damaged, silver inlaid decorative stamps on outer face of each blade.
L 200mm.
Oswald 1962, 129, fig 51.4.

G432 SHEARS
Sulgrave, Northamptonshire.
Second half 11th century, possibly just post-Conquest.
Bow and blades broken. L 212mm.
Excavated by B K Davison.

G433 SHEARS
North Elmham Park, Norfolk.
c1150 to c1600.
Blades broken. L 143mm.
Goodall 1980a, 513, fig 266.56.

G434 SHEARS
Old Sarum, Wiltshire.
Associated with coin of William I.
One arm incomplete. L 217mm.
Stone and Charlton 1935, 184, fig 3.2.

G435 SHEARS
Faxton, Northamptonshire.
Site: 12th to 15th century.
Blades broken. L 190mm.
Excavated by L A S Butler.

G436 SHEARS
Ayton Castle, North Yorkshire.
13th century. Found with sickles, spearhead, axe and pitchfork.
Blades broken. L 220mm.
Rimington and Rutter 1967, 60, fig 11.37/19.

G437 SHEARS
Gomeldon, Wiltshire.
Second half 12th century.
Blade tips broken. L 226mm.
Musty and Algar 1986.

G438 SHEARS
London.
14th century.
Blades and bow damaged. L 248mm.
Museum of London (Guildhall Museum 13079). From 1–3 Little Britain, with 14th-century leather.

KNIVES, SHEARS AND SCISSORS

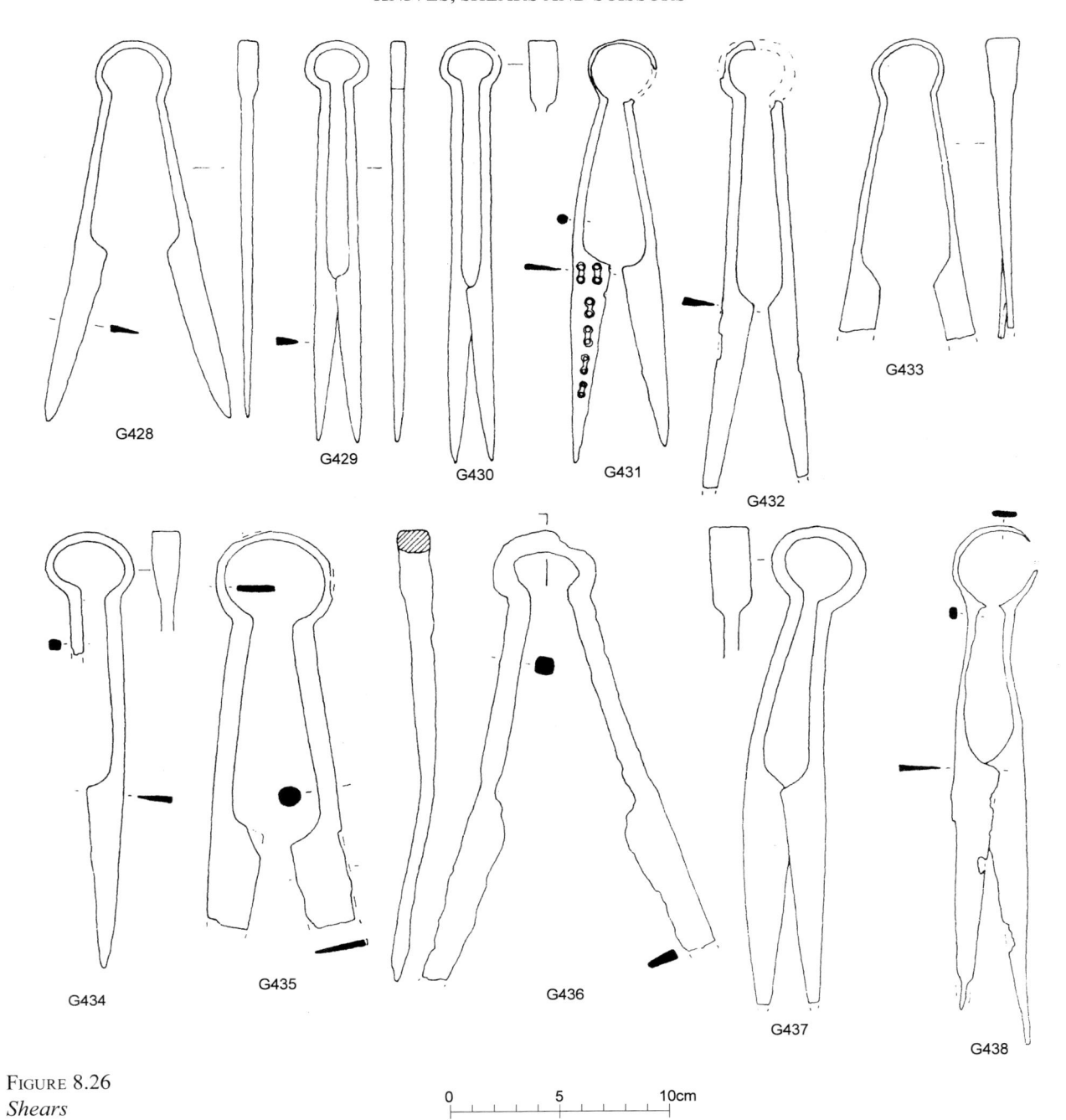

G428 G429 G430 G431 G432 G433

G434 G435 G436 G437 G438

FIGURE 8.26
Shears

G439 SHEARS
Patchway Field, Stanmer Park, East Sussex.
13th century.
Blade tips lost. L 257mm.
Excavated by W C L Gorton.

G440 SHEARS
Northampton.
14th century.
Arm, bow broken. L 258mm.
Goodall et al 1979, 268, fig 118.54.

G441 SHEARS
Brixworth, Northamptonshire.
Late 13th to 14th century. From floor of stokehole of corn-drying kiln.
Complete, bow distorted. L 314mm.
Excavated by P Woods.

G442 SHEARS
Seacourt, Oxfordshire.
Site: mid to late 12th to mid 14th century.
Blades damaged. L 328mm.
Biddle 1961–62, 172, fig 29.1, scale 1:4, not 1:3.

G443 SHEARS
Wallingstones, Hereford and Worcester.
1300–25 to before 1400.
Arm, bow and blade broken. L 114mm.
Bridgewater 1970–72, 102, no. 38.

G444 SHEARS (not illustrated)
Greencastle, Co. Down.
Site: end 13th century to mid 16th century.
Blade and handle broken. Metallurgy: steel-cored blade. L 47mm.
Scott 1976, 45, figs 1.a and 6.3b.

G445 SHEARS (not illustrated)
Woodperry, Oxfordshire.
12to 14th century.
Bow and blade broken. L 67mm.
Ashmolean Museum, Oxford, 1873.98. For site see Wilson 1846.

G446 SHEARS (not illustrated)
Northampton.
Later 15th century.
Arm, blade and handle broken. L 65mm.
Goodall et al 1979, 268, fig 118.55.

G447 SHEARS (not illustrated)
Clarendon Palace, Wiltshire.
Site: c1072 to later 15th century.
Arm, blade and handle broken. L 83mm.
Goodall 1988, 211.

G448 SHEARS (not illustrated)
Pleshey Castle, Essex.
Post-destruction find probably derived from 12th to early–mid 16th century occupation.
Arm, blade and handle broken. L 93mm.
Goodall 1977c, 175, fig 38.12.

G449 SHEARS (not illustrated)
Pleshey Castle, Essex.
Post-destruction find probably derived from 12th- to early–mid 16th-century occupation.
Arm, blade and bow broken. L 98mm.
Goodall 1977c, 176, fig 38.11.

G450 SHEARS (not illustrated)
Thelsford Priory, Warwickshire.
1400 to 1536.
Arm, blade and handle broken. L 71mm.
Excavated by Mrs M Gray.

G451 SHEARS (not illustrated)
Dyserth Castle, Gwynedd.
Site: 1241–63.
Handle broken, cutting edge damaged. L 76mm.
Glenn 1915.

G452 SHEARS (not illustrated)
The Hamel, Oxford.
14th, early 15th century.
Blade and handle broken. L 87mm.
Goodall 1980d.

G453 SHEARS (not illustrated)
Winchester, Hampshire.
Second half 13th century.
Blade and handle fragment. L 94mm.
Goodall 1990-17.

G454 SHEARS (not illustrated)
Upton, Gloucestershire.
Mid to later 13th century.
Blade and handle fragment. L 82mm.
Rahtz 1969a, 108, fig 12.88.

G455 SHEARS (not illustrated)
King's Lynn, Norfolk.
c1150 to 1250.
Arm, blade and handle broken. L 129mm.
Goodall and Carter 1977, 295, fig 133.34.

G456 SHEARS (not illustrated)
Waltham Abbey, Essex.
Site: c1200 to 16th or 17th century. From hearth in forge.
Blade and handle fragment. L 73mm.
Goodall 1973a, 170, fig 11.26.

G457 SHEARS (not illustrated)
Gloucester.
13th century.
Arm, blade and handle broken. L 131mm.
Hassall and Rhodes, 1974, 78, fig 30.14.

G458 SHEARS
Loughor Castle, West Glamorgan.
Site: c1106 to late 13th century.
Arm with broken blade and handle. L 133mm.
Excavated by J M Lewis.

G459 SHEARS (not illustrated)
Winchester, Hampshire.
Late 11th century.
Blade and handle fragment. L 154mm.
Goodall 1990-17, 863, no. 2872.

G460 SHEARS (not illustrated)
Pevensey, East Sussex.
Site: c1200 to c1500.
Arm with broken handle. L 198mm.
Dulley 1967, 228, fig 65.3.

G461 SHEARS
Woodperry, Oxfordshire.
12th–14th century.
Arm, bow broken. L 77mm.
Ashmolean Museum, Oxford, 1873.98. For site see Wilson 1846.

G462 SHEARS
Baginton Castle, Warwickshire.
Castle probably 14th–15th century, desolate in 1535–37.
Bow and blade broken. L 107mm.
Herbert Art Gallery and Museum, Coventry.

G463 SHEARS
Netherton, Hampshire.
Mainly mid 14th century.
Arm with broken bow. L 136mm.
Goodall 1990-28, fig 9.4, no. 174.

G464 SHEARS
Hen Domen, Powys.
13th century.
Arm, bow broken. L 183mm.
Barker and Higham 2000.

G465 SHEARS
Chester.
13th century.
One blade incomplete. L 195mm.
Whitwell and McNamee 1964, 18, fig 13.1.

G466 SHEARS
South Witham, Lincolnshire.
Late 13th century to 1308–13.
Complete. L 211mm.
Goodall 2002, fig 7.1, no. 12.

G467 SHEARS
Northampton.
13th to 14th century.
Complete. L 225mm.
Goodall et al 1979, 268, fig 118.53.

KNIVES, SHEARS AND SCISSORS

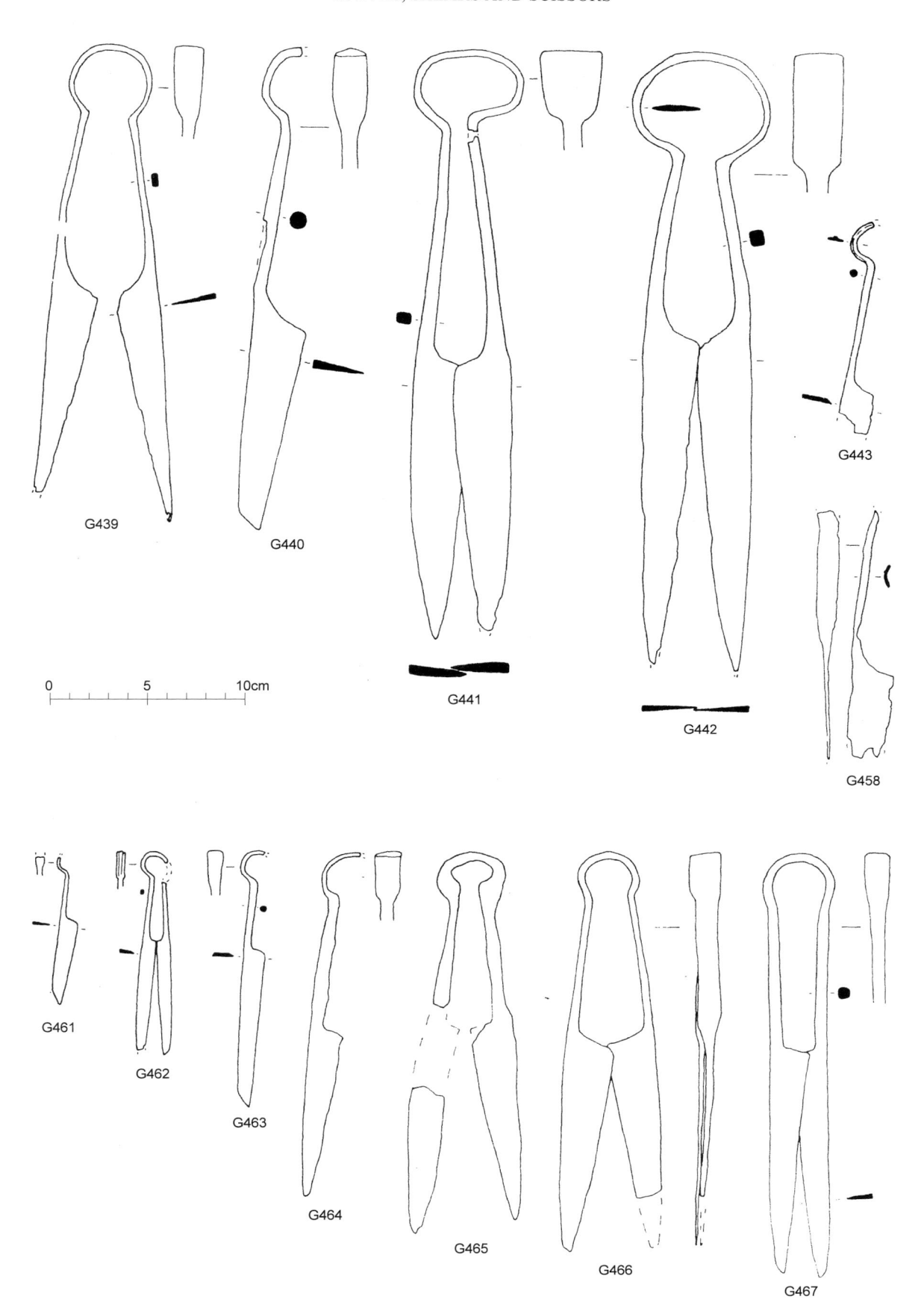

FIGURE 8.27
Shears

G468 SHEARS
Portchester Castle, Hampshire.
13th century.
Blades broken. L 219mm.
Hinton 1977, 198, fig 106.38.

G469 SHEARS
Cambokeels, Durham.
Later 14th to early 16th century.
Bow and one blade broken. L 285mm.
Hildyard 1949, 199, fig 6.4.

G470 SHEARS
Stonar, Kent.
Derived from 13th–14th century levels.
Arm with broken bow and blade. L 73mm.
Excavated by N Macpherson-Grant.

G471 SHEARS
Oxford.
*c*1325 to *c*1400.
Blade fragment. L 50mm.
Goodall 1977e, 142, fig 26.15.

G472 SHEARS
London.
Late 15th to early 16th century.
Shears blade, handle broken. L 110mm.
Excavated by F C Willmot. Site at 66 Foyle Road.

G473 SHEARS
Wharram Percy, North Yorkshire.
Late 15th to early 16th century.
Arm with broken blade and handle.
L 160mm.
Goodall 1979a, 118, fig 62.50.

G474 SHEARS
Waltham Abbey, Essex.
16th/17th-century destruction debris, plus derived material from 13th century onwards.
Fragment of handle and blade with back rib.
L 106mm.
Goodall 1973a, 170, fig 11.27.

G475 SHEARS
West Whelpington, Northumberland.
Medieval, pre-1500.
Blade broken across base of handle.
L 194mm.
Jarrett and Stevens 1962, 221, fig 11.23.

G476 SHEARS
London.
Late 13th to mid 14th century.
Complete. L 92mm.
Henig 1974, 189, fig 37.53.

G477 SHEARS
Old Sarum, Wiltshire.
Principally medieval, to 14th century.
Blades broken, one handle damaged.
L 91mm.
Salisbury and South Wiltshire Museum, Salisbury, O.S.C28.

G478 SHEARS
Stonar, Kent.
*c*1275 to 1385.
Arm with broken bow and blade. L 103mm.
Excavated by N Macpherson-Grant.

G479 SHEARS
Kent's Moat, Sheldon, West Midlands.
12th to 13th century.
One blade broken. L 117mm.
Dornier 1967, 55.

G480 SHEARS
Oxford Castle.
Late 14th to mid 15th century.
Blades broken. L 106mm.
Goodall 1976c.

G481 SHEARS
Benedictine Priory, Coventry, Warwickshire.
Site founded 1043, dissolved 1538.
Complete but for broken blade tip.
L 119mm.
Herbert Art Gallery and Museum, Coventry, 49/227/429. For site see Hobley 1971.

G482 SHEARS
Winchester, Hampshire.
15th century.
One handle and arm missing. L 125mm.
Goodall 1990-17, fig 260.2877.

G483 SHEARS
Dyserth Castle, Gwynedd.
Site: 1241–63.
Complete. L 152mm.
Glenn 1915.

G484 SHEARS
Thelsford Priory, Warwickshire.
Site: 1200–1212 to 1536.
Arm, bow and blade broken. L 141mm.
Excavated by Mrs M Gray.

G485 SHEARS
Winchester, Hampshire.
11th century.
Complete but for fracture in one handle.
L 175mm.
Goodall 1990-17, fig 260.2873.

G486 SHEARS
Stonar, Kent.
*c*1275 to 1385.
One blade missing. L 200mm.
Excavated by N Macpherson-Grant.

G487 SHEARS
Wroughton Copse, Fyfield Down, Wiltshire.
13th century (mid?) to early 14th century.
Complete. L 203mm.
Excavated by P J Fowler.

G488 SHEARS
Castle Acre Castle, Norfolk.
1140s/1150s deposit with derived material.
Site founded soon after 1066.
Blades broken, bow distorted. L 218mm.
Goodall 1982.

KNIVES, SHEARS AND SCISSORS

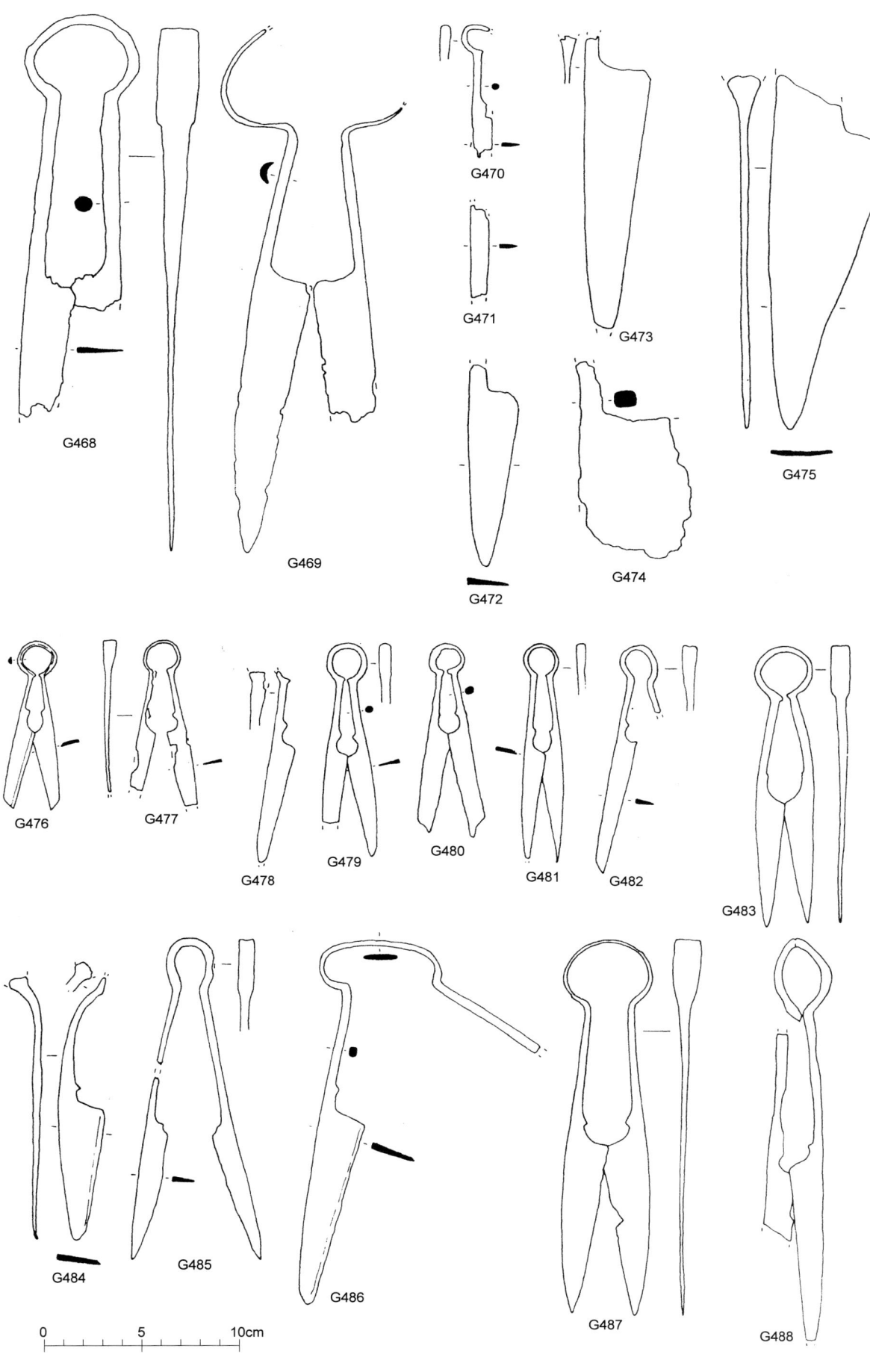

FIGURE 8.28
Shears

G489 SHEARS
Dover Castle, Kent.
Late 12th century to late medieval.
One blade lost. L 158mm.
Rigold 1967, 109, fig 9.Fe7.

G490 SHEARS
Seacourt, Oxfordshire.
Mid to late 14th century.
Arm, blade and handle broken. L 111mm.
Biddle 1961–62, 175, fig 29.8, scale 1:4, not 1:3.

G491 SHEARS
Goltho, Lincolnshire.
Croft A: late Saxon to late 14th or early 15th century.
Arm, blade and handle broken, inlaid mark on blade. L 90mm.
Goodall 1975a, 82, fig 37.44.

G492 SHEARS
Goltho, Lincolnshire.
Croft A: late Saxon to late 14th or early 15th century.
Arm, blade and handle broken. L 95mm.
Goodall 1975a, 82, fig 37.43.

G493 SHEARS
Benedictine Priory, Coventry, Warwickshire.
Site: founded 1043, dissolved 1538.
Complete. L 94mm.
Herbert Art Gallery and Museum, Coventry, 49/227/430. For site see Hobley 1971.

G494 SHEARS
Stonar, Kent.
c1275 to 1385.
Bow and one blade broken. L 100mm.
Excavated by N Macpherson-Grant.

G495 SHEARS
Seacourt, Oxfordshire.
Site: mid to late 12th to mid 14th century.
Complete. L 138mm.
Biddle 1961–62, 172, fig 29.2, scale 1:4, not 1:3.

G496 SHEARS
Goltho, Lincolnshire.
Probably late 14th to early 15th century.
Complete. L 138mm.
Goodall 1975a, 82, fig 37.45.

G497 SHEARS
Wintringham, Cambridgeshire.
Around early 14th century.
Handle broken. L 136mm.
Goodall 1977a.

G498 SHEARS
Clarendon Palace, Wiltshire.
Site: c1072 to later 15th century.
Blade and bow broken. L 144mm.
Goodall 1988, fig 75.27. Borenius and Charlton 1936.

G499 SHEARS
Seacourt, Oxfordshire.
Site: mid to late 12th to mid 14th century.
Complete. L 149mm.
Biddle 1961–62, 172, fig 29.3, scale 1:4, not 1:3.

G500 SHEARS
Goltho, Lincolnshire.
Early 14th century.
Complete. L 144mm.
Goodall 1975a, 82, fig 37.46.

G501 SHEARS
Baginton, Warwickshire.
15th century.
Complete. L 147mm.
Wilkins 1975, 126, fig 8.14.

G502 SHEARS
Waltham Abbey, Essex.
16th century.
Arm with broken blade and handle. L 86mm.
Excavated by P J Huggins. From Romeland.

G503 SHEARS (not illustrated)
Great Yarmouth, Norfolk.
12th century.
Looped bow, one blade tip broken. Heavily corroded. L 231mm.
Rogerson 1976, 166, fig 52.18.

G504 SHEARS (not illustrated)
Lydney Castle, Gloucestershire.
12th century, possibly into 13th century.
Looped bow, blades largely lost. L 175mm.
Casey 1931, 251, pl XXXV.1.

G505 SCISSORS
South Witham, Lincolnshire.
Late 13th century to 1308–13.
Centrally set finger loops, one broken. Blades broken. L 81mm.
Goodall 2002, fig 7.1, no. 11.

G506 SCISSORS
Stonar, Kent.
c1275–1385.
Arm with centrally set finger loop and broken blade. L 151mm.
Excavated by N Macpherson-Grant.

G507 SCISSORS
Avebury, Wiltshire.
Early 14th century.
Centrally set finger loop and blade tip of one arm broken. L 175mm.
Keiller 1965, 178, pl XXVIb.

G508 SCISSORS
Northolt Manor, Greater London.
1350–70.
Blades and remaining centrally set finger loop broken. L 116mm.
Excavated by J G Hurst.

G509 SCISSORS
Woodperry, Oxfordshire.
12th–14th century.
Complete. Centrally set finger loops.
L 120mm.
Ashmolean Museum, Oxford, 1823.58 (illustration from sketch in Accessions Register; object missing).

G510 SCISSORS
Woodperry, Oxfordshire.
12th–14th century.
Centrally set finger loops and blades broken.
L 130mm.
Ashmolean Museum, Oxford, 1873.59. For site see Wilson 1846.

G511 SCISSORS
Criccieth Castle, Gwynedd.
Site: c1230–1404.
Centrally set finger loops. Blade tips broken.
L 141mm.
O'Neil 1944–45, 41, pl IX.14.

G512 SCISSORS
Hadleigh Castle, Essex.
Probably late in occupation from 1230 to mid 16th century.
Broken, centrally set finger loops. Blade tips lost. L 137mm.
King 1869, 77; Drewett 1975, 96–97.

G513 SCISSORS
Beckery Chapel, Glastonbury, Somerset.
Later 13th to ?15th century.
Centrally set finger loops, one broken. Blade tips broken. L 182mm.
Rahtz and Hirst 1974, 61, fig 22.15.

G514 SCISSORS
Winchester, Hampshire.
Late 15th–16th century.
Centrally set finger loops, one broken.
L 169mm.
Goodall 1990-17, fig 260.2878.

G515 SCISSORS
Somerby, Lincolnshire.
Site: 11th to mid 16th century.
Centrally set finger loops and blades all broken. L 116mm.
Mynard 1969, 84, fig 13.1W89.

G516 SCISSORS
Weoley Castle, Birmingham, West Midlands.
Site: c1080–1600.
Centrally set finger loops and blades all broken. L 113mm.
Birmingham City Museum, WC 328. For site see Oswald 1962.

G517 SCISSORS
Gomeldon, Wiltshire.
Topsoil in yard outside late 13th to 14th-century buildings.
Asymmetrically set finger loops. One blade broken. L 101mm.
Excavated by J W G Musty.

G518 SCISSORS
Northolt Manor, Greater London.
1300–50.
Arm with asymmetrically set finger loop.
Blade broken. L 117mm.
Musty and Algar 1986.

G519 SCISSORS
Wharram Percy, North Yorkshire.
Mid 15th to early 16th century.
Asymmetrically set finger loops, blade tips broken. L 99mm.
Goodall 1979a, 123, fig 64.102.

G520 SCISSORS
Cheddar, Somerset.
Early 13th century to c1600.
Aysymmetrically set finger loops, one broken.
L 136mm.
Goodall 1979d, 266, fig 90.3.

G521 SCISSORS
Upton, Gloucestershire.
Mid to later 13th century.
Blade, tip lost, broken across base of handle.
L 94mm.
Rahtz 1969b, 108, fig 12.89A.

KNIVES, SHEARS AND SCISSORS

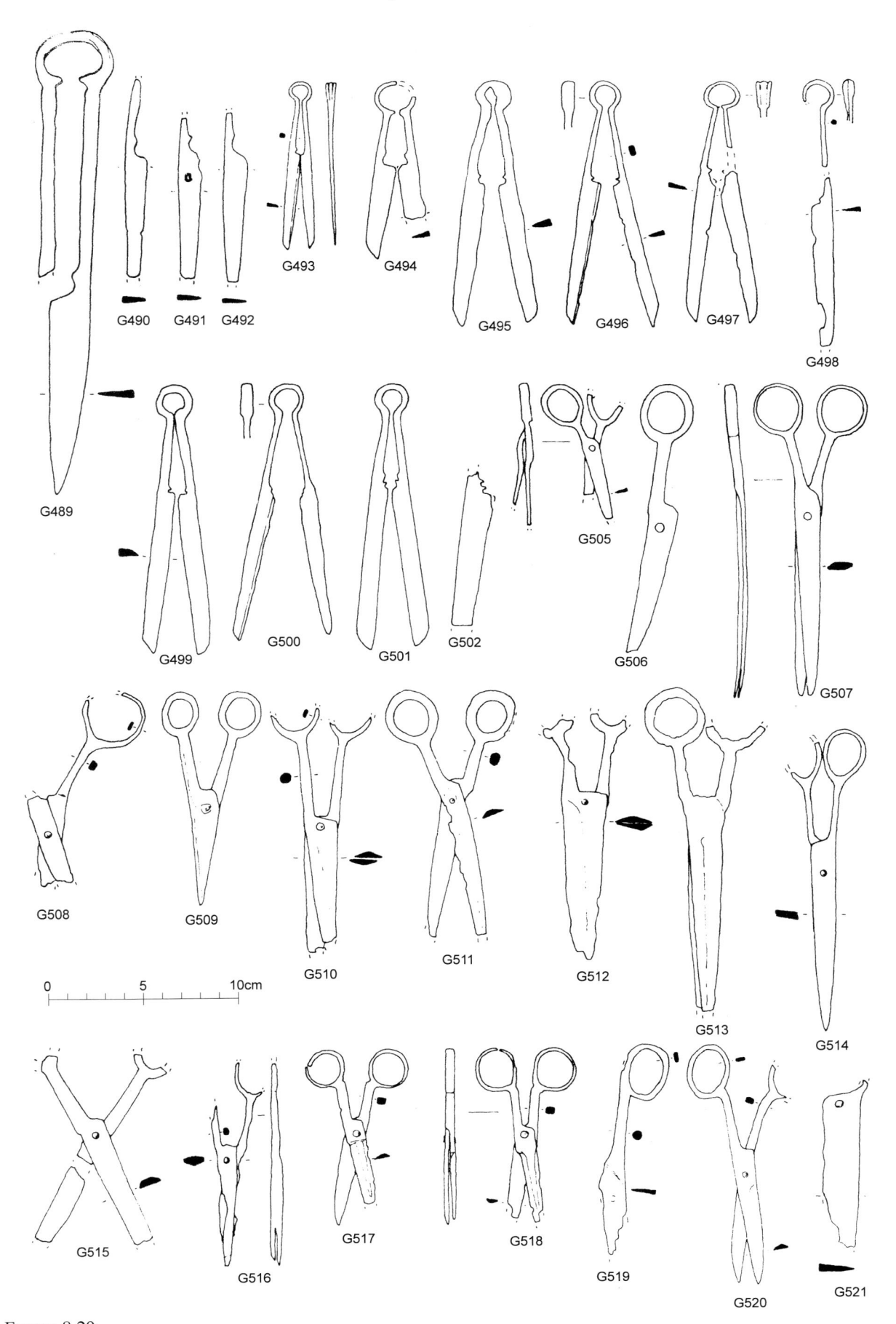

FIGURE 8.29
Shears and scissors

9

BUILDING IRONWORK AND FURNITURE FITTINGS

Standing buildings, surviving furniture, documents and excavated finds combine to provide an overall picture of the ironwork associated with the construction and use of medieval buildings. This chapter is divided into two sections, the first of which considers structural ironwork and includes items such as masonry cramps, timber dogs, ties, staples, wallhooks and nails. The second section deals with door, window and furniture fittings, and includes hinge pivots, hinges, casket fittings, hasps, keyhole plates, latch rests, door bolts, handles and window ironwork. Locks and keys, and household fittings, are discussed in succeeding chapters.

9.1 STRUCTURAL IRONWORK

Masonry cramps

Stones were normally bound together with mortar, but cramps such as the 66 'crampettes of iron made for the cramping and joyning of harde stone togethers' mentioned in the Westminster accounts of 1532 (Salzman 1967, 289) were sometimes used to secure them, particularly those which projected or which were set at an angle at which they might slip. Other documentary references indicate the size and position of cramps. For St Stephen's Chapel, Westminster, for example, payment was made in 1334 'for 18 iron called *tyrauntz*, 2 feet in length and 2 inches in breadth each way, for the work of the gable towers' and for '12 crampons ... for fastening stones of various shapes in the high work of the two towers beside the gables', and in 1399 '126 crampons weighing 143 lb' were bought for the great window in the gable of the King's hall at Westminster (Salzman 1967, 289). These references evidently relate to the main structure of buildings, but cramps were also used for fireplaces, as at Corfe in 1292 where there is payment 'for clamps for the fireplace' (Salzman 1967, 290), and for various other fittings.

Cramps were set in grooves cut between stones with their backs fitting tightly but their arms set in wider holes and secured with lead. Masonry with evidence for iron cramps run in lead includes that from chimneys at Criccieth Castle, Gwynedd (O'Neil 1944–45, 44), and cramp **H4** retains some lead. None of the excavated medieval cramps **H1–9** approaches the two foot length of one of the documented cramps, all being somewhat smaller. In form they are pieces of bar or strip iron with down-turned ends, and all have straight backs with the exception of **H6–9**, distorted by extraction during demolition.

Documents indicate that iron in the form of straps and hoops was also used to bind stonework and strengthen it. A Westminster account of 1531, for example, mentions '2 iron hoops for the top of the western turret of the chapel', and at York in 1364 'iron bars for setting in the mantels of the chymnes' are mentioned (Salzman 1967, 298–290). Perhaps some strap fragments, particularly the larger ones, had such uses and are not from hinges.

Timber dogs

Timber dogs, long rectangular staples with straight backs and pointed down-turned ends, had various uses in woodworking including securing logs onto the frame over a sawing pit and holding heavy timbers in position when they were used as shores on buildings or in shipyards. Salaman (1975, 172, fig 254) notes that modern dogs vary from about 150 to 450mm in length with ends turned down at right angles or pointing in opposing directions and sharpened, often to a chisel-shaped point. Timber dogs were also used in the structure of a building. Salzman (1967, 291) notes that the term 'dog' is frequently used for a bar or band of iron joining or strengthening woodwork, as with '8 dogges of iron for mending the rafters... of the roof, each dogge weighing 15 lb', 'x grete clampes of yron for the bynddyng of the princyples weyng ciiij^{xx} xvj lb' and 8 'dogges of irne' weighing 164 lb with 'pynnes and revettes serving for the same'. Work at Gloucester Castle in 1442 involved '2 iron dogges' used on the repair of the drawbridge (Salzman 1967, 291), and accounts for the erection of King's Hall, Cambridge, in 1338 include payment for '6 crampes of iron for fastening beams to posts' (Salzman 1967, 207).

None of the timber dogs **H10–16** approaches the size of some larger ones quoted, but all have straight backs and the two most complete, down-turned ends (**H10** and **H16**). All surviving ends are pointed rather than chisel-shaped.

Beam stirrups

Beam stirrups were used to bind timbers together or to support them, particularly after alteration. Salzman (1967, 291) quotes payment in 1497 for 'iij stays and a litill sterope and a forth right dogge of iryn for the rodelofte' of St Mary-at-Hill, and for 'two iron instruments called stiroppys for binding the wheel of the well' at Clarendon, Wiltshire, in 1482. Post-medieval stirrups such as those from Chingley, Kent (Goodall 1975d, 68–70, fig 34.68) and Louisbourg, Canada, are typically U-shaped with side straps, either twisted or twisted and bent over, nailed to the beam (Dunton 1972, 211–213, figs 103–104). **H17** is incomplete and has no side twist, but it maybe some type of stirrup.

Hooked bracket

The hooked bracket **H18** may have supported guttering, the projecting stop being used to hammer the pointed shank into timber. Salzman (1967, 266) notes mention of 'iij stiroppes of iron made for the assurance of a gutter of lead' at Westminster in 1532.

Ties

Ties were alternatives to the timber dog and stirrup which were used for binding timbers together and strengthening the junctions between them. The most common type is the angle tie, a right-angled piece of iron with arms tapering to a point, of which **H19–25** are medieval examples. Most are relatively small, but **H24–25** are larger and approach the size of certain timber dogs. **H26–28** are shaped ties, all incomplete, and evidently made for a specific purpose.

Staples

Staples are variously rectangular, U-shaped and looped, and they were used to bind wood together and to attach fittings to wood and stone. The term staple is perhaps not entirely appropriate for all these uses, but it is a convenient one to apply to all these related objects.

Rectangular staples

Rectangular staples have arms which are either longer or shorter than the overall width of the staple. **H29–50** are all of greater length than width, and are between 20 and 96mm in width, the majority exceeding 50mm. The smaller staples must have had many uses, and some for the middle-sized ones may have acted as bolt keepers on door jambs, as the inner shaping on **H40–41** in particular suggests. A number of the larger staples may have been used as timber dogs, not necessarily driven completely into the wood. Salaman (1975, 172, fig 253) notes that modern timber dogs used for driving into the ends of two boards to keep them together while glueing, are between 50 and 100mm wide.

Rectangular staples of greater width than length have arms which are either straight, have inturned ends, or have clenched inturned ends. **H51–81** have straight arms which are generally broken, although complete ones vary from 16 to 48mm in length, and they are 24 to 106mm wide. The arms are either wedge-shaped or tapering and pointed, both suitable for being driven into timber or joints in masonry. The backs have straight or curved sides, some broadening out in the centre in a manner reminiscent of some roves used on doors and hatches (see below).

H82–95 have straight arms with inturned ends which were either driven into wood or wrapped around it like binding. Surviving examples range from the slight (**H83**) to the substantial (**H95**), widths varying from 33 to 114mm, lengths from 14 to 59mm.

H96–106 are rectangular staples with clenched inturned tips which were driven into the wood. They vary in width from 35 to 79mm, although most are over 48mm wide, and nearly all have short arms. **H103** is the only example with arms exceeding 26mm.

U-shaped staples

U-shaped staples are the most numerous of all the different types of staple, and only the most complete examples have been catalogued. U-shaped staples are of two types, the majority (**H107–146**) having straight arms, the remainder (**H147–154**) arms with out-turned tips. These staples were driven into masonry joints or wood, the latter type evidently entirely through the wood since the tips are clenched over, producing a more securely fixed staple. Most of the staples are under 40mm in width, and in length between two and three times their width. These staples must have been used to hold the chains and hasps on doors and gates, and to support tethering rings and various types of handle. **H141** still retains the decoratively twisted ring **H656** which, from its form, must have been a handle.

Looped staples

Looped staples **H155–171** have similarly shaped arms to those of the other staples, those of **H155–159** being straight, of **H160–163** out-turned, and of **H164–165** out-turned and clenched. **H166–171** are incomplete.

Looped staples are ideally shaped for holding chains or handles in position, their arms being driven into, or more often through, wood. **H165** retains one link from a chain, and the two incomplete staples **H166** and **H170**, which retain ring handles, recall those on a 14th-century chest which hold substantial mule slings in position (Jenning 1974, 4–5, pl VI). Several of the staples have broad loops, and it is possible that they held handles on doors or chests in the manner of some on an early 16th-century travelling chest (Jenning 1974, 5, pl VII), or held sliding bolts on doors or on items of furniture such as armoires (Eames 1977, 29–30, pls 14–15).

Wall-hooks

Wall-hooks with tapering shanks are all-purpose hooks which were driven into wood or masonry joints. There are two main types with the hook rising either directly from the end of the shank or before its end.

H172–193 have hooks rising from the end of the shank, and they are found throughout the medieval period. Their size range is considerable, and the hooks are either straight-backed or curved. Wall-hooks **H194–221**, with hooks rising before the end of the shank, are a late medieval type which is found principally in 13th-century and later contexts. Their sizes vary, and the hooks are not commonly recurved. A few are straight backed or merely a single curve.

Hooks

Hooks of various types, of which wall-hooks are the most common, were used in and around medieval buildings. **H222–224** are one of the less common types of hook with shanks which have terminal expansions with shallow depressions. The form of the shank was probably intended to bed firmly in the mortar of a masonry joint. **H222–224** have upright hooks in contrast to the U-shaped hooks of **H225–227**, two of which have looped shanks and the other an angled, pointed one.

Eyed spike and ring

The eyed spike **H228** with a closed eye holding a ring and a long shank driven into a wall is yet another fitting used to attach chains, etc, to walls. Unlike the open hooks of wall-hooks and other hooks, the closed eye would permanently secure any chain forged through it.

Looped straps

H229–230 are straps which were set into walls with the loop projecting beyond the face. **H229** with its lead caulking was evidently set in masonry, whilst **H230** with its clenched tip is from a site with timber-framed buildings. The loop was intended to support fittings or have them inserted into it.

Wall anchors

Wall anchors with tapering shanks and flattened heads were used to attach wood to masonry and brickwork, the shank being driven into a mortar joint and the head resting against the wood, holding it in place. Specific uses for wall anchors include holding door and window frames in walls, and securing the framing to which panelling was attached.

H231 is the only wall anchor with its head in line with the shank, and the head itself broken. **H232–235** have heads at right angles to the shank, that of **H234** perforated for a nail to attach it to the wood and prevent the shank loosening in the wall. The two surviving heads are of flattened oval shape, and **H232** retains horizontal wood graining across its inner face.

Holdfast

H236 resembles a wall anchor but has a flattened terminal on its shank, indicating that it was driven through wood and then spread. It was probably used to hold two pieces of wood together.

S-hooks

H237–241 are small S-shaped hooks which may have been used to secure slipped tiles on roofs.

Nails

Nails are ubiquitous finds on most excavations, as might be expected since documentary references frequently price them in thousands. Purchases made at Wye Fair for the needs to Canterbury Cathedral in 1273, for example, totalled 40,000 nails, and accounts for the erection of part of the college of King's Hall, Cambridge, in 1378 include 18,000 nails (Salzman 1967, 304, 206–207).

Salzman (1967, 303–317) discusses the many types and sizes of nail mentioned in medieval documents, and Figure 9.1 shows the types of timber nail isolated from large assemblages at Waltham Abbey, Essex (Goodall 1973a, 175, fig 13.1–9, Table 3), Ospringe, Kent (Mold 1979, 149–150, fig 30.1–9, Table 2) and Stonar, Kent (excavated by N Macpherson-Grant):

— Type 1: flat head of square, rectangular or rounded shape.
— Type 2: raised head of circular or rounded rectangular shape.
— Type 3: flat head of narrow, rectangular shape.
— Type 4: faceted rectangular head.
— Type 5: flat head of figure-eight shape.
— Type 6: flat rectangular head formed by flaring, wedge-shaped shank.
— Type 7: flat L-shaped head.
— Type 8: headless nail.
— Type 9: stud with long, flat rectangular head.
— Type 10: stud with rectangular or occasionally rounded flat or faceted head.
— Type 11: stud with rectangular pyramidal head.
— Type 12: stud with circular head.

Clench bolts and roves

Clench bolts, which are nails or studs whose shank tips are clenched over shaped plates known as roves, were used in ship-building and for other double thickness timber construction including doors and covers. The rove prevented the nail tip pulling through the wood and made a secure join.

H242–244 are examples of complete medieval clench bolts assembled from variously shaped component parts. **H244** is from the cover **H404** which originally closed the top of the well at Lydford Castle, Devon, and one of many church doors of identical ledge and batten construction is that at Stillingfleet, North Yorkshire (Addyman and Goodall 1979, 84, 90, figs 9, 22). **H245–250** are a series of differently shaped roves, the latter three like that of **H244** being shaped to the profile of the ledge they clasped. **H251–253** indicate the method of forging rectangular and lozenge-shaped roves from strips of iron by punching nail-holes and then cutting off individual roves with a chisel.

9.2 DOOR, WINDOW AND FURNITURE FITTINGS

Hinge pivots

Doors, gates, shutters and windows were hung on iron hinge pivots set either in wood or stone. The range in size and form of surviving hinge pivots reflects these varied circumstances.

Type 1. Vertical hinge pivots

Harr-hung doors which pivoted on the top and bottom ends of their hanging stiles survived in use in recent times on barns and other farm buildings (Innocent 1916, 239–245). The upper end of the stile projected above the top of the door and was worked into a point which turned in a hole in the underside of the lintel. An iron pin set into

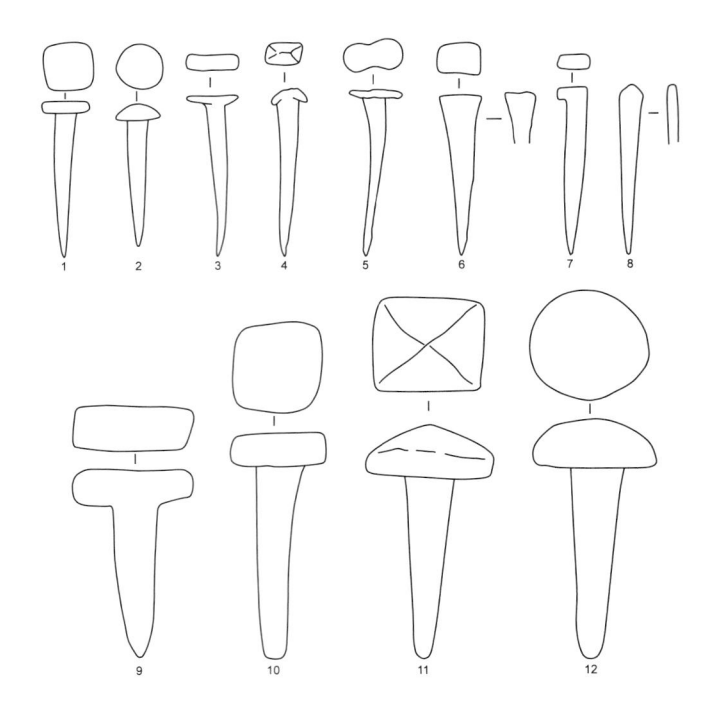

FIGURE 9.1
Types of medieval nail

the base of some hanging stiles turned in a hole in the threshold, and the timber was sometimes strengthened by an iron strap. Salzman (1967, 295) interprets a hoop and gudgeon mentioned in the 1532 accounts of King's Hall, Cambridge, as binding for the spindle or pivot and the socket in which it turned, but notes no other certain entry in medieval building records for this method of hanging.

H254–255 must, however, be related to this method of hanging, particularly since **H254** was found in a gateway through a boundary wall with mortar adhering to its shank. **H255**, which has a cranked shank, must also have been set in the ground.

Type 2. Hinge pivots with tapering shanks

This type of pivot occurs in far greater numbers than any of the other types, and consequently only the more complete or intrinsically interesting examples (**H256–369**) have been catalogued. The type is commonest because of its simple and practical form, which enabled the shank to be driven into wood or into a masonry joint. Most shanks are straight, but the clenched tips of **H256**, **H309**, **H349**, **H360**, **H365** and others imply that they either passed completely through timber or encountered an obstruction when being driven in. Hinge pivots set in masonry rather than in mortar joints had to be secured in lead, and **H297** and **H347**, and probably **H359**, retain this.

The shanks and guide arms of these hinge pivots are frequently of similar width at their junction, although a number, including **H256**, **H299** and **H330** have deepened

164

shanks. The deepening may be the incidental result of forging, or it may have been intended to give an impression of strength, an illusory impression since the shanks are generally of slender cross section. The turning hinge has worn into the top of the shanks of a number of hinge pivots, including **H292**, **H301**, **H323** and **H352**.

The pivots vary considerably in size, and they clearly carried everything from shutters to large doors and gates. **H264**, **H327**, **H341-342**, **H355** and **H367** were found with hinges, and they provide an indication of the possible uses of those found in isolation.

Type 3. Hinge pivots with down-turned shanks

This type of pivot, of which **H370–379** are examples, was set in a mortice cut in masonry and was normally secured with lead, which survives on **H372–375** and **H379**. Salzman (1967, 296) notes entries at Corfe in 1285: 'to a mason making mortices for setting hooks', and 'to Walter Plogge, who made the mortices in which the hooks for doors and windows were set with lead'. Being set in the stonework, such hinges are sometimes called 'stone hinges', as at St Paul's in 1490: 'stonehengis with iron hooks', or at Westminster in 1491: 'a pair of iron stonehokes used for hanging the door at Cheynegate'. 'Hooks' and 'crooks' are the normal words for hinge pivot in medieval documents.

H370–379 characteristically have broad flat shanks which may or may not taper in side view, and which are either parallel-sided or expand towards the down-turned end. **H370–378** may have carried doors or shutters, but the massive shank fragment **H379** must come from a major gateway.

Type 4. Hinge pivots with bifurcated shanks

These hinge pivots were also set in masonry, the bifurcated tip preventing them pulling out as well as anchoring them firmly in place. **H380** and **H381** are complete, the latter as well as the other shank fragments **H382** and **H383** retaining lead caulking. The shanks are all parallel-sided. **H384**, the massive guide arm from a hinge pivot which probably had a bifurcated shank, is from Wolvesey Palace, Winchester, and must have carried a major gate.

Hinges

Hinges were used on doors, gates, window shutters, trapdoors and well covers around buildings, as well as on items of furniture such as chests and armoires, and the varied sizes and types of hinge reflect these many uses. The hinges have been classified according to the way in which they were hung. Strap fragments are discussed separately, as are small hinges and bindings which may be from caskets. Documentary references to hinges are discussed by Salzman (1967, 295–299).

Hinges with looped eyes

The looped eyes of this type of hinge, represented by **H385–410**, generally fitted over a hinge pivot, and while the loops are most commonly closed and either forged in with the strap (**H388**) or butted against its rear face (**H390**, **H393**, **H399**) others are open (**H398**). The looped eye is flush with the rear of the strap on **H385–400**, offset on **H401–409**, and cranked on **H410**. In use the hinge was nailed in place in the way demonstrated by **H404**, and the offset looped eyes are particularly well suited for well covers, trapdoors and large doors.

The majority of these types of hinge have horizontal straps, but **H402–403** are crescent-shaped and **H401** is T-shaped.

Hinges with nailed U-shaped eyes

The nailed U-shaped eye found on hinges **H411–448** provided a secure way of attaching iron to wood since in use both the strap and rear terminal of the eye were nailed in place. The same nail sometimes penetrated both strap and terminal (**H420**), or two separate nails were used (**H417**). The guide arm of the hinge pivot fitted into the void between the edge of the door and the hinge eye.

H411–439 are complete or retain a considerable length of their strap; **H440–445** are U-shaped eyes, **H446–448** are the rear terminals of the eyes. The hinges all have horizontal straps of differing size and form, some parallel-sided, others tapering, some with plain terminals, others bifurcated. To give strength to the eye, the rear arm was almost invariably forged into a terminal which was most frequently lozenge-shaped (**H414**, **H432**, **H446**) but also rounded (**H444**) or rounded and pointed (**H440**, **H448**). The maximum length of most rear arms is 100mm, but added security was given to larger hinges by extending the arm and increasing the number of nail-holes. **H413** has such a rear arm, and **H412** may originally have had one.

Hinges with spiked U-shaped eyes

Hinges with this type of eye (**H449–456**) were used in conjunction with end-looped hinges (**H449–456**) particularly on items of furniture such as chests. **H454** in fact, which retains an end-looped stapled hasp, must be from a chest. In use the spiked end of the eye passed through the loop and was then driven into the wood. Small examples of this type of hinge are discussed under casket fittings below, but otherwise **H449–453** have parallel-sided or tapering straps, **H452** a shaped terminal, **H453** a plain one.

End-looped hinges

End-looped hinges were used in conjunction with spiked U-shaped eyed hinges such as **H449–456**, but they also formed part of some stapled hasps, as **H457** indicates. Incomplete end-looped straps such as **H457a** and **H458** could, therefore, be from either stapled hasps or hinges, and the small size of both suggests that they are from caskets. Larger end-looped straps are identical to bucket handle escutcheons, and the two cannot always be certainly distinguished.

Pinned hinges

The pinned hinge is formed from two straps which turn on a common pin. The single looped projection on the end of one strap fits between a pair on the other, and a pin holds the two together. **H459–471** are pinned hinges, most probably from doors, cupboards or chests, although **H463** carries a stapled hasp which must be from a chest. Several of the pinned hinges are represented by single straps of various shapes, but of those which retain both straps, most (**H469–471**) have identically shaped leaves. **H459**, of a T-shape, is the only one to be certainly asymmetrical.

Strap hinge terminals

A complete study of hinges cannot be made without reference to those surviving on medieval church doors and items of furniture, and the discussion below excludes detailed consideration of ecclesiastical iron-work. The catalogued hinges, however, come from a wide range of buildings, including peasant houses, town houses, manor houses, castles and churches.

C-shaped hinges

C-shaped hinges are not depicted in English manuscripts before the late 11th century, but this form, often with a central strap, is the commonest type in use on 12th-century English church doors, and it continued in use until the 14th-century.

H472, known only form a photograph, must have lost its looped eye. No nail-holes are visible and, like **H402**, it has lost its terminals. The only other C-shaped hinge (**H403**) retains small end-scrolled terminals, and it and the other hinges come from contexts which do not contradict the dating implied by ecclesiastical examples.

Strap hinges

Hinges with straight straps and either parallel or tapering sides are the most common form of medieval hinge, and they occur with a variety of terminal shapes. **H433**, **H436** and **H473–476** taper to plain ends, whilst **H387** and **H426** have square-cut, slightly up-turned ends. The splayed terminal found on hinges **H406**, **H417–418**, **H427**, **H432**, **H464** and **H477–482** was a simple shape for the blacksmith to forge, as was the rounded terminal of **H417–418**, **H434–435** and **H483–486** and lozenge-shape of **H429**, **H438** and **H487–489**. These simple shapes have little chronological value, and they were clearly in common use on town and village house doors and on the lesser doors of the greater houses. It is of interest that the rounded and lozenge-shaped terminals of some of these hinges reappear on the rear terminals of the eyes of some elaborate scrolled hinges.

The end scroll appears as a subsidiary element in some complex hinge terminals, but on **H403**, a C-shaped hinge, and on **H490**, it is a terminal form in its own right. The bifurcated terminal, found throughout the medieval period on all sizes of hinge (**H386**, **H411**, **H419–420**, **H491–497**), most frequently takes the form of a double scroll. **H419** is exceptional in having a round, perforated end to its one complete terminal arm. The fleur-de-lis form of **H498** is common on early church doors and is related to the complex scrolled terminals common on church doors from the late 12th until the 14th century. **H404** has a cluster of four tight scrolls forming its terminal, several combining forward and backward scrolls with a fleur-de-lis motif (**H499–502**). **H503** has two pairs of scrolls, the inner ones recurved, and **H504** pairs of scrolls attached to the sides of the strap. **H505–507** are fragmentary scrolls.

T-shaped hinges

Salzman (1967, 297–298) identifies the 'garnet' of medieval documents as T-shaped hinge whose short crossbar was fastened to the frame of the door. Surviving examples are rare, however. **H401** combines the T-shaped strap with a looped eye, but **H459** is pinned.

Strap shapes

Most hinges have straps with parallel or tapering sides, but a few are shaped. Isolated expansions occur on **H485–486** and **H508–510**, and side scrolls are forged onto **H504**. Several pinned hinges have shaped straps or plates, and **H511** with its three heart-shaped lobes is probably from such a hinge.

The terminal was the most elaborate part of most hinges, but **H501–502** have surface decoration as well. **H502** has a narrow bar with simple geometrical chiselled decoration, and **H501** has raised edges and chiselled lines.

Corner bindings

A number of the strap hinges discussed above must have come from chests or coffins, and these fittings sometimes had their corners reinforced with iron (Eames 1977, pls 38, 41 and 46). **H512** is from a wooden coffin surrounding a lead-encased skeleton, and **H513–514** are of related type, the latter from the position of its nail head evidently set inside the chest or coffin. **H515** and **H516** are lengths of solid corner binding, the latter with holes at the corners for nails.

Casket fittings

In addition to the larger hinge and strap fragments there are smaller hinges and lengths of binding strip which probably come from portable items of furniture such as caskets, coffers and reliquaries. The hinges, binding strips and mounts on these objects are more usually of copper alloy, but iron was an alternative metal, even if it was forged and plated in imitation of the nobler metal.

Hinges

H517–528 are small hinges with, where they are sufficiently complete, looped, spiked and end-looped eyes or pinned hinges. All are shaped in some way, and **H527–528** have elaborate surface decoration as well, the decoration also present on the stapled hasp which the latter supports. Non-ferrous plating has been revealed on several of the hinges, but not analysed.

Binding strip and mounts

The lengths of iron binding strip **H529–559** are generally shaped and moulded, and several also have chiselled decoration. X-radiographs almost invariably reveal non-ferrous plating.

H529–534 are plain lengths of strip, **H534** retaining a complete pointed end and a small domed rivet, but the remainder are incomplete. **H535–540** are further mid-length strips, all straight in side view unless distorted. **H535** has a central ridged section, the others rounded and occasionally moulded expansions. **H541–554** all retain one terminal, but they are otherwise incomplete. **H541–547** have plain strips, **H548–553** have at least one mid-length expansion, and **H554** is bifurcated. The terminals are both rounded and foliate, and a few are moulded, and **H544–545** and **H550** are angled in side view, the others flat. **H555–556** are multi-lobed strips, **H557–559** either sinuous or scrolled, **H558** having surface decoration which recalls that on **H528**.

H560–564 are short mounts or clamps, originally symmetrical with perforated terminals at each end. Smaller copper-alloy examples were used to hold parts of reliquaries together (Pinder-Wilson and Brooke 1973), and these iron examples may have served a similar purpose on slightly larger caskets. All are flat, and only **H564** has any decoration.

Stapled hasps

Stapled hasps **H565–590** were used in conjunction with fixed locks on chests, caskets and doors, and they are either end-looped (Type 1) or have pinned hinges (Type 2).

Type 1. End-looped stapled hasps

Stapled hasps **H565–574** have both rounded and rectangular end loops for attachment to supporting hinges, one of which survives on **H570**. This hinge has a spiked U-shaped eye like those of **H449–456**, the spike being driven into the wood of the chest from which the hasp no doubt came.

Type 2. Stapled hasps with pinned hinges

Stapled hasps **H575–583** all have pinned hinges, which survive in varying degrees of completeness on **H577–578**, **H580–581** and **H583**. The method of assembling the pinned hinge is most clearly demonstrated by **H580**, and this indicates how the single central looped eye of the less complete examples operated.

Incomplete stapled hasps

H584–590 are fragmentary shaped hasps incapable of certain classification.

Discussion

Stapled hasps were used with fixed locks with sliding bolts such as **H142–146**, the bolts passing through the D-shaped staples and closing the lock. Medieval chests show that the straps or hinges to which the stapled hasps were attached were nailed either to the outside or inside of chest lids (Jenning 1974, pls I–V, VII; Eames 1977, pls 36, 37A, 38, 45, 48–52), and that the locks were either set flush with or behind the face of the wood, or projected beyond its face. Most stapled hasps are straight in side view, indicating their use with locks set flush with the wood, but a few (**H572–573** and **H583**) are angled. Many have a hooked or thickened base which enabled them to be lifted out of the lock when released, and this is frequently simply shaped as on **H569**, **H576** and **H581**, but on **H572**, **H574** and **H577** it is moulded. **H571** and **H579** have simple raised bars, **H590** a knob. The hasps vary in shape, some such as **H570**, **H571** and **H581** bring more or less plain rectangles with or without a shaping to the tip, while others taper in one or other direction or expand around the staple. The L-shaped staple hasp **H590** is similar in shape to some plate hasps on a late 14th-century chest at Winchester College (Eames 1977, 165–167, pl 46B). Surface decoration is found on **H577**, **H583** and **H585**, and several have non-ferrous plating.

End-looped stapled hasps are found in contexts of 11th to 14th-century date, whereas pinned stapled hasps are known throughout the medieval period.

Hasps

Hasps were used to hold gates and doors on buildings closed and to fasten the lids of coffers and chests, and they are of two main types: looped or pinned. The former is more commonly found. In use the hasp fitted over a projecting staple, where it was secured by a padlock. On gates in particular, where secure locking was not required, simple wooden sticks may have been used instead.

Type 1. Looped hasps

Looped hasps are most frequently figure-eight shaped (**H591–626**), but a few are of elongated oval shape (**H627-629**). The figure-eight shape is the more secure of the two since one of its two loops was used for suspension while the other closed round the staple to which a padlock could be fixed. The figure-eight shaped hasps characteristically have two unequal loops formed by narrowing the central opening. The degree of narrowness varies, the sides sometimes touching, and a few (**H624–626**) actually have solid or near solid centres which create two independent loops in one hasp. Figure-eight shaped hasps may be further sub-divided; **H591–595** are flat, **H596–618** and **H624** curved, and **H619–623** and **H625–626** angled. This shaping reflects the way in which they were used, and the reconstruction of well cover **H404** shows the curved hasp **H624** in place on the edge. A medieval chest in Lancham church, Nottinghamshire (Mercer 1969, pl 28) has both straight and angled hasps. The elongated and shaped hasps **H627–629** are similarly straight, angled and curved.

The majority of hasps have hooked ends which enabled them to be lifted with greater ease, and **H596** has a ring. It is impossible to be certain that all those without hooks or rings are hasps, since some could be chain links, but **H604** is certainly a hasp since it retains part of the end-looped hinge **H457** which attached it to a chest. The hasps are mainly of plain iron, but a few are spirally twisted. The spirally twisted hasps are restricted to 12th and 13th-century contexts whereas plain ones are found throughout the medieval period.

Type 2. Pinned hasps

H630–631 are pinned hasps, both with pairs of looped eyes which originally joined a pinned strap. Chests with similar hasps include one in the Public Record Office, London (Jenning 1974, 4–5, pl VI).

Incomplete hasps

H632–633 are parts of broken hasps, **H632** from a figure-eight shaped hasp, **H633** not classifiable but of interest for its elongated hooked end which may have held a ring, as do those on a 13th-century chest from Voxtorp, Sweden (Mercer 1969, pl 29).

Keyhole plates

Manuscript illuminations sometimes show shaped metal plates around keyholes on doors, and **H634–638** are excavated examples of triangular, rectangular and elongated oval shape. All have nail-holes at the corners or ends for small nails or studs. **H639** has no deliberate hole and may have been used for decorative effect to balance a keyhole plate such as **H634**.

Handles

Door handles and carrying and lifting handles from chests and caskets are mainly rectangular and circular shape. **H640–648** are rectangular drop handles which were held in place by U-shaped or looped staples around each arm. A number of the small handles may be from caskets, but the others are more likely to be from chests, although actual examples on medieval chests are frequently curved rather than flat in side view (Jenning 1974, pl VI; Eames 1977, pls 49, 51A, 52). The rectangular and U-shaped handles **H649–650** and **H653** have perforated terminals and may be from chest or casket lids. The basal straps of **H651–652** imply that they may come from trapdoors or hatches.

Ring handles such as **H654–657** may be from house doors or from furniture, since a 14th-century representation of a house (Hartley and Elliott 1931, pl 27c) shows one on a door, and they are also found on items of furniture such as armoires (Eames 1977, pls 4–6). On chests similar rings frequently acted as lifting rings, as with two pairs on a chest in Hereford Cathedral (Eames 1977, pls 50A–B) and the rows of rings on one from Voxtorp, Sweden (Mercer 1969, pl 29). Larger lifting rings similar to **H657** but suspended from chains or long iron arms are known on chests from Cound, Shropshire (Eames 1977, pl 42B) and London (Jenning 1974, pl VI). The latter chest also has subsidiary handles similar to **H658–659**.

The precise use of M-shaped handles **H660–662** is uncertain, but **H660** and **H662** appear to have pivoted. The broken flattened end of **H660** may imply a use connected with a lock.

Latches and latch rests

Latches, frequently termed 'haggadays', occur in a number of medieval documents (Salzman 1967, 299–300), and at Hadleigh Castle there is mention in 1363 of '6 rings with lacches and kacches', the rings forming the handle by which the latch was raised. Iron rings of various sizes are known, and no latch has yet been certainly recognised, but **H663–671** are probably the 'kacches' or latch rests.

Latch rests **H663–671** were set in the jambs and reveals of doors and windows to hold latches closed, and all have triangular-shaped heads with blunted ends. **H663–669** have tapering shanks which, like those of hinge pivots, were driven into wood or into masonry joints. The tip of the shank of **H667** is clenched, indicating that is passed completely through the wood it was driven into, and those of **H668–669** are bent through a right angle. **H670** is of unusual form in having a slender split shank, unfortunately incomplete, which may be from a furniture door or an internal door in a building. **H671** was set in a cut stone mortice since its shank retains the lead caulking which secured it in place. The hole in the base of the head may have held a link or chain.

Door flail

Salzman (1967, 301) notes that folding doors and entrance gates were often fastened by means of a 'flail' or 'sweep', an iron bar pivoted at the centre so that when the gates were shut it could be brought horizontally across them, each end fitting into an iron hook or plate which was often provided with a hasp by which the bar could be locked in position. **H672**, a flat strap with tapered ends and central rivet hole, may be such a flail.

Door bolts

H673–681 are sliding door bolts of various types, **H673–679** having straight bolts with single finger grips, shaped and decorated on **H678** and extended on **H679**. **H680** has a cranked, stapled handle which suggests that it was used in conjunction with a projecting fixed lock, as is the bolt on a 12th-century armoire at Obazine, France (Eames 1977, 21–25, pls 10–11). A 15th-century armoire from Malines, Belgium, has straight stapled handles in use with flush-set locks (Eames 1977, 29–30, pls 14–15).

H681 is the most substantial door bolt, and in use its short cranked arm was bedded in the door jamb. One of two U-shaped mounts survives, and **H682** is another from a different site.

Door and window hooks

Hooks **H683–685** may have been used to hold either doors or windows open. All have looped ends which are formed in differing ways and short hook arms.

Window ironwork

Iron used in window construction served the three purposes of strengthening the construction, excluding intruders and supporting any glazing (Salzman 1967, 291–292). The ironwork of a window, consisting of upright and transverse bars, was sometimes known as a 'ferment', and windows of more than one light usually had a horizontal 'stay-bar' running from side to side through the mullion, and a number of smaller bars, parallel to it, in each light. Bars made with eyes to fit round the upright 'standards' are often called 'lockets' in medieval documents, and the smaller bars to which glazing was wired and soldered, 'soudelets' (Salzman 1967, 293).

A number or iron grilles and individual bars from them are known, but a significant find are eight blocks of Totternhoe stone from a window probably inserted in a cellar at the palace in Kings Langley in 1388. The window **H686** originally contained an iron grille with eight horizontal and six vertical bars, but only the mortices now survive. Their position indicates that the horizontal bars must have had eyes for the passage of the vertical ones.

Three iron grilles **H687–689**, distorted and incomplete, are known from Weoley Castle. **H687** has five horizontal bars with lead caulking on each complete arm end and rectangular slots for four vertical bars. **H688–689** have horizontal bars which, where complete, have five eyes for the vertical rods. **H690–693** are further eyed window bar fragments with rounded and rectangular eyes either set centrally or offset. The precise position will have determined how near any shutters could close against them in an unglazed window. **H694–697** are probably incomplete vertical window bars, the last a stub set in lead caulking.

Small windows did not require grills with horizontal and vertical members, and individual horizontal bars such as **H698–705** were used. **H698–699** were probably set in mortices cut in stonework, and the others nailed onto timber window frames.

H706 is the type of window bar found in use in churches, cathedrals and other buildings with large glazed windows. It was nailed against the inner edge of a timber window frame and the leaded panel of glass rested on the backs of the seven internally projecting plates. Wedges through these plates prevented the glass above and below the bar from moving.

Grilles were not restricted to windows. At Launceston in 1460, 86 lb of iron was used 'for mending a grill which lies over le pitte in which thieves and felons are put in ward' (Salzman 1967, 293), and an iron sluice gate was found in a drain at Prestbury Moat, Gloucestershire (O'Neil 1956, 15).

H1 CRAMP
Goltho, Lincolnshire.
Croft A: late Saxon to late 14th or early 15th century.
Back straight, arms complete. L 125mm.
Goodall 1975a, 86, fig 40.78.

H2 CRAMP (not illustrated)
Ospringe, Kent.
Demolition c1550–70 on site founded c1230.
Back broken and distorted, one arm lost.
Goodall 1979c, 129, no. 26.

H3 CRAMP
Clarendon Palace, Wiltshire.
Site: c1072 to later 15th century.
Back straight, arms near complete.
L 125mm.
Goodall 1988, fig 75.29; Borenius and Charlton 1936.

H4 CRAMP
Southampton, Hampshire.
1350–1400.
Broken cramp retaining lead caulking.
L 88mm.
Harvey 1975b, 285, fig 255.2074.

H5 CRAMP
Newminster Abbey, Northumberland.
Site: 1137 to early 16th century.
Back broken, flat curved arm. L 168mm.
Harbottle and Salway 1964, 168, fig 30.83.

H6 CRAMP
Ospringe, Kent.
Demolition c1550–70 on site founded c1230.
Back straight, arms complete. L 146mm.
Goodall 1979c, 129, fig 20.25.

H7 CRAMP
Rievaulx Abbey, North Yorkshire.
Site: 1131–1538 with later robbing.
Distroted straight back, arms complete.
L 116mm.
DAMHB Collection, London, RVA 226(L).

H8 CRAMP
Rievaulx Abbey, North Yorkshire.
Site: 1138–1538 with later robbing.
Distorted, straight back, arms complete.
L 134mm.
DAMHB Collection, London, RVA 226(C).

H9 CRAMP
Rievaulx Abbey, North Yorkshire.
Site: 1138–1538 with later robbing.
Distorted straight back, arms complete.
L 145mm.
DAMHB Collection, London, RVA 226(M).

H10 TIMBER DOG
Wintringham, Cambridgeshire.
Site: late 12th to early 14th century.
Straight back, broken down-turned ends.
L 202mm.
Goodall 1977a, 257, fig 45.53.

H11 TIMBER DOG
Bayham Abbey, East Sussex.
In rubble from frater in southern cloister walk. Medieval.
Broken back, one complete end. L 101mm.
Goodall 1983a, 106, no. 9.

H12 TIMBER DOG
South Witham, Lincolnshire.
1137–85 to c1220.
Broken straight back and down-turned end.
L 72mm.
Goodall 2002, fig 7.3, no. 41.

H13 TIMBER DOG
Winchester, Hampshire.
14th–?15th century.
Incomplete. L 86mm.
Goodall 1990-10, fig 78.513.

H14 TIMBER DOG
Aldingham, Lancashire.
Mid 12th century.
Strap broken. L 145mm.
Excavated by B K Davison.

H15 TIMBER DOG
Princes Risborough, Buckinghamshire.
13th century to late 14th or early 15th century.
Broken straight back, one complete down-turned end. L 114mm.
Pavry and Knocker 1953–60, 163, fig 13.9.

H16 TIMBER DOG
Oxford.
16th century.
One arm broken. W 127mm.
Excavated by N Palmer.

H17 BEAM STIRRUP(?)
Waltham Abbey, Essex.
c1540.
Strap with broken ends pointing in opposite directions. L 183mm.
Huggins 1972. From f64, Building I.

H18 HOOKED BRACKET
Northampton.
c1470 to 1500.
Bracket with tapering shank, projecting stop and semicircular section U-shaped hook.
W 127mm.
Goodall 1978c, 152, fig 24.5.

H19 ANGLE TIE
King's Lynn, Norfolk.
c1350–1500.
Complete. L 67 by 44mm.
Goodall and Carter 1977, 296, fig 134.58.

H20 ANGLE TIE
London.
?Late 13th to mid 14th century.
One arm broken. L 62 by 60mm.
Henig 1974, 195, fig 40.107.

H21 ANGLE TIE
Winchester, Hampshire.
Late 13th–?early 14th century.
Arms complete. L 76 by 57mm.
Goodall 1990-10, fig 79.539.

H22 ANGLE TIE
Criccieth Castle, Gwynedd.
Site: c1220 to 1404.
One arm broken. L 74 by 52mm.
O'Neil 1944–45, 42, pl X.23.

H23 ANGLE TIE
North Elmham Park, Norfolk.
c1150 to c1600.
One arm broken. L 112 by 22mm.
Goodall 1980a, 513, fig 267.84.

H24 ANGLE TIE
Winchester, Hampshire.
Late 12th–?early 13th century.
One arm broken. L 143 by 90mm.
Goodall 1990-10, fig 79.538.

H25 ANGLE TIE
Ospringe, Kent.
c1483 to 1550.
One arm broken. L 175 by 25mm.
Goodall 1979c, 129, fig 20.27.

H26 TIE
Duffield Castle, Derbyshire.
Keep built 1177–90, demolished 1266.
Incomplete shaped tie with clenched tip.
L 157mm.
Derby Museum. Cox 1887.

H27 TIE
Pleshey Castle, Essex.
Post-1140 or possibly 1180 to late 12th or earlier 13th century.
Incomplete shaped tie with clenched tip.
L 43mm.
Goodall 1977c, 177, fig 39.28.

H28 TIE
Clarendon Palace, Wiltshire.
Site: c1072 to later 15th century.
Incomplete shaped tie. L 138mm.
Goodall 1988, fig 80.89. For site Borenius and Charlton 1936.

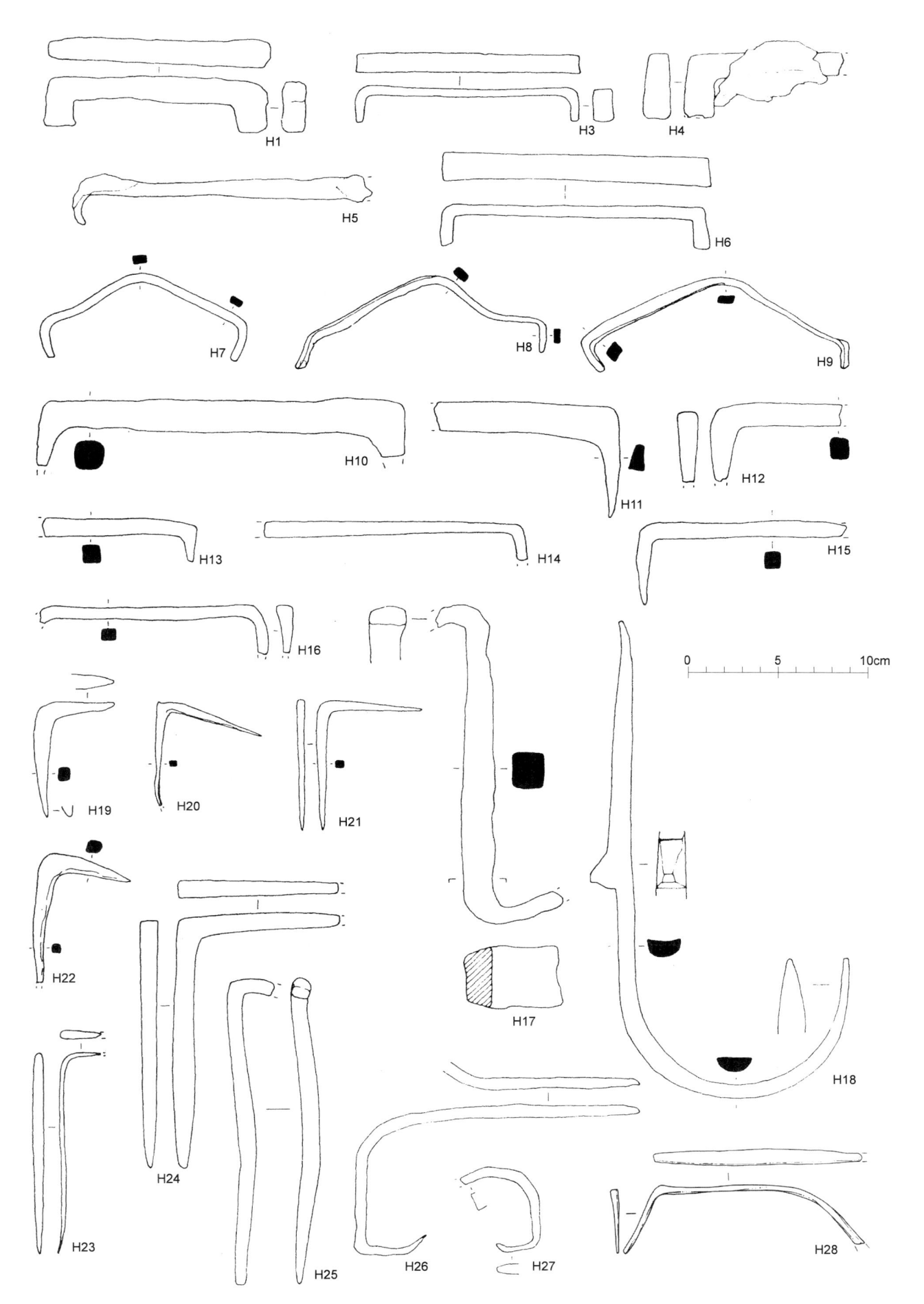

FIGURE 9.2
Cramps, timber dogs, beam stirrup, hooked bracket, angle ties, and ties

H29 STAPLE
Northampton.
Later 15th century.
Rectangular staple, arm broken. L 35mm, W 20mm.
Goodall *et al* 1979, 273, fig 119.72.

H30 STAPLE
Oxford.
Late 12th century to *c*1250.
Rectangular staple. L 23mm, W 22mm.
Goodall 1977e, 142, fig 26.22.

H31 STAPLE
Northampton.
*c*1250 to 15th century.
Rectangular staple, one arm broken. L 30mm, W 24mm.
Goodall *et al* 1979, 273, fig 119, 71.

H32 STAPLE
Goltho Manor, Lincolnshire.
*c*1100–1150.
Rectangular staple, arms broken. L 31mm, W 26mm.
Goodall 1987, fig 158.79.

H33 STAPLE
Strixton, Northamptonshire.
Late 13th century.
Rectangular staple, arm broken. L 46mm, W 26mm.
Hall 1973, 113, fig 4.32.

H34 STAPLE
Clough Castle, Co. Down.
*c*1200 to *c*1225.
Rectangular staple, arms broken. L 51mm, W 34mm.
Waterman 1954, 140, fig 12.7.

H35 STAPLE
Wharram Percy, North Yorkshire.
Late 15th to early 16th century.
Rectangular staple, arms broken. L 45mm, W 46mm.
Goodall 1979a, 118, SF 12423.

H36 STAPLE
Wintringham, Cambridgeshire.
Site: late 12th to early 14th century.
Rectangular staple, arms broken. L 56mm, W 53mm.
Goodall 1977a, 257, fig 45.46.

H37 STAPLE
South Witham, Lincolnshire.
1137–85 to *c*1220.
Rectangular staple, arms broken. L 93mm, W 50mm.
Goodall 2002, fig 7.3, no. 35.

H38 STAPLE
Northampton.
Robbing of late 15th, early 16th-century building.
Rectangular staple, arms broken. L 71mm, W 54mm.
Goodall *et al* 1979, 273, fig 119.73.

H39 STAPLE
Castell-y-Bere, Gwynedd.
Site: *c*1221 to 1295.
Rectangular staple. L 128mm, W 56mm.
Butler 1974, 97, fig 8.22.

H40 STAPLE
Waltham Abbey, Essex.
15th century.
Rectangular staple, internal shaping, arms broken. L 76mm, W 58mm.
Goodall 1978d, 158, fig 21.7.

H41 STAPLE
Criccieth Castle, Gwynedd.
Site: *c*1230 to 1404.
Rectangular staple, broken shaped arms. L 62mm, W 62mm.
O'Neil 1944–45, 41, pl X.21.

H42 STAPLE
Ospringe, Kent.
Demolition *c*1550–70 on site founded *c*1230.
Rectangular staple, arms broken. L 73mm, W 60mm.
Goodall 1979c, 129, fig 20.28.

H43 STAPLE
Waltham Abbey, Essex.
Lower topsoil over destruction debris of 1540.
Rectangular staple. L 101mm, W 63mm.
Huggins 1972, 124.

H44 STAPLE
Wintringham, Cambridgeshire.
Site: late 12th to early 14th century.
Rectangular staple, arms broken. L 96mm, W 64mm.
Goodall 1977a, 257, fig 45.48.

H45 STAPLE
Goltho, Lincolnshire.
Croft A: late Saxon to late 14th or early 15th century.
Rectangular staple, one arm broken. L 67mm, W 65mm.
Goodall 1975a, 86, fig 40.81.

H46 STAPLE
Northolt Manor, Greater London.
1300–1350.
Rectangular staple, arms broken. L 91mm, W 69mm.
Excavated by J G Hurst.

H47 STAPLE
Alsted, Surrey.
*c*1250–1405.
Rectangular staple, arms broken. L 70mm, W 74mm.
From Site 3. See Ketteringham 1976.

H48 STAPLE
Wroughton Copse, Fyfield Down, Wiltshire.
*c*1150 to 1315.
Rectangular staple. L 144mm, W 80mm.
Excavated by P J Fowler.

H49 STAPLE
North Elmham Park, Norfolk.
*c*1150 to *c*1600.
Rectangular staple. L 97mm, W 88mm.
Goodall 1980a, 513, fig 267.75.

H50 STAPLE
North Elmham Park, Norfolk.
*c*1150 to *c*1600.
Rectangular staple, broken arms. L 87mm, W 96mm.
Goodall 1980a, 513, fig 267.76.

H51 STAPLE
Lyveden, Northamptonshire.
*c*1250 to 1350.
Rectangular staple, arms broken. L 5mm, W 33mm.
Steane and Bryant 1975, 132, fig 49.162.

H52 STAPLE
Stonar, Kent.
*c*1275 to 1385.
Rectangular staple. L 29mm, W 40mm.
Excavated by N Macpherson-Grant.

H53 STAPLE
King's Lynn, Norfolk.
*c*1250 to 1350.
Rectangular staple. L 34mm, W 40mm.
Goodall and Carter 1977, 296, fig 134.55.

H54 STAPLE
Lyveden, Northamptonshire.
1475 to 1500.
Rectangular staple, arm broken. L 22mm, W 44mm.
Steane and Bryant 1975, 132, fig 50.171.

H55 STAPLE
Stonar, Kent.
*c*1275 to 1485.
Rectangular staple, back distorted. L 17mm, W 44mm.
Excavated by N Macpherson-Grant.

BUILDING AND FURNITURE FITTINGS

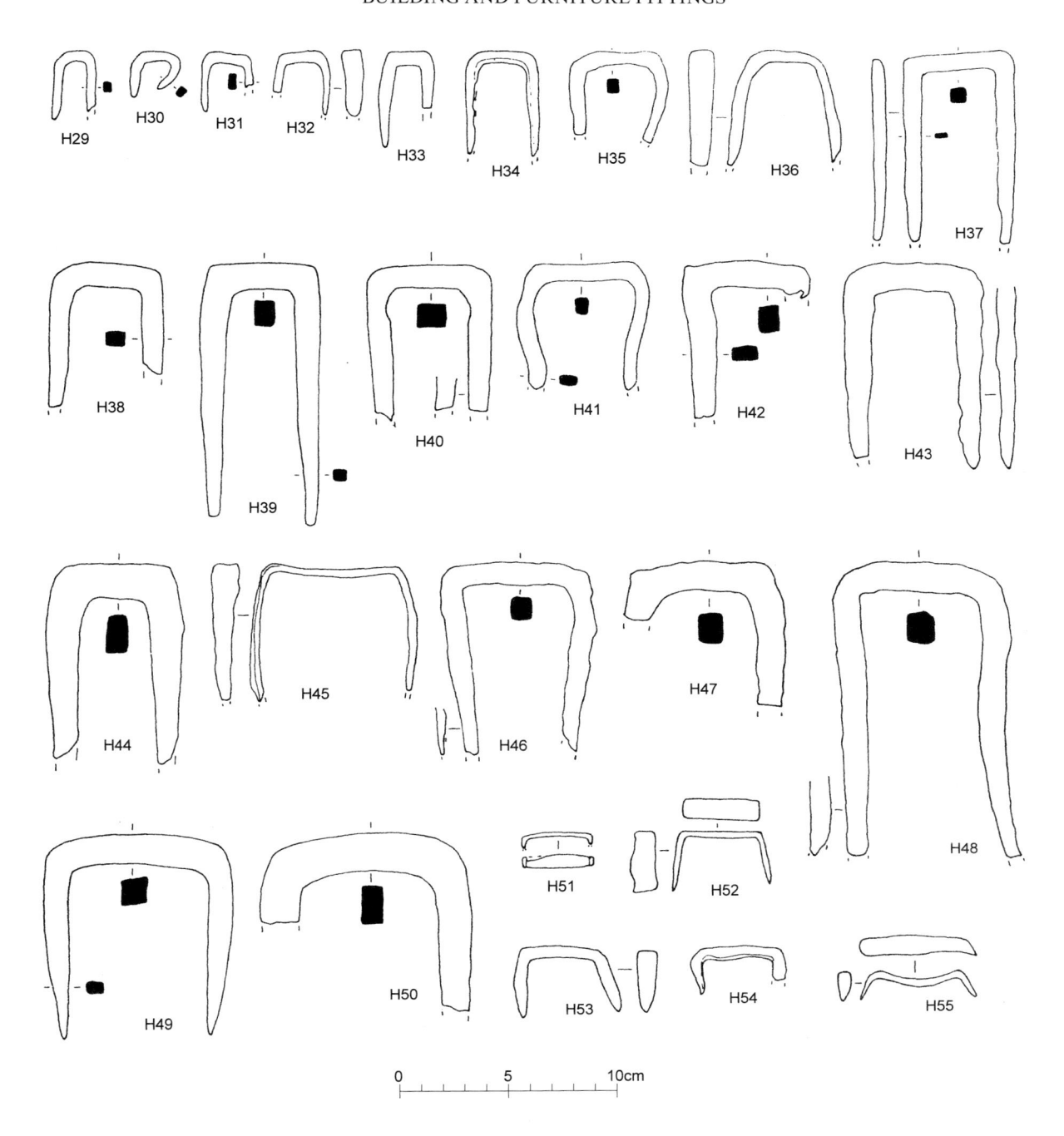

FIGURE 9.3
Staples

H56 STAPLE
Stonar, Kent.
*c*1275 to 1385.
Rectangular staple, arms broken, wood graining across underside. L 20mm, W 44mm.
Excavated by N Macpherson-Grant.

H57 STAPLE
Stonar, Kent.
*c*1275 to 1385.
Rectangular staple. L 29mm, W 48mm.
Excavated by N Macpherson-Grant.

H58 STAPLE
Tattershall College, Lincolnshire.
11th century to 1440.
Rectangular staple, arm broken. L 13mm, W 51mm.
Excavated by L J Keen.

H59 STAPLE
South Witham, Lincolnshire.
Late 13th century to 1308–13.
Rectangular staple, arms broken. L 19mm, W 52mm.
Goodall 2002, fig 7.3, no. 34.

H60 STAPLE
Stonar, Kent.
*c*1275 to 1385.
Rectangular staple, arms broken, wood graining across underside. L 16mm, W 54mm.
Excavated by N Macpherson-Grant.

H61 STAPLE
Stonar, Kent.
*c*1275 to 1385.
Rectangular staple, broken, with wood graining across underside. L 15mm, W 54mm.
Excavated by N Macpherson-Grant.

H62 STAPLE
Stonar, Kent.
*c*1275 to 1385.
Rectangular staple, one arm broken, wood graining across underside. L 25mm, W 58mm.
Excavated by N Macpherson-Grant.

H63 STAPLE
Stonar, Kent.
*c*1275 to 1385.
Rectangular staple. L 19mm, W 58mm.
Excavated by N Macpherson-Grant.

H64 STAPLE
Stonar, Kent.
*c*1225 to 1275.
Rectangular staple, arms broken. L 17mm, W 58mm.
Excavated by N Macpherson-Grant.

H65 STAPLE
Faringdon Clump, Oxfordshire.
Late 13th to 14th century.
Rectangular staple, one arm distorted. W 59mm, L 17mm.
Ashmolean Museum, Oxford. Leeds 1936; 1937.

H66 STAPLE
Lyveden, Northamptonshire.
*c*1350 to 1450.
Rectangular staple, arms broken. L 11mm, W 62mm.
Steane and Bryant 1975, 133, fig 50.175.

H67 STAPLE
Waltham Abbey, Essex.
13th century.
Rectangular staple. L 32mm, W 60mm.
Excavated by P J Huggins. Romeland, F64.

H68 STAPLE
Oxford.
Late 12th century to *c*1250.
Rectangular staple, arms broken. L 11mm, W 61mm.
Goodall 1977e, 142, fig 26.26.

H69 STAPLE
Northampton.
?Late 14th–15th century to 17th century.
Broken rectangular staple. L 35mm, W 64mm.
Goodall 1979b, 71, fig 17.22.

H70 STAPLE
Waltham Abbey, Essex.
Second half 15th century.
Rectangular staple, one arm broken. L 18mm, W 73mm.
Excavated by P J Huggins. Romeland, F111.

H71 STAPLE
Grenstein, Norfolk.
Late 14th, ?early 15th century.
Rectangular staple, arms broken. L 15mm, W 72mm.
Goodall 1980c, fig 77, no. 25.

BUILDING AND FURNITURE FITTINGS

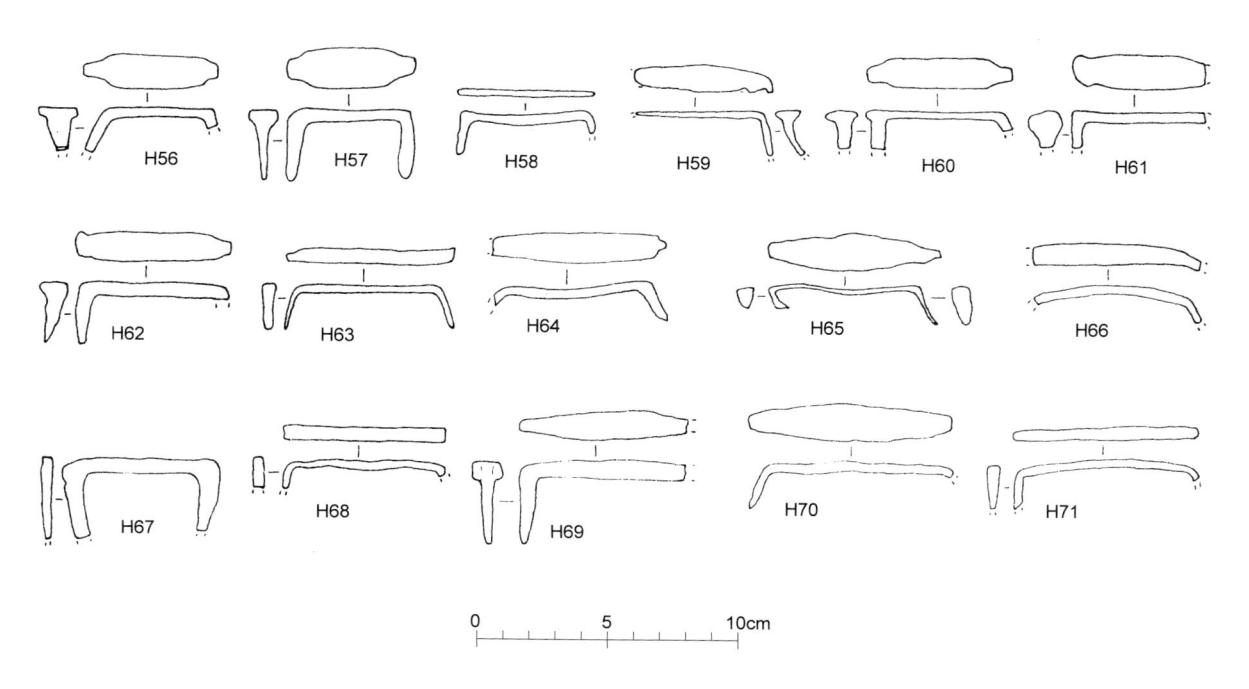

FIGURE 9.4
Staples

H72 STAPLE
Lyveden, Northamptonshire.
Early 13th century to first half 14th century.
Rectangular staple. L 19mm, W 69mm.
Bryant and Steane 1969, 44, fig 18j.

H73 STAPLE
Old Sarum, Wiltshire.
Principally medieval, to 14th century.
Rectangular staple. L 51mm, W 76mm.
Salisbury and South Wiltshire Museum, Salisbury, 8/1932, O.S.C112.

H74 STAPLE
Winchester, Hampshire.
13th century.
Distorted rectangular staple. L 28mm, W 76mm.
Goodall 1990-10, fig 78.527.

H75 STAPLE
Waltham Abbey, Essex.
Destruction level of 1540.
Rectangular staple. L 33mm, W 82mm.
Huggins 1972, 124 (from F64).

H76 STAPLE
Wintringham, Cambridgeshire.
Site: late 12th to early 14th century.
Rectangular staple, arms broken. L 33mm, W 84mm.
Goodall 1977a, 257, fig 45.52.

H77 STAPLE
Wroughton Copse, Fyfield Down, Wiltshire.
c1150 to 1315.
Rectangular staple, arms broken. L 15mm, W 85mm.
Excavated by P J Fowler.

H78 STAPLE
London.
Late 15th to early 16th century.
Rectangular staple, arms distorted or broken. L 33mm, W 88mm.
Excavated by F Willmot. Site at 66 Foyle Road.

H79 STAPLE
North Elmham Park, Norfolk.
c1150 to c1600.
Rectangular staple, arm broken. L 22mm, W 98mm.
Goodall 1980a, 513, fig 267.81.

H80 STAPLE
Upton, Gloucestershire.
Late 13th to late 14th century.
Rectangular staple, one arm broken.
L 48mm, W 105mm.
Hilton and Rahtz 1966, 121, fig 14.20.

H81 STAPLE
London.
Late 15th to early 16th century.
Rectangular staple, one arm broken. L 37mm, W 106mm.
Excavated by F Willmot. Site at 66 Foyle Road.

H82 STAPLE (not illustrated)
Winchester, Hampshire.
13th century.
Distorted and broken rectangular staple with inturned arms. L 37mm, W 33mm.
Goodall 1990-10, 335, no. 531.

H83 STAPLE
London.
Around later 14th century.
Rectangular staple with inturned arms, one broken. L 20mm, W 35mm.
Henig 1974, 195, no. 111.

H84 STAPLE
Dyserth Castle, Clwyd.
Site: 1241 to 1263.
Rectangular staple, inturned arms. L 14mm, W 40mm.
National Museum of Wales, Cardiff, 15–248/14.

H85 STAPLE
Winchester, Hampshire.
13th century.
Rectangular staple with inturned arms.
L 34mm, W 40mm.
Goodall 1990-10, fig 78.532.

H86 STAPLE (not illustrated)
Winchester, Hampshire.
Mid 12th–early 13th century.
Rectangular staple with inturned arms.
L 22mm, W 42mm.
Goodall 1990-10, 335, no. 529.

H87 STAPLE
Wroughton Copse, Fyfield Down, Wiltshire.
c1150 to 1315.
Distorted rectangular staple with inturned arms. L 23mm, W 44mm.
Excavated by P J Fowler.

H88 STAPLE
London.
Late 13th to 14th century.
Rectangular staple, arms ?distorted.
L 22mm, W 45mm.
Henig 1974, 195, no. 115

H89 STAPLE
Goltho Manor, Lincolnshire.
c late 11th century.
Rectangular staple, inturned arms. L 35mm, W 49mm.
Goodall 1987, fig 158.82.

H90 STAPLE
Winchester, Hampshire.
Mid 13th century.
Rectangular staple, one arm broken, other with inturned end. L 16mm, W 92mm.
Goodall 1990-10, 335, no. 530.

H91 STAPLE
London.
Late 13th to 14th century.
Severely distorted rectangular staple with inturned arm. L 17mm approx. W 53mm.
Henig 1974, 195, no. 100.

H92 STAPLE
Faxton, Northamptonshire.
Site: 12th to 15th century.
Rectangular staple with broken inturned arms. L 21mm, W 57mm.
Excavated by L A S Butler.

H93 STAPLE
King's Lynn, Norfolk.
c1250–1350.
Rectangular staple with inturned arms.
L 22mm, W 57mm.
Goodall and Carter 1977, 296, fig 134.56.

H94 CRAMP
Northampton.
Late 13th to 15th century.
Broken rectangular cramp. L 45mm, W 92mm.
Goodall 1979b, 71, fig 17.19.

H95 STAPLE
Ospringe, Kent.
Demolition c1550–70 on site founded c1230.
Rectangular staple with inturned arms.
L 59mm, W 114mm.
Goodall 1979c, 129, fig 20.29.

H96 STAPLE
London.
Late 13th to mid 14th century.
Rectangular staple with clenched inturned arms, one broken. L 20mm, W 34mm.
Henig 1974, 195, fig 40.110.

H97 STAPLE
Goltho, Lincolnshire.
Croft A: late Saxon to late 14th or early 15th century.
Rectangular staple with incomplete clenched, inturned ends. L 19mm, W 42mm.
Goodall 1975a, 86, fig 40.80.

BUILDING AND FURNITURE FITTINGS

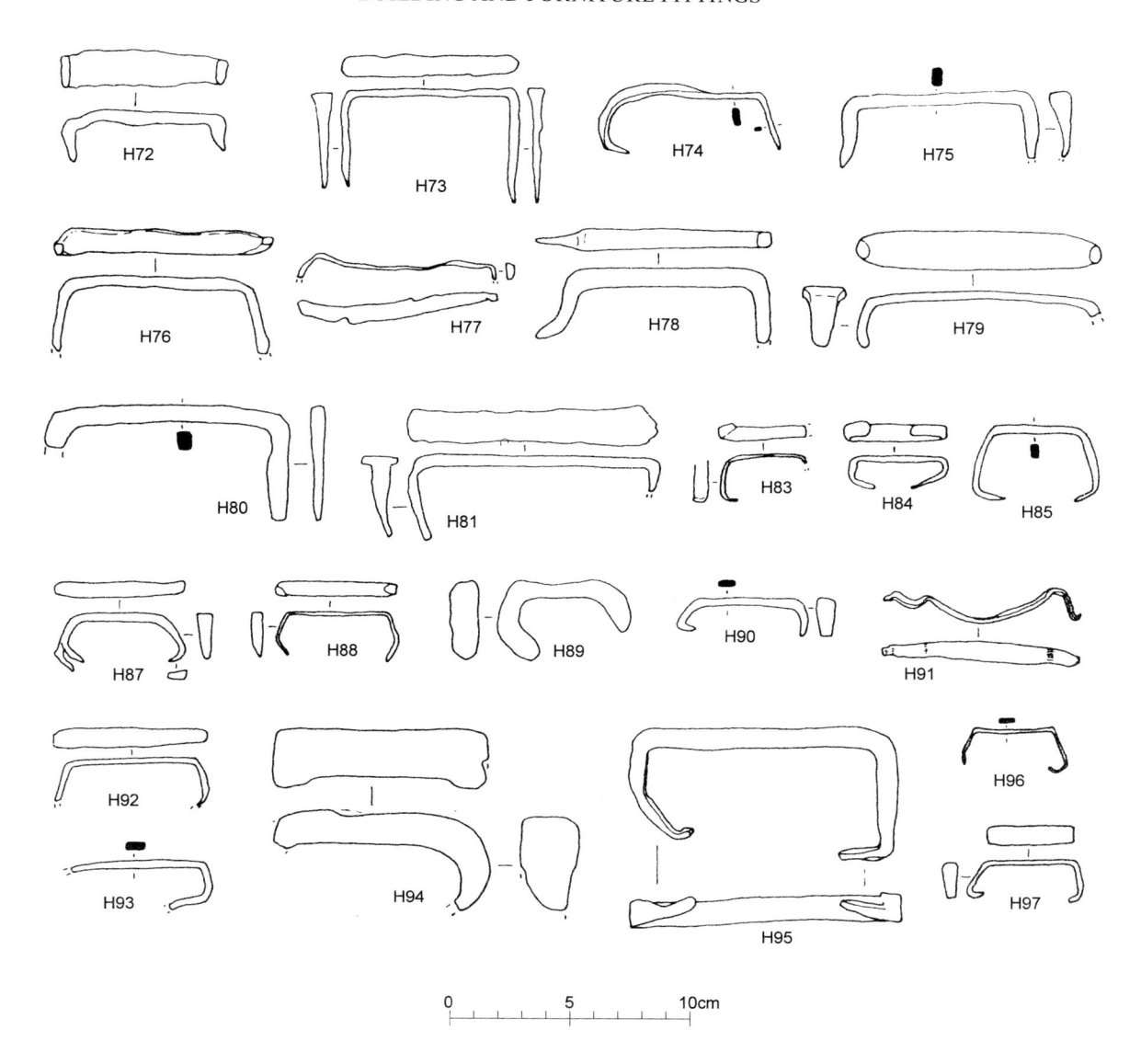

FIGURE 9.5
Staples

H98 STAPLE
Wintringham, Cambridgeshire.
Late 13th century.
Rectangular staple, clenched inturned arms.
L 16mm, W 48mm.
Goodall 1977a, 257, fig 45.51.

H99 STAPLE
Netherton, Hampshire.
Medieval.
Rectangular staple with clenched inturned arms. L 21mm, W 52mm.
Goodall 1990-28, fig 9.4, no. 197.

H100 STAPLE
London.
Roman to 14th century (probably medieval).
Rectangular staple with clenched inturned arms. L 18mm, W 58mm.
Henig 1974, 195, no. 119, from XIV-7, not XXI-7.

H101 STAPLE
Wroughton Copse, Fyfield Down, Wiltshire.
c1150 to 1315.
Rectangular staple with clenched inturned arms, one broken. L 16mm, W 59mm.
Excavated by P J Fowler. WC 460.

H102 STAPLE
Goltho Manor, Lincolnshire.
c1100–1150.
Rectangular staple with clenched inturned arms, one broken. L 24mm, W 59mm.
Goodall 1987, fig 158.83.

H103 STAPLE
Durham.
Later 11th–mid 12th century.
Rectangular staple with clenched inturned arms, one broken. L 62mm, W 43mm.
Carver 1979, 18, fig 13.69/1607.

H104 STAPLE
Winchester, Hampshire.
c1093.
Rectangular staple with inturned arms.
L 22mm, W 65mm.
Goodall 1990-10, fig 78.528.

H105 STAPLE
Burnham Church, Humberside.
c1300–1320 rebuilding.
Rectangular staple with broken, clenched, inturned arms. L 26mm, W 64mm.
Excavated by G Coppack.

H106 STAPLE
London.
Late 13th to 14th century.
Rectangular staple with clenched inturned arm. L 12mm, W 79mm.
Henig 1974, 195, no. 114, from III-16, not II-16.

H107 STAPLE
Lyveden, Northamptonshire.
Second half 13th century.
U-shaped staple, one arm broken. L 33mm, W 14mm.
Bryant and Steane 1971, 65, fig 17t.

H108 STAPLE
Winchester, Hampshire.
13th century.
U-shaped staple, tips distorted. L 37mm, W 18mm.
Goodall 1990-10, fig 78.521.

H109 STAPLE
South Witham, Lincolnshire.
Late 13th century to 1308–13.
U-shaped staple. L 40mm, W 25mm.
Goodall 2002, fig 7.3, no. 37.

H110 STAPLE
Northampton.
14th century.
U-shaped staple. L 44mm, W 28mm.
Goodall et al 1979, 273, fig 119.69.

H111 STAPLE
Grenstein, Norfolk.
Late 14th, ?early 15th century.
U-shaped staple, arms broken. L 45mm, W 24mm.
Goodall 1980c, fig 77, no. 26.

H112 STAPLE
Northampton.
Late Saxon to 15th century.
U-shaped staple. L 47mm, W 22mm.
Goodall et al 1979, 273, fig 119.70.

H113 STAPLE
Rhuddlan, Clwyd.
1241–64.
U-shaped staple. L 48mm, W 17mm.
Goodall 1994, fig 17.3, no. 34.

H114 STAPLE
London.
?Late 13th to mid 14th century.
U-shaped staple, one arm broken. L 50mm, W 12mm.
Henig 1974, 195, fig 40.116.

H115 STAPLE
Bramber Castle, West Sussex.
?14th century.
U-shaped staple, arms broken. L 50mm, W 23mm.
Barton and Holden 1977, 66, fig 20.16.

H116 STAPLE
Goltho, Lincolnshire.
Croft A: late Saxon to late 14th or early 15th century.
U-shaped staple, arm tips broken. L 52mm, W 24mm.
Goodall 1975a, 86, fig 40.84.

H117 STAPLE
Lyveden, Northamptonshire.
c1250 to 1350.
U-shaped staple, one arm broken. L 51mm, W 29mm.
Steane and Bryant 1975, 133, fig 50.176.

H118 STAPLE
London.
Late 13th to mid 14th century.
U-shaped staple, one arm tip broken, other distorted. L 52mm, W 27mm.
Henig 1974, 195, no. 112.

H119 STAPLE
Weoley Castle, Birmingham, West Midlands.
c1200 to 1230.
U-shaped staple. L 53mm, W 26mm.
Oswald 1962, 130, fig 51.7.

H120 STAPLE
Winchester, Hampshire.
13th century.
U-shaped staple, one arm broken. L 55mm, W 23mm.
Goodall 1990-10, fig 78.520.

H121 STAPLE
York.
Later 12th or early 13th century.
U-shaped staple, arms distorted. L 56mm, W 25mm.
Addyman and Priestley 1977, 139, 143, fig 10.18.

H122 STAPLE
Wharram Percy, North Yorkshire.
Early 16th to 20th century.
U-shaped staple, one arm broken. L 58mm, W 29mm.
Goodall 1979a, 118, fig 61.23.

H123 STAPLE
Cheddar, Somerset.
?Late 13th century to c1600.
Distorted U-shaped staple. L 56mm, W 28mm.
Goodall 1979d, 272, fig 91.53.

H124 STAPLE
Northampton.
13th century.
U-shaped staple. L 57mm, W 31mm.
Goodall et al 1979, 273, fig 119.67.

H125 STAPLE
Lochmaben Castle, Dumfries and Galloway.
Late 14th century.
U-shaped staple, arms broken. L 55mm, W 30mm.
Macdonald and Laing 1974–75, 148, fig 11.26.

H126 STAPLE
Kettleby Thorpe, Lincolnshire.
14th to early 15th century.
U-shaped staple, arms broken. L 54mm, W 35mm.
From House 1. See Goodall 1974a.

BUILDING AND FURNITURE FITTINGS

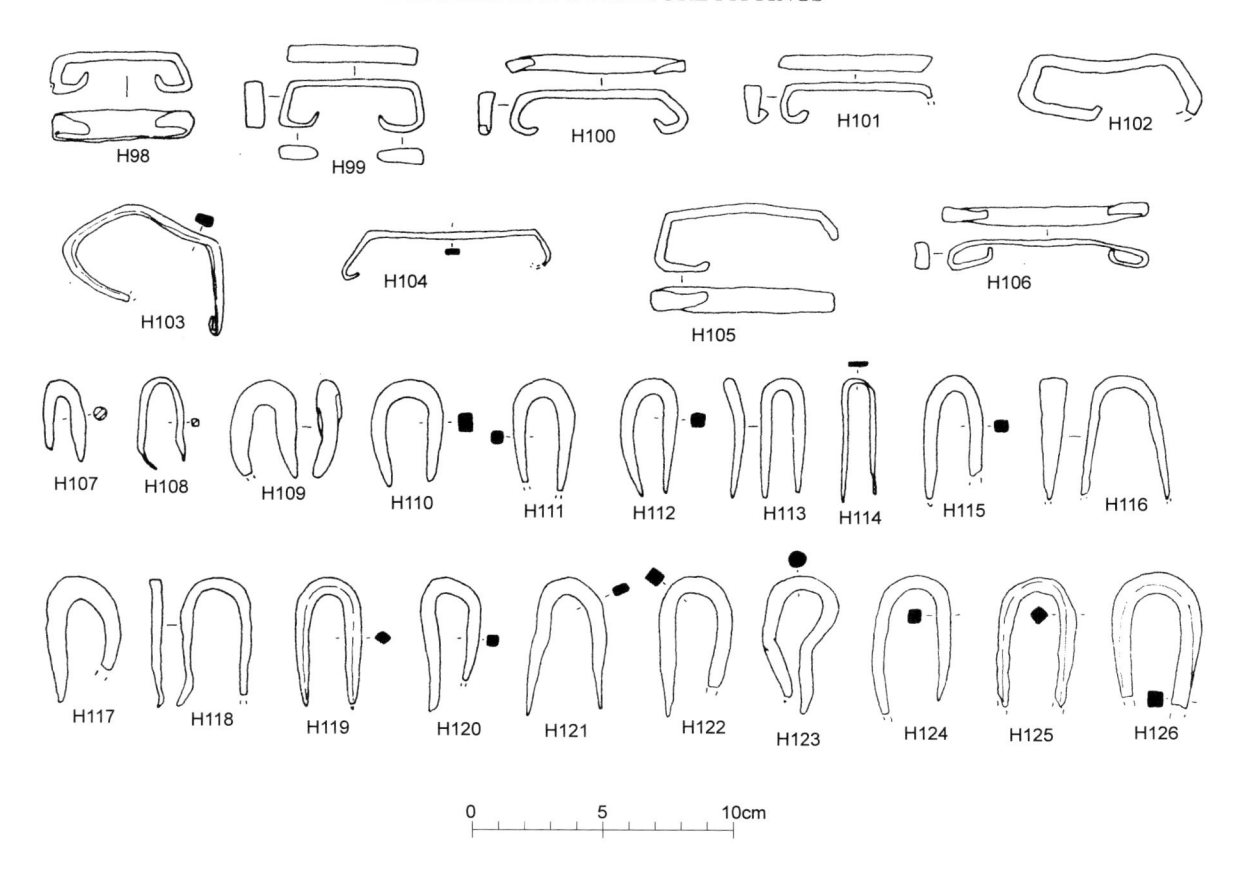

FIGURE 9.6
Staples

H127 STAPLE
Southampton, Hampshire.
11th to 12th century.
Looped staple. L 62mm, W 34mm.
Harvey 1975b, 276, fig 250.1972.

H128 STAPLE
Stonar, Kent.
c1275 to 1385.
U-shaped staple, one arm broken. L 64mm, W 31mm.
Excavated by N Macpherson-Grant.

H129 STAPLE
Gomeldon, Wiltshire.
Site: 13th–14th century.
U-shaped staple. L 67mm, W 39mm.
Musty and Algar 1986.

H130 STAPLE
Chingley Forge, Kent.
Second half 13th to mid 14th century.
U-shaped staple. L 68mm, W 46mm.
Goodall 1975d, 60, fig 27.5.

H131 STAPLE
Lochmaben Castle, Dumfries and Galloway.
Late 14th century.
U-shaped staple, arms broken. L 63mm, W 31mm.
Macdonald and Laing 1974–75, 148, fig 11.25.

H132 STAPLE
Northolt Manor, Greater London.
c1300.
U-shaped staple, distorted, one arm broken. L 68mm, W 35mm.
Excavated by J G Hurst.

H133 STAPLE
South Witham, Lincolnshire.
1137–85 to c1220.
U-shaped staple. L 65mm, W 30mm.
Goodall 2002, fig 7.3, no. 36.

H134 STAPLE
King's Lynn, Norfolk.
c1250 to 1300.
U-shaped staple. L 69mm, W 25mm.
Goodall and Carter 1977, 296, fig 134.52.

H135 STAPLE
Lismahon, Co. Down.
13th or 14th century.
U-shaped staple, one arm broken. L 74mm, W 29mm.
Waterman 1959a, 162, fig 61.4.

H136 STAPLE
Wharram Percy, North Yorkshire.
Late 15th to early 16th century.
U-shaped staple, one arm broken. L 76mm, W 32mm.
Goodall 1979a, 118, SF 11216.

H137 STAPLE
Rhuddlan, Clwyd.
Late 13th or early 14th century.
U-shaped staple, arms broken. L 73mm, W 28mm.
Goodall 1994, fig 17.3, no. 37.

H138 STAPLE
Dyserth Castle, Clwyd.
Site: 1241–63.
U-shaped staple. L 82mm, W 35mm.
National Museum of Wales, Cardiff, 15–248/14.

H139 STAPLE
Wharram Percy, North Yorkshire.
Early 16th to 20th century.
U-shaped staple. L 78mm, W 39mm.
Goodall 1979a, 118, fig 61.24.

H140 STAPLE
Stonar, Kent.
c1275 to 1385.
U-shaped staple. L 86mm, W 37mm.
Excavated by N Macpherson-Grant.

H141 STAPLE
Brandon Castle, Warwickshire.
1226–1266.
U-shaped staple and ring **H656**. Staple L 93mm. For illustration see **H656**.
Chatwin 1955, 81, fig 11.9.

H142 STAPLE
Ospringe, Kent.
c1483 to 1550.
U-shaped staple, one arm broken. L 81mm, W 41mm.
Goodall 1979c, 129, fig 20.30.

H143 STAPLE
Hampton Wafer, Hereford and Worcester.
Site: 11th to early 14th century.
U-shaped staple, arms broken. L 86mm, W 38mm.
Stanford 1967, 87, fig 7.8.

H144 STAPLE
Winchester, Hampshire.
Mid 18th–19th century.
U-shaped staple, one arm broken. L 89mm, W 44mm.
Goodall 1990-10, fig 78.522.

H145 STAPLE
Pleshey Castle, Essex.
Post-1180 to mid 13th/early 14th century.
Complete. L 98mm.
Goodall 1977c, 177, fig 38.27.

H146 STAPLE
Brome, Suffolk.
In mid 14th-century collapse.
U-shaped saple, arm broken. L 123mm, W 45mm.
West 1970, 110, fig 12.6.

H147 STAPLE
King's Lynn, Norfolk.
Later part of period c1150 to 1250.
U-shaped staple, complete arm out-turned. L 52mm, W 22mm.
Goodall and Carter 1977, 296, fig 134.50.

H148 STAPLE
South Witham, Lincolnshire.
Late 13th century to 1308–1313.
U-shaped staple, curved arm tips. L 49mm, W 24mm.
Goodall 2002, fig 7.3, no. 38.

H149 STAPLE
Wintringham, Cambridgeshire.
Site: late 12th to early 14th century.
U-shaped staple, broken out-turned arm. L 54mm, W 30mm.
Goodall 1977a, 257, fig 45.45.

H150 STAPLE
Wharram Percy, North Yorkshire.
Early 16th to 20th century.
U-shaped staple, one arm broken, other with clenched tip. L 55mm, W 35mm.
Goodall 1979a, 123, fig 65.94.

BUILDING AND FURNITURE FITTINGS

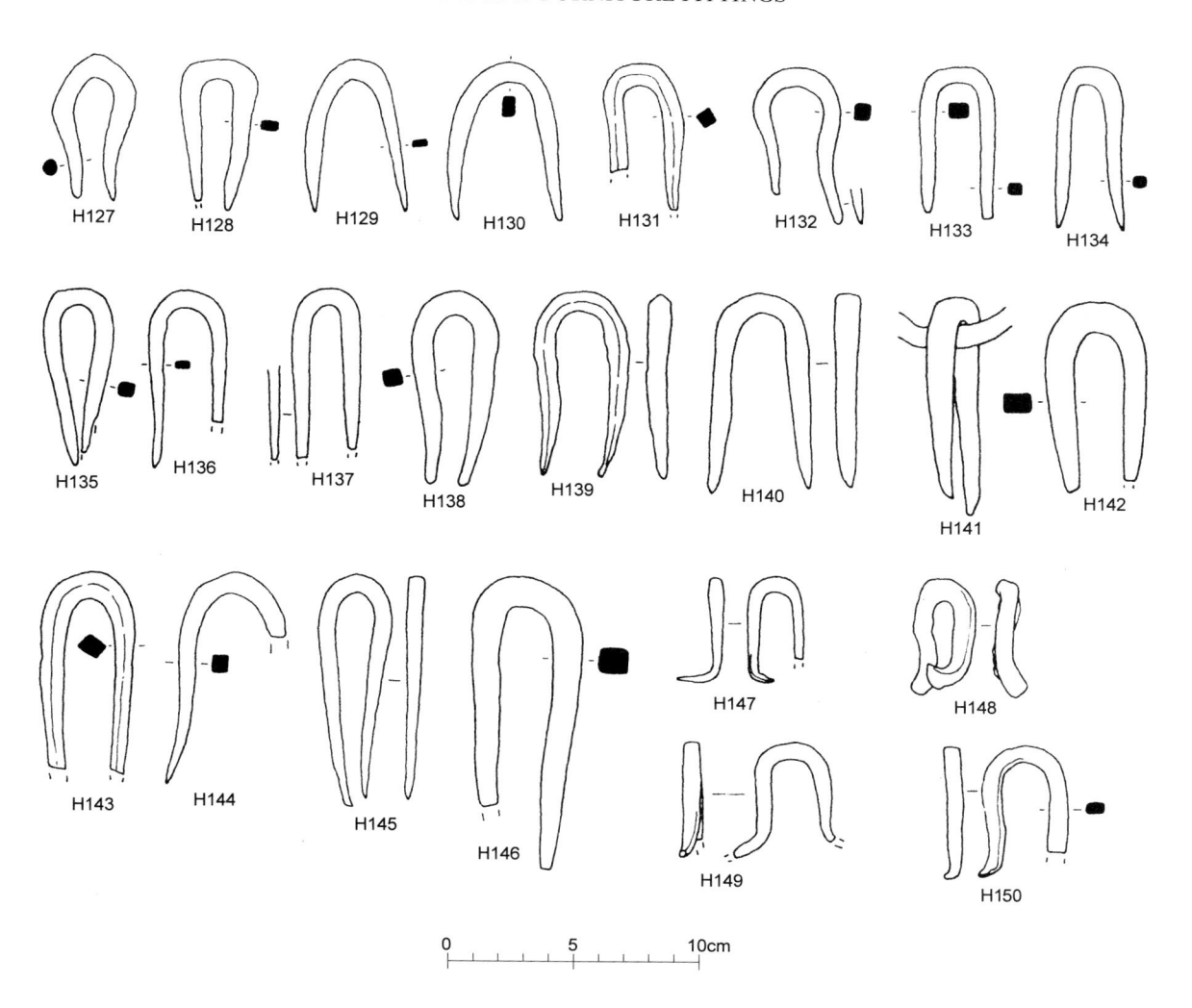

FIGURE 9.7
Staples

H151 STAPLE
Seacourt, Oxfordshire.
Mid 13th–14th century.
U-shaped staple with clenched tips. L 48mm, W 35mm.
Biddle 1961–62, 177, fig 30.6.

H152 STAPLE
Stonar, Kent.
c1150 to c1225.
U-shaped staple, broken out-turned arms. L 60mm, W 26mm.
Excavated by N Macpherson-Grant.

H153 STAPLE
North Elmham Park, Norfolk.
c1150 to c1600.
U-shaped staple, out-turned arms. L 100mm, W 28mm.
Goodall 1980a, 513, fig 267.74.

H154 STAPLE
Chelmsford Priory, Essex.
From destruction debris deposited by c1560 over site founded in mid 13th century, dissolved 1537.
Rectangular staple, long angled arms. L 150mm, W 48mm.
Drury 1974, 59, fig 9.25.

H155 STAPLE
Winchester, Hampshire.
Late 11th–12th century.
Complete looped staple. L 47mm, W 22mm.
Goodall 1990-10, fig 78.523.

H156 STAPLE
Goltho, Lincolnshire.
Croft A: late Saxon to late 14th or early 15th century.
Looped staple. L 58mm, W 15mm.
Goodall 1975a, 86, fig 40.85.

H157 STAPLE
Stonar, Kent.
c1225–1275.
Looped staple, one arm broken. L 66mm, W 21mm.
Excavated by N Macpherson-Grant.

H158 STAPLE
Knaresborough Castle, North Yorkshire.
Early 15th century.
Looped staple. L 86mm, W 20mm.
Le Patourel 1963–66, fig 8.18 (from rubbish pit).

H159 STAPLE
Stonar, Kent.
c1275 to 1385.
Looped staple. L 84mm, W 21mm.
Excavated by N Macpherson-Grant.

H160 STAPLE
Rhuddlan, Clwyd.
14th century, ?earlier part, or conceivably 1290–1300.
Looped staple, broken and distorted clenched arms. L 43mm, W 15mm.
Goodall 1994, fig 17.3, no. 40.

H161 STAPLE
Winchester, Hampshire.
15th–16th century.
Looped staple with out-turned arms. L 67mm.
Goodall 1990-10, fig 78.525.

H162 STAPLE
Staines, Surrey.
1300 to 1500.
Looped staple with broken out-turned arms. L 66mm, W 22mm.
Excavated by K R Crouch.

H163 STAPLE
Rhuddlan, Clwyd.
14th century, ?earlier part, or conceivably 1290–1300.
Looped staple, clenched tips, one broken. L 82mm, W 18mm.
Goodall 1994, fig 17.3, no. 39.

H164 STAPLE
Winchester, Hampshire.
Mid 13th century.
Looped staple with clenched, out-turned arms. L 33mm.
Goodall 1990-10, fig 78.524.

H165 LINK AND STAPLE
Brandon Castle, Warwickshire.
13th century, ?post-1226.
Looped staple with clenched, out-turned arms supporting a link. L 69mm, W 24mm.
Chatwin 1955, 81, fig 11.11.

H166 STAPLE
Hen Domen, Powys.
13th century.
Broken looped staple holding ring **H655**. L 24mm. For illustration see **H655**.
Barker and Higham 2000.

H167 STAPLE
Kilton Castle, Cleveland.
Late 15th century.
Loop staple, arms broken. L 43mm, W 21mm.
Excavated by A Aberg.

H168 STAPLE
Winchester, Hampshire.
16th century.
Staple with deep loop and broken arms. L 41mm.
Goodall 1990-10, fig 78.526.

H169 STAPLE
Wharram Percy, North Yorkshire.
Late 15th to early 16th century.
Looped staple, arms broken. L 64mm, W 29mm.
Goodall 1979a, 118, fig 61.25.

H170 STAPLE
Stonar, Kent.
c1275 to 1385.
Broken looped staple retaining ring **H657**. L 65mm. For illustration see **H657**.
Excavated by N Macpherson-Grant.

H171 STAPLE
Burton-in-Lonsdale, North Yorkshire.
Later 13th to mid 14th century.
Looped staple, arms broken. L 137mm, W 41mm.
Moorhouse 1971, 95, fig 3.19.

BUILDING AND FURNITURE FITTINGS

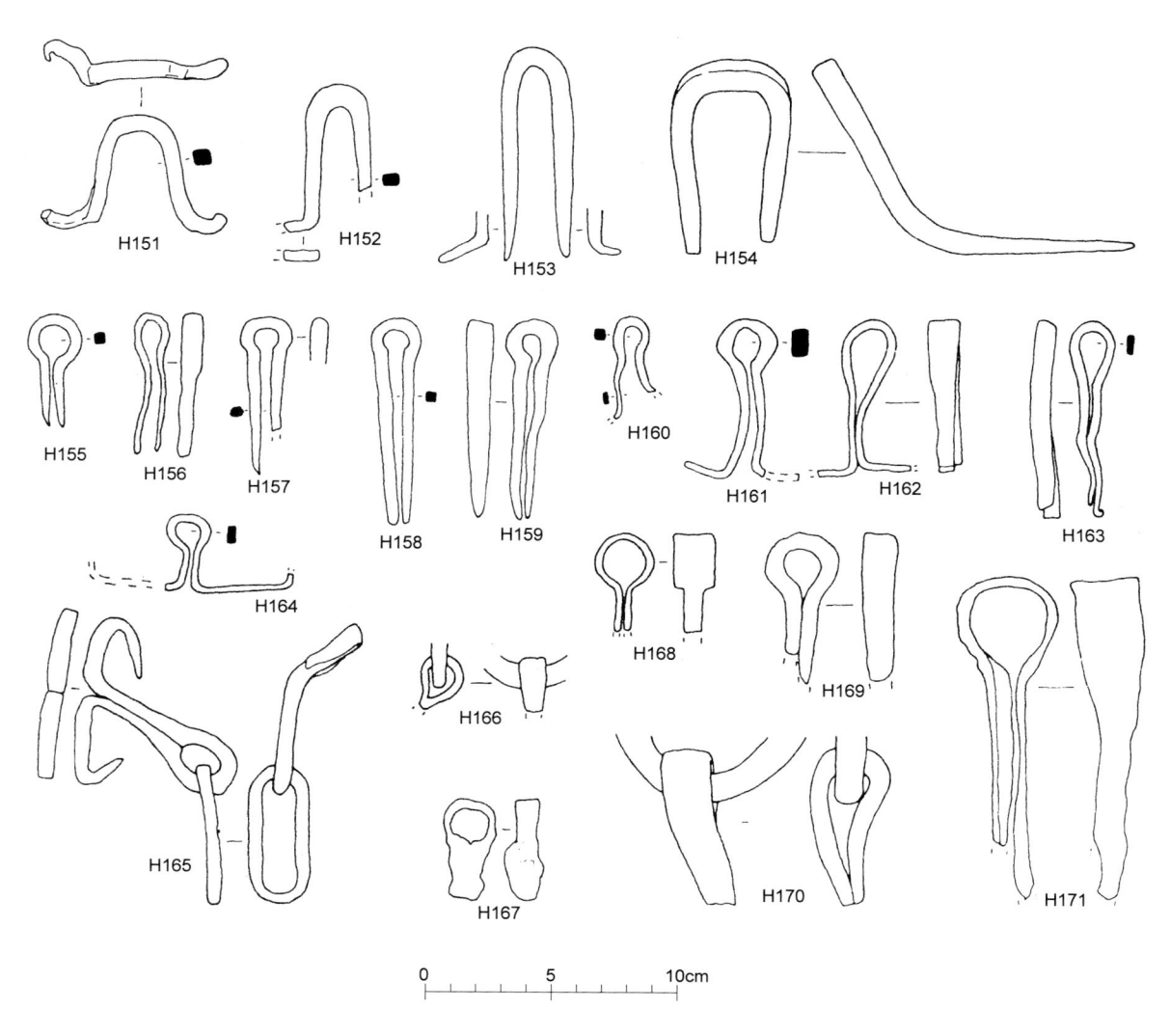

FIGURE 9.8
Staples

H172 WALLHOOK
Portchester Castle, Hampshire.
Immediately prior to construction of building between 1521 and 1527.
Hook broken. L 53mm.
Hinton 1977, 204, fig 209.62.

H173 WALLHOOK
Clarendon Palace, Wiltshire.
Site: c1072 to later 15th century.
Hook broken, shank tip split. L 56mm.
Goodall 1988, fig 75.31; Borenius and Charlton 1936.

H174 WALLHOOK (not illustrated)
Winchester, Hampshire.
15th century.
Shank and hook broken. L 27mm.
Goodall 1990-10, 333, no. 490.

H175 WALLHOOK
Winchester, Hampshire.
Late 11th–12th century.
Hook broken. L 54mm.
Goodall 1990-10, 332, no. 483.

H176 WALLHOOK
Clarendon Palace, Wiltshire.
Site: c1072 to later 15th century.
Shank broken. L 65mm.
Goodall 1988, fig 75.32; Borenius and Charlton 1936.

H177 WALLHOOK (not illustrated)
Winchester, Hampshire.
Early to mid 13th century.
Hook broken. L 47mm.
Goodall 1990-10, 332, no. 485.

H178 WALLHOOK (not illustrated)
Winchester, Hampshire.
1441–42.
Hook and shank broken. L 38mm.
Goodall 1990-10, 333, no. 489.

H179 WALLHOOK
Ospringe, Kent.
c1270 to 1483.
Complete. Shank tip curved. L 65mm.
Goodall 1979c, 129, fig 20.34.

H180 WALLHOOK
Lyveden, Northamptonshire.
c1200–1350.
Hook broken. L 77mm.
Steane and Bryant 1975, 137, fig 51.222.

H181 WALLHOOK
Winchester, Hampshire.
13th century.
Complete. L 92mm.
Goodall 1990-10, fig 77.487.

H182 WALLHOOK
South Witham, Lincolnshire.
Late 13th century to 1308–1313.
Complete. L 77mm.
Goodall 2002, fig 7.3, no. 39.

H183 WALLHOOK
Winchester, Hampshire.
Late 12th–?early 13th century.
Hook and shank broken. L 72mm.
Goodall 1990-10, fig 77.484.

H184 WALLHOOK (not illustrated)
Waltham Abbey, Essex.
In clay floor of smithy of late 12th or early 13th to 16th century date.
Shank broken. L 106mm.
Goodall 1973a, 173, fig 12.49.

H185 WALLHOOK
Norwich.
15th to 17th century.
Complete. L 130mm.
Hurst and Golson 1953–57, 99, fig 24.7.

H186 WALLHOOK
Winchester, Hampshire.
Early 13th–late 14th century.
Hook and shank broken. L 68mm.
Goodall 1990-10, 333, no. 488.

H187 WALLHOOK
Winchester, Hampshire.
Late 13th century.
Hook and shank broken. L 76mm.
Goodall 1990-10, fig 77.486.

H188 WALLHOOK
Northampton.
Site: early Saxon to 15th century.
Hook and shank broken. L 36mm.
Goodall *et al* 1979, 273, fig 119.74.

H189 WALLHOOK
Llantrithyd, South Glamorgan.
Early to mid 12th century.
Shank broken. L 46mm.
Goodall 1977f, 47, iron fig 2.22.

H190 WALLHOOK
Hambleton Moat, Lincolnshire.
1250–1400.
Shank distorted. L 112mm.
Butler 1963, 65, fig 14.3.

H191 WALLHOOK
Stonar, Kent.
c1275 to 1385.
Complete. L 95mm.
Excavated by N Macpherson-Grant.

H192 WALLHOOK
Oxford Castle, Oxford.
Late 14th to mid 15th century.
Hook and shank broken. L 84mm.
Goodall 1976c, 298, fig 26.8.

H193 WALLHOOK
Winchester, Hampshire.
Mid 12th century.
Hook and shank broken. L 97mm.
Goodall 1990-10, fig 77.482.

H194 WALLHOOK
Clarendon Palace, Wiltshire.
Site: c1072 to later 15th century.
Shank broken. L 46mm.
Goodall 1988, fig 75.33; Borenius and Charlton 1936.

H195 WALLHOOK (not illustrated)
Winchester, Hampshire.
Mid to late 13th century.
Hook and shank broken. L 49mm.
Goodall 1990-10, 333, no. 492.

H196 WALLHOOK (not illustrated)
Winchester, Hampshire.
Early to ?mid 16th century.
Hook and shank broken. L 48mm.
Goodall 1990-10, 333, no. 504.

H197 WALLHOOK (not illustrated)
Winchester, Hampshire.
15th–?16th century.
Hook and shank broken. L 65mm.
Goodall 1990-10, 333, no. 501.

H198 WALLHOOK
Goltho, Lincolnshire.
Croft A: late Saxon to late 14th or early 15th century.
Complete but shank distorted. L 75mm.
Goodall 1975a, 86, fig 40.74.

H199 WALLHOOK
Winchester, Hampshire.
15th–16th century.
Complete. L 103mm.
Goodall 1990-10, fig 77.507.

H200 WALLHOOK
Kings Langley, Hertfordshire.
c1300.
Complete. L 92mm.
Neal 1973, 56, fig XV.62.

BUILDING AND FURNITURE FITTINGS

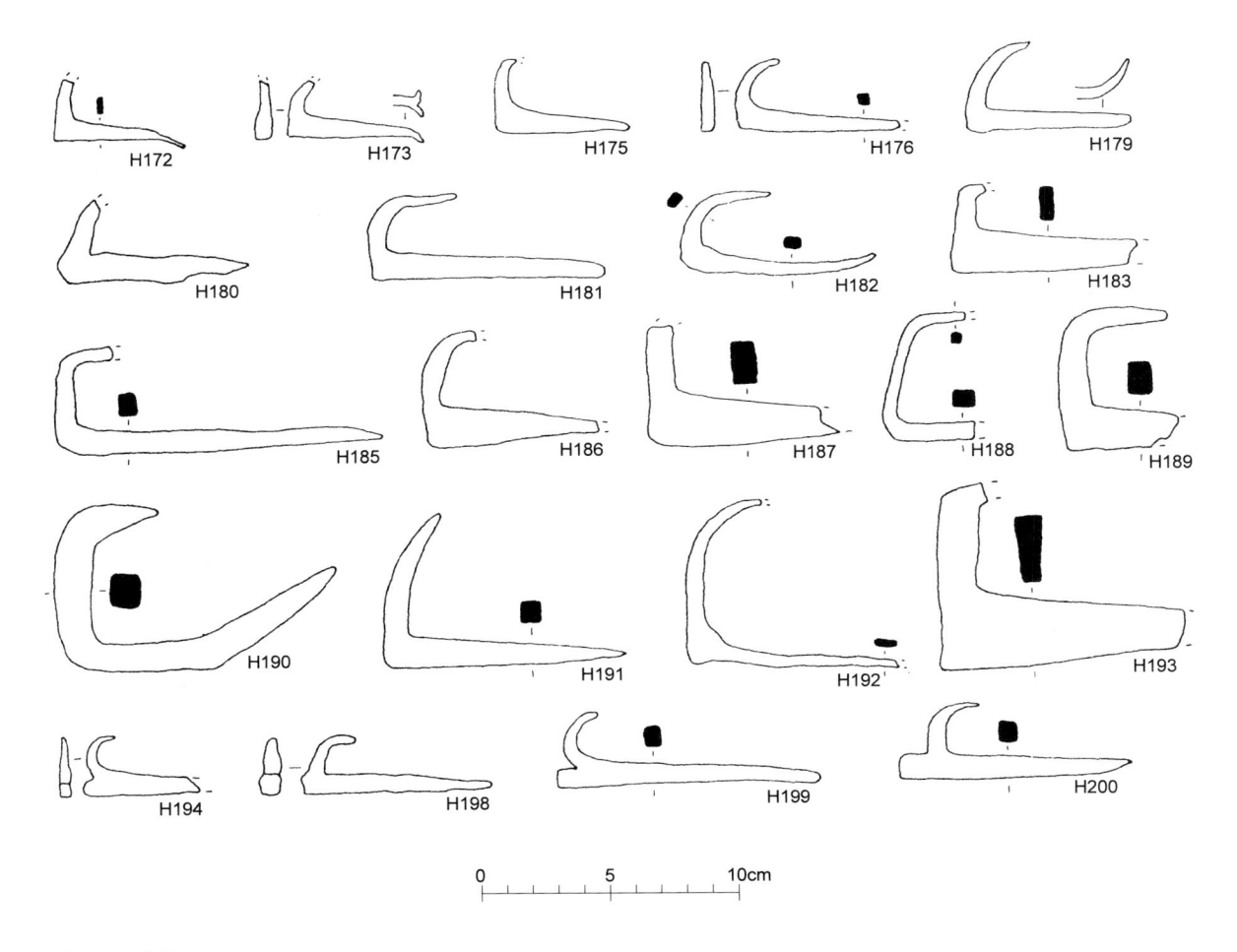

FIGURE 9.9
Wallhooks

H201 WALLHOOK
Winchester, Hampshire.
15th century.
Complete. L 76mm.
Goodall 1990-10, fig 77.500.

H202 WALLHOOK (not illustrated)
Northolt Manor, Greater London.
1350 to 1370.
Hook and shank broken. L 72mm.
Excavated by J G Hurst.

H203 WALLHOOK (not illustrated)
Winchester, Hampshire.
Late 15th–early 16th century.
Hook and shank broken. L 66mm.
Goodall 1990-10, 333, no. 503.

H204 WALLHOOK (not illustrated)
Manor of the More, Rickmansworth, Hertfordshire.
c1426.
Hook and shank broken. L 61mm.
Biddle et al 1959, 185, fig 19.42.

H205 WALLHOOK
Winchester, Hampshire.
Mid 15th century.
Complete. L 78mm.
Goodall 1990-10, 333, no. 497.

H206 WALLHOOK (not illustrated)
Winchester, Hampshire.
Mid 15th century.
Hook and shank broken. L 97mm.
Goodall 1990-10, 333, 499.

H207 WALLHOOK
Winchester, Hampshire.
1441–42 to mid 16th century.
Shank broken. L 70mm.
Goodall 1990-10, 333, no. 506.

H208 WALLHOOK (not illustrated)
Winchester, Hampshire.
14th–?15th century.
Hook and shank broken. L 74mm.
Goodall 1990-10, 333, no. 496.

H209 WALLHOOK
Winchester, Hampshire.
13th–late 14th or ?15th century.
Shank broken. L 80mm.
Goodall 1990-10, fig 77.495.

H210 WALLHOOK
Stonar, Kent.
c1275 to 1385.
Shank broken. L 78mm.
Excavated by N Macpherson-Grant.

H211 WALLHOOK (not illustrated)
Winchester, Hampshire.
Mid 15th century.
Shank broken. L 57mm.
Goodall 1990-10, 333, no. 498.

H212 WALLHOOK (not illustrated)
The Hamel, Oxford.
16th century.
Shank and hook broken. L 66mm.
Goodall 1980d.

H213 WALLHOOK
Pleshey Castle, Essex.
Early/mid 16th century to recent times, but including redeposited material.
Shank broken. L 73mm.
Goodall 1977c, 177, fig 39.23.

H214 WALLHOOK
Portchester Castle, Hampshire.
Immediately prior to construction of building between 1521 and 1527.
Distorted hook. L 94mm.
Hinton 1977, 201, fig 109.61.

H215 WALLHOOK (not illustrated)
Pleshey Castle, Essex.
Mid 13th/early 14th to early/mid 16th century.
Hook and shank broken. L 73mm.
Goodall 1977c, 177, fig 39.24.

H216 WALLHOOK
Winchester, Hampshire.
14th–early 16th century.
Hook and shank broken. L 104mm.
Goodall 1990-10, fig 77.502.

H217 WALLHOOK (not illustrated)
Bodiam Castle, East Sussex.
c1390.
Hook and shank broken. L 109mm.
Excavated by D Martin.

H218 WALLHOOK
Pleshey Castle, Essex.
Mid 13th/early 14th century to recent times.
Shank broken. L 102mm.
Goodall 1977c, 177, fig 38.22.

H219 WALLHOOK
Clarendon Palace, Wiltshire.
Site: c1072 to later 15th century.
Complete. L 119mm.
Goodall 1988, fig 75.34; Borenius and Charlton 1936.

H220 WALLHOOK
Clarendon Palace, Wiltshire.
Site: c1072 to later 15th century.
Complete. L 121mm.
Goodall 1988, fig 75.35; Borenius and Charlton 1936.

H221 WALLHOOK
Old Sarum, Wiltshire.
Principally medieval, to 14th century.
Complete. L 144mm.
Salisbury and South Wiltshire Museum, Salisbury, 8/1932, O.S.C113.

H222 HOOK
Duffield Castle, Derbyshire.
Keep built 1177–1190, demolished 1266.
Shank broken. H 61mm, L 142mm.
Manby 1959.

H223 HOOK
Clough Castle, Co. Down.
c1200 to c1225.
Expanded shank tip with depressions.
H 48mm, L 177mm.
Waterman 1954, 140, fig 12.5.

H224 HOOK
Portchester Castle, Hampshire.
Later medieval.
Shank with expanded end with shallow depressions. L 192mm.
Hinton 1977, 201, fig 109.42.

BUILDING AND FURNITURE FITTINGS

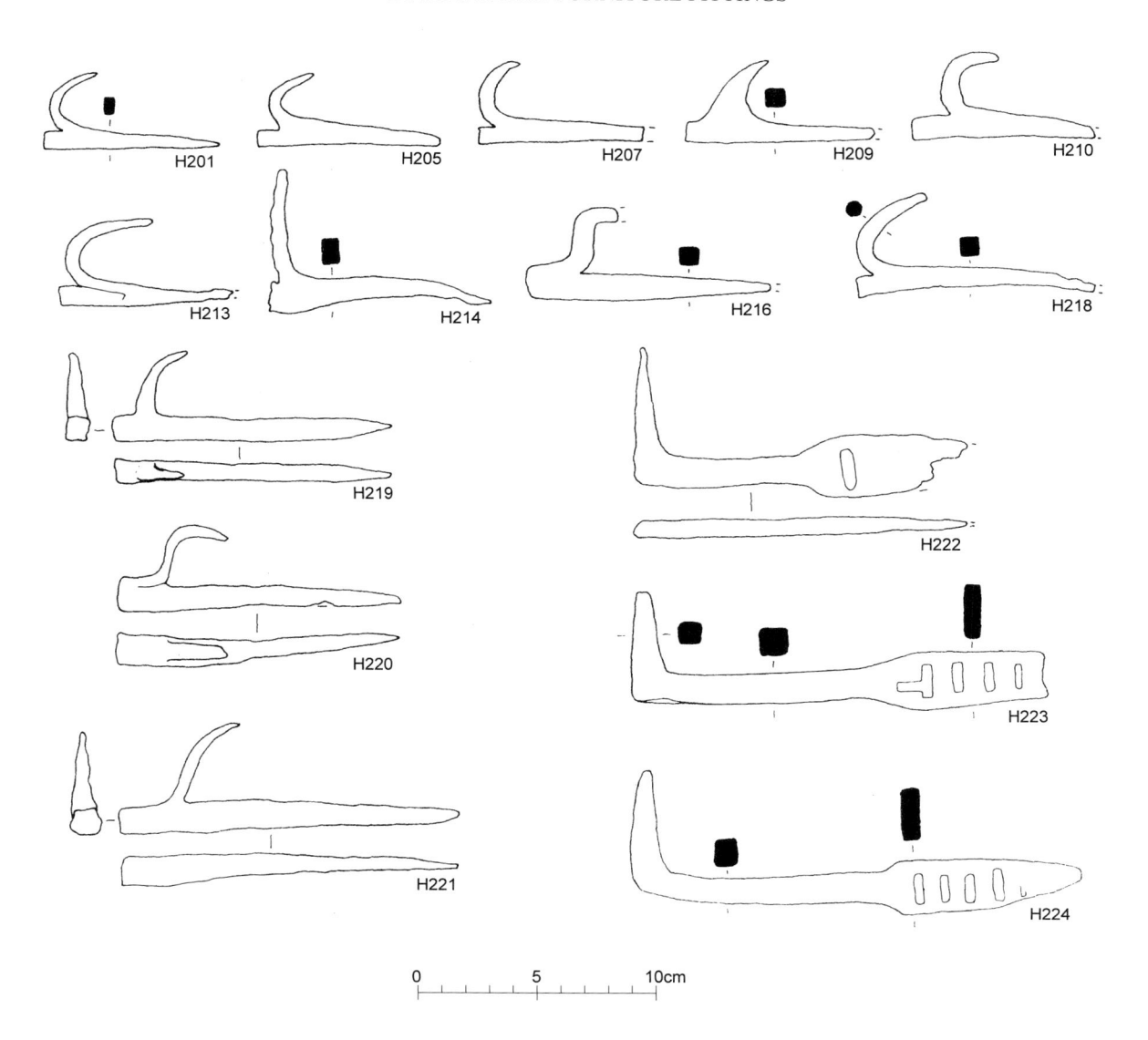

FIGURE 9.10
Wallhooks and hooks

H225 HOOK
King's Lynn, Norfolk.
Mid 13th–14th century.
Broken looped hook. L 47mm.
Goodall and Carter 1977, 296, fig 134.59.

H226 HOOK
Bolton, Fangfoss, Humberside.
Mid 14th century.
Looped hook. L 68mm.
Goodall 1978b, 143, fig 30.32.

H227 HOOK
Stonar, Kent.
c1275 to 1385.
Head broken. L 98mm.
Excavated by N Macpherson-Grant.

H228 EYED SPIKE AND RING
Winchester, Hampshire.
Late 17th to ?18th century.
Eyed spike and ring, both broken. L 194mm.
Goodall 1990-10, fig 79.535.

H229 LOOPED STRAP
Clarendon Palace, Wiltshire.
Site: c1072 to later 15th century.
Loop with upturned shank retaining lead caulking. L 66mm.
Goodall 1988, fig 76.51; Borenius and Charlton 1936.

H230 LOOPED STRAP
Wintringham, Cambridgeshire.
Site: c1175–1340.
Looped strap with clenched tip. L 277mm.
Goodall 1977a, 257, fig 45.59.

H231 WALL ANCHOR
Chelmsford Priory, Essex.
Site founded in mid 13th century, dissolved 1537, destroyed by c1560.
Head broken. L 113mm.
Drury 1974, 59, fig 4.26.

H232 WALL ANCHOR
Tamworth, Staffordshire.
13th century.
Horizontal wood graining on inner face of head. L 81mm.
Excavated by P A Rahtz.

H233 WALL ANCHOR
Ospringe, Kent.
Demolition c1550–70 on site founded c1230.
Head broken. L 141mm.
Goodall 1979c, 129, fig 20.35.

H234 WALL ANCHOR
North Elmham Park, Norfolk.
c1150 to c1600.
Complete. Nail-hole in head. L 145mm.
Goodall 1980a, 514, fig 267.83.

H235 WALL ANCHOR
Clarendon Palace, Wiltshire.
Site: c1072 to late 15th century.
Head broken. L 158mm.
Goodall 1988, fig 75.30; Borenius and Charlton 1936.

H236 HOLDFAST
Red Castle, Thetford, Norfolk.
Site: 11th to early 13th century.
Complete. L 77mm.
Knocker 1966–69, 148, fig 13.4.

H237 S-HOOK
South Witham, Lincolnshire.
1137–85 to c1220.
S-hook, tip broken. L 35mm.
Goodall 2002, fig 7.3, no. 40.

H238 S-HOOK
Wallingstones, Hereford and Worcester.
First half 13th century.
S-hook. L 37mm.
Bridgewater 1970–72, 100, fig 103.8.

H239 S-HOOK
Bodiam, East Sussex.
Late 13th–14th century.
S-hook. L 43mm.
Excavated by D Martin.

H240 S-HOOK
Barry Island, South Glamorgan.
12th to 14th century.
S-hook. L 29mm.
National Museum of Wales, Cardiff, 36–202/78. For site see Fox 1936; 1937.

H241 S-HOOK
Wharram Percy, North Yorkshire.
Late 15th to early 16th century.
S-hook, one end broken. L 51mm.
Goodall 1979a, 118, fig 61.30.

H242 CLENCH BOLT
Winchester, Hampshire.
11th century.
Complete. L 48mm.
Goodall 1990-10, fig 80.540.

H243 CLENCH BOLT
London.
?Late 13th–mid 14th century.
Complete. L 55mm.
Henig 1974, 195, no. 103.

H244 CLENCH BOLT
Lydford Castle, Devon.
Mid 13th century.
Typical clench bolt from well cover **H404**. L 75mm.
Goodall 1980b, fig 17.e.

H245 ROVE
Winchester, Hampshire.
Early 12th century to c1135–38.
Square rove. L 33mm.
Goodall 1990-10, fig 80.542.

H246 ROVE
Clarendon Palace, Wiltshire.
Site: c1072 to later 15th century.
Flat, lozenge-shaped rove with two bevelled edges. L 72mm.
Goodall 1988, fig 76.48; Borenius and Charlton 1936.

H247 ROVE
Winchester, Hampshire.
Early to ?mid 15th century.
Flat, damaged diamond-shaped rove with hollow sides. L 80mm.
Goodall 1990-10, fig 80.550.

H248 ROVE
Goltho manor, Lincolnshire.
c1000–1100.
Curved, shaped rove. L 63mm.
Goodall 1987, fig 158.88.

H249 ROVE
Winchester, Hampshire.
Late 11th century.
Curved, shaped rove with shank fragment. L 62mm.
Goodall 1990-10, fig 80.548.

H250 ROVE
Wintringham, Cambridgeshire.
Site: late 12th to early 14th century.
Rectangular rove with broken side arms and fragment of nail. L 66mm.
Goodall 1977a, 257, fig 45.49.

H251 ROVES
Stonar, Kent.
c1150–c1225.
Strip of two roves. L 48mm.
Excavated by N Macpherson-Grant.

H252 ROVES
London.
Late 13th–14th century.
Strip of three roves. L 86mm.
Henig 1974, 195, fig 40.121.

H253 ROVES
London.
Late 13th–mid 14th century.
Strip of five roves. L 101mm.
Henig 1974, 195, fig 40.119.

BUILDING AND FURNITURE FITTINGS

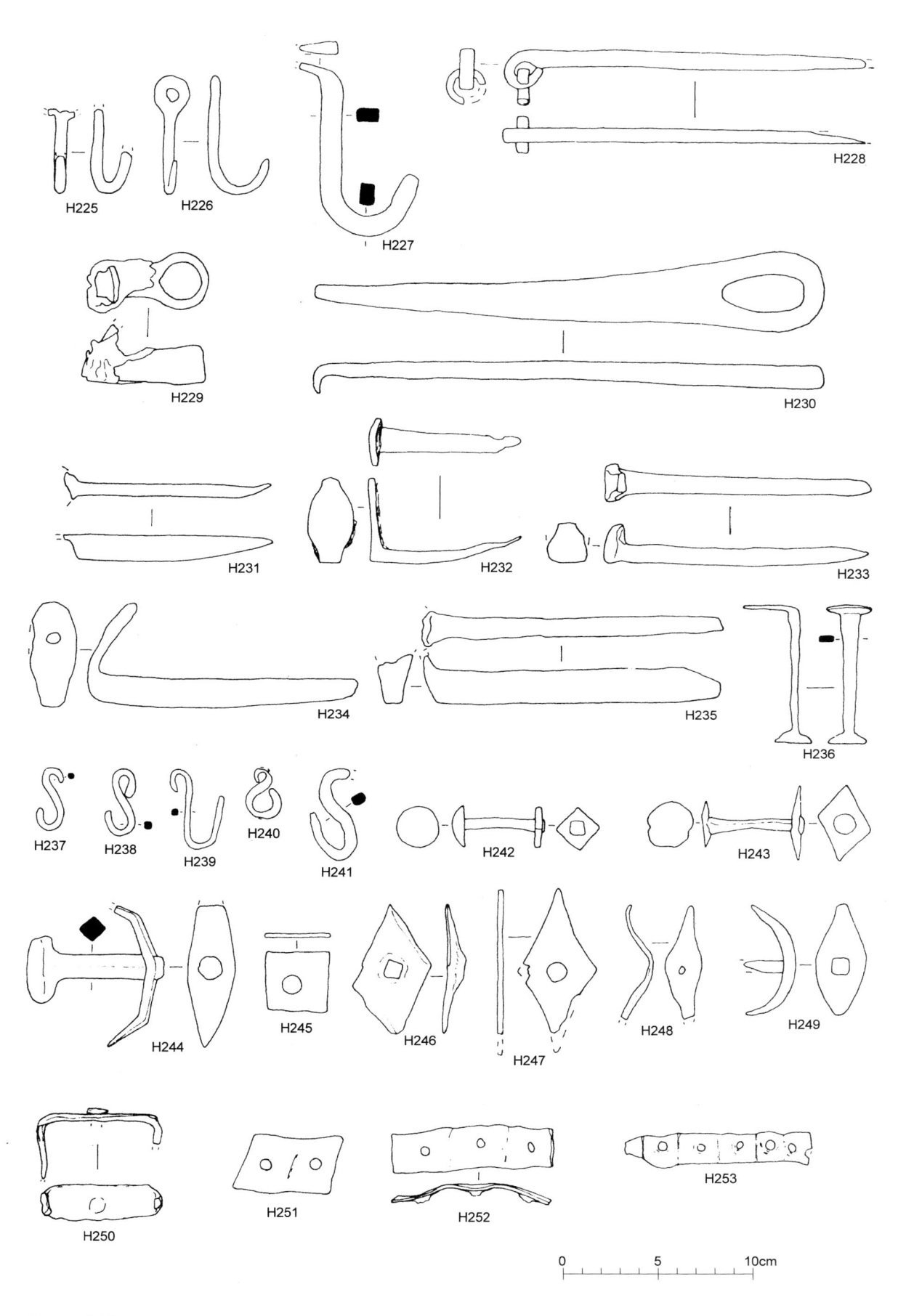

FIGURE 9.11
Hooks, eyed spike and ring, looped straps, wall anchors, holdfast, S-hooks, clench bolts and roves

H254 HINGE PIVOT
Alsted, Surrey.
*c*1250 to 1350. From gateway in boundary wall.
Complete. L 132mm.
Goodall 1976a, 55–56, fig 34.1.

H255 HINGE PIVOT
Rievaulx Abbey, North Yorkshire.
Site: 1131–1538 with later robbing.
Cranked shank, rectangular below ground, circular above. L 169mm.
DAMHB Collection, London, RVA 226(A).

H256 HINGE PIVOT
Winchester, Hampshire.
14th–?15th century.
Shank tip clenched. H 23mm, L 35mm.
Goodall 1990-10, fig 83.633.

H257 HINGE PIVOT
Wintringham, Cambridgeshire.
Mid 13th century.
Complete. H 23mm, L 39mm.
Goodall 1977a, 257, fig 45.35.

H258 HINGE PIVOT (not illustrated)
Dyserth Castle, Clwyd.
Site: 1241–63.
Complete. H 32mm, L 41mm.
Glenn 1915.

H259 HINGE PIVOT (not illustrated)
Oxford.
Late 12th century to *c*1250.
Complete. H 22mm, L 42mm.
Goodall 1977e, 142, fig 27.32.

H260 HINGE PIVOT
Oxford.
Early 14th to mid 15th century.
Complete. H 31mm, L 43mm.
Goodall 1976c, 298, fig 26.7.

H261 HINGE PIVOT (not illustrated)
Riplingham, Humberside.
Late 13th to early 15th century.
Complete. H 23mm, L 44mm.
Wacher 1963–66, 654, fig 20.13.

H262 HINGE PIVOT
Winchester, Hampshire.
Mid to late 13th century.
Complete. H 30mm, L 48mm.
Goodall 1990-10, fig 83.610.

H263 HINGE PIVOT (not illustrated)
Dyserth Castle, Clwyd.
Site: 1241–63.
Shank tip broken. H 36mm, L 48mm.
Glenn 1915.

H264 HINGE PIVOT (not illustrated)
Stonar, Kent.
*c*1275–1385. Found with hinge **H430**.
Complete. H 33mm, L 49mm. For illustration see **H430**.
Excavated by N Macpherson-Grant.

H265 HINGE PIVOT (not illustrated)
Stonar, Kent.
*c*1275 to 1385.
Complete. H 34mm, L 51mm.
Excavated by N Macpherson-Grant.

H266 HINGE PIVOT (not illustrated)
Lyveden, Northamptonshire.
*c*1350 to 1450.
Complete. H 34mm, L 53mm.
Steane and Bryant 1975, 136, fig 51.218.

H267 HINGE PIVOT
King's Lynn, Norfolk.
*c*1350 to 1500.
Complete. H 30mm, L 54mm.
Goodall and Carter 1977, 293, fig 133.16.

H268 HINGE PIVOT (not illustrated)
Northampton.
End 15th century.
Complete. H 34mm, L 54mm.
Goodall *et al* 1979, 268, fig 117.25.

H269 HINGE PIVOT (not illustrated)
Grenstein, Norfolk.
Late 14th to 15th century.
Clenched tip to shank. H 31mm, L 54mm.
Goodall 1980c.

H270 HINGE PIVOT
Wharram Percy, North Yorkshire.
Early 16th to 20th century.
Complete. H 25mm, L 58mm.
Goodall 1979a, 121, fig 64.92.

H271 HINGE PIVOT (not illustrated)
The Hamel, Oxford.
Mid to late 15th century.
Complete. H 38mm, L 58mm.
Goodall 1980d.

H272 HINGE PIVOT (not illustrated)
Winchester, Hampshire.
Early–mid 10th century.
Complete. H 42mm, L 58mm.
Goodall 1990-10, fig 83.564.

H273 HINGE PIVOT
Winchester, Hampshire.
*c*1065–70.
Complete. H 27mm, L 59mm.
Goodall 1990-10, fig 83.578.

H274 HINGE PIVOT
Grenstein, Norfolk.
Late 14th to 15th century.
Complete. H 34mm, L 62mm.
Goodall 1980c, fig 78, no. 39.

H275 HINGE PIVOT (not illustrated)
Wintringham, Cambridgeshire.
Site: *c*1175 to 1340.
Shank broken. H 29mm, L 59mm.
Goodall 1977a, 257, fig 45.36.

H276 HINGE PIVOT (not illustrated)
Winchester, Hampshire.
11th century.
Complete. H 40mm, L 62mm.
Goodall 1990-10, 340, no. 581.

H277 HINGE PIVOT (not illustrated)
Winchester, Hampshire.
18th–19th century.
Shank broken. H 37mm, L 53mm.
Goodall 1990-10, fig 83.648.

H278 HINGE PIVOT (not illustrated)
Wintringham, Cambridgeshire.
Site: *c*1175 to 1340.
Complete, shank distorted. H 33mm, L 62mm.
Goodall 1977a, 257.

H279 HINGE PIVOT
Winchester, Hampshire.
14th century.
Complete. H 42mm, L 63mm.
Goodall 1990-10, 342, no. 626.

H280 HINGE PIVOT
Lyveden, Northamptonshire.
Site: *c*1200 to 1500.
Complete. H 32mm, L 64mm.
Steane and Bryant 1975, 136, fig 51.219.

H281 HINGE PIVOT (not illustrated)
Dyserth Castle, Clwyd.
Site: 1241–63.
Complete. H 27mm, L 65mm.
Glenn 1915, 63, fig 9.A.

H282 HINGE PIVOT (not illustrated)
Winchester, Hampshire.
15th–16th century.
Complete. H 36mm, L 66mm.
Goodall 1990-10, 343, no. 641.

H283 HINGE PIVOT
Seacourt, Oxfordshire.
14th century.
Complete. H 37mm, L 67mm.
Biddle 1961–62, 175, fig 29.14, scale 1:4, not 1:3.

H284 HINGE PIVOT (not illustrated)
Goltho, Lincolnshire.
Site: late Saxon to late 14th or early 15th century.
Complete. H 27mm, L 68mm.
Goodall 1975a, 85, fig 40.69.

H285 HINGE PIVOT
Winchester, Hampshire.
12th–13th century.
Complete. H 32mm, L 68mm.
Goodall 1990-10, fig 83.612.

H286 HINGE PIVOT (not illustrated)
Winchester, Hampshire.
14th century.
Complete. H 32mm, L 68mm.
Goodall 1990-10, fig 83.629.

H287 HINGE PIVOT
Stonar, Kent.
*c*1275 to 1385.
Complete. H 37mm, L 69mm.
Excavated by N Macpherson-Grant.

BUILDING AND FURNITURE FITTINGS

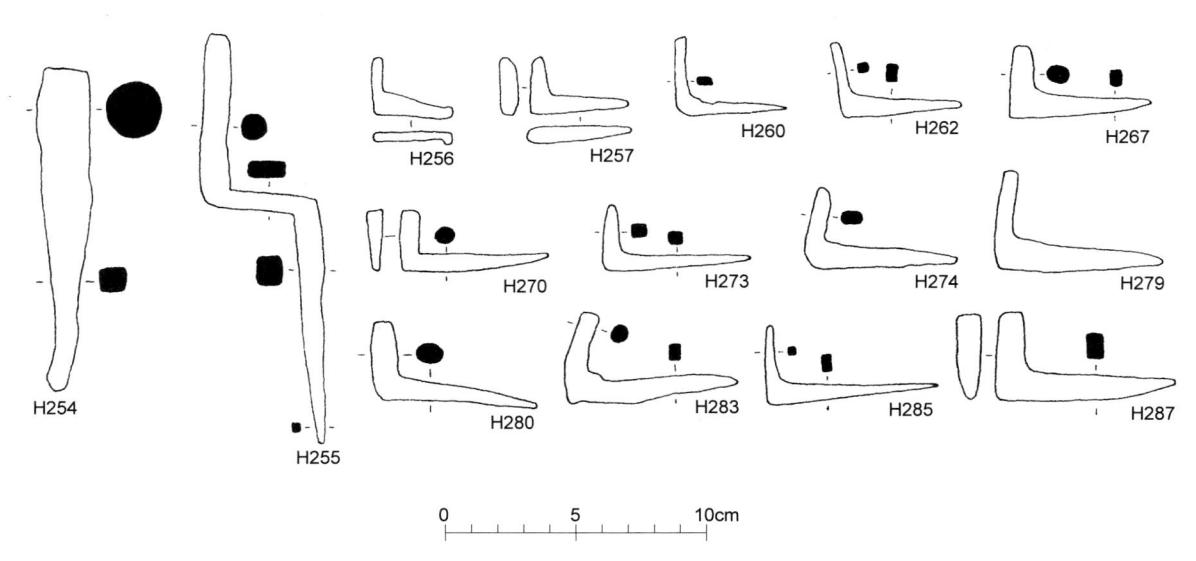

FIGURE 9.12
Hinge pivots

H288 HINGE PIVOT
Winchester, Hampshire.
15th century.
Complete. H 31mm, L 69mm.
Goodall 1990-10, fig 83.638.

H289 HINGE PIVOT (not illustrated)
The Hamel, Oxford.
16th century.
Complete. H 36mm, L 70mm.
Goodall 1980d.

H290 HINGE PIVOT
Winchester, Hampshire.
Mid 11th century.
Worn shank. H 46mm, L 71mm.
Goodall 1990-10, fig 83.577.

H291 HINGE PIVOT
Dyserth Castle, Clwyd.
Site: 1241–1263.
Complete. H 52mm, L 73mm.
Glenn 1915.

H292 HINGE PIVOT
Winchester, Hampshire.
Late 11th–12th century.
Worn shank. H 43mm, L 73mm.
Goodall 1990-10, fig 83.588.

H293 HINGE PIVOT (not illustrated)
Lyveden, Northamptonshire.
c1200 to 1350.
Complete. H 36mm, L 60mm.
Steane and Bryant 1975, 137, fig 51.220.

H294 HINGE PIVOT (not illustrated)
Somerby, Lincolnshire.
15th to 16th century.
Complete. H 35mm, L 75mm.
Mynard 1969, 84.

H295 HINGE PIVOT (not illustrated)
Winchester, Hampshire.
18th–19th century.
Complete. H 44mm, L 75mm.
Goodall 1990-10, 343, no. 649.

H296 HINGE PIVOT (not illustrated)
Holworth, Dorset.
Site: 13th to 15th century.
Shank broken. H 45mm, L 76mm.
Rahtz 1959, 146, fig 12.9.

H297 HINGE PIVOT
Beckery Chapel, Glastonbury, Somerset.
Second half 13th century to Dissolution.
Lead caulking on shank, guide arm ?broken.
H 34mm, L 77mm.
Rahtz and Hirst 1974, 61, fig 22.5.

H298 HINGE PIVOT (not illustrated)
London.
?Late 13th to mid 14th century.
Complete. H 36mm, L 77mm.
Henig 1974, 195, fig 39.105.

H299 HINGE PIVOT
Northampton.
12th to 13th century.
Complete. H 49mm, L 77mm.
Goodall 1979b, 71, fig 17.10.

H300 HINGE PIVOT
Winchester, Hampshire.
Mid–?late 13th century.
Complete. H 43mm, L 78mm.
Goodall 1990-10, fig 83.603.

H301 HINGE PIVOT
North Elmham Park, Norfolk.
c1150 to c1600.
Complete, shank worn. H 32mm, L 78mm.
Goodall 1980a, 513, fig 267.67.

H302 HINGE PIVOT
Glottenham, East Sussex.
Early 14th century.
Complete. H 44mm, L 78mm.
Excavated by D Martin.

H303 HINGE PIVOT (not illustrated)
Northampton.
15th century from c1410–1420.
Complete. H 45mm, L 78mm.
Goodall *et al* 1979, 268, fig 117.30, incorrectly numbered 27 in text.

H304 HINGE PIVOT (not illustrated)
Wharram Percy, North Yorkshire.
Early 15th century.
Complete. H 38mm, L 80mm.
Goodall 1979a, 118, SF 11512.

H305 HINGE PIVOT
Oxford.
Second half 11th century.
Shank tip broken. H 52mm, L 77mm.
Goodall 1977e, 142, fig 27.34.

H306 HINGE PIVOT
Thelsford Priory, Warwickshire.
Site: 1200–1212 to 1536.
Shank tip broken. H 54mm, L 79mm.
Excavated by Mrs M Gray.

H307 HINGE PIVOT
Southampton, Hampshire.
1200–1250.
Shank broken. H 59mm, L 79mm.
Harvey 1975b, 277, fig 250.1989.

H308 HINGE PIVOT
Winchester, Hampshire.
Late 13th–early 14th century.
Complete. H 43mm, L 80mm.
Goodall 1990-10, 342, no. 623.

H309 HINGE PIVOT
Old Sarum, Wiltshire.
12th century.
Complete. H 47mm, L 81mm.
Musty 1958–60, 191, fig 6.

H310 HINGE PIVOT
Seacourt, Oxfordshire.
14th century.
Complete. H 33mm, L 82mm.
Biddle 1961–62, 175, fig 29.13, scale 1:4, not 1:3.

H311 HINGE PIVOT (not illustrated)
Goltho, Lincolnshire.
Site: late Saxon to late 14th or early 15th century
Shank tip broken. H 36mm, L 81mm
Goodall 1975a, 85, fig 40.70

H312 HINGE PIVOT (not illustrated)
Winchester, Hampshire.
Mid 13th century.
Complete. H 40mm, W 82mm.
Goodall 1990-10, 342, no. 602.

H313 HINGE PIVOT (not illustrated)
Wharram Percy, North Yorkshire.
Early 15th century.
Complete. H 43mm, L 81mm.
Goodall 1979a, 118, fig 60.14.

H314 HINGE PIVOT (not illustrated)
The Hamel, Oxford.
Late 15th century.
Complete. H 43mm, L 82mm.
Goodall 1980d.

H315 HINGE PIVOT
Goltho, Lincolnshire.
14th century, occupied until not long of middle of century.
Clenched shank tip. H 39mm, L 84mm.
Goodall 1975a, 85, fig 40.71.

H316 HINGE PIVOT
Stonar, Kent.
c1275 to 1385.
Complete. H 37mm, L 86mm.
Excavated by N Macpherson-Grant.

BUILDING AND FURNITURE FITTINGS

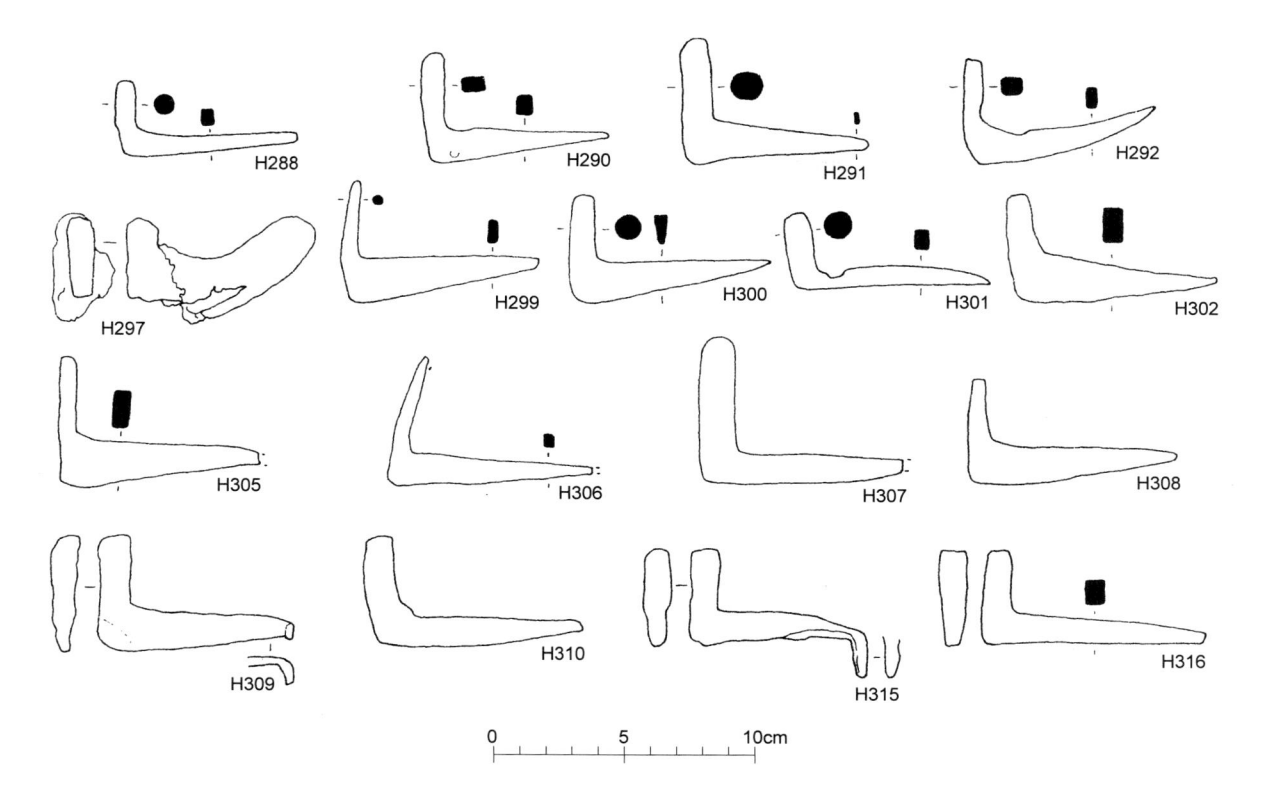

FIGURE 9.13
Hinge pivots

H317 HINGE PIVOT (not illustrated)
North Elmham Park, Norfolk.
*c*1150 to *c*1600.
Complete. H 36mm, L 88mm.
Goodall 1980a, 513, fig 267.68.

H318 HINGE PIVOT
Northampton.
Medieval.
Complete. H 39mm, L 88mm.
Goodall *et al* 1979, 268, fig 117.27,
incorrectly numbered 30 in text.

H319 HINGE PIVOT (not illustrated)
Winchester, Hampshire.
14th century.
Complete. H 40mm, L 88mm.
Goodall 1990-10, 343, no. 632.

H320 HINGE PIVOT (not illustrated)
Winchester, Hampshire.
*c*1110.
Complete. H 49mm, L 89mm.
Goodall 1990-10, fig 83.583.

H321 HINGE PIVOT (not illustrated)
Goltho, Lincolnshire.
Site: late Saxon to late 14th or early 15th
century.
Shank distorted. H 48mm, L 93mm.
Goodall 1975a, 85, fig 40.72.

H322 HINGE PIVOT (not illustrated)
Water Newton, Cambridgeshire.
Medieval, pre-13th century.
Complete. H 38mm, L 95mm.
Green 1962–63, 78, fig 4.4.

H323 HINGE PIVOT
Barrow Mead, Somerset.
13th to 14th century.
Shank worn. H 42mm, L 93mm.
Goodall 1976b, 35, fig 11.19.

H324 HINGE PIVOT
Stonar, Kent.
*c*1275–1385. Found with hinge pivot **H327**
and hinge **H421**.
Complete. H 51mm, L 90mm.
Excavated by N Macpherson-Grant.

H325 HINGE PIVOT
Somerby, Lincolnshire.
Probably derived from 15th to mid
16th-century occupation.
Complete. H 44mm, L 96mm.
Mynard 1969, 84, fig 13.IW77.

H326 HINGE PIVOT
Oxford.
*c*1400 to *c*1550.
Complete. H 47mm, L 96mm.
Goodall 1977e, 142, fig 27.35.

H327 HINGE PIVOT
Stonar, Kent.
*c*1275–1385. Found with hinge pivot **H324**
and hinge **H421**.
Complete. H 34mm, L 98mm.
Excavated by N Macpherson-Grant.

H328 HINGE PIVOT (not illustrated)
Patchway Field, Stanmer Park, East Sussex.
13th century.
Shank tip broken. H 43mm, L 93mm.
Excavated by W C L Gorton.

H329 HINGE PIVOT (not illustrated)
Gomeldon, Wiltshire.
Second half 12th century.
Shank broken. H 45mm, L 92mm.
Musty and Algar 1986.

H330 HINGE PIVOT
Oxford.
Third quarter 12th century.
Complete. H 59mm, L 98mm.
Goodall 1977e, 142, fig 27.36.

H331 HINGE PIVOT (not illustrated)
Goltho Manor, Lincolnshire.
*c*1100–1150.
Shank tip broken. H 47mm, L 97mm.
Goodall 1987, fig 158.89.

H332 HINGE PIVOT
Wroughton Copse, Fyfield Down, Wiltshire.
12th to 13th century.
Shank broken. H 42mm, L 93mm.
Excavated by P J Fowler.

H333 HINGE PIVOT
Clarendon Palace, Wiltshire.
Site: *c*1072 to later 15th century.
Shank tip broken. H 41mm, L 100mm.
Goodall 1988, fig 76.52; Borenius and
Charlton 1936.

H334 HINGE PIVOT
Winchester, Hampshire.
Mid–late 13th century.
Complete. H 64mm, L 95mm.
Goodall 1990-10, fig 83.608.

H335 HINGE PIVOT
Clough Castle, Co. Down.
*c*1250. One of identical pair in same context
as two strap hinges, hasp and barrel
padlock, all perhaps from same door.
Shank worn, tip clenched. H 50mm,
L 100mm.
Waterman 1954, 140, fig 12.4

H336 HINGE PIVOT (not illustrated)
Clough Castle, Co. Down.
*c*1250. One of identical pair in same context
as two strap hinges, hasp and barrel
padlock, all perhaps from same door.
Shank worn, tip clenched. H 50mm,
L 100mm (by comparison with **H333**).
Waterman 1954, 138.

H337 HINGE PIVOT
Ospringe, Kent.
Demolition *c*1550–70 on site founded *c*1230.
Complete. H 45mm, L 102mm.
Goodall 1979c, 132, fig 20.41.

H338 HINGE PIVOT
Wintringham, Cambridgeshire.
Around early 14th century.
Clenched shank tip broken. H 54mm,
L 101mm.
Goodall 1977a, 257.

H339 HINGE PIVOT
Waltham Abbey, Essex.
1500–70.
Complete. H 47mm, L 103mm.
Goodall 1978d, 158, fig 21.6.

H340 HINGE PIVOT (not illustrated)
Somerby, Lincolnshire.
Site: 11th to mid 16th century.
Complete. H 44mm, L 98mm.
Mynard 1969, 84, fig 13.IW78.

H341 HINGE PIVOT (not illustrated)
Wintringham, Cambridgeshire.
Demolition levels of kitchen in use
*c*1275–1300. Found attached to hinge **H417**.
Complete. H 68mm, L 100mm. For
illustration see **H417**.
Goodall 1977a, 257, fig 44.30, scale 1:3,
not 1:4.

H342 HINGE PIVOT
Wintringham, Cambridgeshire.
Demolition levels of kitchen in use *c*1275 to
1300. Found with hinge **H418**.
Hinge identical to **H417**; hinge pivot shank
broken. Hinge L 444mm, hinge pivot H
59mm, L 101mm.
Goodall 1977a, 257.

BUILDING AND FURNITURE FITTINGS

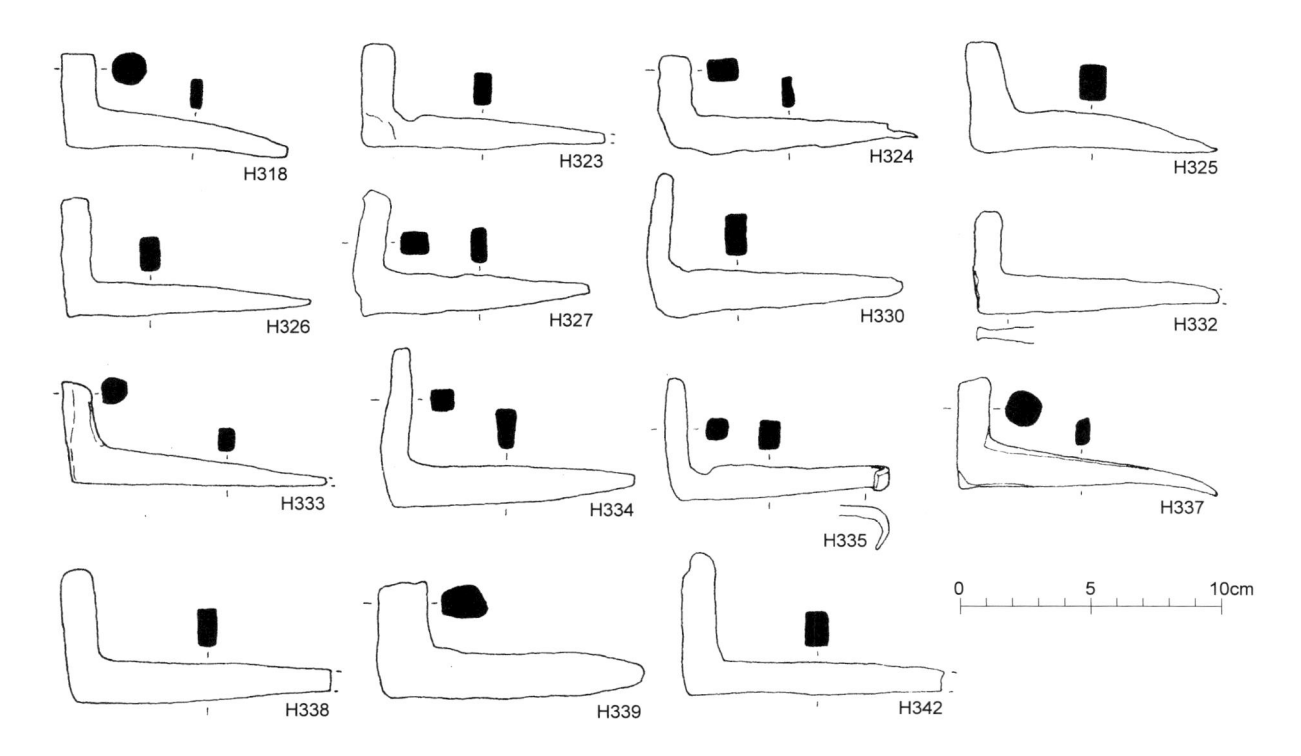

FIGURE 9.14
Hinge pivots

H343 HINGE PIVOT
Wintringham, Cambridgeshire.
Early 14th century.
Worn shank, clenched tip broken. H 67mm,
L 93mm.
Goodall 1977a, 257, fig 45.41.

H344 HINGE PIVOT
Winchester, Hampshire.
Early 13th century.
Distorted pivot, shank broken. H 65mm,
L 83mm.
Goodall 1990-10, fig 83.593.

H345 HINGE PIVOT
Northampton.
Early 15th century from c1410–20.
Complete. H 52mm, L 105mm.
Goodall et al 1979, 268, fig 117.24.

H346 HINGE PIVOT
Brandon Castle, Warwickshire.
1226–66.
Complete. H 60mm, L 107mm.
Chatwin 1955, 81, fig 11.21.

H347 HINGE PIVOT
Clarendon Palace, Wiltshire.
Site: c1072 to later 15th century.
Complete, shank set in lead culking. H 39mm,
L 112mm overall.
Goodall 1988, fig 76.58; Borenius and Charlton 1936.

H348 HINGE PIVOT (not illustrated)
Wintringham, Cambridgeshire.
Early 14th century.
Shank worn, tip broken. H 53mm, L 112mm.
Goodall 1977a, 257, fig 45.39.

H349 HINGE PIVOT
North Elmham Park, Norfolk.
c1150 to c1600.
Shank clenched. H 52mm, L 113mm.
Goodall 1980a, 513, fig 267.69.

H350 HINGE PIVOT
Stonar, Kent.
c1275 to 1385.
Complete. H 50mm, L 119mm.
Excavated by N Macpherson-Grant.

H351 HINGE PIVOT (not illustrated)
Stonar, Kent.
c1275 to 1385.
Broken clenched tip to shank. H 59mm,
L 119mm.
Excavated by N Macpherson-Grant.

H352 HINGE PIVOT
Winchester, Hampshire.
14th century.
Worn, broken shank. H 54mm, L 85mm.
Goodall 1990-10, fig 83.628.

H353 HINGE PIVOT
Oxford.
Early 14th to mid 15th century.
Worn, broken shank. H 55mm, L 118mm.
Goodall 1976c, 298, fig 26.6.

H354 HINGE PIVOT (not illustrated)
Wintringham, Cambridgeshire.
Site: c1175 to 1340.
Shank tip broken. H 57mm, L 119mm.
Goodall 1977a, 257.

H355 HINGE PIVOT (not illustrated)
Wintringham, Cambridgeshire.
Demolition levels of kitchen in use c1275–1300. Found attached to hinge **H412**.
Complete. H 57mm, L 128mm. For illustration see **H412**.
Goodall 1977a, 257, fig 44.31, scale 1:3, not 1:4.

H356 HINGE PIVOT (not illustrated)
Clarendon Palace, Wiltshire.
Site: c1072 to later 15th century.
Complete. H 47mm, L 129mm.
Goodall 1988, fig 76; Borenius and Charlton 1936.

H357 HINGE PIVOT (not illustrated)
Wintringham, Cambridgeshire.
Site: c1175 to 1340.
Complete. H 45mm, L 130mm.
Goodall 1977a, 257.

H358 HINGE PIVOT (not illustrated)
Goltho, Lincolnshire.
Site: late Saxon to late 14th or early 15th century.
Shank worn. H 54mm, L 130mm.
Goodall 1975a, 85, fig 40.73.

H359 HINGE PIVOT (not illustrated)
Kings Langley, Hertfordshire.
In window probably inserted in cellar in 1388.
Single surviving pivot of four set in rebates in window reveal to carry shutters on hinges.
H 60mm, L 130mm.
Neal 1973, 48, fig IX.10.

H360 HINGE PIVOT
Goltho Manor, Lincolnshire.
c1100–1125.
Shank tip clenched. H 47mm, L 135mm.
Goodall 1987, fig 158.90.

H361 HINGE PIVOT
Wintringham, Cambridgeshire.
Around early 14th century.
Worn shank. H 59mm, L 135mm.
Goodall 1977a, 257, fig 45.40.

H362 HINGE PIVOT
Dyserth Castle, Clwyd.
Site: 1241–63.
Complete. H 66mm, L 142mm.
Glenn 1915.

H363 HINGE PIVOT
Kirkcudbright Castle, Dumfries and Galloway.
Site: c1288–1308.
Shank broken. H 61mm, L 135mm.
Dunning et al 1957–58, 138, fig 7.2.

H364 HINGE PIVOT
Wintringham, Cambridgeshire.
Early 14th century.
Shank tip broken. H 68mm, L 144mm.
Goodall 1977a, 257.

H365 HINGE PIVOT
Wintringham, Cambridgeshire.
Site: c1175 to 1340.
Clenched tip to shank broken. H 60mm,
L 146mm.
Goodall 1977a, 257, fig 45.42.

H366 HINGE PIVOT
North Elmham Park, Norfolk.
c1150 to c1600.
Complete. H 44mm, L 160mm.
Goodall 1980a, 513, fig 267.70.

H367 HINGE PIVOT (not illustrated)
Stonar, Kent.
c1275–1385. Found attached to hinge **H435**.
Complete. H 33mm, L 49mm. For illustration see **H435**.
Excavated by N Macpherson-Grant.

H368 HINGE PIVOT
West Hartburn, Durham.
Medieval to later 16th century. One of pair of hinge pivots and hinges from burnt door. See **H369** and **H391–392**.
Shank broken. H 39mm, L 79mm.
Still and Pallister 1967, 146, fig 4.1.

H369 HINGE PIVOT
West Hartburn, Durham.
Site medieval to later 16th century. One of pair of hinge pivots and hinges from burnt door.
See **H368** and **H391–392**.
Shank broken. H 45mm L 66mm.
Still and Pallister 1967, 146, fig 4.1.

H370 HINGE PIVOT
Alsted, Surrey.
c1270 to 1350.
Complete. H 28mm, L 75mm.
Goodall 1976a, 56, fig 34.2.

H371 HINGE PIVOT
Alsted, Surrey.
c1270 to 1350.
Guide arm damaged. H 36mm, L 89mm.
Goodall 1976a, 56, fig 34.3.

H372 HINGE PIVOT
Penhallam, Cornwall.
c1200 to mid 14th century.
Down-turned end to shank which retains some lead caulking. H 37mm, L 94mm.
Goodall 1974c, 139, fig 46.2.

H373 HINGE PIVOT
Penhallam, Cornwall.
c1200 to mid 14th century.
Down-turned end to shank which retains some lead caulking. H 44mm, L 95mm.
Goodall 1974c, 139, fig 46.3.

H374 HINGE PIVOT
Penhallam, Cornwall.
c1200 to mid 14th century.
Down-turned end to shank which retains some lead caulking. H 56mm, L 97mm.
Goodall 1974c, 139, fig 46.4.

H375 HINGE PIVOT
Winchester, Hampshire.
c1222.
Shank with down-turned end retains lead caulking. H 42mm, L 98mm.
Goodall 1990-10, fig 82.559.

BUILDING AND FURNITURE FITTINGS

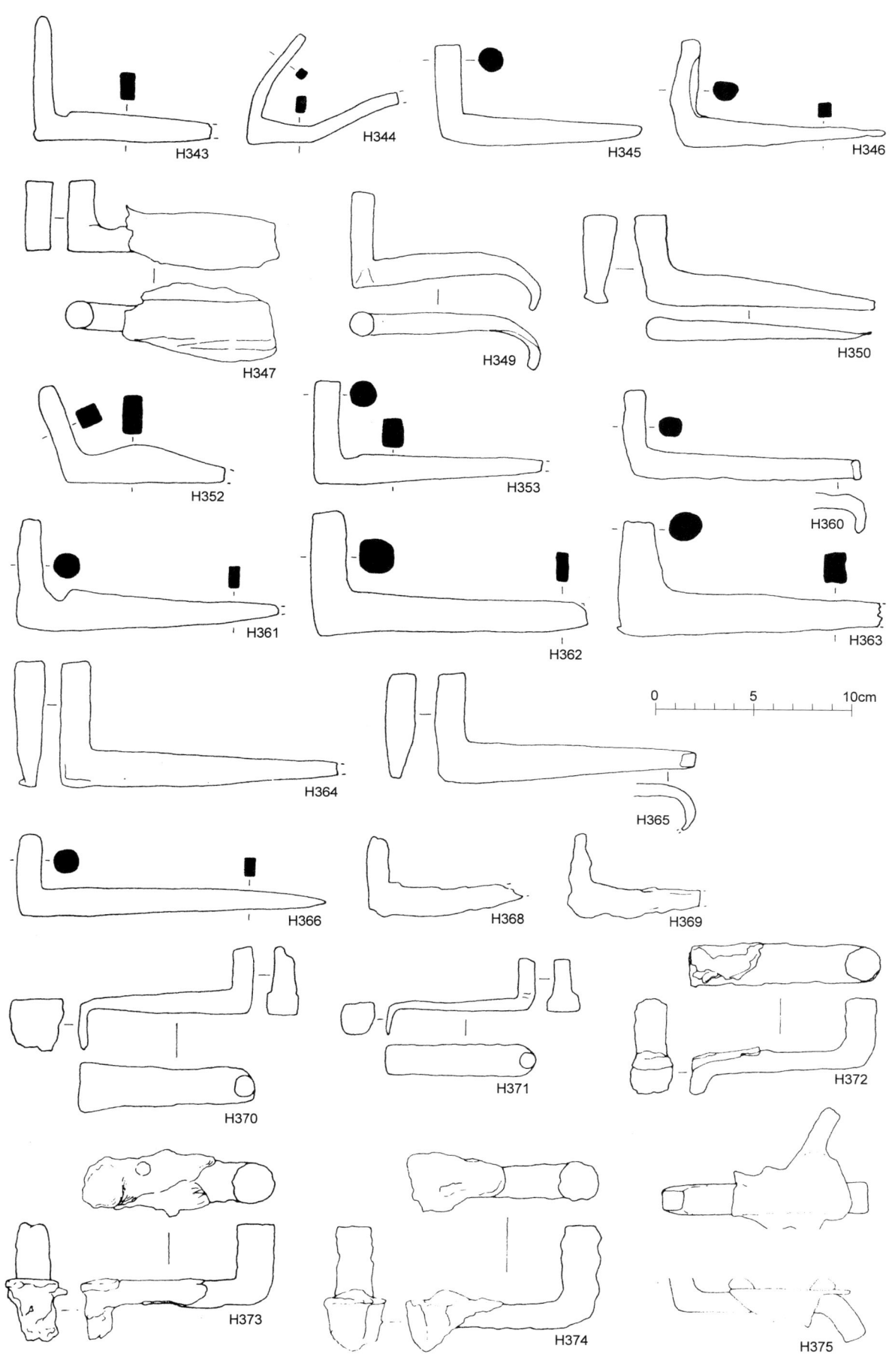

FIGURE 9.15
Hinge pivots

H376 HINGE PIVOT
Northampton.
c1250 to end 14th century.
Down-turned end to shank. H 50mm, L 115mm.
Goodall *et al* 1979, 268, fig 117.23.

H377 HINGE PIVOT
Winchester, Hampshire.
14th century.
Shank broken. H 24mm, L 56mm.
Goodall 1990-10, fig 82.560.

H378 HINGE PIVOT
Somerby, Lincolnshire.
Derived from 11th- to 15th-century occupation.
Shank broken. H 40mm, L 90mm.
Mynard 1969, 84.

H379 HINGE PIVOT
Castell-y-Bere, Gwynedd.
Site: c1221–95.
Shank with down-turned end set in lead, guide arm lost. L 111mm.
Butler 1974, 98, fig 9.28.

H380 HINGE PIVOT
Winchester, Hampshire.
Mid 12th century.
Shank end bifurcated. H 46mm, L 95mm.
Goodall 1990-10, fig 82.558.

H381 HINGE PIVOT (not illustrated)
Bordesley Abbey, Hereford and Worcester.
Site: c1140–1538 and later.
Split shank secured in lead caulking.
L 180mm.
Wright 1976, 195, fig 36.14.

H382 HINGE PIVOT
Hen Blas, Clwyd.
In late 12th-century chapel door jamb.
Broken shank secured in rebate in stone by lead caulking. L 118mm.
Leach 1960, 13–14, fig 10.

H383 HINGE PIVOT (not illustrated)
Winchester, Hampshire.
Mid 16th century.
Substantial, broken shank with bifurcated end set in lead. L 67mm, W 80mm.
Goodall 1990-10, 338, no. 563.

H384 HINGE PIVOT
Winchester, Hampshire.
15th century.
Shank broken. H 127mm, L 88mm.
Goodall 1990-10, fig 82.562.

H385 HINGE
Somerby, Lincolnshire.
15th to mid 16th century.
Looped eye, distorted and broken strap.
L 468mm.
Mynard 1969, 84, fig 13.IW79.

H386 HINGE
Hambleton Moat, Lincolnshire.
Site: 1250–1400.
Looped eye, strap with bifurcated terminal.
L 370mm.
Butler 1963, 67, fig 14.11.

H387 HINGE
Weoley Castle, Birmingham, West Midlands.
c1200–1380.
Looped eye, strap end upturned. L 369mm.
Taylor 1974. For site see Oswald 1962.

H388 HINGE (not illustrated)
Weoley Castle, Birmingham, West Midlands.
c1200–1380.
Looped eye, broken strap. L 336mm, W 32mm.
Taylor 1974. For site see Oswald 1962.

H389 HINGE (not illustrated)
Weoley Castle, Birmingham, West Midlands.
c1200–1380.
Looped eye, broken strap. L 274mm, W 43mm.
Taylor 1974. For site see Oswald 1962.

H390 HINGE (not illustrated)
Winchester, Hampshire.
14th century.
Looped eye, broken strap. L 169mm, W 25mm.
Goodall 1990-10, fig 84.655.

H391 HINGE
West Hartburn, Durham.
Site medieval to later 16th century. One of a pair of hinges and hinge pivots from burnt door. See **H368–369** and **H392**.
Looped eye, broken strap. L 198mm.
Still and Pallister 1967, 141, 146, fig 4.1

H392 HINGE (not illustrated)
West Hartburn, Durham.
Site medieval to later 16th century. One of a pair of hinges and hinge pivots from burnt door. See **H368–369** and **H391**.
Looped eye, broken strap. L 165mm, W unknown.
Still and Pallister 1967, 141, 146, fig 4.1

H393 HINGE
Griff (Sudeley Castle), Warwickshire.
Site: 13th to 14th century.
Looped eye, broken and distorted strap.
L 160mm.
West 1968, 87, fig 4.7.

H394 HINGE
Goltho, Lincolnshire.
Croft A: late Saxon to late 14th or early 15th century.
Looped eye, bifurcated terminal. L 161mm.
Goodall 1975a, 86, fig 40.75.

H395 HINGE (not illustrated)
Somerby, Lincolnshire.
Site: 11th to mid 16th century.
Looped eye, strap broken. L 44mm, W 41mm.
Mynard 1969, 84, fig 13.IW80.

H396 HINGE (not illustrated)
Winchester, Hampshire.
c1135–38.
Looped eye, broken strap. L 37mm, W 30mm.
Goodall 1990-18, fig 303.3454.

H397 HINGE
Goltho, Lincolnshire.
Croft A: late Saxon to late 14th or early 15th century.
Looped eye, broken strap. L 92mm.
Goodall 1975a, 86, fig 40.76.

H398 HINGE
Goltho, Lincolnshire.
Croft A: late Saxon to late 14th or early 15th century.
Looped eye, broken strap. L 52mm, W 18mm.
Goodall 1975a, 86, fig 40.77.

H399 HINGE
Hen Caerwys, Clwyd.
c1450–1520.
Looped eye, broken strap. L 79mm.
Excavated by G B Leach.

H400 HINGE
Cambokeels, Durham.
Site: from last quarter 14th century into 16th century.
Looped eye, broken strap. L 79mm.
Hildyard 1949, 199, fig 4.7.

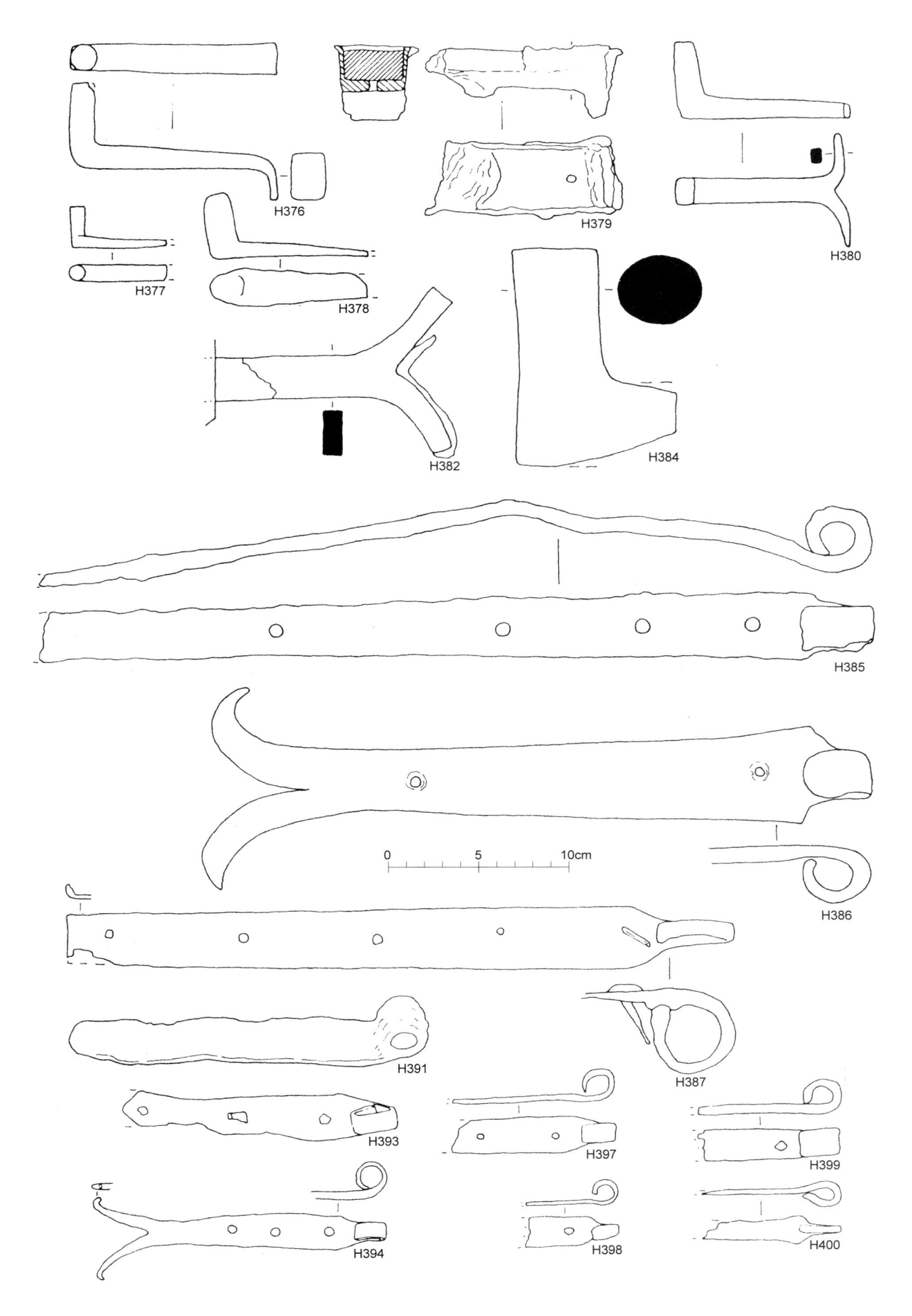

FIGURE 9.16
Hinge pivots and hinges

H401 HINGE
Griff (Sudeley Castle), Warwickshire.
Site: 13th to 14th century.
Looped eye, T-shaped strap. L 98mm.
West 1968, 87, fig 4.8.

H402 HINGE
Alsted, Surrey.
c1270–1350.
C-shaped hinge, both ends broken, with looped eye. W 131mm.
Goodall 1976a, 56, fig 34.7.

H403 HINGE
Rievaulx Abbey, North Yorkshire.
Site: 1131–1538 with later robbing.
C-shaped hinge with shaped terminals and centrally set looped eye. W 214mm.
DAMHB Collection, London. RVA 305.

H404 WELL COVER (Figure 9.17)
Lydford Castle, Devon.
Mid 13th century.
Well cover reconstructed from fragments of ironwork in well. Two strap hinges with scrolled terminals and looped eyes nailed to battens and ledges. Four other ledges held to battens by clench bolts with shaped roves (**H244**). Curved hasp **H624** stapled close to edge. Hinge L 810mm
Goodall 1980b, fig 17.

H405 HINGE
Winchester, Hampshire.
?Mid 14th century.
Looped eye, broken strap. L 440mm.
Goodall 1990-10, fig 84.653.

H406 HINGE
Clarendon Palace, Wiltshire.
Site: c1072 to later 15th century.
Looped eye, strap with simply shaped terminal. L 215mm.
Goodall 1988, fig 77.55; Borenius and Charlton 1936.

H407 HINGE (not illustrated)
Ospringe, Kent.
c1483–1550.
Looped eye, broken strap. L 60mm.
Goodall 1979c, 132, fig 20.47.

H408 HINGE (not illustrated)
Clarendon Palace, Wiltshire.
Site: c1072 to later 15th century.
Looped eye, broken strap. L 35mm, W 28mm.
Goodall 1988, fig 77; Borenius and Charlton 1936.

H409 HINGE
Criccieth Castle, Gwynedd.
Site: c1230–1404.
Looped eye, broken strap. L 61mm.
O'Neil 1944–45, 42, pl X.32.

H410 HINGE
Winchester, Hampshire.
?Mid 14th century.
Looped eye, broken strap. L 91mm.
Goodall 1990-10, fig 84.654.

H411 HINGE (not illustrated)
Eynsford Castle, Kent.
c1250. One of a pair of hinges.
Nailed U-shaped eye, bifurcated terminal. L 574mm.
Rigold 1971, 144, fig 9.1

H412/H355 HINGE AND HINGE PIVOT
Wintringham, Cambridgeshire.
Demolition levels of kitchen in use c1275 to 1300.
Hinge with nailed U-shaped eye and strap, both broken. Hinge pivot complete. Hinge L 538mm, hinge pivot H 57mm, L 128mm.
Goodall 1977a, 257, fig 44.31, scale 1:5, not 1:4.

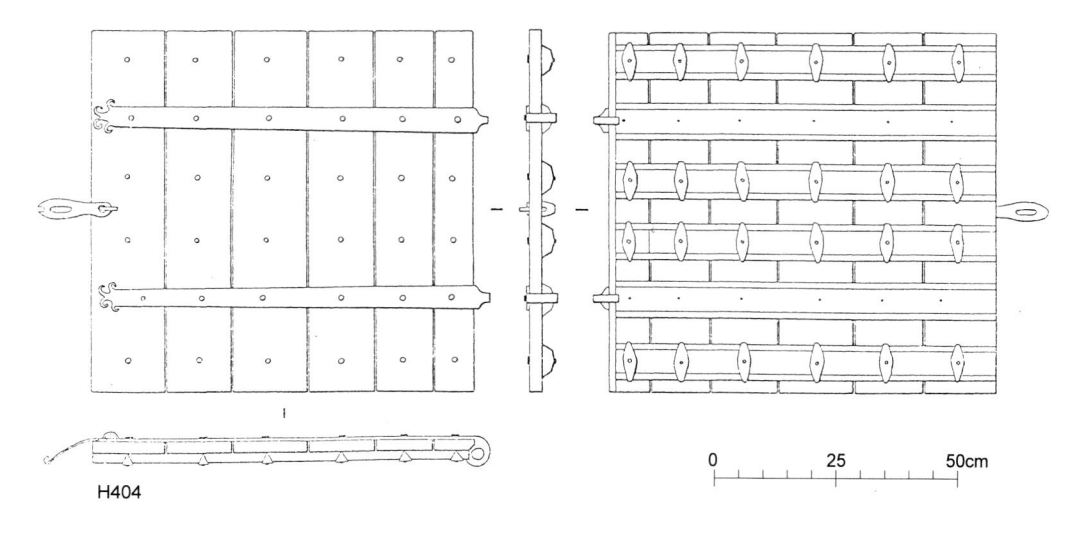

FIGURE 9.17
Well cover

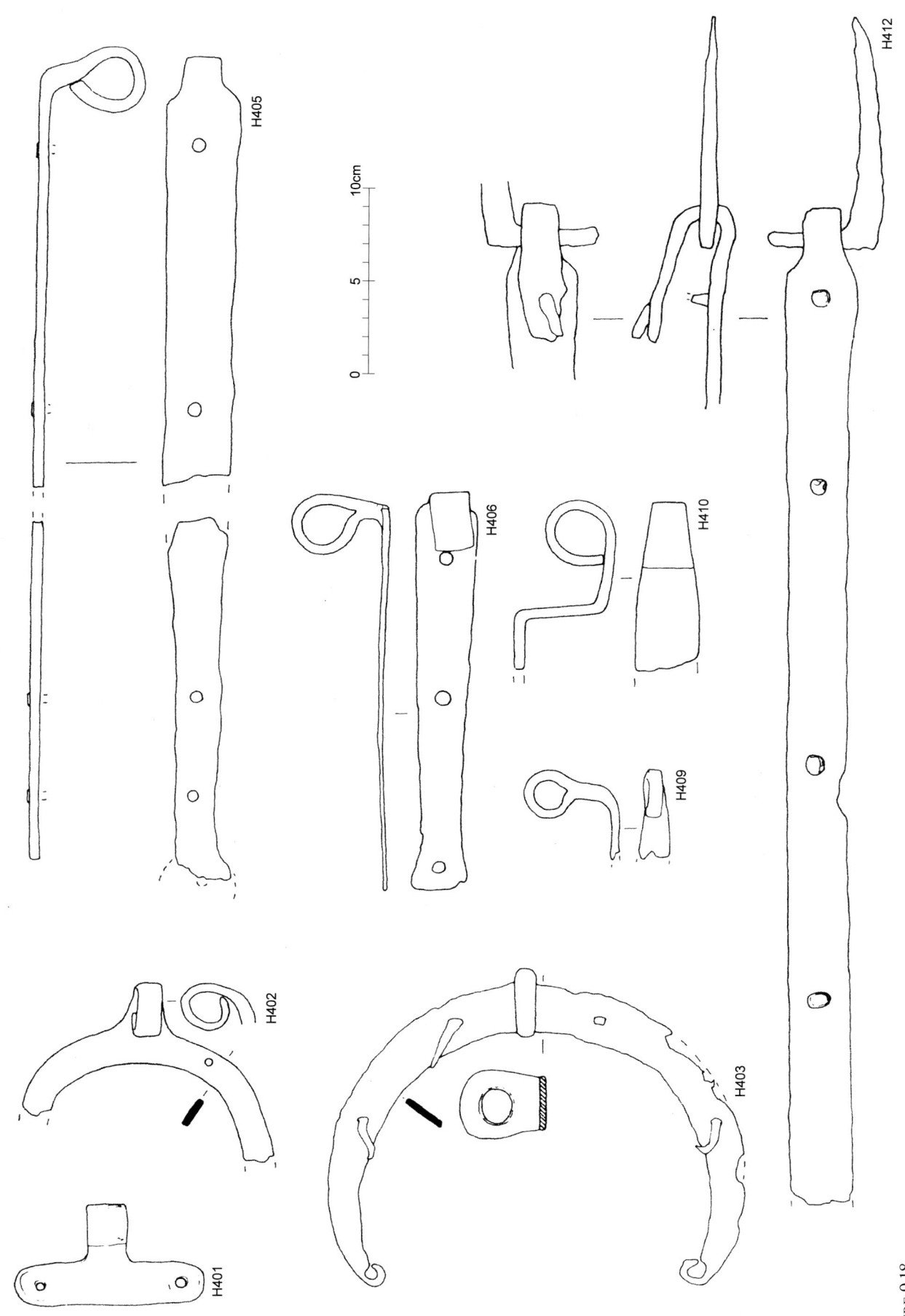

FIGURE 9.18
Hinges

H413 HINGE
Wintringham, Cambridgeshire.
Demolition levels of kitchen in use c1275 to 1300.
Nailed U-shaped eye, strap broken.
L 205mm.
Goodall 1977a, 257, fig 45.32.

H414 HINGE
Alsted, Surrey.
c1270–1400.
Nailed U-shaped eye, broken strap.
L 496mm.
Goodall 1976a, 56, fig 35.34.

H415 HINGE
Huish, Wiltshire.
Site: 12th to mid 15th century.
Nailed U-shaped eye with shaped rear terminal, strap broke. L 302mm.
Shortt 1972, 120, fig 5.31.

H416 HINGE (not illustrated)
Oxford.
Early 14th to mid 15th century.
Nailed U-shaped eye, rear terminal and strap broken. L 128mm, W 38mm.
Goodall 1976c, 298, fig 26.5.

H417/H341 HINGE AND HINGE PIVOT
Wintringham, Cambridgeshire.
Demolition levels of kitchen in use c1275 to 1300. One of a pair.
Hinge with nailed U-shaped eye and shaped terminal; hinge pivot shank broken. Hinge L 444mm, hinge pivot H 68mm, L 10mm.
Goodall 1977a, 257, fig 44.30, scale 1:5, not 1:4.

H418/H342 HINGE AND HINGE PIVOT
(not illustrated)
Wintringham, Cambridgeshire.
Demolition levels of kitchen in use c1275 to 1300.
Hinge identical to **H417**; hinge pivot shank broken. Hinge L 444mm, hinge pivot **H342**, H 59mm, L 101mm.
Goodall 1977a, 257.

H419 HINGE
Clough Castle, Co. Down.
c1250. One of a pair of hinges from same context as two hinge pivots, hasp and barrel padlock, all perhaps from same door.
Nailed U-shaped eye, rear terminal and strap with bifurcated terminal both broken.
L 374mm
Waterman 1954, 138, fig 12.1

FIGURE 9.19
Hinges

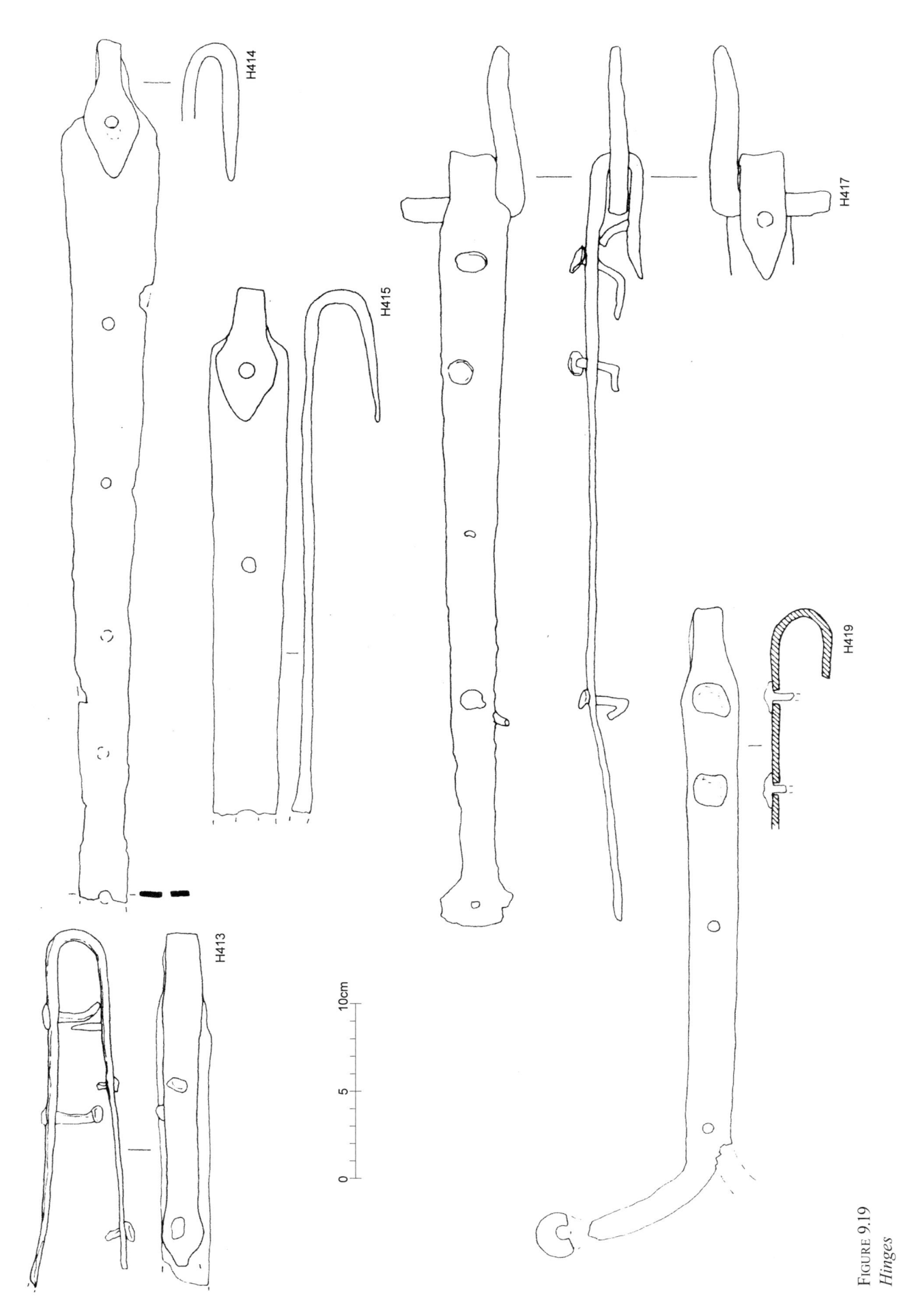

H420 HINGE
Clough Castle, Co. Down.
c1250. One of a pair of hinges from same context as two hinge pivots, hasp and barrel padlock, all perhaps from same door.
Nailed U-shaped eye, strap with broken bifurcated terminal. L 332mm
Waterman 1954, 138, fig 12.2

H421 HINGE
Stonar, Kent.
c1275–1385. Found with hinge pivots **H324** and **H327**.
Nailed U-shaped eye, strap with bifurcated terminal. L 341mm.
Excavated by N Macpherson-Grant.

H422 HINGE (not illustrated)
Northolt Manor, Greater London.
1300–1350 with 13th-century residual material.
Nailed U-shaped eye, broken strap.
L 150mm.
Excavated by J G Hurst.

H423 HINGE (not illustrated)
Northolt Manor, Greater London.
1200–1300.
Nailed U-shaped eye, broken strap.
L 160mm.
Excavated by J G Hurst.

H424 HINGE (not illustrated)
Stonar, Kent.
Around mid to late 14th century.
Nailed U-shaped eye, broken strap. L 291mm, W 31mm.
Excavated by N Macpherson-Grant.

H425 HINGE (not illustrated)
Stonar, Kent.
c1275–1385.
Nailed U-shaped eye, broken strap. L 186mm, W 24mm.
Excavated by N Macpherson-Grant.

H426 HINGE
Huish, Wiltshire.
Site: 12th to mid 15th century.
Nailed U-shaped eye with shaped rear terminal, complete tapering strap. Hinge distorted. L 239mm.
Shortt 1972, 120, fig 5.33.

H427 HINGE
King's Lynn, Norfolk.
c1250–1300.
Nailed U-shaped eye with shaped rear terminal; simply shaped terminal to strap. L 223mm.
Goodall and Carter 1977, 293, fig 133.14.

H428 HINGE
Winchester, Hampshire.
Late 13th–early 14th century.
Nailed U-shaped eye, broken strap.
L 163mm.
Goodall 1990-10, fig 85.669.

H429 HINGE
Stonar, Kent.
c1275–1385.
Nailed U-shaped eye, rear terminal broken. Strap complete with shaped terminal.
L 196mm.
Excavated by N Macpherson-Grant.

H430/H264 HINGE AND HINGE PIVOT
Stonar, Kent.
c1275 to 1385.
Strap hinge with broken nailed U-shaped eye retaining hinge pivot (see **H367**). Hinge L 94mm.
Excavated by N Macpherson-Grant.

H431 HINGE (not illustrated)
Gomeldon, Wiltshire.
13th century.
Nailed, U-shaped eye with broken rear terminal, strap broken. L 118mm.
Musty and Algar 1986.

H432 HINGE
King's Lynn, Norfolk.
c1250–1350.
Nailed U-shaped eye with shaped rear terminal, simply shaped terminal to strap.
L 186mm.
Goodall and Carter 1977, 293, fig 133.15.

H433 HINGE
Castle Acre Castle, Norfolk.
Second half 12th century.
Nailed U-shaped eye, plain strap. L 175mm.
Goodall 1982, fig 39, no. 54.

H434 HINGE
Chew Valley Lake, Somerset.
13th century or later.
Broken nailed U-shaped eye, terminal to strap. L 178mm.
Rahtz and Greenfield 1977, 326, fig 121.5.

H435/H367 HINGE AND HINGE PIVOT
Stonar, Kent.
c1275–1385.
Broken hinge with nailed U-shaped eye clasping hinge pivot with broken shank. Hinge L 103mm, hinge pivot H 45mm, L 57mm.
Excavated by N Macpherson-Grant.

H436 HINGE
Alsted, Surrey.
c1270–1350.
Nailed U-shaped eye with shaped rear terminal and complete tapering strap.
L 147mm.
Goodall 1976a, 56, fig 34.5.

H437 HINGE
Northampton.
Later 15th century.
Nailed U-shaped eye with shaped rear terminal. Strap complete, terminal distorted. L 138mm.
Goodall et al 1979, 268, fig 117.17.

BUILDING AND FURNITURE FITTINGS

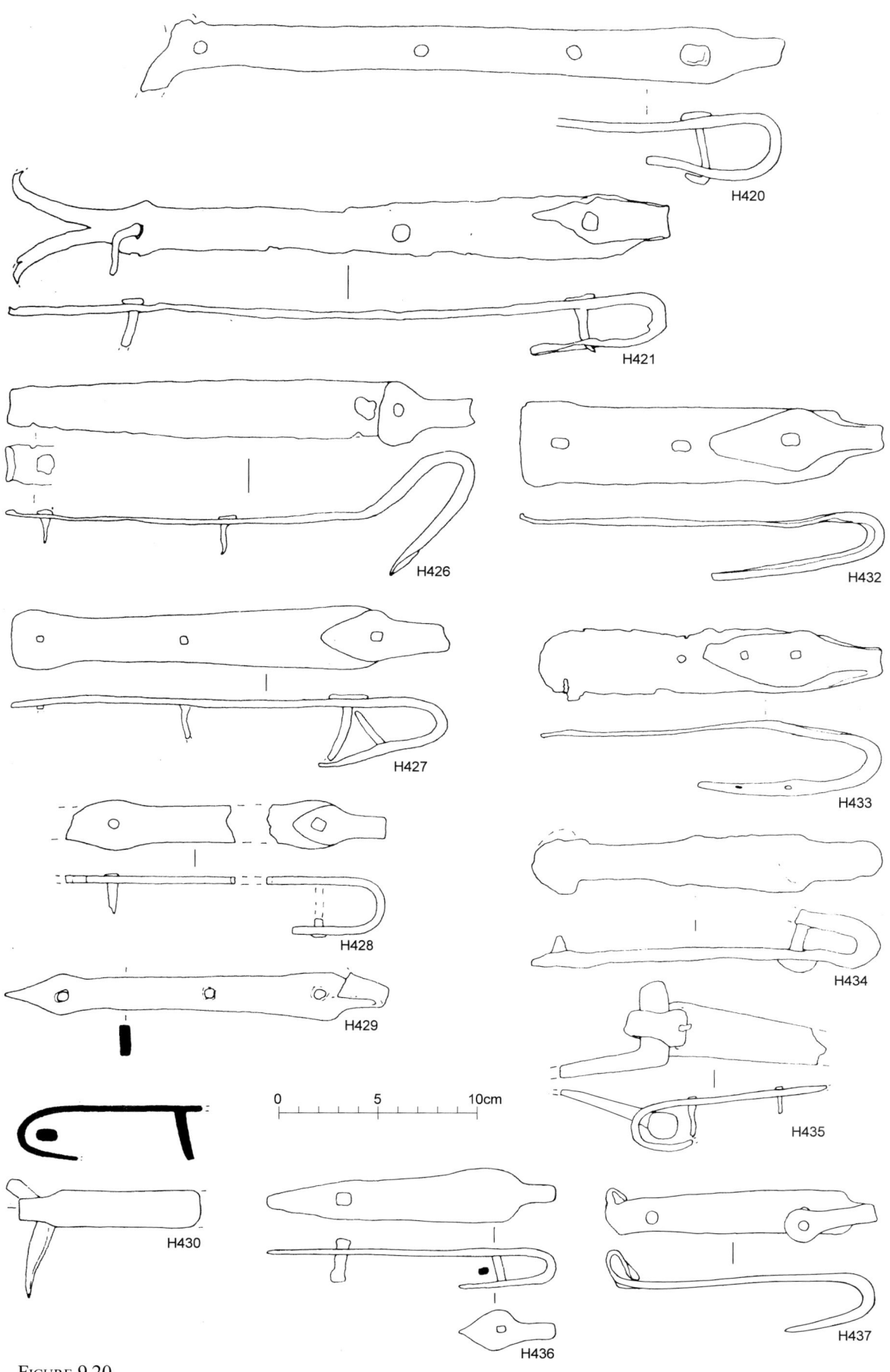

FIGURE 9.20
Hinges

H438 HINGE
Stonar, Kent.
*c*1275–1385.
Broken U-shaped eye, strap with terminal.
L 130mm.
Excavated by N Macpherson-Grant.

H439 HINGE
Northampton.
Early 15th century, from *c*1410–20.
Nailed U-shaped eye, rear terminal and strap broken. L 93mm.
Goodall *et al* 1979, 268, fig 117.16.

H440 HINGE
Badby, Northamptonshire.
1198–1213 to early 14th century.
Nailed U-shaped terminal, strap broken.
L 103mm.
Excavated by Mrs M Gray.

H441 HINGE (not illustrated)
Stonar, Kent.
*c*1150–*c*1225.
Nailed U-shaped eye, strap broken. L 62mm.
Excavated by N Macpherson-Grant.

H442 HINGE (not illustrated)
Grenstein, Norfolk.
Late 14th, 15th century.
Distorted nailed U-shaped eye. L 63mm.
Goodall 1980c.

H443 HINGE (not illustrated)
Oxford.
*c*1325–*c*1400.
Nailed, U-shaped eye with shaped rear terminal, strap broken. L 46mm.
Goodall 1977e, 146, fig 27.40.

H444 HINGE
Ellington, Cambridgeshire.
Mid 12th to second half 13th century.
Nailed U-shaped eye with shaped rear terminal, broken strap. L 50mm.
Goodall 1971, 68, fig 12.20.

H445 HINGE (not illustrated)
Alsted, Surrey.
*c*1250–1350.
Nailed U-shaped eye with shaped rear terminal and broken strap. L 46mm.
Goodall 1976a, 56, fig 34.6.

H446 HINGE
Northampton.
End of 11th to middle of 15th century.
Rear terminal and loop from nailed U-shaped eye of hinge. L 76mm.
Goodall *et al* 1979, 268, fig 117.18.

H447 HINGE (not illustrated)
Wintringham, Cambridgeshire.
Site: *c*1175–1340.
Rear terminal from nailed U-shaped eye, strap broken. L 70mm.
Goodall 1977a, 257, fig 45.34.

H448 HINGE
The Hamel, Oxford.
15th century.
Rear terminal from nailed U-shaped eye.
L 68mm.
Goodall 1980d, fig 29, no. 32.

H449 HINGE
Northampton.
*c*1500.
Spiked U-shaped eye, incomplete. Strap broken.
L 184mm.
Goodall *et al* 1979, 268, fig 117.2.

H450 HINGE
Thelsford Priory, Warwickshire.
Site: 1200–1212 to 1536.
Spiked U-shaped eye, broken strap. L 175mm.
Excavated by Mrs M Gray.

H451 HINGE
Hen Blas, Clwyd.
14th century.
Spiked U-shaped eye, broken strap. L 68mm.
Leach 1960, 23, fig 13.12.

H452 HINGE
Hangleton, East Sussex.
13th–14th century.
Spiked U-shaped eye, complete strap.
L 163mm.
Holden 1963, 169, fig 36.9.

H453 HINGE
North Elmham Park, Norfolk.
*c*1150–*c*1600.
Plain strap, spiked U-shaped eye. L 123mm.
Goodall 1980a, 513, fig 266.62.

H454 HINGE (not illustrated)
Winchester, Hampshire.
Late 13th century.
Broken strap with chisel-cut eye supporting stapled hasp **H570**. Hinge L 53mm. For illustration see **H570**.
Goodall 1990-18, fig 304.3499.

H455 HINGE (not illustrated)
Winchester, Hampshire.
15th century.
Spiked U-shaped eye, broken parallel-sided strap. L 67mm.
Goodall 1990-18, 974, no. 3453.

H456 HINGE (not illustrated)
Winchester, Hampshire.
Late 11th–early 12th.
Spiked U-shaped eye, broken tapering strap.
L 73mm.
Goodall 1990-18, 974, no. 3452.

H456a HINGE (not illustrated)
Winchester, Hampshire.
14th century.
End looped strap, broken. L 38mm, W 17mm.
Goodall 1990-18, 975, no. 3457.

H457 HINGE (not illustrated)
Dover Castle, Kent.
Late 13th century.
Broken end-looped hinge and curved hasp **H604**. Hinge L 71mm. For illustration see **H604**.
Rigold 1967, 109, fig 9.Fe4.

H458 HINGE
Winchester, Hampshire.
Early to mid 13th century.
Broken, angled, end looped strap with non-ferrous plating. L 47mm.
Goodall 1990-18, fig 303.3456.

H459 HINGE
Ospringe, Kent.
*c*1483–1550.
Pinned hinge, originally T-shaped but one strap broken. L 119mm.
Goodall 1979c, 132, fig 21.61.

H460 HINGE
Stonar, Kent.
*c*1275–1385.
Broken plate from pinned hinge. L 100mm.
Excavated by N Macpherson-Grant.

H461 HINGE
Rhuddlan, Clwyd.
Probably very late 13th century or 14th century.
Shaped plate from pinned hinge. L 102mm.
Goodall 1994, fig 17.3, no. 51.

H462 HINGE
Alsted, Surrey.
*c*1250–1405.
Broken plate with single eye from pinned hinge.
L 79mm.
Goodall 1976a, 56, fig 35.33.

H463 HINGE (not illustrated)
Winchester, Hampshire.
16th century
Broken pinned hinge joined to flat stapled hasp **H581**. Hinge L 81mm. For illustration see **H581**.
Goodall 1990-18, fig 304.3506.

H464 HINGE
Ospringe, Kent.
*c*1483–1550.
Pinned hinge with two straight straps, one broken. L 115mm.
Goodall 1979c, 132, fig 21.62.

H465 HINGE (not illustrated)
Winchester, Hampshire.
14th century.
Broken, tapering strap with single eye from pinned hinge. L 96mm, maximum W 22mm.
Goodall 1990-18, 975, no. 3458.

H466 HINGE
Thelsford Priory, Warwickshire.
Site: 1200–1212 to 1536.
Plate with single eye from pinned hinge.
L 81mm.
Excavated by Mrs M Gray.

H467 HINGE
Stonar, Kent.
*c*1275–1385.
Plate with pair of eyes from pinned hinge.
L 68mm.
Excavated by N Macpherson-Grant.

H468 HINGE
Ospringe, Kent.
*c*1483–1550.
Pinned hinge with broken straps, the more complete shaped. L 77mm.
Goodall 1979c, 132, fig 21.63.

H469 HINGE
Winchester, Hampshire.
?Mid 16th century.
Double leaf pinned hinge with non-ferrous plating. L 64mm.
Goodall 1990-18, fig 303.3460.

H470 HINGE
Ospringe, Kent.
*c*1483–1550.
Pinned hinge, one plate incomplete. L 36mm.
Goodall 1979c, 132, fig 21.64.

H471 HINGE
Grenstein, Norfolk.
Late 14th, 15th century.
Strap from pinned hinge. L 79mm.
Goodall 1980c, fig 79, no. 56.

BUILDING AND FURNITURE FITTINGS

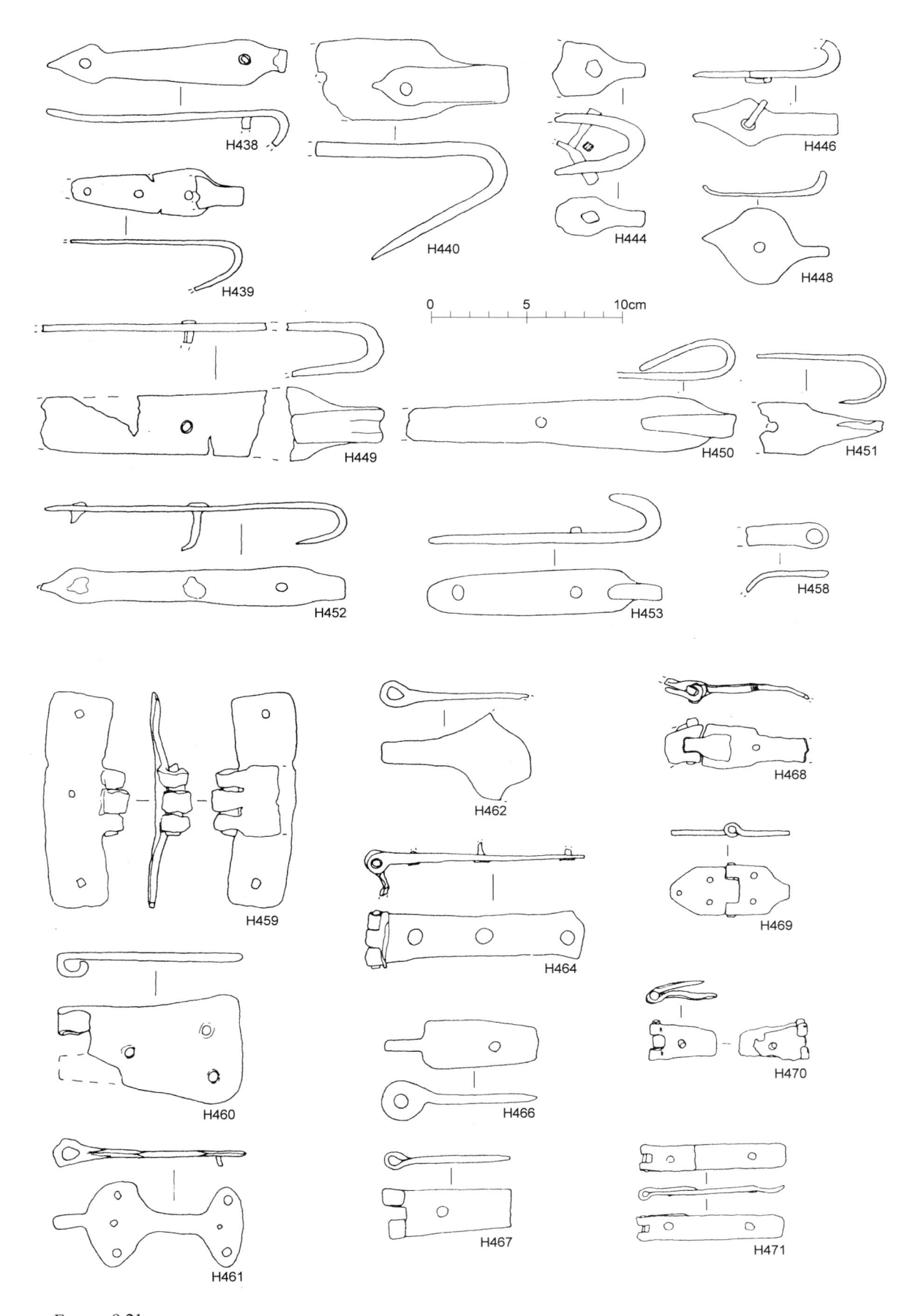

FIGURE 9.21
Hinges

H472 STRAP
Lydney Castle, Gloucestershire.
12th century, possibly into 13th century.
Crescent-shaped strap. D 193mm.
Casey 1931, 254, pl XXXVI.19.

H473 STRAP
Weoley Castle, Birmingham, West Midlands.
c1230–1270.
Broken strap. L 120mm.
Oswald 1962, 130, fig 51.15.

H474 STRAP
Wharram Percy, North Yorkshire.
Late 15th to early 16th century.
Imcomplete strap retaining terminal.
L 129mm.
Goodall 1979a, 118, fig 60.10.

H475 STRAP
South Witham, Lincolnshire.
c1220 to 1308–13.
Broken strap. L 122mm.
Goodall 2002, fig 7.3, no. 46.

H476 STRAP
Wharram Percy, North Yorkshire.
Late 15th to early 16th century.
Broken strap. L 98mm.
Goodall 1979a, 118, SF 12248.

H477 STRAP
King's Lynn, Norfolk.
c1150–1250.
Shaped terminal, strap broken. Wood grain visible across one side. L 236mm.
Goodall and Carter 1977, 293, fig 133.13.

H478 STRAP
Cheddar, Somerset.
Late 10th–12th century.
Shaped terminal, broken and distorted strap.
L 214mm.
Goodall 1979d, 270, fig 91.5.

H479 STRAP (not illustrated)
King's Lynn, Norfolk.
c1250–1300.
Shaped terminal, identical to **H477**, strap broken. Wood grain visible along length.
L 100mm.
Goodall and Carter 1977, 293, BL SF D200.

H480 STRAP
Cheddar, Somerset.
Later 13th century–c1600.
Shaped terminal, broken strap. L 88mm.
Goodall 1979d, 270, fig 91.192.

H481 STRAP
Portchester Castle, Hampshire.
13th century.
Broken, tapering strap with terminal.
L 111mm.
Hinton 1977, 201, fig 108.58.

H482 HINGE
Wharram Percy, North Yorkshire.
Mid 15th to early 16th century.
Broken strap with shaped terminal.
L 120mm.
Goodall 1979a, 121, fig 64.88.

H483 STRAP
Hangleton, East Sussex.
13th century.
Broken strap with terminal. L 192mm.
Holden 1963, 169, fig 36.10.

H484 STRAP (not illustrated)
Eynsford Castle, Kent.
c1250.
Broken strap with edge beading and shaped terminal. L 168mm.
Rigold 1971, 144, fig 9.3.

H485 STRAP
Clough Castle, Co. Down.
c1200–c1225.
Broken strap with terminal. L 131mm.
Waterman 1954, 140, fig 12.3.

H486 STRAP
Winchester, Hampshire.
15th–16th century.
Broken strap with terminal. L 84mm.
Goodall 1990-18, fig 303.3466.

H487 STRAP
Waltham Abbey, Essex.
13th–15th century.
Broken strap retaining terminal. L 264mm.
Goodall 1978d, 158, fig 21.3.

H488 STRAP
Stonar, Kent.
c1275–1385.
Broken strap with terminal. L 144mm.
Excavated by N Macpherson-Grant.

H489 STRAP
The Mount, Princes Risborough, Buckinghamshire.
13th to 15th century.
Broken strap with terminal. L 124mm.
Pavry and Knocker 1953–60, 6, fig 13.6.

H490 STRAP
Somerby, Lincolnshire.
Site: 11th to mid 16th century.
Shaped terminal, broken strap. L 65mm.
Mynard 1969, 84, fig 13.IW82.

H491 STRAP
Winchester, Hampshire.
Late 17th–?early 18th century.
Broken strap and terminal. L 85mm.
Goodall 1990-10, fig 85.677.

H492 STRAP (not illustrated)
Wharram Percy, North Yorkshire.
Late 15th to early 16th century.
Broken strap with bifurcated terminal.
L 89mm.
Goodall 1979a, 118, fig 60.9.

H493 STRAP
Kiln Combe, Bullock Down, East Sussex.
c1200–1500.
Broken bifurcated terminal. L 52mm.
Excavated by P L Drewett.

H494 STRAP
Stonar, Kent.
c1150–c1225.
Broken strap with bifurcated terminal.
L 70mm.
Excavated by N Macpherson-Grant.

H495 STRAP (not illustrated)
Winchester, Hampshire.
Late 13th–early 14th century.
Broken strap with bifurcated terminals.
L 101mm.
Goodall 1990-10, fig 85.676.

H496 STRAP (not illustrated)
Bordesley Abbey, Hereford and Worcester.
Site: c1140–1538 and later.
Broken strap with bifurcated terminal.
L 62mm.
Wright 1976, 195, fig 35.9.

H497 STRAP (not illustrated)
Stonar, Kent.
c1275–1385.
Broken strap and terminal. L 45mm.
Excavated by N Macpherson-Grant.

H498 STRAP
Dyserth Castle, Clwyd.
Site: 1241–63.
Damaged terminal, broken strap. L 39mm.
Glenn 1915.

H499 STRAP
Clarendon Palace, Wiltshire.
Site: c1072 to later 15th century.
Shaped terminal, strap broken. L 138mm.
Goodall 1988, fig 77.57; Borenius and Charlton 1936.

H500 STRAP
Weoley Castle, Birmingham, West Midlands.
c1270–1600.
Broken scrolled terminal. L 73mm.
Birmingham City Museum, WC 415. For site see Oswald 1962.

H501 STRAP
Weoley Castle, Birmingham, West Midlands.
c1270–1600.
Strap with scrolled terminal. Total L 610mm.
Taylor 1974. For site see Oswald 1962.

BUILDING AND FURNITURE FITTINGS

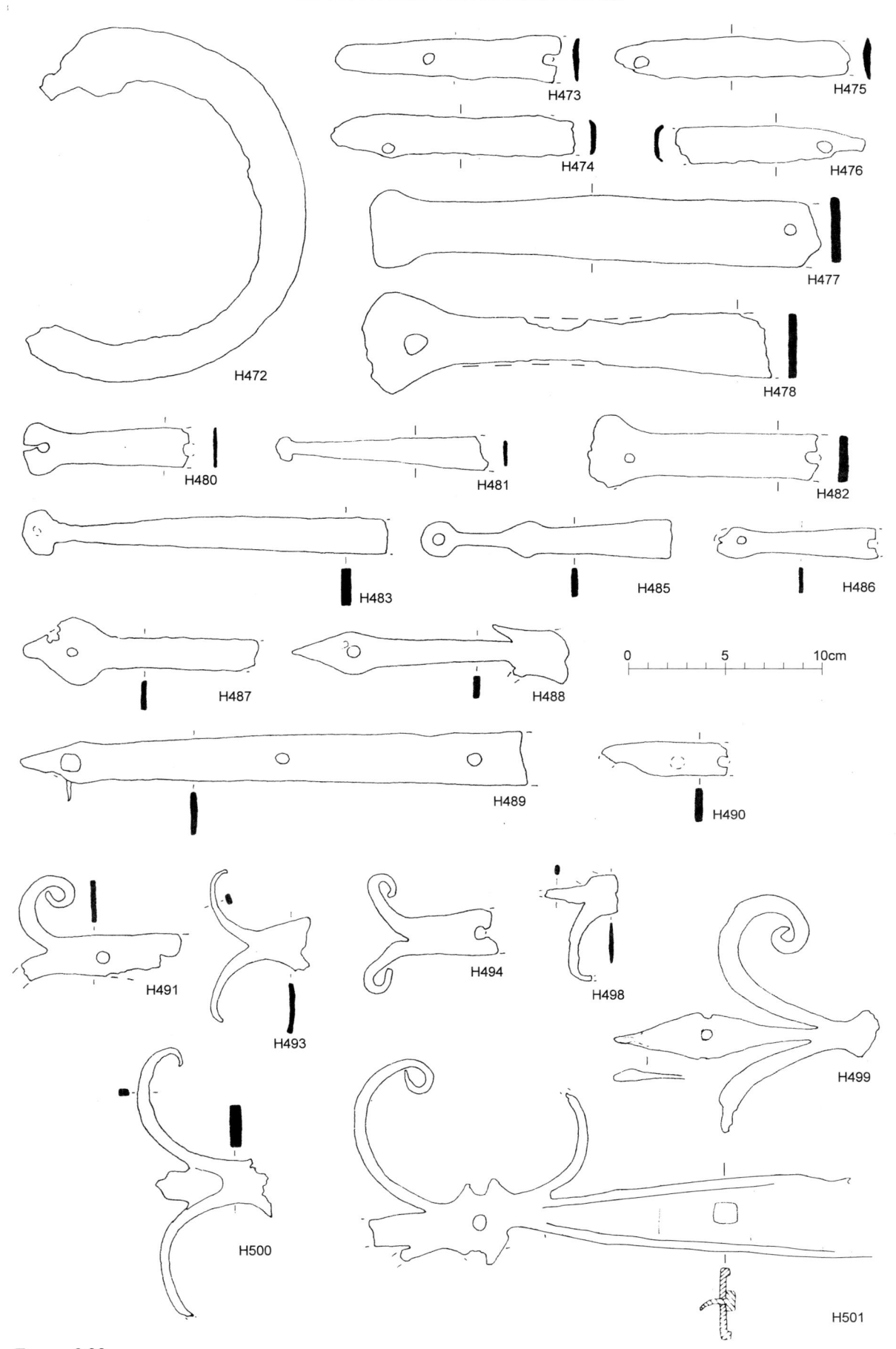

FIGURE 9.22
Straps

H502 STRAP
Winchester, Hampshire.
Late 17th-century context, typologically 13th–14th century.
Broken strap with raised, decorated band and scrolled terminals. L 215mm.
Goodall 1990-10, fig 85.678.

H503 STRAP
Beckery Chapel, Glastonbury, Somerset.
Later 13th to ?15th centuries.
Shaped terminal, strap broken. L 119mm.
Rahtz and Hirst 1974, 61, fig 22.24.

H504 HINGES (not illustrated)
St Neots Priory, Cambridgeshire.
13th century.
Four hinges with broken straight straps with opposed double scrolls. L 170–269mm.
Tebbutt 1966, 39, pl Vc.

H505 STRAP
Winchester, Hampshire.
Mid to late 13th century.
Broken scrolled terminal. L 66mm.
Goodall 1990-10, fig 85.679.

H506 STRAP
South Witham, Lincolnshire.
c1220 to 1308–13.
Scrolled terminal, incomplete. L 69mm.
Goodall 2002, fig 7.5, no. 50.

H507 STRAP
Winchester, Hampshire.
14th century.
Broken scrolled terminal. L 73mm.
Goodall 1990-10, fig 85.680.

H508 STRAP
Northampton.
End of 11th to middle of 15th century.
Shaped strap, distorted. L 64mm.
Goodall et al 1979, 268, fig 117.15.

H509 STRAP
Oxford.
c1325–c1400.
Shaped ?terminal. L 58mm.
Goodall 1977e, 146, fig 27.39.

H510 STRAP
North Elmham Park, Norfolk.
c1500–c1600.
Strap fragment with broken terminal. L 108mm.
Goodall 1980a, 513, fig 266.63.

H511 STRAP
Winchester, Hampshire.
Late 15th–early 16th century.
Broken plate with three heart-shaped lobes. L 68mm.
Goodall 1990-18, fig 303.3459.

H512 CORNER BINDING
Thelsford Priory, Warwickshire.
?14th century.
Corner binding strip, one arm broken, from wooden coffin surrounding lead encased skeleton. L 89 by 84mm.
Excavated by Mrs M Gray.

H513 CORNER BINDING
Clarendon Palace, Wiltshire.
Site: c1072 to later 15th century.
Corner binding with perforations. L 55 by 61mm.
Goodall 1988, fig 80.88; Borenius and Charlton 1936.

H514 CORNER BINDING
Northampton.
c1470–1500 to middle 16th century.
One arm broken, other retains nail. L 75 by 47mm.
Goodall et al 1979, 273, fig 119.75.

H515 CORNER BINDING
Kings Langley, Hertfordshire.
1291–92 to later 14th or first half 15th century.
Incomplete length. L 65mm.
Neal 1973, 56, fig XV.60.

H516 CORNER BINDING
(not illustrated)
Southampton, Hampshire.
14th century.
Complete piece with nail-holes at each corner. L 86mm, W 83mm.
Harvey 1975b, 285, fig 255.2061.

H517 HINGE
Upton, Gloucestershire.
Late 13th to late 14th century.
Looped eye broken. L 76mm.
Hilton and Rahtz 1966, 121, fig 14.38.

H518 HINGE
Castle Acre Castle, Norfolk.
Last quarter 12th century.
Terminal broken. L 85mm.
Goodall 1982, fig 39, no. 62.

H519 HINGE
Faxton, Northamptonshire.
Site: 12th to 15th century.
Looped eye, near complete strap. L 69mm.
Excavated by L A S Butler.

H520 HINGE
Castle Acre Castle, Norfolk.
1140s/1150s deposit with derived material. Site founded soon after 1066.
Hinge, loop broken. Non-ferrous plating. L 56mm.
Goodall 1982, fig 39, no. 61.

H521 HINGE
Goltho Manor, Lincolnshire.
11th century.
Loop broken. L 55mm.
Goodall 1987, fig 158.93.

H522 HINGE
Castle Acre Castle, Norfolk.
1140s deposit with derived material. Site founded soon after 1066.
Hinge, loop broken. Non-ferrous plating. L 43mm.
Goodall 1982, fig 39, no. 60.

H523 HINGE
Winchester, Hampshire.
c1110.
Spiked U-shaped eye, strap with bifurcated terminal. L 70mm.
Goodall 1990-18, fig 303.3449.

H524 HINGE
Winchester, Hampshire.
Early to mid 13th century.
Distorted spiked U-shaped eye, broken strap. L 51mm.
Goodall 1990-18, fig 303.3450.

H525 HINGE
Ospringe, Kent.
c1483–1550.
End-looped hinge with rivet and non-ferrous plating. L 34mm.
Goodall 1979c, 132, fig 21.70.

H526 HINGE
Upton, Gloucestershire.
Late 13th to late 14th century.
Shaped and decorated terminal, broken looped eyes. Non-ferrous plating. L 46mm.
Hilton and Rahtz 1966, 121, fig 13.5.

H527 HINGE
Castle Acre Castle, Norfolk.
Pre c1085. Site founded soon after 1066.
Shaped hinge with inlaid decoration and non-ferrous plating. L 84mm.
Goodall 1982, fig 39, no. 59.

H528 HINGE (not illustrated)
Durham.
Later 11th–mid 12th century.
Broken Y-shaped pinned hinge and angled stapled hasp (**H583**), both with surface decoration. Hinge L 97mm. For illustration see **H583**.
Carver 1979, 19, fig 13.129/1668

BUILDING AND FURNITURE FITTINGS

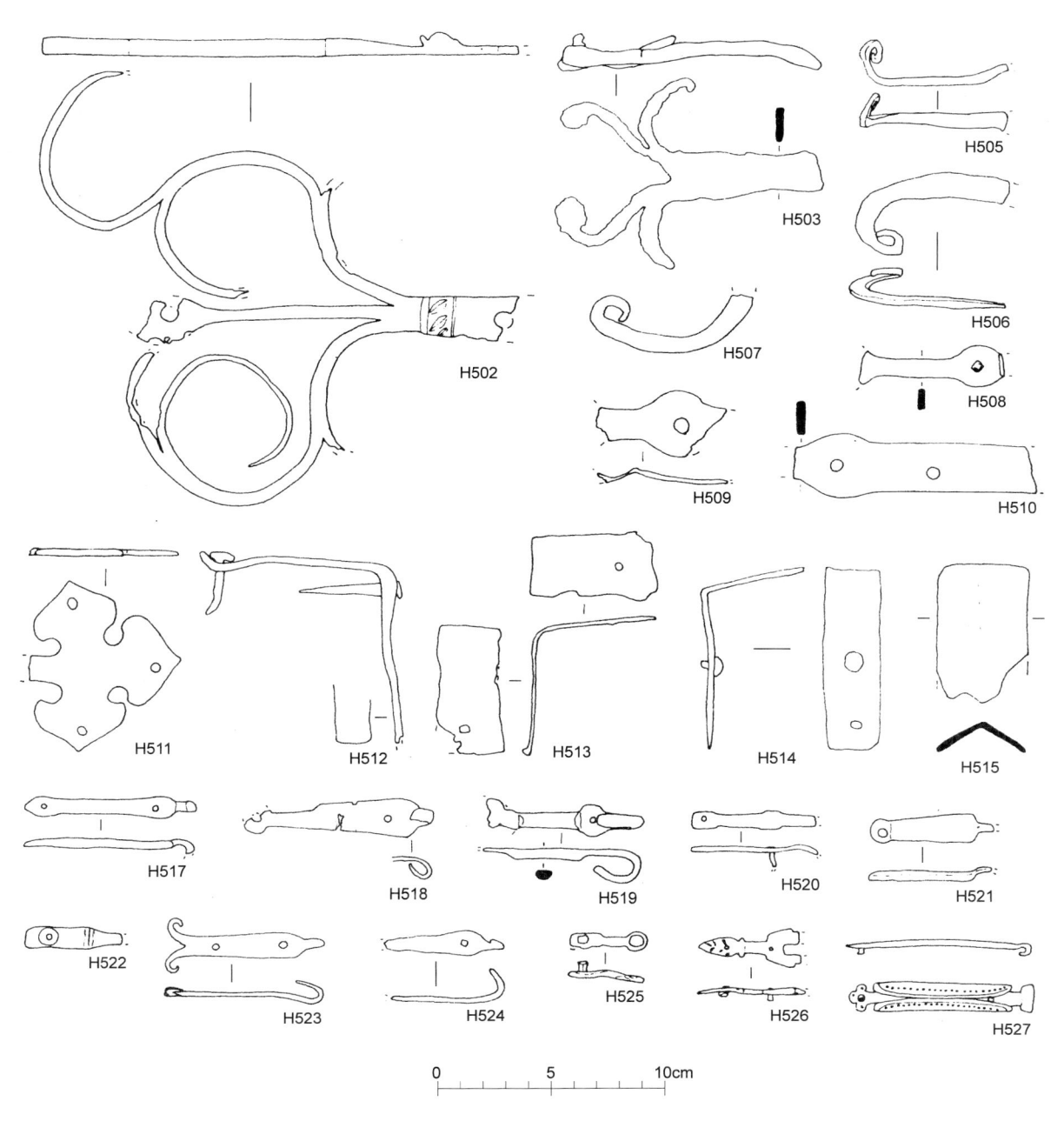

FIGURE 9.23
Hinges, straps and corner bindings

H529 STRIP
Rhuddlan, Clwyd.
End of 13th century
Broken strip, curved at one end. L 117mm.
Goodall 1994, fig 17.3, no. 58.

H530 STRIP (not illustrated)
Grenstein, Norfolk.
Late 14th, 15th century.
Broken strip, rectangular section. L 114mm, W 15mm.
Goodall 1980c, fig 79, no. 55.

H531 BINDING STRIP
Grenstein, Norfolk.
Late 14th, 15th century.
Broken strip retaining single rivet. L 92mm.
Goodall 1980c, fig 79, no. 52.

H532 BINDING STRIP
Brixworth, Northamptonshire.
*c*1100–1400.
Broken strip, D-shaped section. L 72mm, W 7mm.
Goodall 1977g, 94, fig 9.12.

H533 BINDING STRIP (not illustrated)
Rhuddlan, Clwyd.
13th century, ?later part.
Broken strip, rectangular section. L 49mm, W 7mm.
Goodall 1994, fig 17.3, no. 49.

H534 BINDING STRIP
Tattershall College, Lincolnshire.
11th century to 1440.
Broken strip. L 118mm.
Excavated by L J Keen.

H535 BINDING STRIP
Thelsford Priory, Warwickshire.
Site: 1200–1212 to 1536.
Distorted, incomplete strip. L 117mm.
Excavated by Mrs M Gray.

H536 BINDING STRIP
Winchester, Hampshire.
11th century.
Broken strip with simply moulded expansion. Non-ferrous plating. L 77mm.
Goodall 1990-13, fig 229.2442.

H537 BINDING STRIP
Clarendon Palace, Wiltshire.
Site: *c*1072 to later 15th century.
Broken strip with perforated expansion. L 173mm.
Goodall 1988, fig 80.84; Borenius and Charlton 1936.

H538 BINDING STRIP
Bolton, Humberside.
Mid 14th century.
Broken, shaped strip with non-ferrous plating. L 69mm.
Goodall 1978b, 143, fig 30.25.

H539 BINDING STRIP
Bolton, Humberside.
Mid 14th century.
Broken, shaped strip with non-ferrous plating. L 91mm.
Goodall 1978b, 143, fig 30.26.

H540 BINDING STRIP (not illustrated)
Ospringe, Kent.
*c*1483–1550.
Broken strip with perforated expansion. Non-ferrous plating. L 39mm, W 17mm.
Goodall 1979c, 132, fig 21.69.

H541 BINDING STRIP
Wharram Percy, North Yorkshire.
Late 15th to early 16th century.
Riveted terminal, broken shank. L 80mm.
Goodall 1979a, 118, fig 60.18.

H542 BINDING STRIP
Winchester, Hampshire.
Late 14th–?16th century.
Incomplete with moulded terminal. Non-ferrous plating. L 43mm.
Goodall 1990-13, fig 229.2447.

H543 BINDING STRIP
Winchester, Hampshire.
Mid 11th century.
Incomplete strip with double riveted strip. Non-ferrous plating. L 33mm.
Goodall 1990-13, fig 229.2441.

H544 BINDING STRIP
Stonar, Kent.
*c*1275–1385.
Broken, angled strip and terminal. Non-ferrous plating. L 84mm.
Excavated by N Macpherson-Grant.

H545 BINDING STRIP
Stonar, Kent.
*c*1275–1385.
Broken, angled strip with terminal. Non-ferrous plating. L 70mm.
Excavated by N Macpherson-Grant.

H546 BINDING STRIP (not illustrated)
Cambokeels, Durham.
Site: later 14th to early 16th century.
Broken strip and terminal. L 69mm, W 16mm.
Bowes Museum, Barnard Castle. For site see Hildyard and Charlton 1947; Hildyard 1949.

H547 BINDING STRIP (not illustrated)
Oxford.
Second half 11th century.
Broken strip. L 33mm, W 9mm.
Goodall 1977e, 146, fig 27.41.

H548 BINDING STRIP
Old Sarum, Wiltshire.
Principally medieval, to 14th century.
Broken strip with rounded terminal and expansion, both with radiating decorative grooves. Non-ferrous plating. L 126mm.
Salisbury and South Wiltshire Museum, Salisbury, O.S.C2(d).

H549 BINDING STRIP
Netherton, Hampshire.
Mid 14th century.
Broken strip with terminal. L 87mm.
Goodall 1990-18, fig 9.6, no. 335.

BUILDING AND FURNITURE FITTINGS

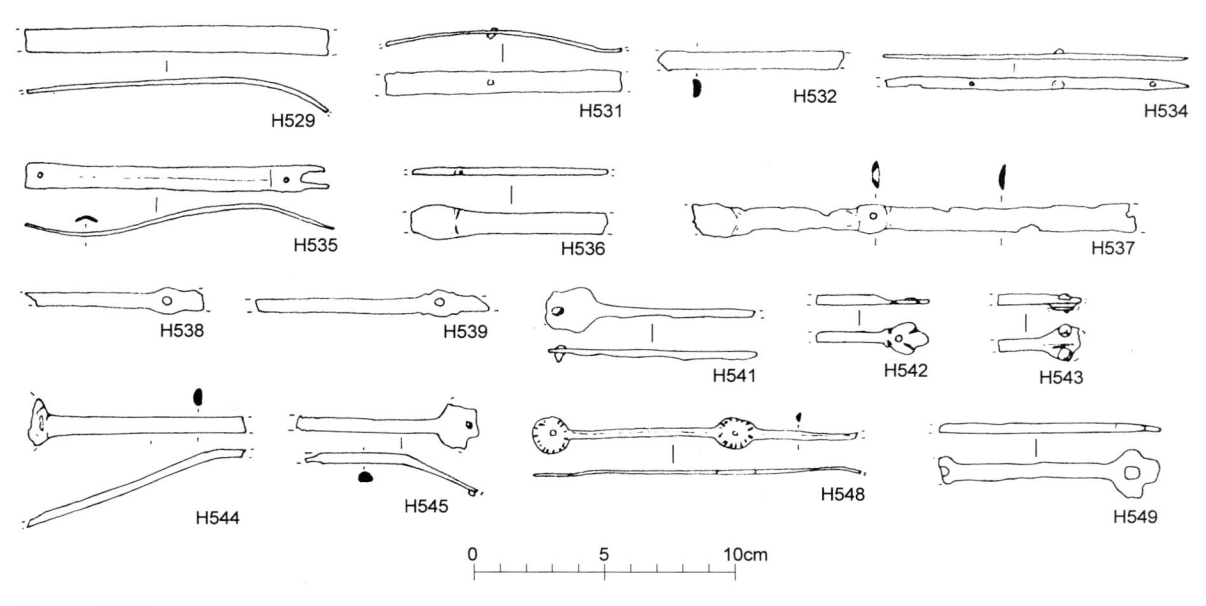

FIGURE 9.24
Strip and binding strips

H550 BINDING STRIP
Wharram Percy, North Yorkshire.
Late 15th to early 16th century.
Broken angled strip with terminal.
Non-ferrous plating. L 88mm.
Goodall 1979a, 118, fig 60.17.

H551 BINDING STRIP (not illustrated)
Stonar, Kent.
c1275–1385.
Broken and distorted strip and terminal.
Non-ferrous plating. L 85mm, W 18mm.
Excavated by N Macpherson-Grant.

H552 BINDING STRIP
Winchester, Hampshire.
Late 11th–early 12th century.
Broken strip and terminal. Decorative grooves. Non-ferrous plating. L 59mm.
Goodall 1990-13, fig 229.2443.

H553 BINDING STRIP
Clarendon Palace, Wiltshire.
Site: c1072 to later 15th century.
Flattened, riveted terminal and broken shank. L 77mm.
Goodall 1988, fig 80.85; Borenius and Charlton 1936.

H554 BINDING STRIP
Winchester, Hampshire.
Late 11th–12th century.
Terminal complete, arms broken. Decorative grooves. Non-ferrous plating. L 92mm.
Goodall 1990-13, fig 229.2444.

H555 BINDING STRIP
Therfield, Hertfordshire.
Saxo-Norman to 12th century.
Incomplete lobed strip with non-ferrous plating. Fragment of mineralised wood noted adhering to object. L 54mm.
Biddle 1964, 81, fig 23.2.

H556 BINDING STRIP
Northampton.
11th century.
Broken, moulded strip retaining non-ferrous plating in decorative grooves. L 49mm.
Goodall *et al* 1979, 273, fig 119.82.

H557 BINDING STRIP
Rhuddlan, Clwyd.
Pre-13th century.
Broken, sinuous strip. L 68mm.
Goodall 1994, fig 17.3, no. 52.

H558 BINDING STRIP
Gloucester.
11th–early 12th century.
Scrolled strip, one end broken and distorted. Traces of simple surface decoration.
L 59mm.
Excavated by H Hurst.

H559 BINDING STRIP
Castle Acre Castle, Norfolk.
Second half 12th century.
Incomplete terminal with fixing stud. Non-ferrous plating. L 32mm.
Goodall 1982, fig 39, no. 58.

H560 BINDING STRIP
Rhuddlan, Clwyd.
11th century.
Broken strip retaining one riveted terminal.
L 49mm.
Goodall 1994, fig 17.3, no. 53.

H561 BINDING STRIP
Wroughton Copse, Fyfield Down, Wiltshire.
12th to (mid?) 13th century.
Near complete strip with riveted terminals.
L 45mm.
Excavated by P J Fowler.

H562 BINDING STRIP
Wroughton Copse, Fyfield Down, Wiltshire.
(Mid?) 13th to early 14th century.
Strip with round, perforated terminals, one broken. L 67mm.
Excavated by P J Fowler.

H563 BINDING STRIP
Goltho, Lincolnshire.
Late 14th to early 15th century.
Broken strip, one terminal complete. L 59mm.
Goodall 1975a, 86, fig 40.82.

H564 BINDING STRIP
Winchester, Hampshire.
Mid 13th century.
Complete strip with shaped and decorated terminals. Non-ferrous plating. L 41mm.
Goodall 1990-13, fig 229.2451.

H565/I143 STAPLED HASP AND LOCK
Upton, Gloucestershire.
Late 13th to late 14th century.
Stapled hasp with hooked end and end loop. Lock **I143** incomplete, but retains bolt which passes through staple of hasp. Non-ferrous plating on hasp. Hasp L 51mm.
For illustration see **I143**.
Hilton and Rahtz 1966, 121, fig 13.5.

H566 STAPLED HASP
Winchester, Hampshire.
13th century.
Flat stapled hasp with end loop. Broken tip. Non-ferrous plating. L 53mm.
Goodall 1990-19, fig 304.3502.

H567 STAPLED HASP
Winchester, Hampshire.
?c1085–c1110
Flat stapled hasp with broken end loop.
L 61mm.
Goodall 1990-19, fig 304.3495.

H568 STAPLED HASP (not illustrated)
Winchester, Hampshire.
Mid to late 13th century.
Flat stapled hasp with near square-cut end. Broken end loop as on **H569**. Non-ferrous plating. L 62mm.
Goodall 1990-19, 977, no. 3498.

H569 STAPLED HASP
Winchester, Hampshire.
13th century.
Flat stapled hasp with thickened tip and broken end loop. Non-ferrous plating.
L 72mm.
Goodall 1990-19, fig 304.3501.

H570/H454 STAPLED HASP AND HINGE
Winchester, Hampshire.
Late 13th century.
Flat stapled hasp with hooked tip and end loop retaining spikes, U-shaped eye of hinge with chisel-cut break. Hasp L 114mm, hinge L 53mm.
Goodall 1990-19, fig 304.3499.

H571 STAPLED HASP
Stonar, Kent.
c1275–1385.
Flat stapled hasp with hooked tip and end loop. L 11mm.
Excavated by N Macpherson-Grant.

H572 STAPLED HASP (not illustrated)
Winchester, Hampshire.
Mid to late 13th century.
Flat stapled hasp similar to **H569** but with transversely set staple and broken circular end loop. L 123mm.
Goodall 1990-19, 977, no. 3497.

H573 STAPLED HASP
The Hamel, Oxford.
Early/mid 13th century.
Angled stapled hasp with moulded tip and end loop. L 153mm.
Goodall 1980d, fig 30, no. 46.

H574 STAPLED HASP
Winchester, Hampshire.
Early to mid 12th century.
Angled stapled hasp with end loop and moulded and thickened tip. Non-ferrous plating. L 178mm.
Goodall 1990-19, fig 304.3496.

H575 STAPLED HASP
Huish, Wiltshire.
Site: 12th to mid 15th century.
Flat stapled hasp with broken looped eye.
L 59mm.
Shortt 1972, 120, fig 5.32.

H576 STAPLED HASP
Wintringham, Cambridgeshire.
Early 14th century.
Flat stapled hasp with hooked tip and broken looped eye. L 80mm.
Goodall 1977a, 257, fig 43.27.

H577 STAPLED HASP AND HINGE
Wallingstones, Hereford and Worcester.
1300–1325 to 1500.
Flat stapled hasp with moulded tip and broken pinned hinge.
Hasp L 87mm, hinge L 29mm.
Bridgewater 1970–72, 103, fig 16.51

BUILDING AND FURNITURE FITTINGS

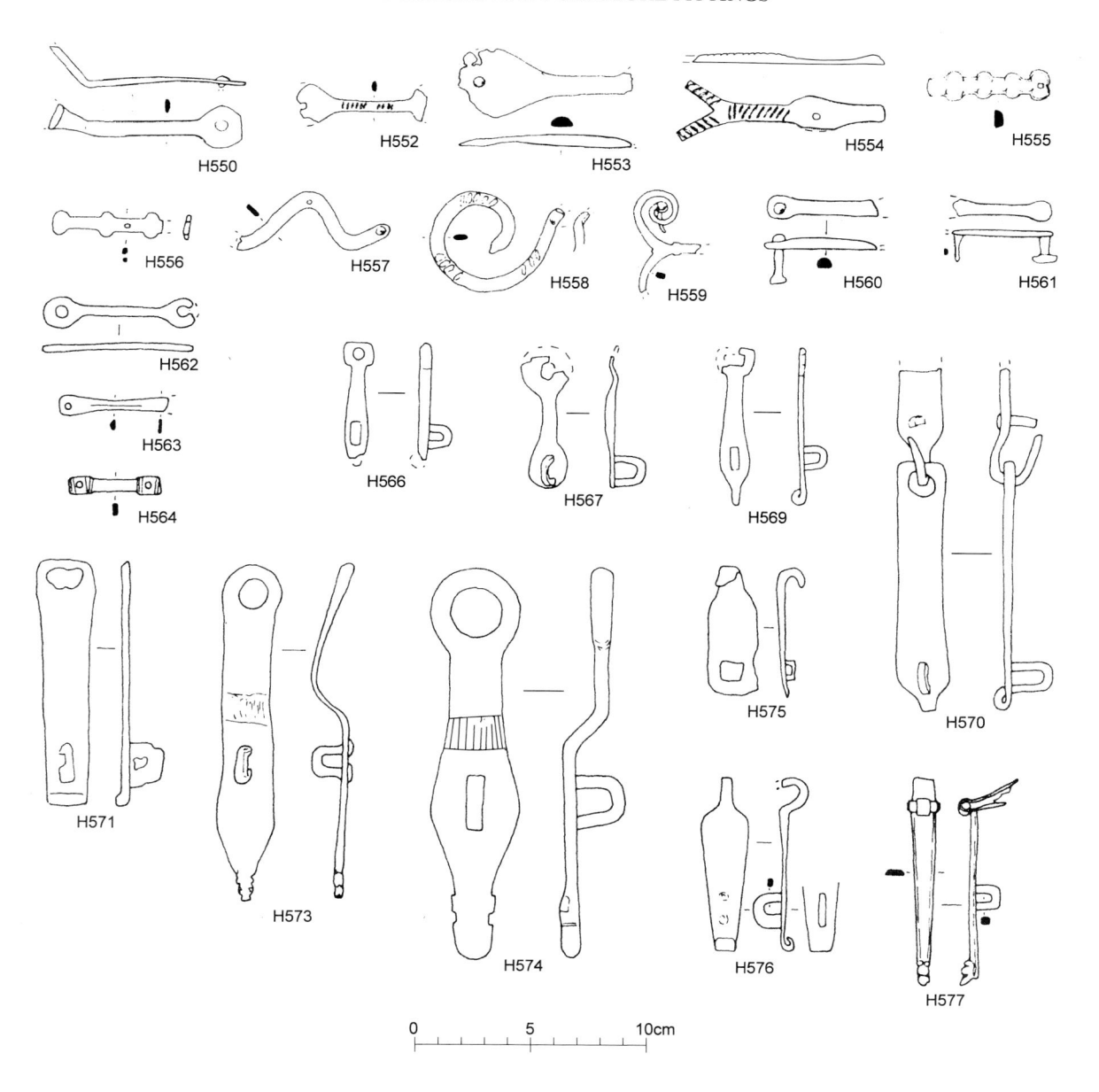

FIGURE 9.25
Binding strips and stapled hasps

H578 STAPLED HASP
Somerby, Lincolnshire.
Site: 11th to mid 16th century.
Flat stapled hasp with pinned hinge fragment. L 94mm.
Mynard 1969, 84, fig 13.IW86.

H579 STAPLED HASP
Gloucester.
11th, early 12th century.
Flat stapled hasp with moulded tip and looped eye. L 127mm.
Excavated by H Hurst.

H580 STAPLED HASP
Barrow Mead, Somerset.
Site: 13th–14th century.
Flat stapled hasp with fragment of pinned hinge. L 135mm.
Rahtz 1960–61, 76, fig 8.1.

H581/H463 STAPLED HASP AND HINGE
Winchester, Hampshire.
16th century.
Flat stapled hasp with thickened tip and broken pinned hinge.
Hasp L 143mm, hinge L 81mm.
Goodall 1990-18, fig 304.3506.

H582 STAPLED HASP
Chew Valley Lake, Avon.
Late 13th to early 14th century.
Flat stapled hasp with looped eye. L 251mm.
Rahtz and Greenfield 1977, 326, fig 121.4.

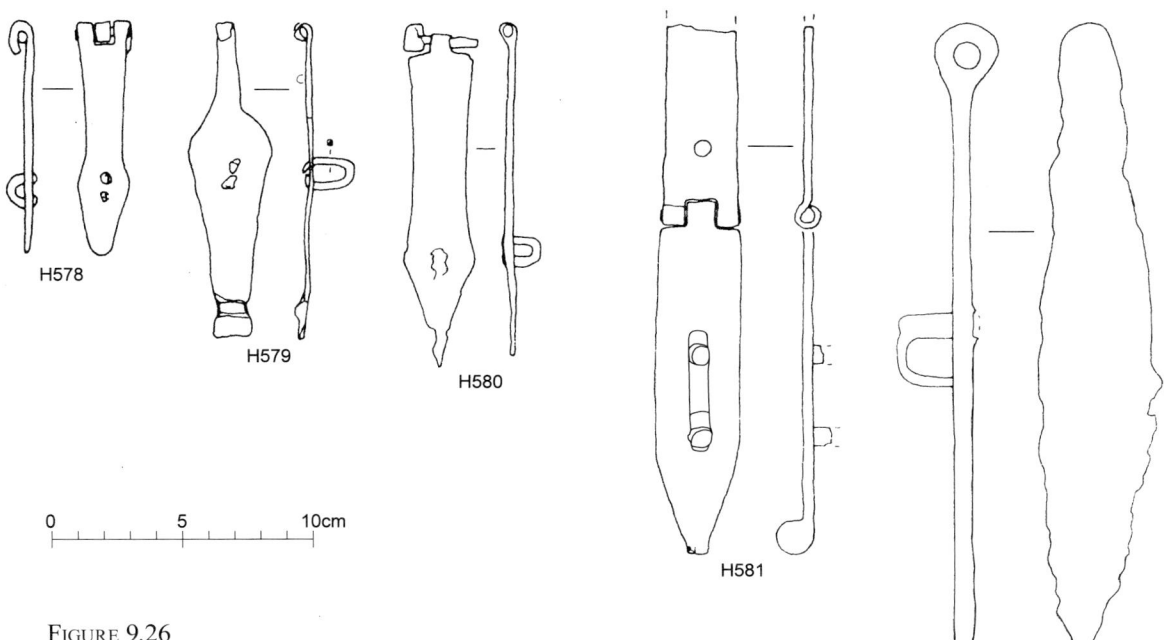

BUILDING AND FURNITURE FITTINGS

FIGURE 9.26
Stapled hasps

H583/H528 STAPLED HASP AND HINGE
Durham.
Later 11th–mid 12th century.
Angled stapled hasp and broken Y-shaped pinned hinge, both with surface decoration. Hasp L 72mm.
Carver 1979, 19, fig 13.129/1668.

H584 STAPLED HASP
Somerby, Lincolnshire.
Site: 11th to mid 16th century.
Flat stapled hasp, incomplete, with hooked tip. L 102mm.
Mynard 1969.

H585 STAPLED HASP
Rhuddlan, Clwyd.
Probably 12th–14th century.
Base of stapled hasp with decorated edges and non-ferrous plating. L 78mm.
Goodall 1994, fig 17.6, no. 97.

H586 STAPLED HASP
Hull, Humberside.
Early to mid 16th century.
Flat but distorted and broken stapled hasp. L 74mm.
Goodall 1997b, 65, fig 27.82.

H587 STAPLED HASP
North Elmham Park, Norfolk.
c1500–c1600.
Broken flat stapled hasp with hooked tip. L 63mm.
Goodall 1980a, 510, fig 265.13.

H588 STAPLED HASP
Upton, Gloucestershire.
Late 13th to late 14th century.
Incomplete hasp, staple missing. L 55mm.
Hilton and Rahtz 1966, 121, fig 14.35.

H589 STAPLED HASP
Winchester, Hampshire.
13th century.
Base of stapled hasp with hooked tip. Non-ferrous plating. L 52mm.
Goodall 1990-19, fig 304.3509.

H590 STAPLED HASP
Chelmsford, Essex.
From destruction debris deposited by c1560 on site founded in mid 13th century, dissolved 1537.
Broken, flat stapled hasp with knobbed base. L 156mm.
Drury 1974, 59, fig 9.23.

H591 HASP
Winchester, Hampshire.
Mid 10th–early 11th century.
Flat hasp with hooked end. L 56mm.
Goodall 1990-19, fig 303.3474.

H592 HASP
Winchester, Hampshire.
Mid 11th century.
Flat hasp with hooked end. L 97mm.
Goodall 1990-19, fig 303.3476.

H593 HASP
Wharram Percy, North Yorkshire.
Mid 15th–early 16th century.
Flat hasp with hooked end. L 102mm.
Goodall 1979a, 121, fig 64.87.

H594 HASP (not illustrated)
Winchester, Hampshire.
Early 16th century.
Broken side from flat hasp. L 116mm.
Goodall 1990-19, 977, no. 3483.

H595 HASP
Northampton.
14th century.
Flat hasp with hooked end. L 152mm.
Central Museum, Northampton. From between Bearwood Street and Silver Street.

H596 HASP AND RING
Northampton.
13th century to c1500.
Curved hasp with broken ring through hooked end. Hasp L 64mm, ring W 26mm.
Goodall *et al* 1979, 268, fig 116.14.

H597 HASP
Winchester, Hampshire.
c1222.
Curved hasp with hooked end. L 92mm.
Goodall 1990-19, 977, no. 3478.

H598 HASP (not illustrated)
Warkworth Castle, Northumberland.
Early medieval. Castle 12th–17th century.
Gently curved hasp with hooked end. L 102mm, W 26mm.
Harbottle 1967, 120, fig 5.38.

H599 HASP
Winchester, Hampshire.
11th century.
Curved hasp with hooked end. L 105mm.
Goodall 1990-19, fig 303.3477.

H600 HASP
Portchester Castle, Hampshire.
Medieval.
Curved hasp with hooked end. L 107mm.
Hinton 1977, 201, fig 108.57.

H601 HASP (not illustrated)
Lyveden, Northamptonshire.
Site: second quarter 13th century to very early 14th century.
Curved hasp with hooked end. L 110mm, W 30mm.
Bryant and Steane 1971, 59, fig 15e.

H602 HASP
Wharram Percy, North Yorkshire.
Late 15th–early 16th century.
Gently curved hasp with hooked end. L 110mm.
Goodall 1979a, 118, fig 60.8.

H603 HASP (not illustrated)
Gloucester.
13th century.
Broken, gently curved hasp. L 103mm, W 26mm.
Hassall and Rhodes 1974, 78, fig 30.13.

H604/H457 HASP AND HINGE
Dover Castle, Kent.
Late 13th century.
Curved hasp and broken end-looped hinge. Hasp L 115mm, hinge L 71mm.
Rigold 1967, 109, fig 9.Fe 4.

H605 HASP
Oxford.
Late 12th century–c1250.
Curved hasp of spirally twisted iron with hooked end. L 115mm.
Goodall 1977e, 142, fig 25.4.

H606 HASP
Castle Acre Castle, Norfolk.
Second half 12th century.
Curved hasp with hooked end. L 118mm.
Goodall 1982, fig 40, no. 106.

BUILDING AND FURNITURE FITTINGS

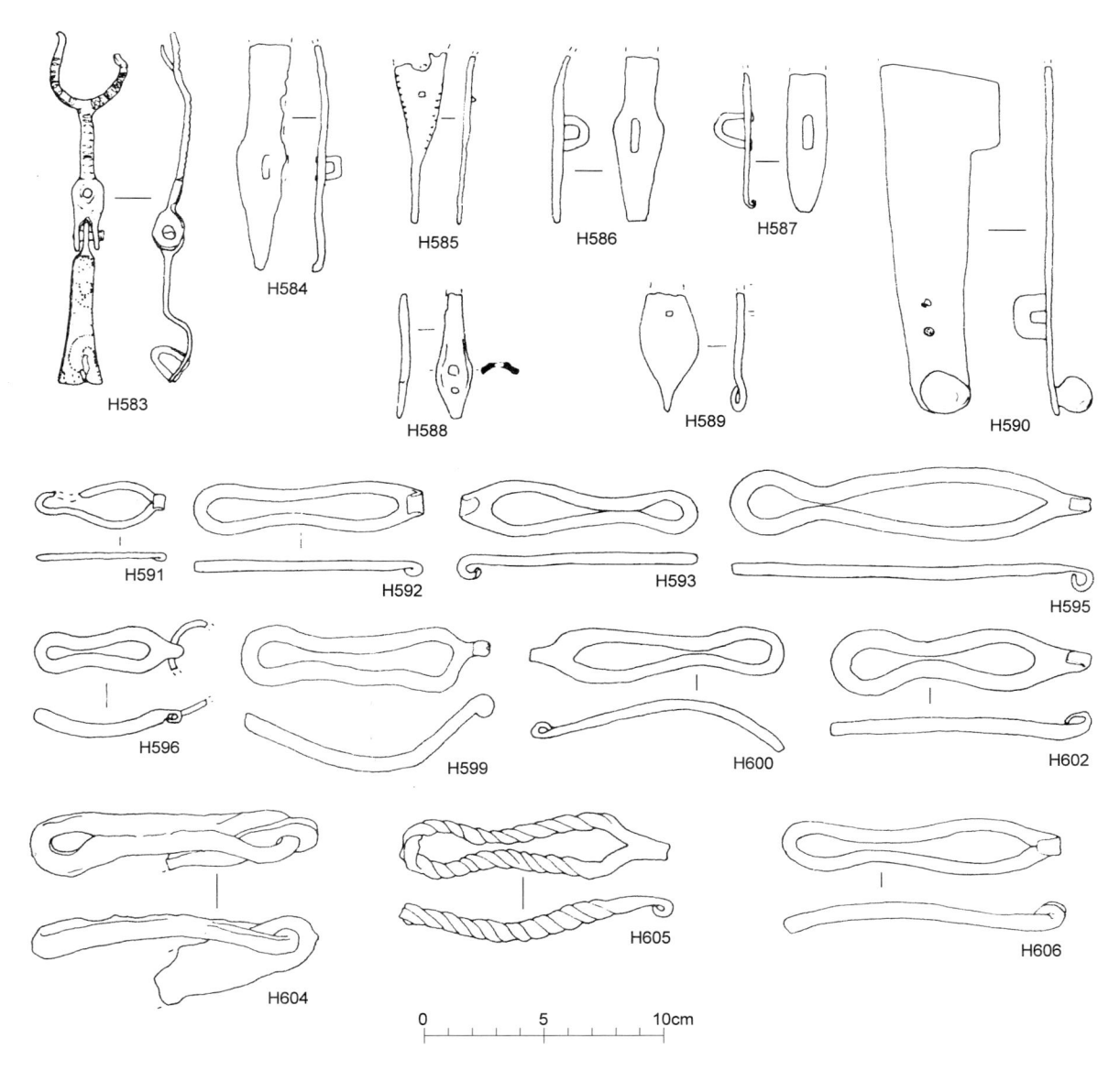

FIGURE 9.27
Stapled hasps and hasps

H607 HASP (not illustrated)
The Hamel, Oxford.
Late 12th–early 13th century.
Broken curved hasp. L 123mm, W 41mm.
Goodall 1980d.

H608 HASP
Llantrithyd, South Glamorgan.
Early to mid 12th century.
Curved hasp with hooked end. L 125mm.
Goodall 1977f, 46, iron object fig 1.12.

H609 HASP
Wroughton Copse, Fyfield Down, Wiltshire.
12th century (?).
Curved hasp with hooked end. L 127mm.
Excavated by P J Fowler.

H610 HASP
Grenstein, Norfolk.
Late 14th, 15th century.
Gently curved hasp with hooked end.
L 136mm.
Goodall 1980c, fig 80, no. 65.

H611 HASP
Llantrithyd, South Glamorgan.
Early to mid 12th century.
Curved hasp partly of spirally twisted iron with hooked end. L 136mm.
Goodall 1977f, 46, iron object fig 1.10.

H612 HASP (not illustrated)
Winchester, Hampshire.
Mid 13th century.
Curved hasp with hooked end. L 138mm.
Goodall 1990-19, 977, no. 3481.

H613 HASP (not illustrated)
North Elmham Park, Norfolk
*c*1500–*c*1600
Curved hasp with hooked end. One side broken. L 138mm, W 31mm
Goodall 1980a, 510, fig 265.17

H614 HASP (not illustrated)
Wintringham, Cambridgeshire.
Around early 14th century.
Curved hasp with hooked end. L 154mm, W 39mm.
Goodall 1977a, 257, fig 43.28.

H615 HASP
Kettleby Thorpe, Licolnshire.
14th to early 15th century.
Curved hasp with hooked end. L 156mm.
Goodall 1974a, 33, fig 18.7.

H616 HASP (not illustrated)
King's Lynn, Norfolk.
*c*1150–1250.
Curved hasp with hooked end. L 160mm, W 27mm.
Goodall and Carter 1977, 293, fig 133.12.

H617 HASP (not illustrated)
Folkestone, Kent.
Mid 12th century.
Curved hasp of twisted iron with hooked end. L 166mm, W unknown.
Pitt-Rivers 1883, 463, pl XVIII.10.

H618 HASP
Winchester, Hampshire.
Early to mid 13th century.
Curved hasp of spirally twisted iron with hooked end. L 178mm.
Goodall 1990-19, fig 303.3480.

H619 HASP
Rhuddlan, Clwyd.
13th century, probably second half.
L-shaped hasp with hooked end. L 76mm.
Goodall 1994, fig 17.6, no. 100.

H620 HASP
Goltho Manor, Lincolnshire.
*c*1100–1150.
L-shaped hasp partly of spirally twisted iron with hooked end. L 101mm.
Goodall 1987, fig 158.92.

BUILDING AND FURNITURE FITTINGS

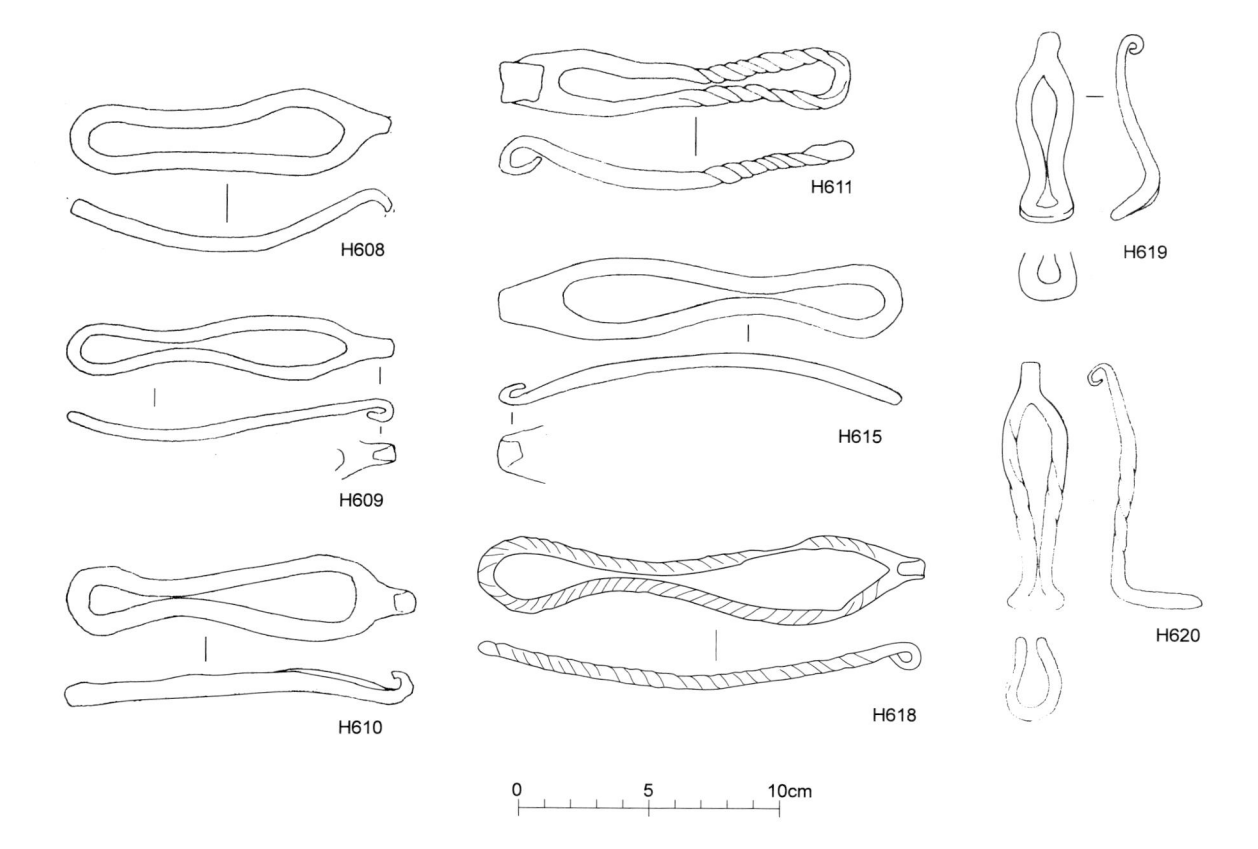

FIGURE 9.28
Hasps

H621 HASP
Grenstein, Norfolk.
Site: 12th to late 14th, 15th century.
Angled hasp with hooked end. L 109mm.
Goodall 1980c, fig 80, no. 66.

H622 HASP
Clough Castle, Co. Down.
c1250, from same context as two hinges, two hinge pivots and barrel padlock, all perhaps from same door.
Angled hasp with broken, hooked end.
L 136mm.
Waterman 1954, 140, fig 12.6.

H623 HASP
Sulgrave, Northamptonshire.
Second half 11th century, possibly just post-Conquest.
Curved hasp with hooked end. L 144mm.
Excavated by B K Davison.

H624 HASP
Lydford Castle, Devon.
Mid 13th century.
Curved hasp with solid centre and hooked end from well cover **H404**. L 158mm.
Goodall 1980b, fig 17.b.

H625 HASP
Winchester, Hampshire.
13th century.
Angled hasp with hooked end. L 157mm.
Goodall 1990-19, fig 303.3486.

H626 HASP
Winchester, Hampshire.
c1065/66–c1110.
Angled hasp. L 124mm.
Goodall 1990-19, fig 303.3485.

H627 HASP
Wythemail, Northamptonshire.
14th century.
Flat hasp with hooked end. L 115mm.
Hurst and Hurst 1969, 200.

H628 HASP
Winchester, Hampshire.
11th–?mid 12th century.
Double angled hasp with hooked end.
L 101mm.
Goodall 1990-19, fig 303.3490.

H629 HASP
Thelsford Priory, Warwickshire.
Site: 1200–1212 to 1536.
Curved hasp with hooked end. L 119mm.
Excavated by Mrs M Gray.

H630 HASP
Glottenham, East Sussex.
Late 13th century.
Pinned hasp with thickened tip. L 78mm.
Excavated by D Martin.

H631 HASP
London.
Late 15th–early 16th century.
Incomplete pinned hasp, tip obscured by corrosion. L 126mm.
Excavated by F C Willmot. Site at 66 Foyle Road.

H632 HASP
Rhuddlan, Clwyd.
Just pre-1280.
Broken hasp with hooked end. L 51mm.
Goodall 1994, fig 17.6, no. 101.

H633 HASP
Winchester, Hampshire.
Mid to late 13th century.
Broken hasp with elongated, hooked end.
L 43mm.
Goodall 1990-19, fig 303.3492.

H634 KEYHOLE PLATE
Castell-y-Bere, Gwynedd.
Site: c1221–95.
Damaged triangular plate. L 99mm.
Butler 1974, 98, fig 9.27.

H635 KEYHOLE PLATE
Brandon Castle, Warwickshire.
1226–66.
Triangular plate with shaped top edge.
L 98mm.
Chatwin 1955, 81, fig 11.10.

H636 KEYHOLE PLATE
Old Sarum, Wiltshire.
Principally medieval, to 14th century.
Damaged triangular plate. L 97mm.
Salisbury and South Wiltshire Museum, Salisbury, 30/1920–21.

H637 KEYHOLE PLATE
Barrow Mead, Somerset.
Site: 13th–14th century.
Rectangular plate, edge damaged. L 53mm.
Goodall 1976b, 35, fig 11.20.

H638 KEYHOLE PLATE
Winchester, Hampshire.
15th century.
Elongated oval plate. L 97mm.
Goodall 1990-19, fig 304.3514.

H639 PLATE
King's Lynn, Norfolk.
c1250–1300.
Broken triangular plate with traces of non-ferrous plating. L 65mm.
Goodall and Carter 1977, 297, fig 134.63.

H640 HANDLE
Eynsford Castle, Kent.
Early 12th century.
Side arms broken. W 63mm.
Rigold 1971, 147, fig 10.21.

H641 HANDLE
Upton, Gloucestershire.
Late 13th–late 14th century.
Complete. W 92mm.
Hilton and Rahtz 1966, 120, fig 14.25.

H642 HANDLE
Effingham, Surrey.
Late 12th to early 14th century.
Side arm broken. W 104mm.
Ruby and Lowther 1955, 14, fig 4.4.

H643 HANDLE
Thuxton, Northamptonshire.
Site: 12th–14th century.
Complete. W 133mm.
Excavated by L A S Butler.

H644 HANDLE
Clarendon Palace, Wiltshire.
Site: c1072 to late 15th century.
Side arms broken. W 123mm.
Goodall 1988, fig 80.91; Borenius and Charlton 1936.

H645 HANDLE
Weoley Castle, Birmingham, West Midlands.
c1230–70.
Complete. W 163mm.
Oswald 1962, 130, fig 51.11. Birmingham City Museum, WC 1115.

H646 HANDLE
Writtle, Essex.
1211–c1306.
One arm broken. W 153mm.
Rahtz 1969b, 87, fig 48.67.

BUILDING AND FURNITURE FITTINGS

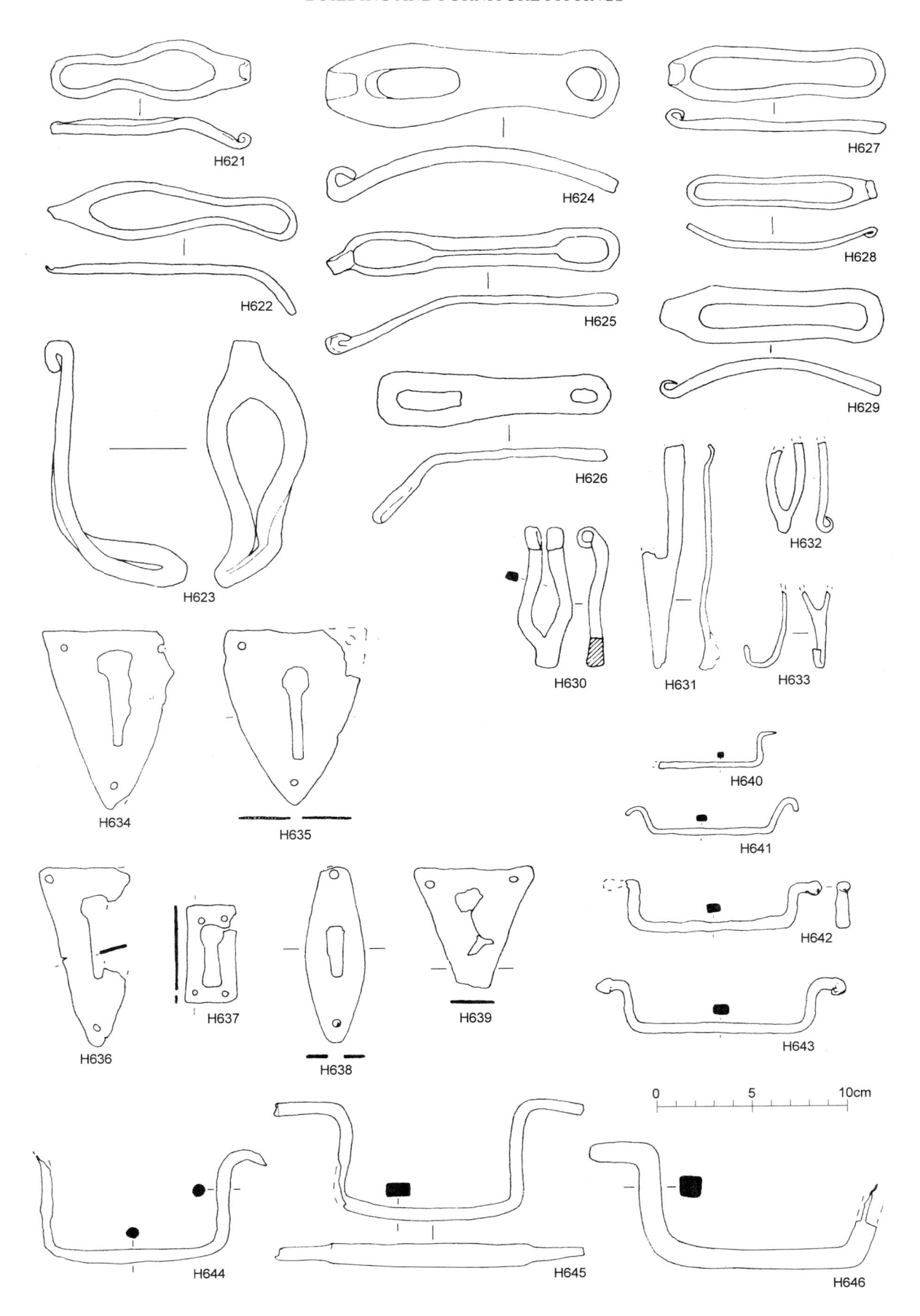

FIGURE 9.29
Hasps, keyhole plates, and handles

H647 HANDLE
Clarendon Palace, Wiltshire.
Site: c1072 to later 15th century.
Complete. W 191mm.
Goodall 1988, fig 80.92; Borenius and Charlton 1936.

H648 HANDLE
Winchester, Hampshire.
16th century.
Arms incomplete. W 267mm.
Goodall 1990-19, fig 304.3520.

H649 HANDLE
Wallingstones, Hereford and Worcester.
1300–25 to 1500.
Complete. W 132mm.
Bridgewater 1970-2, 104, no. 71.

H650 HANDLE
Kilton Castle, Cleveland.
14th century.
Side arms broken. W 117mm.
Excavated by A Aberg.

H651 HANDLE
Stonar, Kent.
c1275–1385.
Basal strap broken. L 192mm.
Excavated by N Macpherson-Grant.

H652 HANDLE
Newbury, Berkshire.
Late 15th century.
Handle and basal strap broken. L 290mm.
Goodall 1997, fig 20, no. 22.

H653 HANDLE
Southampton, Hampshire.
1250–1300.
Broken perforated terminals. W 74mm.
Harvey 1975b, 279, fig 251.2008.

H654 HANDLE
Southampton, Hampshire.
1250–1300.
Ring with broken U-shaped staple. D 50mm.
Harvey 1975b, 279, fig 251.2012.

H655 HANDLE
Hen Domen, Powys.
13th century.
Ring with broken looped staple **H166**.
Overall L 64mm.
Higham and Rouillard 2000, no. 59.

H656 HANDLE
Brandon Castle, Warwickshire.
1226–66.
Ring partly of twisted section with U-shaped staple **H141**. Overall L 159mm.
Chatwin 1955, 81, fig 11.9.

H657 HANDLE
Stonar, Kent.
c1275–1385.
Ring and broken looped staple **H170**.
Overall L 145mm.
Excavated by N Macpherson-Grant.

H658 HANDLE
Alsted, Surrey.
c1250–1405.
Shaped ring and oval link. W 78mm.
Goodall 1976a, 56, fig 36.51.

H659 HANDLE
Winchester, Hampshire.
Late 11th century.
Shaped ring and broken link. W 74mm.
Goodall 1990-19, CG 53.

H660 HANDLE
South Witham, Lincolnshire.
1137–85 to c1220.
M-shaped handle, one arm incomplete.
W 87mm.
Goodall 2002, fig 7.6, no. 66.

H661 HANDLE
Eynsford Castle, Kent.
c1300.
M-shaped handle. W 90mm.
Rigold 1971, 147, fig 9.20.

H662 HANDLE
Writtle, Essex.
c1306–c1425.
M-shaped handle with non-ferrous plating.
W 92mm.
Rahtz 1969b, 85, fig 47.57.

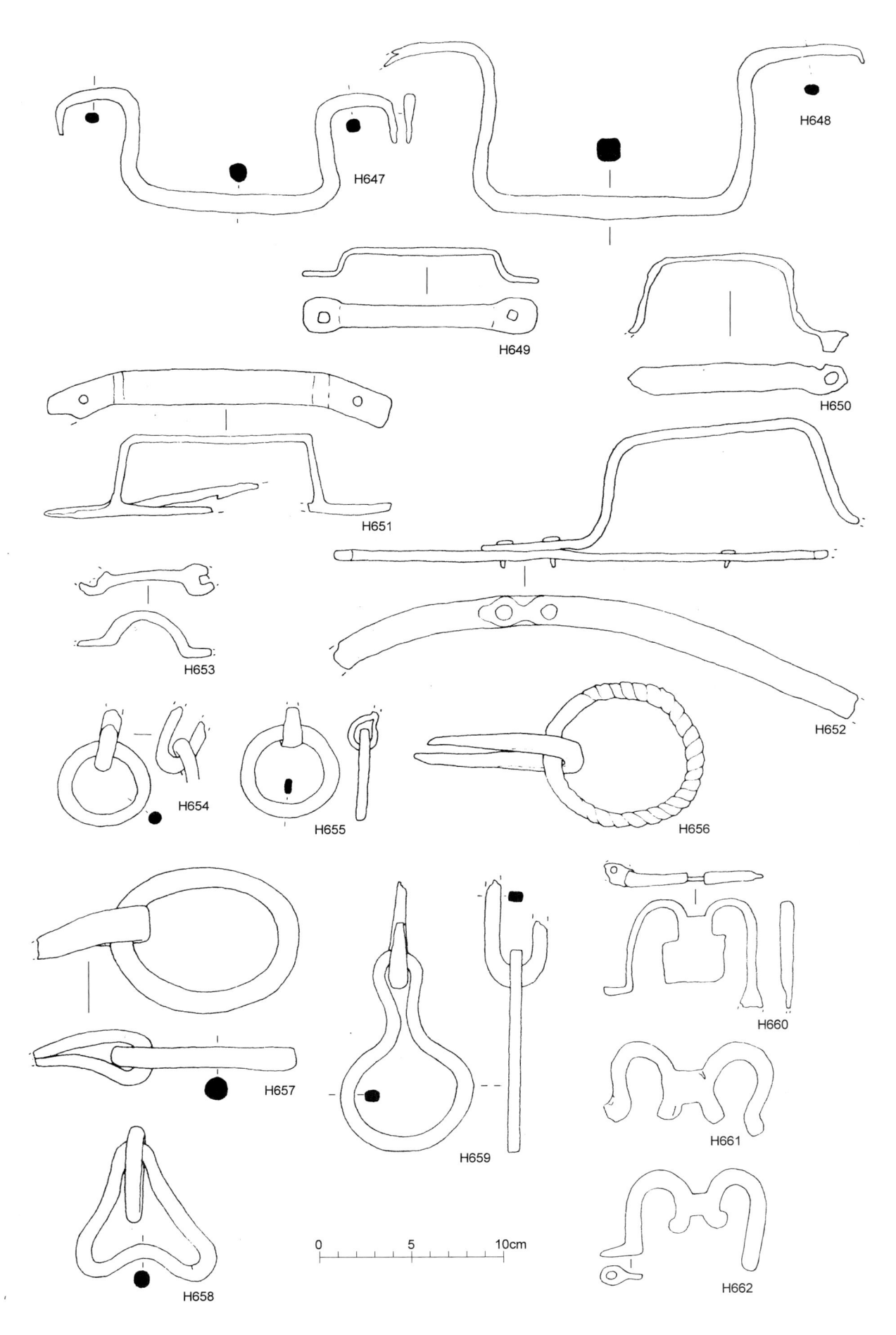

FIGURE 9.30
Handles

H663 LATCH REST
Clarendon Palace, Wiltshire.
Site: c1072 to later 15th century.
Shank distorted. L 96mm.
Goodall 1988, fig 78.65; Borenius and Charlton 1936.

H664 LATCH REST
Alsted, Surrey.
c1250–1350.
Shank broken. L 89mm.
Goodall 1976a, 56, fig 34.4.

H665 LATCH REST
Wintringham, Cambridgeshire.
Early 14th century.
Shank tip broken. L 119mm.
Goodall 1977a, 257, fig 43.29.

H666 LATCH REST
Manor of the More, Rickmansworth, Hertfordshire.
c1426.
Complete. L 150mm.
Biddle et al 1959, 185, fig 19.43

H667 LATCH REST
Kilton Castle, Cleveland.
Late 15th century.
Clenched tip to shank. L 116mm.
Excavated by A Aberg.

H668 LATCH REST
Newbury, Berkshire.
Mid 15th century.
Burred tip, bent shank. L 89mm.
Goodall 1997, fig 20, no. 23.

H669 LATCH REST
Castle Acre Castle, Norfolk.
1140s/1150s deposit with derived material.
Site founded soon after 1066.
Complete, angled shank. L 78mm.
Goodall 1982, fig 40, no. 105.

H670 LATCH REST
London.
Late 13th–mid 14th century.
Broken split shank. L 49mm.
Henig 1974, 191, fig 39.73.

H671 LATCH REST
Winchester, Hampshire.
Late 13th century.
Perforation through base of head, lead caulking on end of shank. L 132mm.
Cunliffe 1964, 154, fig 54.2.

H672 DOOR FLAIL
Lydney Castle, Gloucestershire.
12th century, possibly into 13th century.
Flat bar with tapered ends and central rivet hole. L 403mm.
Casey 1931, 252, pl XXXV.6.

H673 DOOR BOLT
Wroughton Copse, Fyfield Down, Wiltshire.
12th–13th century.
One end broken. L 58mm.
Excavated by P J Fowler.

H674 DOOR BOLT
Sulgrave, Northamptonshire.
End 11th century.
Probably complete. L 83mm.
Excavated by B K Davison.

H675 DOOR BOLT
Wroughton Copse, Fyfield Down, Wiltshire.
13th century (?mid) to early 14th century.
Complete. L 102mm.
Excavated by P J Fowler.

H676 DOOR BOLT
Seacourt, Oxfordshire.
14th century.
One end broken. L 128mm.
Biddle 1961–62, 177–179, fig 30.7, scale 1:4, not 1:3.

H677 DOOR BOLT
Clarendon Palace, Wiltshire.
Site: c1072 to later 15th century.
Complete. L 216mm.
Goodall 1988, fig 79.81; Borenius and Charlton 1936.

H678 DOOR BOLT
Rievaulx Abbey, North Yorkshire.
Site: 1131–1538 with later robbing.
Incomplete bolt with shaped finger grip decorated with an animals' head. L 130mm.
Dunning 1965, 58, fig 5.

H679 DOOR BOLT
Manor of the More, Rickmansworth, Hertfordshire.
c1520.
Circular-sectioned bolt with plain finger grip. L 202mm.
Biddle et al 1959, 185, fig 20.4.

H680 DOOR BOLT WITH STAPLED HANDLE
Winchester, Hampshire.
1141.
Sliding bolt with centrally set, incomplete, cranked stapled handle. Bolt L 152mm.
Goodall 1990-19, fig 304.3513 [Goodall 1980 says COE 3558].

H681 DOOR BOLT
Norwich.
In 1509 fire deposit.
Cranked bolt with finger grip and one of two U-shaped mounts. L 280mm.
Goodall 1993c, fig 113.1207.

H682 U-SHAPED BRACKET
Clarendon Palace, Wiltshire.
Site: c1072 to later 15th century.
Incomplete terminal retains nail. W 83mm.
Goodall 1988, fig 79.82; Borenius and Charlton 1936.

H683 HOOK
Waltham Abbey, Essex.
Well dug c1300, filled in late 15th–early 16th century.
Complete. L 137mm.
Goodall 1973a, 171, fig 11.35.

H684 HOOK
Southampton, Hampshire.
16th century.
Near complete. L 110mm.
Harvey 1975b, 289, fig 257.2114.

H685 DOOR HOOK
Glottenham, East Sussex.
Mid to late 13th century.
Looped hook, incomplete. L 345mm.
Excavated by D Martin.

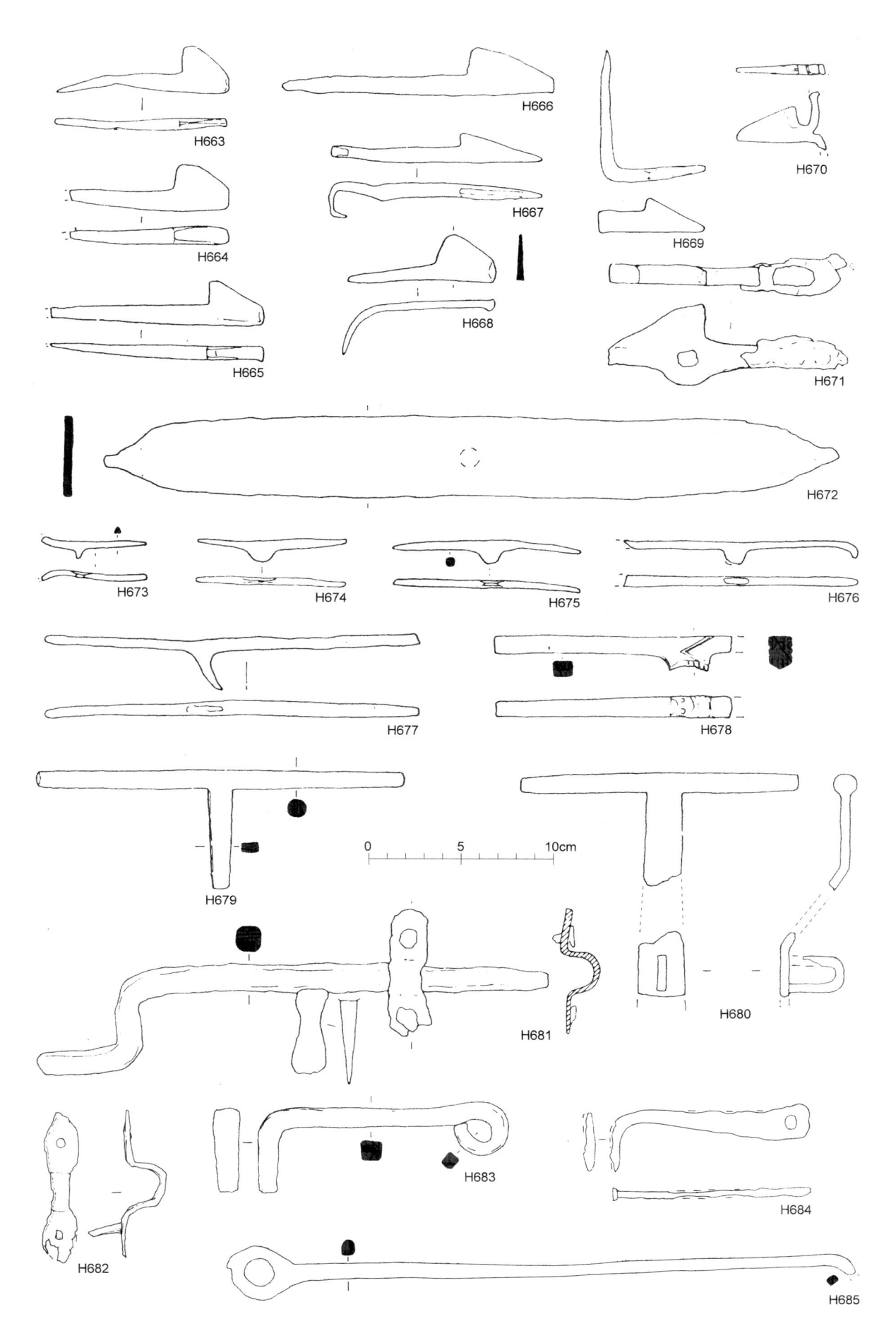

FIGURE 9.31
Latch rests, door flail, door bolts, U-shaped bracket and hooks

H686 GRILLE
Kings Langley, Hertfordshire.
Probably 1388.
Window formed from eight stone blocks with mortices for former iron grille wtih eight horizontal and six vertical bars, and for four hinge pivots, one of which survives.
Neal 1973, 48, fig IX.10.

H687 GRILLE (not illustrated)
Weoley Castle, Birmingham, West Midlands. c1270–1380. One of three grilles from moat. Five horizontal bars, maximum length 883mm, each with four 30 by 33mm holes for vertical rods. The bars have lead caulking at each end, and the longest rod is 1.143m long.
Oswald 1962, 64.

H688 GRILLE (not illustrated)
Weoley Castle, Birmingham, West Midlands. c1270–1380. One of three grilles from moat. Mush distorted grille with four horizontal bars, maximum length 1.080mm, each with five rectangular eyes for vertical rods. The longest rod is 1.448mm long.
Oswald 1962.64.

H689 GRILLE
Weoley Castle, Birmingham, West Midlands. c1270–1380. One of three grilles from moat. Incomplete grille with horizontal bars, maximum length 1.030mm, each with five eyes. Part of one bar drawn, L 270mm.
Oswald 1962, 64.

H690 WINDOW BAR
Griff (Sudeley Castle), Warwickshire.
Site: 13th–14th century.
Broken, straight bar with circular eye. L 217mm.
West 1968, 87, fig 4.9.

H691 WINDOW BAR
Kirkcudbright Castle, Dumfries and Galloway.
Site: c1288–1308.
Straight window bar with rectangular eye. L 348mm.
Dunning et al 1957–58, 138, fig 7.3.

H692 WINDOW BAR
Kilton Castle, Cleveland.
Late 15th century.
Broken bar with rectangular eye. L 222mm.
Excavated by A Aberg.

H693 WINDOW BAR
Ospringe, Kent.
c1483 to 1550.
Broken bar with rectangular eye. L 248mm.
Goodall 1979c, 129–132, fig 20.37.

H694 WINDOW BAR
Castle Acre Castle, Norfolk.
1140s deposit with derived material. Site founded soon after 1066.
Rectangular-sectioned bar. L 424mm.
Goodall 1982, fig 39, no. 51.

H695 WINDOW BAR
Stretham, East Sussex.
Site: 11th century to c1450.
Broken, hexagonal-sectioned bar. L 242mm.
Excavated by A Barr-Hamilton.

H696 WINDOW BAR
Alsted, Surrey
c1250–1350
Broken straight bar, largely of hexagonal section. L 268mm
Goodall 1976a, 56, fig.34.8

H697 WINDOW BAR
Clarendon Palace, Wiltshire.
Site: c1072 to later 15th century.
Stub of bar with lead caulking. L 95mm.
Goodall 1988, fig 77.60.

H698 WINDOW BAR
Clarendon Palace, Wiltshire.
Site: c1072 to later 15th century.
Diamond-sectioned bar with flattened ends. L 400mm.
Goodall 1988, fig 77.61.

H699 WINDOW BAR
South Witham, Lincolnshire.
Late 13th century to 1308–13.
Broken, rounded section bar with flattened terminal. L 178mm.
Goodall 2002, fig 7.3, no. 32.

H700–702 WINDOW BARS
Clarendon Palace, Wiltshire.
Site: c1072 to later 15th century.
Broken, straight, rectangular-sectioned bars with offset terminals. L 135mm, 150mm, 208mm.
Goodall 1988, fig 77.62–64.

H703 WINDOW BAR
Winchester, Hampshire.
14th to mid 15th century.
Terminals broken. L 172mm.
Goodall 1990-10, fig 86.697.

H704 WINDOW BAR (not illustrated)
Alsted, Surrey.
c1395–1405.
Broken bar and offset terminal. L 75mm.
Goodall 1976a, 60, fig 36.56.

H705 WINDOW BAR
Writtle, Essex.
c1425–1521.
Straight, square-sectioned bar with angled, perforated terminals. L 358mm.
Rahtz 1969b, 85, fig 47.44.

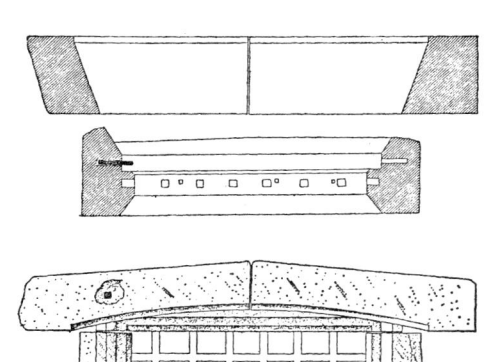

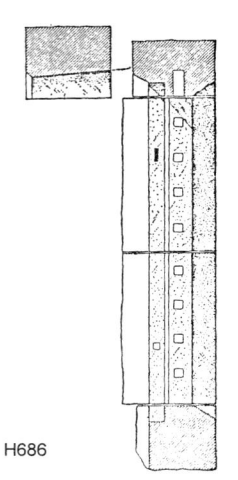

FIGURE 9.32
Window grille

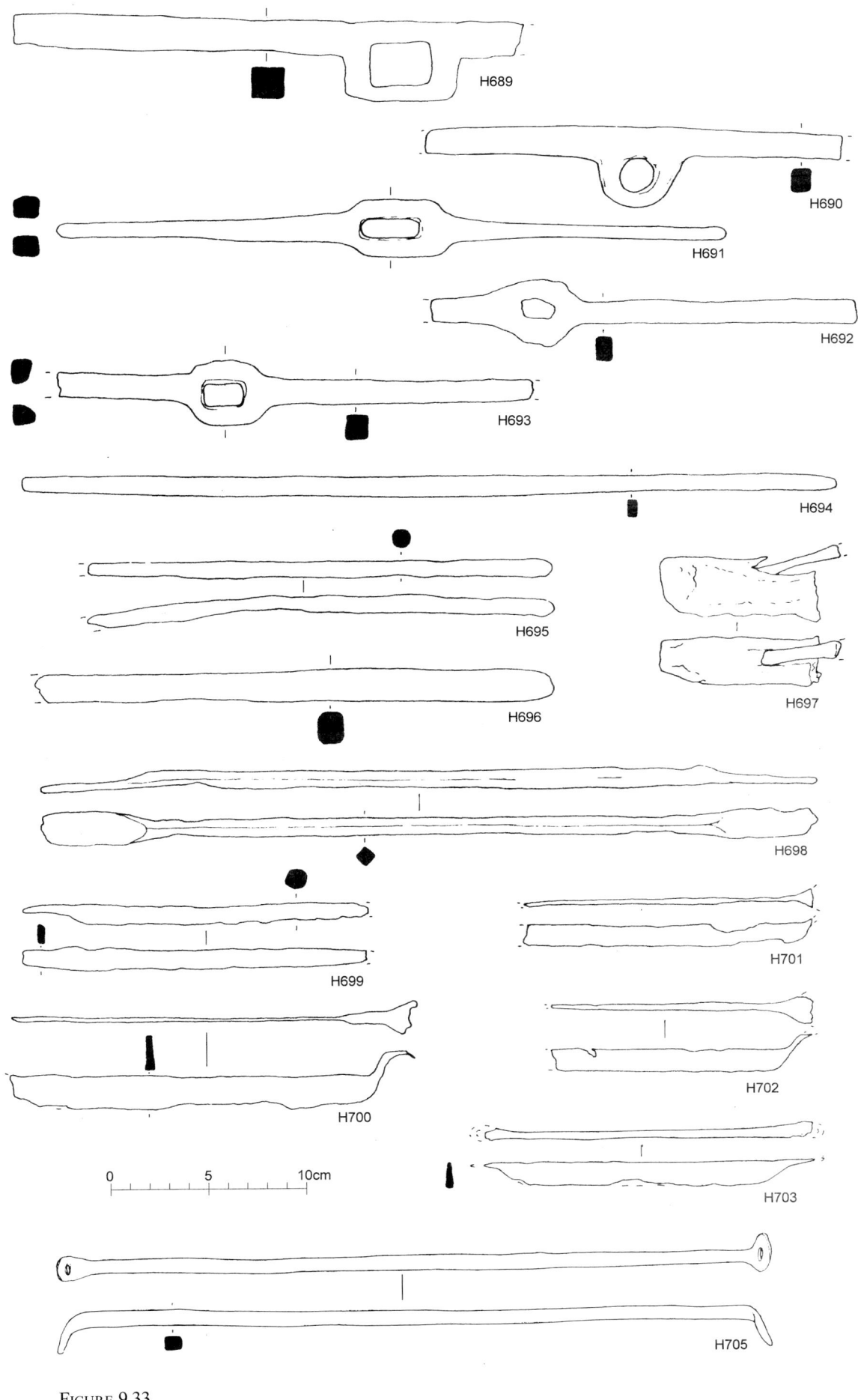

FIGURE 9.33
Window bars

H706 WINDOW BAR
South Witham, Lincolnshire.
*c*1220–late 13th century.
Nailed strap with seven perforated plates, five retaining nails, riveted to it. L 620mm.
Goodall 2002, fig 7.4, no. 31.

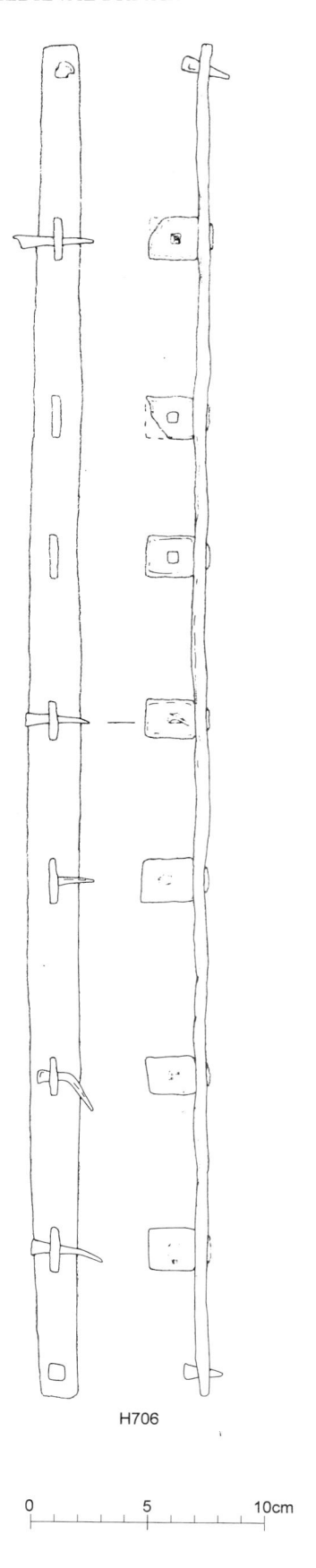

FIGURE 9.34
Window bar

10
LOCKS AND KEYS

Locks and keys, common but complicated finds, are discussed below in the following major sections: box and barrel padlocks; padlocks operated by revolving keys; locks; padlock keys; keys; miscellaneous keys.

10.1 BOX AND BARREL PADLOCKS

Medieval box and barrel padlocks generally have rectangular or cylindrical cases and padlock bolts with springs attached to spines. They were opened by padlock keys which passed over the springs, compressing them against the spine and thereby releasing the bolt. The padlock keys had to be of the appropriate type for the padlock and its keyhole, and the bit had to be of the correct shape to pass along the bolt.

Box padlocks

Box padlocks with rectangular cases are principally of pre-Conquest date, although **I1–3** are incomplete case fragments from medieval contexts. All are of the same basic form with a T-shaped keyhole in one side and a tube on the outer face of the opposite side, and they were used with U-shaped paddock bolts similar to **I4–5** which have rectangular closing plates.

Box padlocks were probably little used after the 11th century. **I3**, although from an early 12th-century context, is from a site occupied since the 8th century, and its twisted rods closely resemble those on a box padlock of probable Viking date from York (Richardson 1959, 81–83, fig 18.4; full size not 1:2). **I5** is probably residual in its context, and **I1–2** are from a castle erected immediately after the Conquest and occupied until about 1350.

Barrel padlocks

The barrel padlock was the most common type of medieval padlock, and five types (A–E) may be isolated, some capable of further subdivision according to the form and position of the keyhole (Figure 10.1).

Type A. Barrel padlocks with attached tubes

This type of barrel padlock has a case to which the tube is directly attached, and it can be divided into Types A1 and A2.
— Type A1 has a case with strengthening rods between the end plates, and **I6** is the only example. It has twisted rods along an otherwise plain case, and lozenge-shaped end plates.
— Type A2 is similarly constructed, but in addition it has pivoting fins set between the end plates. **I7** is the only complete medieval example, and its plain case is strengthened by plain rods. **I8–10** are individual pivoting fins of flattened triangular shape. Barrel padlocks **I6–7** both have keyholes in one end plate and holes for the U-shaped bolt in the other.

Type A barrel padlocks are known from pre-Conquest contexts, and they probably did not continue in use much, if at all, after the 12th century.

Type B. Barrel padlocks with fins and tubes

This type of barrel padlock, one of the most common medieval types, has the case and tube separated by a rectangular or trapezoidal fin. It can be divided into three types according to the position of the keyhole.
— Type B1. Barrel padlocks **I11–19** have a keyhole in one end plate, the other having holes for the entry of the

U-shaped bolt. The barrel padlocks vary in length from 29 to 79mm, and all are decorated, most frequently with longitudinal rods and straps, but occasionally with projecting longitudinal straps. **I16** retains its broken key **I238**.

Type B1 barrel padlocks of iron are known from medieval contexts up to the 14th century, and a 14th-century copper-alloy example comes from Walsall Manor, Staffordshire (Wrathmell and Wrathmell 1974–75, 49, fig 17.1).

— Type B2. Barrel padlocks **I20–21** have T-shaped keyholes which cut across the end plate and underside of the case. Their cases have longitudinal straps and rods, and are from 12th to 14th-century contexts.

— Type B3. Barrel padlocks **I22–35** have a T-shaped keyhole along the underside of the case. The keyhole is generally a plain opening, as on **I28**, **I31** and **I34**, but on **I22–23** and **I29–30** there are cheeks along each side. Those on **I22** are perforated, as also is the fin. Seven of these barrel padlocks have cases with longitudinal and transverse straps, and all but one of the remainder have at least longitudinal straps.

Type B3 padlocks are known from medieval contexts up to and including the 15th century.

A number of barrel padlock fragments incapable of precise classification but of intrinsic interest are known. **I36–38** are case fragments with longitudinal rods, **I39–42** complete fins and tubes of differing size and form. **I39** has wavy line decoration, **I40** is plain, **I41** has a strap and **I42** is perforated.

U-shaped padlock bolts

U-shaped padlock bolts were used with box padlocks and with barrel padlocks of Type A and B. Rectangular or rounded closing plates, where present and recognisable, generally indicate the type of padlock from which the bolts come, but otherwise the context date is a guide. Padlock bolts of 12th-century and later date, unless residual, are unlikely to be from box padlocks, and those of 13th-century and later date are most probably from Type B barrel padlocks.

Padlock bolts, as the surviving barrel padlocks indicate, can have between one and four spines, each with springs, as well as additional rods to increase their complexity. **I43–49** have single spines, most retaining double leaf springs, and of these **I43–45** form a small group of 13th to 14th-century date which have expansions at the head of the spine and an equivalent step on the free arm, where this survives. **I46** has this latter step but no expansion, and it would seem that both features are alternatives to closing plates. **I47** has probably lost its closing plate, which **I48** and **I49** retain. **I48** is unusual in having copper-alloy rather than iron springs.

I50–54 are bolts with double spines arranged in differing ways, all with closing plates. **I55–62** have three spines, although most are incomplete, and **I63** four spines. A feature common to a number of these padlock bolts is the scrolled decoration applied immediately

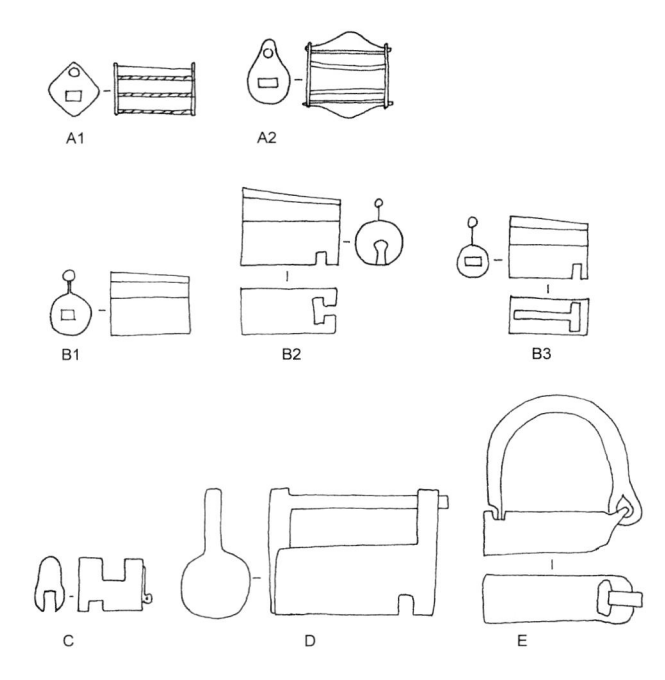

FIGURE 10.1
Types of medieval barrel padlock

above the closing plate, which ranges from the simplicity of **I52** or **I57** to the complexity of **I58**. **I64** is a scrolled bolt fragment.

The method of forging padlock bolts with multiple spines normally involved splitting the spring arm and drawing it out into two spines, and then either brazing the third spine onto the outer or inner edge of the bolt (**I56–57**) or attaching it directly to the main curve of the bolt (**I58**). The latter technique was employed for the two additional spines on **I63**. The scrolled decoration, normally made from iron strip, was also brazed into position and the whole padlock bolt sometimes plated with copper alloy.

Type C. Barrel padlocks with U-shaped housings

Barrel padlocks **I65–72** have cases with inverted U-shaped housings set at each end to house the flat arm of the bolt, itself of a squared U-shape. This arrangement provided a small rectangular opening through which to pass a chain or staple. The compactness of the arrangement was probably intended to give security, and the padlocks must have been difficult and complicated to forge. A gold padlock of this type, only 15mm long and its case rectangular rather than rounded in section, was found with its bolt and key in a hoard of jewellery probably deposited early in 1464 at Fishpool, Nottinghamshire (Cherry 1973, 312–313, pl LXXXVId).

The cases of these iron barrel padlocks are generally plain, only **I65** being decorated, and all have keyholes in an end plate. The padlock bolts have two or three spines, **I65** three additional rods.

Type C barrel padlocks broadly come from 12th to 15th-century contexts.

Type D. Barrel padlocks with L-shaped arms

Barrel padlocks with L-shaped arms over which a looped, L-shaped padlock bolt fitted are found as commonly in copper alloy as in iron, although the former are generally small in size. I73–79 are iron barrel padlocks or bolts; those of copper allow are listed below.

Three iron barrel padlock cases survive, I73 and I74 plain, I75 decorated, and the bolts of I74 and I75 respectively plain and decorated. I78 is another bolt with decorative scrollwork, although more restrained in form. These padlock bolts are of two types, most with circular closing plates, but I76 and I79 without them. The cases of I73 and I74 have keyholes in the end plate, that of I75 a T-shaped keyhole across an end plate and the underside of the case.

Type D barrel padlocks of both iron and copper alloy are found in 12th to 16th-century contexts. Copper-alloy barrel padlocks of Type D:
— Winchester, Hampshire. 1100–25. Broken zoomorphic case. L: 31mm (Goodall 1990-21, BS 4623),
— Norwich, Norfolk. First half of the 13th century. Case. L: 39mm (Hurst 1963, 169, fig 14.8),
— Goltho, Lincolnshire. 13th–mid 14th century. Case. L: 27mm (Goodall 1975a, 93, fig 44.21),
— Rayleigh Castle, Essex. Around 1070–1350. Case retaining iron springs from bolt. L: 32mm (Reader 1913, 163–164, pl B1),
— Old Sarum, Wiltshire. Principally medieval, to 14th century. Bolt. L: 32mm. Salisbury and South Wiltshire Museum, Salisbury, OS C47,
— Brome, Suffolk. Late in period, late 12th to mid 14th century. Bolt. L: 53mm (West 1970, 112, fig 13.21),
— Winchester, Hampshire. 14th century. Case and bolt with iron spines and springs. L: 33mm (Goodall 1990-21, BS 490),
— Northampton. 15th century. Case. L: 33mm (Goodall 1978c, 149, fig 22.2),
— St Helen's, Isles of Scilly. 11th–15th century. Bolt. L: 70mm (Dunning 1964, 66, fig.7.3).

Type E. Barrel padlocks with shackles

Barrel padlocks with shackles were primarily intended to secure and restrain limbs, both human and animal, although their sturdy construction and ease of use led to their having a general purpose use as well. Salzman (1967, 303), for example, records the provision at Collyweston in 1500 of 'horse lokes for the garden yattes'. This type of barrel padlock has an end-looped, curved shackle with an expanded end perforated to allow the passage of a padlock bolt, and in use the expanded end of the shackle passed through a slot in the upper side of the padlock case and was secured within it by a T-shaped bolt.

I80 and its almost identical pair I81 are complete limb shackles with padlock, chain and shackle. None of the others, I82–93, is as complete although I82, I83, I86 and I90 retain their bolts and I83 and I90 also their keys, I251 and I285. I90 was found with a leg bone through the shackle. The padlock cases of I80–93 are all plain, or at most have broad straps around the lower half to strengthen the case without chafing entrapped limbs. All have, or had, keyholes in the end plate below the end loop of the shackle, some of them extending slightly into the underside of the case. The cases have no fixed bolt entry end plate since the expanded and perforated end of the shackle served its function.

I94 is a broken shackle from a Type E barrel padlock.

Many T-shaped padlock bolts of the type used with these barrel padlocks are known, and a selection has been catalogued. I95–96 have single spines, one with a double leaf spring, the other with four springs, and I97–105 all have two spines. I106, the closing plate from a bolt with two countersinkings for spines, is from the forge at Waltham Abbey, Essex, and may be an incomplete forging. I107–117 have, or had, three spines, and I118 has two spines, each with double leaf springs, and two rods.

T-shaped padlock bolts must have been difficult to hold during the opening and closing of the padlocks, and several have looped handles, those of I96 and I102 welded to the rim of the closing plate, while I100–101 and I109–110 have loops made by drawing the end of the spine out and round.

Type E barrel padlocks are found throughout the medieval period.

Indeterminate barrel padlock fragments

I119–123 are unclassifiable barrel padlock fragments of intrinsic interest for their decorative treatment. I124 is part of the spine and spring of a bolt with an inverted U-shaped fitting recalling that of I48.

Barrel padlocks: discussion

Five main types of barrel padlock can be isolated, and of those Type B and E are the commonest. Type E, the more popular of the two, is the only type which was used in any quantity throughout the medieval period, since its form suited its principal use of shackling animals and people. Type B barrel padlocks, however, which are infrequently found after the 14th century, are more likely to have been used on doors and chests and to have been replaced by fixed locks. Types A, C and D are represented by relatively few barrel padlocks. Type A with its attached tube is clearly related to the box padlock, and like it, it only just continued in use into the medieval period. Types C and D are more specialised types, the latter as commonly made in copper alloy as in iron, and both have broad date ranges.

Barrel padlock cases are sometimes plain, but most have decoration of some sort, much of it probably originating as a by-product of the method of assembly. I30, for example, consists of a cylindrical case, two end plates, a rectangular fin and a tapering tube, all brazed together. Straps also bind the case and end plates, and tube and fin, and the decorative straps are an extension of these, strengthening and decorating the case.

The decoration on padlock cases is related to their type, size and date. Plain cases are most frequently found on barrel padlocks with shackles (Type E), which are plain on at least their upper surfaces to avoid chafing limbs. The other plain cases are mainly restricted to small barrel padlocks of Types C and D.

Thirteen barrel padlocks of 11th to 14th-century date have rods along their cases. On I6–7, both of Type A, they run between shaped end plates and are clearly part of the padlocks' construction, but on the other eleven, all of Type B, they are principally a decorative feature. They are almost invariably plain, although those on I6 are twisted.

Straps along padlock cases may serve either to cover the butted edges of the sheet iron case or act as flanges securing the base of a fin in place. Thirteen barrel padlocks have flat straps along the sides of their cases, and some may be considered to be decorative. They are generally applied to otherwise plain cases, although I12 and I28 are corrugated, and I24, I35 and I119 have additional wavy decoration in some panels. These flat side straps are found throughout the medieval period, but the four barrel padlocks with projecting side straps (I14, I16, I33 and I122) are all of 13th to 14th-century date and, where sufficiently complete, of Type B. A type of decoration combining longitudinal and transverse straps is restricted to seven examples of Type B, principally of 11th to 13th-century date.

Decoration was not restricted to padlock cases, and several Type B barrel padlocks have decorated fins. I39 has wavy line decoration, I41 a longitudinal strap, and I22, I28 and I42 are perforated. The perforations on I22 are extended to the cheeks beside the keyhole.

The various types of barrel padlock were used with their own specific type of padlock bolt, and these have been shown to have between one and four spines. A number of bolts, including I113 and I118, and those with padlocks I34, I65 and I75 have rods which never held springs but instead served to complicate the lock. Several, including I48, I98 and I124, have extra fittings or straps attached to the spines.

Examination of two T-shaped padlock bolts from Goltho (I110–111) explained their method of assembly. Many padlock bolts are shown, by their drawings, to have riveted spine tips, and I111 was proved to have had holes punched or drifted through them prior to riveting. One spine on I111 was shown to have been drawn out from the closing plate, but another on I110 had been inserted in a hole and brazed into place. The latter method of assembly is simpler and was probably more generally used since a number of incomplete bolts, including I106, have holes for spines. A number also have these spines drawn out and bent round into handles to enable them to be inserted and withdrawn more easily.

10.2 PADLOCKS OPERATED BY REVOLVING KEYS

Padlocks with separate bolts

I125 is a padlock case which originally had a U-shaped bolt opened by a revolving key. It is from a 12th to 14th-century context and is related to earlier box padlocks opened in a similar way from Birka, Sweden (Arbman 1940, taf 273, 6a–c), and to later medieval box padlocks with hinged shackles. Its case shape with fin and tube is similar to contemporary Type B barrel padlocks, and its wavy line decoration also has medieval parallels.

Padlocks with hinged shackles

Padlocks with hinged shackles and sliding bolts operated by a revolving key were introduced during the late medieval period and became popular during the post-medieval period. Medieval examples I126–128, from 15th to 16th-century contexts, all have plain rectangular cases with U-shaped shackles hinged within the case. I129–130 are hinged shackles found independently of their padlocks.

The keyholes and internal mechanism of I127 is not clear, but I126 and I128 have keyholes in one long side. I126 has a circular mount on the inner face of the opposing side to receive the key tip, while I128 has a hole in the case side to receive it. In use the key bit had to pass a U-shaped spring-cum-ward before sliding the L-shaped bolt out of a recess in the inner edge of the shackle tip and thus freeing it.

Embossed padlocks

I131–141 are embossed padlocks with flanged rectangular cases and U-shaped stapled hasps which were not fixed to doors or items of furniture, despite their appearance, but instead hung freely in the manner of all padlocks. They have flat rectangular backplates and dished cases housing the lock mechanism, the two parts riveted together through a narrow flange with rivets either at each corner (I131 and I138) or all round the case (I139 and I141). The rivets sometimes have raised heads, as on I141, but these are merely decorative and are not from larger studs which fixed the padlock in position.

The stapled hasps used with these padlocks are of a round or flat-headed U-shape, and they have a tapering straight arm which passed vertically through the case and acted as a pivot. The other arm is angled to fit over the outer face of the case. None of the tapering straight arms is complete, and it is impossible to know therefore whether they could be completely withdrawn from the case when not locked, or whether they had clenched tips which retained them within the case, as on an 18th-century embossed padlock from Louisbourg, Canada (Dunton 1972, 116, fig 77.13).

Two types of embossed padlock were in use during the medieval period, one with a sliding bolt and the other a pivoting bolt, each with its appropriate hasp:

— Type 1 has a toothed bolt which operated by sliding in and out of the D-shaped staple of the hasp. **I131–132** are variously incomplete padlocks of this type, **I133–137** the stapled hasps.

— Type 2 has a pivoting bolt, looped at the fixed end, with its tip crossing the hole for the staple of the hasp. **I138–139** are near complete padlocks of this type, the latter retaining its hasp; **I140** is an isolated hasp with the characteristically shaped solid staple with a recess to accommodate the bolt. **I141** is an embossed padlock which has yet to be X-rayed and classified.

Embossed padlocks were opened in the same way as padlocks with hinged shackles, the key revolving in the case and passing all wards before moving the bolt and locking or unlocking it. The sloping edge of staple **I140** would have enabled the padlock to be snapped closed against the pivoting bolt without the use of a key, but the hasps with D-shaped staples must all have required keys for both opening and closing.

Embossed padlocks are of late medieval date, Type 1 probably being introduced during the late 13th or early 14th century, and Type 2 probably during the 15th or 16th century.

10.3 LOCKS

Medieval documents record purchases of clicket locks, plate-locks and stock-locks (Salzman 1967, 301–303), all different types of fixed lock used on doors to buildings and on items of furniture. The plate-lock appears to have had the lock mechanism attached to a visible plate, and the stock-lock to have had it set in a block of wood on the door.

Medieval locks may be divided into two types, Type 1 having a sliding bolt which engaged in one or two stapled hasps, Type 2 having a sliding bolt which engaged in a keeper or staple independent of the lock. Both types of lock worked according to the same principles, differing only in the positioning and shaping of individual components.

Figure 10.2, based on **I146**, shows the method of opening a lock. It shows the lock initially closed, but the stale of the hasp has been omitted from around the bolt end for clarity. The key was first inserted, its tip locating in a hole in the mount (A) which also has a collar on its inner side. It was then turned, and cuts in the bit enabled it to pass the collar (B), L-shaped ward (C), and cross-shaped wards (D) before lifting the tumbler (E) and sliding the bolt (F) open. The tumbler pressed against the upper projection on the lock bolt when closed, but apparently merely rested on top of it when open. In opening and closing, the lock key bit pressed against one or other of the inner sides of the two lower toothed projections of the bolt.

Type 1

Locks with straight or hooked sliding bolts which engaged in one or two stapled hasps respectively.

— Type 1a. This, the most common type of pre-Conquest lock, was operated by keys with projection on their bits and had spring-held sliding bolts with horizontally enlarged and perforated centres set on a flat lockplate. A few keys (**I296–303**) of appropriate type are known from medieval contexts, but they probably barely outlasted the 11th century. No medieval example of this type of lock is known, although earlier ones are discussed by Almgren (1955, 33–40), and one from a late 9th-century context comes from Winchester, Hampshire (Goodall 1990-21, CG 281.37).

— Type 1b. **I142–145** are flat lockplates with the lock mechanism attached to the rear face. **I142** and **I145** are the most complete, and both have holes for the staples of two hasps which were held closed by the ends of hooked sliding bolts. Both bolts slide in U-shaped staples, and are held in place by springs. **I144** has a straight bolt, and **I143** holds a small looped hasp **H565** against the fragmentary lockplate.

— Type 1c. One example of a lock with the mechanism attached to the inner face of a dished or embossed case, is known (**I146**). The lock was nailed to the front of a wooden door or item of furniture and held closed by a hasp with an angled stapled arm such as **H572** or **H574**. The lock has a hole for one hasp and a damaged keyhole, and its operation is described above and illustrated in Figure 10.2.

Components from Type 1 locks

Locks are made from a number of components riveted or brazed together, and these are occasionally found separately. **I147** and **I148** are key tip mounts, **I147** plain but **I148** with two concentric collars on the inner side. The key mounts on locks **I128–129** have single collars. **I149–152** are sliding bolts, **I149** straight and used with a single stapled hasp, **I150–154** hooked and used with two stapled hasps. The cranked ends of **I150–151** enabled the two stapled hasps to be level on the front of the chests that they probably come from, unlike those used with **I142** and **I145**. **I149** is similar in size to the bolts on locks **I145–146**, and could be from a lock of either Type 1b or 1c. **I150–152** are much larger, however, and can only be from the flat lockplates of Type 1b. **I153** is the incomplete spring from a lock which in use, as on **I142** and **I145**, pushed against the top of the bolt and kept it in place.

Type 2

Locks of Type 2 have bolts which engaged in a staple or other keeper outside the lockcase. No complete example is yet known, but a number of the individual components, bolts, tumblers and wards, are known.

I154–166 are lock bolts, the more complete ones having two lower projections and generally one upper notch or projection, **I166**, however, has two upper projections. In operation the key of the lock struck the inner side of one or other of the lower projections, thereby throwing the bolt and either locking or unlocking it. The upper projection acted as a stop against which the tumbler rested when the lock was closed, preventing it being forced open by pressure. The double upper projection on **I166** suggests an arrangement found on post-medieval locks whereby the bolt was held firm when both locked and unlocked (Nöel Hume 1970, fig 77a).

Lock bolts **I154–163** are generally slightly tapered, and thicken towards the outer end. **I164–166** are of similar width throughout, although the inner end is turned through a right angle as if to act as a stop. These latter bolts more closely resemble those found in post-medieval locks (Nöel Hume 1970, fig 77a, b), and they may be a late medieval development of the lock bolt.

I167–168 are tumblers which had to be lifted clear of the top of the bolt by the key before some locks could be opened. **I146** has one in position.

Wards **I169–177** were set in locks to act as barriers which the key bit had to pass, and in locks of Type 2 they were set between side mounts as in extant post-medieval locks (Nöel Hume 1970, fig 77b). **I170** has shaped ends to fit such mounts, but the others are plain. **I169–175** are plain wards which would only require a straight cut in the key bit, but the pin on **I176**, perhaps originally balanced by another now missing, and the collar on **I177**, would have required additional ward cuts. Most of the wards are from 15th to 16th-century contexts.

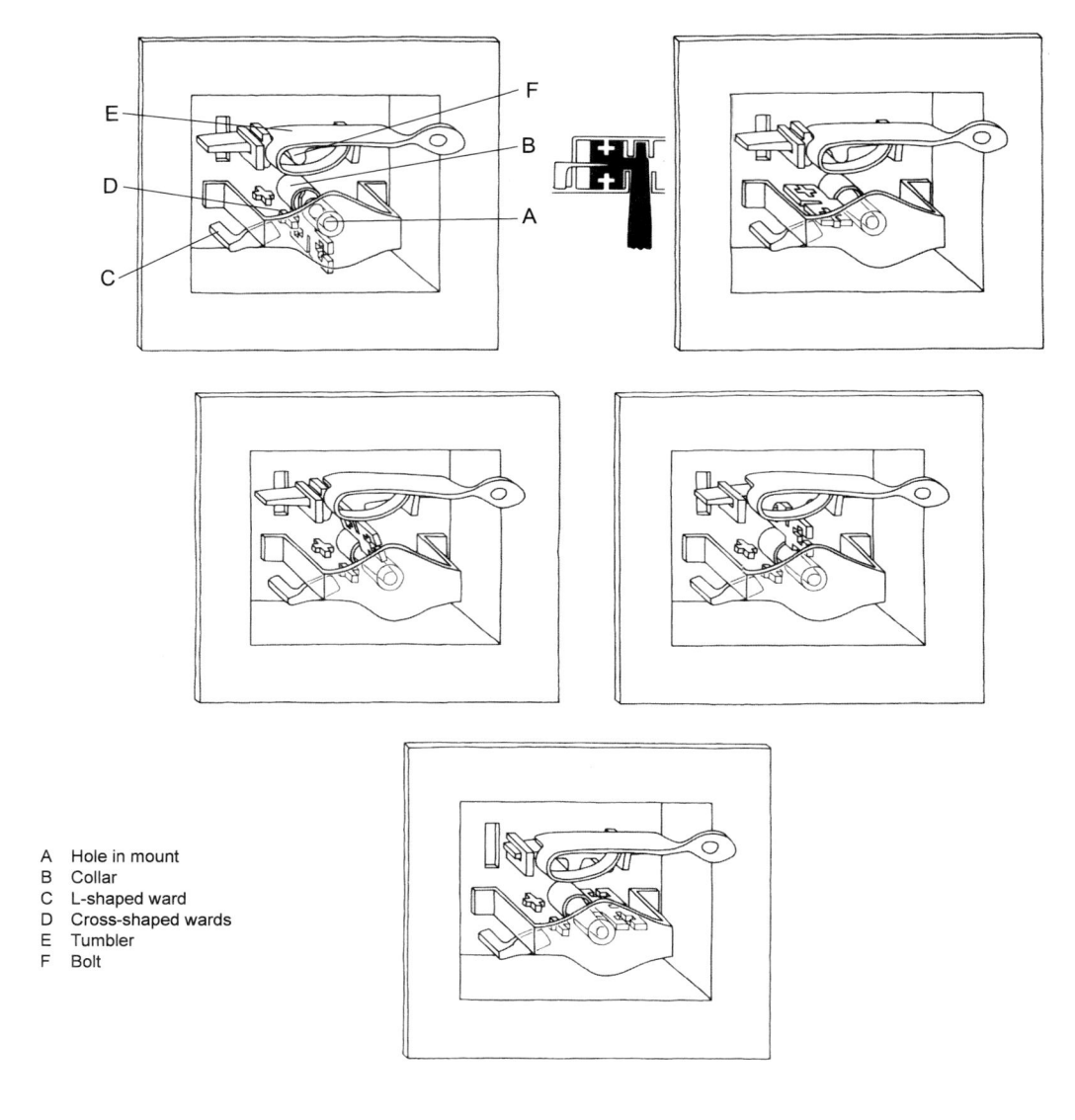

A Hole in mount
B Collar
C L-shaped ward
D Cross-shaped wards
E Tumbler
F Bolt

FIGURE 10.2
*Diagram showing operation of lock **I146** (after original drawing by D V Hyde)*

10.4 PADLOCK KEYS

Box and barrel padlocks with bolts with leaf springs attached to the spines (**I1–124**) were opened by drawing or pushing padlock keys along the springs, compressing them and ejecting the bolt. These padlock keys may be divided into five types (1–5) according to the form and position of the bit in relation to the stem, and some can be further subdivided (Figure 10.3). Box padlocks were probably little used after the 11th century, and most of the keys described must have been used with barrel padlocks.

Type 1

Padlock keys with bit, stem and terminal in line.

Padlock keys of this type (**I178–205**) were inserted into the case and drawn along the bolt, and could only have been used with padlocks with T-shaped keyholes completely in one plane. They could, therefore, have been used with boxed padlocks and certain Type B and C barrel padlocks, but not with any of Types A, D or E. They may be subdivided into Types 1a–d.

— Type 1a. Padlock keys **I178–183** have plain stems, **I181** with a projection immediately above the bit which may have helped to guide the key along the keyhole. All the bits have unbroken outer edges and holes within them to pass the springs of the bolt. The looped terminals are both rounded and lozenge-shaped.

— Type 1b. Padlock keys **I185–202** have swollen stems, eight with spirally inlaid non-ferrous plating, and the remaining eight plain. The wire on **I188** and **I191** has been identified as copper alloy. The looped terminals are either rounded or lozenge-shaped, and **I189**, **I193** and **I197** retain rings. The bits have unbroken outer edges except on **I202**.

— Type 1c. **I203** has a hooked terminal and simply decorated swollen stem.

— Type 1d. Padlock keys **I204–205** have short stems which flatten and expand to a perforated tip. **I204** has a simple decoration, **I205** a small projection on the stem.

Type 1 padlock keys mainly come from 11th to 13th-century contexts, and those of Type 1b, with their swollen stems, are the most common. The bits generally have unbroken outer edges and internal holes to pass over the bolt springs, only **I202–203** have side cuts. This shaping reflects the form of the bolts in use. The looped terminals of Types 1a and 1b are forged in with the stems, and are either in the same plane as the bit or at right angles to it.

Type 2

Padlock keys with wards radiating from the base of the stem.

Padlock keys **I206–212** are of Type 2 and could have been inserted through a keyhole either in the end plate or across the end plate and underside of a padlock. They are therefore capable of being used with certain of the barrel padlocks of Types A–D. There are two variations of Type 2 with either looped or hooked terminals:

— Type 2a. Padlock keys **I206–210** have looped terminals and plain stems, **I208** unusually with a double-looped terminal. The stems are of rectangular section, and on **I207** this thins down just below the handle in part to act as a stop.

— Type 2b. Padlock key **I211** has the expanded stem and hooked terminal more normally found on padlock keys of type 4 and 5, but its bit has radiating wards.

I212 is a stem and bit fragment, probably originally of Type 2a.

Type 2 padlock keys, represented by seven examples, come mainly from 12th to 13th-century contexts. The wards radiating from the base of the stem are generally symmetrical, and those on **I209** and **I212** are each forged round in an unusual way.

Type 3

Padlock keys with elongated sheet metal bits in line with the stem.

This type of padlock key was used with keyholes set in end plates, and it could therefore have been used with certain barrel padlocks of Types A–D. The restricted date range of the British and Continental examples, which include a gold key found with its padlock, suggests nevertheless that it was mainly used with Type C barrel padlocks.

I213, the only Type 3 iron padlock key so far identified from Britain, has a sheet metal bit with thin strips of iron brazed down two sides of a central sheet and a closing plate between it and the stem. The bit occupies about two-thirds of the length of the key, a similar proportion to those on keys from the Continent which all have looped terminals, one combined with a bulbous stem identical to **I213**, the others with longer plain or swollen stems.

I213 is from a 14th-century context, and Continental iron parallels include one from Naesholm Castle, Denmark (La Cour 1961, 132, fig 49.N.806) occupied c1240 to 1340–46, some of 13th to 14th-century date from Lund, Sweden (Blomqvist 1940, 100, figs 20–23), and three from the mass graves at Wisby, Sweden, of 1361 (Thordeman 1939, 129–130, fig 149.1–3).

A gold Type C barrel padlock, 15mm long, has a Type 3 gold key attached by a chain to its bolt. It comes from a hoard of medieval jewellery from Fishpool, Nottinghamshire (Cherry 1973, 312–313, pl LXXXVId) which was probably deposited in the early months of 1464. The key is of a squared U-shaped section.

Type 4

Padlock keys with laterally set bits with radiating wards.

This type of padlock key, represented by **I214–241**, could be pushed along the bolts of barrel padlocks with keyholes in the end plate or across the end plate and

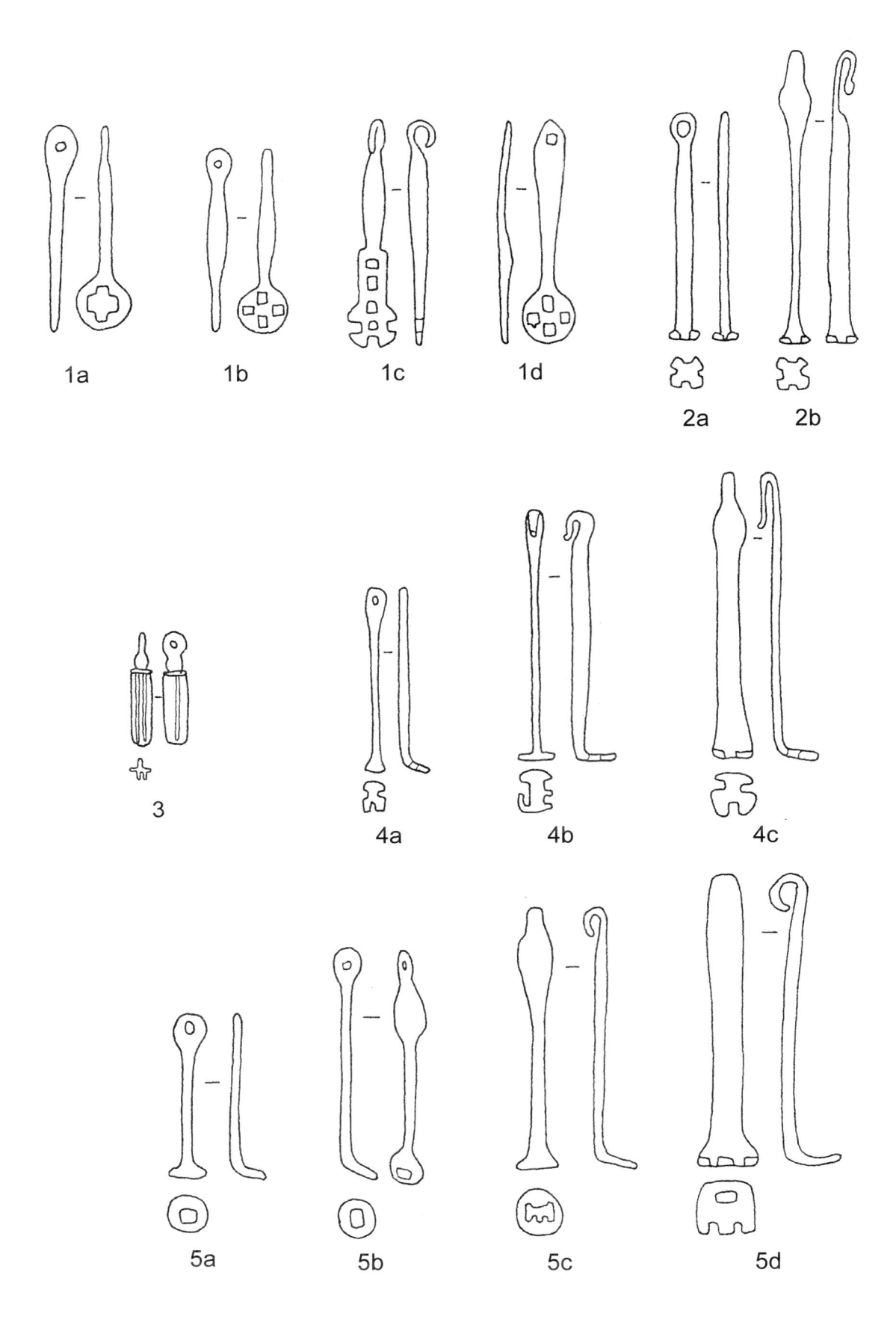

FIGURE 10.3
Types of medieval padlock key

underside of the case, or be drawn along those with T-shaped keyholes along the underside. It could theoretically, therefore, have been used with any type of barrel padlock, although in practice it is especially suitable for those of Types A, B and E. Type 4 padlock keys may be subdivided into Types 4a–c.

— Type 4a. Padlock keys **I214–224** have looped terminals and plain stems, the latter parallel-sided, tapered, part-thickened or part-thinned towards the terminal. The thickened upper parts of **I215–216** and **I220** would have acted as stops against the end-plate of a barrel padlock.

— Type 4b. **I225–228** have plain, parallel-sided stems and hooked terminals, the terminal on **I228** resembling an unforged loop, that on **I226** fully developed.

— Type 4c. Padlock keys **I229–237** have stems with expanded and hooked terminals, the expansion either a flattened lozenge or oval shape.

I238 and **I239–241** are bit and stem fragments incapable of certain classification, **I238** coming from within barrel padlock **I16**.

Type 4 padlock keys are found throughout the medieval period, but most come from 11th to 13th-century contexts. Looped stems are as common as those with hooks, and the bits are fairly standard, most having single ward cuts to the front and in each side. **I232**, however, has only side ward cuts, and **I220–221** and **I226** are more complicated.

Type 5

Padlock keys with looped, laterally set bits.

This type of padlock key, represented by **I242–291**, was used in a similar way to Type 4 keys, and may be subdivided into Types 5a–d:

— Type 5a: **I242** has a looped terminal on a plain stem.
— Type 5b: **I243–245** have expanded terminals with transversely set loops. The expansion are all of a rounded lozenge shape.
— Type 5c: **I246–269** have stems with expanded and hooked terminals, the expansions either of a flattened lozenge or oval shape. The hook is set to the rear on all but **I251**.
— Type 5d: **I270–280** have stems with hooked terminals which are set to the rear on all except **I270**. The stems are generally broad and widen slightly as they curve round into the hook, although **I271**, **I73** and **I77** have narrow stems.

I281–284 have incomplete expanded stems and may be either Type 5b or 5c, whilst **I285** and **I286–291** are Type 5 stem and bit fragments, **I285** coming from within barrel padlock **I90**.

Type 5 padlock keys, like the related Type 4 keys, were in use throughout the medieval period, although most are from 11th to 14th-century contexts. Most have hooked terminals on either plain or expanded stems, but **I242** has the looped terminal more commonly associated with padlock keys of Types 1–3. **I243–245** have a hybrid combination of expanded stem and looped terminal.

The bits vary in form, with from one to three ward cuts. Some have unbroken or closed edges and plain (**I243**) or shaped (**I260**) wards, others combine open and closed wards in various ways (e.g. **I246**, **I259**, **I264**, **I268** and **I278**). **I274** is unique in having a single central open ward cut. The shaping of the cuts of such bits as **I249** and **I272** was to allow the passage of wire brazed along springs, as on padlock bolt **I98**.

Discussion

Padlock keys' forms were determined by those of the box of barrel padlocks to be opened, but the shape of the stem and terminal was subject to the influence of fashion. This is evident amongst the keys, since the plain stem and hooked terminal are found throughout the period, but the shaped and decorated types have restricted chronologies. The terminal of the padlock key acted in part as a handle held when using the key, and in part as a means of suspension. There are two main types, looped and hooked, and **I189**, **I193** and **I197** retain suspension rings, one complete, the others broken.

Five main types of padlock key were used during the medieval period, and Types 4 and 5 with their laterally set bits are the most common. These keys could be used on any type of barrel padlock, given an appropriately shaped keyhole, and they are found throughout the medieval period. Padlock keys of Type 1, the next most common, are largely restricted to 11th to 13th-century contexts, and this dating coincides with that of box padlocks and barrel padlocks with T-shaped keyholes, particularly those of Type B3. Type 2 padlock keys could be used with two keyhole shapes, and were thus more versatile than the complicated Type 3 key, which is rarely found and was probably principally used with Type C barrel padlocks.

Padlock key stems are plain, swollen or expanded, and the plain stem, generally combined with a hooked terminal, is found on all types of keys and was clearly the most practical shape. The swollen stem, only found on padlock keys of Type 1 and on Continental examples of Type 3, was frequently decorated with spiral grooves, some plain, others inlaid with non-ferrous wire. These grooves are found in the 11th to 13th centuries, but the inlay seems to be restricted to keys from 12th-century contexts. **I204–205** are the only other stems with any decoration. The expanded stem is found only in the 11th to 14th centuries, most frequently combined with a hooked terminal but occasionally with a loop.

The differing combinations of ward cuts in bits reflect the various types of padlock bolt construction. The majority of bits are practically shaped, but a few have elaborately shaped holes, or an excessive number. Most ward cuts were intended to pass spines with leaf springs, but a few passed rods added to the bolts to complicate their arrangement and increase security. The shaping of cuts such as **I249** and **I272** reflects springs with attached wire. Padlock keys **I238**, **I251** and **I285** are of interest because they were found with barrel padlocks **I16**, **I83** and **I90**.

10.5 KEYS

Medieval keys have been subjected to considerable study, but their analysis has rarely rested on dated examples, and classification has been heavily dependent on representations and on typological consideration. Penny's study of the Salisbury keys (Penny 1911), all notionally post-dating the foundation of the city in 1227, certainly includes some post-medieval keys, and those classified by J B Ward Perkins (1967, 133–144, pls XXIX–XXXI) include both pre- and post-medieval keys.

Medieval locks **I142–177** and certain types of padlock (**I125–141**) were opened with keys which turned in the lock, passing any ward or collar before throwing or lifting the bolt. The keys have variously shaped bows and either solid or hollow stems whose tips fitted into or over appropriate holes, mounts, or pins within lock cases. The stems and occasionally the bows are moulded or have decorative grooves, and the bits have ward cuts and often collar cuts. Keys may be divided into eight types (A–H) according to the form of the stem and position of the bit, and some can be further subdivided. Types A–H (Figure 10.4) may be correlated with Ward Perkins' classification (1967, 133–144) as follows:

A = I
B = II
C = III
D = incorporated in V but not recognised
E = IV and some VIII
F = V
G = VII
H = V and some VIII.

Incomplete forged keys

Iron keys generally have either solid stems with bits forged in one or hollow stems with bits rolled in one or brazed on. **I292–295** are incompletely forged keys, **I292–293** resembling **I294** with its solid stem, projecting tip and uncut bit. **I295** is even less completely forged, and is made from rectangular-sectioned iron which has been drawn out to form a stem and roughly shaped into a D-shaped bow. The bit has yet to be drawn down and out, and the free end of the bow welded to the stem head before finishing. **I292–294** are Type F or G keys, **I295** Type E. **I294** is from Croft A at Goltho, Lincolnshire, which in the late 14th to early 15th century housed a smithy, and **I295** is from occupation debris in the forge at Waltham Abbey, Essex.

Type A

Keys of Type A, made as commonly in copper alloy as iron, have deep narrow bits which are almost invariably perforated with one or more ward cuts. The bits of the iron keys often also have a divided, upturned fore-edge,

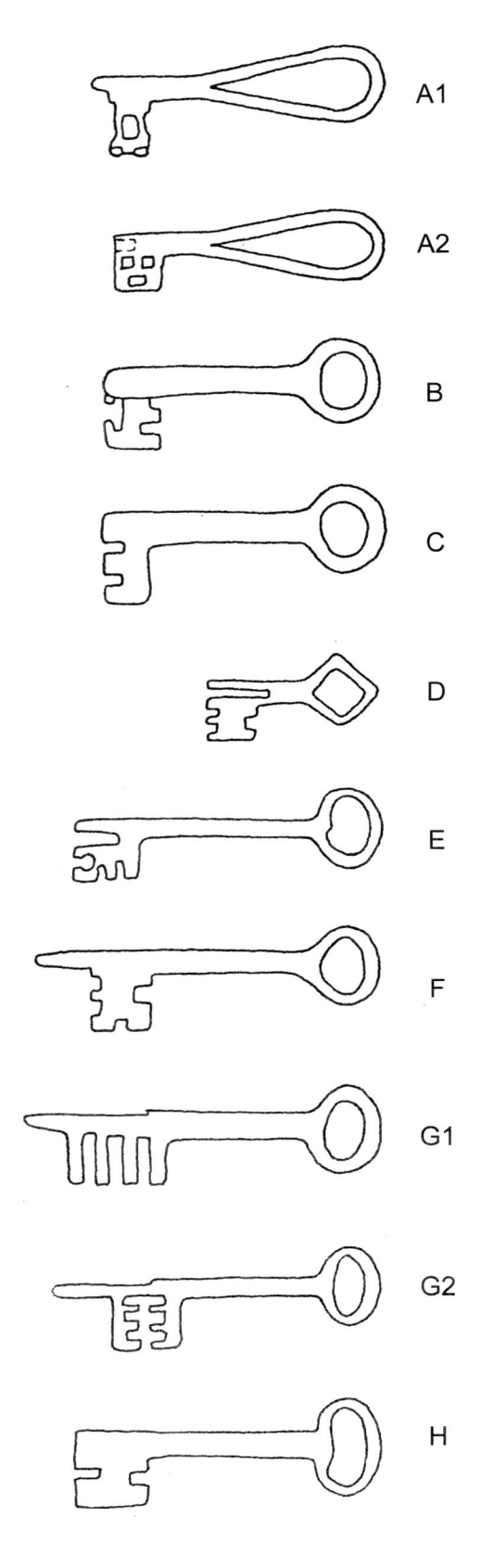

FIGURE 10.4
Types of medieval key

and they (**I296–303**) may be divided into those with projecting stem tips (Type A1) and with hollow stem tips (Type A2). Those of Type A1 are normally of iron, of Type A2 of copper alloy.

I296–303 are all Type A1, **I297** and **I300–301** having bits with upturned fore-edges, the others being flat or incomplete. The bows are all pear-shaped, the stems of **I296–297** grooved and **I300** moulded. Type A2 copper-alloy keys, almost all of pre-Conquest date, have ring and pear-shaped bows which are either plain, solid or have openwork decoration (Almgren 1955, 10–20; Ward Perkins 1967, 134–136, pl XXIX 2–5, 7–10).

Type A keys are principally of pre-Conquest date, and the medieval iron examples suggest that the key and type of lock it operated (see above, Locks Type 1a) barely if at all outlasted the 11th century. **I303** is probably residual, and it is significant that the other examples are all from sites with earlier occupation.

Type B

Keys of Type B, **I304–367**, have hollow stems rolled in one with the bit, and a bow which is either a single-piece forging with the stem or a separate forging set into the head of the stem. Most of the keys have ring bows, but a few are of other shapes, particularly lozenge-shaped. The stems are generally plain, but a number have decorative grooves, occasionally combined with a moulding just below the bow as on **I327** or **I343**. Three of the small keys, **I348–349** and **I352** have a collar at this point to strengthen the junction of the two parts. The bits are almost all flat and have various combinations of ward cuts, but several (**I323, I336** and **I345**) are channelled, and **I352** is of double thickness. The keys vary in size from small examples such as **I307, I333** and **I348** to large ones like **I312** and **I319**. Type B keys were used throughout the medieval period, and their numbers reached a peak during the 13th century.

Type C

Type C keys, with hollow stems and separately made bits welded or brazed in position, are related to those of Type B although they are far less common, probably because they were more difficult to make. **I368–379** are the few examples of the type, and they come from 12th to 16th-century contexts. They vary in size and include some small keys. The bows are variously shaped, and most stems are plain; although **I374** is grooved and **I370** and **I373** are moulded. **I377–378** have collars, and the bit of **I375** is channelled.

I380–391 are keys of either Type B or C, which are too corroded to classify but are of interest for their range of bow form. Their dates complement those of the main types.

Type D

Keys of Type D have solid stems which split close to the bow into one or occasionally two upper arms and into a single lower arm which carries the bit. The tip of the stem and end of the bit are in line. The type is not at all common, and **I392–397** are from 11th to 13th-century contexts. They all have ring or lozenge-shaped bows, and all except **I397** have moulded stems or bows.

Type E

Type E keys **I398–451** have solid stems with tips which end in line with the end of the bit. Many, including **I398–400, I420** and **I411–442**, are small although there are as many again of larger size. A significant number of keys have bits with toothed fore-edges, and several of these are also channelled. The remaining bits have various combinations of ward cut, and some, including **I410–411** and **I419** are complicated. The bows are normally ring-, D- or oval-shaped, but a number of small keys have thistle-shaped bows, several with additional shaping. **I417, I435** and **I442**, also small keys, have plate bows, namely flat sheet bows with small holes. Stems which are moulded or grooved or both are commonplace, ranging for example from the simplicity of **I406, I435** or **I445** to the elaboration of **I410–411**. The moulding invariably occurs at the junction between stem and bit, and takes the form of narrow beads (**I406**), bulbous swellings (**I410–411**) and box mouldings (**I415–435**). The grooves are either concentric (**I407**) or spiral (**I410**).

Keys of Type E were probably introduced during the 13th century, and they continued in use throughout the medieval period.

Type F

Type F keys **I452–493** have solid stems with projecting tips and bits which could be used from only one side of a lock. The bits generally have asymmetrical wards; the few with symmetrical wards in the sides of the bit never have a central ward cut which penetrates the full depth of the bit. Type F keys are found throughout the medieval period, but in greatest numbers in the 12th to 14th centuries. Ring bows are the commonest bow form, but a significant number are lozenge-shaped, **I469** having moulded corner bosses. Several have moulded or grooved stems or both, and the bits vary from simple (**I463** and **I482**) to complex (**I453** and **I475**).

Type G

Type G keys have solid stems with projecting tips and symmetrical bits for use from either side of a lock. They can be subdivided into two groups, Type G1 with the wards generally perpendicular to the stem, and Type G2 with the wards grouped around a central opening. The step on the stem over many of the bits acted as a stop against the ward of the lock, and prevented the key being pushed too far through it.

— Type G1. Keys **I494–535** have one or more ward cuts which run the depth of the bit, dividing it at its simplest into two (**I494, I498, I527**) or four (**I506, I525**) parts. The ward cuts are usually more complicated, and include fore-edge cuts (**I518** and **I521**), side cuts (**I522**) or combinations of the two (**I503, I529**), but yet more complex lock mechanisms with extra wards are implied by cuts within the bits of **I510, I514** and **I520**. In general the earlier bits are the simpler ones, the more complex bits appearing in the 14th century. Most of the bows are D-shaped or oval, and a few stems are moulded or grooved, **I495** having silver inlaid grooves, **I532** white metal plating retained in its grooves. **I497** has a simple moulding at the head of the stem, and **I513** is both moulded and grooved.

— Type G2. Keys **I536–577** have wards grouped symmetrically around a central opening, and although the bits may have other small cuts, they are otherwise undivided. These bits turned round wards with one or more collars, **I538** and **I555** around wards with single horizontal and oblique collars respectively, **I541** and **I550** around wards with paired similarly horizontal and oblique collars. **I544** implies the horizontal collars. The bows are generally oval or D-shaped, but there are a few ring bows and bows incorporating some kidney-shaping.

Type G keys are the most common single type of medieval key, undoubtedly because they were versatile enough to be used from either side of a lock. The type is known from a few early medieval contexts, but is commonest in the late medieval period and continued on to become the principal type of post-medieval key.

Type H

Type H keys have solid stems which have hollow tips. Medieval examples seem almost invariably to have been of copper alloy (Ward Perkins 1967, 140–141, pl XXIX, 11–18), but **I578** is of iron and of 16th-century date. Further post-medieval iron keys of this type are known.

Discussion

Eight main types of medieval key may be identified, most of iron but a very few of copper alloy. The use of each metal was largely determined by their differing properties, iron being wrought and copper alloy normally cast. Keys of Type A are nearly all pre-Conquest in date, and Type A1 is usually of iron, Type A2 of copper alloy. Medieval keys of Type H are also almost entirely of copper alloy, although subsequently iron was used as commonly. Types B–D and G are exclusively of iron, but some copper-alloy keys of Types E and F are known, mostly of small size.

The form of the stems and bits of keys was determined by the various types of lock in use during the medieval period. Keys of Type A were used with locks of comparatively simple type whereas those of Types B–H were used with locks incorporating wards, collars and sometimes tumblers. Types B–F and H could only be used from one side of a lock, but Type G keys were designed for use from either side.

Many keys are of types in use for much of the medieval period (Figure 10.5), although Type A is unlikely to have been used after the 11th century, and the rarely found Type D is restricted to 11th to 13th-century contexts. Keys of Types B and C were used throughout the medieval period, but those of Type E were probably introduced during the 13th century, and they seem to have superseded the longer established and related Type F keys during the late medieval period. The increasing popularity of locks operated by Type G keys, which also have projecting tips, may have affected the use of Type F. Type G keys are found in small numbers in the early medieval period, perhaps having been introduced in the 12th century, and they became the most common form of late medieval key. Iron keys of Type H are mainly of post-medieval date.

The bow forms of keys exhibit certain distinct changes of popularity, no doubt influenced by fashion. The pear-shaped bow is restricted to Type A1 keys and can therefore hardly have outlasted the 11th century. The practical and easily forged ring bow, however, was used throughout the medieval period and between the 11th and 14th centuries was the most popular single bow form. Lozenge-shaped bows are found as late as the 13th century but the form then rapidly went out of fashion and was succeeded by oval and D-shaped bows which only occur in any numbers during and after the 13th century. The forging of bows from solid stems at times incidentally produced an internal shaping of vaguely kidney shape, but properly kidney-shaped bow interiors are only found on a few late medieval keys principally of 15th to 16th-century date. The fully developed kidney-shaped bow appears occasionally at this time, but it did not become popular until the post-medieval period. A few late medieval keys have externally pointed bows, but the pointed heart-shaped bow seems to be a post-medieval form. The Winchester Cathedral roof bosses of 1503–09, and the other examples quoted by Ward Perkins (1967, 141–142) as medieval seem, however, to have pointed bows combined perhaps with an internal kidney shaping. Thistle-shaped bows occur on a few keys, mainly of small size, from 13th-century and later contexts, and a number of other small keys have circular or lozenge-shaped plate bows.

The majority of key bows are plain, although a few lozenge-shaped bows as well as the thistle-shaped bows have additional decoration. The corner bosses on some lozenge-shaped bows are occasionally moulded rather than plain. These decorated bows have the same date range as the plain ones.

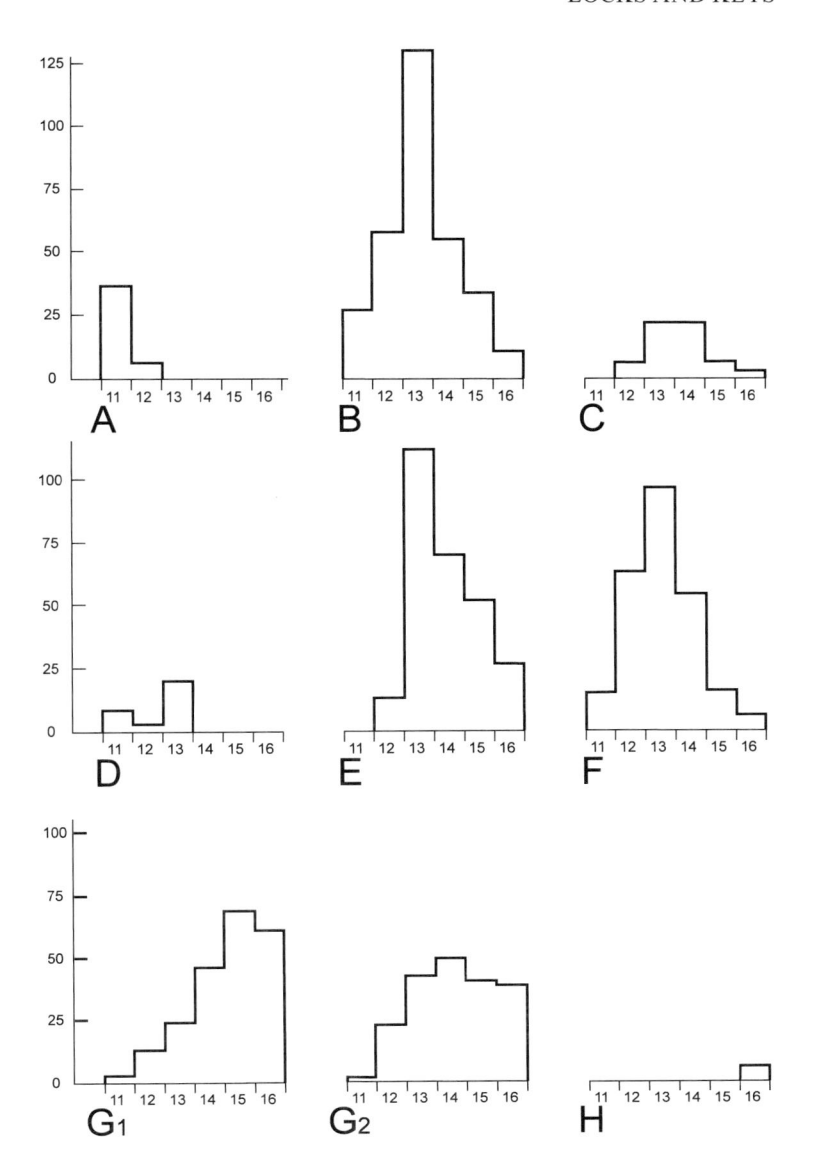

FIGURE 10.5
Chronological range of types of medieval key (the graphs only include objects dated to within three centuries or less, those from a single century being awarded six points, those from two or three centuries three or two points respectively per century)

Mouldings and incised concentric and spiral grooves sometimes decorate key stems. On Type B and C keys this most frequently takes the form of narrow continuous or broken bead mouldings at the junction of their hollow stems with the bow, whilst the solid stems of Types D and G have bulbous or box mouldings at this point. Collars on a few late medieval keys with hollow stems resemble these latter mouldings but are in fact a constructional feature. Decorative grooves occur most frequently on the stems of keys of Types B, E and F, and only rarely on Type G. These decorative elements are often accompanied by non-ferrous plating, which is also found on plain keys, and which served to protect the key from rusting as well as giving it a superior appearance. The plating is normally just that, and not excessive brazing metal since only Type C keys have separately applied, brazed-on bits. Plating is most frequently revealed by X-radiographs, and has rarely been analysed. **1495** has silver inlay however.

10.6 MISCELLANEOUS KEYS

1579–582 are keys with slender stems, hooked terminals and solid plain bits. The spatulate form of the bit is unusual, and its use uncertain.

1583–585 are latch keys from late medieval or 16th-century contexts. They bear a superficial resemblance to certain early medieval padlock keys but differ from them in not having individual holes in their bits but rather an openwork arrangement. They were used like padlock keys, however, being drawn along the lock rather than turned in it.

I1 BOX PADLOCK
Rayleigh Castle, Essex.
Site: c1070–c1350.
Box padlock with fragment of bolt. Case damaged and plain, but with suggestions of former decorative straps. T-shaped keyhole in one narrow side; opposing side with attached tube lost. Case L 75mm.
Reader 1913, 167, fig 3.2–5; Helliwell and Macleod 1965.

I2 BOX PADLOCK
Rayleigh Castle, Essex.
Site: c1070–c1350.
Box padlock with plain case but for strap on one side and tube down another. Damaged. L 43mm.
Excavated by D Macleod.

I3 BOX PADLOCK
Goltho Manor, Lincolnshire.
c1100–50.
Padlock case with attached tube down one side; opposing side with keyhole lost. Twisted rods decorate case. L 34mm.
Goodall 1987, fig 158.100.

I4 PADLOCK BOLT
Oxford.
Second half 11th century.
U-shaped padlock bolt with rectangular closing plate and two spines, each with double leaf springs. L 54mm.
Goodall 1977e, 142, fig 25.1.

I5 PADLOCK BOLT
Glottenham, East Sussex.
Mid to late 13th century.
U-shaped padlock bolt, broken, with rectangular closing plate. Form of springs uncertain. L 61mm.
Excavated by D Martin.

I6 BARREL PADLOCK
Winchester, Hampshire.
c1110.
Padlock case with attached tube set between lozenge-shaped end-plates and reinforced by five spirally twisted rods. Rectangular keyhole in one end-plate, bolt entry in other. Metallurgy: brazing metal attaching tube to case identified as brass. L 42mm.
Goodall 1990-21, fig 311.3643.

I7 BARREL PADLOCK
Christchurch, Hampshire.
12th–13th century.
Padlock case with attached tube set between pear-shaped end-plates and reinforced by four longitudinal plain rods and two pivoting fins. Rectangular keyhole in one end-plate, square bolt entry in other. L 65mm.
Goodall 1983b, fig 34.46.

I8 PIVOTING FIN (not illustrated)
Winchester, Hampshire.
c1093–94.
Broken, flattened, triangular-shaped pivoting fin. L 69mm.
Goodall 1990-21, 1008, no. 3641.

I9 PIVOTING FIN (not illustrated)
Winchester, Hampshire.
11th to ?mid 12th century.
Flattened, triangular-shaped pivoting fin, concave sides. L 79mm.
Goodall 1990-21, 1008, no. 3644.

I10 PIVOTING FIN
Walton, Aylesbury, Buckinghamshire.
12th century.
Broken triangular-shaped pivoting fin. L 75mm.
Farley 1976, 267, fig 49.4.

I11 BARREL PADLOCK (not illustrated)
Winchester, Hampshire.
Late 13th–early 14th century.
Padlock case with fin and tube. Case with plain longitudinal rods; rectangular keyhole in one end-plate, other lost. Fin and tube, bound by three straps, distorted and broken. L 50mm.
Goodall 1990-21, fig 311.3649.

I12 BARREL PADLOCK
Winchester, Hampshire.
12th–13th century.
Padlock case with fin and tube. Corrugated case with central longitudinal straps and added sheet iron repairs. End-plate with keyhole broken, with bolt entry near complete. Fin broken, tube complete. L 75mm.
Goodall 1990-21, fig 311.3647.

I13 BARREL PADLOCK
Lyveden, Northamptonshire.
Second quarter 13th century.
Padlock case with fin, tube lost. Case surface obscured by corrosion, end-plates corroded. Fin incomplete. L 77mm.
Bryant and Steane 1971, 61, fig 16ml.

I14 BARREL PADLOCK
Copt Hay, Tetsworth, Oxfordshire.
Late 13th–14th century.
Padlock case with fin and tube. Projecting longitudinal straps along case. End-plates obscured by corrosion. L 67mm.
Robinson 1973, 104, fig 25.20.

I15 BARREL PADLOCK
Winchester, Hampshire.
15th century.
Padlock case with fin and tube. Case with plain longitudinal rods, end-plates with bolt entry and T-shaped keyhole. Fin and tube bound by straps, broken. L 29mm.
Goodall 1990-21, fig 311.3655.

I16/I238 BARREL PADLOCK AND KEY
Winchester, Hampshire.
Late 14th century.
Padlock case with fin and tube, all broken. Case with projecting longitudinal straps retains padlock key **I238**. L 70mm.
Goodall 1990-21, fig 311.3652.

I17 BARREL PADLOCK (not illustrated)
Winchester, Hampshire.
14th century.
Padlock case, fin and tube, all broken. Case with plain longitudinal rods along and end-plate with broken rectangular keyhole. L 25mm.
Goodall 1990-21, 1010, no. 3654.

I18 BARREL PADLOCK (not illustrated)
Old Sarum, Wiltshire.
Principally medieval, to 14th century.
Padlock case fragment with plain longitudinal rods and base of fin. Tube lost. Fragment of bolt with three spines in case. L 60mm.
Salisbury and South Wiltshire Museum, Salisbury, O.S.C124, 30/1920–21.

I19 BARREL PADLOCK
North Elmham Park, Norfolk.
c1150–c1600.
Padlock case with fin and tube. Case with longitudinal straps and keyhole and bolt entry in end-plates. L 79mm.
Goodall 1980a, 509, fig 265.9.

LOCKS AND KEYS

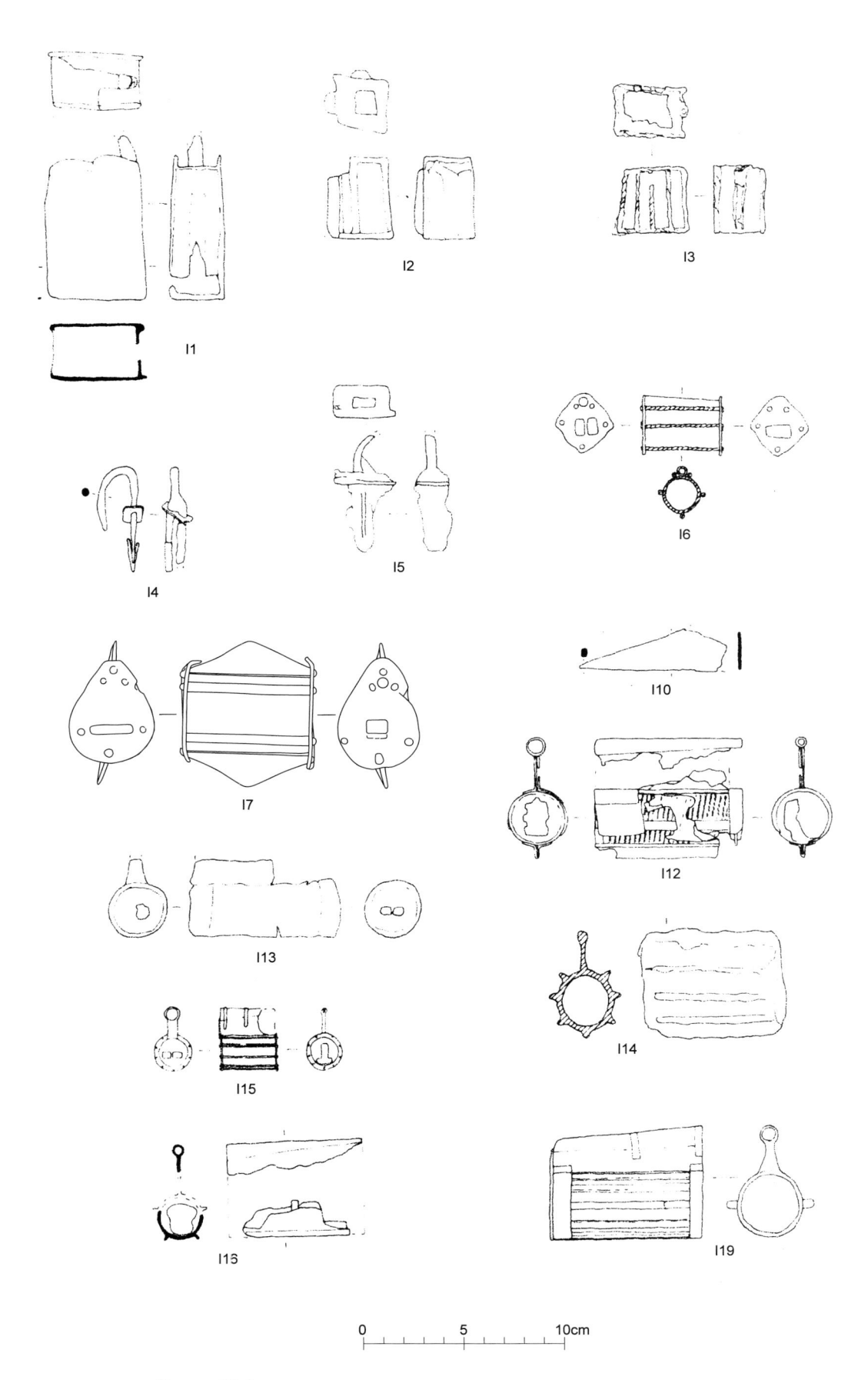

FIGURE 10.6
Box padlocks, barrel padlocks, and pivoting fin

120 BARREL PADLOCK
Eynsford Castle, Kent.
12th century.
Padlock case with fin, tube, and bolt. Case with longitudinal straps and T-shaped keyhole cutting across end-plate and underside. Three rectangular holes in other end-plate for spines of U-shaped bolt, each of which have, or had, double leaf springs. Case L 75mm.
Rigold and Fleming 1973, 105, fig 9.7.

121 BARREL PADLOCK
Seacourt, Oxfordshire.
Mid to late 12th to late 14th century.
Padlock case with fin, tube lost. Case with plain longitudinal rods, T-shaped keyhole across end-plate and underside, and blocked bolt entry. L 57mm.
Biddle 1961–62, 181, fig 31.5, scale incorrect.

122 BARREL PADLOCK
Goltho Manor, Lincolnshire.
Around late 11th century.
Padlock case with fin and distorted tube. Case has longitudinal and transverse straps, T-shaped keyhole along underside, and damaged or lost end-plates. Perforation in fin and in cheeks alongside keyhole. Straps bind tube to fin.
L 62mm.
Goodall 1987, fig 158.102.

123 BARREL PADLOCK
Goltho Manor, Lincolnshire.
c1000–1100.
Padlock case with fin and tube, both distorted. Case has longitudinal and transverse straps and T-shaped keyhole along underside. Form of bolt entry in end-plate unknown. Straps bind fin and tube. L 75mm.
Goodall 1987, fig 158.101.

124 BARREL PADLOCK
Castle Acre Castle, Norfolk.
1140s/1150s deposit with derived material. Site founded soon after 1066.
Padlock case with fin and tube. Case with central longifudinal straps, wavy line decoration and T-shaped keyhole along underside. Bolt entry in end-plate blocked. L 44mm.
Goodall 1982, fig 39, no. 66.

125 BARREL PADLOCK (not illustrated)
Castle Acre Castle, Norfolk.
1140s deposit with derived material. Site founded soon after 1066.
Padlock case with fin and tube. Case with central longitudinal and transverse straps, and T-shaped keyhole along underside. Fin and tube, damaged, bound by straps. L 77mm.
Goodall 1982.

126–27 BARREL PADLOCK
(not illustrated)
Castle Acre Castle, Norfolk.
Second half 12th century.
Padlock cases with fin and tube, identical to **125**. L 77 and 71mm.
Goodall 1982.

128 BARREL PADLOCK
King's Lynn, Norfolk.
c1150–1250.
Padlock case with fin and tube. Corrugated case with longitudinal straps, T-shaped keyhole along underside, and broken bolt entry in end plate. Straps join tube and fin, the latter perforated. L 57mm.
Goodall and Carter 1977, 291, fig 132.1.

129 BARREL PADLOCK
King's Lynn, Norfolk.
13th century.
Padlock case with fin, tube and bolt. Case with longitudinal and transverse straps, damaged T-shaped keyhole along underside, and bolt entry in end-plate. Straps bind tube and fin. U-shaped padlock bolt with circular closing plate and two spines, one with double leaf spring, other with double, leaf spring with forked ends and individual side springs (one lost). Copper-alloy brazing metal overall.
L 104mm.
Goodall and Carter 1977, 291, fig 132.2.

130 BARREL PADLOCK
Winchester, Hampshire.
Late 13th–early 14th century.
Padlock case with fin, tube and bolt. Case with central longitudinal and transverse straps, and T-shaped keyhole along underside. Fin and tube bound by straps. U-shaped padlock bolt with closing plate (probably circular) and single spine with double leaf springs. Overall copper-alloy plating. L 97mm.
Cunliffe 1964, 189, fig 66.8, pl VII.

131 BARREL PADLOCK
Rayleigh Castle, Essex.
Site: c1070–c1350.
Padlock case with fin and tube. Plain case with damaged T-shaped keyhole along underside and bolt entry in end-plate. Narrow fin, damaged tube. U-shaped padlock bolt broken. L 80mm.
Reader 1913, 165–166, fig 2; Helliwell and Macleod 1965.

132 BARREL PADLOCK
Old Sarum, Wiltshire.
Principally medieval, to 14th century.
Padlock case with base of fin, tube lost. Case with longitudinal straps, T-shaped keyhole along underside, and rectangular bolt entry in end plate. L 44mm.
Salisbury and South Wiltshire Museum, Salisbury, O.S.C122a, 8/1932.

133 BARREL PADLOCK (not illustrated)
Portchester Castle, Hampshire.
14th century.
Padlock case with fin and tube. Case has projecting longitudinal rods and T-shaped keyhole along underside. Three square holes for bolt entry in end plate. L unknown,
H 46mm.
Hinton 1977, 196, pl XLIIIb.

134 BARREL PADLOCK
Boston, Lincolnshire.
Mid 15th century.
Padlock case with fin, tube lost. Case with longitudinal straps, T-shaped keyhole along underside, and inset end-plate for bolt entry. U-shaped padlock bolt, broken, has four springs and a rod. L 62mm.
Goodall 1972, fig 7.1, pl 1.

135 BARREL PADLOCK (not illustrated)
Castle Acre Castle, Norfolk.
Medieval.
Padlock case, flattened and distorted, fin and tube lost. Case with central longitudinal straps, wavy line decoration and T-shaped keyhole.
L 55mm.
Goodall 1982.

136 BARREL PADLOCK (not illustrated)
Winchester, Hampshire.
Late 13th–early 14th century.
Padlock case fragment with plain longitudinal rods, end-plate with two rectangular holes for bolt, and stub of fin. Tube lost. L 27mm.
Goodall 1990-21, 1009, no. 3650.

137 BARREL PADLOCK (not illustrated)
Winchester, Hampshire.
13th century.
Padlock case fragment with plain longitudinal rods, broken end-plates and base of fin. Tube lost. L 42mm.
Goodall 1990-21, 1009, no. 3648.

138 BARREL PADLOCK (not illustrated)
Winchester, Hampshire.
Mid 13th century.
Padlock case fragment with plain longitudinal rods, end-plate with three rectangular holes for bolt, and stub of fin. Tube lost. L 37mm.
Goodall 1990-21, 1009, no. 3646.

139 BARREL PADLOCK
King's Lynn, Norfolk.
14th century.
Fin and broken tube bound by straps. Decorative wavy straps on fin. Abundant copper-alloy brazing metal. L 84mm.
Goodall and Carter 1977, 291, fig 132.3.

140 BARREL PADLOCK
Winchester, Hampshire.
14th century.
Fin and tube. L 63mm.
Goodall 1990-21, fig 311.3653.

141 BARREL PADLOCK
Northolt Manor, Greater London.
1350–70.
Fin and tube bound by straps, with intermediate strap along fin. L 101mm.
Excavated by J G Hurst.

142 BARREL PADLOCK
Faxton, Northamptonshire.
Site: 12th–15th century.
Fin and tube, former with perforations.
L 68mm.
Excavated by L A S Butler.

143 PADLOCK BOLT
Rhuddlan, Clwyd.
Later 13th century.
U-shaped padlock bot, broken, with single spine with double leaf spring. L 122mm.
Goodall 1994, fig 17.6, no. 89.

144 PADLOCK BOLT
Rhuddlan, Clwyd.
14th century, ?earlier part or 1290–1300.
U-shaped padlock bolt with single spine with incomplete double leaf spring. L 99mm.
Goodall 1994, fig 17.6, no. 91.

145 PADLOCK BOLT
Lochmaben Castle, Dumfries and Galloway.
Late 14th century.
U-shaped padlock bolt with single spine and double leaf spring. L 102mm.
Macdonald and Laing 1974–75, 148, fig 11.21.

146 PADLOCK BOLT
Hen Caerwys, Clwyd.
c1450–1520.
U-shaped padlock bolt with single spine and broken double leaf spring. L 92mm.
Excavated by G B Leach.

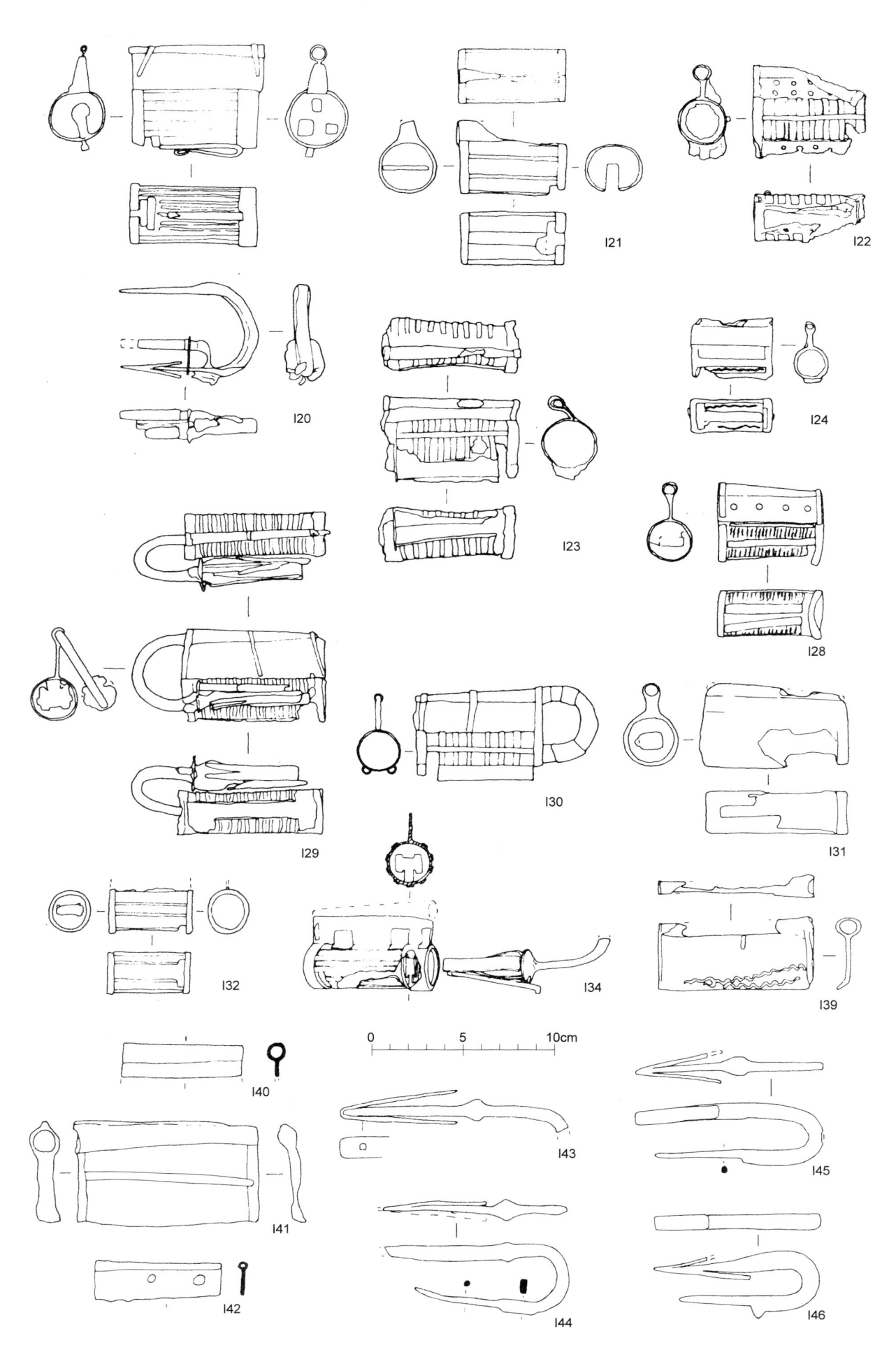

FIGURE 10.7
Barrel padlocks and padlock bolts

I47 PADLOCK BOLT
Southampton, Hampshire.
1200–50.
U-shaped padlock bolt, incomplete, with single spine with double leaf spring.
L 94mm.
Harvey 1975b, 277, fig 250.1988.

I48 PADLOCK BOLT
Rhuddlan, Clwyd.
1280s.
U-shaped padlock bolt with copper-alloy leaf springs riveted to iron spine; staple broken. Holes in each spring accommodate L-shaped fittings (one lost) which acted as barriers for a key. L 74mm.
Goodall 1994, fig 17.6, no. 90.

I49 PADLOCK BOLT (not illustrated)
Winchester, Hampshire.
Early to mid 14th century.
U-shaped padlock bolt, broken, with single spine with double leaf spring and closing plate. L 92mm.
Goodall 1990-21, 1010, no. 3664.

I50 PADLOCK BOLT (not illustrated)
Goltho Manor, Lincolnshire.
c1000–1100.
U-shaped padlock bolt, broken, with stubs of two spines arranged as **I54**. Decorative scroll above circular closing plate. L 41mm.
Goodall 1987, 183.

I51 PADLOCK BOLT
Winchester, Hampshire.
Mid to late 10th century.
U-shaped padlock bolt with oval closing plate and two spines, each with double leaf springs. L 52mm.
Goodall 1990-21, fig 312.3658.

I52 PADLOCK BOLT
Northampton.
12th century.
U-shaped padlock bolt, broken, with two spines each with double leaf springs. Circular closing plate with decorative scrolls on outer surface. L 76mm.
Goodall *et al* 1979, 268, fig 116.4.

I53 PADLOCK BOLT (not illustrated)
Winchester, Hampshire.
11th century.
U-shaped padlock bolt similar to **I51**. Two spines, one broken, the other with a double leaf spring. Rounded rectangular shaped closing plate. L 67mm.
Goodall 1990-21, 1010, no. 3661.

I54 PADLOCK BOLT
Winchester, Hampshire.
Mid 13th century.
U-shaped padlock bolt with two spines, one riveted to the circular closing plate, the other part of the broken, U-shaped staple. The former has a double leaf spring, the latter three separate leaves, the opposed ones with split tops. Case fragment attached to closing plate retains one plain longitudinal rod.
L 68mm.
Goodall 1990-21, fig 312.3663.

I55 PADLOCK BOLT
Lydney Castle, Gloucestershire.
12th, early 13th century.
U-shaped padlock bolt with damaged circular closing plate and three spines, one broken, one with a double leaf spring and one with three springs. L 158mm.
Casey 1931, 251–252, pl XXXV.L.

I56 PADLOCK BOLT
South Witham, Lincolnshire.
1137–85 to c1220.
U-shaped padlock bolt with three broken spines and damaged closing plate. Copper-alloy brazing metal present. L 72mm.
Goodall 2002, fig 7.1, no. 13.

I57 PADLOCK BOLT
Winchester, Hampshire.
Early 13th century.
Broken U-shaped padlock bolt with three spines and decorative scroll fronting pear-shaped closing plate. L 68mm.
Goodall 1990-21, fig 312.3662.

I58 PADLOCK BOLT
Weoley Castle, Birmingham, West Midlands.
c1200–30.
U-shaped padlock bolt with three spines, only two retaining springs. Decorative copper-alloy scrolls above damaged closing plate. L 80mm.
Oswald 1962, 129, fig 51.2.

I59 PADLOCK BOLT
Lyveden, Northamptonshire.
c1150–early 14th century.
U-shaped padlock bolt, broken, with stubs of three spines. Decorative scrolls above circular closing plate. L 49mm.
Steane and Bryant 1975, 130, fig 49.144.

I60 PADLOCK BOLT
Lyveden, Northamptonshire.
Second quarter 13th century to very early 14th century.
U-schaped padlock bolt, broken, with stubs of three spines. Decorative scrolls above circular closing plate. L. 64mm.
Bryant and Steane 1971, 61, fig 16.m3.

I61 PADLOCK BOLT
Netherton, Hampshire.
13th, early 14th century.
U-shaped padlock bolt with closing plate and three spines, one retaining double leaf spring. L 75mm.
Goodall 1990-28, fig 9.7 no. 354.

I62 PADLOCK BOLT
Rayleigh Castle, Essex.
Site: c1070–c1350.
U-shaped padlock bolt, incomplete, with two spines, one with a double leaf spring, the other retaining only one side spring. Scrolled closing plate. L 92mm.
Reader 1913, 167, fig 3.1; Helliwell and Macleod 1965.

I63 PADLOCK BOLT
Clarendon Palace, Wiltshire.
Site: c1072 to later 15th century.
U-shaped padlock bolt, incomplete, with four spines. Copper-alloy brazing metal.
L 66mm.
Goodall 1988, fig 78.68; Borenius and Charlton 1936.

I64 PADLOCK BOLT
Rhuddlan, Clwyd.
Later 13th century.
U-shaped padlock bolt, broken, with scrolled decoration. L 31mm.
Goodall 1994, fig 17.6, no. 88.

I65 BARREL PADLOCK
Netherton, Hampshire.
13th–14th century.
Padlock case with U-shaped housings and bolt. Case with longitudinal straps and keyhole in end-plate. Squared U-shaped bolt with two spines, one retaining a double leaf spring, and three rods. Looped handle.
L 54mm.
Goodall 1990-28, fig 9.7 no. 345.

I66 BARREL PADLOCK
Alvechurch, Hereford and Worcester.
c1350–1400.
Padlock case with U-shaped housings and bolt. Plain case. Squared U-shaped bolt with two spines, each with double leaf springs.
L 39mm.
Oswald 1954, 8, pl 5.4.

I67 BARREL PADLOCK
Kings Langley, Hertfordshire.
1291–92 to later 14th or first half 15th century.
Padlock case with U-shaped housings and bolt. Plain case with keyhole in end-plate. Squared U-shaped bolt with double leaf spring. L 41mm.
Neal 1973, 53, fig XIV.54.

I68 BARREL PADLOCK
London.
From City Ditch, probably dug in 13th century and filled up in 1532.
Padlock case with U-shaped housings, one missing, and bolt. Plain case with broken keyhole across end-plate and underside. Squared U-shaped bolt with projecting U-shaped handle. Two of original three spines with double leaf springs survive. Case L 94mm.
Waddington 1928. (Illustration based on drawing by J Clark.)

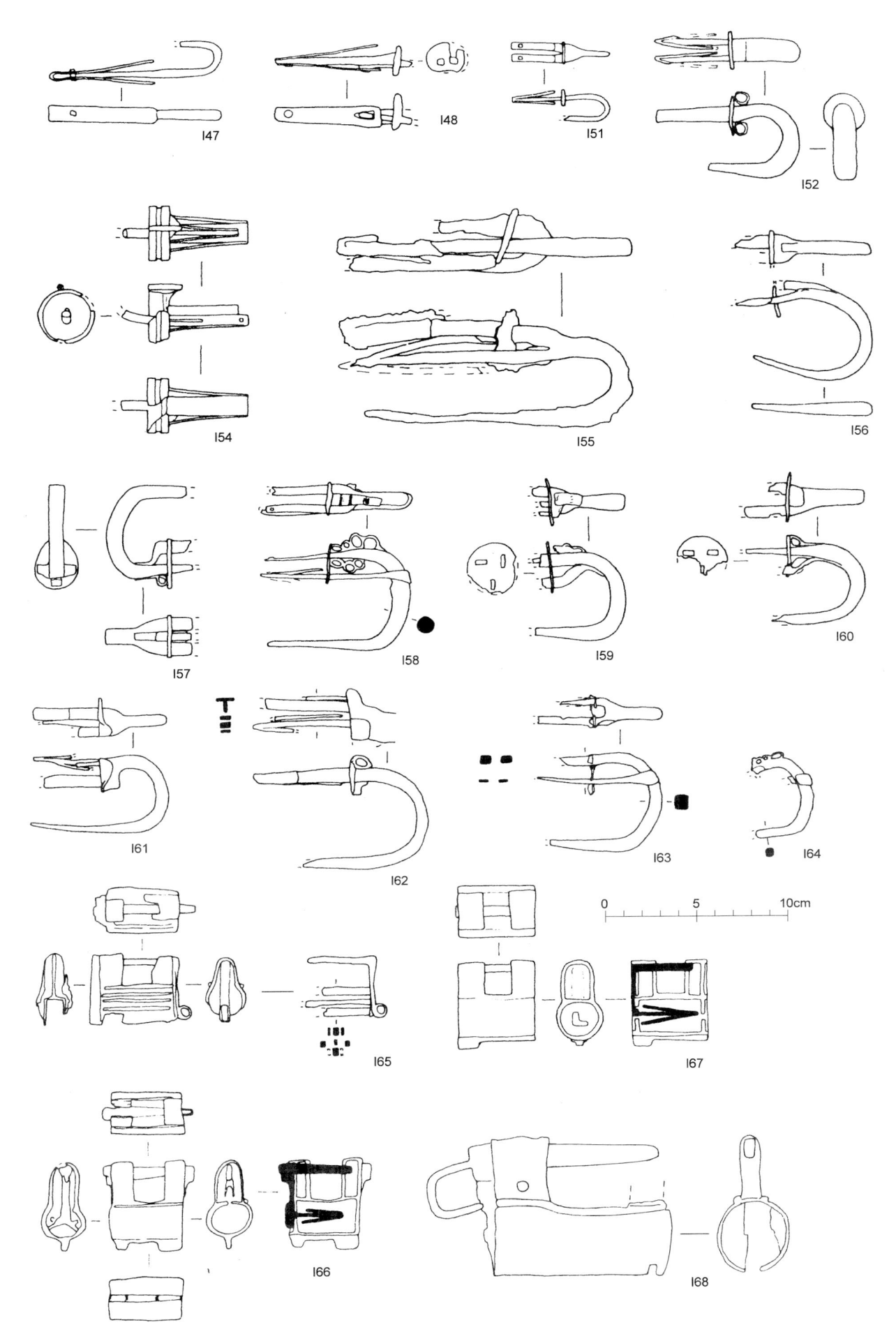

FIGURE 10.8
Padlock bolts and barrel padlocks

I69 BARREL PADLOCK
Weoley Castle, Birmingham, West Midlands.
Site: c1080–1600.
Padlock case with U-shaped housings. Plain case, end-plates damaged. L 37mm.
Birmingham City Museum. For site see Oswald 1962.

I70 PADLOCK BOLT
Lyveden, Northamptonshire.
Late 13th to very early 14th century.
Squared U-shaped padlock bolt, incomplete. Stubs of two spines, third missing. L 70mm.
Bryant and Steane 1969, 43, fig 18d.

I71 PADLOCK BOLT
Lyveden, Northamptonshire.
c1350–1450.
Squared U-shaped padlock bolt with looped handle projection. Three spines each with double leaf springs. L 39mm.
Steane and Bryant 1975, 130, fig 49.148.

I72 PADLOCK BOLT
Lyveden, Northamptonshire.
c1150 to early 14th century.
Squared U-shaped padlock bolt, incomplete. One spine survives, with stub of double leaf spring, other lost. L 74mm.
Steane and Bryant 1975, 130, fig 49.145.

I73 BARREL PADLOCK (not illustrated)
Winchester, Hampshire.
Early to ?mid 16th century.
Padlock case with broken L-shaped arm. Plain case, form of keyhole and bolt entry not clear. L 41mm.
Goodall 1990-21, 1011, no. 3668.

I74 BARREL PADLOCK
Winchester, Hampshire.
15th–?16th century.
Padlock case with L-shaped arm and looped, L-shaped bolt, both perforated. Plain case. Bolt with two spines with double leaf springs. Metallurgy: copper-base alloy plating inside and outside case; steel spring. L 45mm.
Goodall 1990-21, fig 313.3667.

I75 BARREL PADLOCK
London.
From City Ditch, probably dug in 13th century and filled up in 1552.
Padlock case with L-shaped arm and looped, L-shaped bolt. Case has longitudinal straps, spirally twisted rod or thick wire around each end, and T-shaped keyhole across end-plate and underside of case. Bolt entry end-plate incomplete. Padlock bolt has four spines and central red which, like the springs, survive incompletely. Scrolls and loops on case and bolt part utilitarian, part decorative. Case L 106mm.
Waddington 1928, 524, fig on p 525.

I76 PADLOCK BOLT
Winchester, Hampshire.
13th century.
L-shaped bolt, looped arm broken. One spine with double leaf spring. L 108mm.
Goodall 1990-21, fig 313.3669.

I77 PADLOCK BOLT
Waltham Abbey, Essex.
c1200–40.
Looped, L-shaped padlock bolt. L 36mm.
Excavated by P J Huggins. From Sun Street.

I78 PADLOCK BOLT
Grenstein, Norfolk.
Later 14th, 15th century.
Looped, L-shaped padlock bolt retaining the stubs of two of the original three spines. Handle infilled with scrolls. L 55mm.
Goodall 1980c, fig 79, no. 61.

I79 PADLOCK BOLT
Winchester, Hampshire.
Late 17th–?18th century.
Looped, L-shaped bolt with spine retaining only one spring. Head of spine shaped and T-sectioned. L 127mm.
Goodall 1990-21, fig 313.3670.

I80 BARREL PADLOCK WITH SHACKLE, CHAIN AND SHACKLE
Winchester, Hampshire.
Late 10th to late 11th century.
Limb shackles. The looped ends of the U-shaped shackle hold interlocking links which close it and are attached by other links to the barrel padlock shackle. Padlock case plain with T-shaped keyhole in end-plate below shackle loop. T-shaped padlock bolt with two spines, each with double leaf springs, holds shackle closed. Overall L 365mm, padlock L 113mm.
Goodall 1990-21, fig 314.3671.

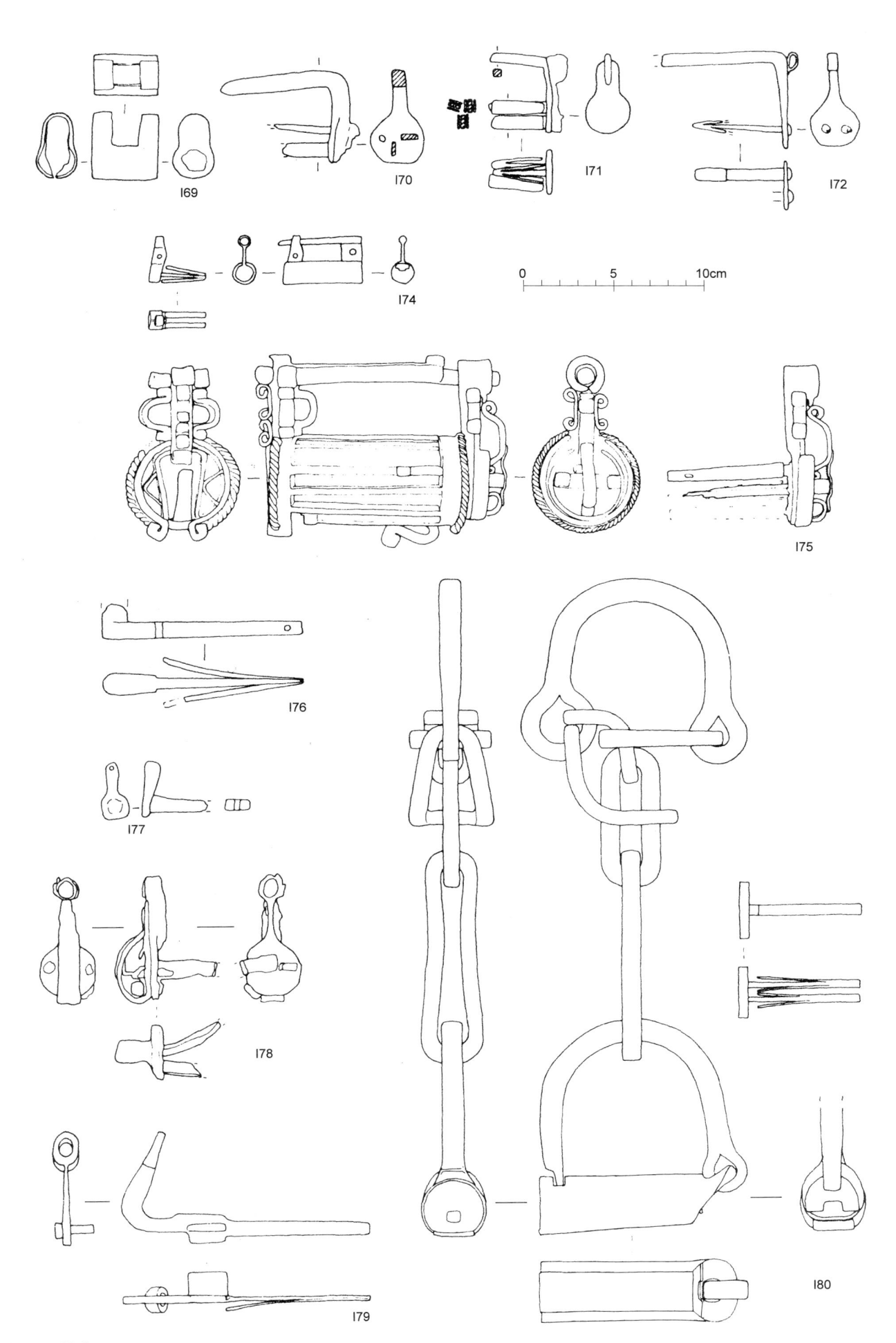

FIGURE 10.9
Barrel padlocks and padlock bolts

I81 BARREL PADLOCK WITH SHACKLE, CHAIN AND SHACKLE (not illustrated)
Winchester, Hampshire.
Late 10th to late 11th century.
Limb shackles, almost identical to **I80** but no longer linked together.
Padlock bolt differs in having the double leaf springs of the spines set in planes at right angles to each other. Metallurgy: shackle, case spines and springs all wrought iron. Padlock L 101mm.
Goodall 1990-21, 1012, no. 3673.

I82 BARREL PADLOCK WITH SHACKLE
Winchester, Hampshire.
Late 10th to late 11th century.
Plain padlock case strengthened by two broad straps around underside. Keyhole in end-plate below loop of shackle, which is held closed by a T-shaped bolt with two spines each with double leaf springs. Padlock L 108mm.
Goodall 1990-21, fig 315.3672.

I83/I251 BARREL PADLOCK WITH SHACKLE AND KEY
Winchester, Hampshire.
11th century.
Plain case with T-shaped keyhole in end-plate below loop of shackle. Shackle closed by T-shaped bolt with two spines each with double leaf springs. Additional strip on one spring. Found with key **I251**. Padlock L 122mm.
Goodall 1990-21, fig 315.3674.

I84 BARREL PADLOCK WITH SHACKLE
West Woodhay, Berkshire.
12th/13th to 14th century.
Plain case with shackle. Keyhole below shackle loop. Case L 100mm.
Jervoise 1954, 65, fig 4.

I85 BARREL PADLOCK WITH SHACKLE
Kettleby Thorpe, Lincolnshire.
14th–early 15th century.
Plain padlock case, damaged, keyhole largely blocked. Shackle broken. Case L 74mm.
Goodall 1974a, 33, fig 18.4.

I86 BARREL PADLOCK WITH SHACKLE
Huish, Wiltshire.
Site: 12th–mid 15th century.
Plain padlock case strengthened by broad strap around underside. T-shaped keyhole beneath shackle loop. Shackle closed by T-shaped padlock bolt with semicircular handle and three spines with corroded springs. Case L 113mm.
Shortt 1972, 116, fig 2.2.

I87 BARREL PADLOCK WITH SHACKLE
King's Lynn, Norfolk.
c1350–1500.
Plain padlock case with three broad straps, now incomplete, around underside. Original extent of straps shown by lines of brazing fluid, stippled on drawing. Keyhole beneath loop of broken shackle, whose expanded end with two holes for the former bolt is corroded within the case. L 91mm.
Goodall and Carter 1977, 291, fig 132.4.

I88 BARREL PADLOCK WITH SHACKLE
Hen Caerwys, Clwyd.
c1450–1520.
Distorted padlock case with broad straps along sides and round underside. Shackle lost. L 105mm.
Excavated by G B Leach.

I89 BARREL PADLOCK WITH SHACKLE
Bicester Priory, Oxfordshire.
Site: end 12th century to 1536.
Plain padlock case damaged, shackle complete but holes for bolt in expanded end obscured. L 66mm.
Hinton 1968, 51, fig 16.1.

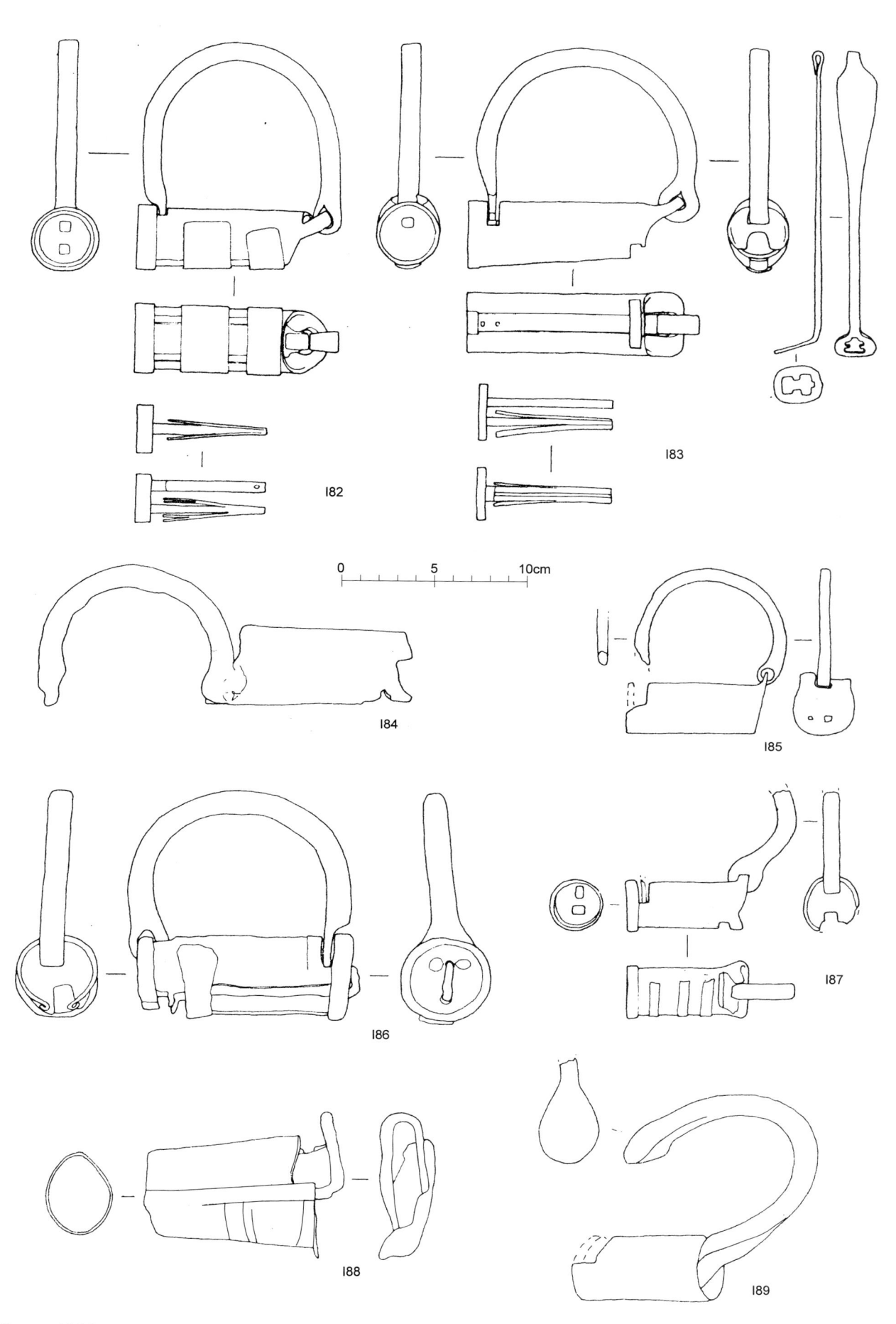

FIGURE 10.10
Barrel padlocks

**I90/I285 BARREL PADLOCK
WITH SHACKLE, KEY AND CHAIN**
Oxford.
13th to 16th century.
Barrel padlock with shackle found in association with link and swivel loop **J247** and with leg bone through shackle. Plain padlock case, with keyhole in end-plate below loop of shackle, buried complete with bolt and key. Bolt T-shaped with two spines each with double leaf spring and additional bar above; only that part of key **I285** within case now survives. Case L 125mm.
Excavated by T G Hassall. From Greyfriars burial ground.

**I91 BARREL PADLOCK
WITH SHACKLE**
Waltham Abbey, Essex.
16th century.
Distorted padlock case, shackle lost. Case with three longitudinal straps and overall copper-alloy brazing metal. L 113mm.
Goodall 1973a, 170, fig 11.28.

I92 BARREL PADLOCK (not illustrated)
Winchester, Hampshire.
Mid 13th century.
Padlock case fragment with three transverse straps. L 98mm.
Goodall 1990-21, 1015, no. 3679.

I93 BARREL PADLOCK
Somerby, Lincolnshire.
11th–15th century.
Padlock case fragment with transverse straps. L 98mm.
Mynard 1969, 83, fig 12.IW71.

**I94 SHACKLE
FROM BARREL PADLOCK**
(not illustrated)
Winchester, Hampshire.
Late 14th–early 15th century.
Incomplete curved shackle. Expanded end with broken rectangular hole for padlock bolt. L 95mm.
Goodall 1990-21, 1012, no. 3675.

I95 PADLOCK BOLT
Castle Acre Castle, Norfolk.
1140s deposit with derived material. Site founded soon after 1066.
T-shaped padlock bolt with single spine with double leaf spring. L 62mm.
Goodall 1082, fig 39, no. 80.

I96 PADLOCK BOLT
Winchester, Hampshire.
15th–16th century.
T-shaped bolt with semicircular handle and single spine with three springs. L 77mm.
Goodall 1990-21, fig 316.3676.

I97 PADLOCK BOLT
Gloucester.
Late 11th, early 12th century.
T-shaped padlock bolt with two spines each with double leaf springs. L 77mm.
Excavated by H Hurst.

I98 PADLOCK BOLT
Wroughton Copse, Fyfield Down, Wiltshire.
12th–13th century.
T-shaped padlock bolt with two spines, each retaining only one spring. More complete spring has rod brazed onto outer face. L 61mm.
Excavated by P J Fowler.

I99 PADLOCK BOLT
Gomeldon, Wiltshire.
Second half 13th century.
T-shaped padlock bolt with two spines each with double leaf springs. L 82mm.
Musty and Algar 1986.

I100 PADLOCK BOLT
Rhuddlan, Clwyd.
Very late 13th or 14th century.
T-shaped padlock bolt with circular closing plate and two spines each with double leaf springs, one projecting as a looped handle. L 67mm.
Goodall 1994, fig 17.6, no. 93.

I101 PADLOCK BOLT
Cheswick Green, West Midlands.
13th–14th century.
T-shaped padlock bolt with two spines, each with a double leaf spring, and one projecting as a looped handle. L 78mm.
Jones 1953, 94–95, fig 4.

I102 PADLOCK BOLT
Brome, Suffolk.
Mid 14th century.
T-shaped padlock bolt with semicircular handle and two spines, both lacking springs. L 73mm.
West 1970, 111, fig 12.11.

I103 PADLOCK BOLT
Lochmaben Castle, Dumfries and Galloway.
Late 14th century.
T-shaped padlock bolt with two spines, each retaining only one spring. L 71mm.
Macdonald and Laing 1974–75, 148, fig 11.22.

I104 PADLOCK BOLT
Goltho, Lincolnshire.
Late 14th–early 15th century. In water-pit with slag from smithy.
T-shaped padlock bolt with both spines broken. L 44mm.
Goodall 1975a, 84, fig 39.62.

I105 PADLOCK BOLT
Wharram Percy, North Yorkshire.
Late 15th–early 16th century.
T-shaped padlock bolt with two spines, springs lost. L 54mm.
Goodall 1979a, 115, fig 60.2.

I106 PADLOCK BOLT
Waltham Abbey, Essex.
13th–16th century. From forge floor.
Closing plate from T-shaped padlock bolt with countersunk holes for two spines. Probably an incomplete forging. D 36mm.
Goodall 1973a, 170, fig 11.29.

I107 PADLOCK BOLT
Faxton, Northamptonshire.
Site: 12th–14th century.
T-shaped padlock bolt with three spines, two retaining springs. L 71mm.
Excavated by L A S Butler.

I108 PADLOCK BOLT
Grenstein, Norfolk.
Site: 12th to later 14th, 15th century.
T-shaped padlock bolt with three spines, all with double leaf springs. L 84mm.
Goodall 1980c, fig 79, no. 60.

I109 PADLOCK BOLT
Goltho, Lincolnshire.
Croft A: late Saxon to late 14th or early 15th century.
T-shaped padlock bolt with rod and two spines with double leaf springs and projecting looped handles. L 76mm.
Goodall 1975a, 84, fig 39.64.

I110 PADLOCK BOLT
Goltho, Lincolnshire.
Late 14th–early 15th century. From smithy floor.
T-shaped padlock bolt with three spines, all with double leaf springs, two projecting to form looped handles. Sectioning showed one of these latter spines to have been inserted into a hole in the closing plate and brazed in place. Metallurgy: closing plate of wrought iron, brass-plated externally. L 74mm.
Goodall 1975a, 84–85, fig 39.60.

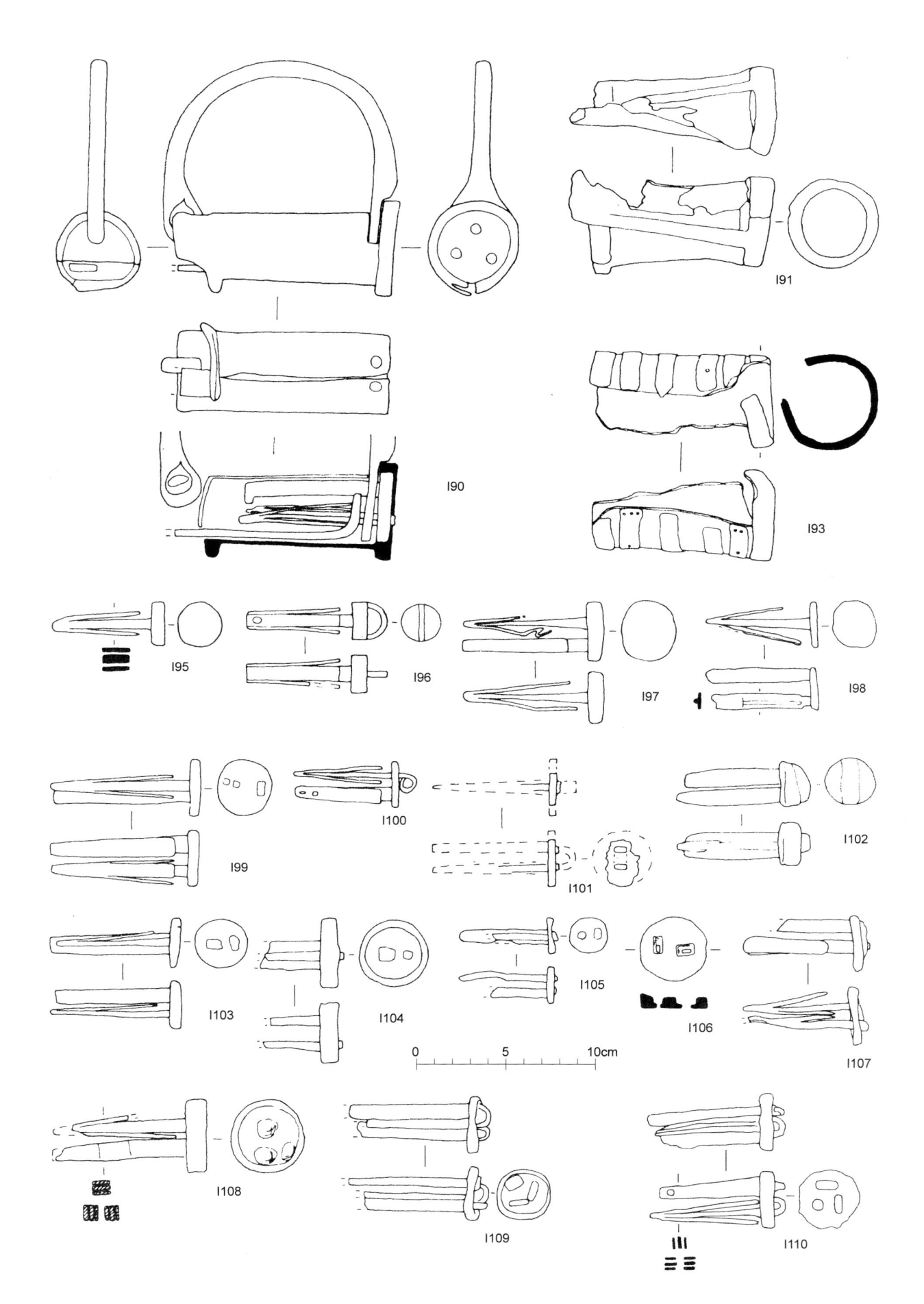

FIGURE 10.11
Barrel padlocks and padlock bolts

I111 PADLOCK BOLT
Goltho, Lincolnshire.
Late 14th–early 15th century. From smithy floor
T-shaped padlock bolt with three spines all with double leaf springs. Metallurgy: bolt made from wrought iron and at least one spine drawn out from closing plate by forging. Leaves assembled on spine by punching square rivet holes in all three and riveting them together. Much of object brass-plated to reduce corrosion. L 72mm.
Goodall 1975a, 84–85, fig 39.61.

I112 PADLOCK BOLT
Goltho, Lincolnshire.
Late 14th–early 15th century. In water-pit with slag from smithy.
T-shaped padlock bolt with two spines, each with double leaf springs and rod. L 65mm.
Goodall 1975a, 84, fig 39.63.

I113 PADLOCK BOLT
Cambokeels, Durham.
Later 14th to early 16th century.
T-shaped padlock bolt with two spines with double leaf springs (one incomplete) and a rod. L 76mm.
Hildyard 1949, 199, fig 3.17.

I114 PADLOCK BOLT
Wharram Percy, North Yorkshire.
Late 14th–mid 15th century.
T-shaped padlock bolt with flanged closing plate. Single spine with double leaf spring survives from three original spines.
L 81mm.
Goodall 1979a, 121, fig 64.84.

I115 PADLOCK BOLT
Hen Caerwys, Clwyd.
c1450–1520.
T-shaped padlock bolt with stubs of three spines. L 55mm.
Excavated by G B Leach.

I116 PADLOCK BOLT
Hen Caerwys, Clwyd.
c1450–1520.
Closing plate from T-shaped padlock bolt with three spines. D 42mm.
Excavated by G B Leach.

I117 PADLOCK BOLT
Huish, Wiltshire.
Site: 12th to mid 15th century.
Closing plate from T-shaped padlock bolt with three spines. D 27mm.
Shortt 1972, 118, fig 2.10.

I118 PADLOCK BOLT
Seacourt, Oxfordshire.
Mid to late 12th to late 14th century.
T-shaped padlock bolt with two spines with double leaf springs and two rods. L 69mm.
Biddle 1961–62, 181, fig 31.4, scale 1:4 not 1:3.

I119 BARREL PADLOCK
Wroughton Copse, Fyfield Down, Wiltshire.
?12th century.
Indeterminate case fragment with straight and wavy longitudinal strips. L 77mm.
Excavated by P J Fowler.

I120 BARREL PADLOCK
Weoley Castle, Birmingham, West Midlands.
c1080–c1200.
Indeterminate case fragment with plain longitudinal rods and copious copper-alloy brazing metal. L 32mm.
Oswald 1962, 129, fig 51.1.

I121 BARREL PADLOCK (not illustrated)
Wintringham, Cambridgeshire.
Immediately before mid 13th century.
Indeterminate case fragment with plain longitudinal straps. L 70mm.
Goodall 1977a, 257, fig 43.18.

I122 BARREL PADLOCK (not illustrated)
Winchester, Hampshire.
Mid 13th century.
Indeterminate padlock case fragment with projecting longitudinal straps. L 76mm.
Goodall 1990-21, 1015, no. 3680.

I123 BARREL PADLOCK
Kettleby Thorpe, Lincolnshire.
14th–early 15th century.
Indeterminate case fragment with longitudinal straps. L 88mm.
Goodall 1974a, 33, fig 18.3.

I124 PADLOCK BOLT
Kettleby Thorpe, Lincolnshire.
14th–early 15th century.
Spine and double leaf spring from padlock bolt. Squared U-shaped fitting set at right angles to spine acted as additional barrier to key. L 50mm.
Goodall 1974a, 30, fig 18.2.

I125 BOX PADLOCK
Northampton.
12th–14th century.
Box padlock with fin and tube and semicircular projection for revolving key. Case made from sheet metal plates brazed and held together by U-shaped binding strips. Both long sides decorated by longitudinal straps and wavy and scrolled strips. Projection has damaged keyhole in one side and hole for key tip in other. L 56mm.
Goodall *et al* 1979, 268, fig 116.2.

I126 BOX PADLOCK WITH SHACKLE
Winchester, Hampshire.
16th century.
Box padlock with hinged, U-shaped shackle. Keyhole in long side of case with circular mount on inner face of opposing side to engage key tip. U-shaped spring, L-shaped sliding bolt. W 54mm.
Goodall 1990-21, fig 316.3684.

I127 BOX PADLOCK WITH SHACKLE
Hen Caerwys, Clwyd.
c1450–1520.
Box padlock with U-shaped shackle.
Excavated by G B Leach.

I128 BOX PADLOCK WITH SHACKLE
Norwich, Norfolk.
In 1507 fire deposit.
Box padlock with U-shaped shackle.
L 39mm.
Goodall 1993d, fig 115.1240.

I129 PADLOCK SHACKLE
Staines, Surrey.
1300–1500.
Hinged, U-shaped shackle, one end broken.
L 62mm.
Excavated by K Crouch.

I130 PADLOCK SHACKLE
Bayham Abbey, East Sussex.
Late 15th–early 16th century.
Hinged, U-shaped shackle, one end broken.
L 68mm.
Goodall 1983a, fig 46.44.

I131 EMBOSSED PADLOCK
Goltho, Lincolnshire.
Croft A: late Saxon to late 14th or early 15th century.
Case and backplate damaged. W 63mm.
Goodall 1975a, 84, fig 39.65.

I132 EMBOOSED PADLOCK
Waltham Abbey, Essex.
Second half 15th century.
Case fragment retaining part of lock mechanism. W 51mm.
Excavated by P J Huggins.

I133 STAPLED PADLOCK HASP
Lyveden, Northamptonshire.
Second quarter 13th to very early 14th century.
One arm broken, staple in other blocked.
L 108mm.
Bryant and Steane 1969, 40, fig 18g.

I134 STAPLED PADLOCK HASP
Brooklands, Weybridge, Surrey.
1200–1325.
Both arms broken, staple lost. L 72mm.
Goodall 1977d, 73–75, fig 45.23.

I135 STAPLED PADLOCK HASP
Rhuddlan, Clwyd.
14th century, ?earlier part, or conceivably 1290–1300.
One arm lost. L 90mm.
Goodall 1994, fig 17.6, no. 94.

I136 STAPLED PADLOCK HASP
Grenstein, Norfolk.
Late 14th–15th centuries.
One arm and staple broken. L 114mm.
Goodall 1980c, fig 79, no. 62.

I137 STAPLED PADLOCK HASP
Newbury, Berkshire.
Late 15th century.
One arm broken. L 102mm.
Goodall 1997, fig 20, no. 28.

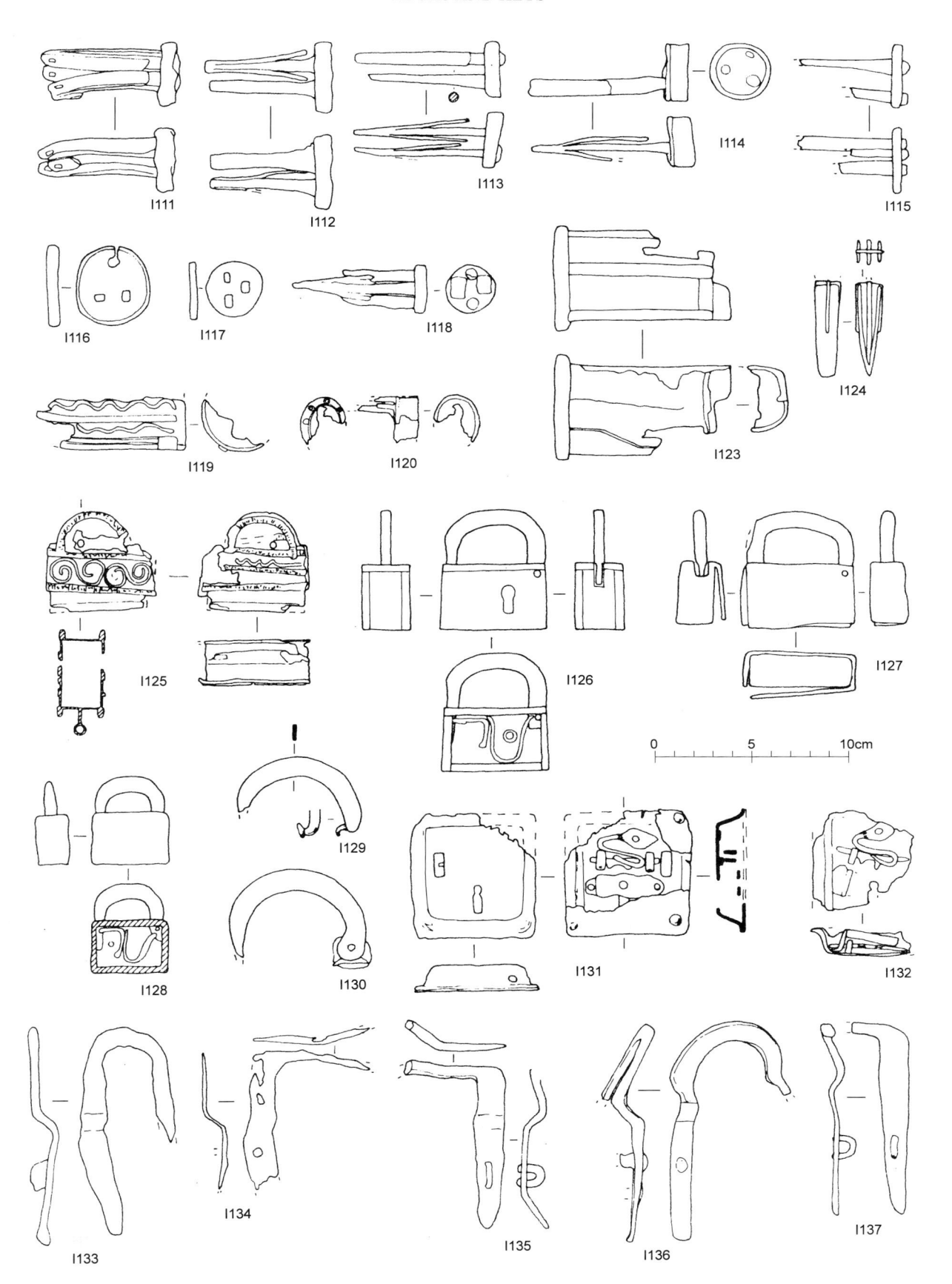

FIGURE 10.12
Padlock bolts, barrel padlocks, box padlocks, padlock shackles, embossed padlocks, and stapled padlock hasps

I138 EMBOSSED PADLOCK
Writtle, Essex.
c1425–1521.
Case and backplate broken. W 85mm.
Rahtz 1969b, 85, fig 47, 48.

I139 EMBOSSED PADLOCK
North Elmham Park, Norfolk.
c1150–c1600.
Case, near complete, retains stapled U-shaped hasp. W 63mm.
Goodall 1980a, 509, fig 265.10.

I140 STAPLED PADLOCK HASP
Hadleigh Castle, Essex.
16th century.
Base of one arm broken. L 76mm.
Goodall 1975c, 141, fig 28.340.

I141 EMBOSSED PADLOCK
Huish, Wiltshire.
Site: 12th–15th century.
Flange damaged. W 86mm.
Shortt 1972, 118, fig 2.12.

I142 LOCK
Winchester, Hampshire.
Mid to late 13th century.
Broken flat lockplate with shaped keyhole and hole for staple of hasp. Toothed bolt with recurved end, secured by spring, slides in two U-shaped staples. Broken mount for key tip. W 48mm.
Goodall 1990-21, fig 321.3688.

I143/H565 LOCK AND STAPLED LOCK HASP
Upton, Gloucestershire.
Late 13th to late 14th century.
Broken flat lockplate retaining end of toothed bolt corroded through stapled of looped hasp. W 30mm.
Hilton and Rahtz 1966, 120, fig 13.6.

I144 LOCK (not illustrated)
Winchester, Hampshire.
14th–?15th century.
Broken flat lockplate retaining straight toothed bolt and little else. L 72mm.
Goodall 1990-21, 1017, no. 3690.

I145 LOCK
Newbury, Berkshire.
Late 15th century.
Broken flat lockplate with two elongated guides for hasps and marks of outer straps on front face, as well as keyhole and holes for staples of hasps. Lock mechanism on rear comprises toothed bolt with recurved end secured by spring and sliding in two U-shaped staples, L-shaped ward, and shaped mount with inner collar and hole for key tip. L 108mm.
Goodall 1997, fig 20, no. 26.

I146 LOCK
Winchester, Hampshire.
Early 12th century.
Dished rectangular lock case with edge binding strips with nail-holes and one nail. Lock mechanism on rear face of projecting case comprises toothed straight bolt, tumbler, one L-shaped and two cross-shaped wards, two collars and a mount for the key tip.
L 180mm.
Goodall 1990-21, fig 319.3687.

I147 KEY TIP MOUNT (not illustrated)
Winchester, Hampshire.
Late 13th–early 14th century.
Shaped mount with hole for key tip, fixing plates broken. Similar to mount in **I128**, but without a collar. L 51mm.
Goodall 1990-21, 1017, no. 3689.

I148 KEY TIP MOUNT
Northampton.
c1250 to end 14th century.
Broken and distorted shaped mount with central recess bearing two concentric collars. L 166mm.
Goodall *et al* 1979, 268, fig 116.7.

I149 LOCK BOLT
Northampton.
12th–13th century.
One end distorted. L 78mm.
Goodall 1979b, 71, fig 17.9.

I150 LOCK BOLT
Joyden's Wood, Kent.
Late 13th, early 14th century.
Complete bolt. L 296mm.
Dunning 1959, 30–31, fig 4.30.

I151 LOCK BOLT
Northolt Manor, Greater London.
c1300.
Distorted bolt with recurved end. L 187mm.
Excavated by J G Hurst.

I152 LOCK BOLT
Southampton, Hampshire.
1300–50.
Broken mid length and at one end, other end recurved. L 236mm.
Harvey 1975b, 285, fig 255.2077.

I153 TUMBLER
Rhuddlan, Clwyd.
Mid 13th century.
Stem broken, fixing plate lost. L 78mm.
Goodall 1994, fig 17.1, no. 96.

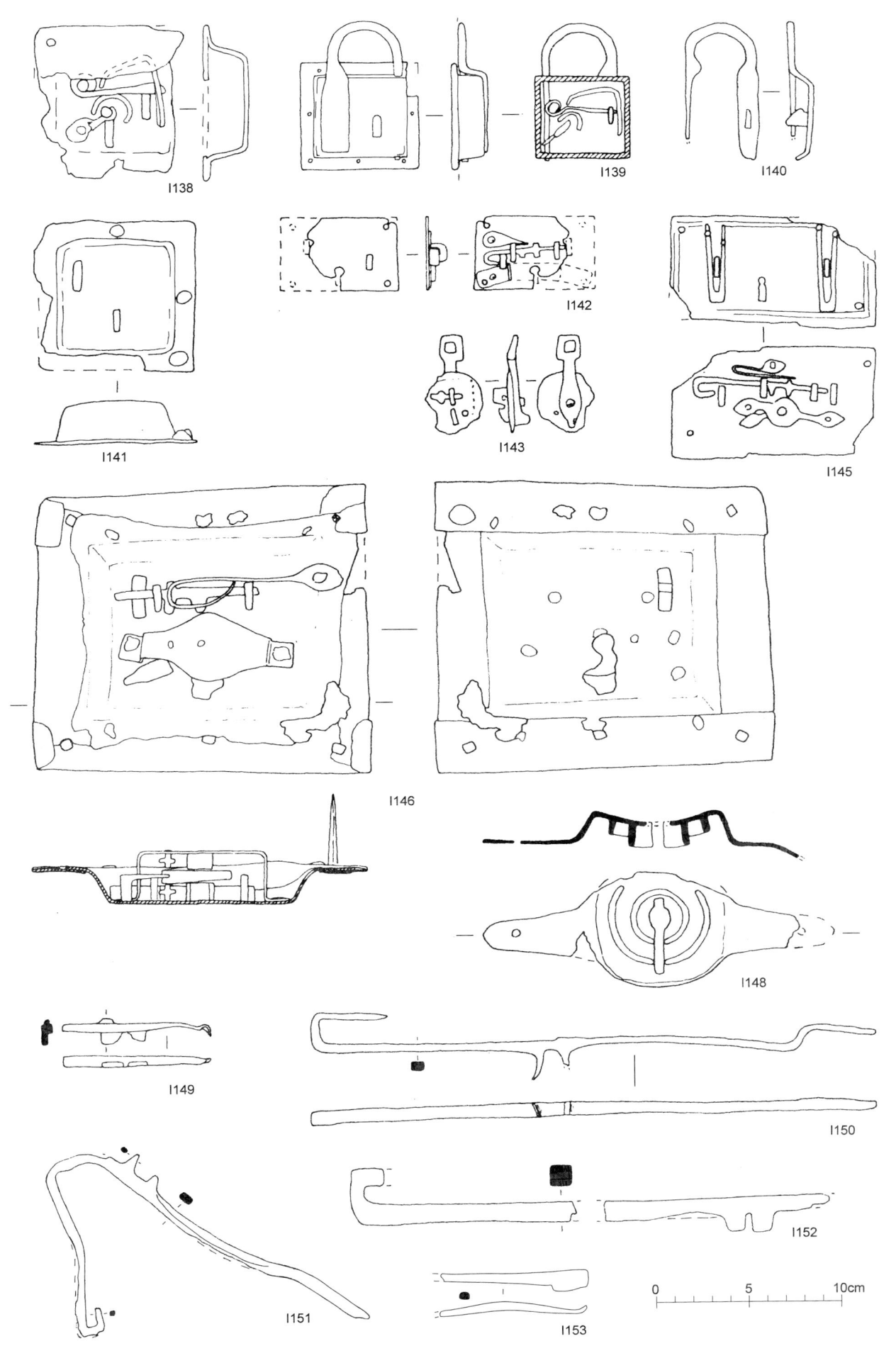

FIGURE 10.13
Embossed padlocks, stapled padlock hasps, locks, key tip mount, lock bolts, and tumbler

I154 LOCK BOLT
Criccieth Castle, Gwynedd.
Site: c1230–1404.
Damaged. L 138mm.
O'Neil 1944–45.

I155 LOCK BOLT
Stonar, Kent.
13th–14th century derived.
One end broken. L 161mm.
Excavated by N Macpherson-Grant.

I156 LOCK BOLT
North Elmham Park, Norfolk.
c1150–c1600.
One end broken. L 114mm.
Goodall 1980a, 510, fig 265.16.

I157 LOCK BOLT
Winchester, Hampshire.
15th century.
Complete. L 252mm.
Goodall 1990-21, fig 321.3692.

I158 LOCK BOLT (not illustrated)
Stonar, Kent.
c1275–1385.
One end broken. L 167mm.
Excavated by N Macpherson-Grant.

I159 LOCK BOLT (not illustrated)
Stonar, Kent.
c1275–1385.
One end broken. Found with part of lockplate. L 175mm.
Excavated by N Macpherson-Grant.

I160 LOCK BOLT
Clarendon Palace, Wiltshire.
Site: c1072 to late 15th century.
One end broken. L 96mm.
Goodall 1988, fig 79.79; Borenius and Charlton 1936.

I161 LOCK BOLT
Kettleby Thorpe, Lincolnshire.
12th to early 15th century.
Both ends broken. L 94mm.
Goodall 1974a, 33, fig 18.6.

I162 LOCK BOLT
Clarendon Palace, Wiltshire.
Site: c1072 to later 15th century.
One end broken. L 146mm.
Goodall 1988, fig 79.80; Borenius and Charlton 1936.

I163 LOCK BOLT
Clarendon Palace, Wiltshire.
Site: c1072 to later 15th century.
One end broken. L 229mm.
Goodall 1988, fig 79.76. Borenius and Charlton 1936.

I164 LOCK BOLT
Goltho, Lincolnshire.
Croft A: late Saxon to late 14th or early 15th century.
One end curved round, other broken. L 143mm.
Goodall 1975a, 84, fig 39.57.

I165 LOCK BOLT
Clarendon Palace, Wiltshire.
Site: c1072 to later 15th century.
Complete. L 222mm.
Goodall 1988, fig 79.77; Borenius and Charlton 1936.

I166 LOCK BOLT
Clarendon Palace, Wiltshire.
Site: c1072 to later 15th century.
Complete. L 156mm.
Goodall 1988, fig 79.78; Borenius and Charlton 1936.

I167 TUMBLER
Barrow Mead, Avon.
13th–14th century.
Broad end broken. L 83mm.
Goodall 1976b, 35, fig 11.21.

I168 TUMBLER
Ospringe, Kent.
Demolition c1550–70 on site founded c1230.
One end broken. L 60mm.
Goodall 1979c, 132, fig 21.77.

I169 WARD
Llantrithyd, South Glamorgan.
Early to mid 12th century.
Plain ward. L 89mm.
Goodall 1977f, 46, iron object fig 1.9.

I170 WARD
Hen Caerwys, Clwyd.
c1450–1520.
Plain ward, complete end shaped. L 68mm.
Excavated by G B Leach.

I171 WARD
Hen Caerwys, Clwyd.
c1450–1520.
Plain ward, one end broken. L 69mm.
Excavated by G B Leach.

I172 WARD
London.
Late 15th–early 16th century.
Plain ward. L 87mm.
Excavated by F C Willmot. Site at 66 Foyle Road.

I173 WARD
Waltham Abbey, Essex.
16th century.
Plain ward. L 80mm.
Goodall 1973a, 171, fig 11.34.

I174 WARD
Waltham Abbey, Essex.
16th century.
Plain ward, one end broken. L 93mm.
Goodall 1973a, 171, fig 11.33.

I175 WARD
Wharram Percy, North Yorkshire.
Early 16th to 20th century.
Both ends broken, top shaped. L 90mm.
Goodall 1979a, 121, fig 64.85.

I176 WARD
Glastonbury Tor, Somerset.
12th–16th century.
Incomplete ward with single pin. L 89mm.
Rahtz 1970, 53, fig 23.17.

I177 WARD
Waltham Abbey, Essex.
16th century.
Ward with collar. L 114mm.
Goodall 1973a, 171, fig 11.32.

I178 PADLOCK KEY
Llantrithyd, South Glamorgan.
Early to mid 12th century.
Plain stem broken across base of looped terminal. Bit broken. L 53mm.
Goodall 1977f, 46, iron object fig 1.5.

I179 PADLOCK KEY
Goltho Manor, Lincolnshire.
Probably mid 12th century; site occupied since 8th century.
Plain stem with looped terminal. L 107mm.
Goodall 1987, fig 158.114.

I180 PADLOCK KEY
Winchester, Hampshire.
13th century.
Plain stem with looped terminal. L 73mm.
Goodall 1990-21, fig 324.3730.

I181 PADLOCK KEY
Seacourt, Oxfordshire.
First quarter 13th century.
Plain stem with looped terminal and projection immediately above bit. L 94mm.
Biddle 1961–62, 180, fig 31.1, scale 1:4, not 1:3.

I182 PADLOCK KEY
Totnes, Devon.
Mid 13th century.
Plain stem, looped terminal. L 70mm.
Rigold 1954, 254, fig 8.8c.

I183 PADLOCK KEY
Bedford.
13th century.
Plain stem with looped terminal, bit lost. L 64mm.
Baker et al 1979, 281, fig 176.1427.

I184 PADLOCK KEY
Brandon Castle, Warwickshire.
13th century.
Plain stem with broken looped terminal. L 133mm.
Chatwin 1955, 83, fig 12.5.

I185 PADLOCK KEY
Winchester, Hampshire.
Late 11th–early 12th century.
Swollen stem with incised decorative grooves and broken looped terminal. Non-ferrous plating. L 90mm.
Goodall 1990-21, fig 324.3727.

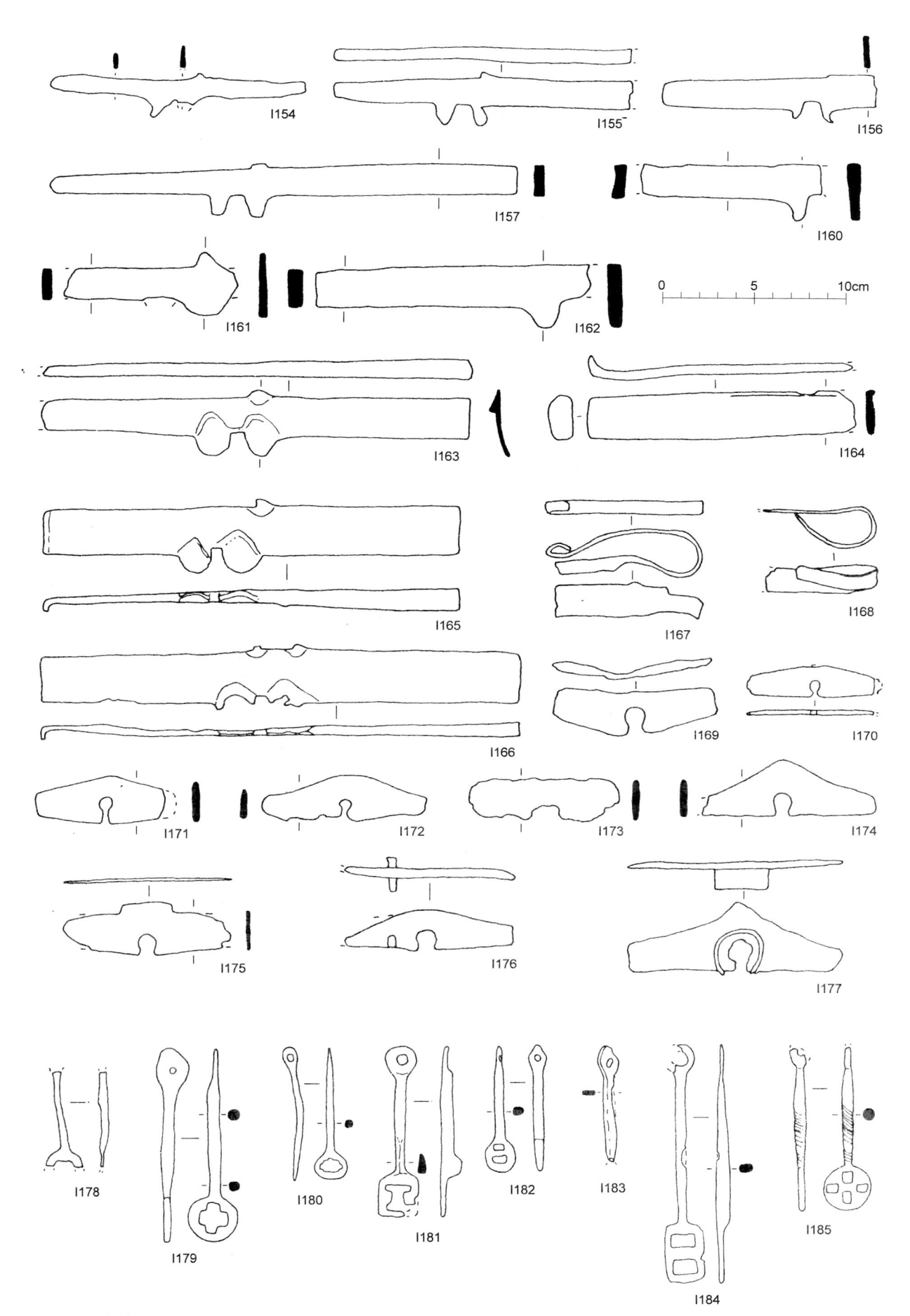

FIGURE 10.14
Lock bolts, tumblers, wards and padlock keys

I186 PADLOCK KEY
Winchester, Hampshire.
Late 11th century.
Swollen stem broken across base of looped terminal. L 98mm.
Goodall 1990-21, fig 324.3725.

I187 PADLOCK KEY (not illustrated)
Winchester, Hampshire.
Early 12th century.
Swollen stem broken across base of loop terminal. Base missing from bit with three rectangular ward cuts. L 72mm.
Goodall 1990-21, 1024, no. 3728.

I188 PADLOCK KEY
Goltho Manor, Lincolnshire.
c1100–25
Swollen stem with spirally inlaid copper-alloy wire. Broken looped terminal and bit. L 99mm.
Goodall 1987, fig 158.112.

I189 PADLOCK KEY
Winchester, Hampshire.
c1130.
Swollen stem with spirally inlaid non-ferrous wire. Broken ring through looped terminal.
L 124mm.
Goodall 1990-21, fig 324.3726.

I190 PADLOCK KEY (not illustrated)
Goltho Manor, Lincolnshire.
c1100–50.
Swollen stem inlaid with copper-alloy wire. Looped terminal and bit both broken. L 77mm.
Goodall 1987, 183.

I191 PADLOCK KEY
Castle Acre Castle, Norfolk.
1140s–50s with derived material. Site founded soon after 1066.
Swollen stem with looped terminal and damaged bit. L 85mm.
Goodall 1982, fig 40, no. 82.

I192 PADLOCK KEY
Castle Acre Castle, Norfolk.
1140s with derived material. Site founded soon after 1066.
Swollen stem with spirally inlaid non-ferrous wire and looped terminal. L 104mm.
Goodall 1982, fig 40, no. 84.

I193 PADLOCK KEY
Castle Acre Castle, Norfolk.
1140s to second half 12th century with derived material. Site founded soon after 1066.
Swollen stem with spirally inlaid non-ferrous wire. Looped terminal with ring. L 100mm.
Goodall 1982, fig 40, no. 85.

I194 PADLOCK KEY
Castle Acre Castle, Norfolk.
1140s to second half 12th century.
Swollen stem with looped terminal. Non-ferrous plating. L 94mm.
Goodall 1982, fig 40, no. 81.

I195 PADLOCK KEY
Castle Acre Castle, Norfolk.
Second half 12th century.
Swollen stem with spirally inlaid non-ferrous wire. Looped terminal broken. L 65mm.
Goodall 1982, fig 40, no. 88.

I196 PADLOCK KEY
Castle Acre Castle, Norfolk.
Second half 12th century.
Swollen stem with looped terminal; bit broken. L 80mm.
Goodall 1982, fig 40, no. 83.

I197 PADLOCK KEY
Castle Acre Castle, Norfolk.
Second half 12th century.
Swollen stem with spirally inlaid non-ferrous wire. Looped terminal with broken ring.
L 85mm.
Goodall 1982, fig 40, no. 87.

I198 PADLOCK KEY
Castle Acre Castle, Norfolk.
Second half 12th century.
Swollen stem with spirally inlaid non-ferrous wire. Looped terminal, broken bit. L 91mm.
Goodall 1982, fig 40, no. 86.

I199 PADLOCK KEY
Winchester, Hampshire.
c1138–c1154.
Swollen stem with incised decorative grooves, looped terminal and non-ferrous plating. L 72mm.
Goodall 1990-21, fig 324.3729.

I200 PADLOCK KEY
Hen Domen, Powys.
After 1200, probably before 1250.
Swollen stem with looped terminal. Bit broken. L 83mm.
Barker and Higham 2000.

I201 PADLOCK KEY
Faxton, Northamptonshire.
Site: 12th–15th century.
Swollen stem. Looped terminal and bit broken. L 54mm.
Excavated by L A S Butler.

I202 PADLOCK KEY
Staines, Surrey.
Medieval, to 15th century.
Swollen stem with looped terminal. L 114mm.
Barker 1976, 124, fig 26.27.

I203 PADLOCK KEY
King's Lynn, Norfolk.
c1250–1350(?).
Swollen stem with incised decorative grooves and hooked-loop terminal. Shaped bit.
L 119mm.
Goodall and Carter 1977, 293, fig 133.7.

I204 PADLOCK KEY
Llantrithyd, South Glamorgan.
Early to mid 12th century.
Short plain stem expanding to perforated tip. Incised decoration on expanded part of stem. Non-ferrous plating. L 117mm.
Goodall 1977f, 46, iron object fig 1.4.

I205 PADLOCK KEY
Brooklands, Surrey.
1200–1325.
Short plain stem with rear projection expanding to perforated tip. L 102mm.
Goodall 1977d, 73, fig 45.21.

I206 PADLOCK KEY
Walton, Aylesbury, Buckinghamshire.
12th century.
Plain stem with looped terminal. L 146mm.
Cocks 1903–09, 285–286, fig on p 285.

I207 PADLOCK KEY
Wroughton Copse, Fyfield Down, Wiltshire.
?12th century.
Plain stem, upper part thickened. Broken looped terminal and bit. L 119mm.
Excavated by P J Fowler.

I208 PADLOCK KEY
Brandon Castle, Warwickshire.
1226–66.
Plain stem with double looped terminal. L 116mm.
Chatwin 1955, 83, fig 12.1.

I209 PADLOCK KEY
Stonar, Kent.
c1275–1385.
Plain stem with looped terminal. Non-ferrous plating. L 96mm.
Excavated by N Macpherson-Grant.

I210 PADLOCK KEY
Rayleigh Castle, Essex.
Site: c1070–c1350.
Plain stem with hooked-loop terminal.
L 119mm.
Reader 1913, 168, pl D.2; Helliwell and Macleod 1965.

I211 PADLOCK KEY
Weoley Castle, Birmingham, West Midlands.
Site: c1080–1500.
Expanded stem with hooked terminal. Bit damaged. L 150mm.
Birmingham City Museum, WC417. For site see Oswald 1962.

LOCKS AND KEYS

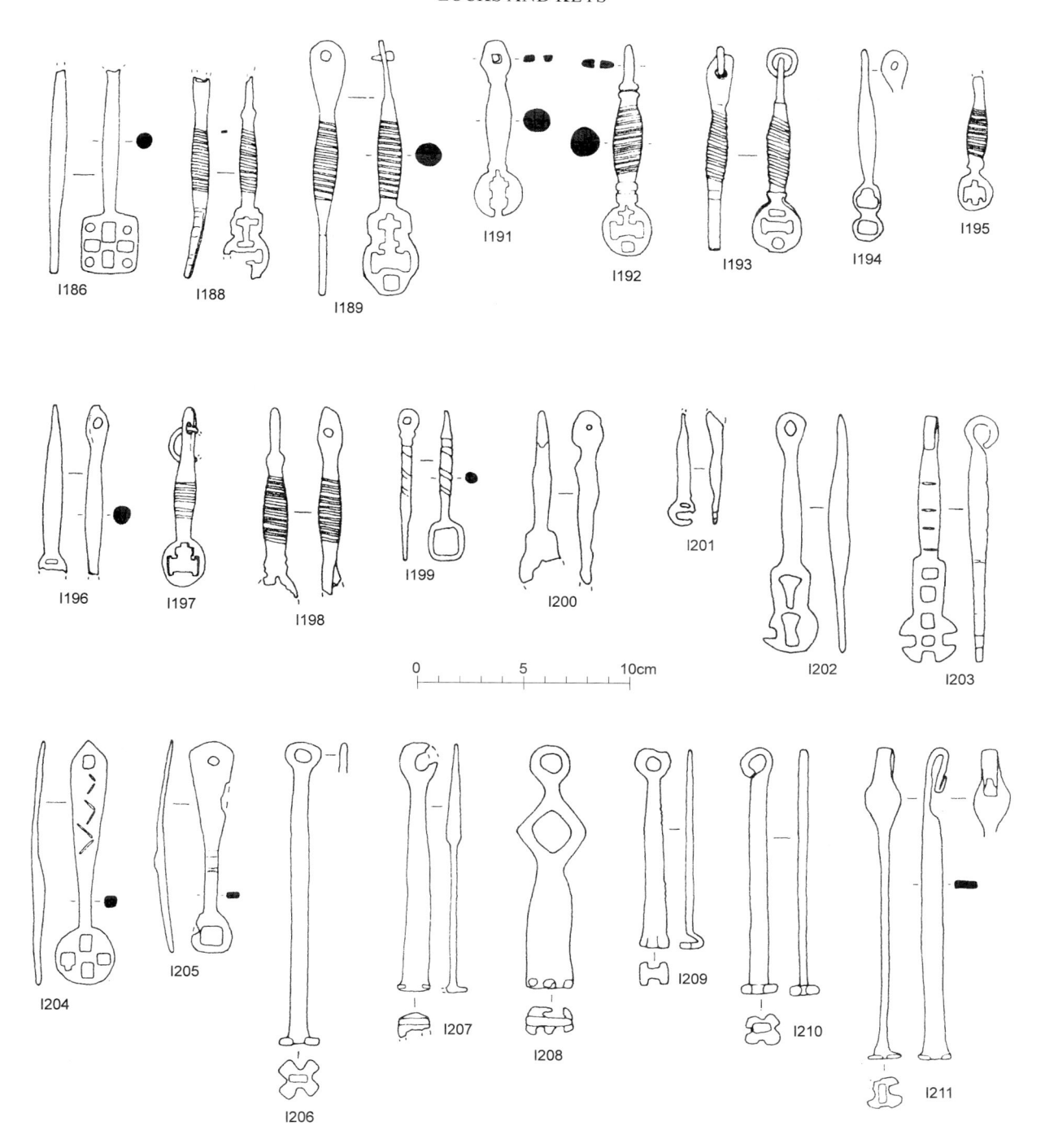

FIGURE 10.15
Padlock keys

I212 PADLOCK KEY
Castle Urquhart, Highlands.
Site: 12th–17th century.
Plain stem broken. L 104mm.
Laing 1974–75, 155, fig 14.15.

I213 PADLOCK KEY
Thelsford Priory, Warwickshire.
14th century.
Bulbous stem with looped terminal. L 58mm.
Excavated by Mrs M Gray.

I214 PADLOCK KEY
Southampton, Hampshire.
1125–50.
Plain stem with looped terminal. L 95mm.
Harvey 1975b, 276, fig 250.1965.

I215 PADLOCK KEY
Ellington, Cambridgeshire.
Second or third quarter 12th to late 13th century.
Plain stem narrowing to looped terminal. L 123mm.
Goodall 1971, 67, fig 12.1.

I216 PADLOCK KEY
Hen Domen, Powys.
After 1200, probably before 1250.
Plain stem, upper part thickened. Looped terminal. L 107mm.
Higham and Rouillard 2000, no. 82.

I217 PADLOCK KEY
Northolt Manor, Greater London.
1225–1300.
Plain stem, upper part thickened. Looped terminal. L 122mm.
Hurst 1961, 289, fig 76.4.

I218 PADLOCK KEY
Seacourt, Oxfordshire.
Mid 13th century.
Plain stem with looped terminal. L 120mm.
Biddle 1961–62, 180, fig 31.2, scale 1:4 not 1:3.

I219 PADLOCK KEY
Winchester, Hampshire.
?13th century.
Plain stem with looped terminal. L 102mm.
Goodall 1990-21, fig 323.3724.

I220 PADLOCK KEY
Brandon Castle, Warwickshire.
13th century.
Plain stem, upper part thickened, broken across base of looped terminal. L 95mm.
Chatwin 1955, 83, fig 12.4.

I221 PADLOCK KEY
Grenstein, Norfolk.
Late 14th–15th century.
Plain, boken stem. L 105mm.
Goodall 1980c, fig 79, no. 59.

I222 PADLOCK KEY
Clarendon Palace, Wiltshire.
Site: c1072 to later 15th century.
Plain stem with looped terminal. L 106mm.
Goodall 1988, fig 78.66; Borenius and Charlton 1936.

I223 PADLOCK KEY
Writtle, Essex.
Site: 1211–1521 with later material.
Plain stem with looped terminal. L 95mm.
Rahtz 1969b, 85, fig 47.45.

I224 PADLOCK KEY
Writtle, Essex.
c1425–1521 but mixed with later levels.
Plain stem with looped terminal. L 105mm.
Rahtz 1969b, 85, fig 47.45.

I225 PADLOCK KEY
Castle Acre Castle, Norfolk.
Second half 12th century.
Plain stem with hooked-loop terminal. L 116mm.
Goodall 1982, fig 40, no. 90.

I226 PADLOCK KEY
Winchester, Hampshire.
Late 12th–early 13th century.
Plain stem with hooked-loop terminal. L 133mm.
Goodall 1990-21, fig 323.3710.

I227 PADLOCK KEY
Walton, Aylesbury, Buckinghamshire.
12th century.
Plain stem with hooked terminal. L 136mm.
Cocks 1903–09, 286; Ward Perkins 1967, 148, fig 45.2.

I228 PADLOCK KEY
Lyveden, Northamptonshire.
Second quarter 13th century.
Plain shank with hooked-loop terminal. L 130mm.
Bryant and Steane 1971, 63, fig 16.n.

LOCKS AND KEYS

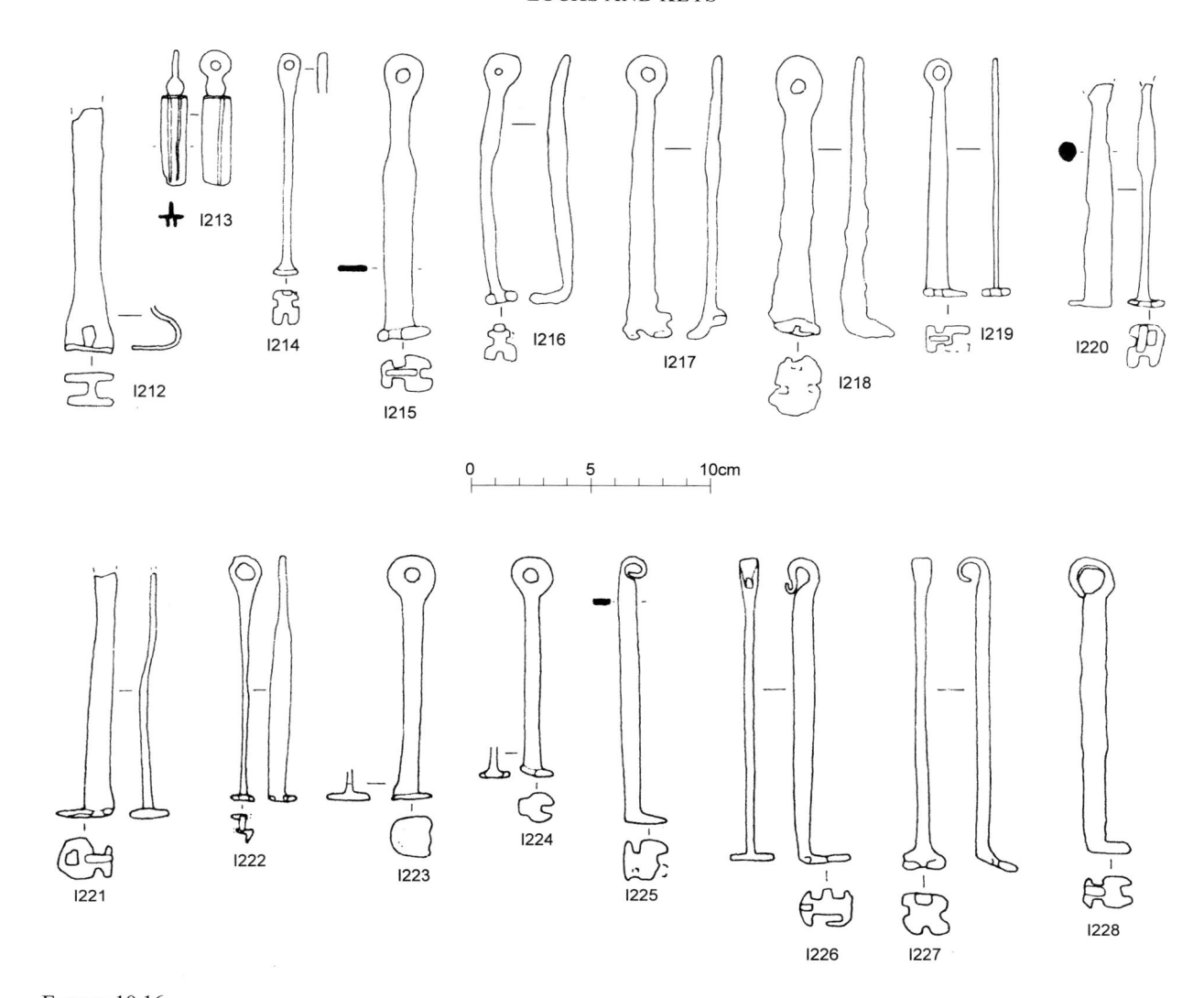

FIGURE 10.16
Padlock keys

I229 PADLOCK KEY
Winchester, Hampshire.
Late 10th–late 11th century.
Expanded stem with hooked terminal.
L 149mm.
Goodall 1990-21, fig 322.3705.

I230 PADLOCK KEY
Winchester, Hampshire.
Late 10th–late 11th century.
Expanded stem with broken hooked terminal. L 172mm.
Goodall 1990-21, fig 322.3704.

I231 PADLOCK KEY
Sulgrave, Northamptonshire.
End 11th to early 12th century.
Expanded stem, hooked terminal and bit broken. L 155mm.
Excavated by B K Davison.

I232 PADLOCK KEY
Winchester, Hampshire.
15th century.
Broken expanded stem. L 97mm.
Goodall 1990-21, fig 323.3720.

I233 PADLOCK KEY
Winchester, Hampshire.
Late 13th century.
Expanded stem, hooked terminal, broken bit, L 136mm.
Goodall 1990-21, fig 323.3713.

I234 PADLOCK KEY
Brandon Castle, Warwickshire.
13th century.
Expanded stem, hooked terminal lost.
L 147mm.
Chatwin 1955, 83, fig 12.6.

I235 PADLOCK KEY
Copt Hay, Tetsworth, Oxfordshire.
Late 13th–14th century.
Expanded stem, with hooked terminal.
L 115mm.
Robinson 1973, 104, fig 25.10.

I236 PADLOCK KEY
Criccieth Castle, Gwynedd.
Site: c1220–1404.
Expanded stem with hooked terminal.
L 150mm.
O'Neil 1944–45, 41, pl IX.8.

I237 PADLOCK KEY
Clarendon Palace, Wiltshire.
Site: c1072 to later 15th century.
Expanded stem with distorted and incomplete hooked terminal. L 178mm.
Goodall 1988, fig 78.67; Borenius and Charlton 1936.

I238/I16 PADLOCK KEY
Winchester, Hampshire.
Late 14th century.
Incomplete and corroded key, found in barrel padlock **I16**. L 29mm.
Goodall 1990-21, fig 311.3652.

I239 PADLOCK KEY (not illustrated)
Winchester, Hampshire.
14th century.
Bit as **I232**. L 77mm.
Goodall 1990-21, 1022, no. 3718.

I240 PADLOCK KEY (not illustrated)
Seacourt, Oxfordshire.
Mid to late 12th to mid 14th century.
L 78mm. Bit as **I218**.
Biddle 1961–62, 181, fig 31.3.

I241 PADLOCK KEY (not illustrated)
Huish, Wiltshire.
Site: 12th to mid 15th century.
Bit as **I232**. L 72mm.
Shortt 1972, 118, fig 2.11.

I242 PADLOCK KEY (not illustrated)
Castle Acre Castle, Norfolk.
Second half 12th century.
Plain stem with looped terminal. L 124mm.
Goodall 1982.

I243 PADLOCK KEY
Castle Acre Castle, Norfolk.
1140s/50s with derived material. Site founded soon after 1066.
Expanded stem with broken looped terminal set in opposing plane. L 83mm.
Goodall 1982, fig 40, no. 93.

I244 PADLOCK KEY (not illustrated)
Castle Acre Castle, Norfolk.
Second half 12th century.
Expanded stem with looped terminal set in opposing plane. L 101mm.
Goodall 1982.

I245 PADLOCK KEY
Winchester, Hampshire.
15th century.
Expanded stem with looped terminal set in opposing plane. Bit broken. L 120mm.
Goodall 1990-21, fig 323.3721.

I246 PADLOCK KEY
Winchester, Hampshire.
Late 10th–late 11th century.
Expanded stem with hooked terminal.
L 148mm.
Goodall 1990-21, fig 322.3703.

I247 PADLOCK KEY
Winchester, Hampshire.
Late 10th–late 11th century.
Expanded stem with hooked terminal.
L 166mm.
Goodall 1990-21, fig 323.3706.

I248 PADLOCK KEY
Gloucester.
11th to early 12th century.
Expanded stem with broken hooked terminal. L 151mm.
Excavated by H Hurst.

LOCKS AND KEYS

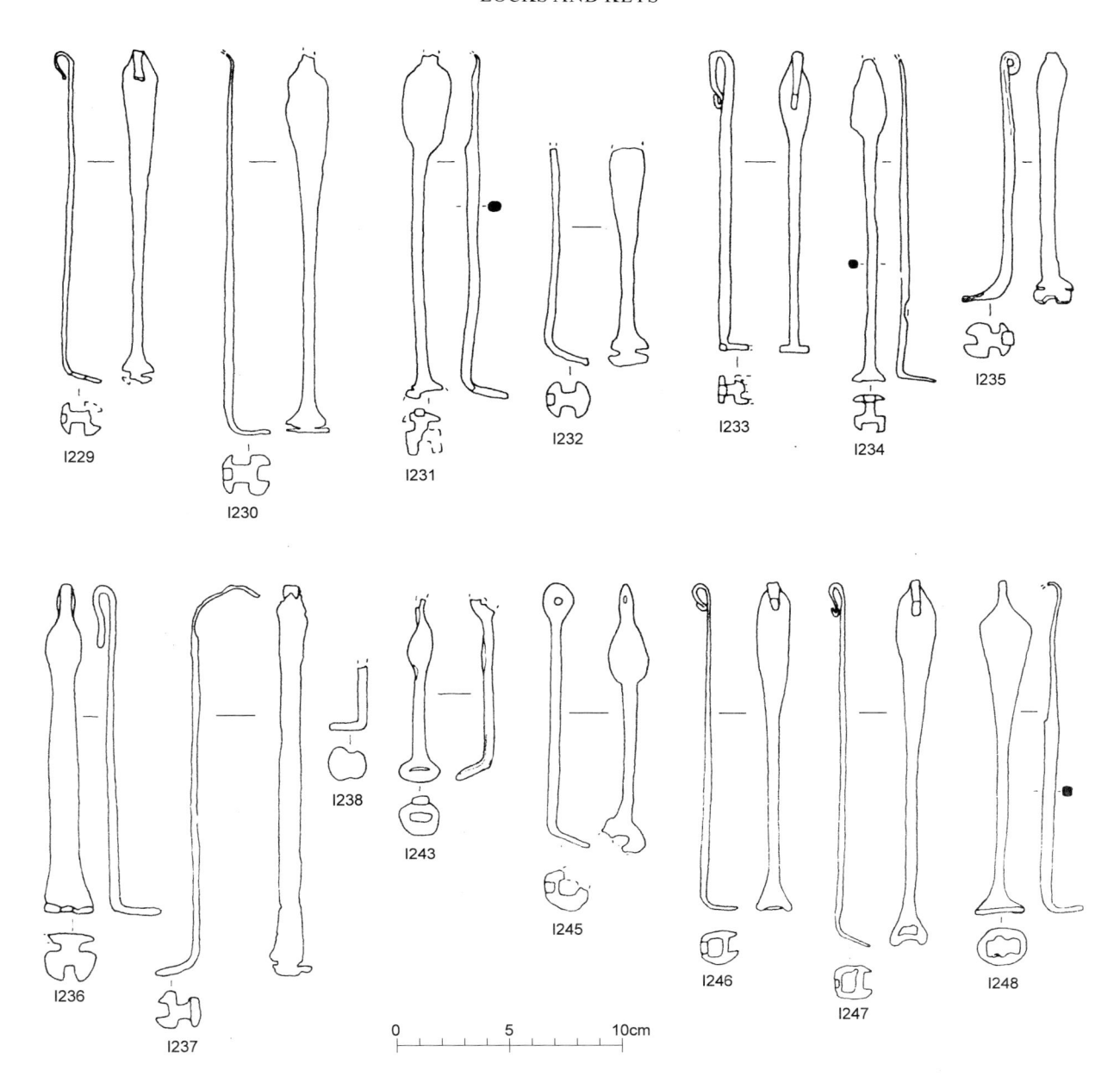

Figure 10.17
Padlock keys

I249 PADLOCK KEY
Gloucester.
11th to early 12th century.
Expanded stem with hooked terminal.
L 220mm.
Excavated by H Hurst.

I250 PADLOCK KEY (not illustrated)
Winchester, Hampshire.
Late 11th–12th century.
Expanded stem with hooked terminal. Bit incomplete. L 93mm.
Goodall 1990-21, 1022, no. 3709.

I251/I83 PADLOCK KEY
Winchester, Hampshire.
11th century.
Key with expanded stem and hooked terminal, found with barrel padlock with shackle and bolt **I83**. L 169mm.
Goodall 1990-21, fig 315.3674.

I252 PADLOCK KEY
Llantrithyd, South Glamorgan.
Early to mid 12th century.
Expanded stem with hooked terminal.
L 142mm.
Goodall 1977f, 46, iron object fig 1.2.

I253 PADLOCK KEY
Llantrithyd, South Glamorgan.
Early to mid 12th century.
Expanded stem, hooked terminal and bit both broken. L 145mm.
Goodall 1977f, 46, iron object fig 1.1.

I254 PADLOCK KEY
Castle Acre Castle, Norfolk.
Second half 12th century.
Expanded stem with hooked terminal.
L 137mm.
Goodall 1982, fig 40, no. 97.

I255 PADLOCK KEY
Castle Acre Castle, Norfolk.
Last quarter 12th century.
Expanded stem with hooked terminal. Bit incomplete.
Goodall 1982, fig 40, no. 98.

I256 PADLOCK KEY
King's Lynn, Norfolk.
c1150–1250.
Expanded stem with hooked terminal.
L 139mm.
Goodall and Carter 1977, 293, fig 133.5.

I257 PADLOCK KEY
Cheddar, Somerset.
Early 13th century.
Expanded stem, hooked terminal and bit broken. L 115mm.
Goodall 1979d, 264, fig 90.143.

I258 PADLOCK KEY
Christchurch, Hampshire.
?13th century.
Expanded stem, hooked terminal and bit broken. L 103mm.
Goodall 1983b, fig 34.47.

I259 PADLOCK KEY
Winchester, Hampshire.
13th century.
Expanded stem with hooked terminal.
L 142mm.
Goodall 1990-21, fig 323.3716.

I260 PADLOCK KEY
Winchester, Hampshire.
13th century.
Expanded stem with hooked terminal.
L 143mm.
Goodall 1990-21, fig 323.3715.

I261 PADLOCK KEY
Brandon Castle, Warwickshire.
13th century.
Expanded stem, hooked terminal and bit broken. L 173mm.
Chatwin 1955, 83, fig 12.7.

I262 PADLOCK KEY
Brandon Castle, Warwickshire.
13th century.
Distorted key with expanded stem and broken hooked terminal and bit. L 204mm.
Herbert Art Gallery and Museum, Coventry. For site see Chatwin 1955.

I263 PADLOCK KEY
King's Lynn, Norfolk.
c1250–1350(?).
Expanded stem with broken hooked terminal. L 129mm.
Goodall and Carter 1977, 293, fig 133.6.

I264 PADLOCK KEY
Upton, Gloucestershire.
Late 13th to late 14th century.
Expanded stem with hooked terminal.
L 177mm.
Hilton and Rahtz 1966, 120, fig 13.2.

I265 PADLOCK KEY
Upton, Gloucestershire.
Late 13th to late 14th century.
Expanded stem with hooked terminal.
L 194mm.
Hilton and Rahtz 1966, 120, fig 13.1.

I266 PADLOCK KEY
East Hill Farm, Houghton Regis, Bedfordshire.
Site: c1000–1400.
Expanded stem, hooked terminal and bit broken. L 83mm.
Luton Museum, L/10/338/38.

I267 PADLOCK KEY
Old Sarum, Wiltshire.
Principally medieval, to 14th century.
Expanded stem with hooked terminal.
L 143mm.
Salisbury and South Wiltshire Museum, Salisbury, O.S.C126, 8/1932.

I268 PADLOCK KEY
Richard's Castle, Hereford and Worcester.
Site: founded c1050 and in disuse by 15th century.
Expanded stem with hooked terminal.
L 198mm.
Curnow and Thompson 1969, 122, fig 8C.

I269 PADLOCK KEY
Kettleby Thorpe, Lincolnshire.
14th to early 15th century.
Expanded stem with hooked terminal.
L 135mm.
Goodall 1974a, 30, fig 18.1.

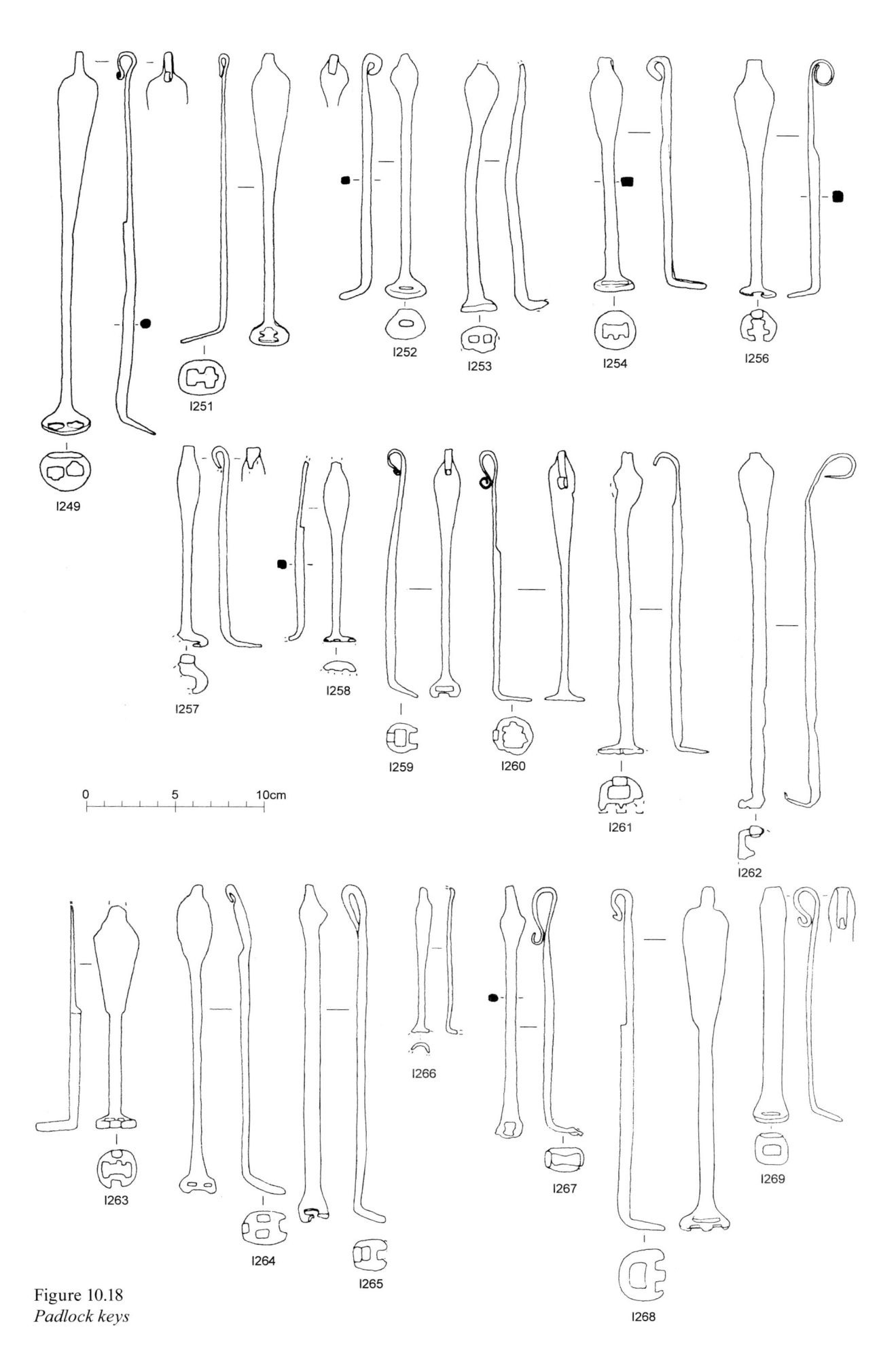

Figure 10.18
Padlock keys

I270 PADLOCK KEY
Dyserth Castle, Clwyd.
1241–63.
Plain stem with hooked terminal. L 141mm.
Glenn 1915.

I271 PADLOCK KEY
Winchester, Hampshire.
Mid to late 13th century.
Plain stem, hooked terminal, broken bit.
L 144mm.
Goodall 1990-21, fig 323.3712.

I272 PADLOCK KEY
Wintringham, Cambridgeshire.
Site: c1175–1340.
Plain stem with hooked terminal. Key distorted but drawn straight. L 157mm.
Goodall 1977a, 257, fig 43.17.

I273 PADLOCK KEY
Rayleigh Castle, Essex.
Site: c1070–c1350.
Plain stem with hooked terminal. L 102mm.
Reader 1913, 167, pl D.3; Helliwell and Macleod 1965.

I274 PADLOCK KEY
Goltho, Lincolnshire.
13th to mid 14th century.
Plain stem with hooked terminal. L 104mm.
Goodall 1975a, 83, fig 39.50.

I275 PADLOCK KEY
Gomeldon, Wiltshire.
Late 13th–14th century.
Plain stem with hooked terminal. L 182mm.
Musty and Algar 1986.

I276 PADLOCK KEY
Lyveden, Northamptonshire.
c1350–1450.
Plain stem with hooked terminal. L 172mm.
Steane and Bryant 1975, 131, fig 49.154.

I277 PADLOCK KEY
Goltho, Lincolnshire.
Croft A: late Saxon to late 14th or early 15th century.
Plain stem with hooked terminal. L 127mm.
Goodall 1975a, 83, fig 39.49.

I278 PADLOCK KEY
London.
Late 15th to early 16th century.
Plain stem with hooked terminal. L 168mm.
Excavated by F C Willmot. Site at 66 Foyle Road.

I279 PADLOCK KEY
Somerby, Lincolnshire.
Site: 11th to mid 16th century.
Plain stem with hooked terminal. L 113mm.
Mynard 1969, 83, fig 12.IW73.

I280 PADLOCK KEY
Somerby, Lincolnshire.
15th to mid 16th century.
Plain stem, hooked terminal, broken bit.
L 171mm.
Mynard 1969, 83, fig 12.IW72.

I281 PADLOCK KEY
Gloucester.
11th to early 12th century.
Broken expanded stem and bit. L 95mm.
Excavated by H Hurst.

I282 PADLOCK KEY
Goltho Manor, Lincolnshire.
c1125–50.
Expanded stem, hooked terminal lost. L 92mm.
Goodall 1987, fig 158.115.

I283 PADLOCK KEY
Llantrithyd, South Glamorgan.
Early to mid 12th century.
Expanded stem broken. L 112mm.
Goodall 1977f, 46, iron object fig 1.3.

I284 PADLOCK KEY
Brandon Castle, Warwickshire.
13th century.
Expanded stem, hooked terminal and bit broken. L 134mm.
Herbert Museum and Art Gallery, Coventry. For site see Chatwin 1955.

I285/I90 PADLOCK KEY
Oxford.
13th–16th century.
Key from barrel padlock with shackle I90 complete with bolt. Broken plain stem, shape of wards of bit conjectured from form of bolt. L 101mm.
Excavated by T G Hassall. From Greyfriars burial ground.

I286 PADLOCK KEY (not illustrated)
Walton, Aylesbury, Buckinghamshire.
11th century.
Bit broken. L 97mm.
Farley 1976, 241, fig 35.4.

I287 PADLOCK KEY (not illustrated)
Montgomery Castle, Powys.
Late 13th to early 14th century.
Bit as I268. L 117mm.
Excavated by J K Knight.

I288 PADLOCK KEY (not illustrated)
Lyveden, Northamptonshire.
Early 13th to first half 14th century.
Bit broken and similar to I253. L 100mm.
Steane 1967, 29, fig 10b.

I289 PADLOCK KEY (not illustrated)
Rayleigh Castle, Essex.
Site: c1070–c1350.
Bit broken. L 90mm.
Francis 1913; Ward Perkins 1967, 149, fig 45.6.

I290 PADLOCK KEY (not illustrated)
Winchester, Hampshire.
Mid 18th–19th century.
Bit as I269. L 73mm.
Goodall 1990-21, 1022, no. 3722.

I291 PADLOCK KEY (not illustrated)
Lyveden, Northamptonshire.
c1350–1450. Bit as I276. L 49mm.
Steane and Bryant 1975, 132, fig 49.157.

I292 KEY (not illustrated)
Winchester, Hampshire.
Late 14th century.
Ring bow, solid stem with projecting tip, uncut bit. L 52mm.
Goodall 1990-21, 1033, no. 3846.

I293 KEY (not illustrated)
Winchester, Hampshire.
14th century.
Lozenge-shaped bow, internally rounded. Solid stem with projecting tip, uncut bit. L 47mm.
Goodall 1990-21, 1033, no. 3847.

I294 KEY
Goltho, Lincolnshire.
Croft A: late Saxon to late 14th or early 15th century. In croft with late 14th, early 15th-century smithy.
Partly forged key with D-shaped bow and uncut bit. Stem tip broken. L 108mm.
Goodall 1975a, 84, fig 39.54.

I295 KEY
Waltham Abbey, Essex.
12th–13th and 16th century pottery in upper occupation debris of forge.
Partly forged key of rectangular-sectioned iron, the stem and bow drawn out but the latter not welded closed. Bit yet to be drawn down and cut. L 93mm.
Goodall 1973a, 170–171, fig 11.30.

I296 KEY
Winchester, Hampshire.
c1065–70.
Pear-shaped bow, moulded stem, broken bit. Non-ferrous plating. L 108mm.
Goodall 1990-21, fig 325.3733.

I297 KEY
Winchester, Hampshire.
c1065–70.
Pear-shaped bow, moulded stem. Non-ferrous plating. L 113mm.
Goodall 1990-21, fig 325.3735.

I298 KEY (not illustrated)
Winchester, Hampshire.
c1065–70.
Pear-shaped bow, broken bit. L 113mm.
Goodall 1990-21, 1024, no. 3734.

I299 KEY
Winchester, Hampshire.
c1065/66 to ?c1085.
Pear-shaped bow, broken bit. Non-ferrous plating. L 117mm.
Goodall 1990-21, fig 325.3736.

I300 KEY
Winchester, Hampshire.
c1065/66 to ?c1085.
Broken pear-shaped bow, moulded stem. Non-ferrous plating. L 103mm.
Goodall 1990-21, fig 325.3737.

I301 KEY
Winchester, Hampshire.
11th to ?mid 12th century.
Pear-shaped bow. Non-ferrous plating. L 118mm.
Goodall 1990-21, fig 325.3738.

I302 KEY
London.
12th century.
Broken, probably pear-shaped bow. L 50mm.
Marsden et al 1975, 206, fig 12.143.

I303 KEY
Northampton.
?12th to late 14th or early 15th century (?residual).
Pear-shaped bow. L 112mm.
Goodall 1979b, 71, fig 17.7.

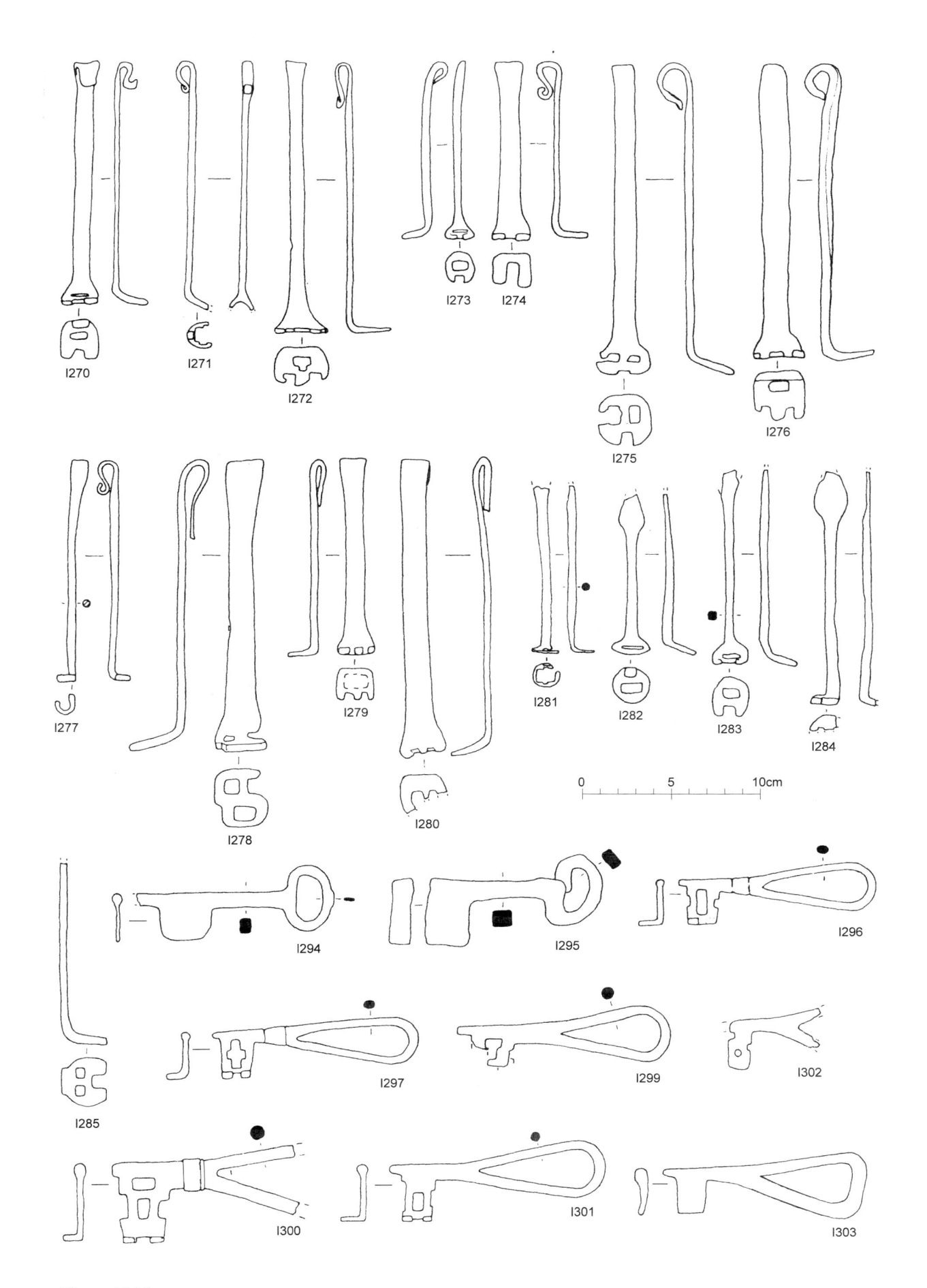

Figure 10.19
Padlock keys and keys

I304 KEY
Great Yarmouth, Norfolk.
Mid to late 11th century.
Ring bow. L 88mm.
Rogerson 1976, 166, fig 52.17.

I305 KEY
Gloucester.
11th, early 12th century.
Lozenge-shaped bow. L 69mm.
Excavated by H Hurst.

I306 KEY
South Cadbury, Somerset.
11th–12th century.
Ring bow, broken bit. L 116mm.
Alcock 1995.

I307 KEY
Winchester, Hampshire.
c1110.
Ring bow, decorative grooves on stem. Non-ferrous plating. L 40mm.
Goodall 1990-21, fig 326.3753.

I308 KEY
Winchester, Hampshire.
Late 11th–early 12th century.
Ring bow. L 49mm.
Goodall 1990-21, fig 326.3755.

I309 KEY
Winchester, Hampshire.
Late 11th–12th century.
Ring bow. L 76mm.
Goodall 1990-21, fig 326.3756.

I310 KEY
York.
12th century.
D-shaped bow, grooved stem. Non-ferrous plating. L 74mm.
Addyman and Priestley 1977, 139, fig 10.13.

I311 KEY
Lydney Castle, Gloucestershire.
12th century, possibly into 13th century.
Ring bow. L 124mm.
Casey 1931, 252–253, pl XXXV.9.

I312 KEY
Lydney Castle, Gloucestershire.
12th century, possibly into 13th century.
Ring bow. L 183mm.
Casey 1931, 252–253, pl XXXV.8.

I313 KEY
South Witham, Lincolnshire.
1137–85 to c1220.
Ring bow, grooved stem, broken bit. Non-ferrous plating. L 133mm.
Goodall 2002, fig 7.2, no. 17.

I314 KEY
Winchester, Hampshire.
13th century.
Ring bow set at right angles to bit. Grooved stem. Non-ferrous plating. L 75mm.
Goodall 1990-21, fig 326.3764.

I315 KEY
Newbury, Berkshire.
c1200–30.
Ring bow. Non-ferrous plating. L 70mm.
Goodall 1997, fig 21, no. 29.

I316 KEY
Winchester, Hampshire.
Mid to ?late 13th century.
Ring bow. Non-ferrous plating. L 69mm.
Goodall 1990-21, fig 326.3761.

I317 KEY
South Witham, Lincolnshire.
c1220 to late 13th century.
Ring bow, broken bit. L 105mm.
Goodall 2002, fig 7.2, no. 20.

I318 KEY
South Witham, Lincolnshire.
c1220 to late 13th century.
Broken ring bow. L 121mm.
Goodall 2002, fig 7.2, no. 18.

I319 KEY
South Witham, Lincolnshire.
c1220 to late 13th century.
Ring bow. L 132mm.
Goodall 2002, fig 7.2, no. 19.

I320 KEY
Wintringham, Cambridgeshire.
Late 13th century.
Ring bow, bit corroded. Non-ferrous plating. L 54mm.
Goodall 1977a, 257, fig 43.22.

I321 KEY
Wintringham, Cambridgeshire.
Late 13th century.
Ring bow, stem and bit broken. Non-ferrous plating. L 71mm.
Goodall 1977a, 257, fig 43.23.

I322 KEY
Winchester, Hampshire.
Mid 13th century.
Ring bow. L 52mm.
Goodall 1990-21, fig 326.3759.

I323 KEY
Winchester, Hampshire.
13th century.
Ring bow, moulded stem, channelled bit. Non-ferrous plating. L 58mm.
Goodall 1990-21, fig 326.3763.

I324 KEY
Winchester, Hampshire.
12th–?13th century.
Ring bow. Grooves on bow and moulded stem. Non-ferrous plating. L 79mm.
Goodall 1990-21, 1026, no. 3757.

I325 KEY
Brandon Castle, Warwickshire.
13th century.
Lozenge-shaped bow. L 112mm.
Chatwin 1955, 83, fig 12.3.

I326 KEY
Writtle, Essex.
13th century.
Ring bow. Non-ferrous plating L 121mm.
Rahtz 1969b, 85, fig 47.49.

I327 KEY
Winchester, Hampshire.
Early to mid 13th century.
Lozenge-shaped bow, moulded and grooved stem. Non-ferrous plating. L 127mm.
Goodall 1990-21, fig 326.3758.

I328 KEY
King's Lynn, Norfolk.
Late 13th and early 14th century.
Ring bow and stem broken. L 97mm.
Goodall and Carter 1977, 293, fig 133.9.

I329 KEY
Burton-in-Lonsdale, North Yorkshire.
Later 13th to mid 14th century.
Ring bow. L 168mm.
Moorhouse 1971a, 93, fig 3.1.

LOCKS AND KEYS

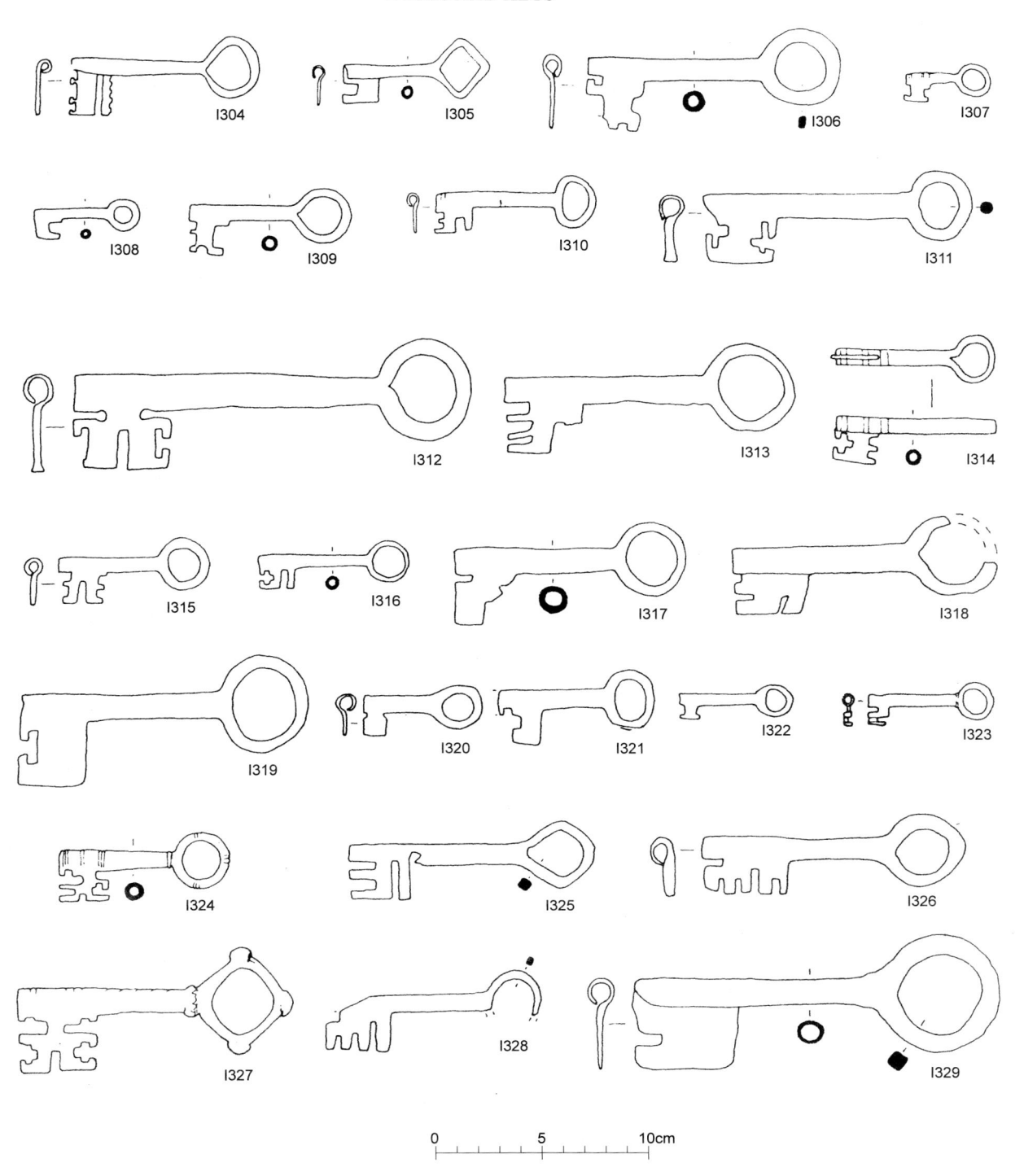

FIGURE 10.20
Keys

I330 KEY
Faringdon Clump, Oxfordshire.
Late 13th to 14th century pottery.
Ring bow. L 94mm.
Leeds 1936; 1937.

I331 KEY
Faringdon Clump, Oxfordshire.
Late 13th to 14th century pottery.
Ring bow. L 111mm.
Leeds 1937, 297, pl LXXXIIa.

I332 KEY
Hadleigh Castle, Essex.
13th–14th century.
Broken lozenge-shaped bow, grooved stem.
Non-ferrous plating. L 79mm.
Goodall 1975c, 138, fig 28.338.

I333 KEY
Winchester, Hampshire.
Mid 13th century.
Circular plate bow, grooved stem.
Non-ferrous plating. L 46mm.
Goodall 1990-21, fig 326.3760.

I334 KEY
Northampton.
Second half 14th century.
Ring bow. Incised grooves on bow and bit.
Non-ferrous plating. L 137mm.
Goodall 1978c, 152, fig 24.1.

I335 KEY
Portchester Castle, Hampshire.
Probably 14th century.
Ring bow. L 79mm.
Hinton 1977, 201, fig 107.48, scale 2:3, not 1:3.

I336 KEY
Winchester, Hampshire.
15th century.
Ring bow, channelled bit. Non-ferrous plating. L 54mm.
Goodall 1990-21, fig 326.3770.

I337 KEY
Woodperry, Oxfordshire.
12th to 14th century pottery.
Oval bow. L 114mm
Ashmolean Museum, Oxford, 1873.72. For site see Wilson 1846.

I338 KEY
Thuxton, Norfolk.
Site: 12th–14th century.
Broken D-shaped bow. L 123mm.
Excavated by L A S Butler.

I339 KEY
King's Lynn, Norfolk.
c1350–1500.
Ring bow. L 118mm.
Goodall and Carter 1977, 293, fig 133.11.

I340 KEY
Wharram Percy, North Yorkshire.
Early 15th century.
Ring bow, broken bit. Non-ferrous plating. L 95mm.
Goodall 1979a, 118, fig 60.4.

LOCKS AND KEYS

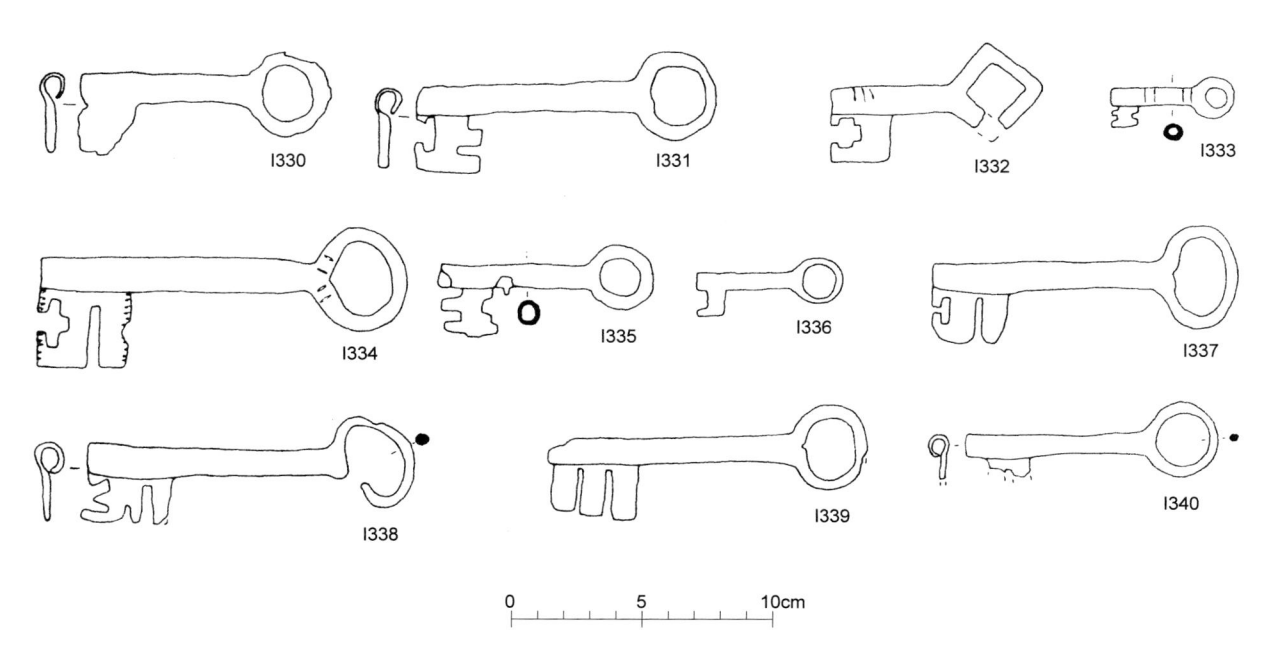

FIGURE 10.21
Keys

I341 KEY
King's Lynn, Norfolk.
15th century onwards.
Ring bow. L 103mm.
Goodall and Carter 1977, 293, fig 133.10.

I342 KEY
Hull, Humberside.
15th century.
D-shaped bow, grooved stem. Non-ferrous plating. L 113mm.
Goodall 1997b, 65, fig 27.74.

I343 KEY
Winchester, Hampshire.
Early to mid 14th century.
Ring bow, moulded and grooved stem, channelled bit. Non-ferrous plating. L 100mm.
Goodall 1990-21, fig 326.3767.

I344 KEY
Holworth, Dorset.
13th–15th century.
Lozenge-shaped bow, damaged bit. L 131mm.
Rahtz 1959, 146, fig 12.15.

I345 KEY
Huish, Wiltshire.
Site: 12th to 15th century.
Ring bow, channelled bit. L 61mm.
Shortt 1972, 116, fig 2.7.

I346 KEY
Grenstein, Norfolk.
Site: 12th to late 14th, 15th century.
Broken ring bow. L 100mm.
Goodall 1980c, fig 80, no. 63.

I347 KEY
Goltho, Lincolnshire.
Croft A: late Saxon to late 14th or early 15th century.
Oval bow. L 102mm.
Goodall 1975a, 84, fig 39.53.

I348 KEY
Goltho, Lincolnshire.
Croft A: late Saxon to late 14th or early 15th century.
Thistle-shaped bow additionally shaped internally and moulded externally. Collar at junction of stem and bit, itself incomplete. L 51mm.
Goodall 1975a, 84, fig 39.56.

I349 KEY
Staines, Surrey.
Medieval, to 15th century.
Oval bow with collar at junction with stem. X-radiography shows stem hollow for full length. L 47mm.
Barker 1976, 124, fig 26.29.

I350 KEY
Wharram Percy, North Yorkshire.
Mid 15th to early 16th century.
Broken ring bow, grooved stem. L 67mm.
Goodall 1979a, 121, fig 64.86.

I351 KEY
Haddlesey, North Yorkshire.
15th to 16th-century destruction level.
Broken oval bow, externally pointed. Non-ferrous plating. L 97mm.
Goodall 1973b, 93, fig 37.12.

I352 KEY
Cambokeels, Durham.
Later 14th to early 16th century.
Ring bow with collar at junction sheet iron bit. Overall copper-alloy brazing. L 61mm.
Hildyard 1949, 199, fig 4.6.

I353 KEY
Weoley Castle, Birmingham, West Midlands.
c1270–1600.
Ring bow, damaged bit. L 101mm.
Birmingham City Museum, WC312. For site see Oswald 1962.

I354 KEY
Weoley Castle, Birmingham, West Midlands.
c1270–1600.
Oval bow. L 86mm.
Taylor 1974. For site see Oswald 1962.

I355 KEY
Weoley Castle, Birmingham, West Midlands.
c1270–1600.
Lozenge-shaped bow. Stem tip broken. L 120mm.
Birmingham City Museum, WC313. For site see Oswald 1962.

I356 KEY (not illustrated)
Winchester, Hampshire.
Mid 10th–early 11th century.
Ring bow. L 107mm.
Goodall 1990-21, 1025, no. 3744.

I357 KEY (not illustrated)
Winchester, Hampshire.
c1110.
Ring bow, grooved stem. Non-ferrous plating. L 40mm.
Goodall 1990-21, fig 326.3753.

I358 KEY (not illustrated)
Lyveden, Northamptonshire.
11th–12th century.
Ring bow, broken bit. L:101mm.
Steane and Bryant 1975, 132, fig 49.159.

I359 KEY (not illustrated)
Winchester, Hampshire.
11th–?12th century.
Broken lozenge-shaped bow, plain bit. L 84mm.
Goodall 1990-21, 1026, no. 3751.

I360 KEY (not illustrated)
Winchester, Hampshire.
c1110.
Ring bow. Non-ferrous plating. L 92mm.
Goodall 1990-21, 1026, no. 3752.

I361 KEY (not illustrated)
Winchester, Hampshire.
Late 13th–early 14th century.
Ring bow, broken bit. L 78mm.
Goodall 1990-21, 1026, no. 3765.

I362 KEY (not illustrated)
Winchester, Hampshire.
Late 13th–early 14th century.
Ring bow. Non-ferrous plating. L 34mm.
Goodall 1990-21, 1026, no. 3766.

I363 KEY (not illustrated)
Winchester, Hampshire.
Late 14th century.
Ring bow, moulded and grooved stem. Non-ferrous plating. L 155mm.
Goodall 1990-21, 1026, no. 3768.

I364 KEY (not illustrated)
Winchester, Hampshire.
Mid to late 13th century.
Ring bow, moulded stem, broken bit. Non-ferrous plating. L 81mm.
Goodall 1990-21, 1026, no. 3762.

I365 KEY (not illustrated)
Winchester, Hampshire.
14th century.
Ring bow. Non-ferrous plating. L 40mm.
Goodall 1990-21, 1026, no. 3769.

I366 KEY
Huish, Wiltshire.
Site: 12th to 15th century.
Ring bow, stem and bit all broken. L 130mm.
Shortt 1972, 116, no. 8.

I367 KEY (not illustrated)
Faxton, Northamptonshire.
Site: 12th to 15th century.
Bow broken. L 100mm.
Excavated by L A S Butler.

I368 KEY
Goltho Manor, Lincolnshire.
c1100–50.
Lozenge-shaped bow. L 87mm.
Goodall 1987, fig 158.116.

I369 KEY
Wintringham, Cambridgeshire.
Mid 13th century.
Ring bow, broken bit. L 116mm.
Goodall 1977a, 257, fig 43.19.

I370 KEY
Wintringham, Cambridgeshire.
Late 13th century.
Ring bow, moulded stem. L 122mm.
Goodall 1977a, 257, fig 43.24.

I371 KEY
Castell-y-Bere, Gwynedd.
Site: c1221–95.
Ring bow. L 123mm.
Butler 1974, 97, fig 9.24.

I372 KEY
Wintringham, Cambridgeshire.
Around early 14th century.
Broken ring bow and bit. Non-ferrous plating. L 83mm.
Goodall 1977a, 257, fig 43.26.

LOCKS AND KEYS

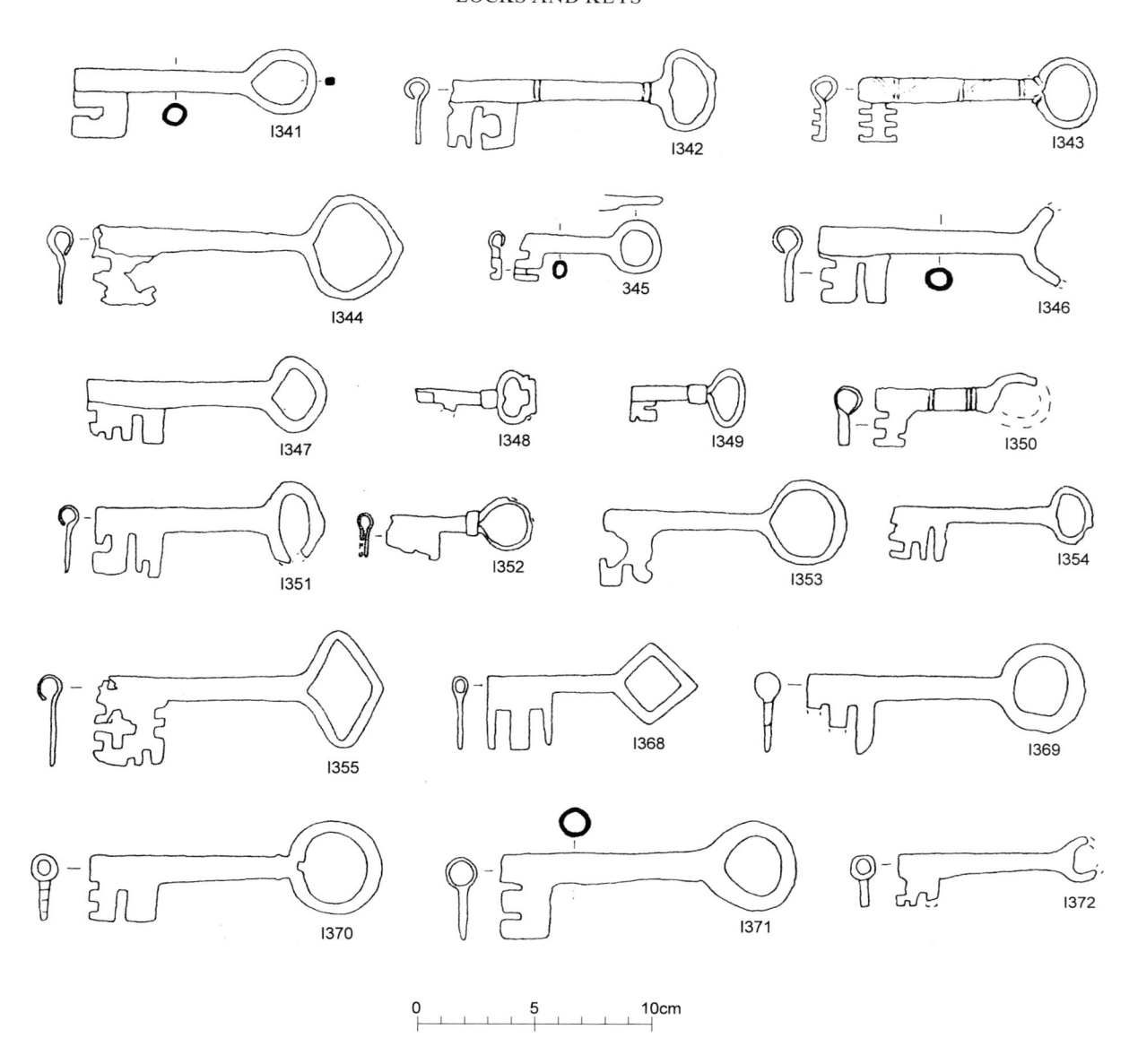

FIGURE 10.22
Keys

I373 KEY (not illustrated)
Winchester, Hampshire.
15th century.
Ring bow, moulded stem with damaged tip.
L 46mm.
Goodall 1990-21, fig 327.3772.

I374 KEY (not illustrated)
Winchester, Hampshire.
Late 13th–?early 14th century.
Bow lost, bit incomplete. Grooved stem.
Non-ferrous plating. L 67mm.
Goodall 1990-21, 1026, no. 3771.

I375 KEY
Alsted, Surrey.
c1250–1405.
Ring bow, channelled bit. L 60mm.
Goodall 1976a, 56, fig 35.30.

I376 KEY
Criccieth Castle, Gwynedd.
Site: c1230–1404.
Broken ring bow and damaged stem tip.
L 116mm.
O'Neil 1944–45, 41, pl IX.5.

I377 KEY
Ospringe, Kent.
c1485–1550.
Oval bow, collar at head of stem. Brazing metal with major constituents tin and copper. L 94mm.
Goodall 1979c, 132, fig 21.72.

I378 KEY
Ospringe, Kent.
Demolition c1550–70 on site founded c1230.
Kidney-shaped bow, collar at head of stem.
Brazing metal with major constituents tin and copper. L 40mm.
Goodall 1979c, 132, fig 21.75.

I379 KEY
Cheddar, Somerset.
?Later 13th century to c1600.
Ring bow. Brazing metal riveted at junction of bit and stem. L 67mm.
Goodall 1979d, 264, fig 90.54.

I380 KEY
Castle Acre Castle, Norfolk.
1140s with derived material. Site founded soon after 1066.
Ring bow, moulded stem, damaged bit.
L 46mm.
Goodall 1982, fig 40, no. 104.

I381 KEY (not illustrated)
Winchester, Hampshire.
Early 12th century.
Ring bow, bit broken. L 58mm.
Goodall 1990-21, 1028, no. 3774.

I382 KEY
Lydney Castle, Gloucestershire.
12th century, possibly into 13th century.
Distorted lozenge-shaped bow retaining one corner boss. L 145mm.
Casey 1931, 252–254, pl XXXV.10.

I383 KEY
Red Castle, Thetford.
Late 11th to early 13th century.
Oval bow, moulded stem, corroded bit.
L 52mm.
Knocker 1966–69, 148, fig 13.5.

I384 KEY
Winchester, Hampshire.
13th century.
Ring bow, moulded and grooved stem. Bit incomplete. L 76mm.
Goodall 1990-21, fig 327.3775.

I385 KEY
Chew Valley Lake, Avon.
13th century or later.
D-shaped bow. L 173mm.
Rahtz and Greenfield 1977, 326, fig 121.5.

I386 KEY
Kirkcudbright Castle, Dumfries and Galloway.
1288–1308.
Oval bow, stem tip and bit broken.
L 100mm.
Dunning et al 1957–58, 138, fig 7.6.

I387 KEY
Hambleton Moat, Lincolnshire.
1250–1400.
Oval bow. L 117.
Butler 1963, 67, fig 14.8.

I388 KEY
Seacourt, Oxfordshire.
Mid to late 12th to before mid to late 14th century.
Broken lozenge-shaped bow, internally rounded. Grooved stem, non-ferrous plating.
L 83mm.
Biddle 1961–62, 181, fig 31.6, scale 1:4, not 1:3.

I389 KEY
Chew Valley Lake, Avon.
13th–14th century.
Oval bow. L 135mm.
Rahtz and Greenfield 1977, 326, fig 121.6.

LOCKS AND KEYS

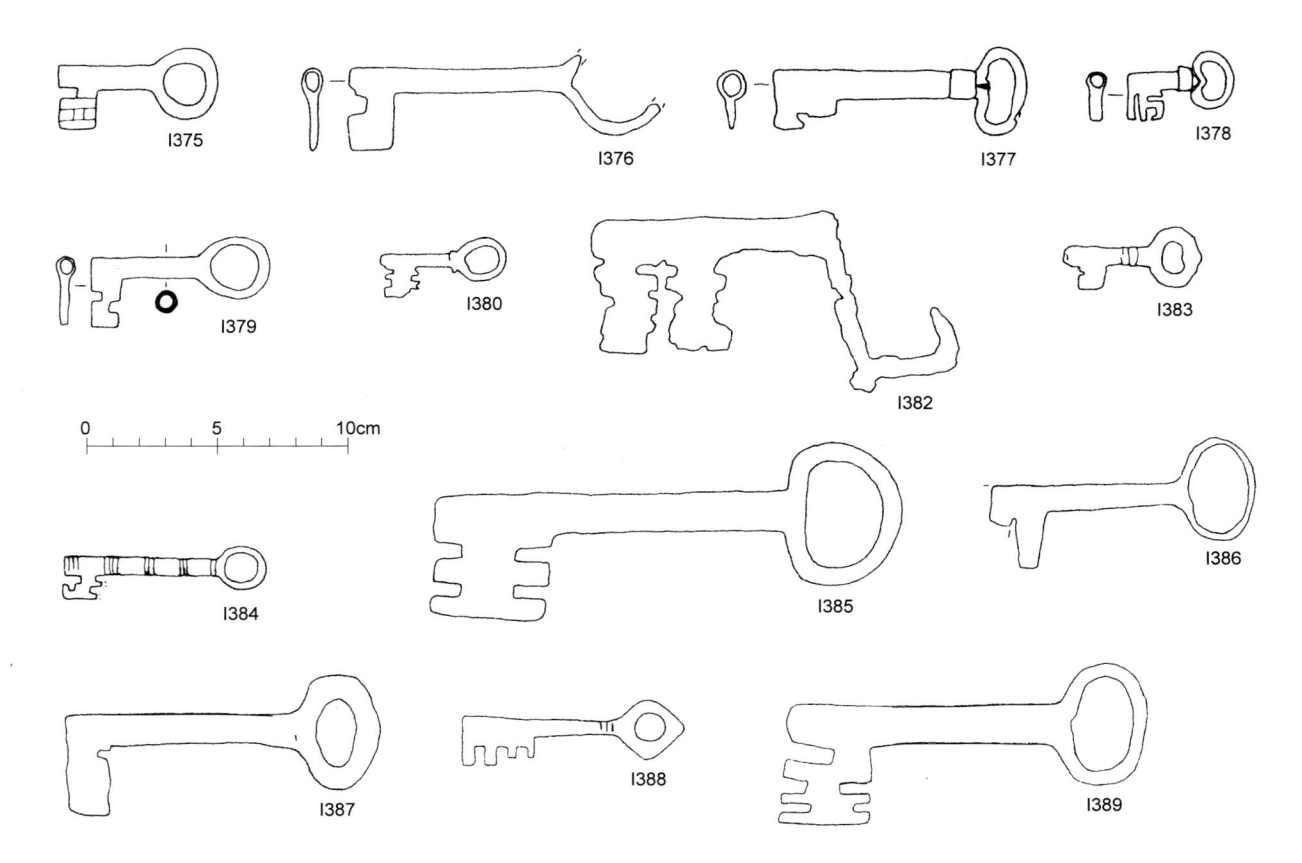

FIGURE 10.23
Keys

I390 KEY
Badby, Northamptonshire.
1198 to mid 14th century.
Ring bow. L 159mm.
Excavated by Mrs M Gray.

I391 KEY
Lyveden, Northamptonshire.
c1350–1450.
Oval bow, corroded bit. L 57mm.
Steane and Bryant 1975, 132, fig 49.158.

I392 KEY (not illustrated)
Winchester, Hampshire.
Late 10th–early 11th century.
Lozenge-shaped bow, internally rounded. Singl top arm to stem and bit both broken. L 75mm.
Goodall 1990-21, 1028, no. 3783.

I393 KEY
Winchester, Hampshire.
c1071–72.
Lozenge-shaped bow with corner bosses. Bit incomplete. L 61mm.
Goodall 1990-21, fig 327.3782.

I394 KEY
Winchester, Hampshire.
12th–early 13th century.
Lozenge-shaped bow, moulded stem, incomplete bit. Non-ferrous plating. L 70mm.
Goodall 1990-21, fig 327.3784.

I395 KEY
Southampton, Hampshire.
Late 13th century.
Broken ring bow, moulded and distorted stem. L 41mm.
Harvey 1975b, 279, fig 252.2022.

I396 KEY (not illustrated)
Winchester, Hampshire.
Mid to late 13th century.
Lozenge-shaped bow, internally rounded. Single top arm to stem, bit lost. Non-ferrous plating. L 71mm.
Goodall 1990-21, 1028, no. 3785.

I397 KEY
Southampton, Hampshire.
1250–1300.
Oval bow. L 65mm.
Harvey 1975b, 279, fig 251.2014.

I398 KEY
Ellington, Cambridgeshire.
Second or third quarter 12th to late 13th century.
Oval bow, moulded and grooved stem. Non-ferrous plating. L 43mm.
Goodall 1971, 68, fig 12.1.

I399 KEY
Lyveden, Northamptonshire.
Second half 13th century.
Oval bow. Copper-alloy plating noted. L 39mm.
Bryant and Steane 1971, 57, fig 1412.

I400 KEY
King's Lynn, Norfolk.
c1250–1300.
Lozenge-shaped bow, moulded stem. L 42mm.
Goodall and Carter 1977, 293, fig 133.8.

I401 KEY (not illustrated)
Winchester, Hampshire.
Mid to late 13th century.
Ring bow, bit broken. L 46mm.
Goodall 1990-21, 1030, no. 3789.

I402 KEY
Wintringham, Cambridgeshire.
Second half 13th century.
Oval bow, stem tip lost. L 125mm.
Goodall 1977a, 257, fig 43.21.

I403 KEY (not illustrated)
Winchester, Hampshire.
14th–?15th century.
Ring bow, moulded and grooved stem. Non-ferrous plating. L 36mm.
Goodall 1990-21, 1030, no. 3792.

I404 KEY
Castell-y-Bere, Gwynedd.
Site: c1221–95.
Thistle-shaped bow with internal shaping. L 55mm.
Butler 1974, 97, fig 9.26.

I405 KEY (not illustrated)
Winchester, Hampshire.
Late 14th century.
Broken ring bow. Moulded and grooved stem. Non-ferrous plating. L 68mm.
Goodall 1990-21, 1030, no. 3791.

I406 KEY
Winchester, Hampshire.
Mid to late 13th century.
Ring bow, moulded stem. Non-ferrous plating. L 76mm.
Goodall 1990-21, 1030, no. 3788.

I407 KEY
Winchester, Hampshire.
Mid 13th century.
Ring bow, moulded and grooved stem. Non-ferrous plating. L 77mm.
Goodall 1990-21, fig 327. 3787.

I408 KEY (not illustrated)
Winchester, Hampshire.
Possibly 13th century.
Ring bow, grooved stem. L 10mm.
Goodall 1990-21, 1030, no. 3804.

I409 KEY (not illustrated)
Winchester, Hampshire.
Late 14th–?15th century.
Ring bow, moulded and grooved stem. Non-ferrous plating. L 101mm.
Goodall 1990-21, 1030, no. 3794.

I410 KEY
Winchester, Hampshire.
Late 13th–early 14th century.
Ring bow, moulded and grooved stem, incomplete bit. Non-ferrous plating. L 103mm.
Goodall 1990-21, 327.3790.

I411 KEY
Gloucester.
13th century.
Ring bow, moulded and grooved stem. Non-ferrous plating. L 104mm.
Hassall and Rhodes 1974, 76, fig 30.5.

I412 KEY
Chingley, Kent.
Second half 13th to mid 14th century.
Ring bow, broken bit. L 46mm.
Goodall 1975d, 60, fig 27.4

I413 KEY
London.
?Late 13h to mid 14th century.
Oval bow. L 57mm.
Henig 1974, 191, fig 39.74.

I414 KEY
Stonar, Kent.
c1275–1385.
D-shaped bow. L 46mm.
Excavated by N Macpherson-Grant.

I415 KEY
Stonar, Kent.
c1275–1385.
Thistle-shaped bow with external shaping. Moulded stem. L 76mm.
Excavated by N Macpherson-Grant.

I416 KEY
Hadleigh Castle, Essex.
13th–14th century.
Ring bow, moulded stem. Non-ferrous plating. L 49mm.
Goodall 1975c, 138, fig 28.337.

I417 KEY
St Catharine's Hill, Winchester, Hampshire.
Second half 14th century.
Lozenge-shaped plate bow, internally rounded. Bit incomplete. L 57mm.
Hawkes et al 1930, 245–246, fig 29.126.

I418 KEY
Wallingstones, Hereford and Worcester.
1300–25 to before 1400.
Thistle-shaped bow with internal and external shaping, moulded stem. L 85mm.
Bridgewater 1970–72, 102, no. 40.

I419 KEY
Winchester, Hampshire.
14th–?15th century.
Lozenge-shaped bow, moulded and grooved stem, broken bit. Non-ferrous plating. L 109mm.
Goodall 1990-21, fig 327.3793.

I420 KEY
Woodperry, Oxfordshire.
12th to 14th centry pottery.
Lozenge-shaped bow, internally rounded. Channelled bit. L 42mm.
Ashmolean Museum, Oxford, 1873.74. For site see Wilson 1846.

I421 KEY
Woodperry, Oxfordshire.
12th to 14th century pottery.
D-shaped bow, corroded bit. L 70mm.
Ashmolean Museum, Oxford, 1873.73. For site see Wilson 1846.

LOCKS AND KEYS

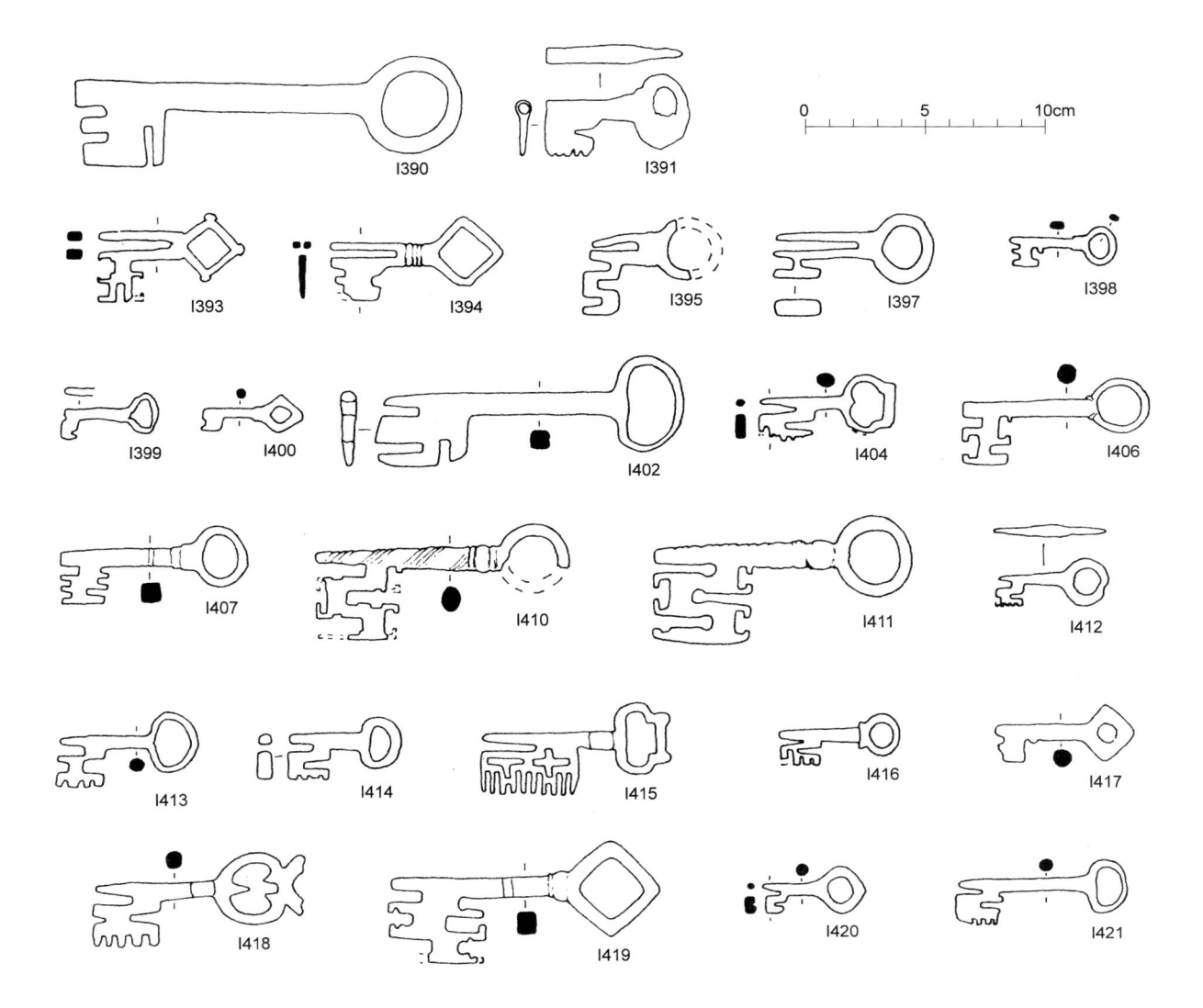

FIGURE 10.24
Keys

I422 KEY
Seacourt, Oxfordshire.
Site: mid to late 12th to late 14th century.
D-shaped bow. L 104mm.
Biddle 1961–62, 182, fig 31.9, scale incorrect.

I423 KEY
Seacourt, Oxfordshire.
Site: mid to late 12th to late 14th century.
D-shaped bow. L 86mm.
Biddle 1961–62, 182, fig 31.8, scale incorrect.

I424 KEY
Seacourt, Oxfordshire.
Site: mid to late 12th to late 14th century.
Oval bow, grooved bit. L 119mm.
Biddle 1961–62, 182, fig 31.10, scale incorrect.

I425 KEY
Criccieth Castle, Gwynedd.
Site: c1230–1404.
Ring bow, corroded bit. L 75mm.
O'Neil 1944–45, 41, pl IX.7.

I426 KEY
Criccieth Castle, Gwynedd.
Site: c1230–1404.
Flattened oval bow, bit corroded. L 99mm.
O'Neil 1944–45, 41, pl IX.6.

I427 KEY
Alsted, Surrey.
c1250–1405.
D-shaped bow. Moulded stem. Non-ferrous plating. L 92mm.
Goodall 1976a, 56, fig 35.29, incorrectly numbered 30 in text.

I428 KEY
Alsted, Surrey.
c1250–1405.
Lozenge-shaped bow, internally rounded. Moulded and grooved stem. Non-ferrous plating. L 96mm.
Goodall 1976a, 56, fig 35.28, incorrectly numbered 29 in text.

I429 KEY
Writtle, Essex.
1306–c1425.
Broken oval bow and bit. L 84mm.
Rahtz 1969b, 87, fig 48.72.

I430 KEY
Princes Risborough, Buckinghamshire.
Late 14th, early 15th century or later.
Oval bow. Non-ferrous plating. L 53mm.
Pavry and Knocker 1953–60, 161, fig 13.2.

I431 KEY
Winchester, Hampshire.
Late14th–early 15th century.
Thistle-shaped bow, moulded stem, incomplete channelled bit. L 40mm.
Goodall 1990-21, fig 327.3795.

I432 KEY
Winchester, Hampshire.
Early to mid 15th century.
Ring bow, moulded and grooved stem. Non-ferrous plating. L 64mm.
Goodall 1990-21, fig 327.3796.

I433 KEY
Huish, Wiltshire.
14th–15th century.
Ring bow, moulded stem. L 95mm.
Shortt 1972, 116, fig 2.5.

I434 KEY
Goltho, Lincolnshire.
Croft A: late Saxon to late 14th or early 15th century.
Ring bow, pointed externally. Moulded stem, broken bit. L 55mm.
Goodall 1975a, 84, fig 39.55.

I435 KEY
Grenstein, Norfolk.
Site: 12th to late 14th, 15th century.
Plate bow, circular, pointed externally. Moulded stem. L 49mm.
Goodall 1980c, fig 80, no. 64.

I436 KEY
Beckery Chapel, Glastonbury, Somerset.
Later 13th–?15th century.
Oval bow, corroded bit. L 41mm.
Rahtz and Hirst 1974, 61, fig 22.12.

I437 KEY
Kiln Combe, Bullock Down, East Sussex.
15th century.
Oval bow, channelled bit. L 50mm.
Excavated by P Drewett.

I438 KEY
Shaftesbury Abbey, Dorset.
?15th century.
Broken oval bow. L 50mm.
Harden 1954, 189, fig 2b.

I439 KEY
Winchester, Hampshire.
Mid 15th century.
Oval bow, moulded stem, grooved and channelled bit. L 98mm.
Goodall 1990-21, fig 327.3797.

I440 KEY
Writtle, Essex.
c1425–1521, mixed with later material.
Broken oval bow, internally kidney-shaped. Bit incomplete. L 79mm.
Rahtz 1969b, 85, fig 47.50.

I441 KEY
Newbury, Berkshire.
c1470–1510.
D-shaped bow, internally kidney-shaped. Non-ferrous plating. L 43mm.
Goodall 1997.

I442 KEY
Winchester, Hampshire.
15th–early 16th century.
Circular plate bow. Non-ferrous plating. L 38mm.
Goodall 1990-21, fig 327.3798.

I443 KEY
Portchester Castle, Hampshire.
c1500–21.
D-shaped bow. L 111mm.
Hinton 1977, 201, fig 107.51, scale 2:3, not 1:3.

I444 KEY
Hull, Humberside.
Early to mid 16th century.
D-shaped bow, externally pointed. L 64mm.
Goodall 1997b, 65, fig 27.85.

I445 KEY
Hull, Humberside.
Mid 16th century.
Thistle-shaped bow, moulded stem. L 73mm.
Goodall 1997b, 65, fig 27.83.

LOCKS AND KEYS

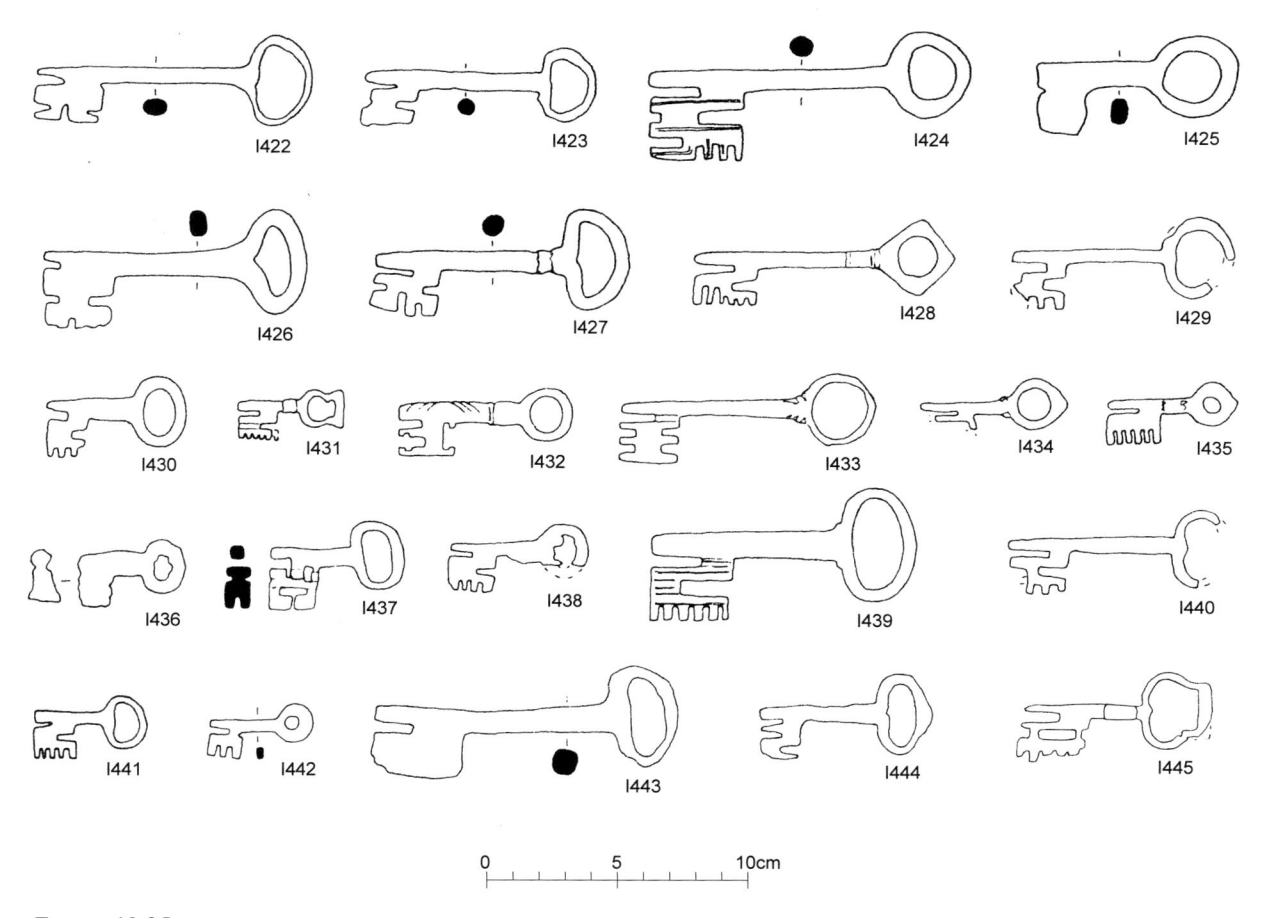

FIGURE 10.25
Keys

I446 KEY
Weoley Castle, Birmingham, West Midlands.
c1080–1600.
D-shaped bow. L 100mm.
Birmingham City Museum, WC315. For site see Oswald 1962.

I447 KEY
Weoley Castle, Birmingham, West Midlands.
c1080–1600.
Broken D-shaped bow, damaged stem and bit. L 119mm.
Birmingham City Museum, WC36. For site see Oswald 1962.

I448 KEY
North Elmham Park, Norfolk.
c1150–c1600.
D-shaped bow, pointed externally.
Non-ferrous plating. L 132mm.
Goodall 1980a, 509, fig 265.4.

I449 KEY
North Elmham Park, Norfolk.
c1150–c1600.
Oval bow. Non-ferrous plating. L 125mm.
Goodall 1980a, 509, fig 265.3.

I450 KEY
Princes Risborough, Buckinghamshire.
Late 13th to 16th century.
Broken D-shaped bow and bit. L 94mm.
Pavry and Knocker 1953–60, 161, fig 13.4.

I451 KEY
Cheddar, Somerset.
Later 13th century to c1600.
Thistle-shaped bow, moulded stem.
L 103mm.
Goodall 1979d, 264, fig 90.62.

I452 KEY
Winchester, Hampshire.
Late 10th to late 11th century.
Ring bow. Non-ferrous plating. L 59mm.
Goodall 1990-21, fig 328.3807.

I453 KEY
Winchester, Hampshire.
c1065–66 to c1110.
Lozenge-shaped bow with corner bosses, internally rounded. Grooved decoration on stem and bit. Non-ferrous plating. L 82mm.
Goodall 1990-21, fig 328.3809.

I454 KEY
Portchester Castle, Hampshire.
11th–12th century.
Ring bow. L 91mm.
Hinton 1977, 201, fig 107.50, scale 2:3, not 1:3.

I455 KEY
Winchester, Hampshire.
c1110.
Lozenge-shaped bow, internally rounded.
Non-ferrous plating. L 96mm.
Goodall 1990-21, fig 328.3810.

I456 KEY
Southampton, Hampshire.
1125–50.
Broken ring bow and stem. L 58mm.
Harvey 1975b, 276, fig 250.1966.

I457 KEY
Llantrithyd, South Glarmorgan.
Early to mid 12th century.
Broken lozenge bow, grooved stem.
Non-ferrous plating. L 35mm.
Goodall 1977f, 46, iron object fig 1.8.

I458 KEY
Llantrithyd, South Glamorgan.
Early to mid 12th century.
Ring bow, bit broken. L 94mm.
Goodall 1977f, 46, iron object fig 1.6.

I459 KEY
Llantrithyd, South Glamorgan.
Early to mid 12th century.
Lozenge bow, grooved stem, broken bit.
Non-ferrous plating. L 96mm.
Goodall 1977f, 46, iron object fig 1.7.

I460 KEY
Winchester, Hampshire.
Late 12th–early 13th century.
Ring bow. L 64mm.
Goodall 1990-21, fig 328.3813.

I461 KEY
Aldingbourne, West Sussex.
12th century.
Lozenge bow. L 154mm.
Brewster and Brewster 1969, 166–169, fig 16.

I462 KEY
Wallingstones, Hereford and Worcester.
Early 13th century.
Broken oval bow. L 138mm.
Bridgewater 1970–72, 100, no. 2.

I463 KEY
Brandon Castle, Warwickshire.
1226–66.
Broken ring bow. L 47mm.
Chatwin 1955, 83, fig 12.2.

I464 KEY
Newbury, Berkshire.
c1230–60.
Lozenge-shaped bow with corner bosses, moulded stem. L 83mm.
Goodall 1997, fig 21, no. 32.

I465 KEY
Winchester, Hampshire.
Late 13th–early 14th century.
Ring bow, moulded and grooved stem.
Non-ferrous plating. L 91mm.
Goodall 1990-21, fig 328.3820.

I466 KEY
Castell-y-Bere, Gwynedd.
Site: c1221–95.
Broken ring bow and bit. L 124mm.
Butler 1974, 97, fig 9.25.

I467 KEY
Oxford.
13th century.
Ring bow, moulded and grooved stem.
Non-ferrous plating. L 67mm.
Excavated by T G Hassall. From Greyfriars.

I468 KEY
Winchester, Hampshire.
Early 13th century.
Ring bow. L 83mm.
Goodall 1990-21, fig 328.3814.

I469 KEY
Winchester, Hampshire.
Mid 13th century.
Broken lozenge-shaped bow with corner bosses. Stem tip broken. Bow and stem moulded and grooved. Non-ferrous plating.
L 75mm.
Goodall 1990-21, fig 328.3817.

I470 KEY
Hangleton, West Sussex.
Late 13th or early 14th century.
Oval bow and bit broken. L 135mm.
Holden 1963, 169, fig 36.11.

I471 KEY
Stonar, Kent.
c1275–1385.
Ring bow, broken bit. L 78mm.
Excavated by N Macpherson-Grant.

I472 KEY
Upton, Gloucestershire.
Late 13th to late 14th century.
Ring bow. L 138mm.
Hilton and Rahtz 1966, 120, fig 13.3.

I473 KEY
Eynsford Castle, Kent.
c1300–1312.
D-shaped bow. L 189mm.
Rigold 1971, 144, fig 10.12.

I474 KEY
Glottenham, East Sussex.
Early 14th century.
Broken ring bow. L 118mm.
Excavated by D Martin.

I475 KEY
Winchester, Hampshire.
16th–18th century.
Incomplete lozenge-shaped bow with corner bosses, moulded and grooved stem.
Non-ferrous plating. L 81mm.
Goodall 1990-21, fig 328.3825.

LOCKS AND KEYS

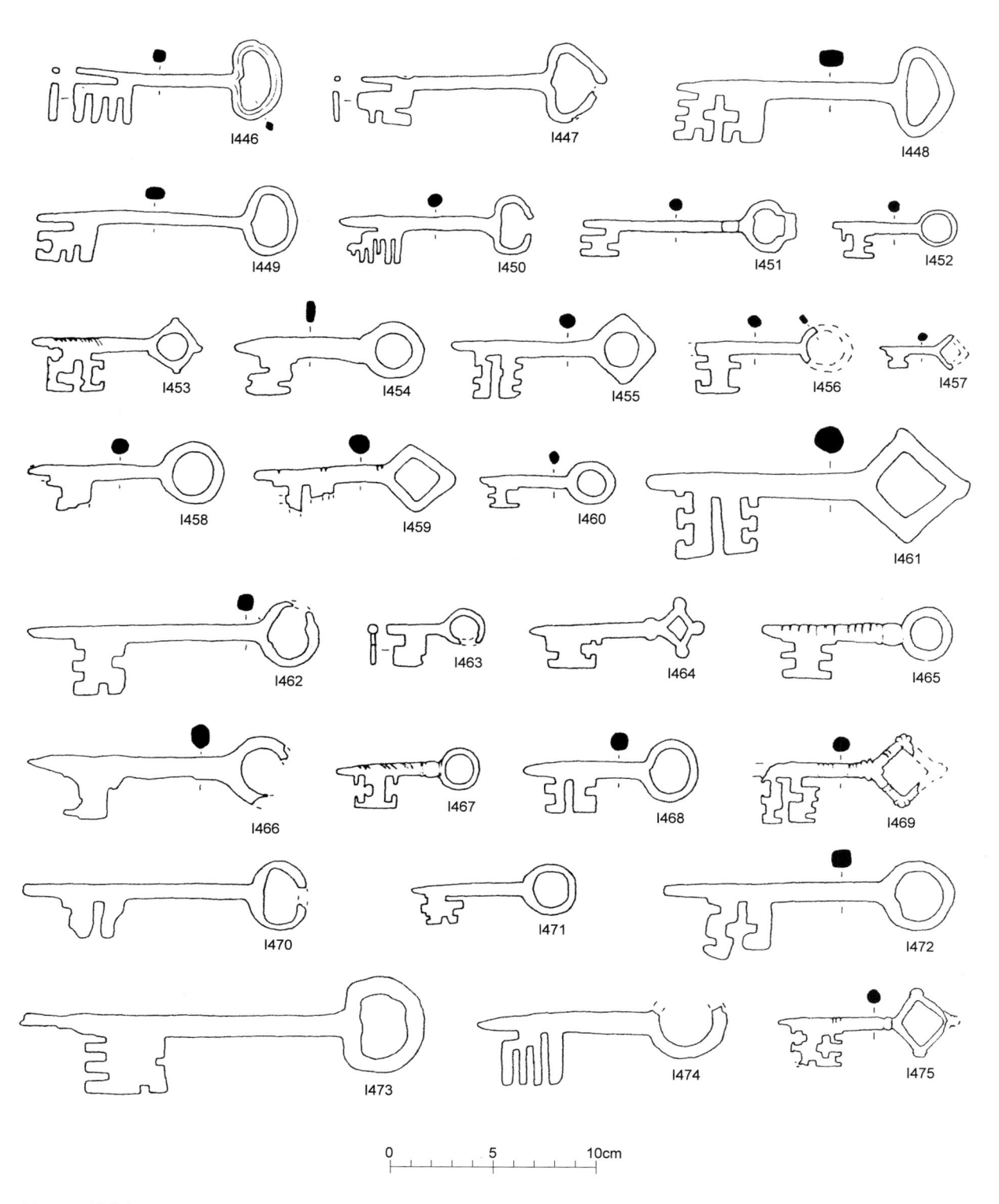

FIGURE 10.26
Keys

I476 KEY
Bramber Castle, West Sussex.
?14th century.
Ring bow. L 96mm.
Barton and Holden 1977, 66, fig 20.8.

I477 KEY
Bramber Castle, West Sussex.
?14th century.
Ring bow, incomplete bit. L 130mm.
Barton and Holden 1977, 66, fig 20.9.

I478 KEY
Brooklands, Weybridge, Surrey.
c1150–1325.
Ring bow, moulded stem, broken bit.
Copper-alloy deposit on stem perhaps the remains of plating. L 129mm.
Goodall 1977d, 73, fig 45.23.

I479 KEY
Seacourt, Oxfordshire.
Site: mid to late 12th to late 14th century.
Ring bow, corroded bit. L 53mm.
Biddle 1961–62, 181, fig 31.7, scale incorrect.

I480 KEY
Woodperry, Oxfordshire.
12th to 14th century pottery.
Ring bow. L 145mm.
Ashmolean Museum, Oxford, 1873.68. For site see Wilson 1846.

I481 KEY
Kettleby Thorpe, Lincolnshire.
14th to early 15th century.
Lozenge-shaped bow. L 49mm.
Goodall 1974a, 33, fig 18.5.

I482 KEY
Winchester, Hampshire.
Early to ?mid 15th century.
Ring bow, moulded and grooved stem.
Non-ferrous plating. L 103mm.
Goodall 1990-21, fig 328.3823.

I483 KEY
Beckery Chapel, Glastonbury, Somerset.
Later 13th–?15th century.
Ring bow, corroded bit. L 42mm.
Rahtz and Hirst 1974, 61, fig 22.13.

I484 KEY
York.
13th–15th century.
Broken ring bow. Moulded stem, tip broken.
L 135mm.
Richardson 1959, 100, fig 28.2.

I485 KEY
Writtle, Essex.
c1425–1521 mixed with later levels.
Broken ring bow and bit. L 172mm.
Rahtz 1969b, 85, fig 47.53.

I486 KEY
Winchester, Hampshire.
16th century.
Ring bow, moulded and grooved stem, broken bit. Non-ferrous plating. L 122mm.
Goodall 1990-21, fig 328.3824.

LOCKS AND KEYS

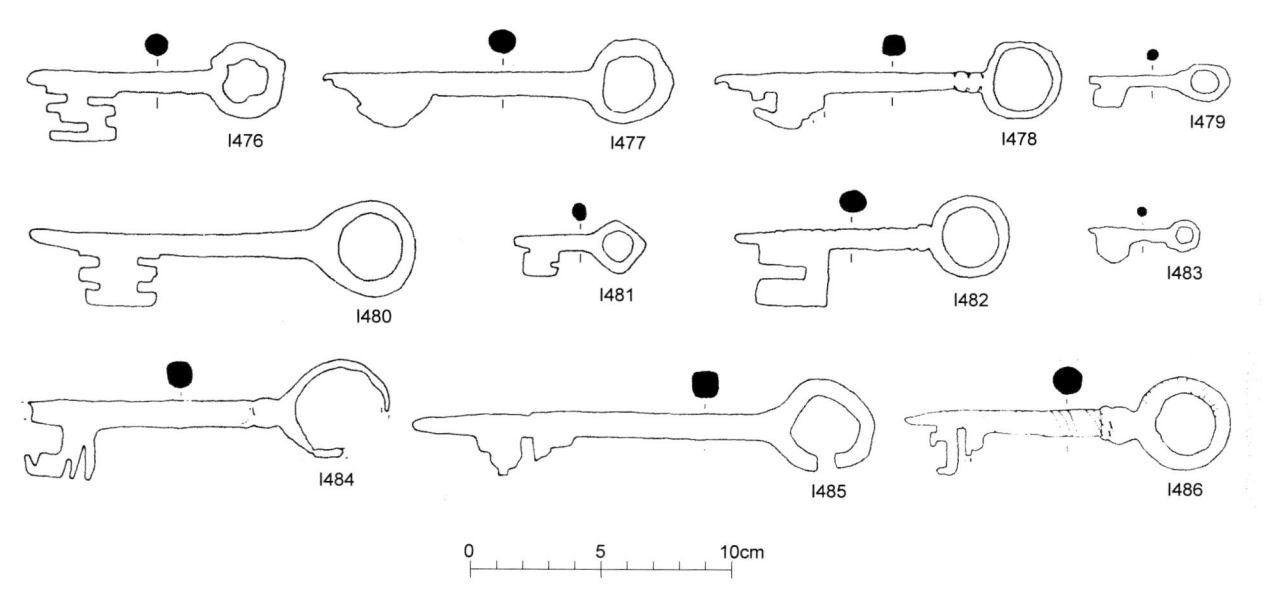

FIGURE 10.27
Keys

I487 KEY (not illustrated)
Winchester, Hampshire.
Late 11th–12th century.
Lozenge-shaped bow. Non-ferrous plating.
L 72mm.
Goodall 1990-21, 1032, no. 3812.

I488 KEY (not illustrated)
Winchester, Hampshire.
Early 12th century.
Lozenge-shaped bow with moulded corner bosses. Bit broken. L 115mm.
Goodall 1990-21, 1032, no. 3811.

I489 KEY (not illustrated)
Winchester, Hampshire.
Late 12th–mid 13th century.
Broken ring bow. Grooved stem. Non-ferrous plating. L 85mm.
Goodall 1990-21, 1032, no. 3815.

I490 KEY (not illustrated)
Winchester, Hampshire.
?Mid 13th century.
Ring bow. Channelled bit. L 29mm.
Goodall 1990-21, 1032, no. 3816.

I491 KEY (not illustrated)
Winchester, Hampshire.
13th century.
Lozenge-shaped bow, internally rounded.
L 67mm.
Goodall 1990-21, 1032, no. 3819.

I492 KEY (not illustrated)
Winchester, Hampshire.
14–?15th th century.
Lozenge-shaped bow, internally rounded. Moulded stem. L 70mm.
Goodall 1990-21, 1032, no. 3822.

I493 KEY (not illustrated)
Winchester, Hampshire.
Late 14th century.
Ring bow, moulded stem and bit broken. Grooved bow and stem. Non-ferrous plating.
L 101mm.
Goodall 1990-21, 1032, no. 3821.

I494 KEY
Durham.
Later 11th to mid 12th century.
Lozenge-shaped plate bow with circular hole. L 74mm.
Carver 1979, 18, fig 13.79/1581.

I495 KEY
Ascot Doilly, Oxfordshire.
12th century.
Ring bow, broken bit. Silver inlaid grooves.
L 92mm.
Jope and Threlfall 1959, 265, fig 20.1.

I496 KEY
Wintringham, Cambridgeshire.
Around mid 13th century.
Broken ring bow and bit. Non-ferrous plating. L 122mm.
Goodall 1977a, 257, fig 43.20.

I497 KEY
Winchester, Hampshire.
13th–14th century.
Ring bow, moulded stem. Non-ferrous plating. L 137mm.
Goodall 1990-21, fig 329.3830.

I498 KEY
South Witham, Lincolnshire.
c1220 to 1308–13.
Ring bow. L 165mm.
Goodall 2002, fig 7.2, no. 21.

I499 KEY
Netherton, Hampshire.
Late 13th–14th century.
Ring bow. L 49mm.
Goodall 1990-28, fig 9.7 no. 397.

I500 KEY
Woodperry, Oxfordshire.
12th to 14th century pottery.
Ring bow, broken bit. L 145mm.
Ashmolean Museum, Oxford, 1873.67. For site see Wilson 1846.

I501 KEY
Durrington, West Sussex.
12th–14th century.
Oval bow. Precise shape of bit uncertain.
L 188mm.
Barton 1964, 32, fig 1.7.

I502 KEY
Alvechurch, Hereford and Worcester.
c1350–1400.
D-shaped bow, damaged stem, broken bit.
L 135mm.
Oswald 1954, 8, pl 5.5.

I503 KEY
Southampton, Hampshire.
1350–1400.
D-shaped bow, internally kidney-shaped.
L 135mm.
Harvey 1975b, 287, fig 256.2085.

I504 KEY
Northolt Manor, Greater London.
1350–70.
Broken D-shaped bow and bit. Non-ferrous plating. L 161mm.
Excavated by J G Hurst.

I505 KEY
Bodiam Castle, East Sussex.
1390 bridge construction.
Oval bow, corroded bit, broken stem tip.
L 164mm.
Excavated by D Martin.

I506 KEY
Writtle, Essex.
1306–c1425.
Broken ?ring bow. L 121mm.
Rahtz 1969b, 87, fig 48.73.

I507 KEY
Baginton Castle, Warwickshire.
Site: probably 14th–15th century.
D-shaped bow, externally pointed.
L 139mm.
Herbert Art Gallery and Museum, Coventry.

I508 KEY
Hereford.
Early 15th century.
Oval bow, broken bit. L 128mm.
Shoesmith 1970–72, 233, fig 5.4.

I509 KEY
Lyveden, Northamptonshire.
1475–1500.
D-shaped bow. L 128mm.
Steane and Bryant 1975, 132, fig 49.156.

I510 KEY
Northampton.
Later 15th century.
D-shaped bow, externally pointed. Non-ferrous plating. L 136mm.
Goodall et al 1979, 268, fig 116.13.

I511 KEY
Hull, Humberside.
15th century.
D-shaped bow, broken bit. Non-ferrous plating. L 120mm.
Goodall 1997b, 65, fig 27.73.

I512 KEY
Hawkesley Moat, West Midlands.
15th century.
D-shaped bow, broken bit. L 137mm.
Oswald 1958, 47. Birmingham City Museum.

I513 KEY
York.
13th–15th century.
Ring bow, moulded and grooved stem, broken bit. L 157mm.
Richardson 1959, 100, fig 28.1.

I514 KEY
Huish, Wiltshire.
Site: 12th to 15th century.
Oval bow, grooved stem. L 179mm.
Shortt 1972, 116, fig 2.4.

I515 KEY
Writtle, Essex.
c1425–1521 mixed with later levels.
Oval bow. Non-ferrous plating. L 142mm.
Rahtz 1969b, 85, fig 47.52.

I516 KEY
Wharram Percy, North Yorkshire.
Late 15th to early 16th century.
Rounded plate bow with circular hole.
L 93mm.
Goodall 1979a, 118, fig 60.5.

LOCKS AND KEYS

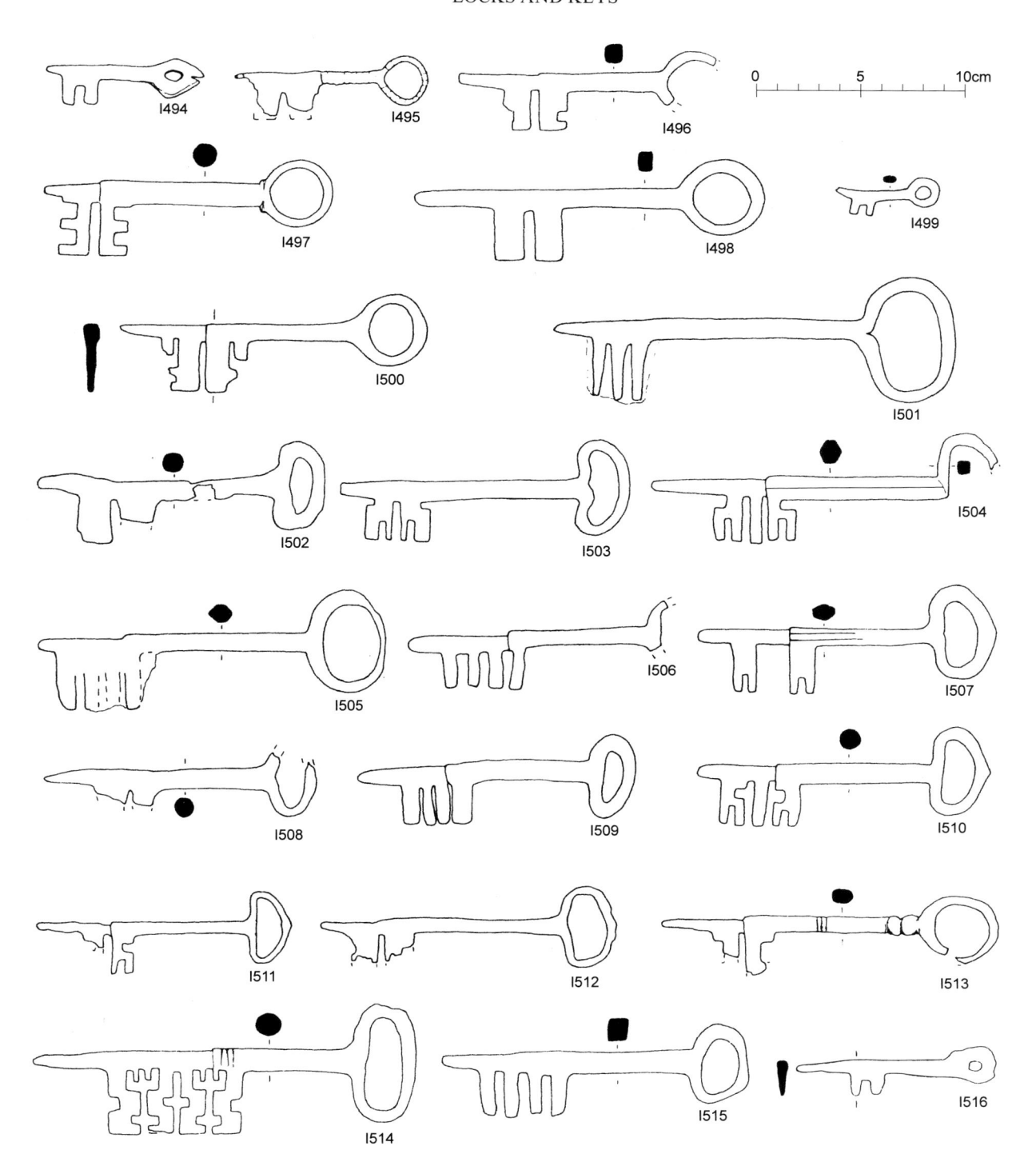

FIGURE 10.28
Keys

I517 KEY
Waltham Abbey, Essex.
From silt of well dug in late 13th, early 14th century and filled in late 15th, early 16th century.
D-shaped bow, incomplete bit, knobbed stem tip. L 140mm.
Goodall 1973a, 171, fig 11.31.

I518 KEY
London.
Late 15th to early 16th century.
D-shaped bow, damaged bit. L 154mm.
Excavated by F C Willmot. Site at 66 Foyle Road.

I519 KEY
St Neots Priory, Cambridgeshire.
Probably 15th, early 16th century.
D-shaped bow, corroded bit. L 116mm.
Tebbutt 1966, 51, fig 4a, scale 1:2, not 1:4.

I520 KEY
Thelsford Priory, Warwickshire.
c1400–1536.
D-shaped bow, grooved stem. L 140mm.
Excavated by Mrs M Gray.

I521 KEY
Ospringe, Kent.
c1483–1550.
Oval bow, damaged bit. L 148mm.
Goodall 1979c, 132, fig 21.71.

I522 KEY
Rest Park, North Yorkshire.
15th to 16th-century destruction levels.
Damaged D-shaped bow, externally pointed. L 166mm.
Goodall 1973b, 93, fig 37.13.

I523 KEY
Hadleigh Castle, Essex.
Probably late in occupation from 1230 to mid 16th century.
Oval bow, corroded bit. L 173mm.
King 1869, 77; Drewett 1975, 96–97.

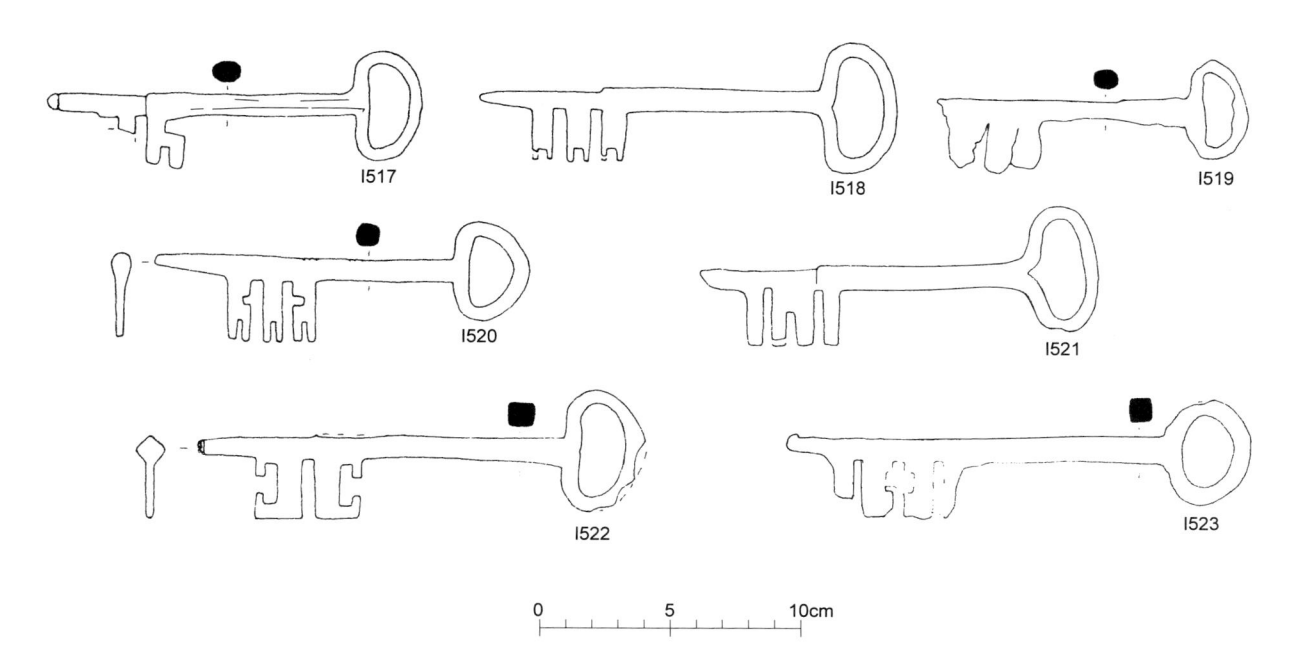

FIGURE 10.29
Keys

1524 KEY
Portchester Castle, Hampshire.
c1500–21.
Distorted bow, broken bit. L 130mm.
Hinton 1977, 204, fig 109.63.

1525 KEY
Waltham Abbey, Essex.
Probably early 16th century.
D-shaped bow, broken bit. L 155mm.
Goodall 1978d, 157, fig 21.1.

1526 KEY
Thelsford Priory, Warwickshire.
Destruction layers of c1536.
Oval bow. L 136mm.
Excavated by Mrs M Gray.

1527 KEY
West Hartburn, Durham.
Probably last occupation of 13th- to 16th-century house.
D-shaped bow, stem tip broken. L 140mm.
Still and Pallister 1964, 197, 200, fig 5.56.

1528 KEY
Abingdon, Oxfordshire.
16th century.
D-shaped bow, internally kidney-shaped.
L 162mm.
Parrington 1976, 77, fig 55.2.

1529 KEY
Winchester, Hampshire.
?Early 14th century.
Broken bow. Non-ferrous plating. L 86mm.
Goodall 1990-21, fig 329.3829.

1530 KEY
Cambokeels, Durham.
Later 14th to early 16th century.
Oval bit, damaged bit. L 126mm.
Hildyard 1949, 199, fig 4.5.

1531 KEY
Weoley Castle, Birmingham, West Midlands.
c1270–1600.
D-shaped bow, incomplete bit. L 142mm.
Taylor 1974. For site see Oswald 1962.

1532 KEY
Weoley Castle, Birmingham, West Midlands.
c1270–1600.
Oval bow, grooved stem. Traces of white metal plating. L 156mm.
Birmingham City Museum, WC319. For site see Oswald 1962.

1533 KEY
North Elmham Park, Norfolk.
c1150–c1600.
D-shaped bow. L 131mm.
Goodall 1980a, 509, fig 265.6.

1534 KEY
North Elmham Park, Norfolk.
c1150–c1600.
D-shaped bow, broken bit. L 121mm.
Goodall 1980a, 509, fig 265.5.

1535 KEY
North Elmham Park, Norfolk.
c1150–c1600.
D-shaped bow. L 189mm.
Goodall 1980a, 509, fig 265.7.

1536 KEY
Winchester, Hampshire.
12th century.
Ring bow, moulded stem, grooves on bit.
Non-ferrous plating. L 155m.
Goodall 1990-21, fig 329.3826.

1537 KEY
Churchill, Oxfordshire.
Late 12th–13th century.
D-shaped bow, corroded bit. L 155mm.
Hinton 1968, 66, fig 18.3.

1538 KEY
Wintringham, Cambridgeshire.
Late 13th century.
D-shaped bow, moulded stem with tip missing. Non-ferrous plating. L 105mm.
Goodall 1977a, 257, fig 43.25.

1539 KEY
Winchester, Hampshire.
?15th century.
D-shaped bow. Bit broken. L 166mm.
Goodall 1990-21, fig 329.3831.

1540 KEY
Beckery Chapel, Glastonbury, Somerset.
Saxon and/or early medieval to later 13th century.
Oval bow. L 173mm.
Rahtz and Hirst 1974, 61, fig 22.9.

1541 KEY
Upton, Gloucestershire.
Late 13th to late 14th century.
D-shaped bow. Non-ferrous plating.
L 131mm.
Hilton and Rahtz 1966, 120, fig 13.4.

1542 KEY
Ayton Castle, North Yorkshire.
13th–14th century.
D-shaped bow. L 106mm.
Rimington and Rutter 1967, 60, fig 13.37/26.

1543 KEY
Eynsford Castle, Kent.
c1300–1312.
Broken oval bow. L 131mm.
Rigold 1971, 144, fig 10.11.

1544 KEY
Seacourt, Oxfordshire.
Early 14th century.
Oval bow. L 132mm.
Biddle 1961–62, 182, fig 31.11, scale 1:4, not 1:3.

1545 KEY
Southampton, Hampshire.
1350–1400.
D-shaped bow. Non-ferrous plating.
L 117mm.
Harvey 1975b, 287, fig 256.2086.

1546 KEY
Seacourt, Oxfordshire.
Site: mid to late 12th to late 14th century.
D-shaped bow. L 130mm.
Biddle 1961–62, 182, fig 31.12, scale 1:4, not 1:3.

1547 KEY
Alsted, Surrey.
c1250–1405, and probably c1395–1405.
Broken ring bow. L 136mm.
Goodall 1976a, 56, fig 35.27, incorrectly numbered 28 in text.

1548 KEY
Baginton Castle, Warwickshire.
Site: probably 14th–15th century.
D-shaped bow. L 129mm.
Herbert Art Gallery and Museum, Coventry.

1549 KEY
Winchester, Hampshire.
Late 15th–early 16th century.
Kidney-shaped bow. Non-ferrous plating.
L 126mm.
Goodall 1990-21, fig 329.3832.

1550 KEY
Baginton Castle, Warwickshire.
Site: probably 14th–15th century.
D-shaped bow, externally pointed.
L 151mm.
Herbert Art Gallery and Museum, Coventry.

1551 KEY
Huish, Wiltshire.
Site: 12th–15th century.
D-shaped bow. L 152mm.
Shortt 1972, 116, fig 2.6.

1552 KEY
Beckery Chapel, Glastonbury, Somerset.
Saxon and/or early medieval to ?15th century.
Oval bow, broken bit. L 132mm.
Rahtz and Hirst 1974, 61, fig 22.10.

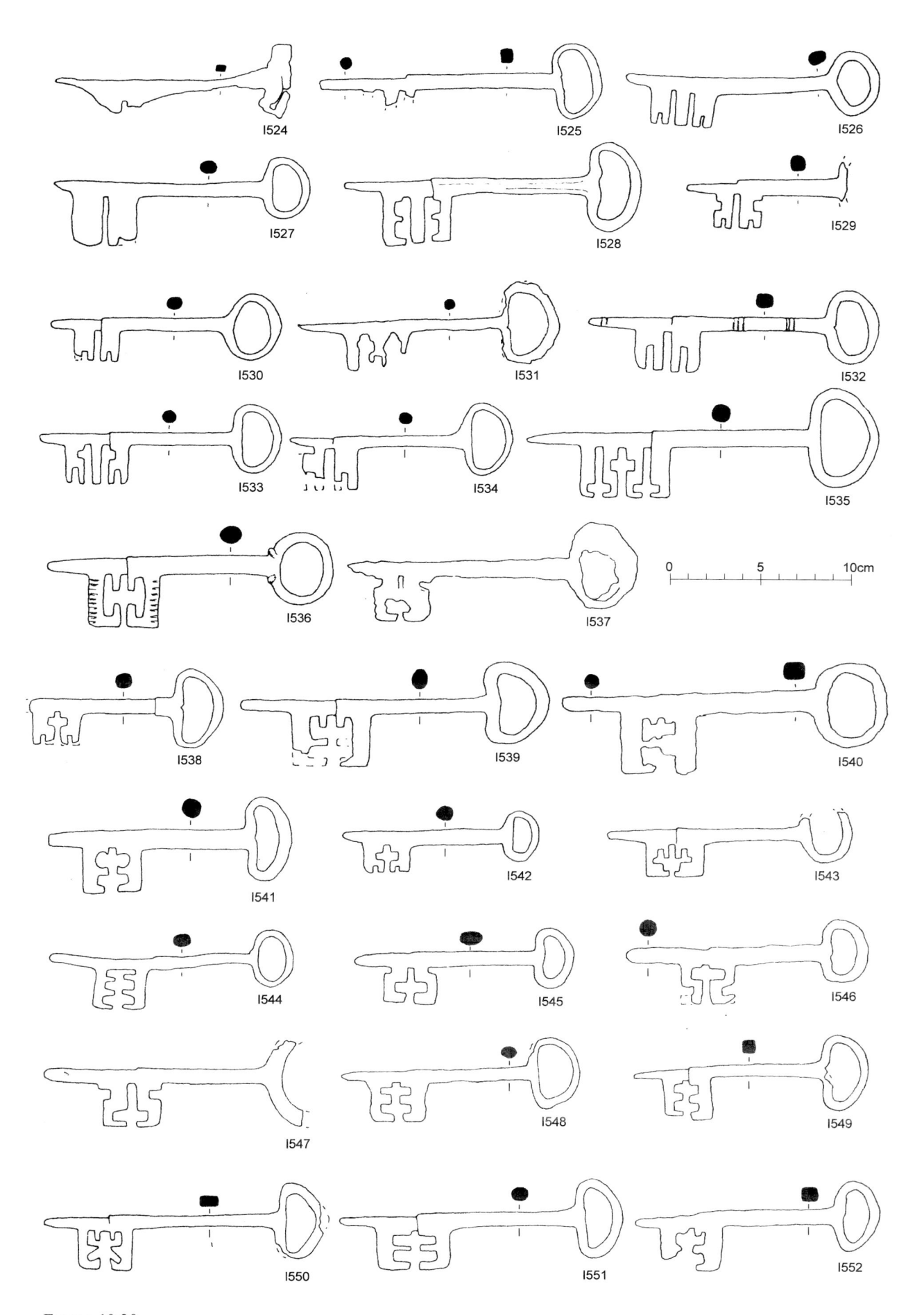

FIGURE 10.30
Keys

I553 KEY
Beckery Chapel, Glastonbury, Somerset.
Later 13th to ?15th century.
Pointed D-shaped bow, possibly with internal mouldings. L 124mm.
Rahtz and Hirst 1974, 61, fig 22.11.

I554 KEY
London.
Late 15th to early 16th century.
Kidney-shaped bow, broken stem tip.
L 134mm.
Excavated by F C Willmot. Site at 66 Foyle Road.

I555 KEY
Thelsford Priory, Warwickshire.
c1400–1536.
Oval bow, externally pointed. L 130mm.
Excavated by Mrs M Gray.

I556 KEY
Winchester, Hampshire.
16th century.
Oval bow set at right angles to bit.
L 137mm.
Goodall 1990-21, fig 329.3837.

I557 KEY
Winchester, Hampshire.
16th–17th century.
D-shaped bow. Non-ferrous plating.
L 136mm.
Goodall 1990-21, fig 329.3838.

I558 KEY
Ospringe, Kent.
Demolition c1550–70 on site founded c1230.
Kidney-shaped bow. Copper base plating.
L 128mm.
Goodall 1979c, 132, fig 21.74.

I559 KEY
Ospringe, Kent.
Demolition c1550–70 on site founded c1230.
Oval bow, broken bit. L 155mm.
Goodall 1979c, 132, fig 21.73.

I560 KEY
Weoley Castle, Birmingham, West Midlands.
c1270–1600.
Oval bow. L 254mm.
Taylor 1974. For site see Oswald 1962.

I561 KEY (not illustrated)
Winchester, Hampshire.
Late 13th–?early 14th century.
Broken ring bow. Moulded stem, tip lost.
Non-ferrous plating. L 125mm.
Goodall 1990-21, 1032, no. 3828.

I562 KEY (not illustrated)
Woodperry, Oxfordshire.
12th to 14th century pottery.
Ring bow. L 172mm.
Ashmolean Museum, Oxford, 1873.65 For site see Wilson 1846.

I563–566 KEYS (not illustrated)
Woodperry, Oxfordshire.
12th to 14th century pottery.
Oval bowl. L 133, 133, 147 and 169mm.
Ashmolean Museum, Oxford, 1873.70, 71, 66 and 64.

I567 KEY (not illustrated)
Northolt Manor, Greater London.
15th century.
Bow and stem broken. L 85mm.
Excavated by J G Hurst.

I568–573 KEYS
Clarendon Palace, Wiltshire.
Site: c1072 to later 15th century.
5 keys with D-shaped bows, one oval.
Second largest key has grooved stem. L 121, 136, 147, 153, 157 and 136mm.
Goodall 1988, fig 78.70–75.

I574 KEY (not illustrated)
Winchester, Hampshire.
16th century.
Broken kidney-shaped bow. L 116mm.
Goodall 1990-21, 1033, no. 3834.

I575 KEY (not illustrated)
Winchester, Hampshire.
16th century.
D-shaped bow, internally kidney-shaped.
Knobbed tip to stem. L 133mm.
Goodall 1990-21, 1033, no. 3835.

I576 KEY (not illustrated)
Haddlesey, North Yorkshire.
15th–16th century.
Bow broken, stem and bit damaged.
Goodall 1973b, 93, fig 37.14.

I577 KEY (not illustrated)
Winchester, Hampshire.
Early 16th century.
Broken oval bow, internally kidney-shaped.
L 112mm.
Goodall 1990-21, 1033, no. 3833.

I578 KEY (not illustrated)
Winchester, Hampshire.
Late 15th–early 16th century
Pointed D-shaped bow, stem tip and base of bit broken. L 62mm.
Goodall 1990-21, 1035, no. 3853.

I579 KEY
Winchester, Hampshire.
Mid to late 13th century.
Hooked terminal, spirally twisted stem, broken bit. L 46mm.
Goodall 1990-21, fig 330.3857.

I580 KEY
Winchester, Hampshire.
Mid to late 13th century.
Hooked terminal, spirally twisted stem, broken bit. L 49mm.
Goodall 1990-21, fig 330.3858.

I581 KEY
Goltho, Lincolnshire.
Late 14th to early 15th century.
Plain stem with hooked terminal and spatulate bit. L 78mm.
Goodall 1975a, 83, fig 39.48.

I582 KEY
Goltho, Lincolnshire.
Croft A: late Saxon to late 14th or early 15th century.
Plain shank with wavy, hooked terminal and spatulate bit. L 118mm.
Goodall 1975a, 83, fig 39.47.

I583 KEY
Bedford.
Late medieval.
Oval bow, internally kidney-shaped
L 67mm.
Baker et al 1979, 281, fig 176.1425.

I584 KEY
Thelsford Priory, Warwickshire.
16th century, before 1536.
Broken ring bow, bit damaged and incomplete. L 63mm.
Excavated by Mrs M Gray.

I585 KEY
Waltham Abbey, Essex.
?16th century.
Oval bow, internally kidney-shaped. Bit broken. L 78mm.
Goodall 1978d, 157, fig 21.2.

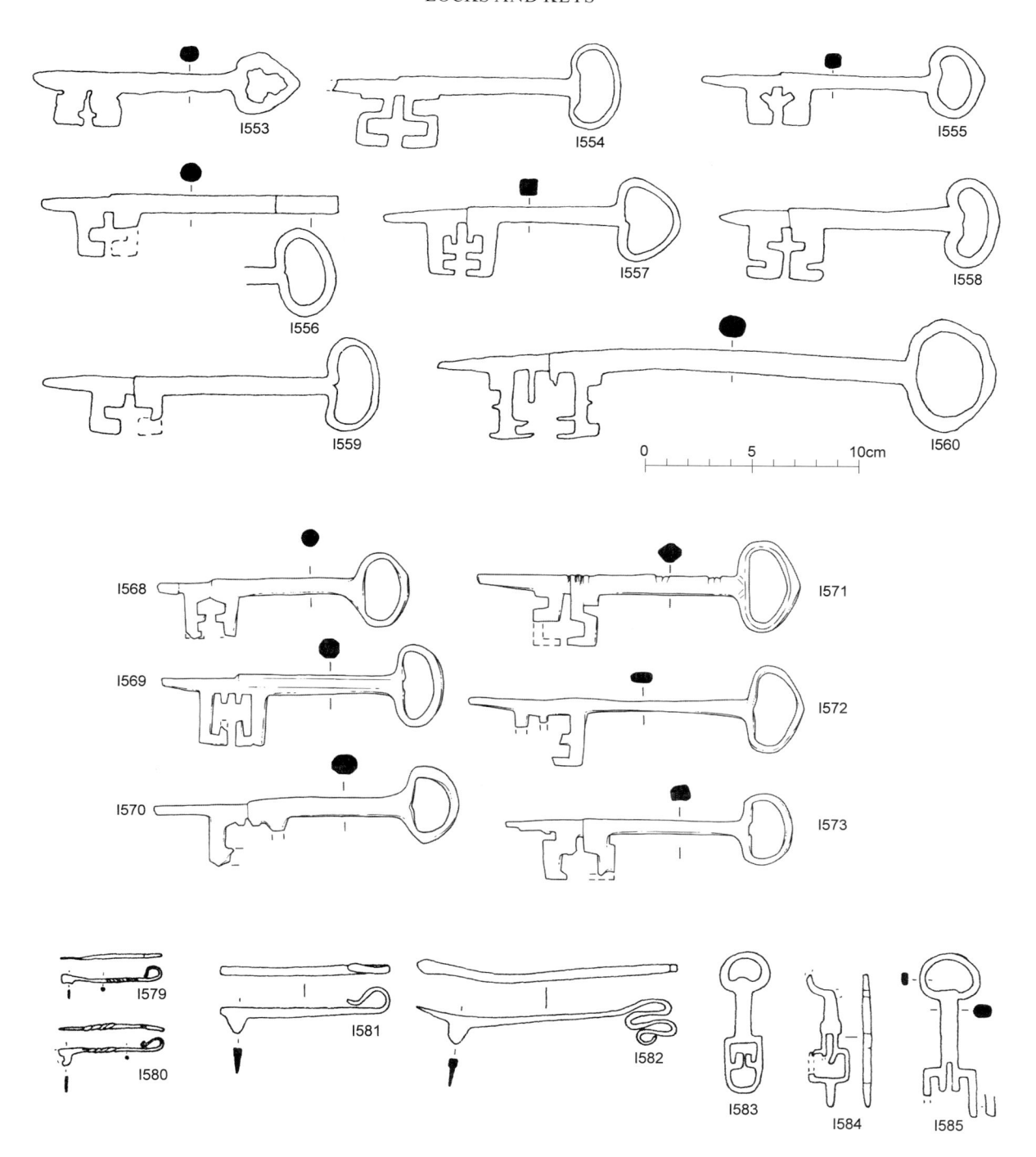

FIGURE 10.31
Keys

11
HOUSEHOLD IRONWORK

Iron had many uses in the day-to-day running of households, particularly those connected with fires and cooking. It was also used for candlesticks and other fittings including buckets, hooks, balances and chains.

11.1 THE HEARTH

Medieval great halls were frequently heated by a central hearth, although this was gradually superseded by the wall fireplace, already known in storeyed buildings in the 11th century (Wood 1965, 257, 261). It remained in universal use in the medieval peasant house, however, in which it comprised either a fire lit directly on the floor or a hearth with a stone or tile base (Beresford and Hurst 1971, 98). Iron fittings associated with fires include fire-dogs, fire-forks and pokers.

Fire-dogs

The fire-dog was probably mainly used in the halls and kitchens of manor houses, castles and monasteries where it supported burning logs on the fire and assisted the flow of air to them. Post-medieval fire-dogs (Lindsay 1964, 7–9, figs 2–16) are of two types with two uprights joined by a horizontal bar or a single upright and an L-shaped bar. **J1**, found in the drain adjacent to the kitchen at Bayham Abbey, East Sussex, is the upright from a fire-dog with two legs, a scrolled top and a hole for a horizontal bar. It is impossible to tell whether it was used alone or was coupled to another upright.

Fire implements

Tongs, fire-forks, pokers and shovels are likely to have been used to maintain and clear away fires. **J2** is a fire-fork, originally mounted on a wooden handle and used to manipulate logs of wood at a distance from the heat of the fire. **A93** is a similarly socketed poker from the same site, although it came from the smithy hearth. **J3** may be a domestic poker. It is entirely of iron and has a suspension hook and ring.

11.2 THE KITCHEN

Representations of cooking and food preparation often include pot-cranes, cauldrons and other vessels, flesh-hooks, ladles and cleavers, and many of these were of iron, although bronze was used for vessels such as skillets, colanders and skimmers. Not all of these classes are as yet represented by objects, gridirons and baker's peels, for example, are as yet absent.

Pot-cranes

Cauldrons are occasionally shown slung from a bar placed across a fire, as in the Bayeux Tapestry (Stenton 1957, 171, pl 48), but they more usually appear suspended from pot-cranes as in the Maciejowski Bible (Hartley and Elliot 1931, pl 4a) or the Holkham Bible (Hartley and Elliot 1928, pl 10d). **J4** is a pot-crane similar to the latter, although it is in three and not two parts and has an upper swivel to give manoeuvrability to the cauldron. The swivel fitting may have been attached directly to the building or have hung by a chain from a bar across the chimney flue.

J5 is probably a suspension link from a pot-crane.

Vessels

Medieval cauldrons seem to have been of copper alloy, the ubiquitous cast-iron cauldron being of post-medieval date, although it is possible that some large iron handles are from cauldrons rather than buckets.

No iron pan like that of the late 9th or first half of the 10th century from Winchester is yet known from a medieval context (Biddle and Quirk 1962, 184–186, fig 8). **J6**, a rectangular pan with an expanding hollow handle, may have had a similar use.

Medieval jugs, ewers, bowls, skillets and strainers are frequently of cast or sheet copper alloy, but occasionally some had iron handles like **J7** which is probably from a strainer. Its curved arms were riveted through the vessel rim.

Trivets and brandreths

Trivets **J8–13** are stands used to support vessels when they are off the fire (Lindsay 1964, 14, figs 51–58), and they comprise a flat plate or ring standing on three or more legs. **J8–10** have circular rings, **J11** is oval, **J12** triangular and **J13** has been reconstructed with five sides. **J8** and **J12** had three legs, **J13** probably five, and the others are incomplete.

Most of the trivets are plain, although **J8** has some simple chiselled decoration. **J12** has a triangular ring, open internally, but the need to give some support to vessels is indicated by the inner forked projections on **J8** and **J9**, and by the probable intersecting arms of **J13**.

The brandreth resembles the trivet in being a ring on legs (Lindsay 1964, 26, figs 122 and 161), but it was intended for use over the fire with the vessel generally sitting within a vertically sided ring. It was also sometimes used to support a griddle plate. No medieval example is yet known.

Griddle plates

Griddle plates used for baking oatmeal and small cakes are flat, circular iron plates used recently either on a brandreth or, if provided with a semicircular handle, suspended from a pot hook. **J14**, a fragmentary griddle plate, was found near a burnt area and had probably been used directly on a fire or on hot ashes derived from one.

Flesh-hooks

Flesh-hooks were mainly used to extract meat and other items from cooking vessels placed over fires, and there are two medieval types: Type 1 with two or three hooked arms set on a short angled stem, Type 2 generally with three hooked arms at the end of a long tanged or socketed stem. Type 1 flesh-hooks **J15–23** are medieval examples of an established pre-Conquest type which was probably little used after the 13th century, which is when the succeeding Type 2 (**J24–30**) appears to have been introduced. **J31–32** are probably socketed arms from Type 2 flesh-hooks.

Flesh-hooks of Type 1 have either two or three hooked arms split from the same tang, but those of Type 2 normally have three arms formed by forging a U-shaped double hook onto the hooked end of the main stem. **J28** is unusual in having only two arms, **J30** in having four. Both types of flesh-hook were generally hafted on wooden handles which enabled them to extract food from vessels over burning fires. The later type is more efficient and hygienic than the earlier, providing a sounder hafting and keeping the wooden handle out of the food. The earlier flesh-hooks were hafted by embedding the hooked or angled tang in the end of the wooden handle, in the manner indicated by an example in the Bayeux Tapestry (Stenton 1957, pl 48, 171), while the handle of the later type was placed well away from the hook (Hartley and Elliot 1931, pl 4a). **J30** had no wooden handle at all and instead a short flattened and looped iron handle forged in one with the stem.

Ladles

Shallow ladles were sometimes used as skimmers, but **J33–35** are true ladles with deep bowls and solid iron handles set either in line with or obliquely to the bowl. **J36** is probably the handle from a ladle, it is too thick to be from a spoon.

Spoons

Medieval spoons were of wood, horn, bone, pewter, latten, and silver, but only rarely of iron. **J37** is of iron, and from a context of c1350–1450, although its form cannot be paralleled amongst spoons of more noble metals until the second half of the 17th century. It is similar, however, to an iron spoon from a mid 16th-century context at Caldecote, Hertfordshire (Cool *et al* 2009), and the contradictory typological dates are best ascribed to the differing properties of the various metals. **J37** is forged in a shape natural to iron, unlike the slender rod-like stems with finials found on other contemporary spoons (Ward Perkins 1967, 128–133).

Cleavers

Cleavers were used to chop up animal and fish meat, and it is probable that **J38–42** were used to cut joints from carcases which had themselves been cut up by cleavers similar to **J43–44**. Several of the cleavers (**J44, J46–47**) have suspension hooks or loops on the blade or handle, and the handles are either solid or have whittle or scale tangs. **J38** and **J45** are both solid handles with depressions close to the end perhaps intended to assist the grip. The substantial blades are all straight-backed and several are burred from hammering.

Fish hooks

Fish bred in fishponds and caught in rivers or the sea were an important item in the medieval diet, and excavations at Great Yarmouth produced 19 species (Wheeler and Jones 1976, 208–224). Fewer were recorded at King's Lynn (Wheeler 1977). Nets may have been used to catch certain fish, but most could have been caught on baited hooks of which **J48–71** are selected medieval examples.

The majority of medieval fish hooks have barbed points, the complete examples (**J48–59**) generally having flattened heads for attachment to the line, although **J60** has an eyed shank, as has the incomplete hook **J64**. **J61–62** and **J70–71** have plain points, the first two retaining flattened heads. **J65** is incomplete, but like the other broken fish hooks included it complements the size range of the complete examples.

Fish hooks **J48–71** vary considerably in size, and the smaller ones may have been used to catch smaller species of fish such as whiting, plaice, small cod, sole and flounder, the larger hooks species such as cod, ling, conger eel, spurdog, large haddock, turbot and halibut. Cod, ling and conger eel are three common fish in medieval contexts, and each can grow to a weight of around 40–50kg.

The hooks have rounded or slightly flattened bends with the point generally either parallel to the shank or slightly open; the incurved point of **J68** is probably distorted. These open hooks are advantageous with active fishing techniques such as lining, which was practised in the medieval period, rather than with passive fishing methods such as fishing with floats. The barbed hook, in the majority amongst medieval fish hooks but although not necessary when a hook was kept in constant tension, was evidently preferred. The barb kept the bait in position and stopped the hook coming out of the fish once it had penetrated. The barbless hook might avoid damage to fish, but it is not well represented amongst medieval fish hooks. When in use for lining, hooks were fastened to a line by means of a short snood whipped onto the commonly found flattened heads, or attached through the eye. The eye, however, is restricted to the larger hooks.

11.3 LIGHTING

Domestic lighting was obtained from lanterns, torches, lamps and candlesticks. Lanterns and torches or flares were used to guide the way, and torches were also set in wall-mounted iron rings to provide illumination, but lamps and candlesticks probably provided most internal lighting.

Cresset lamps with oil and a floating wick take the form of a bowl standing on some form of foot, or of a funnel-shaped bowl with a downward projection to allow suspension (Ward Perkins 1967, 174–176).

Medieval candlesticks are of iron and copper alloy, and of varying types. Tapers may have lit the candles and wicks, but at some stage a steel or strike-a-light must have started the fire.

Candlesticks

An indication of the range of types of medieval candlestick is provided by an entry in the Black Book of the Household of Edward IV (Myers 1958, 90):

> Item, for the king and his chambyr also, when the day shortnyth and no prees of grete straungers, iij torches, j tortayis [very large wax candle], and iij prikettes [candles stuck on pricket candlesticks] for the table and cupbourde, if hit be not fasting day; vj perchers [large wax 'Paris' candles], x candyls wax for syzes of chamber, ij morters wax [bowls with floating wicks] every nyzt.

Candlesticks were used for work as well as for domestic purposes. Accounts (Salzman 1967, 62) record the purchase of candles for work at night, and at Clarendon Palace in 1482 there is payment to Thomas Warmewell for going down into the well to cleanse it and for 'great candles called talowe perchers for lighting the said Thomas at the bottom of the well and burning there for 4 days' (Salzman 1967, 278).

Medieval candlesticks, more commonly of iron than copper alloy, are either of pricket type, the end of the candle being impaled on a spike, socketed, composite or three-armed.

Pricket candlesticks

Pricket candlesticks were used by impaling the candle on the pricket spike which in its simplest form might be no more than a tapered rod set in a wooden beam or on a bracket. A moulded stone bracket at Norrington Manor House, Alvediston, Wiltshire, of c1377, retains two such iron spikes on its upper surface (Wood 1965, 366, pl LVIIG).

Excavated pricket candlesticks **J72–81** have single pricket spikes set on straight stems with either one (**J72**) or two (**J73–81**) side scrolls, **J79** has additional side arms, both unfortunately incomplete.

The stems of **J72–79** are straight, that of **J80** is angled, and each would have been set in a wooden base or appropriate socket. **J82** is altogether more elaborate, and recalls with the form of its moulded stem and tripod base such medieval folding copper-alloy candlesticks as those from York (Wenham 1972, 95, fig 20.7) and Laverstock, Wiltshire (Musty et al 1969, 149, fig 28.3). It has a pair of pricket spikes set to either side of a simple finial and a small wax pan of more aesthetic than practical value. These pricket candlesticks come from 12th to 15th-century contexts.

Socketed candlesticks

Socketed candlesticks are the most common type of iron candlestick, and they take the form of a candle socket set on the end of a straight, angled or cranked stem, or in a wax pan. The socketed candlesticks with straight stems, **J83–93**, vary in length and may have been used in an equivalent way to straight-stemmed pricket candlesticks. Those with angled stems, **J94–112**, have sockets which butt the horizontal bar or are set on short or tall uprights, and their sockets are variously outwardly, inwardly or occasionally centrally set on the upright arm. **J113–115** have cranked stems. Most of these stems are plain, but five are of spirally twisted iron, a simple type of decorative forging also found on objects such as flesh-hooks and hasps.

The three candlesticks with wax-pans **J116–118** differ in detail. **J118**, the most complete, has its handle and candle socket held to the wax-pan by a common rivet, but **J117** has its handle forged in one with the wax pan and a separately welded candle socket. **J116**, a wax pan, evidently resembled **J118**. These three iron candlesticks are quite sophisticated and they resemble some of copper alloy, including that from Writtle, Essex (Rahtz 1969b, 91, fig 51.118).

Socketed candlesticks were in common use from the 13th century onwards, those with angled stems being most common. The more elaborate type with its wax pan is principally of 14th to 15th-century date.

Composite candlesticks

A number of medieval candlesticks combine the pricket spike with a socket, the most elementary being **J119** which has the two arms springing from the same stem and barely separating. **J120** similarly combines a single pricket and socket, but the socket is set on an angled arm. The sockets of **J119–120** are not the fully developed, closed sockets of candlesticks **J83–117**, but rather open sockets onto which candles may have been impaled. The two candlesticks come from 12th to 14th-century contexts.

Three-armed candlesticks

J121–128 are three-armed candlesticks set on central stems, the more complete examples (**J121–122**, **J125** and **J128**) generally having a central pricket between side sockets, although **J126–127** have split terminals. Candles must have been impaled onto all except **J128** which has closed sockets. These three-armed candlesticks are mainly from sites with ecclesiastical connections, **J121–123** from a monastic grange and **J125–127** from Rievaulx Abbey, and it is possible that they at least originated as ecclesiastical rather than domestic fittings. They are found in 12th to 16th-century contexts.

11.4 FIRE-STEELS

Fire-steels were used in conjunction with flints to create sparks and ignite tinder. **J129–133** have rectangular blades, only the latter showing signs of wear, and all have hooked tips or curved arms to allow them to be held and struck. The holes at the inner ends of **J129–130** imply that they were mounted in folding handles. **J134** is a later type of fire-steel comparable to others from the medieval and later site of Urquhart Castle, Highlands (Laing 1974–75, 154, fig 14. 13–14).

11.5 BUCKETS

Medieval wells have produced several complete buckets in addition to some of their component wood and iron parts. **J135–139** are complete wooden buckets of stave-built construction which differ in their detailed methods of assembly, some having iron hoops, others withies, and their variously shaped iron handles may ride in looped or eyed straps nailed to the bucket side. These individual items are described in succession below.

Bucket hoops

The staves of buckets **J135–139** all have plain edges which butted the adjacent staves and were held together by an outer binding. **J137** was evidently bound by withies, but pairs of iron hoops of canted section bind all the other buckets. **J140–143** are variously complete and incomplete individual hoops, all of canted section and therefore from buckets with sloping sides, and none exceeds the diameter of the complete buckets. The hoops were evidently sprung into position since none, not surprisingly, has any evidence of nail-holes.

Handle loops and straps

Iron U-shaped loops and eyed straps frequently strengthened the holes in wooden staves through which bucket handles passed, serving to relieve the wood of some strain and prevent breakage. Complete buckets **J135** and **J138**, however, lack such mounts, although **J138** retains its iron handle. This may imply that **J135** once also had an iron handle, and not a rope one as has been suggested.

J144–147 are individual U-shaped loops similar to those on complete buckets **J136** and **J139**, where they either rise above the rim or are set on the inside of projecting staves. **J148–154** are eyed straps, **J148–149** almost identical in shape to those nailed to the inside of the complete bucket **J137**. It is probable, nevertheless, that some of the eyes projected above bucket rims.

Handles

J155–162 are iron handles, the majority probably from buckets or pails, although some may be from cauldrons or other vessels. **J155–157** resemble those on buckets **J136–139**, all being gently curved and having hooked ends in line with the handle. Most are plain, but **J155** has a central expansion to ease pressure on the hand when being held. **J138–139** and **J157** are specifically intended for use in a well, all having a central perforated expansion housing a swivel hook. Chains associated with the first two buckets were evidently used in conjunction with a rope to haul them up wells.

The small handles **J158–160** with transversely set hooked ends may be from small buckets or pails. **J158**, found near what may have been the hoop from a wooden bucket, has an expanded centre, but **J159–160** are slighter and of spirally twisted iron, and their precise use is uncertain.

11.6 HOOKS

Hooks of a number of types were used in and around buildings, S-hooks like **J163–167** being used to hang meat from hooks or staples in kitchens and pantries. **J168** could be a bag hook or baling hook, and the findspot of **J169** in a well implies that it was used to retrieve buckets. **J170–173**, no doubt hafted on long wooden handles, could have been used as boat hooks, fire hooks or wall hooks, and **J174**, a large draghook, was probably used to clear the moat at Weoley Castle, Birmingham (West Midlands). The use of hooks **J176–179** is uncertain, although in some respects they resemble flesh-hooks.

11.7 BALANCES

The equal-armed balance was the common instrument used for weighing during the medieval period, and small examples such as those from Wallingstones (Bridgewater 1970–72, 104, 112, fig 20) and Goltho (Goodall 1975a, 95, fig 44.37), with rigid and folding beams respectively, are normally of copper alloy. **J180–182** are iron equivalents of the former type, used in conjunction with pans suspended from each end of the beam. **J183** is the suspension stirrup from another balance.

Lead-filled, latten-covered steelyard weights, common finds of 13th-century and later date (Ward Perkins 1967, 171–174), were used with unequal-armed balances like **J184**. This had a wooden beam with graduations along it for the weight and two fulcrums with suspension rings, one or other of which was used according to the weight of the load suspended from the hook. A detailed description of the use of **J184** is given in Shortt 1968.

11.8 CHAINS, LINKS AND RELATED FITTINGS

Chains and links had a multitude of uses, small chains generally of copper alloy forming part of costume, and larger chains being used in horse harness or around buildings supporting cauldrons over fires, holding doors and gates open or closed, tethering animals, or drawing buckets from wells. They are also, but less commonly, found as part of limb shackles, as on **I80**, **I81** and **I90**. Links and chains, some with hooks, rings or swivel fittings, are described according to individual link shape, and isolated examples of their fittings are then catalogued.

Circular links and rings

J185 is part of a chain of small circular links which is probably from costume, although such chains are normally of non-ferrous metal. **J186–196** are individual rings of various sizes, some no doubt from chains like **J185**, or components within them (**J203**, **J206–208**, **J215**), although they could be buckle frames like **K218**, **K221** and **K223**. **J186** with its leather strap is certainly from a shoe, and **J193–194** from a belt. **J190–192** are also large enough to be strap distributors from spurs, as on the effigy of John of Eltham (Ward Perkins 1967, fig 30.5), and rings the size of **J193–195** could be strap distributors from harness like **L103–104**. The partly spirally twisted **J196** may be a ring handle from a cupboard door. Larger rings are discussed below, **J277–287**.

Rectangular links

J197–200 may have acted as strap distributors like **L102** or be belt links.

Oval links

J201–204 are oval links, **J203** unusually having overlapping ends and carrying a small ring.

Straight-sided links

J205–214 are straight-sided links, the smallest forming chain **J206**, the largest, **J214**, a chain with a swivel hook. **J209–210** also have swivel hooks, the latter coming from a hearth in a cooking area and so possibly used in conjunction with a hook to support a cauldron.

U-shaped links

J215 has a chain which combines rings and pivoting U-shaped links. It comes from a hearth in a cooking area where it may have supported a cauldron.

Figure-eight shaped links

J216–239 are figure-eight links of varying size, most flat but **J224** is a chain incorporating one flat and one twisted link. The figure-eights is the most common medieval type of link, the shape giving a strength not necessarily found in the other forms. The shape of individual links varies from the openness of **J225** and **J238** to the tightness of **J229** and **J237**. **J216–217**, **J220** and **J226** support small hooks and may have been used for suspension rather than for linking or closing, whereas **J237** and **J239** come from wells where they were probably used in conjunction with buckets **J138** and **J139**. **J233** retains the U-shaped staple which held it in place.

S-shaped links

J240–243 are chains with S-shaped links, **J240** and **J243** flat, **J241–242** twisted. **J240–241** are small and probably from costume, although they are too coarse to be from jewellery and may be from chatelaines. **J242–243** are large links.

Swivel rings and hooks

Swivel rings and hooks on the ends of chains such as **J209–210** and **J214** gave freedom of movement to whatever was attached to them, and **J244–263** are individual examples. **J244–248** are complete swivel hooks and rings, **J247** coming from a limb shackle, **J248** probably from the shaft of a harrow, plough or cart. **J249–255** are swivel rings, **J256–263** swivel hooks, all of differing sizes. The small swivel hooks may be from harness straps or curb bits, but the larger ones must have supported cauldrons or have had uses similar to those suggested for **J248**.

Double swivel rings

J264–266 are paired swivel rings which may have been used to give movement at the junction between two chains, and some of the swivel rings **J249–255** may be from similar fittings.

Miscellaneous swivel fittings

J267–269 are swivel hooks with extended arms, that of **J269** also angled. The larger ones may be from pot-crane supports, **J268** resembling the upper member of **J4**. **J270** is a swivel rod with a flattened and perforated tip, and **J271** is a swivel loop with opposing knobbed terminals.

J272 is a complicated fitting, the main swivel ring and hook supporting a cage to which two further hooks and side arms are attached. The side arms are unusual in having sprung, hinged clips.

Looped hooks

Chains **J216–217**, **J220** and **J226** have looped hooks attached to the bottom link, and **J273–275** are further individual hooks with hooked or closed looped eyes. **J276** has a sprung loop similar in operation to the side arms of **J272**. It is surprising that this spring closure was not used more widely, since it is merely an adaptation of the spring arrangement of medieval box and barrel padlocks.

11.9 RINGS

Rings **J277–287** are a representative sample of the larger rings from medieval contexts, smaller rings **J185–296** are discussed above. A number of these rings may also be from buckles (cf **K218**, **K221** and **K223**), or from chains (cf **J206–208** and **J215**), and the presence of non-ferrous plating on **J283** is not certain evidence that it is a buckle frame since rings from snaffle bits are frequently plated. **L49** and **L51–52** have such rings, 30, 64 and 32mm in diameter. Some of the largest rings may be from ring handles such as **H654–655** from doors and furnishings.

11.10 WASHERS

J288–290 are flat circular washers which may have been used with bolts.

11.11 COLLARS

J291–311 are circular and rectangular collars used to bind wood and strengthen it, some of them with crudely overlapped ends, others fully forged. The circular collars vary most in width or length, as **J291–306** demonstrate. Small collars on various medieval objects include those on the handles of weedhook **F55** and knives **G96** and **G355**, as well as on curry-combs **L35** and **L44** and snaffle bit **L63**.

J1 FIRE-DOG (not illustrated)
Bayham Abbey, East Sussex.
Late 15th to early 16th century.
Upright from fire-dog with outward-facing pair of scrolls at head of stem which splits towards base to form two straight legs. Hole for former horizontal bar at point where stem divides. H 407mm.
Goodall 1983a, fig 46.35.

J2 FIRE-FORK
Huish, Wiltshire.
Site: 12th–15th century.
Complete two-pronged fork with long stem terminating in a socket with a nail-hole for a former wooden handle. L 742mm.
Shortt 1972, 120, fig 4.29.

J3 POKER
Stonar, Kent.
Very late 13th to early 14th century.
Rectangular-sectioned poker with slender handle terminating in a suspension loop and ring. L 567mm.
Excavated by N Macpherson-Grant.

J4 POT-CRANE (not illustrated)
Norwich.
In 1507 fire deposit.
Pot-crane in three parts, the 765mm long upper arm having a knobbed head to fit in a missing swivel ring. Attached to this arm is a second one, 640mm long, along which the 470mm long pot hook slides. A loop through the lower, hooked end of the intermediate arm can be set in any one of seven ratchets on the pot hook, thereby enabling it to be adjusted.
Goodall 1993a, fig 55.559.

J5 HOOK
Kirkcudbright Castle, Dumfries and Galloway.
c1288–1308.
Double-ended hook. L 301mm.
Dunning et al 1957–58, 138, fig 7.4.

FIGURE 11.1
Fire-fork, poker and hook

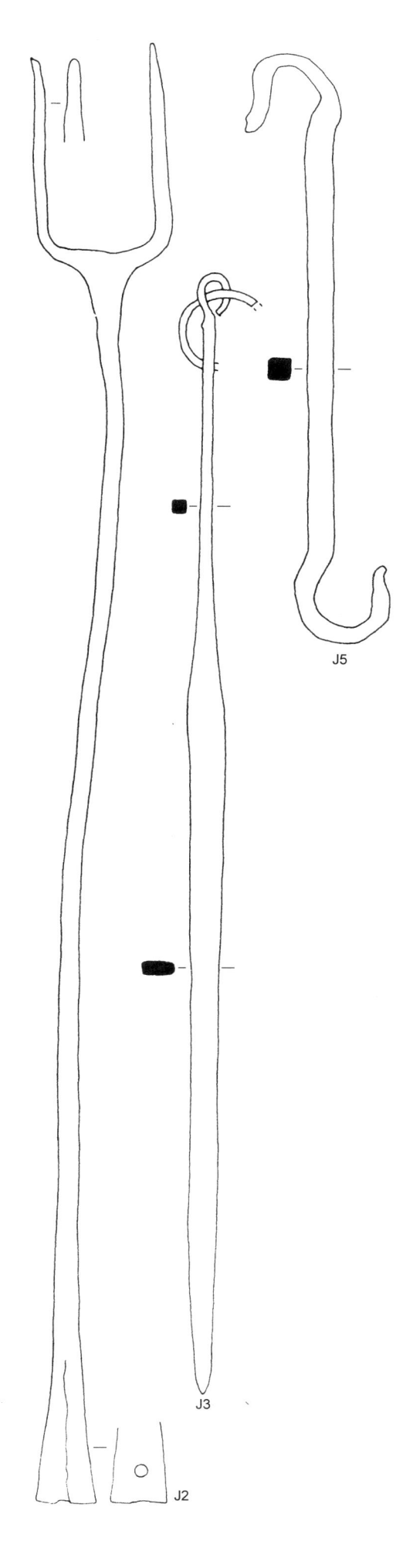

J6 PAN (not illustrated)
Norwich.
In 1509 fire depsit.
Rectangular pan with expanding, hollow, circular-sectioned handle.
Overall length 350mm; pan 193mm by 140mm, 40mm deep.
Goodall 1993a, fig 54.556.

**J7 SKILLET
OR COLANDER HANDLE**
Somerby, Lincolnshire.
15th to mid 16th century.
Broken handle with curved arms riveted to rim flange of non-ferrous skillet or colander. Complete arm has simple terminal. L 124mm.
Mynard 1969, 85, fig 13.IW92.

J8 TRIVET
Cambokeels, Durham.
Later 14th to early 16th century.
Flat circular ring with three broken legs, the most complete a welded-on repair. Top of two original legs and inner forked projection decorated with simple chiselled lines. D 226–242mm.
Hildyard and Charlton 1947, 194, pl VII.

J9 TRIVET
Bolton, Fangfoss, Humberside.
Early 14th century.
Broken flat, circular ring with inner forked projection. L 198mm.
Goodall 1978b, 143, fig 30.20

J10 TRIVET
Thuxton, Northamptonshire.
Site: 12th–14th century.
Broken flat circular ring with stub of one leg.
L 130mm.
Excavated by L A S Butler.

HOUSEHOLD IRONWORK

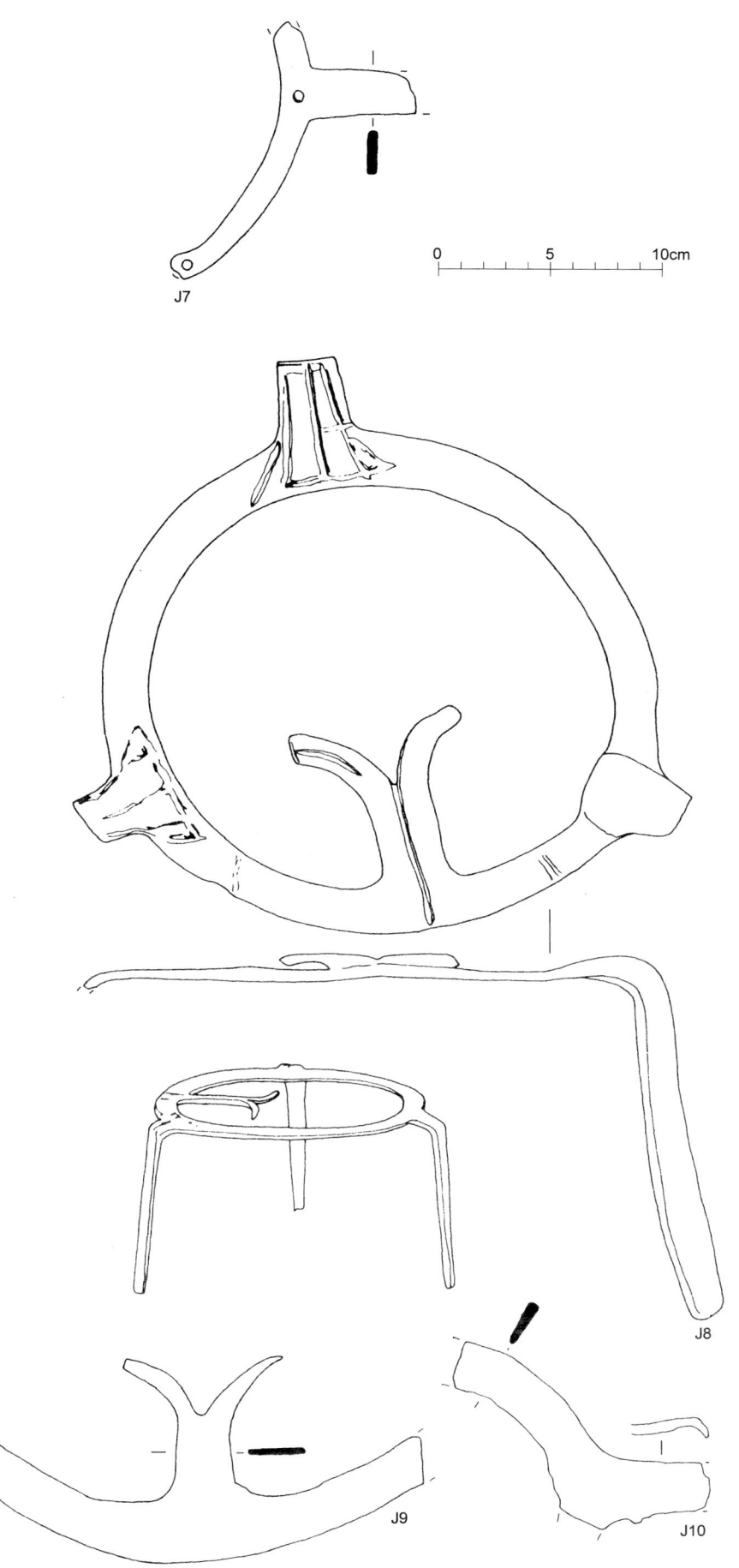

FIGURE 11.2
Skillet or colander handle and trivets

J11 TRIVET
Llawhaden Castle, Dyfed.
Medieval.
Broken, flat, oval ring retaining one leg.
L 142mm.
National Museum of Wales, Cardiff, 40.135/3.

J12 TRIVET
Northampton.
13th–14th century.
Flat, three-sided ring with stubs of three legs.
W 253mm.
Goodall *et al* 1979, 273, fig 120.85.

J13 TRIVET
Winchester, Hampshire.
15th century.
Broken leg and part of flat, five-sided ring with inner projection. L 122mm.
Goodall 1990-14, fig 242.2545.

J14 GRIDDLE PLATE
Beere, Devon.
End 12th to 13th century. Found near burnt area.
Incomplete circular griddle plate, originally about 4mm thick. D 180mm.
Jope and Threlfall 1958, 138, fig 34.1, scale 1:2, not 1:3.

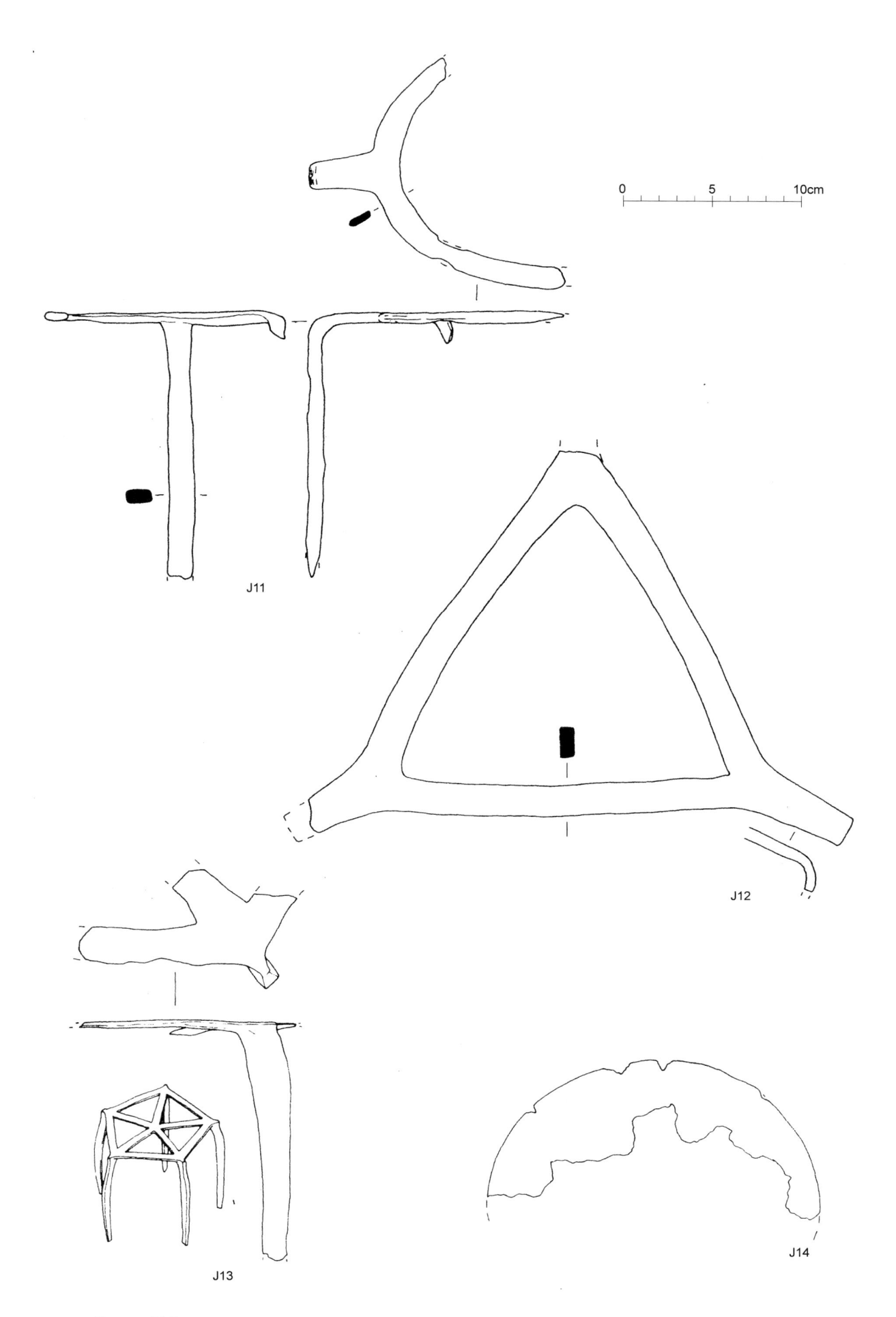

FIGURE 11.3
Trivets and griddle plate

J15 FLESH-HOOK
Goltho Manor, Lincolnshire.
11th century.
Two hooked arms, broken tang. L 80mm.
Goodall 1987, fig 159.119.

J16 FLESH-HOOK
North Elmham, Norfolk.
Early medieval, from 11th century.
Two hooked arms, angled and broken tang. L 112mm.
Rigold 1962–63, 98, fig 35.10.

J17 FLESH-HOOK
Wroughton Copse, Fyfield Down, Wiltshire.
12th–13th century.
Two hooked arms and shank all broken. L 52mm.
Excavated by P J Fowler.

J18 FLESH-HOOK
Goring-by-Sea, West Sussex.
13th century.
Two hooked arms with tang with clenched tip set at right angles. W 62mm.
Barton 1965, 91, fig 3.9

J19 FLESH-HOOK
Brooklands, Weybridge, Surrey.
1200–1325.
Two hooked arms, one incomplete. Tang broken. L 92mm.
Goodall 1977d, 73, fig 45.18.

J20 FLESH-HOOK
Clough Castle, Co. Down.
c1250 to early 14th century.
Two hooked arms, one distorted and straight. Tang broken. L 70mm.
Waterman 1954, 140, fig 12.8.

J21 FLESH-HOOK
Winchester, Hampshire.
c1070–71.
Three hooked arms, tips broken. Tang broken and distorted. L 111mm.
Goodall 1990-14, fig 242.2548.

J22 FLESH-HOOK
Old Sarum, Wiltshire.
Principally medieval, to 14th century.
Three hooked arms, tang tip hooked round and broken. L 83mm.
Salisbury and South Wiltshire Museum, Salisbury, O.S.C144, 30/1920–21.

J23 FLESH-HOOK
Huish, Wiltshire.
Site: 12th to 15th century.
Three hooked arms and tang all broken. L 66mm.
Shortt 1972, 120, fig 4.30.

J24 FLESH-HOOK
Winchester, Hampshire.
13th century.
Broken, spirally twisted stem. One of three original hooked arms survives. L 176mm.
Goodall 1990-14, fig 242.2551.

J25 FLESH-HOOK
Wythemail, Northamptonshire.
Early 13th century. From post-hole in C3.
Three hooked arms, broken shank. L 121mm.
Hurst and Hurst 1969.

J26 FLESH-HOOK
Northolt Manor, Greater London.
1300–50.
Three hooked arms and tang. L 204mm.
Hurst 1961, 289, fig 76.16.

J27 FLESH-HOOK
Cambokeels, Durham.
Later 14th to early 16th century.
Three hooked arms, two broken. Spirally twisted shank with socket. L 273mm.
Hildyard 1949, 196, fig 5.2.

J28 FLESH-HOOK
Writtle, Essex.
c1425–1521.
Two hooked arms, one broken. L 116mm.
Rahtz 1969b, 87, fig 48.76.

J29 FLESH-HOOK
Northampton.
15th–16th centuries to post-18th century.
One hooked arm and part of shank from flesh-hook originally with three hooked arms. L 150mm.
Goodall 1979b, 71, fig 17.27.

J30 FLESH-HOOK (not illustrated)
Norwich.
In 1509 fire deposit.
Broad, looped handle tapering to slender shank with four hooked arms, one complete. Overall length 543mm. Looped handle 170mm long, complete arm 50mm wide.
Goodall 1993b, fig 83.740.

J31 FLESH-HOOK
Lyveden, Northamptonshire.
Site: second quarter 13th to very early 14th century.
Socket with nail-hole and broken shank, probably from flesh-hook. L 101mm.
Bryant and Steane 1969, 43, fig 18f.

J32 FLESH-HOOK
Staines, Surrey.
1300–1500.
Socket and broken shank, probably from flesh-hook. L 117mm.
Excavated by K Crouch.

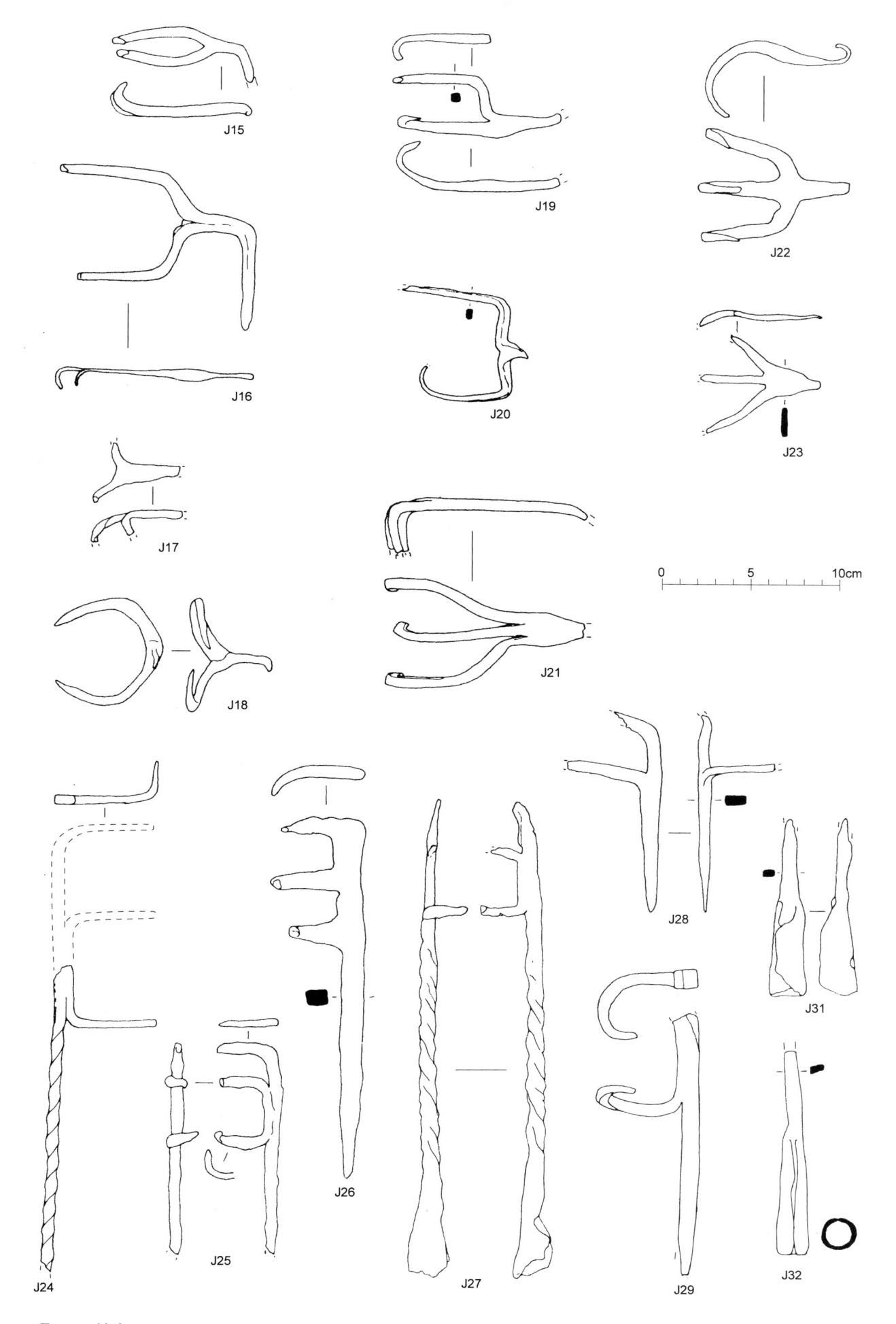

FIGURE 11.4
Flesh-hooks

J33 LADLE
Winchester, Hampshire.
Late 12th–early 13th century.
Oval bow and shaped horizontal handle bolt broken. L 111mm.
Goodall 1990-14, fig 243.2554.

J34 LADLE
Winchester, Hampshire.
Mid to ?late 13th century.
Oval bowl and angled handle both broken. L 91mm.
Goodall 1990-14, fig 243.2555.

J35 LADLE
Baconsthorpe Castle, Norfolk.
c1440–1650.
Damaged oval bowl, broken handle set at a slight angle. L 258mm.
DAMHB Collection, London, BAC 4.

J36 LADLE
Staines, Surrey.
1300–1500.
Plain handle, bowl lost. L 137mm.
Excavated by K Crouch.

J37 SPOON
Broughton, Lincolnshire.
c1350–1450.
Broken bowl and stem, the latter expanding towards a simply shaped, slightly downturned terminal. L 182mm.
Goodall 1974d, 11, fig 3.25.

J38 CLEAVER
Goltho Manor, Lincolnshire.
c1100–50.
Blade tip lost, solid handle with two shallow depressions towards end. L 265mm.
Goodall 1987, fig 157.66.

J39 CLEAVER
Aldringham, Lancashire.
Mid 12th century.
Blade damaged, handle solid. L 230mm.
Excavated by B K Davison.

J40 CLEAVER
Weoley Castle, Birmingham, West Midlands.
c1230–1270.
Whittle tang incomplete, blade back burred. L 135mm.
Oswald 1962–63, 132, fig 51.16.

J41 CLEAVER
Clough Castle, Co. Down.
c1200–c1225.
Blade complete, with thin projection running from upper, inner corner to underside of handle. Handle of square section, thinning to probable scale tang broken across a rivet hole. L 204mm.
Waterman 1954, 137, fig 11.3.

J42 CLEAVER
St Catharine's Hill, Winchester, Hampshire.
Early 12th to 14th century.
Complete, cutting edge damaged, blade back burred. L 214mm.
Hawkes et al 1930, 246, fig 29.I20.

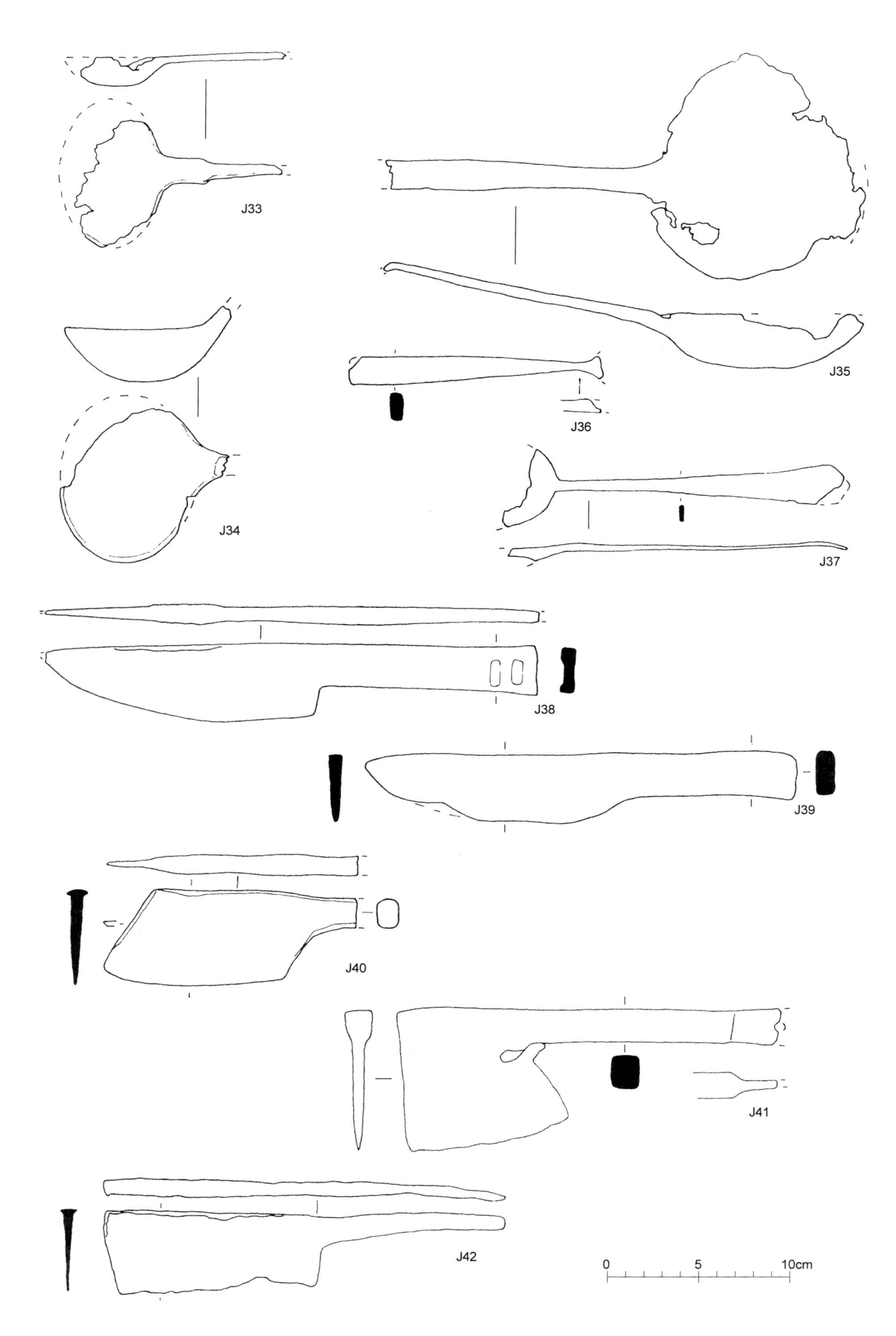

FIGURE 11.5
Ladles, spoon, and cleavers

J43 CLEAVER
Northolt Manor, Greater London.
1350–1370.
Complete, end-plate and two rivets in scale tang which retains thin mineralised slivers of the wooden handle. L 538mm.
Hurst 1961, 291, fig 76.19.

J44 CLEAVER
Huish, Wiltshire.
Site: 12th to 15th century.
Suspension loop and burred back to blade, riveted tang. L 366mm.
Shortt 1972, 120, fig 4.24.

J45 CLEAVER
Loughor Castle, West Glamorgan.
Site: c1106 to late 13th century.
Broken handle with three shallow depressions. L 100mm.
Excavated by J M Lewis.

J46 CLEAVER
Winchester, Hampshire.
?13th century.
Solid handle with hole for suspension. L 161mm.
Goodall 1990-14, fig 240.2542.

J47 CLEAVER
Winchester, Hampshire.
15th–16th century.
Handle with hooked terminal and stub of blade. L 73mm.
Goodall 1990-14, fig 240.2543.

J48 FISH HOOK
Stonar, Kent.
c1275–1385.
Flat-headed shank, broken barb. L 31mm.
Excavated by N Macpherson-Grant.

J49 FISH HOOK
London.
?Late 13th–mid 14th century.
Flat-headed shank, barbed point. L 36mm.
Henig 1974, 189, fig 37.52.

J50 FISH HOOK
Stonar, Kent.
c1275–1385.
Flat-headed shank, barbed point. L 40mm.
Excavated by N Macpherson-Grant.

J51 FISH HOOK
Stonar, Kent.
c1225–1275.
Flat-headed shank, barbed point. L 45mm.
Excavated by N Macpherson-Grant.

J52 FISH HOOK
Stonar, Kent.
c1275–1385.
Incomplete flat-headed shank, barbed point. L 53mm.
Excavated by N Macpherson-Grant.

J53 FISH HOOK
Holworth, Dorset.
13th–14th century.
Flat-headed shank, barbed point. L 53mm.
Rahtz 1959, 146, fig 12.7.

J54 FISH HOOK
Great Yarmouth, Norfolk.
Late 11th or early 12th century.
Flat-headed shank, barbed point. L 61mm.
Rogerson 1976, 166, fig 53.3.

J55 FISH HOOK
Pevensey, East Sussex.
13th century.
Flat-headed shank, barbed point. L 62mm.
Dulley 1967, 228, fig 65.5.

J56 FISH HOOK
Kilton Castle, Cleveland.
Late 15th century.
Flat-headed shank, broken barbed point. L 66mm.
Excavated by A Aberg.

J57 FISH HOOK
Stonar, Kent.
c1100–c1225.
Flat-headed shank, barbed point. L 69mm.
Excavated by N Macpherson-Grant.

J58 FISH HOOK
Kilton Castle, Cleveland.
Late 15th century.
Flat-headed shank, barbed point. L 68mm.
Excavated by A Aberg.

J59 FISH HOOK
Stonar, Kent.
c1225–1275.
Flat-headed shank, broken barbed point. L 96mm.
Excavated by N Macpherson-Grant.

J60 FISH HOOK
Stonar, Kent.
c1225–1275.
Eyed shank, barbed point. L 90mm.
Excavated by N Macpherson-Grant.

J61 FISH HOOK
Great Yarmouth, Norfolk.
Late 11th or early 12th century.
Flat-headed shank, plain point. L 66mm.
Rogerson 1976, 166, fig 53.1.

J62 FISH HOOK
Upton, Gloucestershire.
Mid to late 13th century.
Flat-headed shank, plain point. L 59mm.
Rahtz 1969a, 108, fig 12.85.

J63 FISH HOOK
Great Yarmouth, Norfolk.
Late 11th or early 12th century.
Flat-headed shank, point broken. L 75mm.
Rogerson 1976, 166, fig 53.2.

J64 FISH HOOK
Great Yarmouth, Norfolk.
Mid 11th century.
Eyed shank, broken point. L 123mm.
Rogerson 1976, 162, fig 52.13.

J65 FISH HOOK
Great Yarmouth, Norfolk.
Mid to late 11th century.
Shank and point broken. L 69mm.
Rogerson 1976, 166, fig 53.12.

J66 FISH HOOK
Winchester, Hampshire.
Mid 13th century.
Shank broken, barbed point. L 25mm.
Goodall 1990-14, fig 240.2540.

J67 FISH HOOK
Stonar, Kent.
c1225–75.
Shank broken, barbed point. L 38mm.
Excavated by N Macpherson-Grant.

J68 FISH HOOK
London.
Later 13th–14th century.
Shank broken, barbed point. L 50mm.
Henig 1974, 189, fig 37.51.

J69 FISH HOOK
Castle Acre Castle, Norfolk.
1140s deposit with derived material. Site founded soon after 1066.
Shank broken, barbed point. L 92mm.
Goodall 1982, fig 40, no. 112.

J70 FISH HOOK
Upton, Gloucestershire.
Late 13th to late 14th century.
Shank broken, plain point. L 46mm.
Hilton and Rahtz 1966, 120, fig 14.32.

J71 FISH HOOK
Pevensey, East Sussex.
13th century.
Shank broken, plain point. L 145mm.
Dulley 1967, 228, fig 65.4.

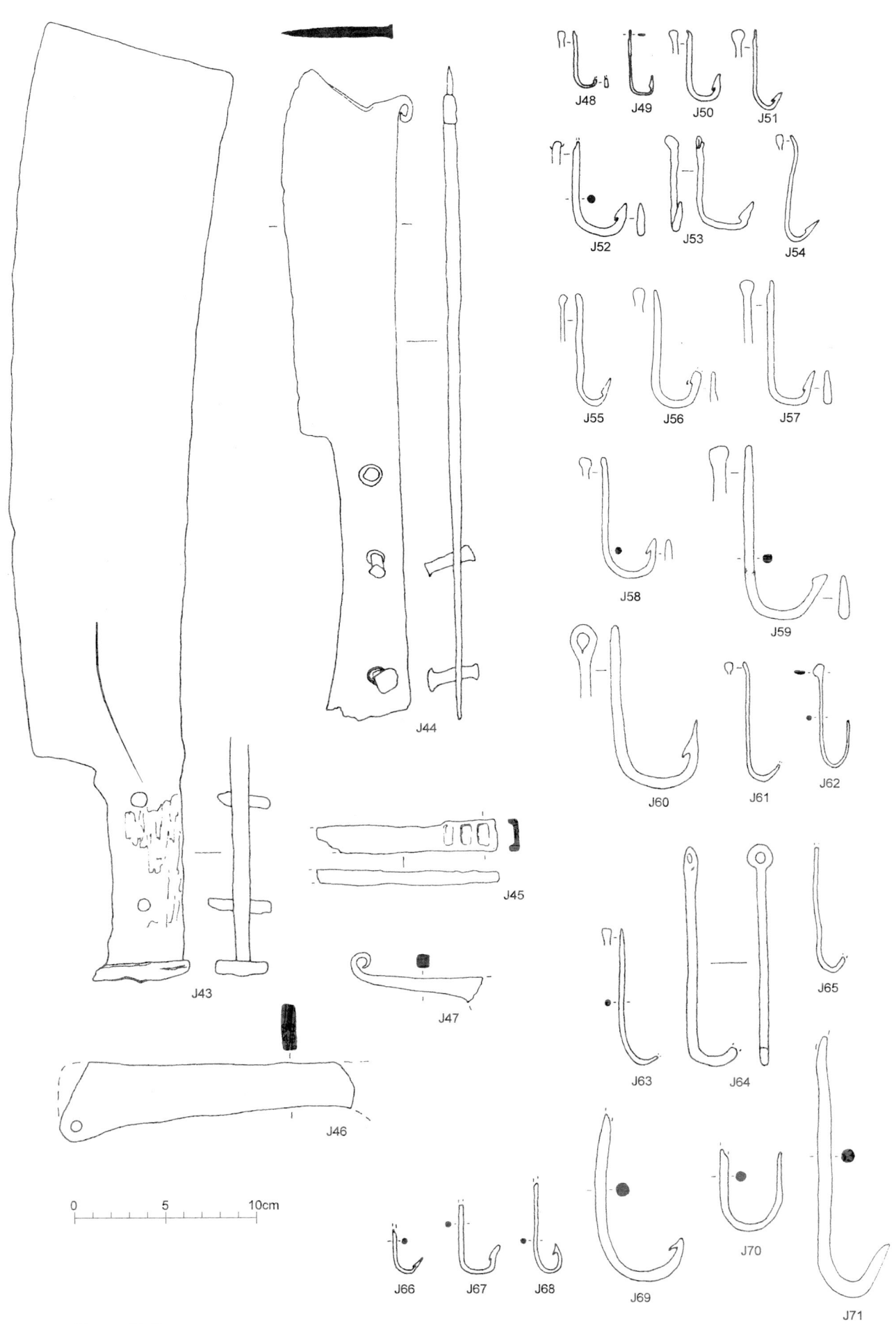

FIGURE 11.6
Cleavers and fish hooks

J72 CANDLESTICK
London.
13th century.
Pricket with single side scroll. L 110mm.
Museum of London. Former Guildhall Museum 17760. From Austin Friars, pit 1012.

J73 CANDLESTICK
Waltham Abbey, Essex.
12th–13th century.
Pricket with side scrolls. Stem broken. L 98mm.
Excavated by P J Huggins. From Church Street.

J74 CANDLESTICK
London.
Late 13th–mid 14th century.
Broken pricket with side scrolls. L 143mm.
Henig 1974, 191, fig 38.70.

J75 CANDLESTICK
London.
Late 13th to later 14th century.
Distorted pricket with side scroll. L 125mm.
Henig 1974, 191, fig 38.69.

J76 CANDLESTICK
Stonar, Kent.
c1275–1385.
Broken pricket with side scrolls, stem incomplete. L 110mm.
Excavated by N Macpherson-Grant.

J77 CANDLESTICK
Lochmaben Castle, Dumfries and Galloway.
Late 14th century.
Pricket broken, rest corroded. L 76mm.
Macdonald and Laing 1974–75, 149, fig 11.32.

J78 CANDLESTICK
London.
13th century to late medieval.
Pricket with side scrolls. Stem broken. L 113mm.
Museum of London. Former Guildhall Museum 24172. From Upper Thames Street.

J79 CANDLESTICK
Wharram Percy, North Yorkshire.
Early 15th century.
Pricket and side arms broken, side scrolls and stem complete. L 83mm.
Goodall 1979a, 118, fig 61.20.

J80 CANDLESTICK
London.
Around later 14th century.
Pricket with side scrolls and broken, angled stem. L 74mm.
Henig 1974, 191, fig 38.71.

J81 CANDLESTICK
Pleshey Castle, Essex.
Post-1140 or 1180 to late 12th or earlier 13th century.
Pricket and stem broken, side scrolls complete. L 41mm.
Goodall 1977c, 177, fig 39.34.

J82 CANDLESTICK
Winchester, Hampshire.
Early 13th century.
Three-legged base supports wax pan and distorted stem with knop moulding, shaped finial and two side prickets. Tinned. L 299mm.
Goodall 1990-20, fig 306.3530.

J83 CANDLESTICK
Winchester, Hampshire.
Late 11th–12th century.
Socketed with straight stem. L 59mm.
Goodall 1990-20, fig 306.3531.

J84 CANDLESTICK
Goltho, Lincolnshire.
Early to mid 14th century.
Socketed with straight stem. L 74mm.
Goodall 1975a, 87, not illustrated but as 100.

J85 CANDLESTICK
Goltho, Lincolnshire.
Early to mid 14th century.
Socketed with straight stem. L 88mm.
Goodall 1975a, 87, fig 41.100.

J86 CANDLESTICK
Criccieth Castle, Gwynedd.
Site: c1230–1404.
Socketed, base of stem probably distorted. L 105mm.
O'Neil 1944–45, 41, pl IX.11.

J87 CANDLESTICK
Seacourt, Oxfordshire.
Mid to late 12th to late 14th century.
Socketed with straight, spirally twisted stem. L 172mm.
Biddle 1961–62, 177, fig 30.1, scale 1:4, not 1:3.

J88 CANDLESTICK
Newcastle-upon-Tyne, Tyne and Wear.
Probably late medieval.
Socketed with short straight stem. L 78mm.
Harbottle 1968, 220, fig 18.149.

J89 CANDLESTICK
Faxton, Northamptonshire.
Site: 12th–15th century.
Socketed with straight stem. L 121mm.
Excavated by L A S Butler.

J90 CANDLESTICK
Grafton Regis, Northamptonshire.
Probably 15th century.
Socket broken, straight stem. L 124mm.
Excavated by Miss C M Mahany.

J91 CANDLESTICK
London.
Late 15th–early 16th century.
Socketed with broken, straight stem. L 97mm.
Excavated by F C Willmot. Site at 66 Foyle Road.

J92 CANDLESTICK
Lyveden, Northamptonshire.
1475–1500.
Socketed with broken, straight, spirally twisted stem. L 136mm.
Steane and Bryant 1975, 119, fig 45.15.

J93 CANDLESTICK
Wharram Percy, North Yorkshire.
Early 16th century to 20th century.
Socketed with gently curved, spirally twisted stem. L 130mm.
Goodall 1979a, 118, fig 61.22.

J94 CANDLESTICK
Wintringham, Cambridgeshire.
Mid 13th century.
Socketed with broken, angled stem. L 97mm.
Goodall 1977a, 258, fig 46.66.

J95 CANDLESTICK
Wintringham, Cambridgeshire.
Second half 13th century.
Socketed with broken, angled stem. L 74mm.
Goodall 1977a, 258, fig 46.68.

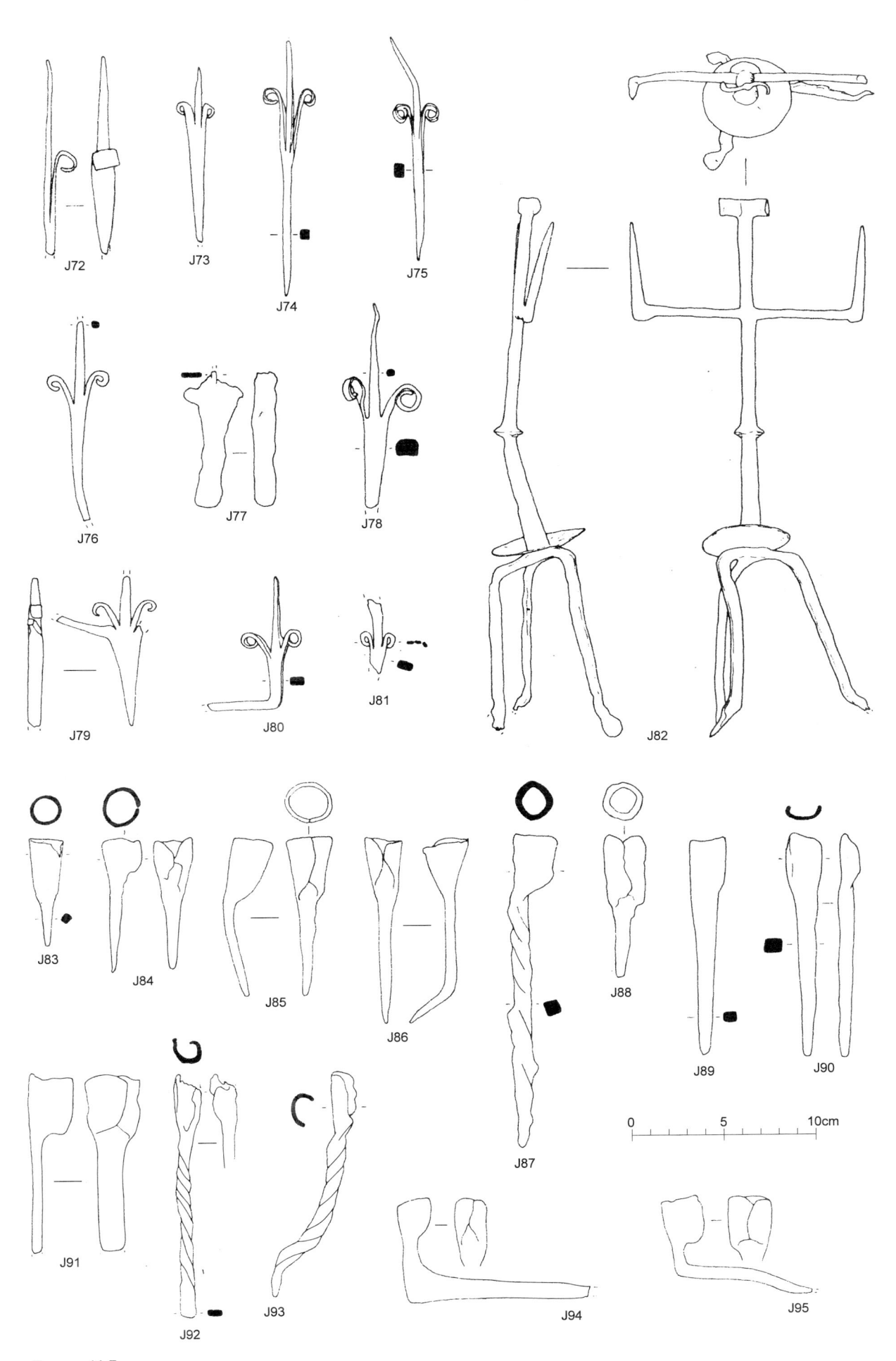

FIGURE 11.7
Candlesticks

J96 CANDLESTICK
Wintringham, Cambridgeshire.
Second half 13th century.
Socketed with angled stem. L 88mm.
Goodall 1977a, 258, fig 46.67.

J97 CANDLESTICK
Wintringham, Cambridgeshire.
Late 13th to early 14th century.
Socketed with broken, spirally twisted, angled arm. L 70mm.
Goodall 1977a, 258, fig 46.70.

J98 CANDLESTICK
London.
?Late 13th–14th century.
Socketed with side scroll on angled stem. L 105mm.
Henig 1974, 191, fig 39.72.

J99 CANDLESTICK
Stonar, Kent.
c1275–1385.
Socketed with broken, angled stem. L 63mm.
Excavated by N Macpherson-Grant.

J100 CANDLESTICK
Wintringham, Cambridgeshire.
Around early 14th century.
Socketed with broken, angled stem. L 79mm.
Goodall 1977a, 258, fig 46.71.

J101 CANDLESTICK
Goltho, Lincolnshire.
Croft B: late Saxon to mid 14th century.
Socketed with broken, angled stem. L 52mm.
Goodall 1975a, 87, fig 41.102.

J102 CANDLESTICK
Lochmaben Castle, Dumfries and Galloway.
Late 14th century.
Socketed with broken, angled stem. L 76mm.
Macdonald and Laing 1974–75, 148, fig 11.20.

J103 CANDLESTICK
Goltho, Lincolnshire.
Croft A: late Saxon to late 14th or early 15th century.
Socketed with broken, angled stem. L 79mm.
Goodall 1975a, 87, fig 41.101.

J104 CANDLESTICK
Goltho, Lincolnshire.
Croft A: late Saxon to late 14th, early 15th century.
Socketed with angled stem of spirally twisted iron. L 98mm.
Goodall 1975a, 87, fig 41.103.

J105 CANDLESTICK
Grenstein, Norfolk.
Late 14th–15th century.
Socketed with broken, angled stem. L 75mm.
Goodall 1980c, fig 81, no. 68.

J106 CANDLESTICK
Grenstein, Norfolk.
Late 14th–15th century.
Socketed with angled stem. L 77mm.
Goodall 1980c, fig 81, no. 69.

J107 CANDLESTICK
Wharram Percy, North Yorkshire.
Early 15th century.
Socketed with broken, angled stem. L 56mm.
Goodall 1979a, 118, fig 61.21.

J108 CANDLESTICK
Kilton Castle, Cleveland.
Late 15th century.
Socketed with angled stem. L 94mm.
Excavated by A Aberg.

J109 CANDLESTICK
Northampton.
Later 15th century.
Socketed with angled stem. L 108mm.
Goodall et al 1979, 273, fig 119.84.

J110 CANDLESTICK
Winchester, Hampshire.
15th century.
Socketed with broken, angled stem. L 68mm.
Goodall 1990-20, fig 306.3534.

J111 CANDLESTICK
Writtle, Essex.
c1425–1521.
Socketed with angled stem. L 74mm.
Rahtz 1969b, 85, fig 47.55.

J112 CANDLESTICK
Cambokeels, Durham.
Site: later 14th to early 16th century.
Socketed with broken, angled stem. L 80mm.
Hildyard 1949, 199, fig 6.3.

J113 CANDLESTICK
Rhuddlan, Clwyd.
1280s.
Socketed with broken, cranked stem. L 52mm.
Goodall 1994, fig 17.4, no. 73.

J114 CANDLESTICK
Oxford.
c1325–c1400.
Socketed with cranked, incomplete stem. L 53mm.
Goodall 1977e, 146, fig 27.43.

J115 CANDLESTICK
Winchester, Hampshire.
14th century.
Socketed with cranked stem. L 119mm.
Goodall 1990-20, fig 306.3532.

J116 CANDLESTICK
Goltho, Lincolnshire.
Croft B: late Saxon to mid 14th century.
Rectangular wax-pan with corner spout and central hole. L 69mm.
Goodall 1975a, 87, fig 41.105.

J117 CANDLESTICK
Oxford.
14th–early 15th century.
Rectangular wax-pan with broken handle and central candle socket. L 86mm.
Excavated by N Palmer.

J118 CANDLESTICK
Grenstein, Norfolk.
Late 14th–15th century.
Rectangular wax-pan with common rivet through handle and candle socket. L 158mm.
Goodall 1980c, fig 81, no. 73.

J119 CANDLESTICK
South Witham, Lincolnshire.
1137–85 to c1220.
Pricket and socket spring from single, broken stem. L 117mm.
Goodall 2002, fig 7.6, no. 68.

J120 CANDLESTICK
Rhuddlan, Clwyd.
14th century, ?earlier part, or conceivably 1290–1300.
Pricket and socket set on broken, angled stem. H 89mm.
Goodall 1994, fig 17.4, no. 74.

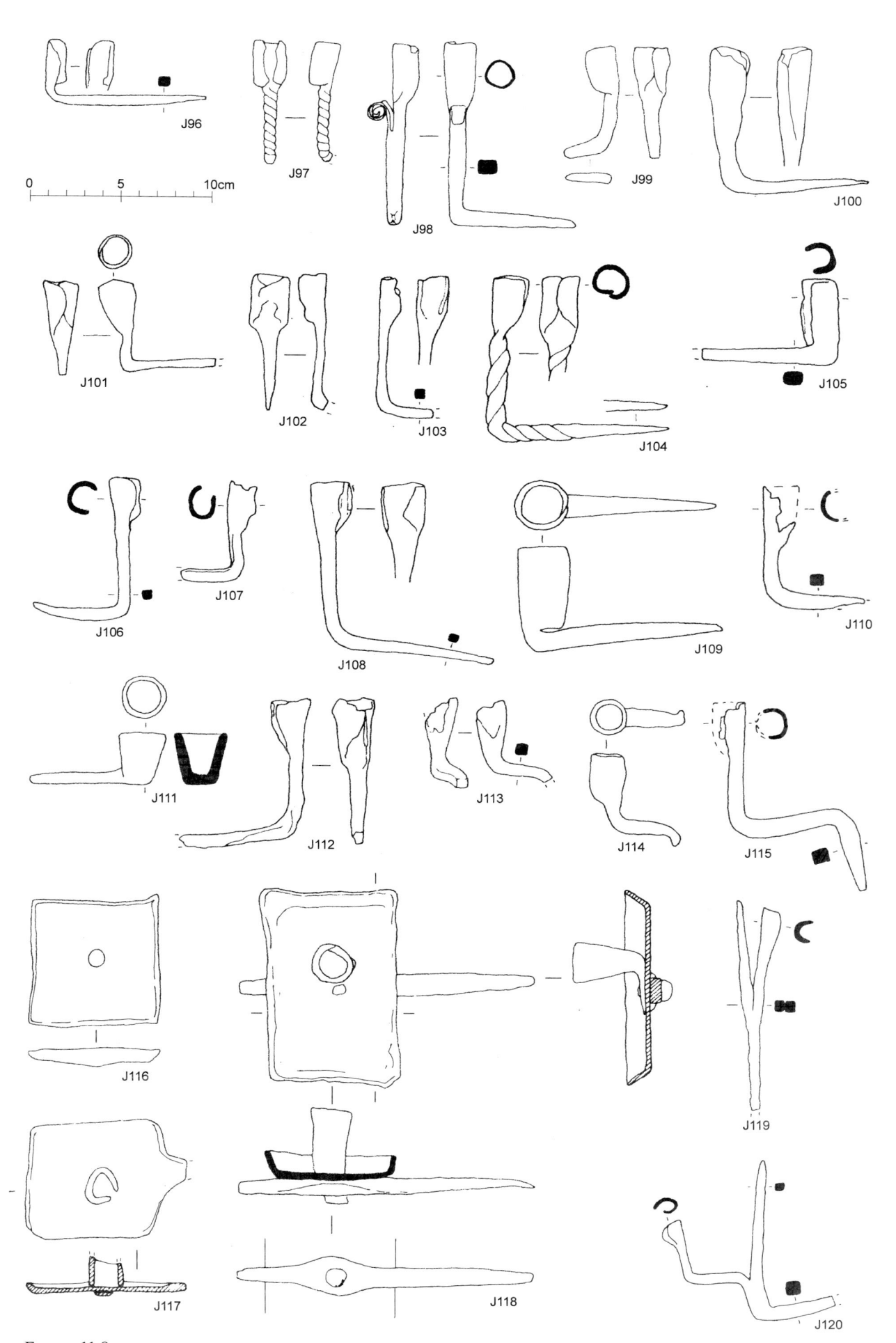

FIGURE 11.8
Candlesticks

J121 CANDLESTICK
South Witham, Lincolnshire.
1137–85 to c1220.
Three-armed candlestick with socketed side arms and broken central pricket and stem. L 132mm.
Goodall 2002, fig 7.6, no. 71.

J122 CANDLESTICK
South Witham, Lincolnshire.
c1220–late 13th century.
Three-armed candlestick with one of two socketed side arms broken, broken central pricket and stem. L 129mm.
Goodall 2002, fig 7.6, no. 73.

J123 CANDLESTICK
South Witham, Lincolnshire.
1137–85 to c1220.
Broken socketed side arm from three-armed candlestick. L 60mm.
Goodall 2002, fig 7.6, no. 72.

J124 CANDLESTICK
Goltho, Lincolnshire.
Croft A: late Saxon to late 14th or early 15th century.
Broken socketed side arm from three-armed candlestick. L 37mm.
Goodall 1975a, 87, fig 41.104.

J125 CANDLESTICK
Rievaulx Abbey, North Yorkshire.
Site: 1131–1538 with later robbing.
Three-armed candlestick with socketed side arms, one broken, central pricket, broken stem. L 115mm.
DAMHB Collection, London.

J126 CANDLESTICK
Rievaulx Abbey, North Yorkshire.
Site: 1131–1538 with later robbing.
Three-armed candlestick with side arms with split ends, broken central arm and stem. L 102mm.
DAMHB Collection, London.

J127 CANDLESTICK
Rievaulx Abbey, North Yorkshire.
Site: 1131–1538 with later robbing.
Three-armed candlestick with side arms with split ends, broken central arm and stem. L 105mm.
DAMHB Collection, London.

J128 CANDLESTICK
London.
Late 15th or early 16th century.
Three-armed candlestick with socketed side arms, central pricket and broken stem. L 114mm.
Hammerson 1975, 242, fig 19.5.

J129 FIRE-STEEL
Winchester, Hampshire.
Mid to late 11th century.
Rectangular blade with hooked tip and perforated inner end. L 98mm.
Goodall 1990-20, fig 306.3538.

J130 FIRE-STEEL
Winchester, Hampshire.
Mid 12th century.
Rectangular blade with hooked tip and broken, perforated inner end. L 103mm.
Goodall 1990-20, fig 306.3539.

J131 FIRE-STEEL
Brooklands, Weybridge, Surrey.
c1150–1325.
Blade and handle broken. L 71mm.
Goodall 1977d, 73, fig 45.17.

J132 FIRE-STEEL
Pleshey Castle, Essex.
Post 1180 to mid 13th, early 14th century.
Blade broken. L 68mm.
Goodall 1977c, 176, fig 38.13.

J133 FIRE-STEEL
Thelsford Priory, Warwickshire.
Site: 1200–1212 to 1536.
Shank broken. L 71mm.
Excavated by Mrs M Gray.

J134 FIRE-STEEL
Loughor Castle, West Glamorgan.
Site: c1106 to late 13th century.
Open rectangular fire-steel, the long sides convex. L 83mm.
Excavated by J M Lewis.

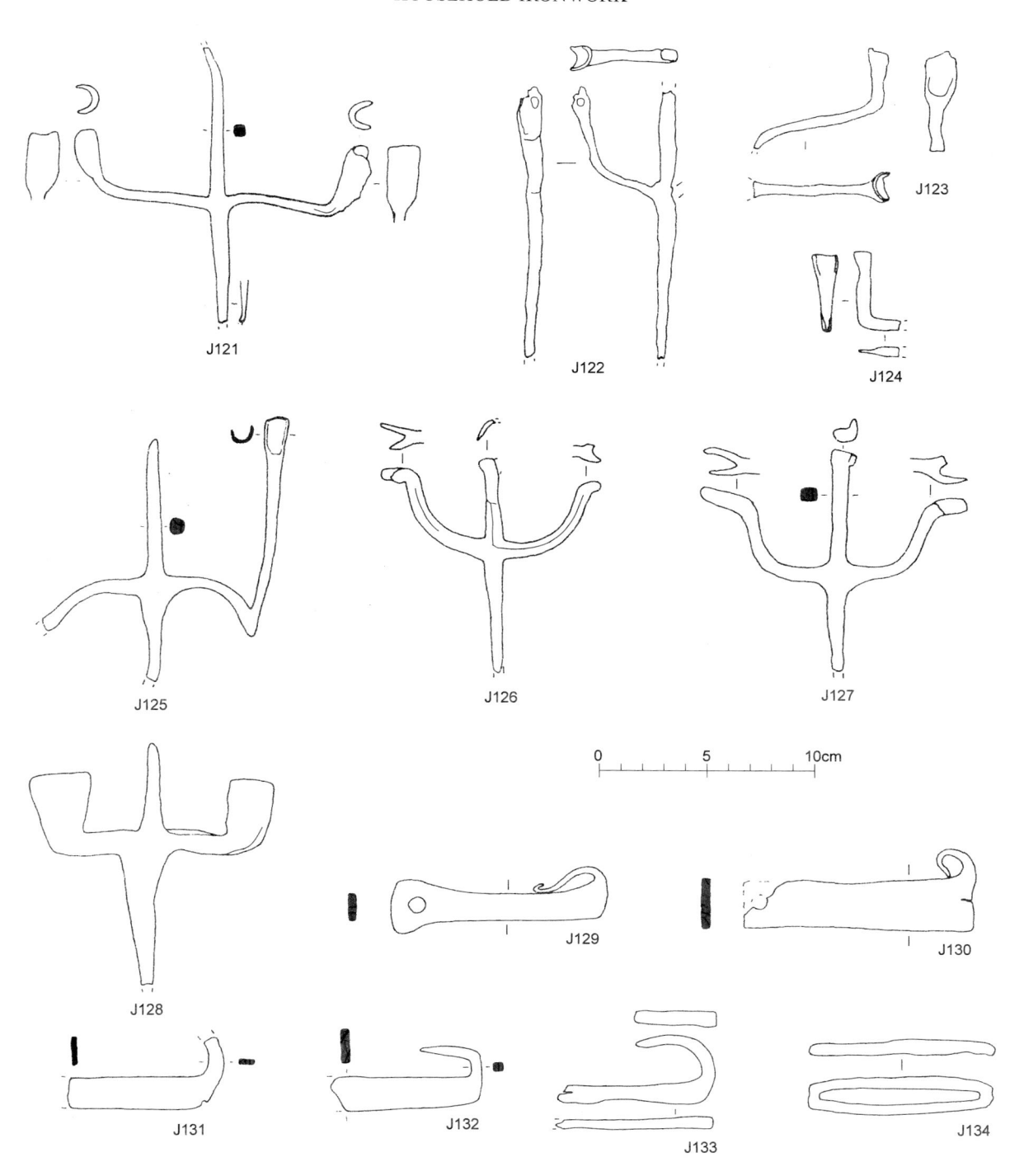

FIGURE 11.9
Candlesticks and fire-steels

J135 BUCKET
Taunton Castle, Taunton, Somerset.
*c*1150. From well.
Stave-built wooden bucket bound by two iron hoops, about one quarter of which survives. No handle found. Bucket diameter at rim: 334mm. Mean internal diameters of iron hoops: 328mm and 294mm.
Gray 1930; 1941, 68; Dunning 1974, 103–104, fig 12.

J136 BUCKET
Duffield Castle, Derbyshire.
Keep 1177–90 to 1266. From well.
Stave-built wooden bucket found by two iron hoops which survived in a fragmentary state. Iron handle rides in U-shaped handle loops nailed to inside of bucket. Bucket diameter at rim: 303mm. Handle W 303mm. Handle loop W 67mm.
Cox 1887, 160–161, fig on page 161; Dunning 1974, 104–105, fig 13.

J137 BUCKET
Castell-y-Bere, Gwynedd.
From well fill of 1283–95.
Stave-built wooden bucket originally boud by withies. Iron handle rides in eyed straps nailed to insides of opposing tall staves. Bucket diameter at rim: 356mm. Handle W 382mm. Eyed straps L 200mm.
Butler 1974, 100–101, figs 10–11, pl XXIV.

HOUSEHOLD IRONWORK

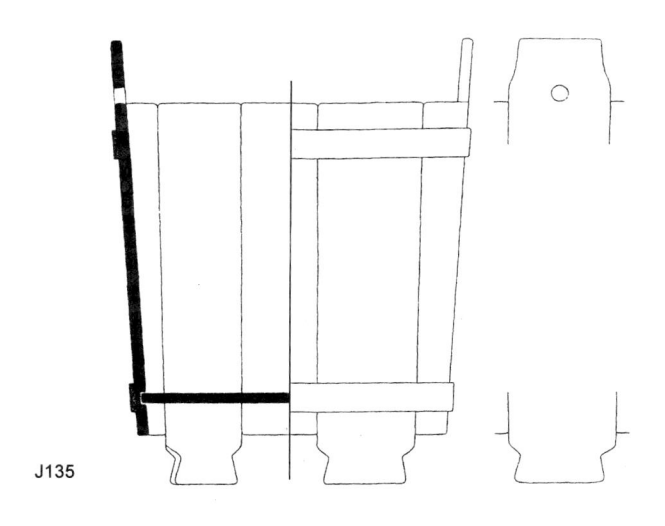

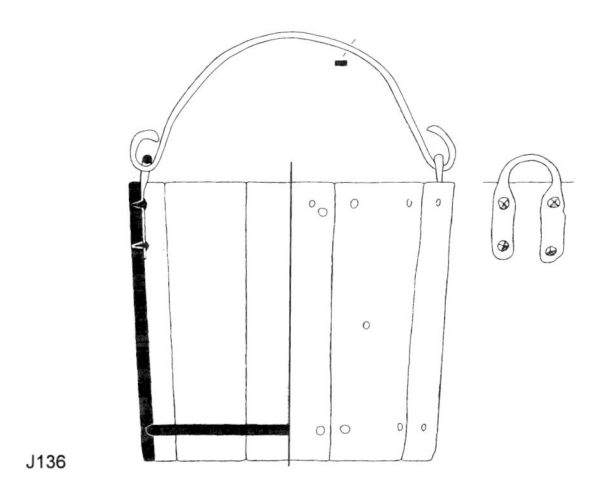

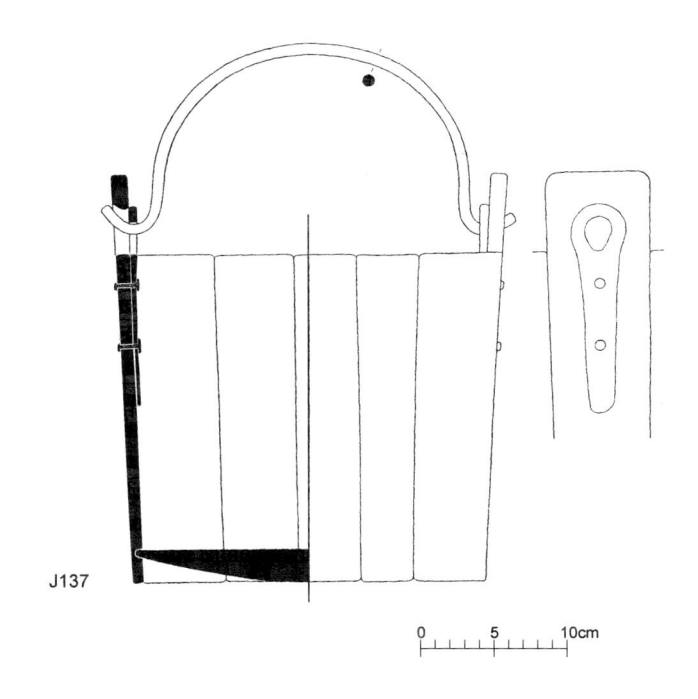

FIGURE 11.10
Buckets

J138 BUCKET (not illustrated)
Weoley Castle, Birmingham, West Midlands.
c1270–1600. From well.
Stave-built wooden bucket bound by two iron hoops. Iron handle with central expansion carrying swivel hook and chain **J239** of three figure-eight links rides in holes in opposing tall staves. Bucket diameter at rim: 340mm.
Taylor 1974. For site see Oswald 1962.

J139 BUCKET
Kilton Castle, Cleveland.
Late 15th century. From well.
Stave-built wooden bucket bound by two iron hoops. Iron handle with central expansion around corroded swivel loop rides in U-shaped handle loops (one lost) nailed to insides of opposing tall staves. Bucket not restored or conserved when examined. Handle width approximately 463mm. Three links **J237** from chain found with bucket.
Excavated by A Aberg.

J140 BUCKET HOOP
Winchester, Hampshire.
?Mid 14th century.
Incomplete, canted hoop. External D 209mm.
Goodall 1990-18, fig 300.3435.

J141 BUCKET HOOP
Oxford.
c1400–c1550.
Near complete canted hoop, distorted diameter 40mm.
Goodall 1977e, 142, fig 26.31.

J142 BUCKET HOOP
Waltham Abbey, Essex.
15th–16th century. From well.
Complete circular hoop of canted, rectangular section with vertical wood graining from staves on inner side. Mean internal diameter 250mm.
Goodall 1973a, 173, fig 12.45.

J143 BUCKET HOOP (not illustrated)
Waltham Abbey, Essex.
15th–16th century. From well.
Complete hoop of canted section. Mean internal diameter 230mm.
Goodall 1973a, 173, 45 (unillustrated example).

J144 HANDLE LOOP
Newbury, Berkshire.
Mid 15th century. From well.
U-shaped handle loop, straps incomplete. L 106mm.
Goodall 1997, fig 21, no. 34.

J145 HANDLE LOOP
Newbury, Berkshire.
Mid 15th century. From well.
U-shaped handle loop. L 110mm.
Goodall 1997, fig 21, no. 33.

J146 HANDLE LOOP
Newbury, Berkshire.
Mid 15th century.
U-shaped handle loop, incomplete. L 79mm.
Goodall 1997, fig 21, no. 35.

J147 HANDLE LOOP
Waltham Abbey, Essex.
1500–70.
U-shaped handle loop, side straps broken. L 126mm.
Goodall 1978d, 158, fig 22.15.

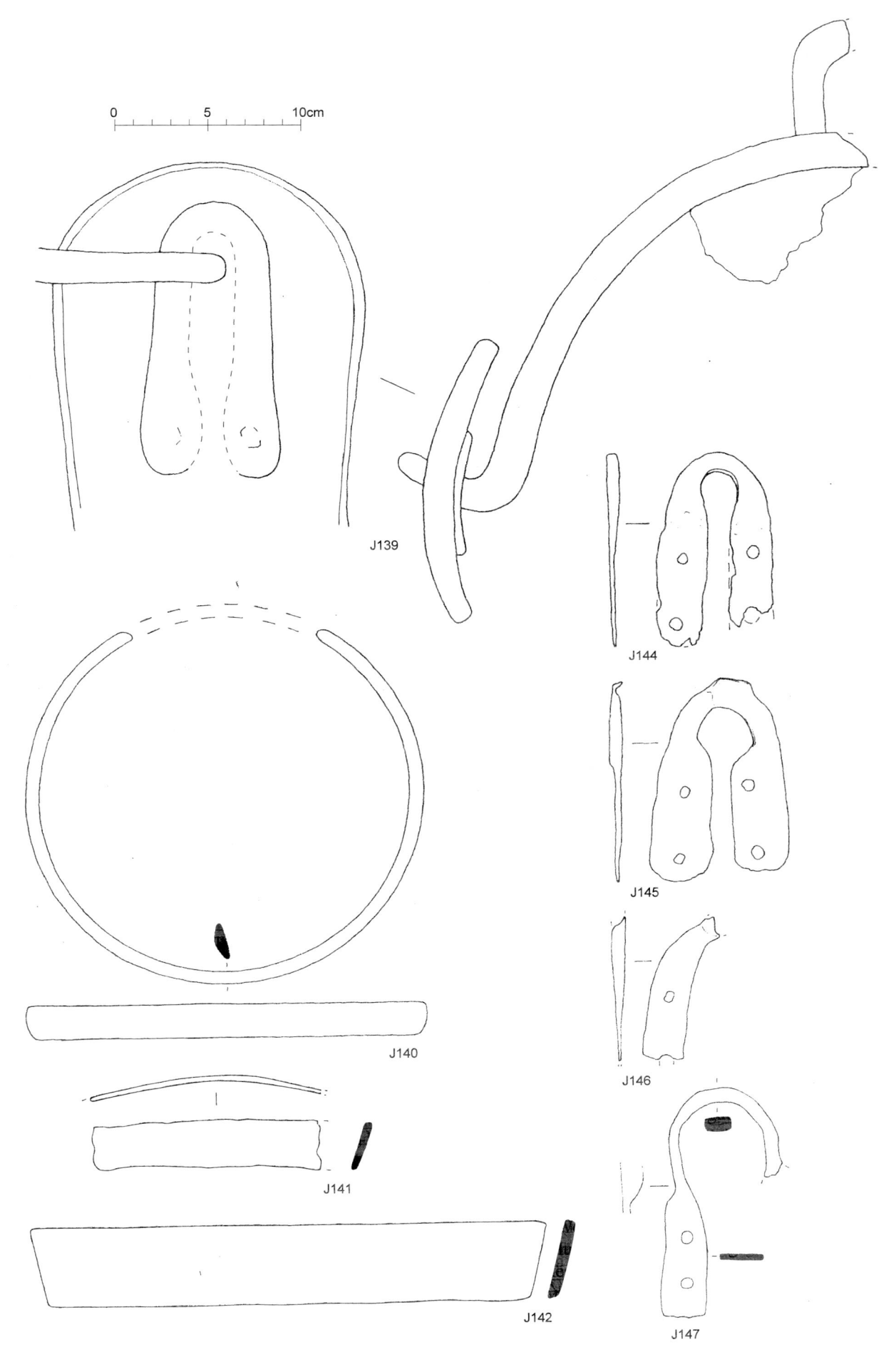

FIGURE 11.11
Bucket, bucket hoops and handle loops

J148 HANDLE STRAP
Llantwit Major, South Glamorgan.
12th to early 16th century.
Eyed strap, damaged. L 130mm.
Nash-Williams 1952, 331, pl X1(2).9.

J149 HANDLE STRAP
Ospringe, Kent.
c1483–1550.
Eyed handle strap. L 181mm.
Goodall 1979c, 132, fig 21.66.

J150 HANDLE STRAP
Newbury, Berkshire.
Mid 15th century. From well.
Eyed strap, broken. L 52mm.
Goodall 1997, fig 21, no. 38.

J151 HANDLE STRAP
Newbury, Berkshire.
Mid 15th century. From well.
Eyed strap, base incomplete. L 117mm.
Goodall 1997, fig 21, no. 37.

J152 HANDLE STRAP
Waltham Abbey, Essex.
From well dug; c1300, filled late 15th to early 16th century.
Eyed handle strap, broken. L 75mm.
Goodall 1973a, 173, fig 12.46.

J153 HANDLE STRAP
Newbury, Berkshire.
c1430–70.
Eyed handle strap. L 176mm.
Goodall 1997.

J154 HANDLE STRAP
Pivington, Kent.
Early 16th century.
Eyed handle strap. L 107mm.
Rigold 1962, 46, fig 8ii.

J155 HANDLE
Gloucester.
12th century.
Complete handle, flattened at the centre. W 340mm.
Excavated by H Hurst.

J156 HANDLE
Rhuddlan, Clwyd.
?Mid 13th century, or late 11th–12th century.
One end broken. W 287mm.
Goodall 1994, fig 17.4, no. 75.

J157 HANDLE
Llanstephan Castle, Dyfed.
Site: 12th–15th century. From well.
Broken handle with central expansion with swivel hook. W 319mm.
DAMHB Collection, Cardiff.

J158 HANDLE
Criccieth Castle, Gwynedd.
Site: c1230–1404.
Handle, flattened and expanded at the centre. Found near part of what may have been a bucket or bucket hoop. W 169mm.
O'Neil 1944–45, 41, pl IX.17.

J159 HANDLE
Goltho Manor, Lincolnshire.
c1100–1150.
Broken handle. W 42mm.
Goodall 1987, fig 159.120.

J160 HANDLE
Winchester, Hampshire.
14th century.
Broken handle. W 39mm.
Goodall 1990-18, fig 300.3431.

J161 HANDLE
Winchester, Hampshire.
14th century.
Distorted, spirally twisted handle. W 242mm.
Goodall 1990-19, fig 304.3518.

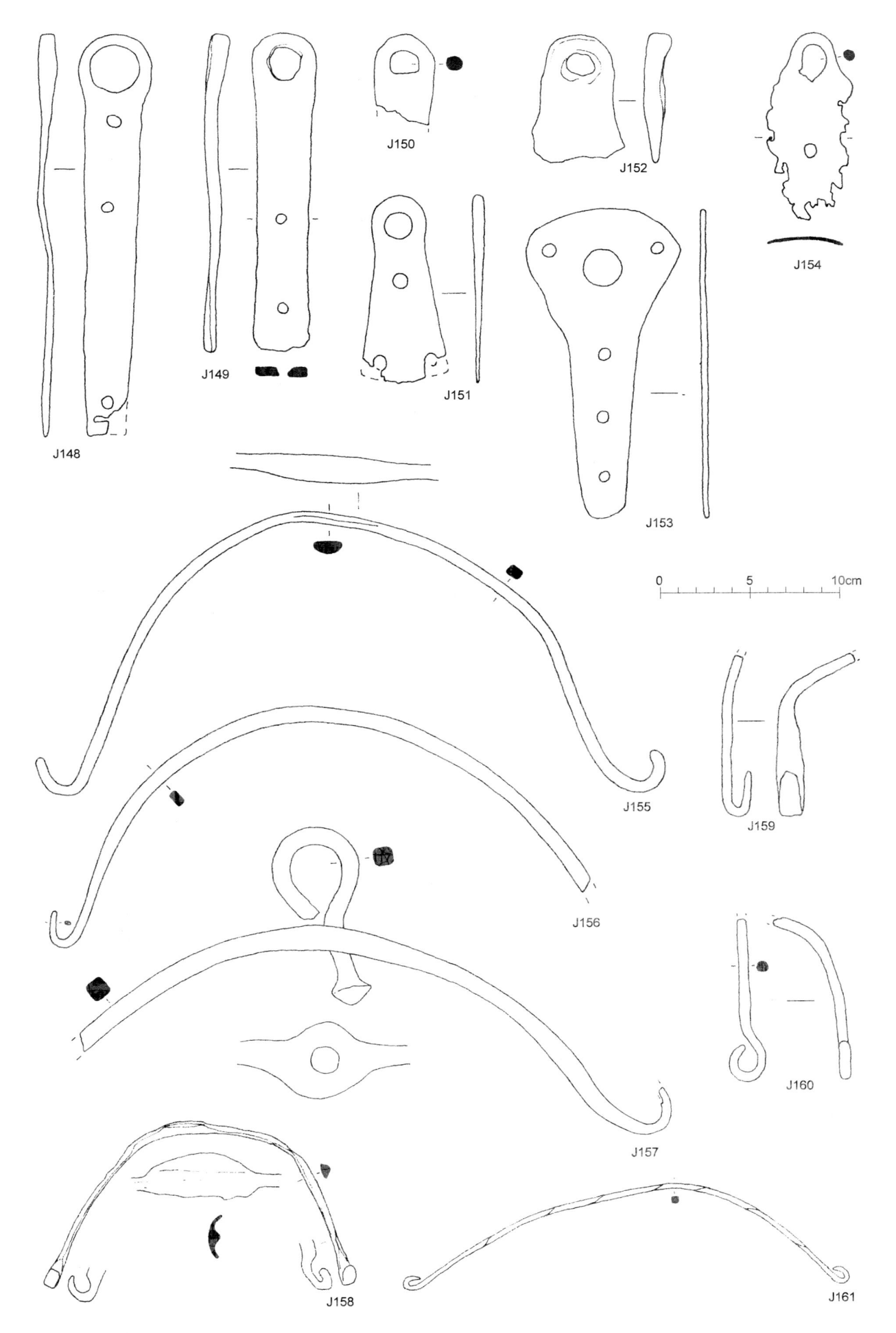

FIGURE 11.12
Handle straps and handles

J162 HANDLE (not illustrated)
Winchester, Hampshire.
14th century.
Handle of spirally twisted iron with hooked ends, one broken. W 152mm. Compare with **J161**.
Goodall 1990-19, 978, no. 3519.

J163 HOOK
South Witham, Lincolnshire.
1137–85 to c1220.
S-hook. L 103mm.
Goodall 2002, fig 7.5, no. 62.

J164 HOOK
The Mount, Princes Risborough, Buckinghamshire.
14th, early 15th century.
S-hook. L 138mm.
Pavry and Knocker 1953–60, 163, fig 13.8.

J165 HOOK
The Mount, Princes Risborough, Buckinghamshire.
14th, early 15th century.
S-hook. L 178mm.
Pavry and Knocker 1953–60, 163, fig 13.7.

J166 HOOK
Weoley Castle, Birmingham, West Midlands.
Site: c1080–1600.
S-hook. L 287mm.
Birmingham City Museum, WC 434. For site see Oswald 1962.

J167 HOOK
Weoley Castle, Birmingham, West Midlands.
Site: c1080–c1600.
S-hook. L 288mm.
Birmingham City Museum. For site see Oswald 1962.

J168 HOOK
Manor of the More, Rickmansworth, Hertfordshire.
c1350–1426.
Hook with flattened, looped handle. L 110mm.
Biddle et al 1959, 185, fig 20.5.

J169 HOOK
Waltham Abbey, Essex.
c1300. From well.
Incomplete hook with socket and strap extension, both formerly nailed. L 212mm.
Goodall 1973a, 173, fig 12.47.

J170 HOOK
Thelsford Priory, Warwickshire.
13th–14th, possibly 15th century.
Socketed hook. L 307mm.
Excavated by Mrs M Gray.

J171 HOOK
Hambleton Moat, Lincolnshire.
Site: 1250–1400.
Hook with broken stem. L 165mm.
Butler 1963, 67, fig 14.7.

J172 HOOK
Clarendon Palace, Wiltshire.
Site: c1072 to later 15th century.
Hook with nailed, flanged arm. L 178mm.
Goodall 1988, fig 81.94; Borenius and Charlton 1936.

J173 HOOK
Norwich.
In 1507 fire deposit.
Hook with socket and nailed extension strap. L 231mm.
Goodall 1993a, fig 54.557.

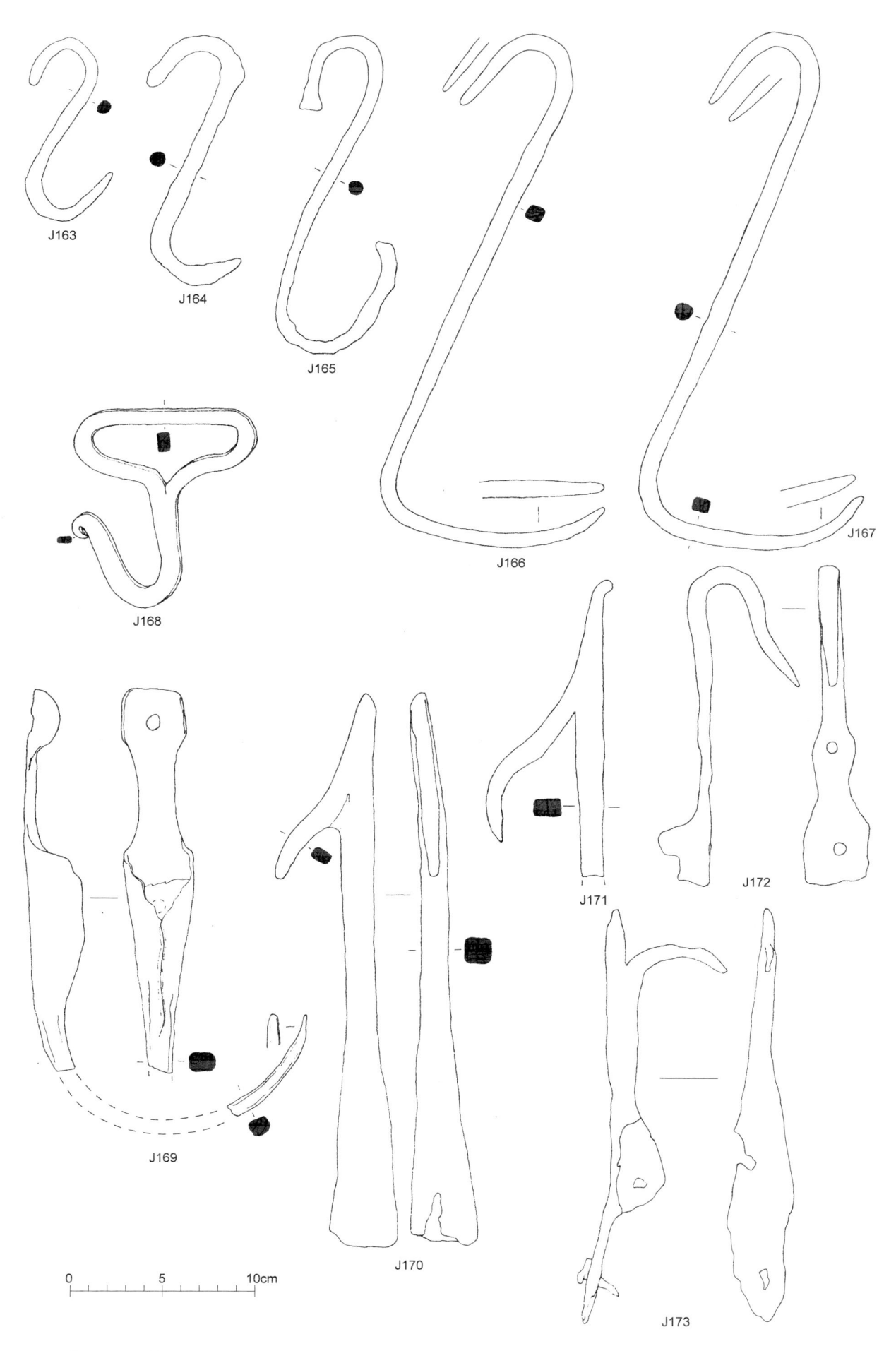

FIGURE 11.13
Hooks

J174 DRAGHOOK (not illustrated)
Weoley Castle, Birmingham, West Midlands.
Site c1080–1600.
Eyed shank with loop and four outward curving arms each terminating in four back-facing barbs. Larger central arm (length not known).
Birmingham City Museum, WC 368.

J175 HOOK
Weoley Castle, Birmingham, West Midlands.
Site: c1080–1600.
Closed loop, flattened hooked end. L 390mm.
Birmingham City Museum, WC 435. For site see Oswald 1962.

J176 HOOK
Wisley, Surrey.
12th–13th century.
Two hooked arms and tang. L 95mm.
Excavated by Mrs A Watson.

J177 HOOK
Winchester, Hampshire.
Mid to ?late 13th century.
Two hooked arms broken, tang complete. L 66mm.
Goodall 1990-14, fig 242.2549.

J178 HOOK (not illustrated)
Winchester, Hampshire.
14th–?15th century.
Two hooked arms broken, tang complete. As J177. L 45mm.
Goodall 1990-14, 820, no. 2552.

J179 HOOK
Winchester, Hampshire.
Mid to late 13th century.
Two hooked arms, one broken. Tang tip damaged. L 47mm.
Goodall 1990-14, fig 242.2550.

J180 BALANCE
Oxford.
14th–18th century.
Equal-armed balance retaining one eyed terminal, stub of central upright pointer, and pivoting suspension stirrup. L 256mm.
Goodall 1976c, 300, fig 28.89.

J181 BALANCE
Copt Hay, Tetsworth, Oxfordshire.
Late 13th–14th century.
Equal-armed balance with near-complete beam and central U-shaped mount supporting broken ring. L 328mm.
Robinson 1973, 106, fig 25.23.

J182 BALANCE
Copt Hay, Tetsworth, Oxfordshire.
Mid 13th century.
Arm tip from equal-armed balance. Length unknown.
Robinson 1973, 106, fig 25.24.

J183 BALANCE
Theodoric's Hermitage, Margam, West Glamorgan.
Site: 13th–15th century.
Stirrup from equal-armed balance. H 143mm.
National Museum of Wales, Cardiff, 49.140.21.

J184 BALANCE
Huish, Wiltshire.
Site: 12th–15th century.
Unequal-armed balance with wooden beam, iron fittings and latten weight. The beam, almost entirely lost, has a 98mm long, 8mm diameter sheet iron sleeve at one end. Two fulchrums and the bar for the load pass through the sleeve and wood, and are held firm at their outer ends by rectangular plates with out-turned ends. U-shaped loops from the fulchrums support suspension rings, and from the load bar support a swivel ring and looped hook with chisel-cut decoration. An iron swivel hook supports the weight at the opposing end, which is of latten filled with lead.
Shortt 1968.

HOUSEHOLD IRONWORK

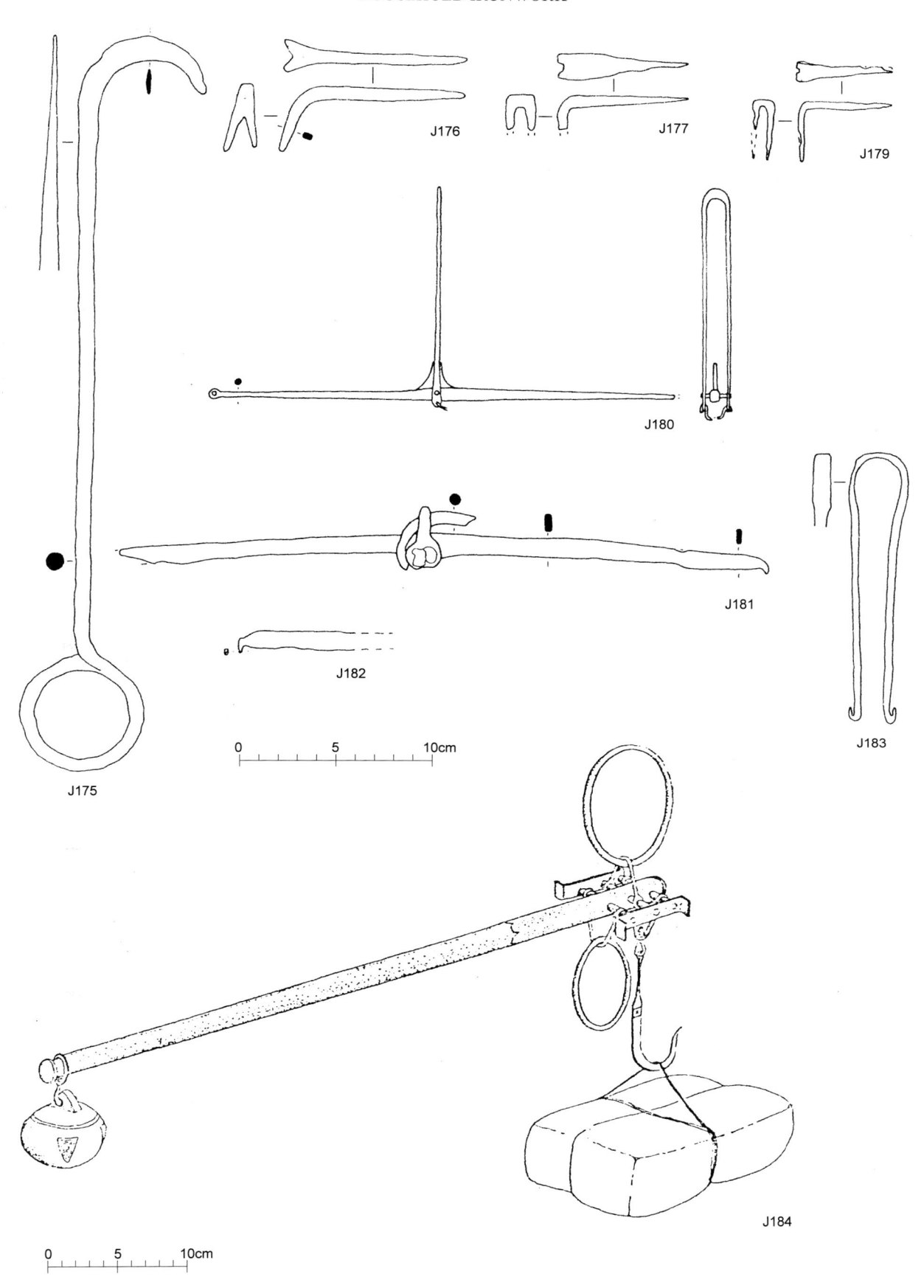

FIGURE 11.14
Hooks and balances

J185 CHAIN
Gomeldon, Wiltshire.
Second half 13th century.
Chain of several circular lings, 12mm diameter, L 41mm.
Excavated by J W G Musty.

J186 RING
Tarring, West Sussex.
c1490–1510. From well with shoe leather.
Ring with fragment of leather strap from shoe. D:12mm.
Barton 1963, 34, fig 4.12.

J187 RING
Wallingstones, Hereford and Worcester.
First half 13th century.
D 12mm.
Bridgewater 1970–72, 102, no. 16.

J188 RING
Winchester, Hampshire.
12th–early 13th century.
Distorted. D 13mm.
Goodall 1990-12, fig 140.1325.

J189 RING
Hangleton, West Sussex.
13th–14th century.
D 14mm.
Holden 1963, 171, fig 37.5.

J190 RING
Kings Langley, Hertfordshire.
15th century.
D 15mm.
Neal 1973, 56, fig XV.76.

J191 RING
Northampton.
Later 15th century.
Broken ring with non-ferrous plating. D 17mm.
Goodall et al 1979, 273, fig 120.92.

J192 RING
Castle Acre Castle, Norfolk.
1140s–50s with derived material from c1066.
D 20mm.
Goodall 1982, fig 41, no. 119.

J193–194 RINGS
Stockbridge Down, Hampshire.
Late 11th century. Found with buckle **K2** near skeleton in position suggesting they were attached one in front and one on either side of a belt.
Two rings, one broken. D 33 and 30mm.
Hill 1935–37, 250, pl 1.

J195 RING
Goltho Manor, Lincolnshire.
c1100–50.
D 39mm.
Goodall 1987, fig 159.126.

J196 RING
Brandon Castle, Warwickshire.
13th century.
Overlapped ends, part-twisted circumference.
D 46mm.
Chatwin 1955, 81, fig 11.24.

J197 LINK
Thuxton, Norfolk.
Site: 12th–14th century.
Rectangular link. W 23mm.
Excavated by L A S Butler.

J198 LINK
Castle Acre Castle, Norfolk.
1140s deposits with derived material from c1066.
Broken rectangular link. W 24mm.
Goodall 1982, fig 41, no. 115.

J199 LINK
Grafton Regis, Northamptonshire.
Probably 15th century.
Rectangular link. W 26mm.
Excavated by Miss C Mahany.

J200 LINK
Goltho Manor, Lincolnshire.
c1100–30.
Rectangular link. W 30mm.
Goodall 1987, fig 159.141.

J201 LINK (not illustrated)
Winchester, Hampshire.
Mid to late 13th century.
Distorted oval link. L 39mm.
Goodall 1990-15, 824, no. 2557.

J202 LINK
South Witham, Lincolnshire.
Late 13th century to 1308–13.
Broken oval link. L 68mm.
Goodall 2002, fig 7.5, no. 58.

J203 CHAIN
Winchester, Hampshire.
13th century.
Oval flat link and ring. L 73mm.
Goodall 1990-15, fig 245.2558.

J204 CHAIN
Alsted, Surrey.
c1270–1350.
Two oval links, one broken and distorted.
L 133mm.
Goodall 1976a, 56, fig 34.20.

J205 CHAIN
Cambokeels, Durham.
Later 14th to early 15th century.
Fifteen straight-sided links, some distorted.
Length of four links. 138mm.
Hildyard and Charlton 1947, 194, fig 3.3.

J206 CHAIN
Winchester, Hampshire.
14th–15th century.
Circular flat ring and straight-sided link.
L 65mm.
Goodall 1990-15, fig 245.2563.

J207 CHAIN
Winchester, Hampshire.
15th–16th century.
Circular flat ring and straight-sided link.
L 60mm.
Goodall 1990-15, fig 245.2564.

J208 CHAIN
Clarendon Palace, Wiltshire.
Site: c1072 to later 15th century.
Ring and two straight-sided links. L 133mm.
Goodall 1988, fig 81.95; Borenius and Charlton 1936.

J209 CHAIN WITH SWIVEL RING
Wintringham, Cambridgeshire.
Late 13th–early 14th century.
Two flat straight-sided links with swivel hook and ring. L 175mm.
Goodall 1977a, 257, fig 45.56.

J210 CHAIN WITH SWIVEL RING
Northolt Manor, Greater London.
1300–50. Found near hearth.
Fragments of chain of straight-sided links and swivel ring and hook. Swivel L 50mm.
Hurst 1961, 289, fig 76.9–12.

J211 CHAIN
Hen Blas, Clwyd.
13th–14th century.
Five flat straight-sided links, two drawn.
L 122mm.
Leach 1960, 23, fig 13.18.

J212 LINK
Newbury, Berkshire.
c1430–70.
Straight-sided link, worn one end, broken at the other. L 89mm.
Goodall 1997, fig 21, no. 39.

J213 LINK
South Witham, Lincolnshire.
Late 13th century to 1308–13.
Broken straight-sided link. L 110mm.
Goodall 2002, fig 7.5, no. 59.

J214 CHAIN WITH SWIVEL LOOP
Winchester, Hampshire.
Late 13th century.
Chain of two straight-sided links, the lower supporting a swivel loop. L 465mm.
Cunliffe 1964, 157, fig 54.5, scale incorrect.

J215 CHAIN AND RING
Northolt Manor, Greater London.
1300–50. From hearth in cooking area.
Chain and copper-alloy ring, with large bottom ring. Iron links pivoting on a common bar.
L 183mm.
Hurst 1961, 289, fig 76.17.

J216 CHAIN AND HOOK
London.
?Late 13th–mid 14th century.
Three flat figure-eight links and looped hook.
L 125mm.
Henig 1974, 191, fig 38.66.

J217 CHAIN AND HOOK
Llantrithyd, South Glamorgan.
Early to mid 12th century.
Broken flat, figure-eight link and looped hook.
L 52mm.
Goodall 1977f, 47, iron object fig 2.35.

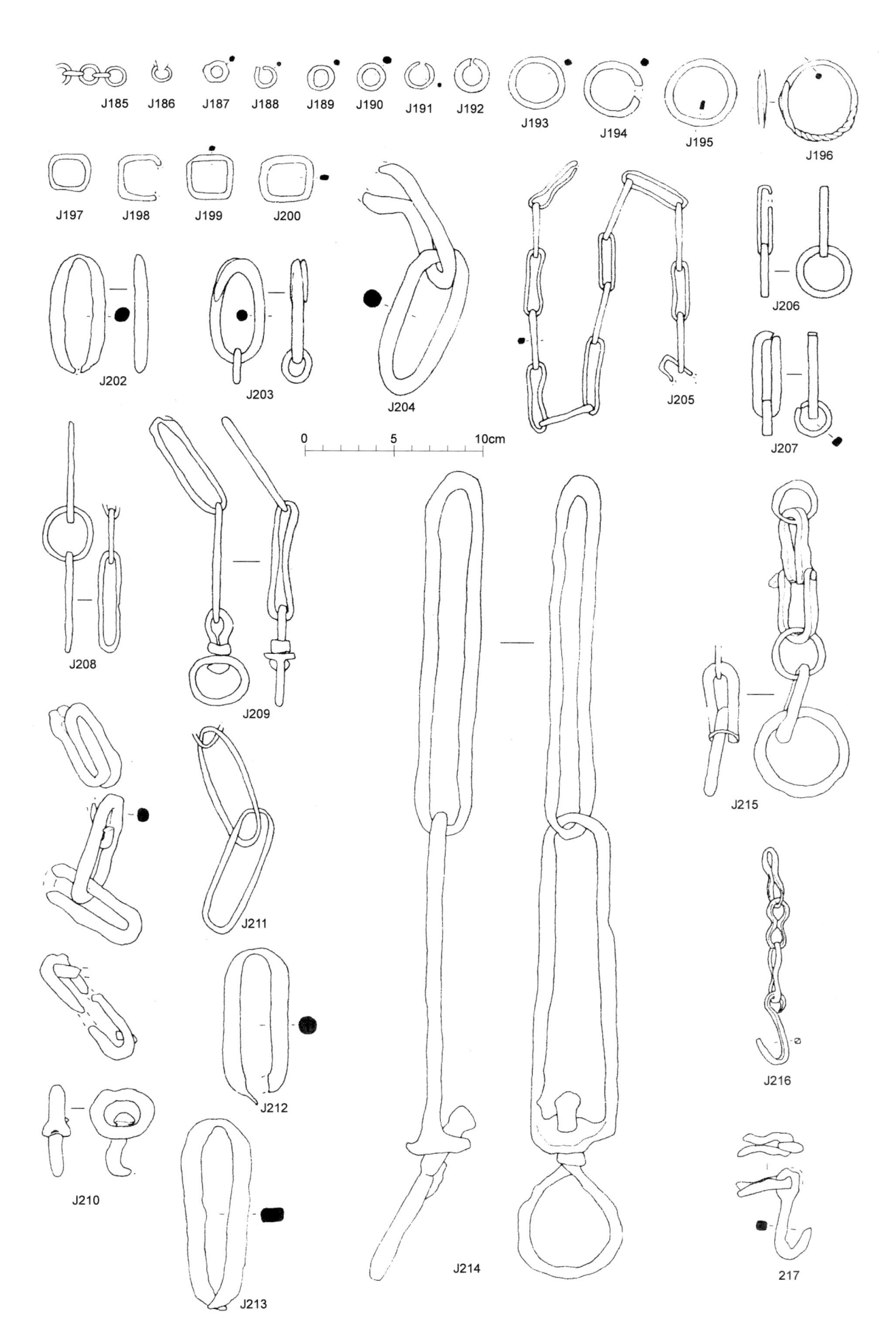

FIGURE 11.15
Chains, rings, and links

J218 CHAIN
South Witham, Lincolnshire.
1137–85 to c1220.
Three flat figure-eight links. L 102mm.
Goodall 2002, fig 7.5, no. 56.

J219 CHAIN
Winchester, Hampshire.
14th–?15th century.
Two flat, figure-eight links, one broken. L 47mm.
Goodall 1990-15, fig 245.2571.

J220 CHAIN AND HOOK
Dyserth Castle, Clwyd.
Site: 1241–63.
Three flat figure-eight links and looped hook. L 145mm.
Glenn 1915, 65, fig 10.

J221 LINK
Norwich.
13th century.
Flat figure-eight link. L 51mm.
Hurst 1963, 168, fig 14.3.

J222 CHAIN
Northampton.
?Second half 13th century.
Two flat figure-eight links. L 83mm.
Goodall 1978c, 152, fig 24.3.

J223 LINK
Weoley Castle, Birmingham, West Midlands.
Site: c1080–1600.
Broken, tinned, flat figure-eight link. L 58mm.
Birmingham City Museum, WC 329. For site see Oswald 1962.

J224 CHAIN
Winchester, Hampshire.
Late 11th–early 12th century.
Two figure-eight links, one flat, one twisted. L 103mm.
Goodall 1990-15, fig 245.2567.

J225 LINK
Oxford.
c1250–c1325.
Flat, figure-eight link. L 68mm.
Goodall 1977e, 142, fig 26.28.

J226 CHAIN AND HOOK
Portchester, Hampshire.
13th century.
Chain of figure-eight links and hook. L 126mm.
Hinton 1977, 204, fig 109.70, scale 2:3, not 1:3.

J227 CHAIN
Clough Castle, Co. Down.
c1250–early 14th century.
Two broken flat figure-eight shaped links, one with collar. L 61mm.
Waterman 1954, 141, fig 13.3.

J228 LINK
Winchester, Hampshire.
12th–?13th century.
Broken flat, figure-eight link. L 66mm.
Goodall 1990-15, fig 245.2568.

J229 CHAIN
Glastonbury Tor, Somerset.
12th–16th century.
Four flat figure-eight links. L 155mm.
Rahtz 1970, 53, fig 23.14.

J230 LINK
Writtle, Essex.
1211–c1306.
Flat figure-eight link. L 113mm.
Rahtz 1969b, 87, fig 48.78.

J231 LINK
Wintringham, Cambridgeshire.
Second half 13th century.
Flat figure-eight link. L 116mm.
Goodall 1977a, 257, fig 45.57.

J232 LINK
South Witham, Lincolnshire.
Late 13th century to 1308–13.
Broken flat rectangular link. L 123mm.
Goodall 2002, fig 7.5, no. 57.

J233 LINK AND STAPLE
Winchester, Hampshire.
Late 13th–early 14th century.
Curved figure-eight link and U-shaped staple. Link L 109mm, staple W 18mm, L 35mm.
Goodall 1990-19, fig 303.3482.

J234 CHAIN
Waltham Abbey, Essex.
c1540.
Two flat figure-eight links. L 125mm.
Huggins 1972, 124. From F64.

J235 LINK
Lochmaben Castle, Dumfries and Galloway.
Late 14th century.
Broken figure-eight link. L 142mm.
Macdonald and Laing 1974–75, 148, fig 11.23.

J236 CHAIN
Hangleton, West Sussex.
13th–14th century.
Two flat figure-eight links. L 224mm.
Holden 1963, 169–171, fig 37.1.

J237 CHAIN
Kilton Castle, Cleveland.
Late 15th century.
Three flat figure-eight links found in well with bucket **J139**. L 305mm.
Excavated by A Aberg.

J238 LINK
Brandon Castle, Warwickshire.
13th century, ?post-1226.
Flat figure-eight link. L 173mm.
Chatwin 1955, 81, fig 11.16.

J239 CHAIN
Weoley Castle, Birmingham, West Midlands.
c1270–1600. Probably from well.
Three flat figure-eight links, only one drawn. Probably associated with bucket **J138**. Total L 560mm.
Birmingham City Museum, 835. For site see Oswald 1962.

J240 CHAIN
Winchester, Hampshire.
Late 11th–12th century.
Six flat, S-shaped links. L 98mm.
Goodall 1990-15, fig 245.2574.

J241 CHAIN
Gomeldon, Wiltshire.
Second half 13th century.
S-shaped links. L 44mm.
Musty and Algar 1986.

J242 LINK AND HOOK
Wroughton Copse, Fyfield Down, Wiltshire.
13th century (?mid) to 14th century.
S-shaped link and looped hook. L 82mm.
Excavated by P J Fowler.

J243 CHAIN
King's Lynn, Norfolk.
c1250–1300.
Four variously complete links with opposed ends. L 59mm.
Goodall and Carter 1977, 296, fig 134.60.

J244 SWIVEL RING AND HOOK
Wharram Percy, North Yorkshire.
Late 15th to early 16th century.
Complete. L 47mm.
Goodall 1979a, 118, fig 61.31.

J245 SWIVEL RING AND HOOK
Somerby, Lincolnshire.
15th–mid 16th century.
Complete. L 108mm.
Mynard 1969, 81, fig 11.IW29.

J246 SWIVEL HOOK AND RING
Goltho, Lincolnshire.
Near fire-pit in croft A: late Saxon to late 14th or early 15th century. Complete. L 120mm.
Goodall 1975a, 87, fig 41.108.

J247 SWIVEL RING AND HOOK
Oxford.
13th–16th century.
Swivel hook, broken ring and fragmentary link (not drawn), found with barrel padlock with shackle **I90**. L 118mm.
Excavated by T G Hassall. From Greyfriars burial ground.

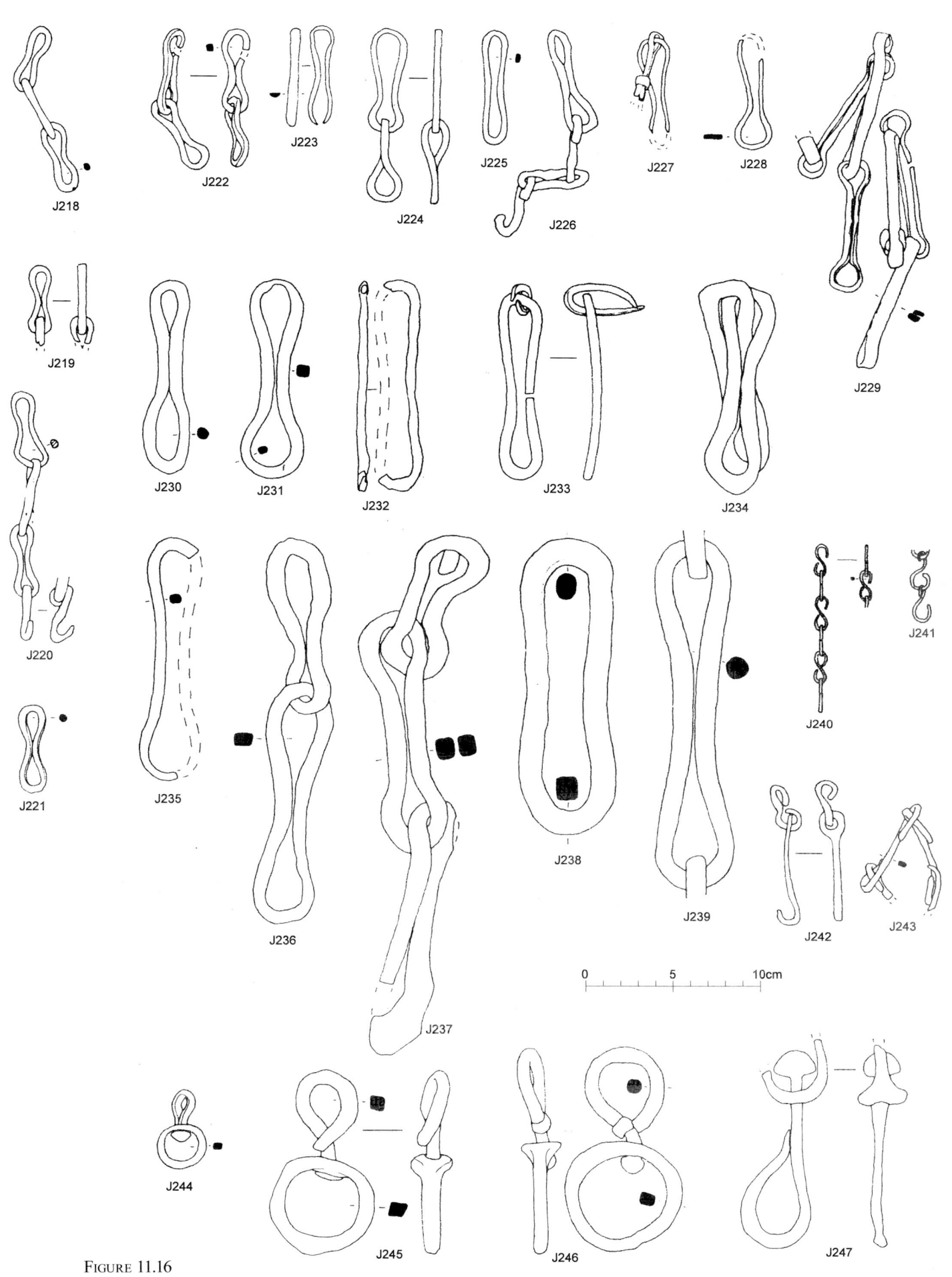

FIGURE 11.16
Chains, links, and chain fittings

J248 SWIVEL RING, HOOK AND SHAFT FITTING
Badby, Northamptonshire.
Mid to late 14th century.
Complete. Length of swivel: 155mm.
Excavated by Mrs M Gray.

J249 SWIVEL RING AND HOOK
Llantrithyd, South Glamorgan.
Early to mid 12th century.
Swivel hook broken. D 31mm.
Goodall 1977f, 47, iron object fig 226.

J250 SWIVEL RING
Llantrithyd, South Glamorgan.
Early to mid 12th century.
Ring broken. D 31mm.
Goodall 1977f, 47, iron object fig 227.

J251 SWIVEL RING
Winchester, Hampshire.
15th–16th century.
Complete. D 32mm.
Goodall 1990-15, fig 246.2591.

J252 SWIVEL RING
Wharram Percy, North Yorkshire.
Late 15th–early 16th century.
Complete. D 34mm.
Goodall 1979a, 118, fig 61.33.

J253 SWIVEL RING
Kirkcudbright Castle, Dumfries and Galloway.
c1288–1308.
Complete. D 50mm.
Dunning 1957–58, 138, fig 7.5.

J254 SWIVAL RING
Hangleton, West Sussex.
13th–14th century.
Complete. D 59mm.
Holden 1963, 171, fig 37.3.

J255 SWIVEL RING
Upton, Gloucestershire.
Late 13th to late 14th century.
Complete. D 68mm.
Hilton and Rahtz 1966, 121, fig 14.37.

J256 SWIVEL HOOK
Lyveden, Northamptonshire.
Second half 13th century.
Complete. L 28mm.
Bryant and Steane 1971, 65, fig 17s.

J257 SWIVEL HOOK
Goltho Manor, Licolnshire.
c1125–50.
Hook tip broken. L 35mm.
Goodall 1987, fig 159.125.

J258 SWIVEL HOOK
Northampton.
End 15th century.
Complete. L 40mm.
Goodall *et al* 1979, 273, fig 119.77.

J259 SWIVEL HOOK
London.
Late 13th to mid 14th century.
Complete. L 47mm.
Henig 1974, 195, fig 39.95.

J260 SWIVEL HOOK
Wharram Percy, North Yorkshire.
Early 15th century.
Swivel hook and bar. L 52mm.
Goodall 1979a, 118, fig 61.32.

J261 SWIVEL HOOK
Hangleton, West Sussex.
13th–14th century.
Complete. L 53mm.
Holden 1963, 171, fig 37.4.

J262 SWIVEL HOOK
South Witham, Lincolnshire.
Late 13th century to 1308–13.
Hook distorted. L 102mm.
Goodall 2002, fig 7.5, no. 61.

J263 SWIVEL HOOK
Newbury, Berkshire.
Mid 15th century.
Complete. L 109mm.
Goodall 1997, fig 21, no. 40.

J264 SWIVEL RINGS
West Whelpington, Northumberland.
Medieval.
Pair of swivel rings. L 74mm.
For site see Jarrett 1962; 1970.

J265 SWIVEL RINGS
Clarendon Palace, Wiltshire.
Site: c1072 to later 15th century.
Pair of rings. L 63mm.
Goodall 1988, fig 81.97; Borenius and Charlton 1936.

J266 SWIVEL RINGS
Sawtry, Cambridgeshire.
15th–early 16th century.
Pair of rings. L 61mm.
Moorhouse 1971b, 85, fig 4.4.

J267 SWIVEL HOOK
Winchester, Hampshire.
12th–early 13th century.
Hook broken. L 89mm.
Goodall 1990-15, fig 246.2585.

J268 SWIVEL ROD AND LOOP
Stonar, Kent.
c1275–1385.
Loop broken. L 245mm.
Excavated by N Macpherson-Grant.

J269 SWIVEL HOOK
Wallingstones, Hereford and Worcester.
Post-1500 destruction layer on site occupied from c1200.
Swivel hook with angled shank. L 193mm.
Bridgewater 1970–72, 104, no. 95.

J270 SWIVEL ROD
Goltho, Lincolnshire.
Late 14th–early 15th century.
Complete, tip perforated. L 100mm.
Goodall 1975a, 87, fig 41.106.

J271 SWIVEL LOOP
Winchester, Hampshire.
?1432–33.
Loop with opposing knobbed terminals. Non-ferrous plating. D 38mm.
Goodall 1990-15, fig 246.2587.

J272 CHAIN FITTING
Winchester, Hampshire.
Late 15th–early 16th century.
Swivel ring and hook support openwork, barrel-shaped cage with further swivel hooks through the end-plates holding looped arms with hinged clips closed by springs. Tinned. W 79mm.
Goodall 1990-15, fig 246.2590.

J273 HOOK
Keighton, Nottinghamshire.
Site: mid 12th to late 15th century.
Looped hook. L 125mm.
Coppack 1971, 58, fig 8.8.

J274 HOOK
Clough Castle, Co. Down.
c1250–75.
Looped hook. L 86mm.
Waterman 1954, 137, fig 11.7.

J275 HOOK
Stretham, East Sussex.
Site: 11th century to c1450.
Looped hook. L 79mm.
Excavated by A Barr-Hamilton.

J276 HOOK
Winchester, Hampshire.
15th century.
Hook with sprung loop. L 55mm.
Goodall 1990-15, fig 246.2588.

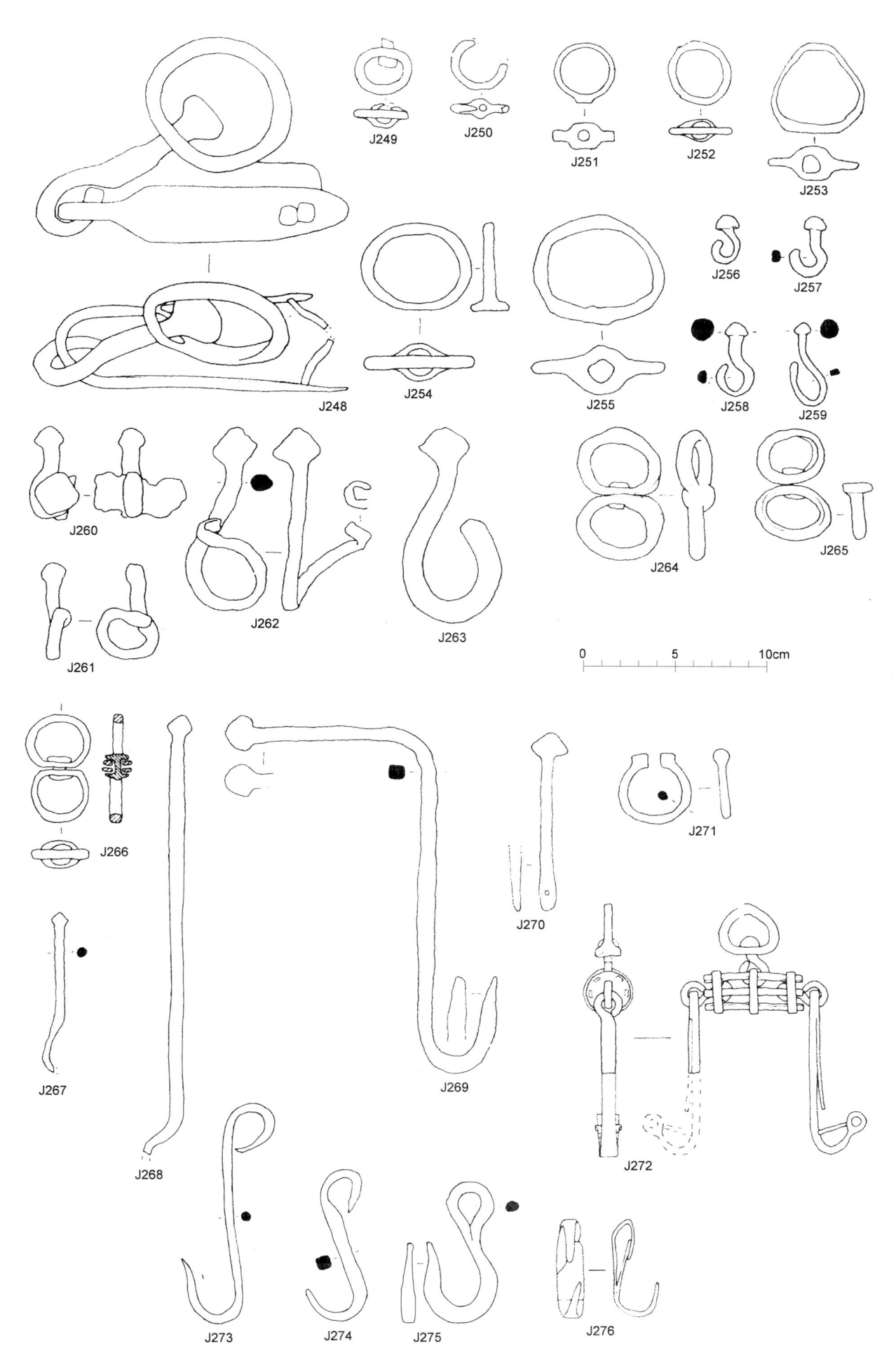

FIGURE 11.17
Chain fittings and hooks

J277 RING
Winchester, Hampshire.
?Mid 14th century.
Circular ring. D 24mm.
Goodall 1990-15, fig 246.2605.

J278 RING
Wharram Percy, North Yorkshire.
Early 15th century.
Circular ring. D 26mm.
Goodall 1979a, 118, SF 12676.

J279 RING
Bolton, Fangfoss, Humberside.
Mid 14th century.
Circular ring. D 29mm.
Goodall 1978b, 143, fig 30.30.

J280 RING
Winchester, Hampshire.
Late 11th–12th century.
Circular ring. D 31mm.
Goodall 1990-15, fig 246.2599.

J281 RING
Winchester, Hampshire.
12th century.
Circular ring. D 36mm.
Goodall 1990-15, fig 246.2602.

J282 RING
Winchester, Hampshire.
13th–14th century.
Circular ring. D 39mm.
Goodall 1990-15, fig 246.2606.

J283 RING
Winchester, Hampshire.
?Late 14th–15th century.
Circular ring. Non-ferrous plating. D 43mm.
Goodall 1990-15, fig 246.2609.

J284 RING
Winchester, Hampshire.
?Late 14th century.
Circular ring. D 47mm.
Goodall 1990-15, fig 246.2607.

J285 RING
Alsted, Surrey.
c1250–1405.
Circular ring. D 60mm.
Goodall 1976a, 56, fig 36.47.

J286 RING
Winchester, Hampshire.
Probably 13th–14th century.
Broken circular ring. D 79mm.
Goodall 1978a, 28, fig 9.11.

J287 RING (not illustrated)
Upton, Gloucestershire.
Late 13th–late 14th century.
Near circular ring. D 86mm.
Hilton and Rahtz 1966, 120.

J288 WASHER
Staines, Surrey.
1300–1500.
Flat circular washer. D 41mm.
Excavated by K R Crouch.

J289 WASHER
Winchester, Hampshire.
15th–early 16th century.
Flat, circular washer. D 50mm.
Goodall 1990-15, fig 246.2619.

J290 WASHER
Winchester, Hampshire.
15th–early 16th century.
Flat, circular washer. D 66mm.
Goodall 1990-15, fig 246.2616.

J291 COLLAR
Castell-y-Bere, Gwynedd.
Site: c1221–1295.
Circular collar. D 27mm.
Butler 1974, 98, fig 9.31.

J292 COLLAR
Strixton, Northamptonshire.
Late 13th century.
Circular collar, broken. D 31mm.
Hall 1973, 113, fig 4.29.

J293 COLLAR
London.
Late 13th to mid 14th century.
Circular collar with overlapping ends. D 30mm.
Henig 1974, 195, no. 101.

J294 COLLAR
Northampton.
Medieval.
Circular collar. D 34mm.
Goodall *et al* 1979, 273, fig 119.76.

J295 COLLAR
Grenstein, Norfolk.
Late 14th or possibly early 15th century.
Irregular, nailed collar. D 39mm.
Goodall 1980c, fig 77, no. 23.

J296 COLLAR
Winchester, Hampshire.
Late 13th to 14th century.
Circular collar. D 38mm.
Goodall 1990-10, fig 81.555.

J297 COLLAR
Waltham Abbey, Essex.
Early 16th century.
Circular collar. D 38mm.
Excavated by P J Huggins. From Romeland.

J298 COLLAR
Clarendon Palace, Wiltshire.
Site: c1072 to later 15th century.
Circular collar with welded, overlapping ends. D 40mm.
Goodall 1988, fig 81.101; Borenius and Charlton 1936.

J299 COLLAR
Waltham Abbey, Essex.
Destruction level of 1540.
Oval collar with overlapping ends. D 45mm.
Huggins 1972, 124 (from F64).

J300 COLLAR
Old Sarum (east suburb), Wiltshire.
Principally medieval, to 14th century.
Circular collar, vertical wood graining inside. D 41mm.
Salisbury and South Wiltshire Museum, Salisbury 8/1932, O.S.C117.

J301 COLLAR
Wintringham, Cambridgeshire.
Early 14th century.
Circular collar. D 46mm.
Goodall 1977a, 257, fig 45.55.

J302 COLLAR
South Witham, Lincolnshire.
1137–85 to c1220.
Circular collar. D 62mm.
Goodall 2002, fig 7.5, no. 53.

J303 COLLAR
Lyveden, Northamptonshire.
1475 to 1500.
Cylindrical collar. D 19–22mm.
Steane and Bryant 1975, 138, fig 52.239.

J304 COLLAR
Folkestone, Kent.
Mid 12th century.
Cylindrical collar. D 50mm.
Pitt-Rivers 1878, 463, pl XVIII.12.

J305 COLLAR
Pleshey Castle, Essex.
Early/mid 16th century to recent times, but including redeposited material.
Cylindrical collar. D 30–32mm.
Goodall 1977c, 177, fig 39.30.

J306 COLLAR
Grenstein, Norfolk.
Site 12th to late 14th or early 15th century.
Cylindrical collar. D 45mm.
Goodall 1980c, fig 77.

J307 COLLAR
South Witham, Lincolnshire.
c1220 to 1308–13.
Sub-rectangular collar with overlapping ends, one side lozenge-shaped. W 37mm.
Goodall 2002, fig 7.5, no. 54.

J308 COLLAR
Lyveden, Northamptonshire.
Second half 13th century.
Rectangular collar. W 51mm.
Bryant and Steane 1971, 57, fig 14k.

J309 COLLAR
King's Lynn, Norfolk.
c1280–1350.
Sub-rectangular collar. W 55mm.
Goodall 1977, 296, fig 134.57.

J310 COLLAR
Wharram Percy, North Yorkshire.
Early 15th century.
Rectangular collar with overlapping ends, broken. W 58mm.
Goodall 1979, 118, fig 61.28.

J311 COLLAR
Lyveden, Northamptonshire
c1200 to 1350.
Rectangular collar. W 94mm.
Steane and Bryant 1975, 134–135, fig 50.200.

HOUSEHOLD IRONWORK

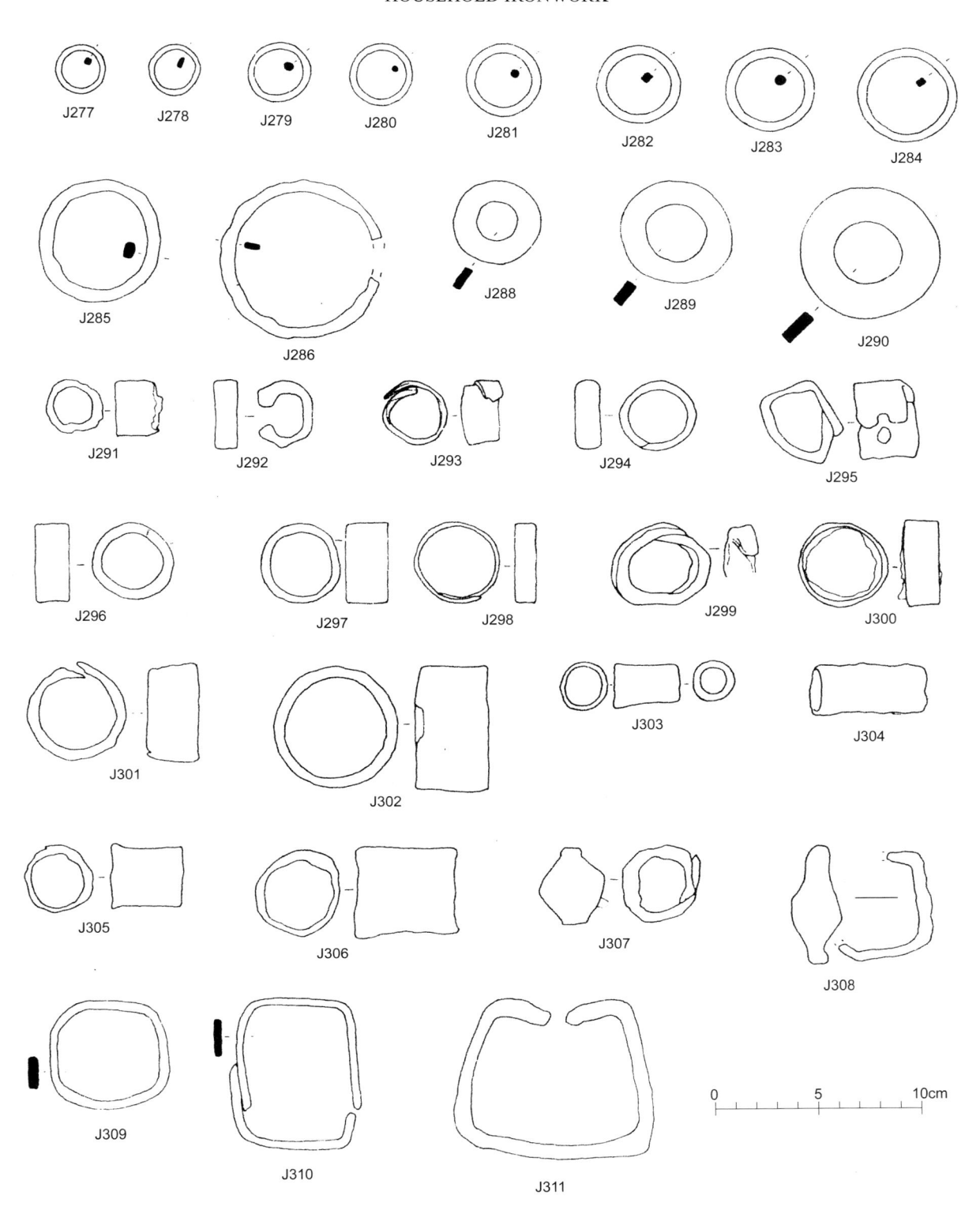

FIGURE 11.18
Rings, washers, and collars

12
BUCKLES AND PERSONAL EQUIPMENT

12.1 BUCKLES

Medieval buckles were made of iron, copper alloy, pewter, gold, silver, and occasionally bone, and of all these the iron buckles are generally the largest, plainest and most numerous. Some do, however, have decorative grooves or shaping, and a substantial number retain traces of non-ferrous plating, probably tinning. Iron buckles **K1–274**, many of which retain their pins, and some their buckle plates, have been classified according to their frame shapes. They are grouped chronologically within each type.

D-shaped buckles

D-shaped buckles such as **K1–82** and **K83–108** are the most common medieval iron buckles, their frames varying in shape from the flattened D-shape of **K20** or **K54**, through a rounded (**K9** or **K56**) or pointed (**K12** or **K19**) D-shape, to the elongated D-shape of **K3** or **K65**. The variety of shape seems to have little chronological significance, one merging into another and defying detailed subdivision.

Belts or straps were attached round the straight pin bars of these buckles, many undoubtedly without any other metal fitting, although **K18**, **K40**, **K58**, **K59**, **K76** and possibly **K57** have iron buckle plates which were riveted in place. The buckle frames are generally forged in one piece, but **K7**, **K32**, **K38** and **K66** have free, overlapping ends. The corners of the pin bars of **K24**, **K39** and **K82** are flattened and expanded, and **K7**, **K9**, **K21**, **K25**, **K38**, **K73** and **K87** have grooved decoration on the frame and almost invariably, when it is present, on the pin as well. The pins frequently rest directly against the plain frame, but on **K25**, **K27–28** and **K38** they rest in shallow depressions, and on **K21**, **K24**, **K39**, **K60** and **K62** in expanded pin rests.

D-shaped buckles are found throughout the medieval period.

Flattened oval buckles

The four buckles of this type, **K109–112**, are from contexts which span the medieval period. **K110** has decorative grooves.

Rectangular buckles

Rectangular buckles **K113–138** vary in shape from the near square shape of **K116** or **K121** to the true rectangular shape of **K117** or **K138**, the pin set in these latter cases on either a long or short side of the frame. The cylinders on **K113**, **K116**, **K134** and **K137** imply that these buckles in particular may come from a harness, the revolving cylinders allowing straps to pass through or round without excessive chafing. A number of the buckles must, because of their elaboration, come from dress belts. These include **K119** and **K126**, which have elaborate frames and buckle plates, and **K120** and **K125** which have simply shaped buckle plates.

Rectangular buckles are not particularly common but enough survive to indicate that the type was used throughout the medieval period.

Trapezoidal buckles

Buckles **K139–153** have frames of trapezoidal shape with the pin, where it survives, almost invariably mounted on the longer of the parallel arms. Half of the buckles retain the sheet iron cylinders against which their pins rested, suggesting that they come from harness. The

FIGURE 12.1
Main types of buckle

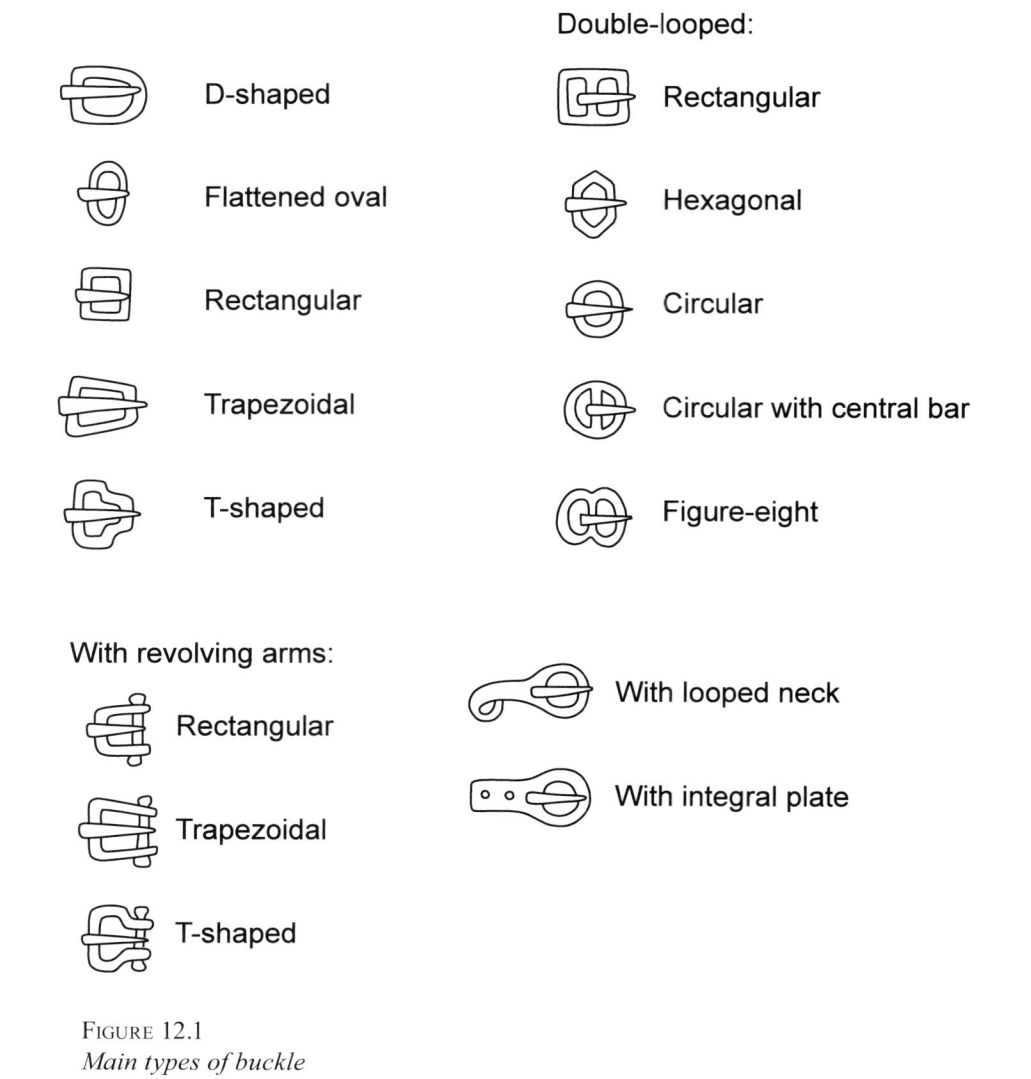

closely dated examples of the type come from 14th to 16th-century contexts.

T-shaped buckles

T-shaped buckles **K154–159** come principally from 13th to 14th-century contexts, although few examples are known. None of the buckles retains its pin, although **K157** has a sheet iron cylinder on the narrower of the parallel arms, implying that the pin was set on the longer arm. Most of the buckles are plain, but **K156** has decorative grooves. It is possible that some examples come from armour, since a number of 15th-century helms have such buckles to attach them to the body armour (Mann 1933, 153).

Buckles with revolving arms

Buckles **K160–203** have rectangular, trapezoidal and T-shaped frames incorporating a revolving arm set between the looped ends of the side arms. These buckles, most of them quite large, are probably from harness, their revolving arms equivalent to the sheet iron cylinders of other buckles in allowing the free passage of a strap with a minimum of chafing.

Rectangular buckles with revolving arms

K160–188 have rectangular frames with the same varieties of square and rectangular shapes found on buckles **K113–138**. The frames are generally plain, although **K162** and **K169** have decorative grooves, and the type is found in contexts throughout the medieval period.

Trapezoidal buckles with revolving arms

K189–196 are buckles with trapezoidal frames whose pin bar forms either the long or short of the parallel side, the other being the revolving arm. The frames vary considerably in size, from the smaller **K190–191** to the larger **K192**. **K195** is unusual in having a rigid 'revolving' arm. The buckles come from 12th to 16th-century contexts.

BUCKLES AND PERSONAL EQUIPMENT

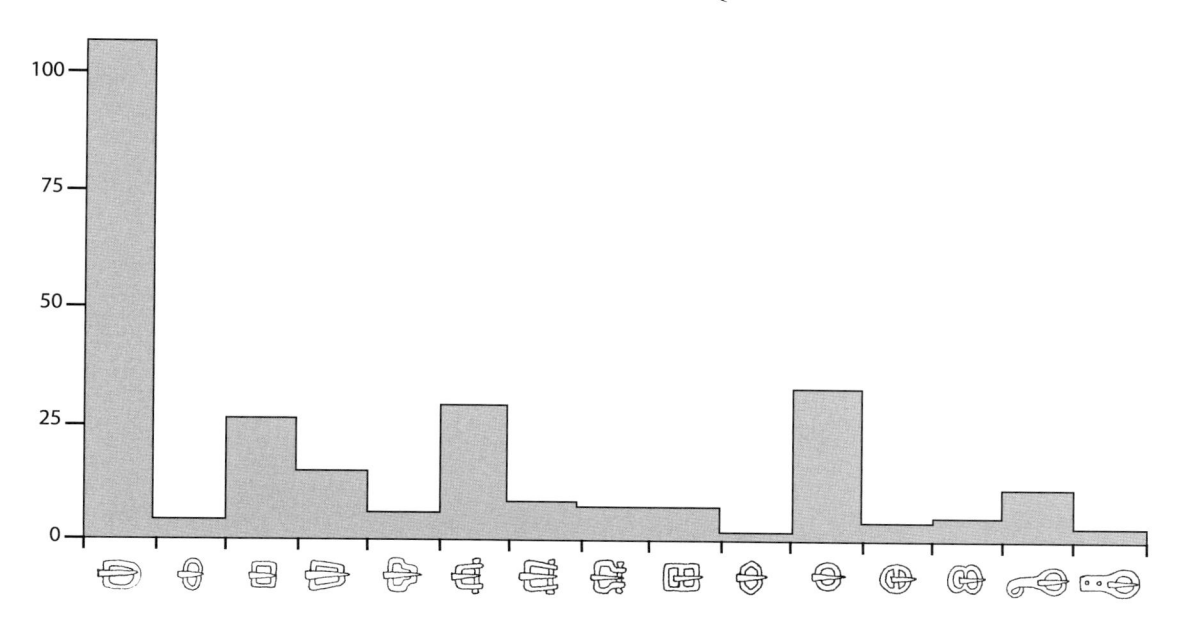

FIGURE 12.2
Frequency of types of medieval buckle

T-shaped buckles with revolving arms

Buckles **K197–203** are mostly incomplete, although **K197** and **K200** are complete and retain pins on their longer arms. The buckles come from 12th to 15th-century contexts.

Revolving arms from buckles

Several of the buckles noted above have incomplete frames which lack revolving arms similar to **K204–208**. Most are straight-sided, **K208** unusually having a central pin tip groove. Some of the arms which still form parts of buckles are swollen or baluster-shaped.

Rectangular double-looped buckles

The few examples of this type of buckle, **K209–215**, vary greatly in size, as **K214** and **K211** demonstrate. All have pins set on the middle arm, with the exception of **K212** which has lost its pin, and on **K211** this arm also carries a buckle plate for attachment to a broad strap. **K215**, with its shaped attachment plate, is from a spur. The frames are generally flat and plain, although **K210** and **K213** are slightly shaped in side view, and **K210** is also decorated. These buckles are almost all of late medieval date.

Hexagonal buckles

Buckles with hexagonal frames are occasionally forged in iron (**K216–217**), and they are clearly related to copper-alloy buckles of the type known from Upton (Hilton and Rahtz 1966, 122, fig 15.4), Lyveden (Steane and Bryant 1975, 109, fig 42.17) and elsewhere. **K216** in particular, which retains its buckle plate but lacks its iron pin, appears to be a copy of a frame shape more appropriate to copper alloy.

Circular buckles

K218–250 are circular iron buckles, the larger ones (**K218**, **K221** and **K223**) resembling the size of many of those of copper alloy. The other buckles are smaller, generally under 20mm in diameter, and most between 12 and 15mm. These small buckles are from 13th-century and later contexts, and come from shoes and clothing. **K220**, **K222** and **K232** are on straps, or on the uppers of leather shoes, and a small buckle from London (Russell-Smith 1956) comes from a 'breche' belt.

Circular buckles with central bars

K251–254 are circular buckles with central bars, all probably from spurs, **K251–252** retaining the looped attachment plates which were originally joined to spur terminals. A broken rowel spur from Southampton (Harvey 1975b, 287, fig 257.2106–07) has a buckle of similar size to **K253–254**, although it has a looped attachment plate, omitted from the drawing. These buckles are of late medieval date.

Figure-eight shaped buckles

Buckles **K255–260**, sometimes called spectacle buckles, are a late medieval type often used with rowel spurs, including some of 15th-century date from London (Ward Perkins 1967, fig 35.5–7).

Buckles with looped necks

K261–271, all buckles with looped necks, were mainly used with spurs, the loop being attached to the terminal on the outer side of the spur and the buckle used to adjust the straps. **K261–266** have short necks, that on **K263** with an additional side ring, and **K267–271** have elongated necks, **K268** attached to a Y-shaped, looped fitting. An early 14th-century rowel spur from London (Ward Perkins 1967, fig 30.7) has a buckle not unlike **K263–266**. The short-necked buckles come principally from 11th to 14th-century contexts, those with elongated necks from 13th-century and later contexts.

Buckles with integral plates

Buckles **K272–274** have integral plates which were riveted directly to a strap. **K274** has a copper-alloy pin, but the others merely have the holes for them. These buckles may have been used with spurs, and come from contexts spanning the 12th to 16th centuries.

Buckle pins

K275–278 are selected buckle pins which are flat or curved in side view with straight or down-turned tips. **K277** has non-ferrous plating and is probably from a buckle with a frame with decorative grooves.

Buckle plates

K279–282 are buckle plates used to attach certain types of buckle to belts and straps. They have either one or two rivet holes; **K282** has closed sides and **K281** a shaped, decorated edge.

Discussion

Buckles were used to fasten dress belts, sword belts, harness straps and spurs, and the size and shape of the medieval buckles reflects this range of use. Many must be from harness, as the sheet iron cylinders and revolving bars of certain buckles imply. Figure 12.1 shows the number of buckles of each type.

Most medieval buckles are plain, but a number with D-shaped frames and several of other shapes have decorative grooves. They come mainly from 12th to 13th-century contexts. **K216** appears to be a copy of a buckle shape more appropriate to copper alloy, and it is of interest that no other frames attempt to copy any complicated mouldings, surface decoration being restricted to simple grooves.

Buckles were frequently attached directly to belts or straps, but a number have riveted buckle plates, particularly those used with spurs.

12.2 STRAP-ENDS

Belts worn as part of dress, and probably straps in harness, often had a strap-end riveted to the loose end. Most are of copper alloy and are moulded or shaped, but **K283–285** are plain iron examples. In shape they are either trapezoidal or rectangular, with one or two rivets, and at least two have non-ferrous plating intended to counter corrosion and present a better appearance.

12.3 BELT SLIDES

After fastening with a buckle, the free end of a belt was sometimes held firm by a belt slide, of which **K286–288** may be examples. If so they were probably used with broad belts.

12.4 BELT HOOKS

Belt hooks **K289–291** were used to support metal-framed purses, the belt passing through the rectangular loop in the shorter arm and the central loop of the purse frame over the longer upright arm. The hooked tops of these upright arms were intended to prevent the purse becoming detached from the hook. **K289** is plain but **K290–291** have moulded upright arms. None of these belt hooks is certainly medieval.

12.5 PURSE FRAMES

Medieval metal purse frames, not introduced to Britain until the late medieval period, are of iron or copper alloy, or of iron with copper-alloy fittings. They commonly consist of a purse bar, suspended from the belt by its central loop, which supported from its end one or two roughly semicircular metal arms from which the bag hung (Ward Perkins 1967, 158–171).

K292–294 are of iron and of the most basic type, having a centrally placed, swivelling suspension hook or loop supporting a circular or oval ring frame to which the bag was attached. **K292** is from a context of c1350–1500, and the others are 15th to 16th century.

K295–297, from 15th to 16th-century contexts, belong to more elaborate types of purse frame which consist of straight purse bars supporting pendent frames, one of which survives incompletely on **K295**. The bags were either attached directly through holes in the iron frame, or through copper-alloy mounts fitted to the purse bar. **K295** has holes in both bar and frame, one of those in the bar retaining a fragment of wire, whereas **K296–297** are plain and may have lost copper-alloy fittings similar to those on some purse bars from London (Ward Perkins 1967, pl XXXIV, 1, 3). Neither of these latter two bars has been X-rayed, however, and corrosion could obscure either brazing metal from non-ferrous plating or holes. **K296–297** may, therefore, be of Ward Perkins' Type A3, and **K295** is probably related to Type A4 or A5 (Ward Perkins 1967, 165–166).

K298 is the decorative pin from the purse bar of one of the more complex types of iron purse frame, Type A6 (Ward Perkins 1967, 166–167, pl XXXVI).

12.6 SCABBARD FITTINGS

Later medieval scabbards were attached to sword belts by mounts similar to **K299**, which was found with part of a single-edged blade from a sword or dagger. It is of iron, but similar mounts of copper alloy from the tops of scabbards include one from London (Ward Perkins 1967, 37, 271, pl V).

Chapes are normally also of copper alloy, but **K300** is a sheet iron example with a simple knobbed terminal.

12.7 JEW'S HARPS

Jew's harps are small musical instruments with looped frames and reeds which were played within the mouth by the tongue. **K301–304** are of iron, **K302** the most complete, and all with the characteristically shaped frame of lozenge section. Some copper-alloy jew's harps are also known, but with iron reeds.

K1 BUCKLE
Meon Hill, Hampshire.
Late 11th century. Found beside left hip of skeleton.
Frame and broken pin. W 30mm.
Liddell 1932–34, 154, fig 15.MB.

K2 BUCKLE
Stockbridge Down, Hampshire.
Late 11th century. Found with two rings (**J193–194**) on skeleton in position suggesting they came from belt.
Frame and broken pin. W 34mm.
Hill 1935–37, 250, pl 1.

K3 BUCKLE
Stockbridge Down, Hampshire.
Late 11th century. Found within pelvis of skeleton.
Frame and pin. W 34mm.
Hill 1935–37, 250, pl 1e.

K4 BUCKLE
Stockbridge Down, Hampshire.
Late 11th century. In grave near disturbed skeletons.
Frame and pin. W 37mm.
Hill 1935–37, 250, pl 1f.

K5 BUCKLE
Stockbridge Down, Hampshire.
Late 11th century. From near hip joint of skeleton.
Frame and pin. W 38mm.
Hill 1935–37, 250, pl 1d.

K6 BUCKLE
Goltho Manor, Lincolnshire.
11th century.
Frame. W 53mm.
Goodall 1987, fig 159.133.

K7 BUCKLE
Winchester, Hampshire.
11th–mid 12th century.
Frame with overlapping free ends forming pin bar. Decorative grooves. Non-ferrous plating. W 33mm.
Goodall 1990-12, fig 136.1266.

K8 BUCKLE
Goltho Manor, Lincolnshire.
c1100–50.
Frame and pin. W 59mm.
Goodall 1987, fig 159.138.

K9 BUCKLE
Goltho Manor, Lincolnshire.
c1100–50.
Frame and pin, frame with grooved decoration. W 61mm.
Goodall 1987, fig 159.139.

K10 BUCKLE
Llantrithyd, South Glamorgan.
Early to mid 12th century.
Frame and pin. W 32mm.
Goodall 1977f, 48, iron object fig 2.40.

K11 BUCKLE
Llantrithyd, South Glamorgan.
Early to mid 12th century.
Frame and pin. W 39mm.
Goodall 1977f, 48, iron object fig 2.41.

K12 BUCKLE
Folkestone, Kent
Mid 12th century.
Buckle and broken pin. W 70mm.
Pitt-Rivers 1883, 463, pl XVIII.9.

K13 BUCKLE
Winchester, Hampshire.
Mid to late 12th century.
Frame, ends of pin bar shaped. W 57mm.
Goodall 1990-12, fig 136.1270.

K14 BUCKLE
Walton, Aylesbury, Buckinghamshire.
12th century.
Frame and pin. W 36mm.
Cocks 1904–09, 285.

K15 BUCKLE
Walton, Aylesbury, Buckinghamshire.
12th century.
Frame. W 55mm.
Cocks 1904–09, 285.

K16 BUCKLE
Walton, Aylesbury, Buckinghamshire.
12th century.
Frame and pin. W 57mm.
Cocks 1904–09, 285.

K17 BUCKLE
Winchester, Hampshire.
c1138–1141.
Frame and pin. W 60mm.
Goodall 1990-12, fig 136.1267.

K18 BUCKLE
Lydney Castle, Gloucestershire.
12th century, possibly into 13th century.
Buckle, frame and plate. L 53mm.
Casey 1931, 252, pl XXXV.5.

K19 BUCKLE
Lydney Castle, Gloucestershire.
12th century, possibly into 13th century.
Frame and pin. W 68mm.
Casey 1931, 252, pl XXXV.4.

K20 BUCKLE
Wroughton Copse, Fyfield Down, Wiltshire.
12th–13th century.
Frame. W 66mm.
Excavated by P J Fowler.

K21 BUCKLE
Old Sarum, Wiltshire.
Possibly 12th–13th century.
Frame and pin. Frame with pin rest and decorative grooves. W 84mm.
Salisbury and South Wiltshire Museum, Salisbury, 8/1932. O.S.C107.

K22 BUCKLE
Ellington, Cambridgeshire.
Second or third quarter 12th to late 13th century.
Frame and pin. W 60mm.
Goodall 1971, 68, fig 12.10.

K23 BUCKLE
Wallingstones, Hereford and Worcester.
First half 13th century.
Frame. W 34mm.
Bridgewater 1970–72, 102, no. 21.

K24 BUCKLE
Dyserth Castle, Clwyd.
Site: 1241–63.
Frame and pin, the frame shaped and with pin rest. W 101mm.
Glenn 1915, fig 9D.

K25 BUCKLE
Winchester, Hampshire.
Mid 13th century.
Frame and pin, both with decorative grooves and non-ferrous plating. W 46mm.
Goodall 1990-12, fig 136.1274.

K26 BUCKLE
Upton, Gloucestershire.
Mid to later 13th century.
Frame and pin. W 27mm.
Rahtz 1969a, 108, fig 12.121.

K27 BUCKLE
Winchester, Hampshire.
14th century.
Frame and pin, both with decorative grooves and non-ferrous plating. W 51mm.
Goodall 1990-12, fig 136.1282.

K28 BUCKLE
Winchester, Hampshire.
Early to mid 13th century.
Broken frame with decorative grooves and non-ferrous plating. W 38mm.
Goodall 1990-12, fig 136.1273.

K29 BUCKLE
Portchester Castle, Hampshire.
13th century.
Frame and pin. W 55mm.
Hinton 1977, 201, fig 108.52, scale 2:3, not 1:3.

K30 BUCKLE
Southampton, Hampshire.
c1300.
Frame and pin possibly with non-ferrous plating. W 70mm.
Harvey 1975b, 279, fig 251.2006.

K31 BUCKLE
South Witham, Lincolnshire.
Late 13th century to 1308–13.
Frame. W 34mm.
Goodall 2002, fig 7.8, no. 97.

K32 BUCKLE
Winchester, Hampshire.
1250–1320.
Frame and pin, latter incomplete, both with non-ferrous plating. Overlapping free ends form pin bar. W 45mm.
Goodall 1990-12, fig 136.1277.

K33 BUCKLE
Goltho, Lincolnshire.
Late 13th–early 14th century.
Frame and pin with non-ferrous plating. W 50mm.
Goodall 1975a, 89, fig 41.115.

K34 BUCKLE
Winchester, Hampshire.
12th to 13th century.
Frame and pin. W 33mm.
Goodall 1990-12, fig 136.1275.

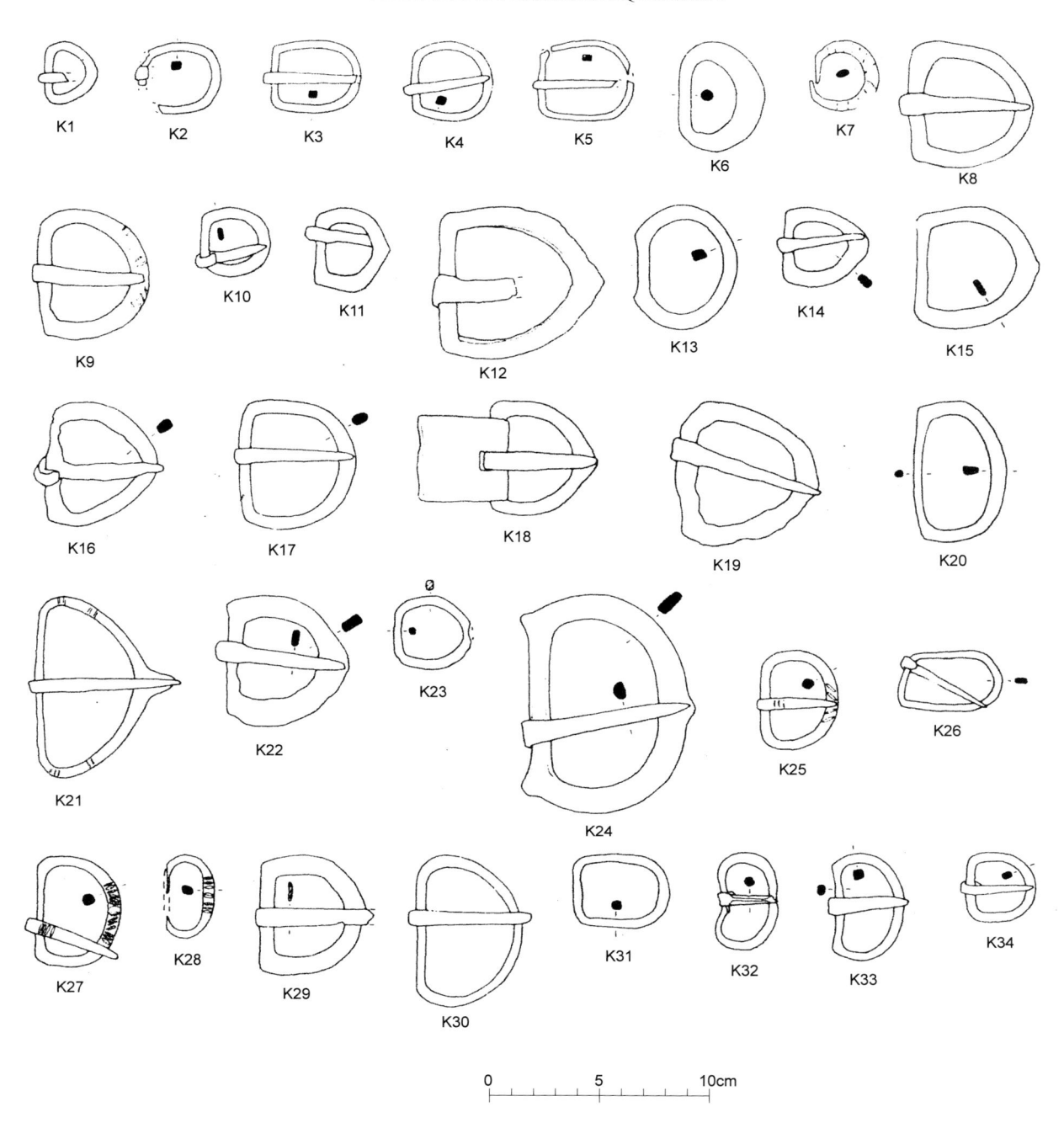

FIGURE 12.3
Buckles

K35 BUCKLE
Alsted, Surrey.
c1250–1350.
Frame. W 35mm.
Goodall 1976a, 56, fig 34.21.

K36 BUCKLE
Lyveden, Northamptonshire.
c1200–1350.
Frame. W 31mm.
Steane and Bryant 1975, 128, fig 48.110.

K37 BUCKLE
London.
Late 13th–mid 14th century.
Frame and pin. W 36mm.
Henig 1974, 191, fig 39.79.

K38 BUCKLE
London.
?Late 13th to mid 14th century.
Frame with distorted free ends and grooved decoration. W 51mm.
Henig 1974, 195, fig 39.82.

K39 BUCKLE
London.
Late 13th–mid 14th century.
Frame, shaped, with pin rest. W 66mm.
Henig 1974, 191, fig 39.80.

K40 BUCKLE
Upton, Gloucestershire.
Late 13th to late 14th century.
Frame, pin and broken plate with non-ferrous plating. W 32mm.
Hilton and Rahtz 1966, 120, fig 14.24.

K41 BUCKLE
Upton, Gloucestershire.
Late 13th to late 14th century.
Frame and broken pin with non-ferrous plating. W 38mm.
Hilton and Rahtz 1966, 117, fig 14.18.

K42 BUCKLE
Seacourt, Oxfordshire.
Mid–late 13th to late 14th century.
Frame and pin. W 30mm.
Biddle 1961–62, 179, fig 30.16, scale wrong.

K43 BUCKLE
Seacourt, Oxfordshire.
Mid–late 13th to late 14th century.
Frame and pin. W 36mm.
Biddle 1961–62, 179, fig 30.15, scale wrong.

K44 BUCKLE
Seacourt, Oxfordshire.
Mid–late 12th to late 14th century.
Frame and pin. W 72mm.
Biddle 1961–62, 179, fig 30.17, scale 1:4, not 1:3.

K45 BUCKLE
Badby, Northamptonshire.
1198–1213 to late 14th century.
Frame and pin. W 76mm.
Excavated by Mrs M Gray.

K46 BUCKLE
Criccieth Castle, Gwynedd.
Site: c1230–1404.
Frame and broken pin. W 33mm.
O'Neil 1944–45.

K47 BUCKLE
Criccieth Castle, Gwynedd.
Site: c1230–1404.
Frame and pin. W 32mm.
O'Neil 1944–45, 41, pl IX.19.

K48 BUCKLE
Criccieth Castle, Gwynedd.
Site: c1230–1404.
Frame. W 49mm.
O'Neil 1944–45.

K49 BUCKLE
Wintringham, Cambridgeshire.
Early 14th century.
Frame and pin. W 35mm.
Goodall 1977a, 258, fig 46.86.

K50 BUCKLE
Avebury, Wiltshire.
Early 14th century.
Frame and pin. W 35mm.
Keiller 1965, 178.

K51 BUCKLE
Netherton, Hampshire.
Early to mid 14th century.
Frame and pin. W 69mm.
Goodall 1990-28, fig 9.9 no. 473.

K52 BUCKLE
Bolton, Fangfoss, Humberside.
Mid 14th century.
Frame with non-ferrous plating. W 41mm.
Goodall 1978b, 143, fig 30.29.

K53 BUCKLE
Goltho, Lincolnshire.
Mid 14th century.
Frame and pin. W 47mm.
Goodall 1975a, 89, fig 41.117.

K54 BUCKLE
Badby, Northamptonshire.
Mid to late 14th century.
Frame and pin with non-ferrous plating. W 57mm.
Excavated by Mrs M Gray.

K55 BUCKLE
Winchester, Hampshire.
Late 14th century.
Frame and broken pin. Non-ferrous plating. W 40mm.
Goodall 1990-12, fig 137.1296.

K56 BUCKLE
Lochmaben Castle, Dumfries and Galloway.
Late 14th century.
Frame and pin. W 79mm.
Macdonald and Laing 1974–75, 146, fig 1.6.

BUCKLES AND PERSONAL EQUIPMENT

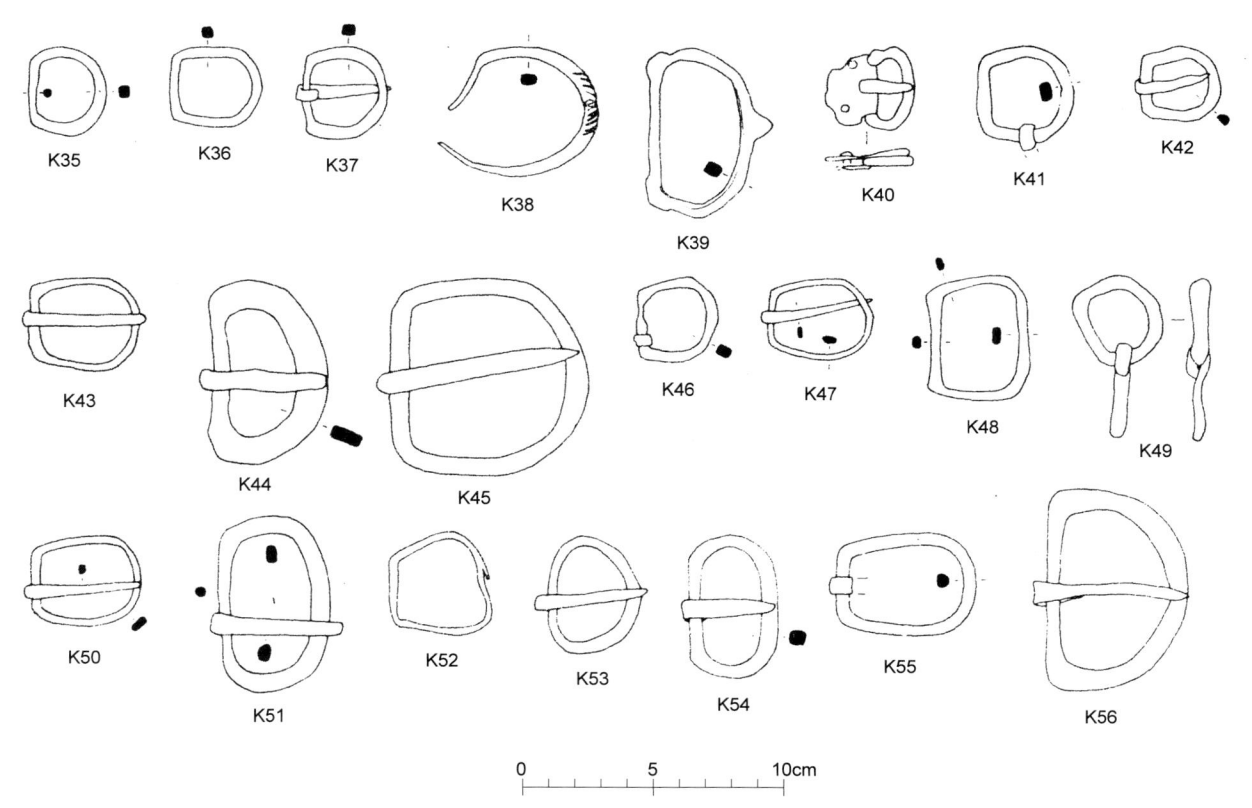

FIGURE 12.4
Buckles

K57 BUCKLE
London.
14th century.
D-shaped buckle attached to leather strap. Pin broken. W 14mm.
Henig 1974, 199, fig 42.240.

K58 BUCKLE
Winchester, Hampshire.
14th century.
Frame, pin and broken plate with one rivet. Non-ferrous plating. W 38mm.
Goodall 1990-12, fig 136.1280.

K59 BUCKLE
Boston, Lincolnshire.
14th century.
Frame, pin and plate. Frame and pin broken. W 38mm.
Mayes 1965, 103, fig 6.

K60 BUCKLE
Winchester, Hampshire.
14th century.
Frame and pin, the frame with an expanded pin rest. W 36mm.
Goodall 1990-12, fig 136.1281.

K61 BUCKLE
Northolt Manor, Greater London.
14th century.
Frame. W 52mm.
Excavated by J G Hurst.

K62 BUCKLE
Winchester, Hampshire.
15th century.
Frame and pin, frame with expanded pin rest, pin broken. W 63mm.
Goodall 1990-12, fig 137.1285.

K63 BUCKLE
Southampton, Hampshire.
Probably 14th century, but possibly 15th century.
Frame and pin with non-ferrous plating. W 42mm.
Harvey 1975b, 285, fig 255.2070.

K64 BUCKLE
Kettleby Thorpe, Lincolnshire.
14th–early 15th century.
Frame. W 33mm.
Goodall 1974a, 33, fig 18.11.

K65 BUCKLE
Goltho, Lincolnshire.
Late 14th–early 15th century.
Frame and pin. W 28mm.
Goodall 1975a, 89, fig 41.111.

K66 BUCKLE
Northampton.
Late 14th or 15th century.
Frame with distorted, free ends. W 44mm.
Goodall 1979b, 71, fig 17.21.

K67 BUCKLE
Wharram Percy, North Yorkshire.
Early 15th century.
Frame. W 49mm.
Goodall 1979a, 121, fig 63.75.

K68 BUCKLE
Northampton.
Later 15th century.
Frame and pin. W 66mm.
Goodall *et al* 1979, 273, fig 120.93.

K69 BUCKLE
Winchester, Hampshire.
15th century.
Frame and pin. W 74mm.
Goodall 1990-12, fig 137.1286.

K70 BUCKLE
Wharram Percy, North Yorkshire.
Late 15th to early 16th century.
Frame. W 48mm.
Goodall 1979a, 121, fig 63.76.

K71 BUCKLE
London.
Late 15th–early 16th century.
Frame and pin. W 61mm.
Excavated by F C Willmot. Site at 66 Foyle Road.

K72 BUCKLE
London.
Late 15th–early 16th century.
Frame and pin. W 45mm.
Excavated by F C Willmot. Site at 66 Foyle Road.

K73 BUCKLE
Winchester, Hampshire.
Mid 15th–early 16th century.
Frame and pin with non-ferrous plating. Decorative grooves on frame. W 47mm.
Goodall 1990-12, fig 137.1287.

K74 BUCKLE
Winchester, Hampshire.
Mid 15th–early 16th century.
Frame and pin broken. Non-ferrous plating. W 39mm.
Goodall 1990-12, fig 137.1298.

K75 BUCKLE
Cambokeels, Durham.
Later 14th to early 16th century.
Frame. W 55mm.
Hildyard and Charlton 1947; Hildyard 1949.

K76 BUCKLE
Portchester Castle, Hampshire.
15th or early 16th century.
Frame and broken plate. W 25mm.
Hinton 1977, 201, fig 108.55, scale 2:3, not 1:3.

K77 BUCKLE
Somerby, Lincolnshire.
15th–mid 16th century.
Broken frame. W 58mm.
Mynard 1969, 81, fig 11.IW32.

K78 BUCKLE
Underbank, Sedbergh, Cumbria.
15th–16th century.
Frame. W 58mm.
Addyman *et al* 1963–66, 39, fig 6.3.

K79 BUCKLE
Winchester, Hampshire.
15th–16th century.
Frame and pin. W 31mm.
Goodall 1990-12, fig 137.1293.

K80 BUCKLE
Winchester, Hampshire.
Early to ?mid 16th century.
Frame and pin with non-ferrous plating. W 40mm.
Goodall 1990-12, fig 137.1290.

K81 BUCKLE
Winchester, Hampshire.
Early to ?mid 16th century.
Frame and pin. W 38mm.
Goodall 1990-12, fig 137.1289.

K82 BUCKLE
Southampton, Hampshire.
*c*1550.
Frame and pin with non-ferrous plating. W 67mm.
Harvey 1975b, 287, fig 257.2101.

BUCKLES AND PERSONAL EQUIPMENT

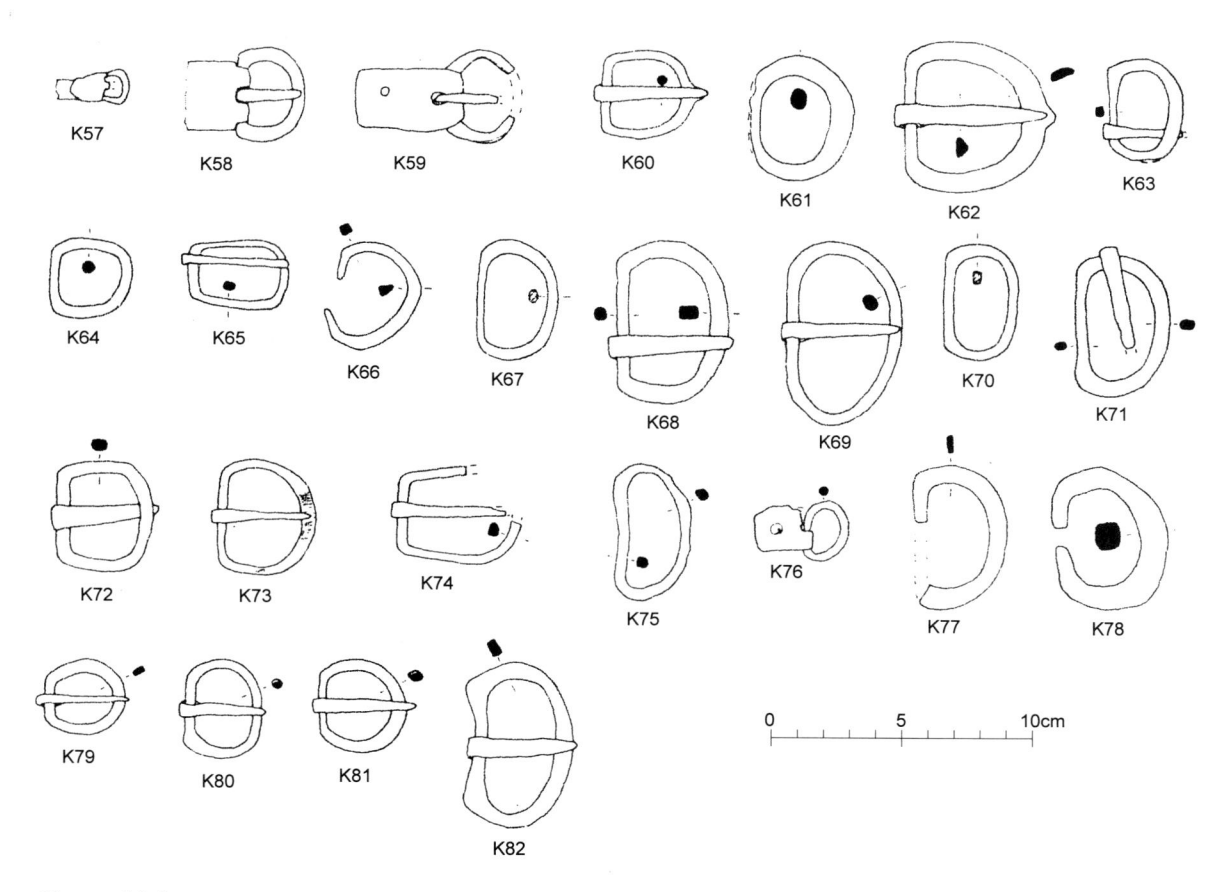

FIGURE 12.5
Buckles

Not illustrated:
K83 Castle Acre Castle, Norfolk. 1140s from c1066. Broken frame, W 59mm, L 52mm. Goodall 1982.
K84 Water Newton, Cambridgeshire. Probably 11th–12th century. Frame and pin. W 59mm, L 43mm. Green 1962–63, 78, fig 4.3.
K85 Goltho Manor, Lincolnshire. c1100–50. Frame and pin. W 32mm, L 33mm. Goodall 1987, 184.
K86 Goltho Manor, Lincolnshire. c1100–50. Frame and broken pin with non-ferrous plating. W 57mm, L 48mm. Goodall 1987, 184.
K87 Goltho Manor, Lincolnshire. c1100–50. Broken frame with grooved decoration and non-ferrous plating. W 57mm, L 53mm. Goodall 1987, 184.
K88 Castle Tower, Penmaen, West Gla-morgan. 12th century into early 13th century. Broken frame and pin. W 22mm, L 38mm. Alcock 1966, 199, fig 9.2.
K89 South Witham, Lincolnshire. 1137–85 to c1220. Frame and pin. W 36mm, L 45mm. Goodall 2002, fig 7.8, no. 94.

K90–91 Loughor Castle, West Glamorgan. Site: c1106 to late 13th century. Broken frames and pins. W 54mm, L 53mm; W 46mm, L 48mm. Excavated by J M Lewis.
K92 Brandon Castle, Warwickshire. 13th century. Broken frame. W 77mm, L 35mm. Chatwin 1955, 81, fig 11.13.
K93–94 South Witham, Lincolnshire. Late 13th century to 1308–13. Frame. W 34mm, L 42mm; W 31mm, L 30mm. Goodall 2002, fig 7.8.
K95 Lyveden, Northamptonshire. 1200–1350. Broken frame. W 58mm, L 41mm. Steane and Bryant 1975, 129, fig 48.126.
K96 Hadleigh Castle, Essex. 13th–14th century. Frame. W 52mm, L 33mm. Goodall 1975c, 142, fig 28.349.
K97 Lyveden, Northamptonshire. c1150 to early 14th century. Frame and pin. W 40mm, L 43mm. Steane and Bryant 1975, 128, fig 48.109.
K98 Somerby, Lincolnshire. 11th–15th century. Frame and broken pin. W 35mm, L 28mm. Mynard 1969, 82, fig 11.IW39.

K99 Somerby, Lincolnshire. 11th–15th century. Frame. W 65mm, L 44mm. Mynard 1969, 81, fig 11.IW3.
K100 Clarendon Palace, Wiltshire. Site: c1072 to later 15th century. Frame. W 49mm, L 35mm. Salisbury and South Wiltshire Museum, Salisbury, 47/1957.
K101 Faxton, Northamptonshire. Site: 12th–15th century. Frame. W 42mm, L 24mm. Excavated by L A S Butler.
K102–104 London. Late 15th to early 16th century. Three buckle frames and pins. W 55, 50 and 42mm, L 42, 36 and 36mm respectively. Excavated by F C Willmot at 66 Foyle Road.
K105 Hadleigh Castle, Essex. 16th century. Frame and pin. W 75mm, L 45mm. Goodall 1975c, 142, fig 28.354.
K106 Weoley Castle, Birmingham, West Midlands. c1080–1600. Frame and broken pin. W 38mm, L 30mm. Birmingham City Museum, WC 333.
K107 Weoley Castle, Birmingham, West Midlands. c1270–1600. Frame and pin, tinned. W 62mm, L 52mm. Birmingham City Museum, WC 343.
K108 Somerby, Lincolnshire. 11th–mid 16th century. Frame. W 65mm, L 60mm. Mynard 1969, 81, fig 11.IW30.

K109 BUCKLE
Winchester, Hampshire.
Late 11th century.
Frame and pin. W 43mm.
Goodall 1990-12, fig 138.1308.

K110 BUCKLE
Winchester, Hampshire.
Late 12th–13th century disturbance.
Frame with decorative grooves and non-ferrous plating. W 51mm.
Goodall 1990-12, fig 138.1310.

K111 BUCKLE
Bolton, Fangfoss, Humberside.
Mid 14th century.
Broken frame. W 45mm.
Goodall 1978b, 143, fig 30.18.

K112 BUCKLE
London.
Late 15th–early 16th century.
Frame and pin. W 50mm.
Excavated by F C Willmot. Site at 66 Foyle Road.

K113 BUCKLE
Llantrithyd, South Glamorgan.
Early to mid 12th century.
Frame and pin, the frame with a broken sheet iron cylinder. W 36mm.
Goodall 1977f, 48, iron object fig 2.32.

K114 BUCKLE
Newbury, Berkshire.
c1170–1200.
Frame and pin. W 25mm.
Goodall 1997, fig 22, no. 44.

K115 BUCKLE
Ascot Doilly, Oxfordshire.
12th century.
Frame and broken pin. W 31mm.
Jope and Threlfall 1959, 266, fig 20.4.

K116 BUCKLE
Wroughton Copse, Fyfield Down, Wiltshire.
12th century.
Frame with sheet iron cylinder. W 65mm.
Excavated by P J Fowler.

K117 BUCKLE
Knaresborough Castle, North Yorkshire.
12th century.
Frame and pin. W 86mm.
Waterman 1953, 213, fig 1.23.

K118 BUCKLE
Clough Castle, Co. Down.
c1200–25.
Broken frame and pin. W 72mm.
Waterman 1954, 141, fig 13.2.

K119 BUCKLE
Stonar, Kent.
c1225–75.
Frame, pin and plate. Shaped frame and plate both decorated. W 36mm.
Excavated by N Macpherson-Grant.

K120 BUCKLE
Newbury, Berkshire.
13th century.
Frame, pin and plate with non-ferrous plating. Shaped pin rest on frame; shaped end to plate. W 33mm.
Goodall 1997, fig 22, no. 45.

K121 BUCKLE
Waltham Abbey, Essex.
Probably 13th century.
Frame and pin. W 33mm.
Excavated by P J Huggins. From Romeland.

K122 BUCKLE
Lyveden, Northamptonshire.
c1400.
Frame with sheet iron cylinder. W 44mm.
Steane and Bryant 1975, 59, fig 15.c1.

K123 BUCKLE
Strood, Kent.
Probably early 14th century.
Frame and pin. W 37mm.
Rigold 1965, 125, fig 12.7.

K124 BUCKLE
Wintringham, Cambridgeshire.
Around early 14th century.
Frame. W 73mm.
Goodall 1977a, 258, fig 46.85.

K125 BUCKLE
The Hamel, Oxford.
Mid 14th century.
Buckle, pin and incomplete plate with shaped end. W 33mm.
Goodall 1980d, fig 31, no. 70.

K126 BUCKLE
Winchester, Hampshire.
15th century.
Frame, pin and plate with non-ferrous plating. Shaped pin rest on frame, plate shaped, decorated and held by two rivets. W 32mm.
Goodall 1990-12, fig 137.1300.

K127 BUCKLE
Thuxton, Norfolk.
Site: 12th–14th century.
Frame. W 52mm.
Excavated by L A S Butler.

K128 BUCKLE
Goltho, Lincolnshire.
Late 14th, early 15th century.
Frame. W 38mm.
Goodall 1975a, 89, fig 41.110.

K129 BUCKLE
Kings Langley, Hertfordshire.
1291–92 to late 14th or first half 15th century.
Frame. W 54mm.
Neal 1973, 56, fig XV.61.

K130 BUCKLE
Bramber Castle, West Sussex.
?15th century.
Frame and pin. W 47mm.
Barton and Holden 1977, 66, fig 20.10.

K131 BUCKLE
Portchester Castle, Hampshire.
Medieval to 15th century.
Frame and pin. W 59mm.
Hinton 1977, 201, fig 108.53, scale 2:3, not 1:3.

K132 BUCKLE
Hen Caerwys, Clwyd.
c1450–1520.
Frame and pin. W 34mm.
Excavated by G B Leach.

K133 BUCKLE
London. Late 15th–early 16th century.
Frame and pin. W 47mm.
Excavated by F C Willmot.

K134 BUCKLE
London.
Late 15th–early 16th century.
Frame with sheet iron cylinder. W 43mm.
Excavated by F C Willmot. Site at 66 Foyle Road.

K135 BUCKLE
Somerby, Lincolnshire.
15th–mid 16th century.
Frame and pin. W 24mm.
Mynard 1969, 81, fig 11.JW34.

K136 BUCKLE
Somerby, Lincolnshire.
15th–16th century.
Frame. W 34mm.
Mynard 1969, 81, fig 11.IW35.

K137 BUCKLE
Cambokeels, Durham.
Later 14th to early 16th century.
Frame and pin, the frame with sheet iron cylinder. W 30mm.
Hildyard and Charlton 1947, 194, fig 3.8.

K138 BUCKLE
Rochester, Kent.
16th century.
Frame and pin. W 42mm.
Harrison and Flight 1968, 100, fig 18.5.

BUCKLES AND PERSONAL EQUIPMENT

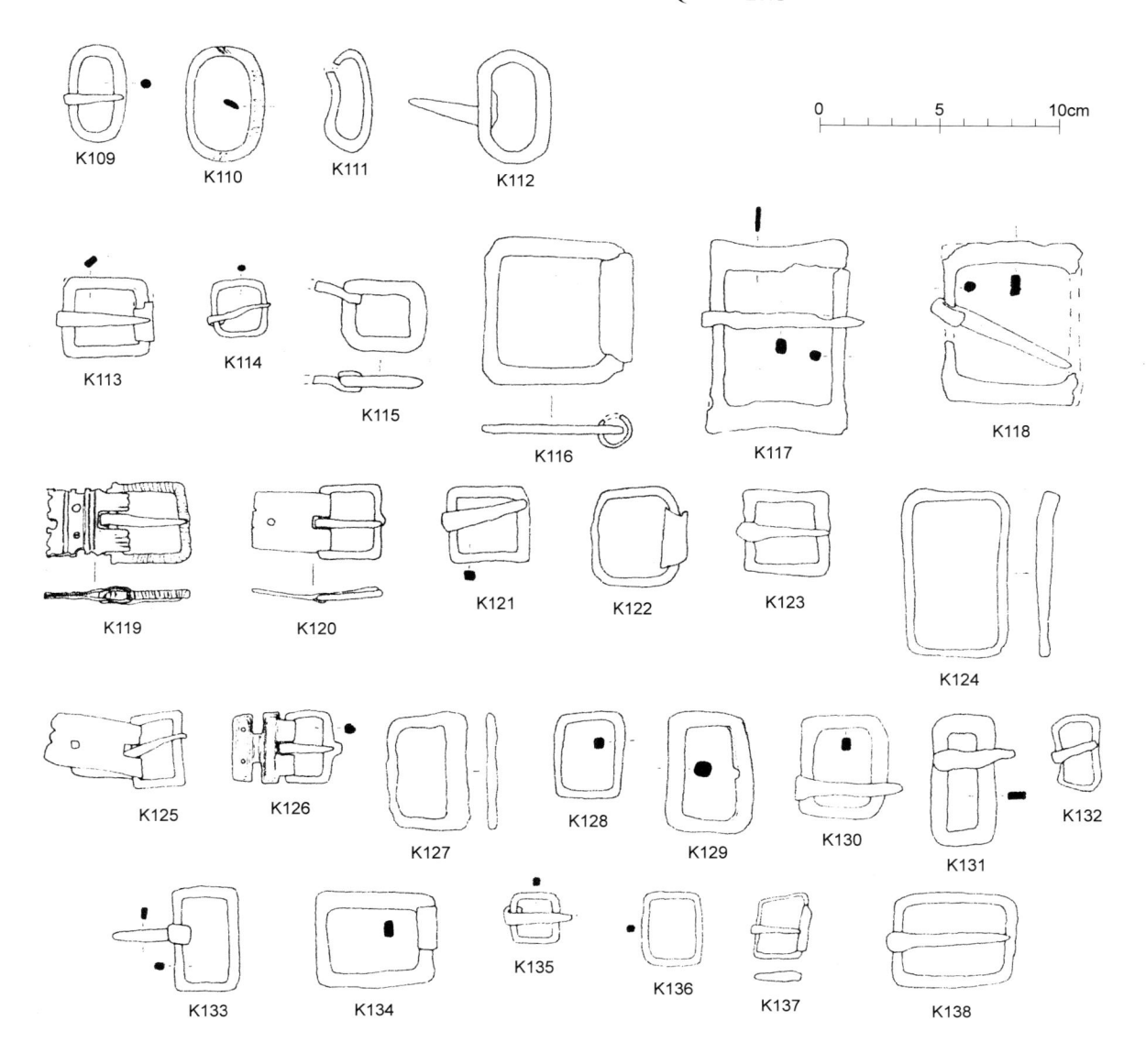

FIGURE 12.6
Buckles

K139 BUCKLE
Winchester, Hampshire.
?15th century.
Frame. W 38mm.
Goodall 1990-12, fig 139.1312.

K140 BUCKLE
Lochmaben Castle, Dumfries and Galloway.
Late 14th century.
Frame. W 50mm.
Macdonald and Laing 1974–75, 146, fig 10.7.

K141 BUCKLE
London.
Around late 14th to early 15th century.
Frame and pin with decorative grooves.
W 83mm.
Blurton 1977, 88, fig 31.605.

K142 BUCKLE
Sawtry, Cambridgeshire.
15th–early 16th century.
Frame and broken pin. W 50mm.
Moorhouse 1971b, 85, fig 4.3.

K143 BUCKLE
East Haddlesey, North Yorkshire.
15th–early 16th century.
Frame and pin, the pin resting against a broken sheet iron cylinder. W 45mm.
Goodall 1973b, 93, fig 37.22.

K144 BUCKLE
Sawtry, Cambridgeshire.
15th–early 16th century.
Broken frame and pin, the frame with sheet iron cylinder. W 50mm.
Moorhouse 1971b, 85, fig 4.2.

K145 BUCKLE
Somerby, Lincolnshire.
15th–mid 16th century.
Frame. W 40mm.
Mynard 1969, 82, fig 11.IW37.

K146 BUCKLE
Cambokeels, Durham.
Later 14th to early 16th century.
Frame and pin. W 45mm.
Hildyard 1949, 195.

K147 BUCKLE
Ospringe, Kent.
Demolition c1550–70 on site founded c1230.
Frame with sheet iron cylinder and broken pin.
W 47mm.
Goodall 1979c, 132, fig 22.93.

K148 BUCKLE
Staines, Surrey.
Medieval, to 15th century.
Frame and pin, the frame with sheet iron cylinder. W 46mm.
Barker 1976, 124, fig 26.31.

K149 BUCKLE
Clarendon Palace, Wiltshire.
Site: c1072 to later 15th century.
Frame with sheet iron cylinder. W 45mm.
Goodall 1988, fig 81.103; Borenius and Charlton 1936.

K150 BUCKLE
Weoley Castle, Birmingham, West Midlands.
Site: c1080–1600.
Frame with sheet iron cylinder and pin.
W 43mm.
Birmingham City Museum, WC 332. Taylor 1974. For site see Oswald 1962.

Not illustrated:
K151 Lyveden, Northamptonshire. 1475–1500. Frame and pin. W 47mm, L 56mm. Steane and Bryant 1975, 128, fig 48.108.
K152 West Hartburn, Durham. Medieval to later 16th century. Frame and pin. W 38mm, L 52mm. Still and Pallister 1967, 146, fig 4.3.
K153 Clarendon Palace, Wiltshire. Site: c1072 to later 15th century. Broken frame with sheet iron cylinder. W 43mm, L 53mm. Salisbury and South Wiltshire Museum, Salisbury, 47/1957.

K154 BUCKLE
Glottenham, East Sussex.
Mid to late 13th century.
Broken frame. W 62mm.
Excavated by D Martin.

K155 BUCKLE
Rhuddlan, Clwyd.
c1280.
Frame. W 68mm.
Goodall 1994, fig 17.7, no. 102.

K156 BUCKLE
Brandon Castle, Warwickshire.
13th century.
Decorated frame. W 71mm.
Chatwin 1955, 81, fig 11.12. Herbert Art Gallery and Museum, Coventry.

K157 BUCKLE
Clarendon Palace, Wiltshire.
Site: c1072 to later 13th century.
Frame with sheet iron cylinder. W 82mm.
Goodall 1988, fig 81.105; Borenius and Charlton 1936.

K158 BUCKLE
Winchester, Hampshire.
15th century.
Frame with non-ferrous plating. W 70mm.
Goodall 1990-12, fig 139.1315.

K159 BUCKLE
Durrance Moat, Warwickshire.
Site: c1200–1450.
Frame. W 73mm.
Birmingham City Museum. For site see Oswald and Taylor 1964.

K160 BUCKLE
Castle Neroche, Somerset.
Late 11th–12th century.
Frame. W 79mm.
Gray 1903, 45, pl III.S.

K161 BUCKLE
Southampton, Hampshire.
11th–12th century.
Frame with non-ferrous plating. W 43mm.
Harvey 1975b, 277, fig 250.1973.

K162 BUCKLE
Goltho Manor, Lincolnshire.
c1100–50.
Frame and pin with non-ferrous plating.
Decorative grooves on frame. W 75mm.
Goodall 1987, fig 159.144.

K163 BUCKLE
Llantrithyd, South Glamorgan.
Early to mid 12th century.
Distorted frame and pin. W 69mm.
Goodall 1977f, 48, iron object fig 2.44.

K164 BUCKLE
Ipswich, Suffolk.
12th century.
Frame and broken pin. W 78mm.
West 1963, 274, fig 54.11.

K165 BUCKLE
Loughor Castle, West Glamorgan.
Site: c1106 to late 13th century.
Broken frame. W 67mm.
Excavated by J M Lewis.

K166 BUCKLE
Winchester, Hampshire.
12th–13th century.
Frame and pin. W 75mm.
Goodall 1990-12, fig 138.1304.

K167 BUCKLE
Dyserth Castle, Clwyd.
Site: c1241–63.
Frame and pin. W 90mm.
Glenn 1915, fig 90.

K168 BUCKLE
Dyserth Castle, Clwyd.
Site: 1241–63.
Broken frame. W 98mm.
Glenn 1915.

K169 BUCKLE
London.
13th century.
Frame and pin with decorative grooves.
W 75mm.
Wood et al 1975, 260, fig 3.55.

K170 BUCKLE
Brandon Castle, Warwickshire.
13th century.
Frame and pin. W 79mm.
Chatwin 1955, 81, fig 11.14.

K171 BUCKLE
Winchester, Hampshire.
Late 13th century.
Frame and pin. W 85mm.
Goodall 1990-12, fig 138.1303.

K172 BUCKLE
Bramber Castle, West Sussex.
Late 13th–14th century.
Frame and pin. W 74mm.
Barton and Holden 1977, 63, fig 19.15.

K173 BUCKLE
Gomeldon, Wiltshire.
13th–14th century.
Frame and pin. W 60mm.
Musty and Algar 1986.

K174 BUCKLE
Glottenham, East Sussex.
Early 14th century.
Frame and broken pin. W 54mm.
Excavated by D Martin.

K175 BUCKLE
Lochmaben Castle, Dumfries and Galloway.
Late 14th century.
Frame and pin. W 65mm.
Macdonald and Laing 1974–75, 146, fig 10.5.

BUCKLES AND PERSONAL EQUIPMENT

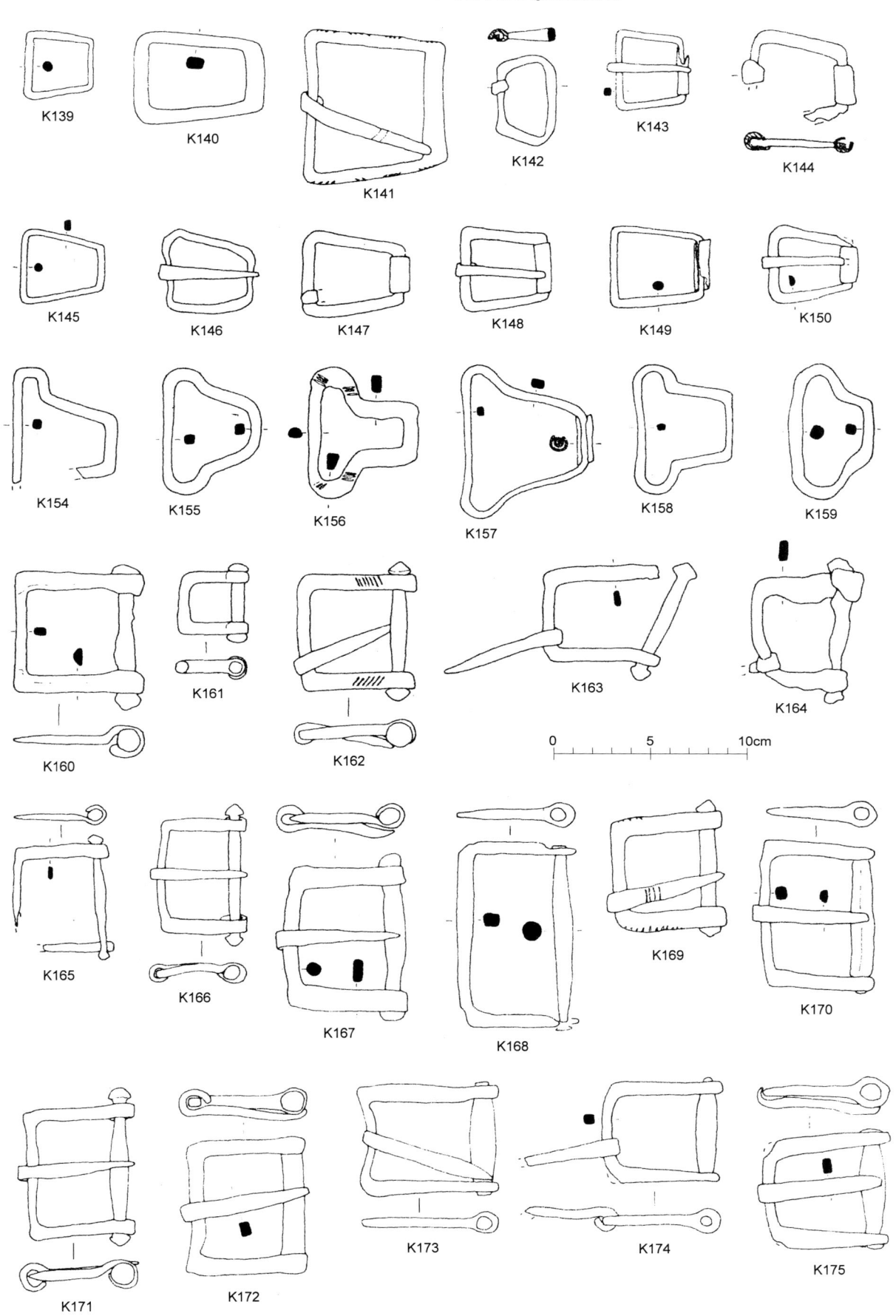

FIGURE 12.7
Buckles

K176 BUCKLE
Goltho, Lincolnshire.
Late 14th, early 15th century.
Frame and pin. W 46mm.
Goodall 1975a, 89, fig 41.121.

K177 BUCKLE
Alsted, Surrey.
c1250–1405.
Frame. W 58mm.
Goodall 1976a, 56, fig 36.52.

K178 BUCKLE
Wallingstones, Hereford and Worcester.
1300–25 to 1500.
Frame. W 65mm.
Bridgewater 1970-2, 104, no. 70.

K179 BUCKLE
Wallingstones, Hereford and Worcester.
Post-1500 destruction layer with residual objects. Site occupied from c1200.
Broken frame. W 80mm.
Bridgewater 1970-72, 104, no. 93.

K180 BUCKLE
Writtle, Essex.
c1425–1521.
Frame and pin. W 71mm.
Rahtz 1969b, 85, fig 47.54.

K181 BUCKLE
London.
Late 15th–early 16th century.
Frame and pin. W 77mm.
Excavated by F C Willmot. Site at 66 Foyle Road.

K182 BUCKLE
Cambokeels, Durham.
Later 14th–early 16th century.
Frame damaged. W 64mm.
Hildyard 1949, 195.

Not illustrated:
K183 Bramber Castle, West Sussex. 1075–1180. Frame and pin. W 77mm, L 66mm. Barton and Holden 1977, 63, fig 19.15.
K184 Woodperry, Oxfordshire. 12th to 14th century pottery. Frame and pin. W 86mm, L 71mm. Ashmolean Museum, Oxford, 1873.63.
K185 Seacourt, Oxfordshire. Mid to late 12th to late 14th century. Frame and pin. W 81mm, L 61mm. Biddle 1961–62, 179, fig 30.14, scale 1:4, not 1:3.
K186 Staxton, North Yorkshire. Later 12th to mid 15th century. Frame and pin. W 68mm, L 53mm. Brewster 1952, 12, fig IX.4
K187 Huish, Wiltshire. 12th–15th century. Frame and pin. W 69mm, L 61mm. Shortt 1972, 120, fig 5.36
K188 Hadleigh Castle, Essex. 16th century. Frame and pin. W 75mm, L 72mm. Goodall 1975c, 142, fig 28.352.

K189 BUCKLE
Goltho Manor, Lincolnshire.
c1100–50.
Frame and pin. W 67mm.
Goodall 1987, fig 159.143.

K190 BUCKLE
South Witham, Lincolnshire.
1137–85 to c1220.
Frame and pin. W 44mm.
Goodall 2002, fig 7.8, no. 92.

K191 BUCKLE
South Witham, Lincolnshire.
1137–85 to c1220.
Frame and pin. W 42mm.
Goodall 2002, fig 7.8, no. 91.

K192 BUCKLE
Northampton.
c1250 to end 14th century.
Frame with sheet iron cylinder and pin. W 92mm.
Goodall et al 1979, 273, fig 120.90.

K193 BUCKLE
Criccieth Castle, Gwynedd.
Site: c1230–1404.
Frame and pin. W 66mm.
O'Neil 1944–45, 41, pl IX.16.

K194 BUCKLE
Theodoric's Hermitage, Margam, West Glamorgan.
Site: 13th–15th century.
Frame. W 71mm.
National Museum of Wales, Cardiff, 49.140.6.

K195 BUCKLE
Hen Caerwys, Clwyd.
c1450–1520.
Frame and pin. Non-ferrous plating.
W 74mm.
Excavated by G B Leach.

K196 BUCKLE
North Elmham Park, Norfolk.
c1150–c1600.
Incomplete frame. W 63mm.
Goodall 1980a, 516, fig 267.124.

K197 BUCKLE
Old Sarum, Wiltshire.
Possible 12th–13th century.
Frame and pin. W 91mm.
Salisbury and South Wiltshire Museum, Salisbury, 8/1932, O.S.C106.

K198 BUCKLE
Wintringham, Cambridgeshire.
Late 13th century.
Broken frame with non-ferrous plating.
W 92mm.
Goodall 1977a, 258, fig 46.83.

K199 BUCKLE
Hangleton, West Sussex.
Near 13th-century building.
Broken frame. W 118mm.
Holden 1963, 171, fig 37.17.

K200 BUCKLE
Netherton, Hampshire.
Late 13th–early 14th century.
Frame and pin. W 102mm.
Goodall 1990-28, fig 9.9 no. 485.

K201 BUCKLE
Lochmaben Castle, Dumfries and Galloway.
Late 14th century.
Broken frame. W 96mm.
Macdonald and Laing 1974–75, 146, fig 10.8.

K202 BUCKLE
Woodperry, Oxfordshire.
12th to 14th century pottery.
Frame and pin. W 132mm, L 68mm.
Ashmolean Museum, Oxford, 1873.62. For site see Wilson 1846.

K203 BUCKLE
Winchester, Hampshire.
16th century.
Frame. W 101mm.
Goodall 1990-12, fig 139.1316.

K204 BUCKLE BAR
Castle Acre Castle, Norfolk.
1140s deposit with derived material. Site founded soon after 1066.
Complete. L 74mm.
Goodall 1982, fig 41, no. 118.

K205 BUCKLE BAR
South Witham, Lincolnshire.
1137–85 to c1220.
Complete. L 76mm.
Goodall 2002, fig 7.8, no. 93.

K206 BUCKLE BAR
Upton, Gloucestershire.
Late 13th to late 14th century.
Complete. L 72mm.
Hilton and Rahtz 1966, 121, fig 14.30.

K207 BUCKLE BAR
London.
?Late 13th to mid 14th century.
Complete. L 74mm.
Henig 1974, 195, fig 39.81.

K208 BUCKLE BAR
Alsted, Surrey.
c1250–1405.
Complete. L 70mm.
Goodall 1976a, 56, fig 36.53.

BUCKLES AND PERSONAL EQUIPMENT

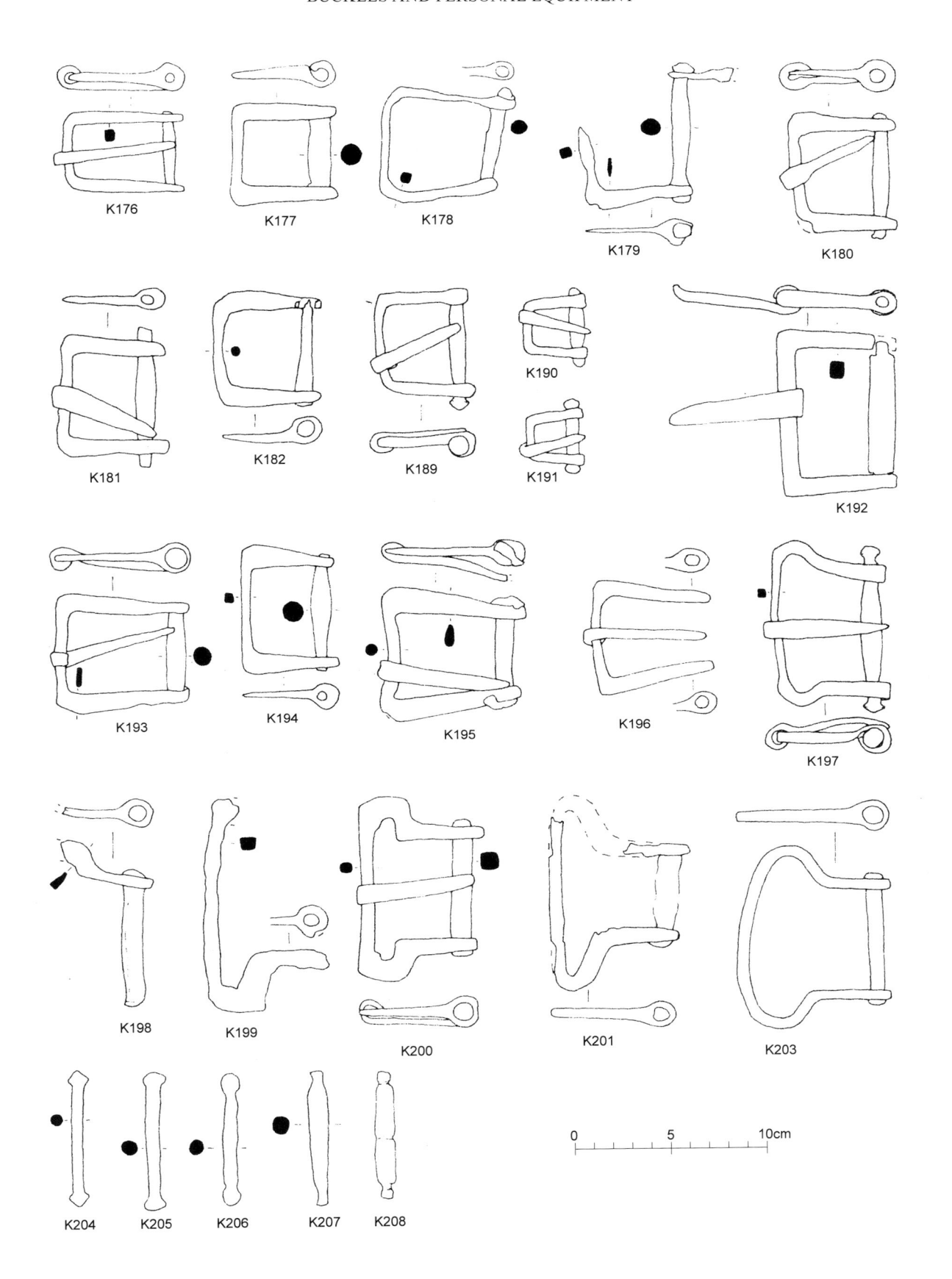

FIGURE 12.8
Buckles

K209 BUCKLE
Wintringham, Cambridgeshire.
Second half 13th century.
Frame and pin. W 39mm.
Goodall 1977a, 258, fig 46.82.

K210 BUCKLE
Lyveden, Northamptonshire.
1350–1450.
Decorated frame, angled in side view, with pin.
W 39mm.
Steane and Bryant 1975, 129, fig 48.136.

K211 BUCKLE
Baginton, Warwickshire.
Late 14th–early 15th century.
Frame, pin and plate. W 72mm.
Wilkins 1975, 126, fig 8.17.

K212 BUCKLE
Grenstein, Norfolk.
Late 14th–15th century.
Frame. W 30mm.
Goodall 1980c, fig 82, no. 87.

K213 BUCKLE
Lyveden, Northamptonshire.
1475–1500.
Broken, angled frame with pin. W 22mm.
Steane and Bryant 1975, 129, fig 48.137.

K214 BUCKLE
Winchester, Hampshire.
15th–16th century.
Frame slightly angled in side view. Pin rests against sheet metal cylinder. W 16mm.
Goodall 1990-12, fig 140.1332.

K215 BUCKLE
Thelsford Priory, Warwickshire.
16th century destruction deposit.
Frame and pin with broken attachment plate round central bar. W 22mm.
Excavated by Mrs M Gray.

K216 BUCKLE
Grafton Regis, Northamptonshire.
13th–15th century.
Frame and plate with non-ferrous plating.
W 22mm.
Excavated by Miss C Mahany.

K217 BUCKLE
Glenluce, Dumfries and Galloway.
Late 13th–early 14th century.
Frame. W 34mm.
Jope and Jope 1959, 269, fig 94.9.

K218 BUCKLE
Brandon Castle, Warwickshire.
1226–66.
Broken frame and pin. D 30mm.
Chatwin 1955, 83, pl 8a.

K219 BUCKLE
Netherton, Hampshire.
Late 13th century.
Frame and pin. D 13mm.
Goodall 1990-28, fig 9.9 no. 493.

K220 BUCKLE
London.
?Late 13th–early 14th century.
Frame and pin in part of projecting leather strap from shoe upper. D 13mm.
Jones 1975, 161, fig 28.97.

K221 BUCKLE
London.
Late 13th–mid 14th century.
Broken iron frame wrapped round with fine copper-alloy wire. D 30mm.
Henig 1974, 196, fig 40.134.

K222 BUCKLE
Oakham Castle, Leicestershire.
13th–14th century.
Large leather front upper from shoe (part drawn) with two straps, one retaining tinned buckle and pin. Buckle D 12mm.
Gathercole 1958, 33, fig 9.9.

K223 BUCKLE
Riplingham, Humberside.
Second half 14th century.
Frame and pin, possibly with non-ferrous plating. D 34mm.
Wacher 1963–66, 655, fig 21.22.

K224 BUCKLE
Lyveden, Northamptonshire.
1350–1450.
Frame and pin. D 12mm.
Steane and Bryant 1975, 118, fig 45.7.

K225 BUCKLE
Grenstein, Norfolk.
Late 14th to 15th century.
Frame and pin. D 14mm.
Goodall 1980c, fig 82, no. 83.

K226 BUCKLE
Thelsford Priory, Warwickshire.
14th–15th century.
Frame and pin. D 15mm.
Excavated by Mrs M Gray.

K227 BUCKLE
Somerby, Lincolnshire.
11th–15th century.
Frame and pin. D 17mm.
Mynard 1969, 82, fig 11.IW44.

K228 BUCKLE
Faxton, Northamptonshire.
Site: 12th–15th century.
Frame and pin. D 21mm.
Excavated by L A S Butler.

K229 BUCKLE
Wharram Percy, North Yorkshire.
Late 15th to early 16th century.
Frame and broken pin. D 20mm.
Goodall 1979a, 121, fig 63.78.

K230 BUCKLE
Ospringe, Kent.
c1483–1550.
Frame and broken pin. D 17mm.
Goodall 1979c, 132, fig 22.91.

K231 BUCKLE
St Catharine's Hill, Winchester, Hampshire.
12th century to 1538–40.
Frame and broken pin. D 14mm.
Hawkes et al 1930, 246, fig 29.17.

Not illustrated:
K232 London. Late 13th–mid 14th century. Leather-covered metal (?iron) buckle and pin in end of strap from leather shoe upper. D 3mm. Jones 1975, 161, fig 28.101.

K233–243 Lyveden, Northamptonshire. 1350–1450. Eleven buckles with pins from Site J.
D 12–15mm. For selection see Steane and Bryant 1975, 118, fig 45.1–6, 8.
K244–246 Grenstein, Norfolk. Late 14th–15th century. Three buckles, two with pins. D 13–15mm. Goodall 1980c.
K247–250 Wharram Percy, North Yorkshire. Late 15th–early 16th century. Four buckles, three with pins. D 14–15mm. Goodall 1979a, 121.

K251 BUCKLE
Cambokeels, Durham.
Later 14th to early 16th century.
Frame with expanded pin rest and broken, looped attached plate round central bar.
D 32mm.
Hildyard 1949, 195, fig 4.9.

K252 BUCKLE
Hen Caerwys, Clwyd.
c1450–1520.
Frame with broken, looped attachment round central bar. Pin lost. Non-ferrous plating.
D 24mm.
Excavated by G B Leach.

K253 BUCKLE
East Haddlesey, North Yorkshire.
15th–early 16th century.
Damaged frame. D 48mm.
Goodall 1973b, 93, fig 37.25.

K254 BUCKLE
London.
Late 15th–early 16th century.
Frame. D 53mm.
Excavated by F C Willmot

K255 BUCKLE
Bolton, Fangfoss, Humberside.
Early 14th century.
Frame and pin with non-ferrous plating. Frame gently curved in side view. W 16mm.
Goodall 1978b, 143, fig 30.21.

K256 BUCKLE
Goltho, Lincolnshire.
14th–early 15th century.
Frame and pin. W 43mm.
Goodall 1975a, 89, fig 41.118.

K257 BUCKLE
Wharram Percy, North Yorkshire.
Late 15th–early 16th century.
Frame and pin. W 18mm.
Goodall 1979a, 121, fig 63.77.

K258 BUCKLE
Hull, Humberside.
Early to mid 16th century.
Broken frame and pin with non-ferrous plating. Frame slightly angled in side view. W 25mm.
Goodall 1997b, 65, fig 27.86.

K259 BUCKLE
West Hartburn, Durham.
13th–16th century.
Frame and pin. L 22mm.
Still and Pallister 1964, 197, fig 5.15.

K260 BUCKLE
West Hartburn, Durham.
13th–16th century.
Frame. W 29mm.
Still and Pallister 1964, 197, fig 5.13.

BUCKLES AND PERSONAL EQUIPMENT

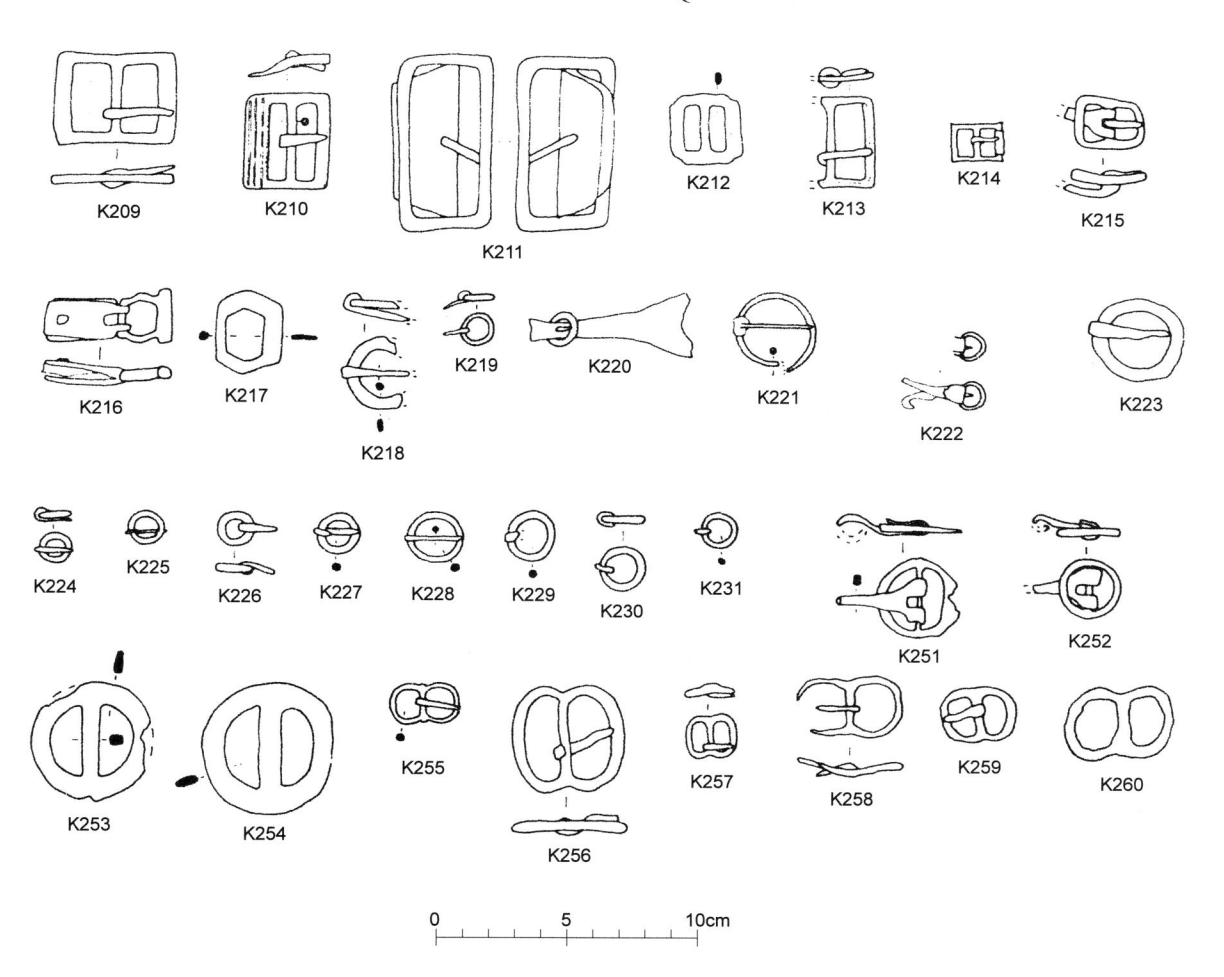

FIGURE 12.9
Buckles

K261 BUCKLE
Winchester, Hampshire.
1050–1150.
Frame and pin. Decorated neck with broken loop. Non-ferrous plating. W 36mm.
Goodall 1990-12, fig 139.1317.

K262 BUCKLE
Winchester, Hampshire.
12th century.
Frame and elongated neck, both broken. Pin lost. W 16mm.
Goodall 1990-12, fig 139.1318.

K263 BUCKLE
Seacourt, Oxfordshire.
Mid 13th century.
Frame with looped neck to which side-ring attached. W 19mm.
Biddle 1961–62, 180, fig 30.23, scale 1:4, not 1:3.

K264 BUCKLE
Winchester, Hampshire.
Mid to late 13th century.
Frame with elongated neck and pin both broken. Non-ferrous plating. W 17mm.
Goodall 1990-12, fig 139.1320.

K265 BUCKLE
Seacourt, Oxfordshire.
14th century.
Broken frame with looped neck. Possible non-ferrous plating. W 25mm.
Biddle 1961–62, 180, fig 30.22, scale 1:4, not 1:3.

K266 BUCKLE
Criccieth Castle, Gwynedd.
Site: c1230–1404.
Frame with elongated, looped neck and pin. L 43mm.
O'Neil 1944–45.

K267 BUCKLE
Castell-y-Bere, Gwynedd.
Site: c1221–95.
Buckle with looped, elongated neck and broken pin. W 37mm.
Butler 1974, 97, fig 8.23.

K268 BUCKLE
Winchester, Hampshire.
Mid to late 13th century.
Frame with elongated, looped neck and pin set on looped strap. W 37mm.
Goodall 1990-12, fig 139.1319.

K269 BUCKLE
Clarendon Palace, Wiltshire.
Site: c1072 to later 15th century.
Frame with elongated, looped neck and pin. L 106mm.
Goodall 1988, fig 81.108; Borenius and Charlton 1936.

K270 BUCKLE
Glastonbury Tor, Somerset.
12th–16th century.
Frame with broken, elongated looped neck and pin. L 78mm.
Rahtz 1970, 53, fig 12.10.

K271 BUCKLE
Writtle, Essex.
c1425–1521 and later.
Frame with elongated, looped neck and pin. L 80mm.
Rahtz 1969b, 85, fig 47.56.

K272 BUCKLE
Thuxton, Norfolk.
Site: 12th–14th century.
Frame with integral plate. Incomplete. L 37mm.
Excavated by L A S Butler.

K273 BUCKLE
Stonar, Kent.
c1275–1385.
Frame with integral plate and broken pin. Non-ferrous plating. W 19mm.
Excavated by N Macpherson-Grant.

K274 BUCKLE
East Haddlesey, North Yorkshire.
15th–early 16th century.
Frame with copper-alloy pin and broken integral plate. Non-ferrous plating. W 27mm.
Goodall 1973b, 93, fig 37.23.

K275 BUCKLE PIN
Goltho Manor, Lincolnshire.
c1100–50.
Loop broken. L 60mm.
Goodall 1987, fig 159.151.

K276 BUCKLE PIN
The Hamel, Oxford.
Early to mid 13th century.
Loop broken. L 55mm.
Goodall 1980d, fig 31, no. 72.

K277 BUCKLE PIN
Oakley, Hampshire.
Mid 13th century.
Grooved decoration and non-ferrous plating. L 67mm.
Excavated by S Moorhouse.

K278 BUCKLE PIN
Winchester, Hampshire.
Mid 13th century.
Complete. L 53mm.
Goodall 1990-12, fig 141.1338.

K279 BUCKLE PLATE
The Hamel, Oxford.
Late 12th–early 13th century.
Complete. W 37mm.
Goodall 1980d, fig 31, no. 73.

K280 BUCKLE PLATE
King's Lynn, Norfolk.
c1280–1350.
Broken plate. W 15mm.
Goodall and Carter 1977, 295, fig 134.49.

K281 BUCKLE PLATE
The Hamel, Oxford.
Mid to late 15th century.
Broken plate with punched decoration and non-ferrous plating. W 18mm.
Goodall 1980d, fig 31, no. 74.

K282 BUCKLE
Winchester, Hampshire.
Late 15th century.
Frame and pin broken. Buckle plates linked by side sheets form rectangular case. W 25mm.
Goodall 1990-12, fig 141.1343.

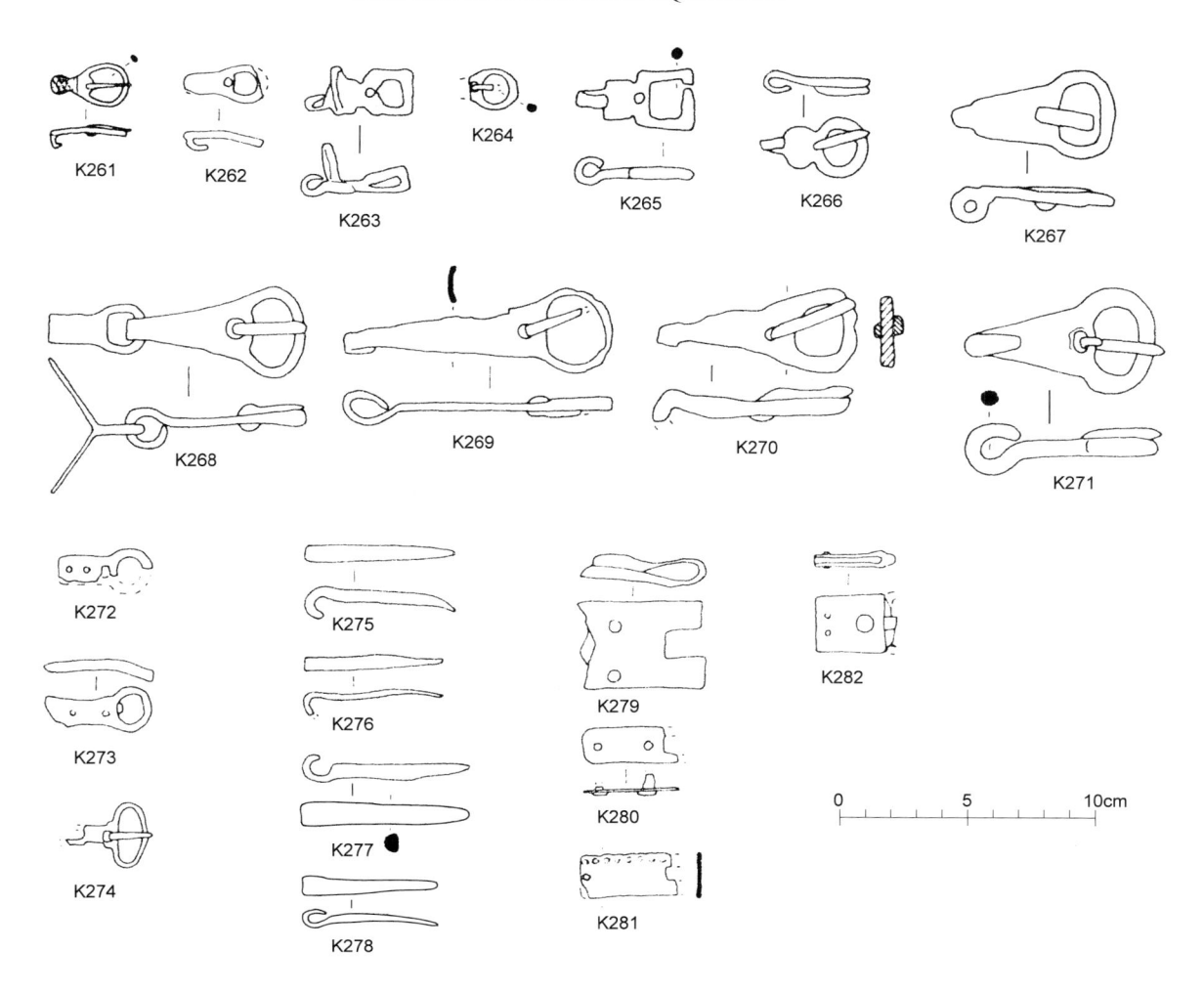

FIGURE 12.10
Buckles

K283 STRAP-END
Thuxton, Norfolk.
Site: 12th–14th century.
Strap-end with shaped terminal and non-ferrous plating. L 31mm.
Excavated by L A S Butler.

K284 STRAP-END
Oxford.
c1325–c1400.
Plain strap-end with non-ferrous plating. L 29mm.
Goodall 1977e, 146, fig 28.53.

K285 STRAP-END
Lyveden, Northamptonshire.
Early 15th century.
Plain strap-end with single, ?iron rivet. L 17mm.
Steane and Bryant 1975, 139, fig 52.242.

K286 BELT SLIDE
Winchester, Hampshire.
Early 13th century.
Rectangular belt slide. L 75mm.
Goodall 1990-12, fig 334.3901.

K287 BELT SLIDE
Clough Castle, Co. Down.
c1250 to early 14th century.
Curved sides, shouldered ends. L 65mm.
Waterman 1954, 141, fig 13.5.

K288 BELT SLIDE
Beckery Chapel, Glastonbury, Somerset.
Later 13th to ?15th century.
Curved-sided belt slide with indented ends. L 97mm.
Rahtz and Hirst 1974, 61, fig 22.16.

K289 BELT HOOK
Salisbury, Wiltshire.
After 1227.
Rectangular belt loop with plain upright arm. L 76mm.
Salisbury and South Wiltshire Museum, Salisbury, Drainage Collection.

K290 BELT HOOK
Salisbury, Wiltshire.
After 1227.
Rectangular belt loop with shaped and upright arm. L 65mm.
Salisbury and South Wiltshire Museum, Salisbury, Drainage Collection.

K291 BELT HOOK
Wharram Percy, North Yorkshire.
Early 16th to 20th century.
Rectangular belt loop above perforation. Shaped and moulded upright arm. L 64mm.
Goodall 1979a, 123, fig 65.116.

K292 PURSE FRAME
King's Lynn, Norfolk.
c1350–1500.
Broken frame with suspension loop. Non-ferrous plating. W 113mm.
Goodall and Carter 1977, 295, fig 134.48.

K293 PURSE FRAME
Somerby, Lincolnshire.
Destruction levels of 15th to mid 16th-century occupation.
Broken frame with suspension loop. W 192mm.
Mynard 1969, 82, fig 11.IW48.

K294 PURSE FRAME
Portchester Castle, Hampshire.
c1500–21.
Oval purse frame with suspension loop. W 229mm.
Hinton 1977, 198, fig 106.39.

K295 PURSE FRAME
Ospringe, Kent.
c1483–1550.
Near complete bar with suspension loop mount decorated on one face. Broken pendent loop. W 145mm.
Goodall 1979c, 132, fig 22.90.

K296 PURSE BAR
London.
Late 15th–early 16th century.
Near complete bar with fragment of pendent frame. Suspension loop lost. L 147mm.
Excavated by F C Willmot. Site at 66 Foyle Road.

K297 PURSE BAR
Waltham Abbey, Essex.
12th–13th century, but ?16th century, from floor above.
Complete bar, suspension loop and pendent frames lost. L 143mm.
Goodall 1973a, 173, fig 12.43.

K298 PURSE FRAME FITTING
Thuxton, Norfolk.
Site: 12th–14th century.
Decorated and shaped pin formerly inset in iron purse bar. L 37mm.
Excavated by L A S Butler.

K299 SCABBARD MOUNT
Hambleton Moat, Lincolnshire.
1250–1400.
Simply shaped scabbard mount found with 260mm long tip of single edged sword or knife-dagger. W 91mm.
Butler 1963, 67, fig 14.12–13.

K300 SCABBARD CHAPE
Norht Elmham Park, Norfolk.
c1150–c1600.
Incomplete chape with knobbed terminal. L 148mm.
Goodall 1980a, 516, fig 267.129.

K301 JEW'S HARP
Woodperry, Oxfordshire.
12th to 14th century pottery.
Reed distorted and broken. L 65mm.
Ashmolean Museum, Oxford, 1873.97. For site see Wilson 1846.

K302 JEW'S HARP
London.
Late 13th–mid 14th century.
Distorted and broken reed. L 67mm.
Henig 1974, 195, fig 39.83.

K303 JEW'S HARP
Wharram Percy, North Yorkshire.
Late 15th to early 16th century.
Reed broken. L 50mm.
Goodall 1979a, 121, fig 63.83.

K304 JEW'S HARP
Wharram Percy, North Yorkshire.
Late 15th to early 16th century.
Distorted and incomplete frame, reed lost. L 35mm.
Goodall 1979a, 121, SF 13083.

BUCKLES AND PERSONAL EQUIPMENT

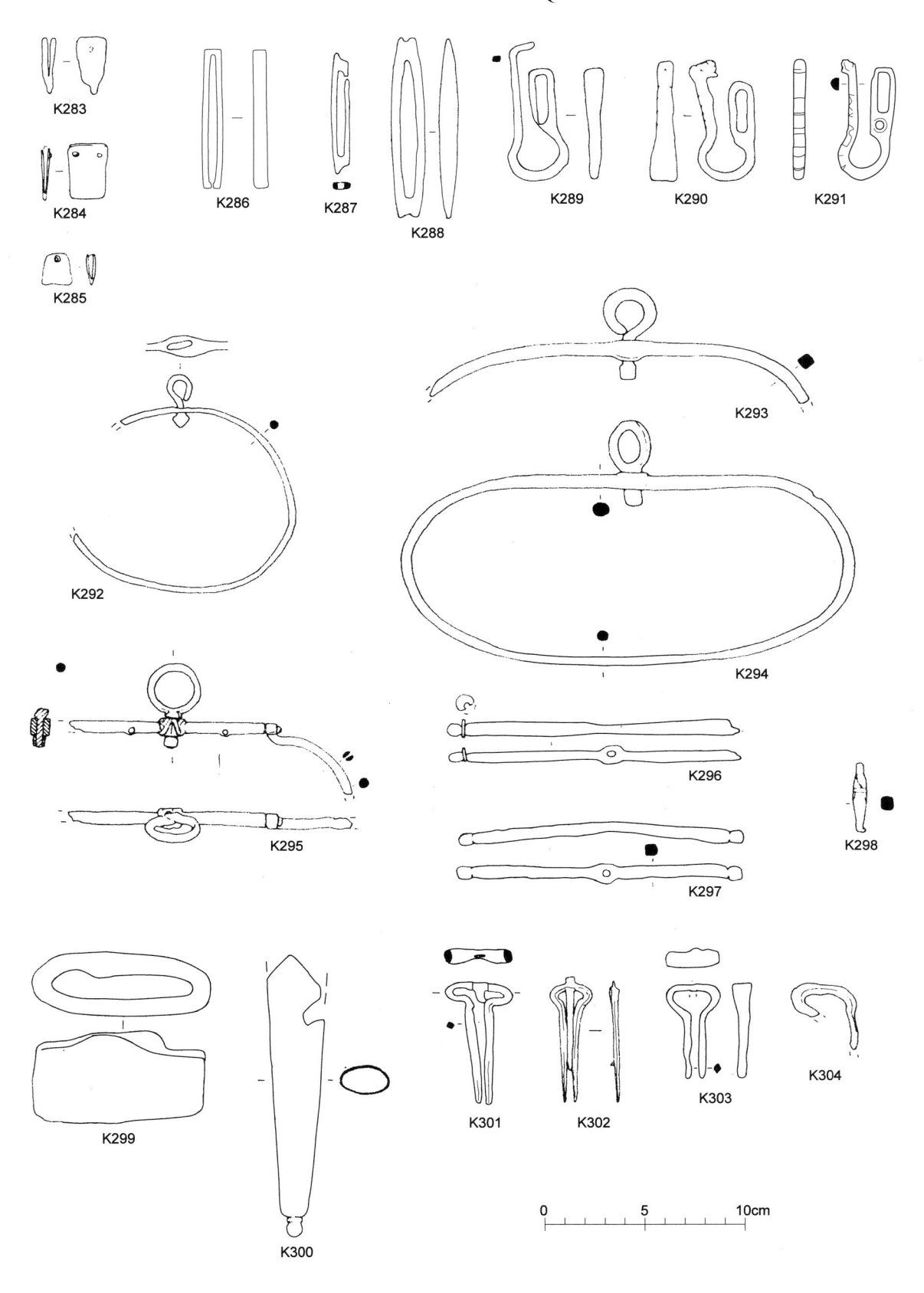

FIGURE 12.11
Strap-ends, belt slides, belt hooks, purse frames, scabbard mount, scabbard chape, and jew's harps

13
HORSE EQUIPMENT

13.1 HORSESHOES

Horseshoes have attracted the attention of many writers, but in the absence of securely dated examples most of their texts are at best merely speculation. Ward Perkins' study (1967, 112–117) is the first to be based on dated horseshoes, although most of the later medieval examples are drawn from Continental sites.

Horseshoes of pre-Conquest date are known from sites including Ipswich, Cheddar, Goltho Manor and Winchester, and they are of identical form to the early medieval type which has countersunk nail-holes whose punching commonly produced a sinuous or wavy edge. **L1–9** are examples of this type, most with up-turned or thickened ends known as calkins. The waviness of the edge varies, and depends largely on the breadth and thickness of the iron bar from which the horseshoe is forged, and on the position of the nail-holes within it. **L3** and **L6**, for example, have only slightly sinuous edges in comparison with **L1–2**. Many examples of this type of horseshoe are forged from comparatively narrow bar iron, and they commonly have a U-shaped inner profile. **L4** is unusual, its one broad and other narrow arm implying that it is a surgical horseshoe. These early medieval horseshoes were normally used with fiddle-key horseshoe nails of Type A (see below).

The transition to the later type of medieval horseshoe took place during the 13th century. **L10–14** all have countersunk nail-holes, like the earlier horseshoes, but they are set within broader arms which consequently have a more or less plain outline. **L10** and **L14**, in contrast to the earlier horseshoes, have nails of Type B (see below) which were introduced during the 13th century. These intermediate horseshoes resemble some earlier medieval specimens such as **L6**, but these are atypical at their date.

The later medieval horseshoes, typified by **L15–27**, have a plain edge and rectangular nail-holes, and are generally of broader iron than preceding horseshoes. The inner profile is sometimes U-shaped, but as commonly V-shaped, and fewer arms have calkins. These shoes were fitted with nails of Types B–D.

13.2 OXSHOES

The bailiff's accounts of the Manor of Dorking in the time of Richard II (quoted in Dunning 1932, 291–292) include the entry 'the forefeet of Oxen used in plowing, and heifers in harrowing, were shod, at 3d each'. The cloven feet of oxen were each shod with pairs of shoes which characteristically have clips, present on **L29** and **L31**, but missing on **L30** and **L32**. Nail-holes on these oxshoes are more closely spaced than they are on horseshoes.

13.3 HORSESHOE AND OXSHOE NAILS

Medieval horseshoe nails (Figure 13.1), some probably also used with oxshoes, are of four main types (A–D). This classification follows that proposed for horseshoe nails from the forge at Waltham Abbey, Essex (Goodall 1973a, 173–175, fig 13A–D), and other significant groups include those from Seacourt, Oxfordshire (Biddle 1961–62, 176), Bramber Castle, West Sussex (Barton and Holden 1977, 64, fig 20) and Ospringe, Kent (Mold 1979, 150–152, fig 30A–C).

Type A

Fiddle-key nails with head no thicker in side view than the shank.

Nails of this type were used with horseshoes with countersunk nail-holes, the base of the head set in the countersinking. Complete nails either have semicircular

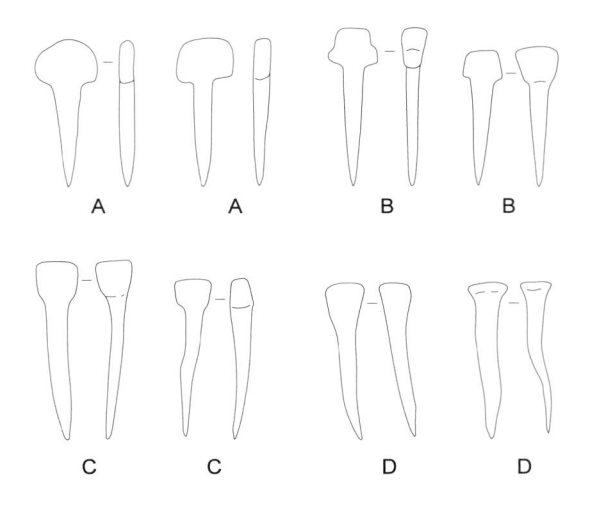

FIGURE 13.1
Types of medieval horseshoe nail

or more rectangular-shaped heads, both of which can be worn down to a T-shape. Type A nails occur in 11th to 13th-century contexts, but they also come from some of the 14th century which are not necessarily residual, including the smithing and working area at Bramber Castle, West Sussex (Barton and Holden 1977, 64, fig 20, Nails 1a,b).

Type B

Nails with trapezoidal heads which expand in side view to a flat top.

Type B nails, some of which have well-defined ears, were used in the 13th and 14th centuries, some in horseshoes such as **L10** and **L14** with countersunk nail-holes, others including **L16** and one from Seacourt, Oxfordshire (Biddle 1961–62, 180, fig 30.19) in horseshoes with plain nail-holes. Nearly all the many individual horseshoe nails from Dyserth Castle, Clwyd, occupied 1241–63 (Glenn 1915, fig 9), are of Type B, as are those from the end of the 13th century at Rhuddlan, Clwyd (Goodall 1994).

Type C

Nails with shouldered heads, thickened in side view, with near-vertical sides.

Nails of Type C were used with later medieval horseshoes, and examples include those from a late 13th to 14th century context at Hambleton Moat, Lincolnshire (Butler 1963, 67, fig 14.14) and from one of the late 14th century at Lochmaben Castle, Dumfries and Galloway (Macdonald and Laing 1974–75, 147, fig 10.13). Later examples come from Waltham Abbey, Essex (Goodall 1973a, 174–175, fig 13.C), and horseshoe **L22** retains one.

Type D

Nails with heads which expand in front and side views to a flat top.

Nails of Type D were used with later medieval horseshoes and oxshoes, although only the smaller examples are suitable for oxshoes. They are probably mainly of 15th to 16th-century date, and horseshoes **L21**, **L24** and **L27** retain them, as well as an incomplete horseshoe from Cambokeels, Durham (Hildyard and Charlton 1947, 193, fig 3.2). Seacourt, Oxfordshire, produced 14th-century nails of the type (Biddle 1961–62, 176, Type 1.iii).

13.4 CURRY-COMBS

Curry-combs were used in conjunction with body brushes in grooming horses, and the surviving medieval examples have two or three-armed handles riveted to the backs of sheet-iron combs. **L33–36** are all fairly complete and have U-sectioned combs with straight sides and serrated edges. **L33** and **L35** retain two-armed handles, **L36** a three-armed handle, all of which were originally inserted into wooden hand-grips. **L33** retains part of an iron impregnated wooden hand-grip. Curry-comb handles **L37–40** have two arms, **L41–45** three arms, and **L46** is an isolated arm fragment. The two-armed handle is found throughout the medieval period, but the three-armed form comes principally from 14th-century and later contexts.

Horse harness was frequently fitted with jangling bells and pendants, and the loose rings on the arms of **L35** and **L44** are their equivalent on curry-combs.

Post-medieval curry-combs included a type with a flat back-plate to which individual serrated plates were riveted, as well as examples resembling medieval types but with an additional central serrated plate. The curry-comb from Rickinghall Superior, Suffolk (Knocker 1961–63) is of this latter type, and is more probably post-medieval than medieval.

13.5 BRIDLE BITS

Snaffle bits and curb bits were used throughout the medieval period, snaffle bits having mouth-pieces and simple looped cheek-pieces, curb bits and complex cheek-pieces with additional loops for extra reins, linking bars and chains. The snaffle bit is the milder bit, the curb bit giving greater control of a horse and being used by competent riders. Ward Perkins comments that the curb bit bulks disproportionately large in contemporary illustration, to the detriment of the snaffle bit (Ward Perkins 1967, 77), but there are now at least a few more dated medieval bits to set against these representations.

Curb bits

Curb bits **L47–50** compare well with the forms shown in contemporary representations. Earlier medieval illustrations, including the mid 13th-century Maciejowski Bible and early 14th-century Luttrell Psalter show curb bits with more or less plain straight cheek-pieces projecting downwards and linked by transverse bars near the bottom (Ward Perkins 1967, 79, fig 18. 4–6), and **L47–48** are of this type. Both are of 11th-century date, **L47**, which has lost its bottom transverse bar, having a rigid mouth-piece forged in one with the looped and hooked L-shaped cheek-pieces. **L48** is a transverse bottom bar with bossed terminals which were mounted in the bottom ends of cheek-pieces, their corner perforations holding rings or small swivel hooks to which reins were attached.

L49–50 are examples of the more elaborate later type of curb bit with multiple-looped and perforated cheek-pieces to which reins, straps and chains were attached. The hole in the lower part of one of the cheek-pieces of **L49** retains a link from a chain which held the cheek-pieces together, reins and the headstall straps passed through or were attached to the other loops. **L50** would have been used in a similar way, and the small hole between the two upper loops may originally have held a mount for a bridle boss (see below). These two curb bits are from 15th-century and later contexts, although **L49** resembles one from Tannenberg Castle, Germany, apparently destroyed in 1399 (Ward Perkins 1967, 79, fig 18.2).

Snaffle bits

The medieval snaffle bit, like earlier and later examples, consisted of a mouth-piece with simple cheek-pieces at either end to which reins and the headstall were attached. The classification of snaffle bit cheek-pieces into Type A–E (Figure 13.2) proposed by Ward Perkins (1967, 80–81, fig 19a) is adopted here, although no certainly medieval example of Type D is yet known. The details about the origins of the various types is not repeated below, and mouth-pieces found independently of cheek-pieces are discussed later.

Type A

The ring snaffle is the simplest type of all snaffle bits, although unless ring and mouth-piece are attached the former might be incorrectly identified. **L51–52** are complete snaffle bits with unusually shaped jointed mouth-pieces, and with rings of markedly different sizes.

Type B

L53, of 12th-century date, has a centrally set loop and arms with out-turned tips.

Type C

This, the most common medieval type of cheek-piece, is found in contexts throughout the medieval period. **L54–62** exhibit minor differences of form, but the centrally placed, side-set loops are rounded except on **L56**, and the arms have either knobbed, expanded or moulded tips.

Type D

No stratified medieval cheek-piece of this type is yet known, and it is possible that it is a post-medieval development of Type C. The supposed medieval examples (Ward Perkins 1967, 81, 83, fig 20) may all be of later date.

Type E

L63 is a near complete snaffle bit with flaring cheek-pieces and a jointed mouth-piece which is unusual in having three small rings or collars on each link.

Mouth-pieces from curb bits and snaffle bits

A number of the more complete curb bits and snaffle bits retain their mouth-pieces, but more mouth-piece links

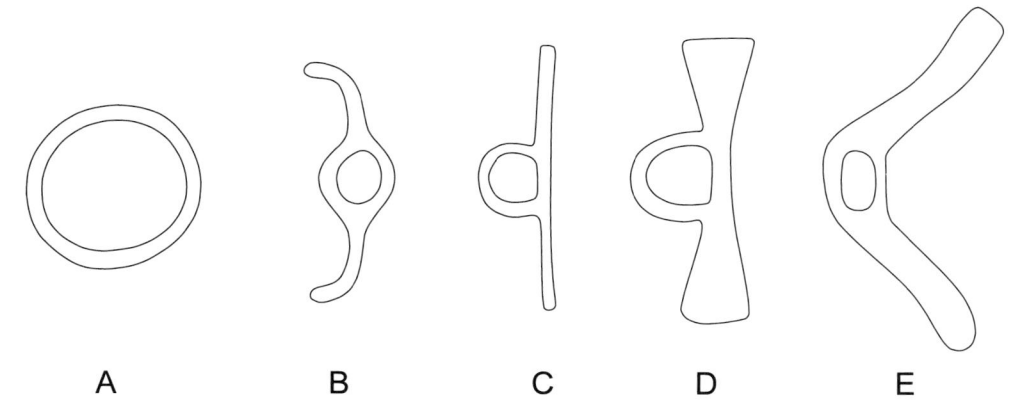

FIGURE 13.2
Types of medieval bridle bit cheek-piece

are known as isolated finds. The rigid, one-piece mouth-piece is rarely found, curb bit **L47** having the only example. The other sufficiently complete bits, all snaffle bits, have jointed mouth-pieces with either two links, as on **L56** and **L63**, or two links and a central ring (**L49**). **L64** is another two link mouth-pieces, but **L65–73** are all broken single links, as are those on bits **L59**, **L60** and **L62**. The hollow conical mouth-piece found on post-medieval bits, including the early 17th-century curb bit from Basing House, Hampshire (Moorhouse and Goodall 1971, 47–49, fig 21.89), is rarely recognised in medieval contexts, although **L74** is an example.

Curb chains

Chains fitted between the upper loops of curb bits passed behind the lower jaw of the horse and exerted pressure on it when the lower rein was pulled. Modern bits generally have a simple link chain, but medieval chains sometimes incorporated a curved, U-sectioned fitting such as **L75–77**. These fittings were used in conjunction with links like **L78**, as **L75** and **L77** demonstrate, and others like **L79**. The latter link resembles one through the upper loop of an early 17th-century bit from Basing House, Hampshire (Moorhouse and Goodall 1971, 47–49).

13.6 BRIDLE BOSSES

The junction between mouth-piece and cheek-piece on the more elaborate curb bits was sometimes hidden by a bridle boss of iron or copper alloy, and cheek-piece **L50** has a hole between its two upper loops which may have held the mount for such a boss. The early 17th-century curb bit from Basing House, Hampshire (Moorhouse and Goodall 1971, 47–49) retains one form of mount. **L80–82** are iron bridle bosses, all probably secured by rivets through their flanges. At least two bosses have traces of non-ferrous plating, and all are shaped or decorated in some way. The beaded flange of **L82** recalls a gilt copper-alloy boss from Goltho, Lincolnshire (Goodall 1975a, 95, fig 44.38).

13.7 HARNESS FITTINGS

Buckles formed part of both the bridle and saddle, enabling each to be adjusted, and other iron fittings also have a place in the bridle.

Strap links

Viking or late Saxon bridle bits were sometimes linked to the reins by double-looped strap links similar to **L83–87**, as a complete bit from York indicates (Waterman 1959b, 74–75, fig 8.1). **L84–86** are from 11th to 12th-century contexts, and unless residual as **L87** probably is, they imply that the type may have continued in use into the very early medieval period.

L88 may have been used as a link between the headstall straps which kept the bit in place; this may be an alternative use for some of the other strap links.

Strap loops and distributors

Strap loops with extended, riveted plates were used to join straps to cheek-pieces, and to items of dress such as belts, as well as to support swivel fittings or simply to join straps together.

L89–97 are large strap loops, **L97** U-shaped but the others looped, and any or all could be from harness, as are a pair on a snaffle bit from London (Ward Perkins 1967, 83, fig 21.3). The smaller strap loops **L98–100**, particularly the decorated gilt example **L98**, are more probably personal objects. **L101** comprises a pair of strap loops evidently joining two straps together, a function also performed by the strap distributor **L102**. **L013–104** are other strap distributors, unless **L104** is the circular Type A cheek-piece of a snaffle bit. The ring, though small, is not unlike that of the ring snaffle **L52**.

Looped strap guides

Few medieval curb bits retain any of their smaller associated fittings, but two Continental examples (Ward Perkins 1967, 79, fig 18.1, 2) retain looped strap guides similar to **L105–111** in their cheek-pieces. The hooked ends of these guides were attached to the bit, and the leather harness strap passed freely through the loop.

Swivel fittings

Harness incorporated various elements which had to be free to move about loosely and independently, and if strap loops or guides did not provide sufficient freedom, swivel fittings were employed. **L112–116** may be from harness, certainly none of those with a swivel hook and ring is robust enough to be from a cauldron chain.

Harness pendants

Elaborate pendant fittings were an important part of the finer sets of horse equipment, but the pendants and their mounts are usually of copper alloy (Ward Perkins 1967, 118–122). **L117–118** are circular hooked iron pendants, both with non-ferrous plating.

13.8 STIRRUPS

Stirrups are probably the least well represented item of

medieval horse equipment, although iron stirrups **L119–124** and the few additional copper-alloy examples do enable an outline development sequence to be described.

Ward Perkins (1967, 86–87) describes the types of stirrups in use during the Viking period, and notes that representations of early medieval stirrups are sufficient only to show that both loop-stirrups and squared forms with flattened foot-rests were current. Iron stirrups **L119–122** are either examples or developments of these types, **L119** of 11th to early 12th-century date and closely resembling Viking types with its boss and twisted round loop for the stirrup-leather. **L120**, of 13th-century date, is broadly similar in shape although it has lost its loop, whereas the later stirrups **L121–122** exhibit the developed rounded body with integrated loop which may be typical of the 13th and 14th centuries. The squat, rounded shape of **L122** developed into the trapezoidal shape of the later medieval period. **L123** is of this latter shape, but is not closely dated, but of three similar copper-alloy stirrups from East Haddlesey, North Yorkshire (Goodall 1973b, 91, fig 36.1–2a, b), one is unstratified and the other two probably 15th or early 16th century. The asymmetrical form of **L124**, from a 16th-century context, is known from 14th-century sites on the Continent (Ward Perkins 1967, 89, fig 23.9–10).

L1 HORSESHOE
Goltho Manor, Lincolnshire.
11th century.
Complete. W 101mm.
Goodall 1987, fig 160.155.

L2 HORSESHOE
Goltho Manor, Lincolnshire.
c1100–1150.
Complete. W 107mm.
Goodall 1987, fig 160.156.

L3 HORSESHOE
Winchester, Hampshire.
Late 11th to 12th century.
One arm damaged. W 94mm.
Goodall 1990-25, fig 340.3945 [Goodall 1980 says BSSC 3888].

L4 HORSESHOE
Winchester, Hampshire.
12th–early 13th century.
Complete. One arm broader than other.
W 110mm.
Goodall 1990-25, fig 340.3953.

L5 HORSESHOE
Winchester, Hampshire.
Late 12th–?early 13th century.
Toe damaged. W 99mm.
Goodall 1990-25, fig 340.3951.

L6 HORSESHOE
Dover Castle, Kent.
Mid 13th century.
Complete. W 100mm.
Rigold 1967, 109, fig 9.Fe6.

L7 HORSESHOE
Winchester, Hampshire.
Mid to late 13th century.
One arm damaged. W 95mm.
Goodall 1990-25, fig 341.3959.

L8 HORSESHOE
Dyserth Castle, Clwyd.
Site: 1241–63.
Complete. W 99mm.
Glenn 1915, fig 10.

L9 HORSESHOE
Rhuddlan, Clwyd.
End 13th century.
Complete. W 104mm.
Goodall 1994, fig 17.7, no. 108.

L10 HORSESHOE
Dyserth Castle, Clwyd.
Site: 1241–63.
Complete. W 102mm.
Glenn 1915, fig 10.

L11 HORSESHOE
Castell-y-Bere, Gwynedd.
Site: c1221–95.
Complete. W 104mm.
Butler 1974, 97, fig 8.9.

L12 HORSESHOE
Brandon Castle, Warwickshire.
13th century.
Complete. W 106mm.
Chatwin 1955, 81, fig 11.6.

L13 HORSESHOE
Rhuddlan, Clwyd.
1280s.
Complete. W 113mm.
Goodall 1994, fig 17.7, no. 116.

L14 HORSESHOE
Rhuddlan, Clwyd.
1280s.
Complete. W 100mm.
Goodall 1994, fig 17.7, no. 117.

L15 HORSESHOE
London.
Late 13th–mid 14th century.
Complete. W 114mm.
Henig 1974, 191, fig 38.61.

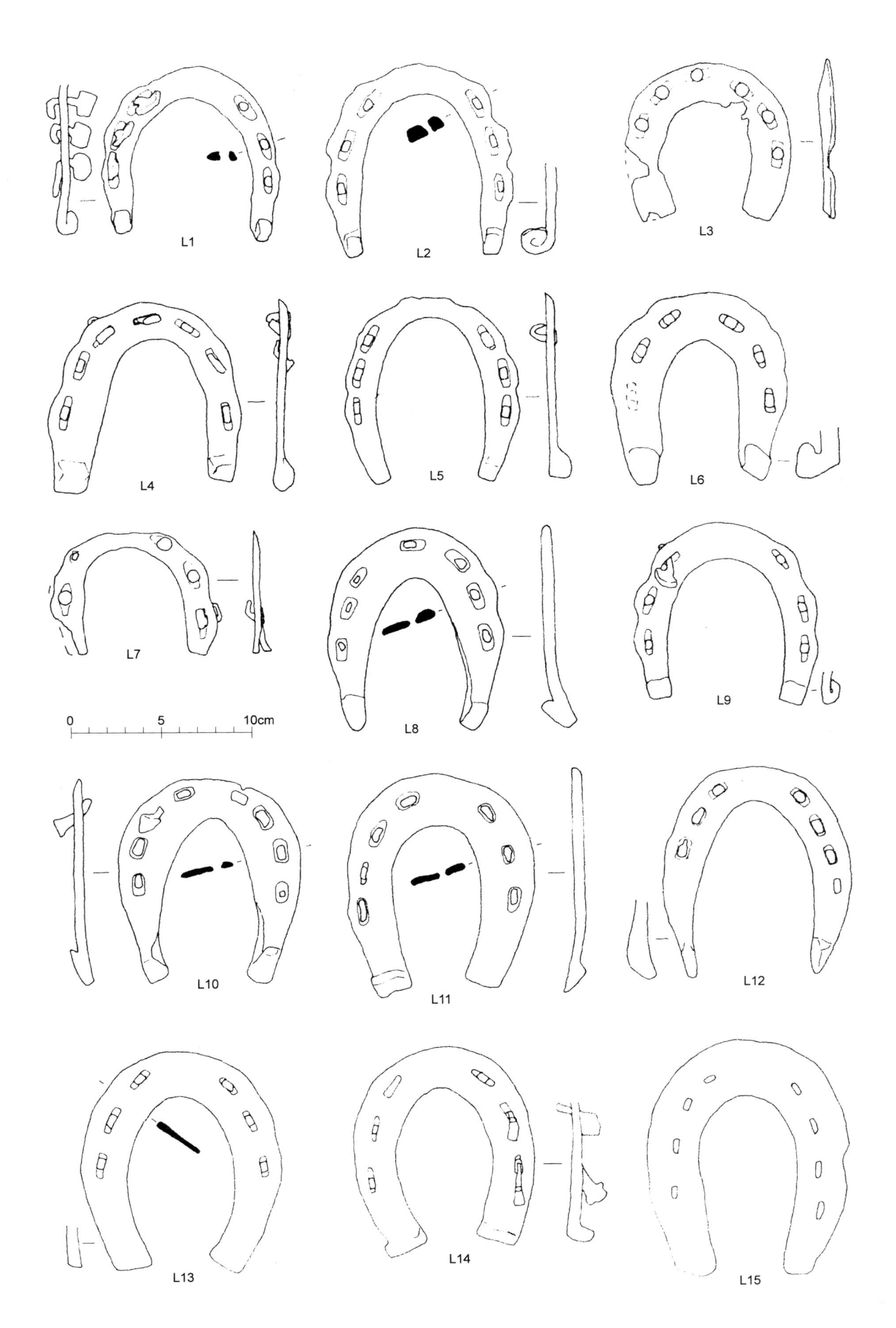

FIGURE 13.3
Horseshoes

L16 HORSESHOE
London.
Late 13th–mid 14th century.
One arm broken. W 93mm.
Henig 1974, 191, no. 63.

L17 HORSESHOE
Seacourt, Oxfordshire.
14th century.
Complete. W 100mm.
Biddle 1961–62, 179, fig 30.18, scale 1:4, not 1:3.

L18 HORSESHOE
Winchester, Hampshire.
14th century.
Arms damaged. W 124mm.
Goodall 1990-25, fig 342.3967 [Goodall 1980 says CG 2714].

L19 HORSESHOE
Oxford.
c1325–c1400.
Complete. WL109mm.
Goodall 1977e, 148, fig 29.59.

L20 HORSESHOE
Lochmaben Castle, Dumfries and Galloway.
Late 14th century.
Complete. W 113mm.
Macdonald and Laing 1974–75, 146–147, fig 10.9.

L21 HORSESHOE
Cambokeels, Durham.
Later 14th to early 16th century.
Complete. W 105mm.
Hildyard 1949, 195, fig 3.13.

L22 HORSESHOE
Cambokeels, Durham.
Later 14th to early 16th century.
One arm broken. W 106mm.
Hildyard and Charlton 1947, 193, fig 3.1.
Bowes Museum, Barnard Castle.

L23 HORSESHOE
Huish, Wiltshire.
In hearth of smithy, burnt in mid 15th century.
Complete. W 98mm.
Shortt 1972, 124, fig 6.41.

L24 HORSESHOE
Winchester, Hampshire.
Mid 15th century.
One arm and toe damaged. W 105mm.
Goodall 1990-25, fig 342.3968.

L25 HORSESHOE
Ospringe, Kent.
c1483–1550.
One arm broken. W 81mm.
Goodall 1979c, 132, fig 22.102.

L26 HORSESHOE
Alvechurch, Hereford and Worcester.
c1500.
Toe worn. W 113mm.
Oswald 1954, 9, pl 5.14.

L27 HORSESHOE
Alvechurch, Hereford and Worcester.
c1500.
Toe worn. W 110mm.
Oswald 1954, 9, pl 5.14.

L28 HORSESHOE
Southampton, Hampshire.
16th century.
One arm damaged. W 118mm.
Harvey 1975b, 287, fig 257.2104.

L29 OXSHOE
Eynsford Castle, Kent.
First half 13th century.
Complete. L 111mm.
Rigold and Fleming 1973, 105, fig 9.11.

L30 OXSHOE
Hangleton, West Sussex.
14th–15th century.
Broken. L 79mm.
Holden 1963, 173, fig 38.7.

L31 OXSHOE
London.
Late 15th–early 16th century.
Complete. L 112mm.
Excavated by F C Willmot. Site at 66 Foyle Road.

L32 OXSHOE
Waltham Abbey, Essex.
13th and 16th century.
Clip broken. L 86mm.
Goodall 1973a, 171, fig 12.38.

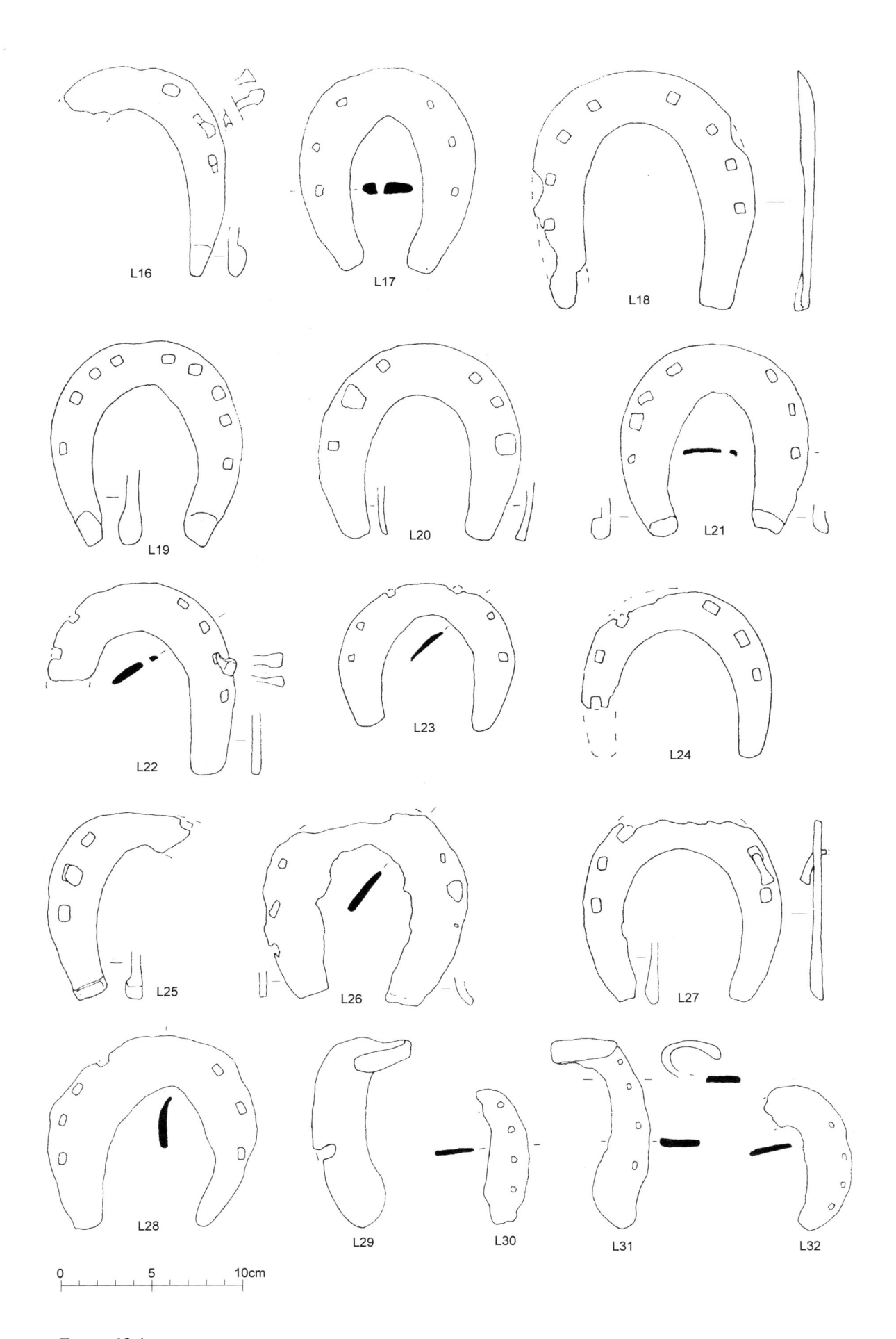

FIGURE 13.4
Horseshoes

L33 CURRY-COMB
Southampton, Hampshire.
1300–50.
Curry-comb with two-armed handle riveted to U-shaped comb. Broken tang retains part of former wooden handle. Comb incomplete. L 182mm, W 176mm.
Harvey 1975b, 282, fig 254.1049.

L34 CURRY-COMB
Thuxton, Norfolk.
Site: 12th–14th century.
U-shaped comb fragment with rivet from handle. W 130mm.
Excavated by L A S Butler.

L35 CURRY-COMB
Wharram Percy, North Yorkshire.
Late 15th to early 16th century.
Curry-comb with two-armed handle riveted to U-shaped comb. Comb near complete, handle tang broken. Two loose rings on handle arms. L 95mm, W 165mm.
Goodall 1979a, 121, fig 63.65.

L36 CURRY-COMB
Oxford.
Mid 16th century.
Fragment of incomplete and distorted U-shaped comb with part of three-armed handle. W 97mm.
Excavated by N Palmer.

L37 CURRY-COMB HANDLE
Winchester, Hampshire.
13th to early 14th century.
Two-armed handle, near complete. L 165mm.
Goodall 1990-24, fig 338.3936.

L38 CURRY-COMB HANDLE
(not illustrated)
Winchester, Hampshire.
Late 12th century.
Two arms and tang broken. L 65mm.
Goodall 1990-24, 1053, no. 3934.

L39 CURRY-COMB HANDLE
Castell-y-Bere, Gwynedd.
Site: c1221–95.
Two-armed handle, complete. L 128mm.
National Museum of Wales, Cardiff, 21–24/1957. For site see Butler 1974.

L40 CURRY-COMB HANDLE
Oxford.
c1325–c1400.
Incomplete two-armed handle. L 68mm.
Goodall 1977e, 148, fig 29.67.

L41 CURRY-COMB HANDLE
Winchester, Hampshire.
14th century.
Incomplete three-armed handle. L 103mm.
Goodall 1990-24, fig 338.3938.

L42 CURRY-COMB HANDLE
The Mount, Princes Risborough, Buckinghamshire.
14th, early 15th century.
Three-armed handle, near complete, with fragments of former U-shaped comb riveted to undersides of terminals, not to split terminals as published. L 119mm.
Pavry and Knocker 1953–60, 161, fig 12.5.

L43 CURRY-COMB HANDLE
West Hartburn, Durham.
16th century.
Near complete, distorted three-armed handle. L 149mm.
Excavated by L Still.

L44 CURRY-COMB HANDLE
Winchester, Hampshire.
Late 15th–early 16th century.
Three-armed handle, incomplete, with loose ring on central arm. L 106mm.
Goodall 1990-24, fig 338.3937.

L45 CURRY-COMB HANDLE
Waltham Abbey, Essex.
16th century.
Incomplete three-armed handle. L 90mm.
Goodall 1973a, 171, fig 12.39.

L46 CURRY-COMB HANDLE
King's Lynn, Norfolk
c1350–1500.
Riveted arm from handle. L 95mm.
Goodall and Carter 1977, 295, fig 134.47.

HORSE EQUIPMENT

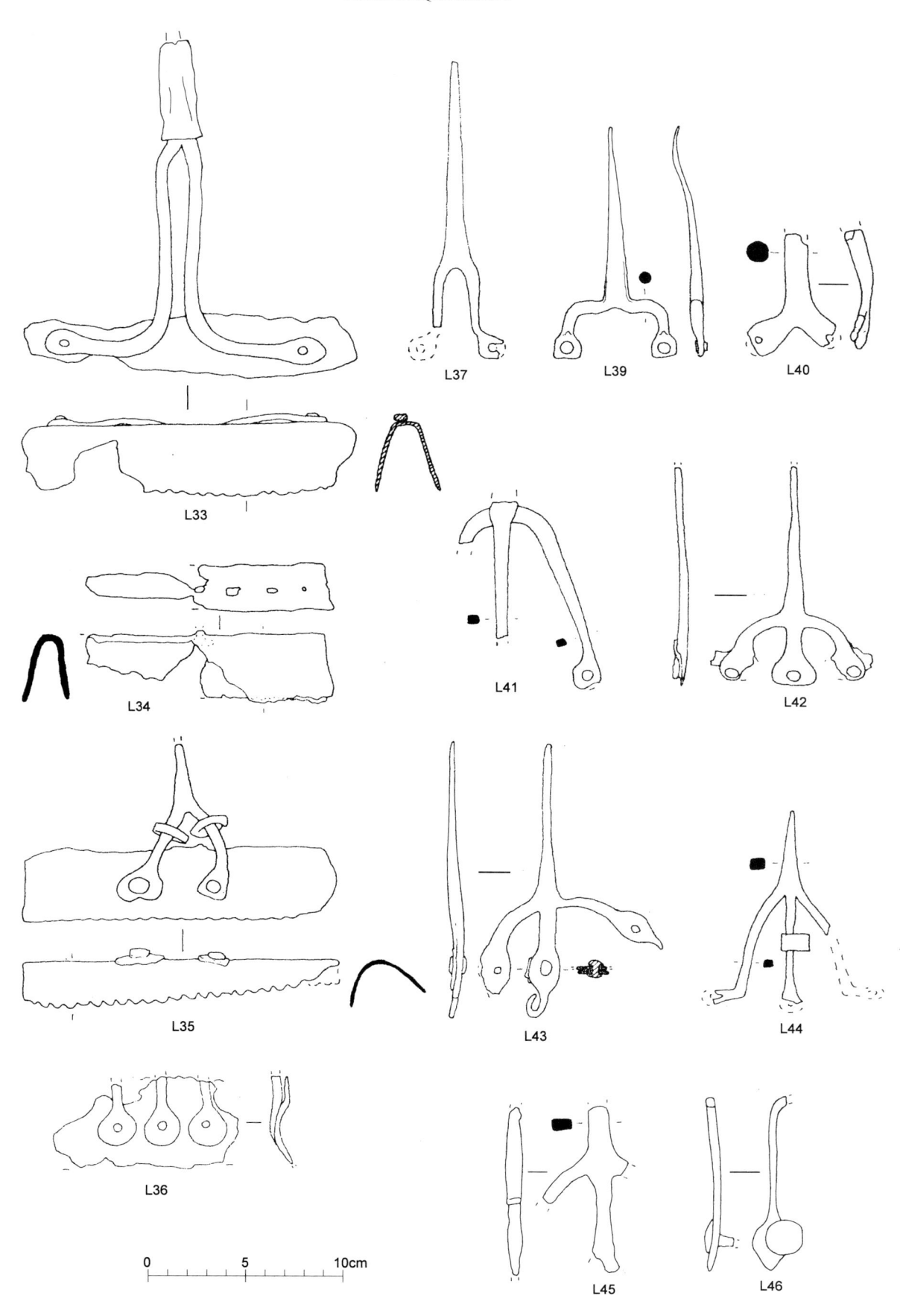

FIGURE 13.5
Curry-combs

L47 CURB BIT
Sulgrave, Northamptonshire.
Second half 11th century, possibly just post-Conquest.
Incomplete curb bit. W 125mm.
Excavated by B K Davison.

L48 CURB BIT
King's Lynn, Norfolk.
Late 11th century.
Bar with side arms terminating in swivel bosses. Non-ferrous plating. W 119mm.
Goodall and Carter 1977, 295, fig 143.44.

L49 CURB BIT
Weoley Castle, Birmingham, West Midlands.
*c*1400–50.
Jointed mouth-piece complete, cheek-piece near complete. W 104mm, L 151mm.
Taylor 1974. For site see Oswald 1962.

L50 CHEEK-PIECE
Somerby, Lincolnshire.
15th to mid 16th century.
Near complete cheek-piece with non-ferrous plating. L 156mm.
Mynard 1969, 81, fig 11.IW28.

L51 SNAFFLE BIT
Lochmaben Castle, Dumfries and Galloway.
Late 14th century.
Complete snaffle bit with jointed mouth-piece, one link end with incised decoration. W 206mm.
Macdonald and Laing 1974–75, 146, fig 10.1.

L52 SNAFFLE BIT
Ospringe, Kent.
*c*1483–1550.
Complete snaffle bit with jointed and twisted mouth-piece. Tinned. W 102mm.
Goodall 1979c, 132, fig 23.111.

L53 CHEEK-PIECE
Weaverthorpe, North Yorkshire.
12th century.
Complete. L 96mm.
Brewster 1972, 132, fig 14.A.

L54 SNAFFLE BIT
Lyveden, Northamptonshire.
Site: *c*1150–*c*1350.
Broken knobbed cheek-piece and link from jointed mouth-piece. W 91mm.
Steane and Bryant 1975, 127–128, fig 48.105.

L55 CHEEK-PIECE
Lyveden, Northamptonshire.
Site: *c*1150–*c*1350.
Broken, knobbed cheek-piece. L 86mm.
Steane and Bryant 1975, 128, fig 48.107.

L56 SNAFFLE BIT
Criccieth Castle, Gwynedd.
Site: *c*1230–1404.
Complete snaffle bit with jointed mouth-piece. W 190mm.
O'Neil 1944–45, 41, pl IX.1.

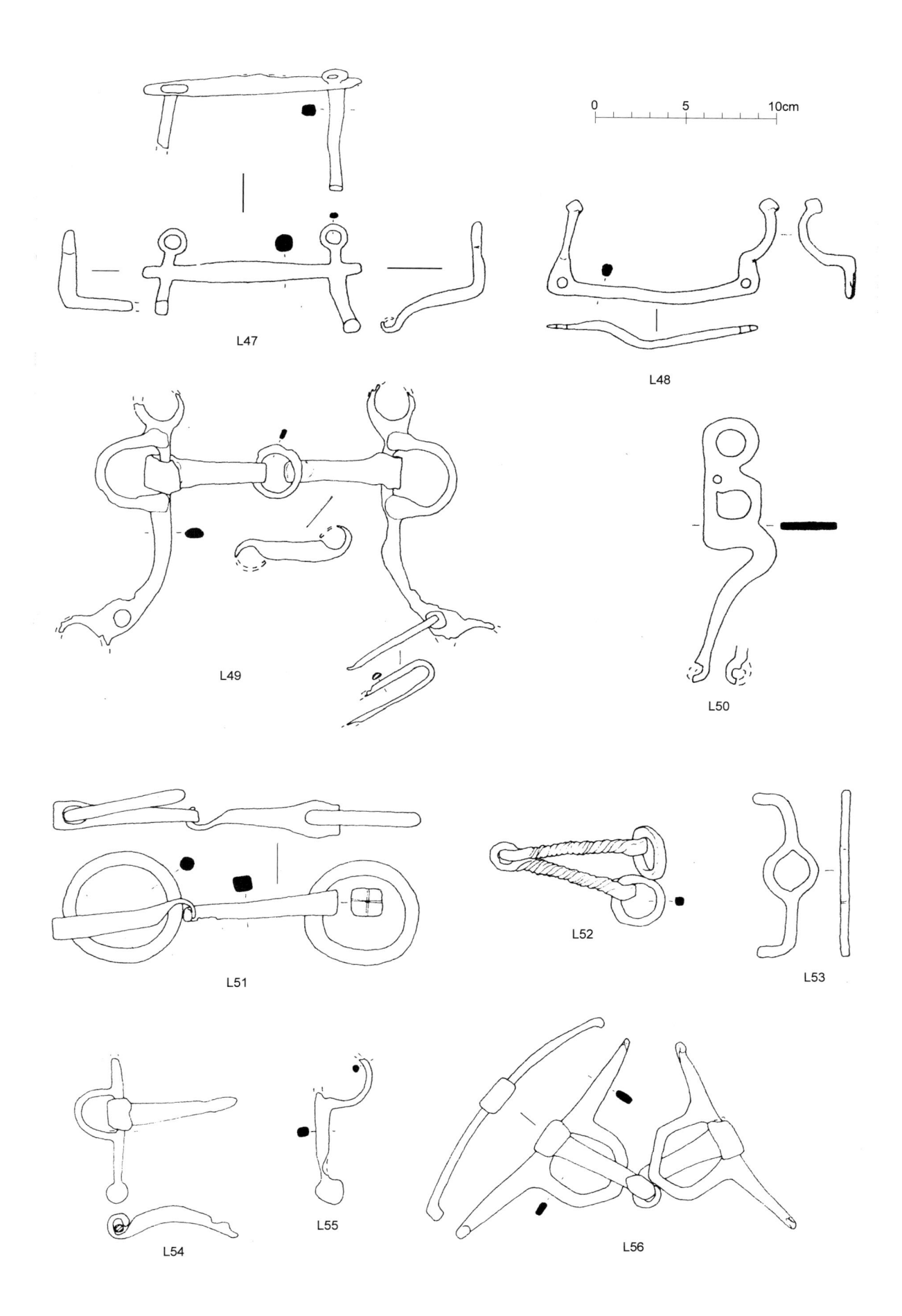

FIGURE 13.6
Bridle bits

L57 CHEEK-PIECE
Somerby, Lincolnshire.
15th to mid 16th century.
Knobbed terminals. Non-ferrous plating.
L 157mm.
Mynard 1969, 82, fig 11.IW47.

L58 CHEEK-PIECE
Newbury, Berkshire.
c1470–1510.
Broken and distorted cheek-piece with knobbed terminal. L 83mm.
Goodall 1997, fig 22, no. 56.

L59 SNAFFLE BIT
Ospringe, Kent.
c1483–1550.
Cheek-piece and link from jointed mouth-piece. Tinned. W 55mm.
Goodall 1979c, 132, fig 23.110.

L60 SNAFFLE BIT
Rest Park, North Yorkshire.
15th–16th century.
Cheek-piece and link from jointed mouth-piece. W 114mm.
Goodall 1973b, 93, fig 36.3.

L61 CHEEK-PIECE
West Hartburn, Durham.
Medieval to later 16th century.
Complete. L 149mm.
Still and Pallister 1967, 146, fig 4.5.

L62 SNAFFLE BIT
West Hartburn, Durham.
13th–16th century.
Cheek-piece and broken link from jointed mouth-piece. W 85mm.
Still and Pallister 1964, 200, fig 6.21.

L63 SNAFFLE BIT
Weoley Castle, Birmingham, West Midlands.
c1270–1600.
One cheek-piece incomplete. Jointed mouth-piece, each link with three collars.
W 181mm, L 158mm.
Taylor 1974. For site see Oswald 1962.

L64 MOUTH-PIECE
Castell-y-Bere, Gwynedd.
Site: c1221–95.
Jointed mouth-piece. W 169mm.
Butler 1974, 97, no. 8A.

L65 MOUTH-PIECE
Llantrithyd, South Glamorgan.
Early to mid 12th century.
Broken link from jointed mouth-piece.
W 64mm.
Goodall 1977f, 48, iron object fig 3.62.

L66 MOUTH-PIECE
Winchester, Hampshire.
12th–mid 13th century.
Broken link from jointed mouth-piece.
W 73mm.
Goodall 1990-23, fig 334.3889.

L67 MOUTH-PIECE
Rhuddlan, Clwyd.
Earlier part 14th century or 1290–1300.
Broken link from jointed mouth-piece.
W 78mm.
Goodall 1994, fig 17.7, no. 135.

L68 MOUTH-PIECE
Alsted, Surrey.
c1270–1340.
Broken link from jointed mouth-piece.
W 95mm.
Goodall 1976a, 60, fig 36.57.

L69 MOUTH-PIECE
Alsted, Surrey.
c1250–1405.
Broken link from jointed mouth-piece.
W 113mm.
Goodall 1976a, 60, fig 36.58.

L70 MOUTH-PIECE
Brooklands, Weybridge, Surrey.
c1150–1325.
Broken link from jointed mouth-piece.
W 106mm.
Goodall 1977d, 73, fig 45.13.

L71 MOUTH-PIECE
Lyveden, Northamptonshire.
Site: c1150–c1350.
Broken link from jointed mouth-piece.
W 78mm.
Steane and Bryant 1975, 128, fig 48.114.

L72 MOUTH-PIECE
Bolton, Fangfoss, Humberside.
End 14th to mid 15th century.
Broken link from jointed mouth-piece.
W 125mm.
Goodall 1978b, 143, fig 30.39.

L73 MOUTH-PIECE
Wharram Percy, North Yorkshire.
Late 15th to early 16th century.
Broken link from jointed mouth-piece.
W 75mm.
Goodall 1979a, 121, fig 63.66.

L74 MOUTH-PIECE (not illustrated)
Waltham Abbey, Essex.
c1540.
Hollow conical mouth-piece.
Huggins 1972, 117.

L75 CURB CHAIN FITTING
Wallingstones, Hereford and Worcester.
Site: c1200–c1500.
Broken fitting and figure-eight link.
L 110mm.
Bridgewater 1970–72.

L76 CURB CHAIN FITTING
Weoley Castle, Birmingham, West Midlands.
Site: c1080–1600.
Broken fitting. L 102mm.
Birmingham City Museum, WC 436. For site see Oswald 1962.

L77 CURB CHAIN FITTING
Lyveden, Northamptonshire.
First half 15th century.
Broken fitting and figure-eight link.
L 67mm.
Steane and Bryant 1975, 129, fig 48.128.

L78 CURB CHAIN LINK
Lyveden, Northamptonshire.
c1350–1450.
Complete. L 40mm.
Steane and Bryant 1975, 129, fig 48.127.

L79 CURB CHAIN LINK
South Witham, Lincolnshire.
c1220 to 1308–13.
Complete. L 53mm.
Goodall 2002, fig 7.8, no. 85.

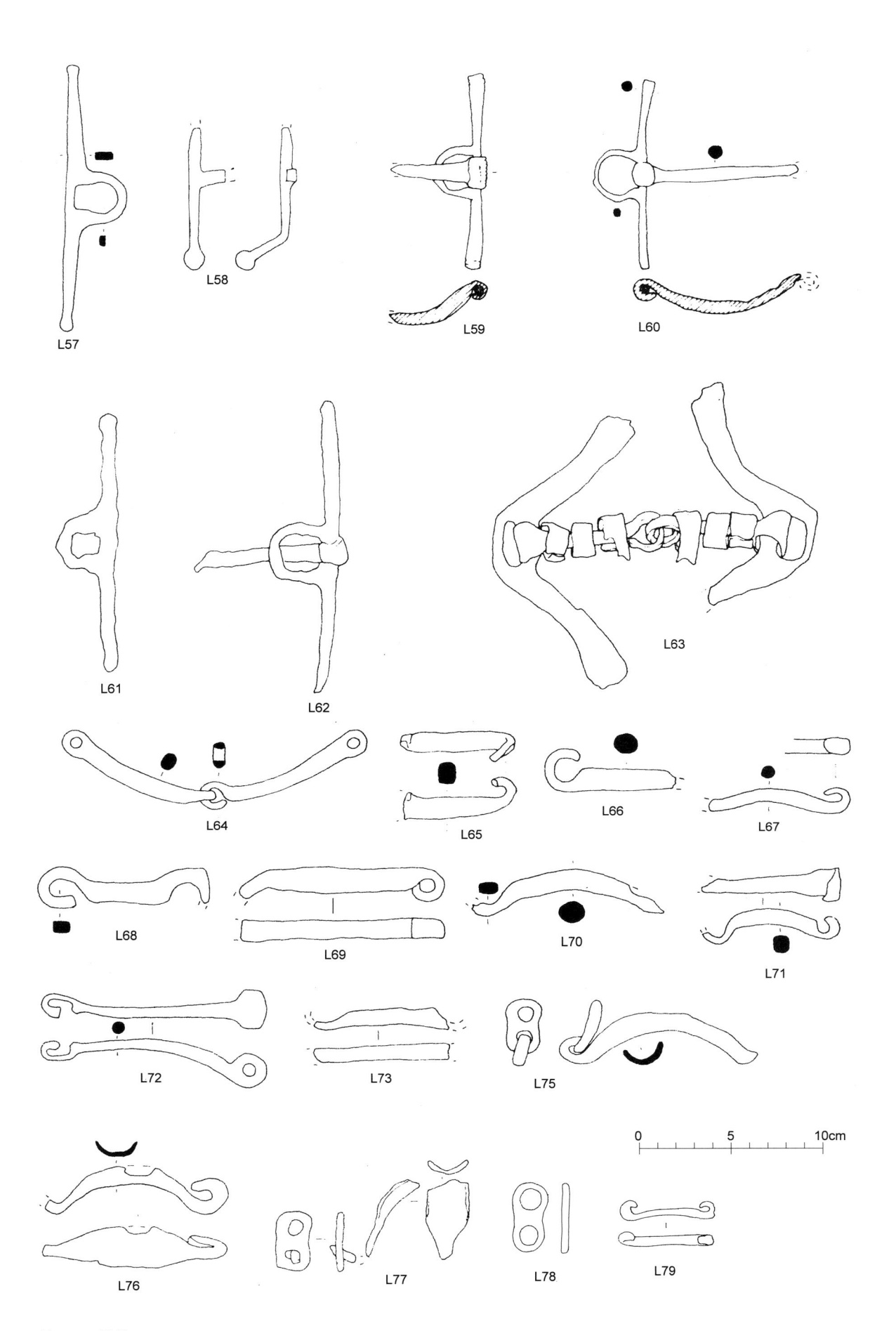

FIGURE 13.7
Bridle bits

L80 BRIDLE BOSS
King's Lynn, Norfolk.
c1250–1300.
Circular boss with flat flange and domed centre. Three holes through flange, filed decoration around edge. Non-ferrous plating. D 55–59mm.
Goodall and Carter 1977, 295, fig 143, 45, pl V.E.

L81 BRIDLE BOSS
Badby, Northamptonshire.
Mid to late 14th century.
Circular boss with flat, petalled flange and domed centre. Non-ferrous plating. D 61mm.
Excavated by Mrs M Gray.

L82 BRIDLE BOSS
Ospringe, Kent.
Demolition c1550–70 on site founded c1230.
Circular boss with flange with outer bead and domed, flat-topped centre. Two of original three rivets through flange survive. D 70mm.
Goodall 1979c, 132, fig 23.114.

L83 STRAP LINK
Winchester, Hampshire.
1050–75.
Moulded, flat-backed strap link. Non-ferrous plating. L 81mm.
Goodall 1990-23, fig 334.3882.

L84 STRAP LINK
Goltho Manor, Lincolnshire.
11th century.
Flat strap link, punched decoration on loops. Non-ferrous plating. L 101mm.
Goodall 1987, fig 160.160.

L85 STRAP LINK
Walton, Aylesbury, Buckinghamshire.
12th century.
Broken, moulded strap link with non-ferrous plating. L 84mm.
Farley 1976, 267, fig 49.5.

L86 STRAP LINK
Winchester, Hampshire.
Early 13th century.
Broken flat strap link. Non-ferrous plating. L 41mm.
Goodall 1990-23, fig 334.3884.

L87 STRAP LINK
Winchester, Hampshire.
14th century, probably residual.
Broken flat strap link. L 100mm.
Goodall 1990-23, fig 334.3885.

L88 STRAP LINK
Hambleton Moat, Lincolnshire.
1250–1400.
Broken strap link. L 74mm.
Butler 1963, 65, fig 14.6.

L89 STRAP LOOP
Castle Acre Castle, Norfolk.
After 1066, before c1085.
Plates broken. L 35mm.
Goodall 1982, fig 41, no. 122.

L90 STRAP LOOP
Castle Acre Castle, Norfolk.
1140s to second half 12th century.
Loop broken. L 44mm.
Goodall 1982, fig 41, no. 124.

L91 STRAP LOOP
Winchester, Hampshire.
Late 12th–early 13th century.
Complete. L 44mm.
Goodall 1990-23, fig 334.3895.

L92 STRAP LOOP
Dyserth Castle, Clwyd.
Site: 1241–63.
Complete. L 58mm.
Glenn 1915.

L93 STRAP LOOP
South Witham, Lincolnshire.
c1220 to 1308–13.
Plates broken and distorted. L 49mm.
Goodall 2002.

L94 STRAP LOOP
Wroughton Copse, Fyfield Down, Wiltshire.
(Mid?) 13th to early 14th century.
Plates broken. L 42mm.
Excavated by P J Fowler.

L95 STRAP LOOP
Winchester, Hampshire.
Second quarter 14th century.
One plate broken. Non-ferrous plating. L 44mm.
Goodall 1990-23, fig 334.3897.

L96 STRAP LOOP
Lyveden, Northamptonshire.
Site: c1400.
Complete. L 56mm.
Bryant and Steane 1971, 65, fig 17.0.

L97 STRAP LOOP
Winchester, Hampshire.
Early 12th century.
U-shaped strap loop, distorted. L 58mm
Goodall 1990-23, fig 334.3894.

L98 STRAP LOOP
Waltham Abbey, Essex.
12th century.
Incomplete strap loop with gilt surface decoration. L 25mm.
Excavated by P J Huggins.

L99 STRAP LOOP
Rayleigh Castle, Essex.
Site: c1070–c1350.
Complete. L 21mm.
Excavated by L Helliwell and D G Macleod.

L100 STRAP LOOP
Rayleigh Castle, Essex.
Site: c1070–c1350.
One plate broken. L 38mm.
Excavated by L Helliwell and D G Macleod.

L101 STRAP LOOP
Lyveden, Northamptonshire.
Second quarter 13th to very early 14th century.
Pair of broken strap loops. L 51mm.
Bryant and Steane 1971, 61, fig 15f.

L102 STRAP DISTRIBUTOR
Wharram Percy, North Yorkshire.
Early 15th century.
Two broken strap loops attached to square link. L 29mm.
Goodall 1979a, 121, fig 63.80.

L103 STRAP DISTRIBUTOR
Goltho Manor, Lincolnshire.
Around late 11th century.
Three strap loops attached to ring. L 52mm.
Goodall 1987, fig 160.165.

L104 RING AND STRAP LOOP
Castle Acre Castle, Norfolk.
1140s to second half 12th century.
Circular ring and broken strap loop. L 42mm.
Goodall 1982, fig 41, no. 123.

L105 LOOPED STRAP GUIDE
Wallingstones, Hereford and Worcester.
First half 13th century.
Complete. L 33mm.
Bridgewater 1970–72, 100, fig 16.9.

L106 LOOPED STRAP GUIDE
Lyveden, Northamptonshire.
c1350–1450.
Complete. L 28mm.
Steane and Bryant 1975, 129, fig 48.134.

L107 LOOPED STRAP GUIDE
Goltho, Lincolnshire.
Croft A: late Saxon to late 14th or early 15th century.
Complete. Non-ferrous plating. L 41mm.
Goodall 1975a, 89, fig 42.129.

L108 LOOPED STRAP GUIDE
Lyveden, Northamptonshire.
1475–1500.
Complete. L 36mm.
Steane and Bryant 1975, 129, fig 48.135.

L109 LOOPED STRAP GUIDE
Northampton.
c1250 to end 14th century.
Loop broken. L 52mm.
Goodall *et al* 1979, 273, fig 120.103.

L110 LOOPED STRAP GUIDE
Wintringham, Cambridgeshire.
Mid 13th century.
Complete. L 65mm.
Goodall 1977a, 258, fig 46.81.

L111 LOOPED STRAP GUIDE
Cambokeels, Durham.
Later 14th to early 16th century.
Complete. L 63mm.
Hildyard 1949, 195, fig 4.8.

HORSE EQUIPMENT

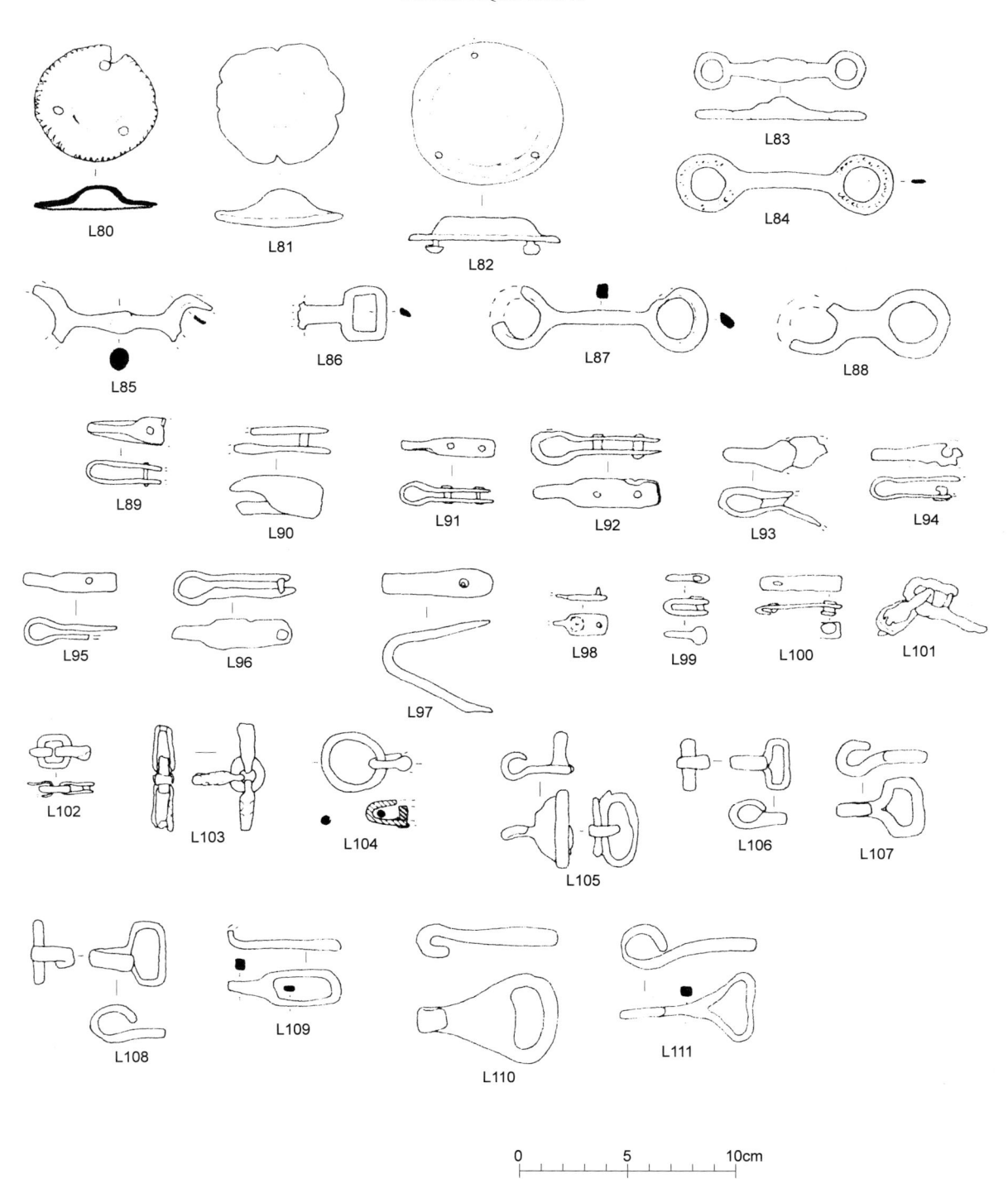

FIGURE 13.8
Bridle bosses and harness fittings

L112 SWIVEL FITTING
Dyserth Castle, Clwyd.
Site: 1241–63.
Incomplete link, oval flat link and swivel hook and rink. L 91mm.
Glenn 1915.

L113 SWIVEL FITTING
London.
14th century.
Oval link with swivel hook and ring and two looped fittings riveted to the ends of leather straps. Overall L 100mm.
Henig 1974, 191, fig 38.65.

L114 SWIVEL FITTING
Newbury, Berkshire.
c1320–50.
Strap loop with swivel hook and ring.
L 36mm.
Goodall 1997, fig 22, no. 57.

L115 SWIVEL FITTING
Ospringe, Kent.
c1483–1550.
Strap guide with cylinder and a pair of S-links and swivel hooks. L 90mm.
Goodall 1979c, 132, fig 23.115.

L116 SWIVEL FITTING
Winchester, Hampshire.
1220–75.
Shaped, perforated fitting with two swivel bosses. W 58mm.
Goodall 1990-23, fig 334.3900.

L117 HARNESS PENDANT
South Witham, Lincolnshire.
Late 13th century to 1308–13.
Hooked pendant with non-ferrous plating.
L 51mm.
Goodall 2002, fig 7.8, no. 86.

L118 HARNESS PENDANT
Lyveden, Northamptonshire.
c1200–1350.
Hooked pendant with non-ferrous plating.
L 37mm.
Steane and Bryant 1975, 127, fig 48.104.

L119 STIRRUP
Gloucester.
11th to early 12th century.
Semicircular-shaped stirrup with D-sectioned sides, flattened and expanded foot-rest, and broken loop for stirrup leather set at right angles to the body and separated from it by a boss. W 100mm.
Excavated by H Hurst.

L120 STIRRUP
Rabley Heath, Knebworth, Hertfordshire.
13th century.
Squat triangular-shaped stirrup with ex-panded and pierced foot-rest. Loop for stirrup leather lost. Traces of silver plating on side. W 120mm.
Andrews and Dunning 1939, 303–305, fig 2.

L121 STIRRUP
South Witham, Lincolnshire.
Late 13th century to 1308–13.
Broken roughly circular stirrup. W 83mm.
Goodall 2002, fig 7.8, no. 84.

L122 STIRRUP
West Hartburn, Durham.
13th to 16th century.
Squat rounded stirrup with flattened and expanded foot-rest and rectangular box for stirrup leather. W 128mm.
Still and Pallister 1964, 197, fig 6.20.

L123 STIRRUP
North Elmham Park, Norfolk.
c1150–c1600.
Trapezoidal stirrup with sides widening toward base. Broad, curved foot-rest, rectangular studded box for stirrup leather.
W 114mm.
Goodall 1980a, 516, fig 267.116.

L124 STIRRUP
Winchester, Hampshire.
Mid 16th–late 17th century.
Asymmetrical body with expanded foot-rest and rectangular box for stirrup leather with suspension bar. W 105mm.
Goodall 1990-22, fig 332.3879.

HORSE EQUIPMENT

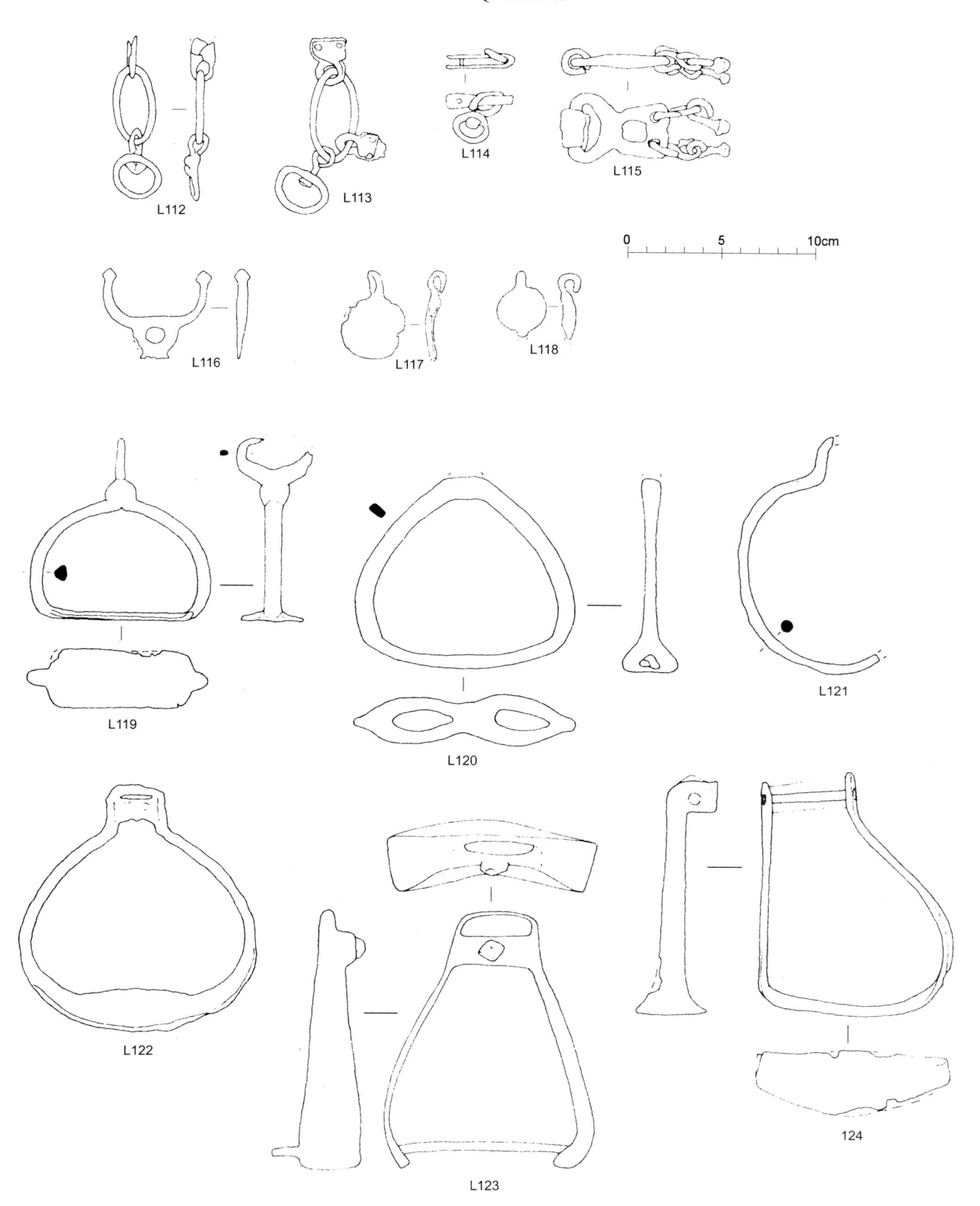

FIGURE 13.9
Bridle bosses, harness fittings and stirrups

BIBLIOGRAPHY

Addyman, P V, 1965 'Late Saxon settlements in the St Neots area: the Saxon settlement and Norman castle at Eaton Socon, Bedfordshire', *Proceedings of the Cambridge Antiquarian Society* 58, 38–73

Addyman, P V, 1973 'Late Saxon settlements in the St Neots area: the village or township at St Neots', *Proceedings of the Cambridge Antiquarian Society* 64, 45–99

Addyman, P V, and Biddle, M, 1965 'Medieval Cambridge: recent finds and excavations', *Proceedings of the Cambridge Antiquarian Society* 58, 122–124

Addyman, P V and Goodall, I H, 1979 'The Norman church and door at Stillingfleet, North Yorkshire', *Archaeologia* 106, 75–105

Addyman, P V and Priestley, J, 1977 'Baile Hill, York: a report on the Institute's excavations', *Archaeological Journal* 134, 115–156

Addyman, P V, Simpson, W G and Spring, P W H, 1963–66 'Two medieval sites rear Sedbergh, West Riding' *Yorkshire Archaeological Journal* 41, 27–42

Alcock, L, 1966 'Castle Tower, Penmaen: a Norman ring-work in Glamorgan', *Antiquaries Journal* 46, 178–210

Alcock, L, 1967 'Excavations at Deganwy Castle, Caernarvonshire, 1961–66', *Archaeological Journal* 124, 190–201

Almgren, B, 1955 *Bronsnycklar och djurornamentik vid overgangen fran Vendeltid till vikingatid*, Uppsala

Andersen, H H, Crabb, P J and Madsen, H J, 1971 *Århus Søndervold: En Byarkæologisk Undersøgelse*, Jysk Arkæologisk Selkabs Skrifter IX, Århus

Andrews, D D and Milne, G (eds), 1979 *Wharram. A study of settlement on the Yorkshire Wolds 1: domestic settlement, Areas 10 and 6*, The Society for Medieval Archaeology Monograph 8, London

Andrews, H C and Dunning, G C, 1939 'A thirteenth-century stirrup and storage-jar from Rabley Heath, Herts', *Antiquaries Journal* 19, 303–312

Anon, 1953 'Medieval spade found near the Eastgate', *Journal of the Chester and North Wales Architectural, Archaeological and Historic Society* 40, 65–66

Anstee, J W, 1970–72 'Weed hooks', in N P Bridgewater, 'The medieval homestead of Wallingstones', *Transactions of the Woolhope Naturalists' Field Club* 40, 114–115 (75–116)

Anstee, J W and Biek, L, 1961 'A study in pattern-welding', *Medieval Archaeology* 5, 71–93

Arbman, H, 1940 *Birka I. Die Graber*, Uppsala

Arkell, W J, 1947 *Oxford stone*, Faber & Faber, London

Aston, M, 1974 *Stonesfield slate*, Department of Museum Services, Oxford Council, Oxford

Attwater, W A, 1961 *Leathercraft*, Batsford, London

Baker, D, Baker, E, Hassall, J and Simco, A, 1979 'Excavations in Bedford 1967–1977', *Bedfordshire Archaeological Journal* 13, 1–309

Barker, A F, 1957 'Woollen manufacture', in *Encyclopaedia Britannica* 23, 733–734

Barker, D, 1976 'Small finds', in K Crouch, 'The archaeology of Staines and the excavation at Elmsleigh House', *Transactions of the London and Middlesex Archaeological Society* 27, 121–127 (71–134)

Barker, P A, 1964 'Excavation of the moated site at Shifnal, Shropshire, 1962', *Transactions of the Shropshire Archaeological Society* 57, 194–205

Barr-Hamilton, A, 1970 'Excavations at Lullington Church', *Sussex Archaeological Collections* 108, 1–22

Barton, K J, 1963 'A late 15th century well at Tarring', *Sussex Archaeological Collections* 101, 28–34

Barton, K J, 1964 'Worthing Museum Archaeology Report for 1962', *Sussex Archaeological Collections* 102, 31–32

Barton, K J, 1965 'A medieval site at Goring-by-Sea', *Sussex Archaeological Collections* 103, 88–103

Barton, K J and Holden, E W, 1977 'Excavations at Bramber Castle, Sussex, 1966–67', *Archaeological Journal* 134, 11–79

Beresford, G, 1971 'Tresmorn, St Gennys', *Cornish Archaeology* 10, 55–73

Beresford, G, 1975 *The medieval clay-land village: excavations at Goltho and Barton Blount*, The Society for Medieval Archaeology Monograph 6, London

Beresford, M W and Hurst, J G (eds), 1971 *Deserted medieval villages*, Lutterworth Press, London

Beresford, M W and St Joseph, J K S, 1979 *Medieval England: an aerial survey* (2nd edition)

Biddle, M, 1961–62 'The deserted medieval village of Seacourt, Berkshire', *Oxoniensia* 26–27, 70–201

Biddle, M, 1964 'The excavation of a motte and bailey castle at Therfield, Hertfordshire', *Journal of the British Archaeological Association* 3rd series 27, 53–91

Biddle, M (ed), 1990 *Winchester Studies. Artefacts from medieval Winchester. Part i. Object and economy in medieval Winchester*, Clarendon Press, Oxford

Biddle, M, Barfield, L and Millard, A, 1959 'The excavation of the Manor of the More, Rickmansworth, Hertfordshire', *Archaeological Journal* 116, 136–199

Biddle, M and Quirk, R N, 1962 'Excavations near Winchester Cathedral, 1961', *Archaeological Journal* 119, 150–194

Blomqvist, R, 1940 'Medeltida bultas och bultas-nyklar fran Lund', *Kulturen* (1940), 92–104

Blurton, T R, 1977 'Excavations at Angel Court, Walbrook, 1974', *Transactions of the London and Middlesex Archaeological Society* 28, 14–100

Borenius, T and Charlton, J, 1936 'Clarendon Palace: an interim report', *Antiquaries Journal* 16, 55–84

Brewster, T C M, 1952 *Two mediaeval habitation sites in the Vale of Pickering*, Studies in Yorkshire Archaeology 1, Scarborough

Brewster, T C M, 1972 'An excavation at Weaverthorpe Manor, East Riding, 1960', *Yorkshire Archaeological Journal* 44, 114–133

Brewster, T C M and Brewster, A, 1969 'Tote Copse Castle, Aldingbourne, Sussex', *Sussex Archaeological Collections* 107, 141–179

Bridgewater, N P, 1970–72 'The medieval homestead of Wallingstones', *Transactions of the Woolhope Naturalists' Field Club* 40, 75–116

Browne, R H, 1913 'Rayleigh Castle', *Transactions of the Essex Archaeological Society* new series 12, 353–354

Bryant, G C and Steane, J M, 1969 'Excavations at the deserted medieval settlement at Lyveden. A second interim report', *Journal of the Northamptonshire Museums and Art Gallery* 5, 3–50

Bryant, G F and Steane, J M, 1971 'Excavations at the deserted medieval settlement at Lyveden. A third interim report', *Journal of the Northamptonshire Museums and Art Gallery* 9, 1–94

Butler, L A S, 1963 'Hambleton Moat, Scredington, Lincolnshire', *Journal of the British Archaeological Association* 3rd series 26, 51–78

Butler, L A S, 1964 'An excavation in the Vicarage Garden, Conway, 1961', *Archaeologia Cambrensis* 113, 97–128

Butler, L A S, 1974 'Medieval finds from Castell-y-Bere, Merioneth', *Archaeologia Cambrensis* 123, 78–112

Carter, A, 1977 'Wooden objects', in H Clarke and A Carter, *Excavations in King's Lynn 1963–1970*, The Society for Medieval Archaeology Monograph 7, 366–374

Carter, A, Roberts, J P and Sutermeister, H, 1974–77 'Excavations in Norwich, 1973. The Norwich Survey, third interim report', *Norfolk Archaeology* 36, 39–71

Carus-Wilson, E, 1957 'The significance of the secular sculptures in the Lane Chapel, Cullimpton', *Medieval Archaeology* 1, 104–117

Carver, M O H, 1979 'Three Saxo-Norman tenements in Durham City', *Medieval Archaeology* 23, 1–80

Casey, D A, 1931 'Lydney Castle', *Antiquaries Journal* 11, 240–261

Chatwin, P B, 1955 'Brandon Castle, Warwickshire', *Transactions of the Birmingham and Warwickshire Archaeological Society* 73, 63–83

Cherry, J, 1973 'The medieval jewellery from the Fishpool, Nottinghamshire, Hoard', *Archaeologia* 104, 307–321

Christie, P M and Coad, J G 1980 'Excavations at Denny Abbey', *Archaeological Journal* 137, 138–279

Clapham, A W, 1934 *English Romanesque architecture after the Conquest*, Clarendon Press, Oxford

Cocks, A H, 1904–09 'Semi-underground hut, Walton Road, Aylesbury', *Records of Buckinghamshire* 9, 282–296

Coffey, G, 1909 *Royal Irish Academy Collection. Guide to the Celtic Antiquities of the Christian Period in the National Museum*, Dublin

Colvin, H M, 1953 'A medieval drawing of a plough', *Antiquity* 27, 165–167

Colvin, H M (ed), 1971 *Building accounts of King Henry III*, Clarendon Press, Oxford

Cool, H, Ellis, B, Pearce, J and Zeepvat, R, 2009 'Medieval and post-medieval artefacts', in G Beresford, *Caldecote: the development and desertion of a Hertfordshire Village*, The Society for Medieval Archaeology Monograph 28, 179–209

Coppack, G, 1971 'The deserted medieval village of Keighton', *Transactions of the Thoroton Society of Nottinghamshire* 75, 41–58

Coppack, G, 1974 'Low Caythorpe, East Yorkshire: the manor site', *Yorkshire Archaeological Journal* 46, 34–41

COSIRA 1955: Council for Small Industries in Rural Areas 1955, *The Blacksmith's Craft*, Rural Industries Bureau, London

Cowen, J D, 1971 'The Southwark knife reconsidered', *Antiquaries Journal* 51, 281–286

Cox, J C, 1887 'Duffield Castle: its history, site, and recently found remains; with some account of the seven earl ferrers who held it', *Journal of the Derbyshire Archaeological and Natural History Society* 9, 118–178

Craster, O E, 1970 *Skenfrith Castle, Monmouthshire*, HMSO, London

Crossley, D W, 1981 'Medieval iron smelting', in D W Crossley (ed), *Medieval Industry*, Council for British Archaeology Research Report 40, 29–41

Cunliffe, B, 1964 *Winchester Excavations 1949-60. Volume I*, Winchester

Curnow, P E and Thompson, M W, 1969 'Excavations at Richard's Castle, Herefordshire, 1962–1964', *Journal of the British Archaeological Association* 3rd series 32, 105–127

Dalton, O M, 1907 'On a set of table-knives in the British Museum made for John the Intrepid, Duke of Burgundy', *Archaeologia* 60, 423–430

Davison, B K, 1972 'Castle Neroche: an abandoned Norman fortress in South Somerset', *Proceedings of the Somerset Archaeological and Natural History Society* 116, 16–58

Dawson, G J, 1976 *The Black Prince's Palace at Kennington, Surrey*, British Archaeological Reports 26, Oxford

Dornier, A, 1967 'Kent's Moat, Sheldon, Birmingham', *Transactions and Proceedings, Birmingham Archaeological Society* 82, 45–57

Drewett, P L, 1975 'Excavations at Hadleigh Castle, Essex, 1971–72', *Journal of the British Archaeological Association* 3rd series 38, 90–154

Drury, P J, 1974 'Chelmsford Dominican Priory: The excavation of the reredorter 1973', *Essex Archaeology and History* 6, 40–81

Dulley, A J F, 1967 'Excavations at Pevensey, Sussex, 1962–6', *Medieval Archaeology* 11, 209–232

Dunning, G C, 1932 'Bronze Age settlements and a Saxon hut near Bourton-on-the-Water, Gloucestershire', *Antiquaries Journal* 12, 279–393

Dunning, G C, 1939 'A thirteenth-century midden at Windcliff, near Niton', *Proceedings of the Isle of Wight Natural History and Archaeological Society* 3.2, 128–137

Dunning, G C, 1958 'A Norman pit at Pevensey Castle and its contents', *Antiquaries Journal* 38, 205–217

Dunning, G C, 1959 'Report on medieval pottery from Joyden's Wood, near Bexley', in P J Tester and J E L Caiger, 'Medieval buildings in the Joyden's Wood Square Earthwork', *Archaeologia Cantiana* 72, 30–31 (18–40)

Dunning, G C, 1964 'Objects of metal, stone and bone, and ridge-tiles from St Helen's, Isles of Scilly', *Archaeological Journal* 121, 66–68

Dunning, G C, 1965 'Heraldic and decorated metalwork and other finds from Rievaulx Abbey, Yorkshire', *Antiquaries Journal* 45, 53–63

Dunning, G C, 1974 'Comparative material', in L A S Butler, 'Medieval finds from Castell-y-Bere, Merioneth', *Archaeologia Cambrensis* 123, 101–106 (78–112)

Dunning, G C, Hodges, H W M and Jope, E M, 1957–58. 'Kirkcudbright Castle, its pottery and ironwork', *Proceedings of the Society of Antiquaries of Scotland* 91, 117–138

Dunton, J, 1972 *Building hardware excavated at the Fortress of Louisbourg*, Manuscript Report No. 97, Parks Canada, dept. Indian Affairs and Northern Development, Louisbourg

Dyson, B R, 1936 *A glossary of words and dialect formerly used in the Sheffield trades*, Society for Preservation of Old Sheffield Tools, Sheffield

Eames, P, 1977 *Furniture in England, France and the Netherlands from the twelfth to the fifteenth century*, The Furniture History Society, London

Evison, V I, 1961 'The Saxon objects', in J G Hurst, 'The kitchen area of Northolt Manor, Middlesex', *Medieval Archaeology* 5, 226–230 (211–299)

Evison, V I, 1970 'The Anglo-Saxon cemetery', in B N Eagles and V I Evison, 'Excavations at Harrold, Bedfordshire, 1951–53', *Bedfordshire Archaeological Journal* 5, 38–46 (17–55)

Farley, M, 1976 'Saxon and medieval Walton, Aylesbury: excavations 1973–4', *Records of Buckinghamshire* 20, 153–290

Ford, S D, 1979 'Excavations in Newbury town centre 1971–74. Part II', *Transactions of the Newbury and District Field Club* 12(5), 19–40

Fowler, P J and Walthew, C V (eds), 1971 'Archaeology and the M5 Motorway. First Report', *Transactions of the Bristol and Gloucestershire Archaeological Society* 90, 22–63

Fox, A, 1936 'An account of John Storrie's excavations on Barry Island in 1894–5', *Transactions of the Cardiff Natural Society* 69, 12–38

Fox, A, 1937 'Medieval pottery from Barry Island, Glamorgan', *Antiquaries Journal* 17, 314–317

BIBLIOGRAPHY

Fox, C and Radford, C A R, 1933 'Kidwelly Castle, Carmarthenshire; including a survey of the polychrome pottery found there and elsewhere in Britain', *Archaeologia* 83, 93–138

Fox, R and Barton, K H, 1986 'Excavations at Oyster Street, Portsmouth, Hampshire, 1968–71', *Post-Medieval Archaeology* 20, 31–255

Francis, E B, 1913 'Rayleigh Castle: new facts in its history and recent explorations on its site', *Transactions of the Essex Archaeological Society* new series 12, 147–185

Freese, S, 1957 *Windmills and millwrighting*, Cambridge University Press, Cambridge

Gathercole, P W, 1958 'Excavations at Oakham Castle, Rutland, 1953–54', *Transactions of the Leicestershire Archaeological and Historical Society* 34, 17–38

Glenn, T A, 1915 'Prehistoric and historic remains at Dyserth Castle', *Archaeologia Cambrensis* 15, 47–86

Goodall, I H, 1971 'Iron objects', in C F Tebbutt, G T Rudd, and S Moorhouse, 'Excavation of a moated site at Ellington, Huntingdonshire', *Proceedings of the Cambridge Antiquarian Society* 63, 67–68 (31–73)

Goodall, I H, 1972 'Iron barrel padlock', in S Moorhouse, 'Finds from excavations in the refectory at the Dominican Friary, Boston', *Lincolnshire History and Archaeology* 1, 40–41 (21–53)

Goodall, I H, 1973a 'Iron objects', in P J Huggins and R M Huggins, 'Excavation of monastic forge and Saxo-Norman enclosure, Waltham Abbey, Essex, 1972–73', *Essex Archaeology and History* 5, 168–175 (127–184)

Goodall, I H, 1973b 'Metalwork', in H E J Le Patourel, *The moated sites of Yorkshire*, The Society for Medieval Archaeology Monograph 5, 91–95

Goodall, I H, 1974a 'Iron objects', in E Russell, *Excavations on the site of the deserted medieval village of Kettleby Thorpe, Lincolnshire*, Journal of the Scunthorpe Museum Society Series 3 (Archaeology) 2, 30–36

Goodall, I H, 1974b 'Iron objects', in E C Klingelhöfer, *Broadfield Deserted Medieval Village*, British Archaeological Report 2, Oxford, 56–58

Goodall, I H, 1974c 'Appendix VI: Metalwork', in G Beresford, 'The medieval manor of Penhallam, Jacobstow, Cornwall', *Medieval Archaeology* 18, 139–140 (90–145)

Goodall, I H, 1974d 'Barrel padlock', in S Moorhouse, 'A late medieval domestic rubbish deposit from Broughton, Lincolnshire', *Lincolnshire History and Archaeology* 9, 40–41 (21–53)

Goodall, I H, 1975a 'Iron objects', in G Beresford, *The medieval clay-land village: excavations at Goltho and Barton Blount*, The Society for Medieval Archaeology Monograph 6, 79–91

Goodall, I H, 1975b 'Metalwork from Barton Blount', in G Beresford, *The medieval clay-land village: excavations at Goltho and Barton Blount*, The Society for Medieval Archaeology Monograph 6, 96–98

Goodall, I H, 1975c 'Metalwork', in P L Drewett, 'Excavations at Hadleigh Castle, Essex, 1971–1972', *Journal of the British Archaeological Association* 3rd series 38, 138–146 (89–154)

Goodall, I H, 1975d 'Chingley Forge metalwork', in D Crossley, *The Bewl Valley ironworks, Kent, c1300–1730*, Royal Archaeological Institute Monograph, 59–84

Goodall, I H, 1976a 'Iron objects', in L Ketteringham, *Alsted: excavation of a thirteenth-fourteenth century sub-manor house with its ironworks in Netherne Wood, Merstham, Surrey*, Surrey Archaeological Society Research 2, Guildford, 55–60

Goodall, I H, 1976b 'Iron', in J Woodhouse, *Barrow Mead, Bath, 1964 excavation*, British Archaeological Report 28, Oxford, 33–35

Goodall, I H, 1976c 'Metalwork', in T G Hassall, 'Excavations at Oxford Castle, 1965–73', *Oxoniensia* 41, 298–303 (232–308)

Goodall, I H, 1977a 'Metalwork', in G Beresford, 'Excavation of a moated house at Wintringham in Huntingdonshire', *Archaeological Journal* 134, 257–258 (194–286)

Goodall, I H, 1977b 'Iron', in P Armstrong, *Excavations in Sewer Lane, Hull 1974*, East Riding Archaeologist 3, Hull Old Town Report Series 1, 63–67

Goodall, I H, 1977c 'Iron objects', in F Williams, *Pleshey Castle, Essex (XII–XIV century): excavations in the bailey, 1959–1963*, British Archaeological Reports 42, 174–183

Goodall, I H, 1977d 'Medieval iron objects', in R Hanworth D J Tomalin, *Brooklands, Weybridge: the excavation of an Iron Age and medieval site 1964–5 and 1970–71*, Surrey Archaeological Society Research Volume 4, Guildford, 73–75

Goodall, I H, 1977e 'Iron objects', in B Durham, 'Archaeological investigations in St Aldates, Oxford', *Oxoniensia* 42, 142–148 (82–203)

Goodall, I H, 1977f 'The metalwork', in P Charlton, J Roberts, and V Vale, *Llantrithyd. A ringwork in South Glamorgan*, Cardiff, 46–51

Goodall, I H, 1977g 'Iron objects', in P Everson, 'Excavations in the Vicarage Garden at Brixworth, 1972', *Journal of the British Archaeological Association* 130, 94 (55–122)

Goodall, I H, 1978a 'The iron objects' and 'Medieval iron objects', in J Collis, *Winchester Excavations. Volume II. 1949-1960. Excavations in the suburbs and the western part of the town*, Winchester, 28 and 139

Goodall, I H, 1978b 'Iron objects', in G Coppack, 'An excavation at Chapel Garth, Bolton, Fangfoss, Humberside', *Yorkshire Archaeological Journal* 50, 140–145 (93–150)

Goodall, I H, 1978c 'The iron-work', in J H Williams, 'Excavations at Greyfriars, Northampton 1972', *Northamptonshire Archaeology* 13, 152 (96–160)

Goodall, I H, 1978d 'Iron objects', in A E S Musty, 'Exploratory excavation within the monastic precinct, Waltham Abbey, 1972', *Essex Archaeology and History* 10, 157–160 (127–173)

Goodall, I H, 1979a 'Iron objects', in D D Andrews and G Milne, *Wharram. A study of settlement on the Yorkshire Wolds 1: domestic settlement, Areas 10 and 6*, The Society for Medieval Archaeology Monograph 8, 115–123

Goodall, I H, 1979b 'The iron objects', in F Williams, 'Excavations on Marefair, Northampton, 1977', *Northamptonshire Archaeology* 14, 70–71 (38–79)

Goodall, I H, 1979c 'Iron objects', in G H Smith, 'The excavation of the hospital of St Mary of Ospringe, commonly called Maison Dieu', *Archaeologia Cantiana* 95, 129–137 (81–184)

Goodall, I H, 1979d 'Iron objects', in P A Rahtz, *The Saxon and Medieval Palaces at Cheddar*, British Archaeological Reports British Series 65, 263–274

Goodall, I H, 1980a 'The iron objects', in P Wade-Martins, *Excavations in North Elmham Park, 1967–1972*, East Anglian Archaeology 9, 509–516

Goodall, I H, 1980b 'Iron objects', in A D Saunders, 'Lydford Castle, Devon', *Medieval Archaeology* 24, 165–167 (123–186)

Goodall, I H, 1980c 'Objects of iron', in P Wade-Martins (ed), *Fieldwork and excavations on village sites in Launditch Hundred, Norfolk*, East Anglian Archaeology Monograph 10, 129–141

Goodall, I H, 1980d 'Iron objects', in N Palmer, 'A Beaker burial and medieval tenements in The Hamel, Oxford', *Oxoniensia* 45, 189–191 (124–225)

Goodall, I H, 1982 'Iron objects', in J G Coad and A D F Streeten, 'Excavations at Castle Acre Castle, Norfolk, 1972–77, County House and Castle of the Norman Earls of Surrey', *Archaeological Journal* 139, 227–235 (138–301)

Goodall, I H, 1983a 'Iron objects', in A Streeten, *Bayham Abbey: Recent research, including a report on excavations (1973–76) directed by the late Helen Sutermeister*, Sussex Archaeological Society Monograph 2, 105–109

Goodall, I H, 1983b 'The small finds', in K Jarvis, *Excavations in Christchurch 1969 to 1980*, Dorset Natural History and Archaeological Society Monograph 5, 76–77

Goodall, I H, 1984 'Iron objects', in A Rogerson and C Dallas, *Excavations in Thetford 1948–59 and 1973–80*, East Anglian Archaeological Report 22, 77–105

Goodall, I H, 1987 'Objects of iron', in G Beresford, *Goltho: the development of an early medieval manor c850–1150*, English Heritage Archaeological Report 4, 177–187

Goodall, I H, 1988 'Iron objects', in T J James and A M Robinson, *Clarendon Palace*, Society of Antiquaries of London Research Report 45, 208–223

Goodall, I H, 1990-1 'The medieval iron objects from Winchester', in M Biddle (ed), *Winchester Studies. Artefacts from medieval Winchester. Part i. Object and economy in medieval Winchester*, Clarendon Press, Oxford, 36–41

Goodall, I H, 1990-2 'Tools', in M Biddle (ed), *Winchester Studies. Artefacts from medieval Winchester. Part i. Object and economy in medieval Winchester*, Clarendon Press, Oxford, 130

Goodall, I H, 1990-3 'Metal-working tools', in M Biddle (ed), *Winchester Studies. Artefacts from medieval Winchester. Part i. Object and economy in medieval Winchester*, Clarendon Press, Oxford, 198–199

Goodall, I H, 1990-4 'Heckle or woolcomb teeth', in M Biddle (ed), *Winchester Studies. Artefacts from medieval Winchester. Part i. Object and economy in medieval Winchester*, Clarendon Press, Oxford, 214–216

Goodall, I H, 1990-5 'Weaving comb', in M Biddle (ed), *Winchester Studies. Artefacts from medieval Winchester. Part i. Object and economy in medieval Winchester*, Clarendon Press, Oxford, 234

Goodall, I H, 1990-6 'Tenter-hooks', in M Biddle (ed), *Winchester Studies. Artefacts from medieval Winchester. Part i. Object and economy in medieval Winchester*, Clarendon Press, Oxford, 234–239

Goodall, I H, 1990-7 'Tanning, currying and leather-working tools', in M Biddle (ed), *Winchester Studies. Artefacts from medieval Winchester. Part i. Object and economy in medieval Winchester*, Clarendon Press, Oxford, 247–250

Goodall, I H, 1990-8 'Wood-working tools', in M Biddle (ed), *Winchester Studies. Artefacts from medieval Winchester. Part i. Object and economy in medieval Winchester*, Clarendon Press, Oxford, 273–277

Goodall, I H, 1990-9 'Stone-working tools', in M Biddle (ed), *Winchester Studies. Artefacts from medieval Winchester. Part i. Object and economy in medieval Winchester*, Clarendon Press, Oxford, 299–302

Goodall, I H, 1990-10 'Building ironwork', in M Biddle (ed), *Winchester Studies. Artefacts from medieval Winchester. Part i. Object and economy in medieval Winchester*, Clarendon Press, Oxford, 328–349

Goodall, I H, 1990-11 'Horticultural tools', in M Biddle (ed), *Winchester Studies. Artefacts from medieval Winchester. Part i. Object and economy in medieval Winchester*, Clarendon Press, Oxford, 450–452

Goodall, I H, 1990-12 'Iron buckles and belt-fittings', in M Biddle (ed), *Winchester Studies. Artefacts from medieval Winchester. Part ii. Object and economy in medieval Winchester*, Clarendon Press, Oxford, 526–538

Goodall, I H, 1990-13 'Iron binding strips and mounts', in M Biddle (ed), *Winchester Studies. Artefacts from medieval Winchester. Part ii. Object and economy in medieval Winchester*, Clarendon Press, Oxford, 787–788

Goodall, I H, 1990-14 'Iron domestic implements', in M Biddle (ed), *Winchester Studies. Artefacts from medieval Winchester. Part ii. Object and economy in medieval Winchester*, Clarendon Press, Oxford, 818–821

Goodall, I H, 1990-15 'Chains, links, chain fittings, rings, and washers', in M Biddle (ed), *Winchester Studies. Artefacts from medieval Winchester. Part ii. Object and economy in medieval Winchester*, Clarendon Press, Oxford, 821–827

Goodall, I H, 1990-16 'Knives', in M Biddle (ed), *Winchester Studies. Artefacts from medieval Winchester. Part ii. Object and economy in medieval Winchester*, Clarendon Press, Oxford, 835–860

Goodall, I H, 1990-17 'Shears and scissors', in M Biddle (ed), *Winchester Studies. Artefacts from medieval Winchester. Part ii. Object and economy in medieval Winchester*, Clarendon Press, Oxford, 861–863

Goodall, I H, 1990-18 'Iron fittings from vessels', in M Biddle (ed), *Winchester Studies. Artefacts from medieval Winchester. Part ii. Object and economy in medieval Winchester*, Clarendon Press, Oxford, 967–968

Goodall, I H, 1990-19 'Iron fittings from furniture', in M Biddle (ed), *Winchester Studies. Artefacts from medieval Winchester. Part ii. Object and economy in medieval Winchester*, Clarendon Press, Oxford, 971–979

Goodall, I H, 1990-20 'Iron fittings for lights', in M Biddle (ed), *Winchester Studies. Artefacts from medieval Winchester. Part ii. Object and economy in medieval Winchester*, Clarendon Press, Oxford, 981–983

Goodall, I H, 1990-21 'Locks and keys', in M Biddle (ed), *Winchester Studies. Artefacts from medieval Winchester. Part ii. Object and economy in medieval Winchester*, Clarendon Press, Oxford, 984–1036

Goodall, I H, 1990-22 'Stirrups', in M Biddle (ed), *Winchester Studies. Artefacts from medieval Winchester. Part ii. Object and economy in medieval Winchester*, Clarendon Press, Oxford, 1042

Goodall, I H, 1990-23 'Bridle bits and associated strap-fittings', in M Biddle (ed), *Winchester Studies. Artefacts from medieval Winchester. Part ii. Object and economy in medieval Winchester*, Clarendon Press, Oxford, 1043–1046

Goodall, I H, 1990-24 'Curry-combs', in M Biddle (ed), *Winchester Studies. Artefacts from medieval Winchester. Part ii. Object and economy in medieval Winchester*, Clarendon Press, Oxford, 1053–1054

Goodall, I H, 1990-25 'Horseshoes', in M Biddle (ed), *Winchester Studies. Artefacts from medieval Winchester. Part ii. Object and economy in medieval Winchester*, Clarendon Press, Oxford, 1054–1067

Goodall, I H, 1990-26 'Arrowheads', in M Biddle (ed), *Winchester Studies. Artefacts from medieval Winchester. Part ii. Object and economy in medieval Winchester*, Clarendon Press, Oxford, 1070–1074

Goodall, I H, 1990-27 'Iron sheet-binding', in M Biddle (ed), *Object and economy in medieval Winchester*, Clarendon Press, Oxford, 1102

Goodall, I H, 1990-28 'Iron objects', in J R Fairbrother, *Faccombe Netherton. Excavations of a Saxon and medieval manorial complex*, British Museum Occasional Paper 74, 403–425

Goodall, I H, 1993a 'Iron hearth equipment', in S Margeson, *Norwich households: the medieval and post-medieval finds from Norwich survey excavations 1971–1978*, East Anglian Archaeology 58, 86–89

Goodall, I H, 1993b 'Implements', in S Margeson, *Norwich households: the medieval and post-medieval finds from Norwich survey excavations 1971–1978*, East Anglian Archaeology 58, 118–136

Goodall, I H, 1993c 'Iron door, window and furniture fittings', in S Margeson, *Norwich households: the medieval and post-medieval finds from Norwich survey excavations 1971–1978*, East Anglian Archaeology 58, 148–155

Goodall, I H, 1993d 'Lock furniture, hasps and keys', in S Margeson, *Norwich households: the medieval and post-medieval finds from Norwich survey excavations 1971–1978*, East Anglian Archaeology 58, 155–163

Goodall, I H, 1993e 'Iron woodworking tools', in S Margeson, *Norwich households: the medieval and post-medieval finds from Norwich survey excavations 1971–1978*, East Anglian Archaeology 58, 177–181

Goodall, I H, 1993f 'Textile manufacture and needlework', in S Margeson, *Norwich households: the medieval and post-medieval finds from Norwich survey excavations 1971–1978*, East Anglian Archaeology 58, 182–189

Goodall, I H, 1993g 'Iron horticultural and agricultural tools', in S Margeson, *Norwich households: the medieval and post-medieval finds from Norwich survey excavations 1971–1978*, East Anglian Archaeology 58, 193–195

Goodall, I H, 1994 'Iron work and metallurgy', in H Quinnell and M R Blockley with P Berridge, *Excavations at Rhuddlan, Clwyd 1969–73, Mesolithic to Medieval*, Council for British Archaeology Research Report 95, 178–190

Goodall, I H, 1997 'Iron objects', in A G Vince, S J Lobb, J C Richards and L Mepham, *Excavations in Newbury, Berkshire, 1979–1990*, Wessex Archaeology Report 13, 36–42

Goodall, I H, 2002 'The metalwork', in P Mayes, *Excavations at a Templar preceptory. South Witham, Lincolnshire 1965–67*, The Society for Medieval Archaeology Monograph 19, 96–110

Goodall, I H, and Carter, A, 1977 'Iron objects', in H Clarke and A Carter, *Excavations in King's Lynn 1963–1970*, The Society for Medieval Archaeology Monograph 7, 291–298

Goodall, I H, Ellis, B and Oakley, G E, 1979 'The iron objects', in J H Williams, *St Peter's Street, Northampton, Excavations 1973–6*, Northampton, 268–277

BIBLIOGRAPHY

Goodall, I H and Keene, D, 1990 'Harbicks (shear-board hooks)', in M Biddle (ed), *Winchester Studies. Artefacts from medieval Winchester. Part i. Object and economy in medieval Winchester*, Clarendon Press, Oxford, 239–240

Goodall, I H, Rigold, S E and Christie, P M, 1980 'Metalwork and bone objects', in P M Christie and J G Coad, 'Excavations at Denny Abbey', *Archaeological Journal* 138, 253–263 (138–279)

Goodman, W L, 1964 *The history of woodworking tools*, G Bell, London

Gray, H St G, 1903 'Excavations at Castle Neroche, Somerset, June–July 1903', *Proceedings of the Somerset Archaeological and Natural History Society* 49, 23–53

Gray, H St G, 1930 'A medieval spoon found at Taunton Castle', *Antiquaries Journal* 10, 156

Gray, H St G, 1941 'Gorbel, etc found at Taunton Castle', *Antiquaries Journal* 21, 67–68

Green, C, 1962–63 'Excavations on a medieval site at Water Newton, in the count of Huntingdon, in 1958', *Proceedings of the Cambridge Antiquaries Society* 56–57, 68–87

Groves, S, 1966 *The history of needlework tools and accessories*, Country Life, London

Hall, D N, 1973 'A thirteenth century windmill site at Strixton, Northamptonshire', *Bedfordshire Archaeological Journal* 8, 109–118

Hammerson, M J, 1975 'Excavations on the site of Arundel House in the Strand, W.C.2, in 1972', *Transactions of the London and Middlesex Archaeological Society* 26, 209–251

Harbottle, B, 1967 'An excavation at Warkworth Castle, Northumberland, 1966', *Archaeologia Aeliana* 4th series 45, 105–121

Harbottle, B, 1968 'Excavations at the Carmelite Friary, Newcastle upon Tyne, 1965 and 1967', *Archaeologia Aeliana* 4th series 46, 163–223

Harbottle, B and Salway, P, 1964 'Excavations at Newminster Abbey, Northumberland, 1961–1963', *Archaeologia Aeliana* 4th series 42, 85–171

Harden, D B, 1954 'A glass bowl of Dark Age date and some medieval grave-finds from Shaftersbury Abbey', *Antiquaries Journal* 34, 188–194

Harrison, A C, 1970 'Excavations in Rochester', *Archaeologia Cantiana* 85, 95–112

Harrison, A C and Flight, C, 1968 'The Roman and medieval defences of Rochester in the light of recent excavations', *Archaeologia Cantiana* 83, 55–104

Hartley, D and Elliot, M M, 1928 *Life and work of the people of England. The fourteenth century*, Batsford, London

Hartley, D and Elliot, M M, 1931 *Life and work of the people of England. 11th to 13th centuries*, Batsford, London

Harvey, J, 1975a *Medieval craftsmen*, London

Harvey, Y, 1975b 'The small finds catalogue', in C Platt and R Coleman-Smith, *Excavations in medieval Southampton 1953–1969. Volume 2: The finds*, Leicester University Press, 254–293

Hassall, M and Rhodes, J, 1974 'Excavations at the new Market Hall, Gloucester, 1966–7', *Transactions of the Bristol and Gloucestershire Archaeological Society* 93, 15–100

Hassall, W O, 1954 *The Holkham Bible picture book*, Dropmore Press, London (2nd ed)

Hassall, W O, 1970 'Notes on medieval spades', in A Gailey and A Fenton (eds), *The spade in Northern and Atlantic Europe*, Belfast, 30–34

Hawkes, C F C, Myres, J N L and Stevens, C G, 1930 'St Catharine's Hill, Winchester', *Proceedings of the Hampshire Field Club and Archaeological Society* 11, 1–286

Hayward, J F, 1957 *English cutlery*, Her Majesty's Stationery Office, London

Hellier, R and Moorhouse, S, 1978 *Medieval agriculture*, Medieval Section, Yorkshire Archaeological Society, Leeds

Helliwell, L and Macleod, D G, 1965 *Rayleigh Mount*, Rayleigh

Henig, M, 1974 'Small finds', in T Tatton-Brown, 'Excavations at the Custom House Site, City of London, 1973', *Transactions of the London and Middlesex Archaeological Society* 25, 186–201 (117–219)

Higgs, J W Y, 1965 *English rural life in the Middle Ages*, Bodleian Picture Book no. 14, Oxford

Hildyard, E J W, 1949 'Further excavations at Cambokeels in Weardale', *Archaeologia Aeliana* 4th series 27, 177–205

Hildyard, E J W and Charlton, J, 1947 'A medieval site in Weardale', *Archaeologia Aeliana* 4th series 25, 181–196

Hill, N G, 1935–37 'Excavations on Stockbridge Down, 1935–36', *Proceedings of the Hampshire Field Club and Archaeological Society* 13, 246–259

Hilton, R H and Rahtz, P A, 1966 'Upton, Gloucestershire, 1959–1964', *Transactions of the Bristol and Gloucestershire Archaeological Society* 85, 70–146

Hinton, D A, 1968 'Bicester Priory', *Oxoniensia* 33, 22–52

Hinton, D A, 1977 'Objects of iron', in B Cunliffe, *Excavations at Portchester Castle. Volume III: Medieval, the Outer Bailey and its Defences*, Society of Antiquaries Research Report 34, 196–204

Hobley, B, 1971 'Excavations at the cathedral and Benedictine priory of St Mary, Coventry', *Transactions of the Birmingham and Warwickshire Archaeological Society* 84, 46–139

Holden, E Q, 1963 'Excavations at the deserted medieval village of Hangleton, Part I', *Sussex Archaeological Collections* 101, 54–181

Holmes, M, 1966 'An unrecorded map of London', *Archaeologia* 100, 105–128

Huggins, P J, 1972 'Monastic grange and outer close excavations, Waltham Abbey, Essex, 1970–1972', *Essex Archaeology and History* 4, 30–127

Huggins, P J and Huggins, R M, 1973 'Excavation of Monastic Forge and Saxo-Norman Enclosure, Waltham Abbey, Essex, 1972–73', *Essex Archaeology and History* 5, 127–184

Hurst, J G, 1961 'The kitchen area of Northolt Manor, Middlesex', *Medieval Archaeology* 5, 211–299

Hurst, J G, 1965 'Excavations at Barn Road, Norwich, 1954–55', *Norfolk Archaeology* 33, 131–179

Hurst, J G and Golson, J, 1953–57 'Excavations at St Benedict's Gates, Norwich, 1951 and 1953', *Norfolk Archaeology* 31, 1–112

Hurst, J G and Hurst, D G, 1964 'Excavations at the deserted medieval village of Hangleton, Part II', *Sussex Archaeological Collections* 102, 94–142

Hurst, D G and Hurst, J G, 1969 'Excavations at the medieval village of Wythemail, Northamptonshire', *Medieval Archaeology* 13, 167–203

Innocent, C F, 1916 *The development of English building construction*, Cambridge University Press, Cambridge

Jarrett, M G, and Stevens D G, 1962 'Metal', in M G Jarrett, 'The deserted village of West Whelpington, Northumberland', *Archaeologia Aeliana* 4th series 40, 219–222 (189–226)

Jarrett, M G, 1962 'The deserted village of West Whelpington, Northumberland', *Archaeologia Aeliana* 4th series 40, 189–225

Jarrett, M G, 1970 'The deserted village of West Whelpington, Northumberland: second report', *Archaeologia Aeliana* 4th series 48, 183–302

Jenkins, J G, 1965 *Traditional country craftsmen*, Routledge, London

Jenning, C, 1974 *Early chests in wood and iron*, Her Majesty's Stationery Office, London

Jervoise, E, 1954 'Norman motte at West Woodhay, Second Report', *Transactions of the Newbury and District Field Club* 10.2, 65–68

Jones, J, 1975 'Medieval leather', in T Tatton-Brown, 'Excavations at the Custom House Site, City of London, 1973: Part 2', *Transactions of the London and Middlesex Archaeological Society* 26, 154–167 (103–170)

Jones, T L, 1953 'Excavations at The Mount, Cheswick Green, Shirley, Birmingham', *Transactions and Proceedings, Birmingham Archaeological Society* 71, 80–95

Jope, E M, 1958 'The Clarendon Hotel, Oxford. Part I. The Site', *Oxoniensia* 23, 1–83

Jope, E M and Jope, H M, 1959 'A hoard of fifteenth-century coins from Glenluce sand-dunes and their context', *Medieval Archaeology* 3, 259–279

Jope, E M and Threlfall, R I, 1958 'Excavation of a medieval settlement at Beere, North Tawton, Devon', *Medieval Archaeology* 2, 112–140

Jope, E M and Threlfall, R I, 1959 'The twelfth-century castle at Ascot Doilly, Oxfordshire: its history and excavation', *Antiquaries Journal* 39, 219–273

Keiller, A, 1965 *Windmill Hill and Avebury*, Clarendon Press, Oxford

Ketteringham, L, 1976 *Alsted: excavation of a thirteenth-fourteenth century sub-manor house with its ironworks in Netherne Wood, Merstham, Surrey*, Surrey Archaeological Society Research Volume 2, Guildford

King, D J C, 1963 *Llanstephan Castle*, Ancient Monuments Inspectorate Guide, London

King, H W, 1869 'Notes on recent excavations at Hadleigh Castle', *Transactions of the Essex Archaeological Society* 4, 70–81

Knight, J K, 1994 'Excavations at Montgomery Castle. Part II: the finds', *Archaeologia Cambrensis* 142, 182–242

Knocker, G M, 1961–63 'A medieval curry-comb from Rickinghall Superior', *Proceedings of the Suffolk Institute of Archaeology and History* 29, 222–223

Knocker, G M, 1966–69 'Excavations at Red Castle, Thetford', *Norfolk Archaeology* 34, 119–186

La Cour, V, 1961 *Naesholm*, Copenhagen

Laing, L R, 1974–75 'Appendix C. Some medieval ironwork from Castle Urquhart, Inverness', in A D S Macdonald and L R Laing, 'Excavations at Lochmaben Castle, Dumfriesshire', *Proceedings of the Society of Antiquaries of Scotland* 106, 154–156 (124–157)

Le Patourel, H E J, 1963–66. 'Knaresborough Castle', *Yorkshire Archaeological Journal* 41, 591–607

Le Patourel, H E J, 1973 *The moated sites of Yorkshire*, The Society for Medieval Archaeology Monograph 5, London

Leach, G B, 1960 'Excavations at Hen Blas, Coleshill Fawr, near Flint, Second Report', *Journal of the Flintshire Historical Society* 18, 13–48

Leeds, E T, 1936 'An adulterine castle on Faringdon Clump, Berkshire', *Antiquaries Journal* 16, 165–178

Leeds, E T, 1937 'An adulterine castle on Faringdon Clump, Berkshire (second report)', *Antiquaries Journal* 17, 294–298

Lewis, E, 1985 'Excavations in Bishops Waltham 1967–78', *Proceedings of the Hampshire Field Club and Archaeological Society* 41, 82–126

Liddell, D M, 1932–34 'Excavations at Meon Hill', *Proceedings of Hampshire Field Club and Archaeological Society* 12, 126–162

Lindsay, J S, 1964 *Iron and brass implements of the English House*, Alec Tiranti, London

Lowther, A W G, 1948 'The Mounts, Pachesham. Second interim report on the excavations', *Proceedings of the Leatherhead and District Local History Society* 1.2, 5–8

Luff, R, 1990 'Iron bell', in M Biddle (ed), *Winchester Studies. Artefacts from medieval Winchester. Part ii. Object and economy in medieval Winchester*, Clarendon Press, Oxford, 728–729

Macdonald, A D S and Laing, L R, 1974–75 'Excavations at Lochmaben Castle, Dumfriesshire', *Proceedings of the Society of Antiquaries of Scotland* 106, 124–157

Manby, T G, 1959 'Duffield Castle excavations 1957', *Journal of the Derbyshire Archaeological and Natural History Society* 79, 1–21

Mann, J G, 1933 'The Coleshill helm', *Antiquaries Journal* 13, 152–154

Manning, W H, 1976 *Catalogue of Romano-British Ironwork in the Museum of Antiquities, Newcastle upon Tyne*, Newcastle

Marsden, P, Dyson, T and Rhodes, M, 1975 'Excavations on the site of St Mildred's Church, Bread Street, London, 1973–74', *Transactions of the London and Middlesex Archaeological Society* 26, 171–208

Mayes, P, 1965 'A medieval tile kiln at Boston, Lincs', *Journal of the British Archaeological Association* 3rd series 28, 86–106

McGrail, S, 1977 'Axe, adze, hoe, or slice?', *International Journal of Nautical Archaeology* 6, 62–64

Mercer, E, 1969 *Furniture 700-1700*, Weidenfeld and Nicolson, London

Mercer, H C, 1968 *Ancient carpenters' tools*, Buckinghamshire County Historical Society, Doylestown (4th ed)

Millar, E G, 1932 *The Luttrell Psalter*, British Museum, London

Mold, Q, 1979 'The iron nails', in G H Smith, 'The excavation of the Hospital of St Mary of Ospringe, commonly called Maison Dieu', *Archaeologia Cantiana* 95, 148–152 (81–184)

Moorhouse, S, 1971a 'Excavations at Burton-in-Lonsdale: a reconsideration', *Yorkshire Archaeological Journal* 43, 85–98

Moorhouse, S, 1971b 'Excavation of a moated site near Sawtry, Huntingdonshire', *Proceedings of the Cambridge Antiquarian Society* 63, 75–86

Moorhouse, S and Goodall, I H, 1971 'Iron', in S Moorhouse, 'Finds from Basing House, Hampshire (c1540–1645): Part two', *Post-Medieval Archaeology* 5, 36–57

Musty, J and Algar, D J, 1986 'Excavations at the deserted medieval village of Gomeldon, near Salisbury', *Wiltshire Archaeological and Natural History Magazine* 80, 127–169

Musty, J and Rahtz, P A, 1964 'The suburbs of Old Sarum', *Wiltshire Natural History and Archaeological Magazine* 59, 130–154

Musty, J and Algar, D J, 1986 'Excavations at the deserted medieval village of Gomeldon near Salisbury, Wilts', *Wiltshire Archaeological Magazine* 80, 127–169

Musty, J, Algar, D J and Ewence, P F, 1969 'The medieval pottery kilns at Laverstock, near Salisbury, Wiltshire', *Archaeologia* 102, 83-150

Myers, A R, 1958 *The household of Edward IV. The Black Book and the Ordinance of 1478*, Manchester University Press, Manchester

Mynard, D C, 1969 'Excavations at Somerby, Lincolnshire, 1957', *Lincolnshire History and Archaeology* 4, 63–91

Nash-Williams, V E, 1952 'The medieval settlement at Llantwit Major, Glamorgan', *Bulletin of the Board of Celtic Studies* 14, 313–333

Neal, D S, 1973 'Excavations at the Palace and Priory at Kings Langley, 1970', *Hertfordshire Archaeology* 3, 31–72

Nöel Hume, I, 1970 *A guide to artifacts of Colonial America*, New York

O'Neil, B H St J, 1944–45 'Criccieth Castle, Caernarvonshire', *Archaeologia Cambrensis* 98, 1–51

O'Neil, H, 1956 'Prestbury Moat, a manor house of the Bishops of Hereford in Gloucestershire', *Transactions of the Bristol and Gloucestershire Archaeological Society* 75, 5–34

Oswald, A, 1954 'Excavation at Alvechurch, Worcestershire, 1951–2', *Transactions and Proceedings, Birmingham Archaeological Society* 72, 5–9

Oswald, A, 1958 'Hawkesley Farm, Longbridge, Birmingham', *Transactions and Proceedings, Birmingham Archaeological Society* 76, 36–50

Oswald, A, 1962 'Interim report on excavations at Weoley Castle, 1955–60', *Transactions and Proceedings, Birmingham Archaeological Society* 78, 61–85

Oswald, A and Taylor, G S, 1964 'Durrance Moat, Upton Warren, Worcestershsire', *Transactions and Proceedings, Birmingham Archaeological Society* 79, 61–75

Parrington, M, 1976 'Excavations at the Old Gaol, Abingdon', *Oxoniensia* 40, 59–78

Patterson, R, 1957 'Spinning and weaving', in C Singer (ed), *A History of Technology, Volume II. The Mediterranean Civilizations and the Middle Ages, c700 BC to cAD 1500*, Clarendon Press, Oxford, 191–220

Pavry, F H and Knocker, G M, 1953–60 'The Mount, Princes Risborough, Buckinghamshire', *Records of Buckinghamshire* 16, 131–178

Penny, W E W, 1911 'The medieval keys in Salisbury Museum', *Connoisseur* 29 (January–April 1911), 11–16

Pinder-Wilson, R H and Brooke, C N L, 1973 'The reliquary of St Petroc and the ivories of Norman Sicily', *Archaeologia* 104, 261–305

Pitt-Rivers, A H L F, 1883 'Excavations at Caesar's Camp near Folkestone, conducted in June and July 1878', *Archaeologia* 47, 429–465

Platt, C and Coleman-Smith, R, 1975 *Excavations in medieval Southampton*, 2 volumes, Leicester

Purcell, D, 1967 *Cambridge stone*, Faber, London

Raby, F J E and Reynolds, P K B, 1952 *Castle Acre Priory*, Her Majesty's Stationery Office, London (2nd edition)

Radford, C A R, 1962 *White Castle, Monmouthshire*, Her Majesty's Stationery Office, London

Rahtz, P, 1959 *Excavations at the Medieval Village of Holworth, 1958*, Dorset Natural History and Archaeological Society 80, 103–105

Rahtz, P, 1960–61 'Barrow Mead, Bath, Somerset', *Proceedings of the Somersetshire Archaeological and Natural History Society* 105, 61–76

Rahtz, P, 1969a 'Upton, Gloucestershire, 1964–1968. Second Report', *Transactions of the Bristol and Gloucestershire Archaeological Society* 88, 74–126

BIBLIOGRAPHY

Rahtz, P A, 1969b *Excavations at King John's Hunting Lodge, Writtle, Essex, 1955–57*, The Society for Medieval Archaeology Monograph 3, London

Rahtz, P A, 1970 'Excavations on Glastonbury Tor, Somerset, 1964–6', *Archaeological Journal* 127, 1–81

Rahtz, P A and Greenfield, E, 1977 *Excavations at Chew Valley Lake, Somerset*, Department of the Environment Archaeological Report 8, Her Majesty's Stationery Office, London

Rahtz, P and Hirst, S, 1974 *Beckery Chapel, Glastonbury, 1967–8*, Glastonbury

Reader, F W, 1913 'On the miscellaneous objects found', in E B Francis, 'Rayleigh Castle: new facts in its history and recent explorations on its site', *Transactions of the Essex Archaeological Society* new series 12, 162–171 (147–185)

Renn, D F, 1973 *Norman castles in Britain*, J Baker, London (2nd edition)

Richardson, K M, 1959 'Excavations in Hungate, York', *Archaeological Journal* 116, 51–114

Rifkin, B A, 1973 *The Book of Trades. Jost Amman and Hans Sachs*, New York

Rigold, S E, 1954 'Totnes Castle. Recent excavations by the Ancient Monuments Department, Ministry of Works', *Transactions of the Devonshire Association* 86, 228–256

Rigold, S E, 1962 'Excavation of a moated site at Pivington's, *Archaeologia Cantiana* 77, 27–47

Rigold, S E, 1962–63 'The Anglian Cathedral of North Elmham, Norfolk', *Medieval Archaeology* 6–7, 67–108

Rigold, S E, 1965 'Two camerae of the military orders: Strood Temple, Kent, and Harefiled, Middlesex', *Archaeological Journal* 122, 86–132

Rigold, S E, 1967 'Excavations at Dover Castle 1964–1966', *Journal of the British Archaeological Association* 3rd series 30, 87–121

Rigold, S E, 1971 'Eynsford Castle and its excavation', *Archaeologia Cantiana* 86, 109–171

Rigold, S E and Fleming, A J, 1973 'Eynsford Castle: the moat and bridge', *Archaeologia Cantiana* 88, 87–116

Rimington, F C and Rutter, J G, 1967 *Ayton Castle. Its history and excavation*, Scarborough District Archaeological Society Research Report 5, Scarborough

Robinson, M, 1973 'Excavations at Copt Hay, Tetsworth, Oxon', *Oxoniensia* 38, 41–115

Rogerson, A, 1976 'Excavations on Fuller's Hill, Great Yarmouth', *East Anglian Archaeology* 2, 131–245

Rose, J K, 1957 'Wool', in *Encyclopaedia Britannica* 23, 730–731

Ruby, A T and Lowther, A W G, 1955 'A report on the investigation of the moated site in 'Greatlee Wood', Effingham (1952–1953)', *Proceedings of the Leatherhead and District Local History Society* 1, no. 9, 4–17

Russell-Smith, F, 1956 'The medieval *brygyrdyl*', *Antiquaries Journal* 36, 218–221

Salaman, R A, 1975 *Dictionary of tools used in the woodworking and allied trades, c1700-1970*, Scribner, New York

Salzman, L F, 1957 'Some notes on shepherds' staves', *Agricultural History Review* 5, 91–94

Salzman, L F, 1964 *English industries of the Middle Ages*, H Pordes, London (new edition)

Salzman, L F, 1967 *Building in England down to 1540. A documentary history*, Clarendon Press, Oxford (2nd edition)

Schubert, H R, 1957 *History of the British iron and steel industry from c450 BC to AD 1775*, Routledge & Kegan Paul, London

Scott, B G, 1976 'Metallographic and chemical studies on a group of iron artifacts from the excavations at Greencastle, County Down', *Ulster Journal of Archaeology* 39, 42–52

Shoesmith, R, 1970–72 'Hereford city excavations 1970', *Transactions of the Woolhope Naturalist Field Club* 40, 225–240

Shortt, H, 1968 'A thirteenth-century "steelyard" balance from Huish', *Wiltshire Archaeological and Natural History Magazine* 63, 66–71

Shortt, H, 1972 'Catalogue of metal objects', in N P Thompson, 'Excavation on a medieval site at Huish, 1967–68', *Wiltshire Archaeological Magazine* 67, 116–124 (112–131)

Smith, H R B, 1966 *Blacksmiths' and farriers' tools at Shelburne Museum*, Museum Pamphlet Series 7, Shelburne, Vermont

Spry, N, 1971 'The material', in P J Fowler and C V Walthew (eds), 'Archaeology and the M5 Motorway. First Report', *Transactions of the Bristol and Gloucestershire Archaeological Society* 90, 38–42 (22–63)

Stanford, S C, 1967 'The deserted medieval village of Hampton Wafer, Herefordshire', *Transactions of the Woolhope Naturalist Field Club* 39, 71–92

Steane, J M, 1967 'Excavations at Lyveden, 1965–1967', *Northampton Museum and Art Gallery* 2, 3–37

Steane, J M and Bryant, G F, 1975 'Excavations at the deserted medieval settlement at Lyveden. Fourth Report', *Northampton Museum and Art Gallery* 12, 1–160

Stenton, F (ed), 1957 *The Bayeux Tapestry: a comprehensive survey*, Phaidon Publishers, New York

Still, L and Pallister, A, 1964 'The excavation of one house site in the deserted village of West Hartburn, Co. Durham', *Archaeologia Aeliana* 4th series 42, 187–206

Still, L and Pallister, A, 1967 'West Hartburn 1965. Site C', *Archaeologia Aeliana* 4th series 45, 139–148

Stone, J F S and Charlton, J, 1935 'Trial excavations in the East Suburb of Old Sarum', *Antiquaries Journal* 15, 174–192

Streeten, A, 1983 *Bayham Abbey: Recent research, including a report on excavations (1973–76) directed by the late Helen Sutermeister*, Sussex Archaeological Society Monograph 2, Lewes

Taylor, R, 1974 *Weoley Castle. Handlist of exhibits*, Birmingham

Tebbutt, C F, 1966 'St Neots Priory', *Proceedings of the Cambridge Antiquaries Society* 59, 33–74

Thompson, M W, 1956 'Trial excavation on the West Bailey of a ring motte and bailey at Long Buckby, Northants', *Journal of the Northamptonshire Natural History Society* 33, 55–66

Thompson, N P, 1972 'Excavation on a medieval site at Huish, 1967–68', *Wiltshire Archaeological Magazine* 67, 112–131

Thompson, R, 1978 'The industrial archaeology of leather', *Leather* (September 1978), 189–193

Thordeman, B, 1939 *Armour from the Battle of Wisby 1361*, Stockholm

Tylecote, R F, 1962 *Metallurgy in Archaeology*, Arnold, London

Tylecote, R F, 1975 'Metallurgical report', in G Beresford, *The medieval clay-land village: excavations at Goltho and Barton Blount*, The Society for Medieval Archaeology Monograph 6, 81–82

Tylecote, R F, 1976 *A History of Metallurgy*, Metals Society, London

Wacher, J, 1963–66 'Excavations at Riplingham, East Yorkshire, 1956–7', *Yorkshire Archaeological Journal* 41, 608–669

Wade, K, 1980 'A settlement site at Bonhunt Farm, Wicken Bonhunt, Essex', in D G Buckley (ed), *Archaeology in Essex to AD 1500*, Council for British Archaeology Research Report 34, 96–102

Waddington, Q, 1928 'Padlocks from the City', *Antiquaries Journal* 8, 524–526

Ward Perkins, J B, 1967 *London Museum medieval catalogue*, Her Majesty's Stationery Office, London

Waterer, J W, 1957 'Leather', in C Singer, E J Holmyard, A R Hall and T I Williams (eds), *A history of technology. Volume II: the Mediterranean civilizations and the Middle Ages, c700 BC to cAD 1500*, 147–190

Waterer, J W, 1968 *Leather craftsmanship*, G Bell and Sons, London

Waterman, D M, 1954 'Excavations at Clough Castle, Co. Down', *Ulster Journal of Archaeology* 17, 103–163

Waterman, D M, 1959a 'Excavations at Lismahon, Co. Down', *Medieval Archaeology* 3, 139–176

Waterman, D M, 1959b 'Late Saxon, Viking and early medieval finds from York', *Archaeologia* 97, 59–105

Waterman, E, 1953 'A group of twelfth-century pottery and other finds from Knaresborough Castle', *Antiquaries Journal* 33, 211–213

Webber, R, 1971 *The village blacksmith*, David and Charles, Newton Abbot

Webster, L E and Cherry, J, 1975 'Medieval Britain in 1974', *Medieval Archaeology* 19, 220–260

Welch, C, 1916 *History of the Cutlers' Company of London and of the minor cutlery crafts. Vol 1: from earlier times to... 1500*, Cutlers' Company, London

Wenham, P, 1972 'Excavations in Low Petergate, York. 1957–58', *Yorkshire Archaeological Journal* 44, 65–113

West, S E, 1963 'Excavations at Cox Lane (1958) and the Town defences, Shire Hall Yard, Ipswich (1959)', *Proceedings of the Suffolk Institute of Archaeology* 29, 233–303

West, S E, 1968 'Griff Manor House (Sudeley Castle), Warwickshire', *Journal of the British Archaeological Association* 3rd series 31, 76–101

West, S E, 1970 'Brome, Suffolk. The excavation of a moated site, 1967', *Journal of the British Archaeological Association* 3rd series 33, 89–121

Wheeler, A and Jones, A, 1976 'Fish remains', in A Rogerson, 'Excavations on Fuller's Hill, Great Yarmouth', *East Anglian Archaeology* 2, 208–224 (131–245)

Wheeler, A, 1977 'Fish bone', in H Clarke and A Carter, *Excavations in King's Lynn 1963–1970*, The Society for Medieval Archaeology Monograph 7, 403–409

Whitwell, J B and McNamee, S M, 1964 'Excavations in Foregate Street', *Journal of the Chester Archaeological Society* 51, 1–19

Wilkins, G G, 1975 'A section of a gravel pit at Baginton, Coventry', *Transactions of the Birmingham and Warwickshire Archaeological Society* 87, 111–127

Williams, F, 1977 *Pleshey Castle, Essex (XII–XVI century): excavations in the bailey, 1959–1963*, British Archaeological Reports 42, Oxford

Wilson, D M (ed) 1976 *The archaeology of Anglo-Saxon England*, Methuen, London

Wilson, J, 1846 'Antiquities found at Woodperry, Oxon', *Archaeological Journal* 3, 116–128

Wood, M, 1965 *The English medieval house*, Phoenix House, London

Wood, D, Rhodes. M and Dyson, T, 1965 'Africa house sections, London, 1973', *Transactions of the London and Middlesex Archaeological Society* 26, 252–266

Wood, E S, 1965 'A medieval glasshouse at Blunden's Wood, Hambledon, Surrey', *Surrey Archaeological Collections* 62, 54–79

Woodhouse, T, 1957 'Linen and linen manufactures', in *Encyclopaedia Britannica* 14, 159–161

Wrathmell, S and Wrathmell, S P, 1974–75 'Excavations at the Moat Site, Walsall, Staffs. 1972–74', *Transactions of the South Staffordshire Archaeological and Historical Society* 16, 19–53

Wright, S, 1976 'The finds', in P Rahtz and S Hirst, *Bordesley Abbey, Redditch, Hereford- Worcestershire. First report on excavations 1969–1973*, British Archaeological Report 23, Oxford, 138–221

INDEX

Abingdon, Oxfordshire 45, 92, 292
Abingdon Abbey 45
accounts 3, 7, 23–24, 26, 43–45, 77–78, 161–64, 299, 363
adzes 22–23, 32–33
agricultural tools 77, 79, 81, 83, 85, 87, 89, 91–93, 95, 97, 99, 101, 103
Aldingbourne, West Sussex 284
Aldringham, Lancashire 310
Alsted, Surrey 2, 7, 18, 27, 36, 38, 40, 94, 172, 190, 196, 200, 202, 204, 206, 224, 226, 228, 278, 282, 292, 330, 336, 346, 354, 376
Alvechurch, Hereford and Worcester 38, 248, 288, 370
Amman, Jost 21, 24
Andover, Wiltshire 25
angle tie 162, 170–171
angled hasp 168, 222
Anglo-Saxon 14, 16, 21, 30, 36, 38, 40, 59, 62, 64, 70, 77, 90, 92, 94, 102, 109, 114, 122, 128, 134, 136, 138, 140, 142, 146, 148, 150, 158, 170, 172, 176, 178, 182, 184, 190, 192, 194, 196, 198, 254, 256, 260, 270, 276, 282, 292, 294, 316, 318, 332, 366, 378
Anglo-Saxon, Late 16, 21, 30, 38, 62, 70, 77, 92, 94, 102, 114, 122, 128, 134, 136, 140, 142, 146, 148, 150, 158, 170, 172, 176, 178, 182, 184, 190, 192, 194, 196, 198, 254, 256, 260, 270, 276, 282, 294, 316, 318, 332, 378
Anglo-Saxon, Middle 36, 59, 138
anvil 2–3, 7–10
Århus, Denmark 59
armoires 163, 165, 168–69
Ascot Doilly, Oxfordshire 288, 350
ashes 11, 45, 50, 79
Ashmolean Museum, Oxford 56, 92, 148, 154, 158, 174, 274, 280, 286, 288, 294, 354, 360
augers 22–24, 26, 46
Avebury, Wiltshire 158, 346
Avon 126, 136, 216, 260, 278

awls 67–68, 72–75
axes 2, 21–23, 25, 27–33, 43, 45, 47, 52–53, 80, 82, 96, 98, 100, 152
  terminology 23
  types 21
Aylesbury, Buckinghamshire 62, 244, 262, 264, 270, 344, 378
Ayton Castle, North Yorkshire 28, 96, 98, 100, 152, 292

Baconsthorpe Castle, Norfolk 28, 310
Badby, Northamptonshire 32, 72, 88, 100, 102, 134, 206, 280, 334, 346, 378
Baginton, Warwickshire 34, 130, 154, 158, 288, 292, 356
balances 301, 328
Baltic 107, 110
bar 4, 8, 46, 60, 161, 169, 228, 254, 297, 328, 334, 343, 374
  iron 1–5, 9, 106, 161, 169, 363
barbed point 299, 312
Barnack, Northamptonshire 43
barrel padlock 194, 202, 204, 222, 231–34, 237, 239, 244–57, 266, 268, 270, 302, 332
  types 237
Barrow Mead, Bath, Somerset 100, 126, 136, 194, 216, 222, 260
Barton Blount, Derbyshire 25, 52, 102, 122, 130, 136
Bayeux Tapestry 21–23, 25, 297–98
Bayham Abbey, East Sussex 18, 48, 170, 256, 297, 303
beam 77, 162, 301, 328
beam stirrups 162, 170–171
Beckery Chapel, Glastonbury, Somerset 56, 158, 192, 210, 282, 286, 292, 294, 360
Bedford 260, 294
Beere, Devon 306
bell clappers 102–3
bell-pits 1
bells 82–83, 102–3
belt 301, 330, 339, 342, 344, 366
belt slides 342, 360–361
bevel 23, 32

billhooks 80–81, 90–91
binding 25–26, 59, 162, 164–65, 300
binding strip 167, 212–15
Birmingham 28, 38, 48, 56, 90, 152, 178, 198, 228, 248, 256, 294, 301, 310, 322, 374
Birmingham City Museum 12, 14, 18, 30, 32, 36, 52, 144, 158, 208, 222, 250, 262, 276, 284, 288, 292, 326, 328, 332, 349, 352, 376
Bishops Waltham, Hampshire 86
bits 24–25, 34, 36, 231, 235, 237, 239–43, 260, 262, 266, 268, 270, 272, 274, 276, 278, 280, 282, 284, 286, 288, 292, 294, 302, 364–66, 374
  auger 3, 23–26
  bridle 364, 375, 377
  complex 242
  key 234, 236
  lanceolate 34
  spatulate 294
  uncut 240, 270
blacksmith 1–3, 7–11, 27, 44, 47, 111, 166
  equipment 3–4, 9, 12, 14, 30
blade 9, 14, 18, 21–26, 28, 32, 34, 36, 38, 45, 47–48, 52, 60–61, 67–68, 70, 77–82, 86, 88, 90, 92, 94, 96, 98, 100, 105–14, 116, 118, 120, 122, 124, 126, 128, 130, 132, 134, 136, 138, 140, 142, 144, 146, 148, 150, 152, 154, 156, 158, 298, 310, 312, 318
  asymmetrical 28, 30, 77–78
  axe 50, 52
  broad 22, 113
  crescent-shaped 80–81, 90, 92
  curved 26, 32, 38, 74, 80–81, 92
  distorted iron shovel 88
  flaring 9, 21–23, 48, 52
  flat 23, 32
  half-moon 80–81
  iron 120
  iron-cored 111, 128, 150
  iron-shod 11
  pattern-welded 110, 114, 124, 144
  plain 23, 32
  round 74

391

shaped 16, 92
sickle 81–82, 96
slender 68, 107–8, 113
spoon bit 34, 36, 70
steel-cored 32, 111, 114, 118, 120, 128, 130, 134, 150, 154
steel-edged 111, 114, 116, 120, 122, 124, 126, 128, 130, 136, 150
symmetrical 21, 28, 77
tapering 24, 54
toothed 64
triangular-shaped 22, 92
wedge-shaped 80–81, 92
blade edge 86
blade form 22, 45, 80–81, 106–7, 111
blade fragment 22, 32, 70, 82, 98, 100, 113–14, 118, 144, 148, 150, 156
blade shapes 80–81
blade steel 126, 132
blade tip 36, 40, 82, 92, 98, 100, 116, 120, 124, 138, 150, 152, 154, 158, 310
blanks 24, 106
blocks 7, 43, 45, 47, 59, 79, 169, 235
bloomery 1
blooms 1, 3, 8, 67
Blunden's Wood, Hambledon 88
Bodiam Castle, East Sussex 186, 288
bolsters 11, 109
bolt 161, 169, 214, 226–27, 231–37, 239–40, 244, 246, 248, 250, 252, 254, 256, 270, 302, 310
L-shaped 234, 250
pivoting 235
T-shaped 233, 252, 254
toothed 235, 258
U-shaped 231–32, 234, 246
bolt entry 244, 246, 250
Bolton, Fangfoss, Humberside 100, 146, 188, 212, 304, 336, 346, 350, 356, 376
bone scales 111, 142, 146, 148
bosses, bridle 365–66, 378–79, 381
Boston, Lincolnshire 246, 348
bow 111–12, 150, 152, 154, 156, 158, 240–243, 270, 272, 274, 276, 278, 284, 294
looped 64, 111–12, 158
oval 274, 276, 278, 280, 282, 284, 288, 290, 292, 294, 310
pear-shaped 241–42, 270
ring 241, 270, 272, 274, 276, 278, 280, 282, 284, 286, 288, 292, 294
thistle-shaped 241–42, 276, 280, 282, 284
Bowes Museum, Barnard Castle 18, 98, 212, 370
box padlock 231–33, 237, 239, 244–45, 256–57
bracket 162, 170–171, 226–27, 299
hooked 162, 170–171, 226–27
U-shaped 226–27
Bramber Castle, West Sussex 2, 18, 34, 36, 38, 56, 122, 134, 178, 286, 350, 352, 354, 363–64
Brampton, Cambridgeshire 60
Brandon Castle, Warwickshire 90, 98, 180, 182, 196, 222, 224, 260, 262, 264, 266, 268, 270, 272, 284, 330, 332, 349, 352, 356, 368
brandreth 298
brass 146, 148, 150, 244, 254, 256
brazing fluid 110–111, 138, 140, 142, 144, 146, 148, 252
bricklayers 46

Brixworth, Northamptonshire 62, 64, 90, 154, 212
Broadfield, Hertfordshire 90, 142, 148
Brome, Suffolk 128, 140, 142, 180, 233, 254
bronze 2, 9, 140, 297
bronzesmiths 9
Brooklands, Weybridge, Surrey 34, 76, 116, 122, 134, 256, 262, 286, 308, 318, 376
Broughton, Lincolnshire 310
bucket 166, 297, 300–301, 320–324
handle loop 322
handle strap 324
hoops 300, 322–24
buckle 302, 339–45, 347, 349–51, 353, 355–59, 361, 366
circular 341
D-shaped 339, 348
elongated neck 342, 358
figure-eight shaped 342
frequency of medieval types 340
hexagonal 341
integral plates 342, 358
looped attachment plates 341
looped neck 342, 358
rectangular 339–40
T-shaped 340
trapezoidal 339–40
buckle bar 354
buckle frame 301–2, 339, 349
buckle pins 342, 358
buckle plate 339–42, 358
building, timber-framed 22–23, 163
building and furniture fittings 163, 165, 167, 169, 171, 173, 175, 177, 179, 181, 183, 185, 187, 189, 191, 193, 195, 197, 199, 205, 207, 209, 211, 213, 215, 217, 219, 221, 223, 225, 227, 229
building work 43–44
Burgundy, Duke of 108
Burnham Church, Humberside 40, 72, 102, 178
Burton-in-Lonsdale, North Yorkshire 30, 48, 102, 126, 182, 272

cabinet makers 26
Caedmon manuscript 7, 77
Caldecote, Hertfordshire 298
Cambokeels, Durham 18, 72, 98, 100, 114, 138, 156, 198, 212, 256, 276, 292, 304, 308, 316, 330, 348, 350, 352, 354, 356, 364, 370, 378
Cambridge 46, 146, 162–64
Cambridge Castle 46
candles 299–300
candlesticks 297, 299–300, 315, 317, 319
pricket 299
socketed 300
three-armed 318
Canterbury 77, 163
Canterbury Cathedral 163
Cardiff 12, 14, 18, 130, 132, 176, 180, 188, 306, 324, 328, 354, 372
carpenters 8–9, 11, 21–23, 27, 46
cartulary 77
carving 23, 46, 108
casket 161, 165–68
fittings 165, 167
Castell-y-Bere, Gwynedd 18, 48, 54, 124, 172, 198, 222, 276, 280, 284, 320, 336, 358, 368, 372, 376
Castle Acre Castle, Norfolk 32, 40, 102,

116, 118, 150, 152, 156, 204, 210, 214, 218, 226, 228, 246, 254, 262, 264, 266, 268, 278, 312, 330, 349, 354, 378
Castle Acre Priory, Norfolk 48, 50
Castle Neroche, Somerset 36, 352
Castle Tower, Penmaen, West Glamorgan 349
cauldrons 297, 301
caulking 163, 165, 169–70, 188, 192, 196, 198, 226, 228
Central Museum, Northampton 30, 128, 140, 218
chain 77, 144, 162–63, 168–69, 232–33, 237, 250, 252, 297, 301–2, 322, 330–333, 364–66
fittings 333–35, 376
links 168, 376
Cheddar, Somerset 32, 34, 100, 102, 132, 158, 178, 208, 268, 278, 284, 363
cheek-piece 365–66, 374, 376
Chelmsford, Essex 182, 188, 218
Chertsey Abbey 45, 47
Chester 78–79, 154
chests 23, 163, 165–68, 233, 235
Cheswick Green, West Midlands 254
Chew Valley Lake, Somerset 86, 204, 216, 278
Chingley, Kent 3, 40, 114, 126, 150, 162, 180, 280
chisels 2–4, 7, 9, 22–23, 26, 32–33, 43, 45, 52–53, 164
cold 9–10, 14–15, 44
expanded head 14, 52
hot 9–10, 14–17
octagonal-sectioned stem 14, 16, 52
single bevel 23, 32
Christchurch, Hampshire 36, 244, 268
Churchill, Oxfordshire 292
clapper 82, 102
Clarendon Palace, Wiltshire 36, 94, 138, 144, 146, 150, 154, 158, 162, 170, 184, 186, 188, 194, 196, 200, 208, 210, 212, 214, 222, 224, 226, 228, 248, 260, 264, 266, 294, 299, 326, 330, 334, 336, 349, 352, 358
claws 27
claw hammer 2, 8–9, 26–27, 38–41
cleavers 108, 297–98, 310–313
clench bolts 164, 188–89, 200
Cleveland 18, 182, 224, 226, 228, 312, 316, 322, 332
closing plate 233, 246, 248, 254
cloth 59–61, 111
cloth shears 59–61, 112
Clough Castle, Co. Down 32, 34, 36, 38, 48, 92, 172, 186, 194, 202, 204, 208, 222, 308, 310, 332, 334, 350, 360
coin 152
colander 297, 304–5
collar 10, 54, 110, 120, 140, 146, 235–36, 240–243, 258, 260, 276, 278, 302, 332, 337, 365, 376
circular 302, 336
cylindrical 336
rectangular 302, 336
sub-rectangular 336
Collyweston 233
comb
carding 59–60
weaving 59–60, 64–65
compasses 27, 40
Conway, Gwynedd 54, 94
coopers 27
copper 105

INDEX

copper alloy 61, 68, 110–111, 134, 144, 167, 232–33, 237, 240–242, 297, 299–301, 339, 341–43, 366
    brazing metal 246, 248, 254
    rivets 76, 138, 140, 146, 148
coppicing 80
Copt Hay, Tetsworth, Oxfordshire 48, 90, 92, 98, 120, 126, 244, 266, 328
Corfe, Dorset 3, 161, 165
corner bindings 166, 210–211
corner bosses 242, 278, 280, 284
coulter 77, 84
Coventry 34, 50, 154, 156, 158, 268, 270, 288, 292, 352
cramp 161, 170–171, 176
Crane Godrevy, Cornwall 32
creaser 67–68, 72–73, 75
cresset lamps 299
Criccieth Castle, Gwynedd 12, 40, 52, 70, 122, 136, 150, 158, 161, 170, 172, 200, 260, 266, 278, 282, 314, 324, 346, 354, 358, 374
cross-pane hammer 9, 14
crotch 80
crows 43
crucible 7
Cullompton, Devon 61
curry-combs 364, 372–73
currying 67–68
Cutlers' Company 111
cutler's mark 70, 105, 107, 116, 122, 126, 128, 130, 140, 142, 148
    inlaid 122, 126, 128, 130, 132, 136, 138, 140, 142, 144, 146, 148
cutlery 105–6, 108, 111
cutting edge 9, 21–23, 26, 28, 30, 32, 47, 56, 68, 70, 80–82, 90, 105–8, 111, 114, 122, 124, 134, 154, 310
    curved 70
    double bevelled 23
    parallel 106–7
    straight 70, 80–81
    vertical 45, 50, 52
cylinder, sheet iron 339–40, 342, 350, 352, 354

DAMHB Collection, London 28, 48, 50, 52, 54, 170, 190, 200, 310, 318, 324
decoration 21, 110, 144, 166–67, 210, 218, 233–34, 239, 242, 328
    grooves 64
    incised 260, 262
    openwork 241
    wavy line 232, 234, 246
Deganwy Castle, Gwynedd 2–4, 12, 14, 30
Denny Abbey, Cambridgeshire 12
diamond-shaped blades 46, 54
distorted padlock case 252, 254
dividers 27, 40–41, 46
documents 44–46, 77, 79, 82, 161
dolabra 45
door 162–69, 233–35, 301–2
    bolt 226
    fittings 16
    flail 169, 226–27
    hook 226
Dover 3
Dover Castle, Kent 7, 158, 206, 218, 368
drawknife 26, 38–39
drifts 10, 18–19
Duffield Castle, Derbyshire 78, 120, 132, 134, 170, 186, 320
Durham 26, 44, 74, 178, 210, 218, 288
Durrance Moat, Hereford and Worcester 98, 352
Durrington, West Sussex 288
Dyserth Castle, Clwyd 16, 18, 38, 40, 52, 92, 98, 102, 150, 154, 156, 176, 180, 190, 192, 196, 208, 270, 332, 344, 352, 364, 368, 378, 380

East Haddlesey, North Yorkshire 352, 356, 358, 367
East Hill Farm, Houghton Regis, Bedfordshire 28, 30, 150, 268
Eaton Socon, Cambridgeshire 62
Edward III 111
Edward IV 299
Effingham, Surrey 222
Ellington, Cambridgeshire 14, 206, 264, 280, 344
end-plate 146, 239, 244, 246, 248, 250, 252, 254, 312, 334
escutcheons 166
eye 9–10, 14, 21–22, 24, 27–28, 30, 32, 38, 40, 44–45, 47, 50, 52, 56, 68, 74, 76, 165–66, 169, 206, 299–300
    rectangular 9, 14, 169, 228
    spiked 206, 210
    U-shaped 165, 200, 202, 204, 206
Eynsford Castle, Kent 118, 200, 208, 222, 224, 246, 284, 292, 370

Faringdon Clump, Oxfordshire 174, 274
farriers 2, 9, 11, 27
Faxton, Northamptonshire 72, 136, 152, 176, 210, 246, 254, 262, 276, 314, 349, 356
fibres 59–60
files 11, 18–19, 26
finger loops 113, 158
fire-dogs 297, 303
fire-forks 297, 303
fire-steel 300, 318–19
fire tools 11
fish hooks 299, 312–13
Fishpool, Notthinghamshire 232, 237
fittings 21, 60, 161–64, 166, 169, 297, 301, 366
    doors 164
    furniture 164
flanges 81, 92, 234, 258, 366, 378
flatters 9
flesh-hooks 297–98, 300, 308–9
floats 26, 38–39, 299
Folkestone, Kent 52, 118, 220, 336, 344
forceps 59–60, 64–65
Forest of Dean 1
forge 1–4, 7–8, 10, 24, 154, 166, 232–33, 240, 270, 363
forging 2, 7–10, 110, 165, 242, 256, 298
forks 79, 88–89, 108
Fountains Abbey, North Yorkshire 52
Foyle Road, London 34, 40, 94, 102, 116, 130, 138, 148, 156, 176, 222, 260, 270, 290, 294, 314, 348–50, 354, 360, 370
frame 26, 80, 161, 166, 339–40, 342–44, 348, 350, 352
    buckle 344, 346, 348–50, 352, 354, 356, 358
frame saw 26
fullers 10
furnace 1–2

furniture fittings 161, 164
Fyfield Down, Wiltshire 30, 38, 56, 70, 72, 254, 256, 262, 308, 332

gad 3
garderobe 79–80, 88, 90
gates 162, 164–65, 167–69, 301
gavelocks 43–44
gimlet bits 25
Glastonbury Tor, Somerset 16, 32, 124, 260, 332, 358
Glenluce, Dumfries and Galloway 356
Glottenham, East Sussex 34, 192, 222, 226, 244, 284, 352
Gloucester 3, 12, 34, 62, 118, 124, 132, 154, 162, 214, 216, 218, 254, 266, 268, 270, 272, 280, 324, 380
Gloucester Castle 162
glovers 113
gold 110, 144, 232, 237, 339
Goldsborough, North Yorkshire 56
Goltho, Lincolnshire 2–4, 10, 14, 16, 32, 34, 38, 62, 64, 70, 72, 92, 114, 118, 122, 124, 128, 134, 136, 140, 142, 144, 146, 148, 150, 152, 158, 170, 172, 176, 178, 182, 184, 188, 190, 192, 194, 196, 198, 210, 214, 220, 233–34, 240, 244, 246, 248, 254, 256, 260, 262, 270, 276, 282, 294, 301, 308, 310, 314, 316, 318, 324, 330, 332, 334, 344, 346, 348, 349, 350, 352, 354, 356, 358, 366, 368, 378
Gomeldon, Wiltshire 16, 138, 152, 158, 180, 194, 204, 254, 270, 330, 332, 352
Goring-by-Sea, West Sussex 308
gouge bits 24–25, 36–37
Grafton Regis, Northamptonshire 314, 330, 356
Great Yarmouth 114, 122, 158, 272, 299, 312
Greencastle, Co. Down 116, 148, 150, 154
Gregory of Tours 109
Grenstein, Norfolk 34, 40, 74, 76, 88, 128, 138, 148, 174, 178, 190, 206, 212, 220, 222, 250, 254, 256, 264, 276, 282, 316, 336, 356
griddle plates 298, 306–7
grilles 169, 228
grinder 111
grooved stem 241, 272, 274, 276, 278, 280, 282, 284, 286, 288, 290, 292, 294
guide arm 164–65, 192, 196, 198
Guildford 38

Haddlesey, North Yorkshire 276, 294, 358
Hadleigh Castle, Essex 140, 146, 158, 168, 258, 274, 280, 290, 349, 354
haft 9–10, 14, 44, 80
hafter 111
hafting 9, 67, 80, 108–9
Hambleton Moat, Lincolnshire 126, 184, 198, 278, 326, 360, 364, 378
The Hamel, Oxford 40, 136, 154, 186, 190, 192, 206, 214, 220, 350, 358
hammer 3, 7–9, 14–15, 21, 27, 43–45, 47, 52, 56–57, 162
    arms 9, 12, 40, 45, 50, 77, 150, 154, 156, 158, 162, 165, 168, 170, 172, 174, 176, 178, 180, 182, 210, 214, 222, 224, 234, 256, 258, 298, 303, 340, 342, 363–65, 368, 370, 372
    cross-pane 9, 14
    curved claws 27, 38, 40
    flat claw 38, 40

393

hammer-axes 43, 45, 50–53
hammer scale 1–2, 7
Hampton Court 25, 46
Hampton Wafer, Hereford and Worcester 40, 70, 90, 120, 180
hand hammer 9
handle 8–12, 14, 21–24, 26–28, 30, 32, 36, 38, 45–48, 50, 52, 54, 59–62, 67–68, 70, 72, 74, 76, 78–82, 90, 92, 102, 105, 107–8, 110–113, 116, 118, 120, 124, 126, 128, 132, 134, 138, 140, 142, 146, 148, 150, 154, 156, 158, 162, 166, 168–69, 222, 224, 226, 237, 239, 248, 250, 252, 254, 297–98, 300–301, 303–5, 308, 310, 312, 316, 318, 320, 322–26, 364, 372
   loop 254, 322
   M-shaped 168, 224
   stapled 169, 226
   strap 324
   wooden 11, 14, 23–24, 26–27, 32, 36, 38, 46–48, 50, 54, 67, 70, 76, 79–81, 90, 92, 116, 118, 120, 124, 126, 128, 132, 134, 142, 146, 148, 150, 297–98, 303, 312, 372
Hangleton, West Sussex 28, 38, 98, 148, 206, 208, 284, 330, 332, 334, 354, 370
harbicks 59–61
harness 301, 339–40, 342, 366
Harrold, Bedfordshire 59
harrows 80, 302
hasp 161–62, 167–69, 194, 202, 204, 214, 216, 218–19, 221, 223, 235, 258, 300
   angled 168, 222
   curved 218, 220, 222
   looped 168, 258
   pinned 168, 222
   shaped 167–68
   stapled padlock 256–59
Hawkesley Moat, West Midlands 288
hearth 2, 7–8, 11, 18, 79, 154, 297, 301, 330
heckles 59–60, 62–63, 65
hedge-bill 80
Hen Blas, Clwyd 16, 40, 198, 206, 330
Hen Caerwys, Clwyd 16, 18, 90, 122, 138, 142, 198, 246, 252, 256, 260, 350, 354, 356
Hen Domen, Powys 28, 38, 40, 56, 92, 154, 182, 224, 262, 264
Hen Gaerwys, Clwyd 40
Hengrave Hall 25
Henry III 2
Herbert Art Gallery and Museum, Coventry 34, 154, 156, 158, 268, 270, 288, 292, 352
hes 3
hides 47
hilt plates 105, 107, 110
hinge 165–67, 194, 198, 200–207, 210–211, 214
   C-shaped 166, 200
   end-looped 165
   pinned 166, 206
   with nailed U-shaped eyes 165
hinge pivots 164–65, 191, 193, 195–97, 199–200
hoes 43, 79–80, 90–91
hoisting equipment 46
holdfast 163, 188–89
Holkham Bible 7, 77, 297
Holworth, Dorset 192, 276, 312
hook 3, 46, 60–61, 64, 81, 92–93, 163, 165, 168–69, 184, 186–89, 226–27, 239, 297–99, 301–3, 326–30, 332, 334–35, 342
   belt 342, 360–361

looped 188, 226, 302, 328, 330, 332, 334
   S-shaped 163, 188–89, 301, 326
   shearboard 60, 64–65
   suspension 102, 297–98, 342
hooked bracket 162, 170–171
hoops 10, 161, 164, 300–301, 320, 322
horse equipment 363, 365–67, 369, 371, 373, 375, 377, 379, 381
horseshoe 2, 8, 10, 27, 363–64, 368–71
horseshoe nails 2, 8, 363–64
household ironwork 46, 297, 299, 301, 303, 305, 307, 309, 311, 313, 315, 317, 319, 321, 323, 325, 327, 329, 333, 335, 337
Huish, Wiltshire 2, 8, 11, 18, 27, 40, 84, 90, 136, 138, 142, 144, 202, 204, 214, 252, 256, 258, 266, 276, 282, 288, 292, 303, 308, 312, 328, 354, 370
Hull, Humberside 28, 109, 148, 218, 276, 282, 288, 356

inlay 105, 110–111, 116, 122, 128, 140, 142, 144, 148, 239
inventory 7–8, 10–11, 26
Ipswich, Norfolk 352, 363
iron 1, 3–4, 7–10, 22, 24, 26, 40, 44, 46, 59, 61, 68, 76–77, 82, 94, 105–6, 110–111, 124, 134, 150, 161–62, 164, 166–67, 169, 232–33, 237, 240–242, 252, 254, 256, 297–301, 320, 322, 339, 341–43, 356, 363–64, 366
   hot 9–10
   scrap 2–3
   Spanish 3
iron ore 1
iron slag 2–4, 9, 12, 14, 30
iron smelting 1, 5
iron spines 233, 248
ironworking site 18

jew's harps 343, 360–361
John of Eltham 301
joiners 26
Joyden's Wood, Kent 258

Keighton, Nottinghamshire 98, 334
Kennington, Greater London 52
Kettleby Thorpe, Lincolnshire 16, 92, 178, 220, 252, 256, 260, 268, 286, 348
keyhole 168, 231–34, 237, 244, 246, 248, 250, 252, 254, 256, 258
   plates 161, 168, 222–23
keys 3, 161, 231–33, 235–37, 239–44, 248, 254, 256, 268, 270–295
   channelled bit 272, 274, 276, 278, 280, 282, 288
   D-shaped bow 240, 242, 270, 272, 274, 276, 278, 280, 282, 284, 288, 290, 292, 294
   gold 237
   grooved stem 241, 272, 274, 276, 278, 280, 282, 284, 286, 288, 290, 292, 294
   lozenge-shaped bow 241–42, 270, 272, 276, 280, 282, 284, 286, 288
   oval bow 274, 276, 278, 280, 282, 284, 288, 290, 292, 294, 310
   pear-shaped bow 242, 270
   plain stem 239, 260, 262, 264, 266, 270, 294
   post-medieval 240, 242
   types 240–242
Kidwelly Castle, Dyfed 70, 124, 126

Kiln Combe, Bullock Down, East Sussex 132, 208, 282
Kilton Castle, Cleveland 18, 182, 224, 226, 228, 312, 316, 322, 332
King's Hall, Westminster, London 161–64
Kings Langley, Hertfordshire 150, 169, 184, 196, 210, 228, 248, 330, 350
King's Lynn, Norfolk 52, 56, 70, 76, 78, 100, 114, 120, 122, 124, 132, 134, 144, 154, 170, 172, 176, 180, 188, 190, 204, 208, 220, 222, 246, 252, 262, 268, 272, 274, 276, 280, 299, 332, 336, 358, 360, 372, 374, 378
Kirkcudbright Castle, Dumfries and Galloway 56, 196, 228, 278, 303, 334
Knaresborough Castle 44, 70, 182, 350
knife-daggers 108, 360
knife moods 3, 106, 114
knives 11, 23–24, 67–68, 70, 81, 105–11, 113–51, 153, 155, 157, 159
   blade decoration 110
   blades 111
   carving 108
   chronological range 109
   copper-alloy shoulder plates 142, 146
   dating 108
   frequency of medieval types 109
   handles 24, 110
   non-ferrous shoulder plates 130, 138, 140, 142, 146
   paring 67–68
   terminology 105
   types 107–8
ladles 297–98, 310–311
lamps 299
Lancham Church, Nottinghamshire 168
lanterns 299
latch rest 226
latches 161, 168, 227
latten 298, 301, 328
Laverstock, Wiltshire 299
lead 46, 161–62, 164–65, 198, 328
lead caulking 163, 169, 192, 196, 198, 226, 228
leather 61, 67–68, 152
leatherworkers 108
leatherworking tools 67, 71, 73, 75–76
lewises 43, 46
lighting 299
limb shackles 250, 252, 301–2
Lismahon, Co. Down 2, 74, 126, 180
Llanstephan Castle, Dyfed 50, 62, 324
Llantrithyd, South Glamorgan 40, 62, 64, 74, 76, 118, 130, 184, 220, 260, 262, 268, 270, 284, 330, 334, 344, 350, 352, 376
Llantwit Major, South Glamorgan 324
Llawhaden Castle, Dyfed 306
Lochmaben Castle, Dumfries and Galloway 72, 90, 178, 180, 246, 254, 314, 316, 332, 346, 352, 354, 364, 370, 374
lock bolt 235–36, 258–61
lock mechanism 234–35, 256, 258
locks 10, 161, 167–68, 214, 231, 233–37, 239–43, 245, 247, 249, 251, 253, 255, 257–59, 261, 263, 265, 267, 269, 271, 273, 275, 277, 279, 281, 283, 285, 287, 289, 291, 293, 295
   fixed 167, 233, 235
   types 235–36
London 36, 60, 62, 84, 88, 94, 102, 116,

INDEX

246, 248, 250, 258, 260, 264, 270, 280, 288, 290, 294, 308, 310, 312, 314, 316, 318, 330, 334, 336
London Bridge 23, 26
Long Buckby, Northamptonshire 118
loop 8, 11, 46, 102, 163, 165, 167–68, 182, 188, 206, 210, 214, 233, 239, 250, 252, 262, 298, 300, 303, 320, 322–23, 328, 334, 342, 358, 364–67, 378, 380
   suspension 303, 312, 360
Loppington, Shropshire 77, 79
Loughor Castle, West Glamorgan 16, 154, 312, 318, 349, 352
Louisbourg, Canada 162, 234
Low Caythorpe, Humberside 40, 92
Lullington, East Sussex 144
Lund, Sweden 237
Luton Museum and Art Gallery 28, 30
Luttrell Psalter 8, 77, 365
Lydford Castle, Devon 50, 79, 86, 164, 188, 200, 222
Lydney Castle, Gloucestershire 48, 54, 158, 208, 226, 248, 272, 278, 344
Lyveden, Northamptonshire 2–3, 34, 38, 62, 74, 86, 88, 90, 92, 98, 116, 120, 126, 128, 130, 132, 138, 148, 172, 174, 176, 178, 184, 190, 192, 218, 244, 248, 250, 256, 264, 270, 276, 280, 288, 308, 314, 334, 336, 341, 346, 349–50, 352, 356, 360, 374, 376, 378, 380

Magdalen College, Oxford 43–44
Maison Dieu, Ospringe, Kent 74
mallets 22–23, 45
mandrel 10–11, 18–19
Manor of the More, Rickmansworth, Hertfordshire 18, 186, 226, 326
manuscripts 7–8, 24, 46, 77, 79–80, 82, 166, 168
masonry 46, 120, 132, 134, 161–65
masons 9, 21, 43–47, 165
mattocks 43–45
mauls 43–44
Meon Hill, Hampshire 344
metallurgy 32, 62, 106, 111, 114, 116, 118, 120, 122, 124, 126, 128, 130, 132, 134, 136, 140, 144, 146, 148, 150, 154, 244, 250, 252, 254, 256
metalworkers 11, 26
metalworking tools 7, 9, 11, 13, 15, 17, 19, 27
Mileham, Norfolk 36
millstone dressing tools 47
millwright 21
Montgomery Castle, Powys 30, 36, 270
moods 3, 106, 114
mortices 22–24, 26, 165, 169, 228
The Mount, Princes Risborough, Buckinghamshire 146, 208, 235, 326, 366, 372
mounts 79, 146, 167, 208, 235–36, 240, 258, 300, 326, 343, 365–66, 372
mouthpieces 364–66, 374, 376

Naesholm Castle, Denmark 237
nail 8–9, 11, 22, 25, 27, 38, 52, 90, 161, 163–66, 188, 210, 226, 258, 363–64
   types 363–64
National Museum of Wales 12, 14, 130, 132, 176, 180, 188, 306, 328, 354, 372
needle 61, 67–68, 73, 75–76

Netherton, Hampshire 12, 70, 72, 74, 86, 90, 92, 120, 124, 126, 132, 134, 154, 178, 212, 248, 288, 346, 354, 356
Newbridge, Sussex 1
Newbury, Berkshire 3–4, 64, 70, 72, 92, 128, 130, 132, 144, 224, 226, 256, 258, 272, 282, 284, 322, 324, 330, 334, 350, 376, 380
non-ferrous plating 167, 206, 210, 212, 214, 218, 222, 224, 243, 260, 262, 270, 272, 274, 276, 278, 280, 282, 284, 286, 288, 292, 294, 330, 334, 336, 342–44, 346, 348–50, 352, 354, 356, 358, 360, 366, 374, 376, 378, 380
Norrington Manor House, Alvediston, Wiltshire 299
North Elmham Park, Norfolk 28, 34, 40, 70, 90, 94, 116, 130, 140, 144, 152, 170, 172, 176, 182, 188, 192, 194, 196, 206, 210, 218, 220, 244, 258, 260, 284, 292, 308, 354, 380
Northampton 14, 16, 30, 36, 38, 40, 60, 62, 64, 72, 74, 76, 122, 128, 130, 138, 140, 142, 146, 154, 170, 172, 174, 176, 178, 184, 190, 192, 194, 196, 198, 204, 206, 210, 214, 218, 233, 248, 256, 258, 270, 274, 288, 306, 308, 316, 330, 332, 334, 336, 348, 354, 378
Northampton Central Museum 30
Northolt Manor, Greater London 16, 38, 88, 94, 124, 142, 144, 158, 172, 180, 186, 204, 246, 258, 264, 288, 294, 308, 312, 330, 348
Norton, Simon de 47
Norwich, Norfolk 12, 28, 54, 62, 90, 184, 226, 233, 256, 303–4, 308, 326, 332
Nottingham 25
Nun Cotham, Humberside 77

Oakham Castle, Leicestershire 70, 148, 356
Old Manor, Askett 88
Old Sarum, Wiltshire 12, 14, 98, 118, 140, 146, 152, 156, 176, 186, 192, 212, 222, 233, 244, 246, 268, 308, 336, 344, 354
Ospringe, Kent 14, 72, 74, 122, 130, 138, 140, 142, 146, 150, 163, 170, 172, 176, 180, 184, 188, 194, 200, 206, 210, 212, 228, 260, 278, 290, 294, 324, 352, 356, 360, 363, 370, 374, 376, 378, 380
ox goads 82, 102–3
Oxford Castle 156, 184
oxshoes 2, 8, 363–64, 370

Pachesham, Surrey 79
padlocks 168, 231–35, 237, 240, 250, 252
   barrel 194, 202, 204, 222, 231–34, 237, 239, 244–57, 266, 268, 270, 302, 332
   bolt 231–34, 244, 246–52, 254–57
   box 231–33, 237, 239, 244–45, 256–57
   embossed 234–35, 256–59
   key 231, 237, 239, 243, 260–271
   shackles 256–57
pan 298–300, 304, 314, 316
paring knives 67–68
Patchway Field, Stanmer Park, East Sussex 154, 194
pattern-welding 110
personal equipment 339, 341, 343, 345, 347, 349, 351, 353, 355, 357, 359, 361
Pevensey, East Sussex 77–79, 154, 312
pewter 111, 140, 298, 339
pickaxes 27, 43–45, 49–51

picks 43
piled blade 111, 114, 118, 120, 128, 130, 140, 146, 148, 150
pin 111, 142, 166, 236, 240, 339–40, 344, 346, 348–50, 352, 354, 356, 358
pincers 7–8, 12–13, 27
Pinsley, Southwick, Hampshire 38
pitchfork 82, 96, 98, 100–103, 152
Pivington, Kent 146, 324
pivots 161, 164–65, 168, 194, 196, 198, 200, 202, 204, 222, 228, 234
plane 9, 26, 38, 67, 237, 252, 266
plate-locks 235
plates 108, 110, 146, 166, 169, 206, 222, 231–35, 237, 246, 344, 348, 350, 356, 378
   iron 11, 44, 111
plating 83, 102, 167, 206, 210, 212, 214, 218, 222, 224, 237, 242–43, 246, 250, 260, 262, 270, 272, 274, 276, 278, 280, 282, 284, 286, 288, 292, 294, 302, 330, 334, 336, 339, 342–44, 346, 348–50, 352, 354, 356, 358, 360, 366, 374, 376, 378, 380
Pleshey Castle 34, 36, 76, 109–10, 130, 144, 154, 170, 180, 186, 314, 318, 336
ploughs 77, 82, 302
ploughshares 77, 84–85
plumb-bob 46, 54–55
plumb-lines 43, 46
pokers 2, 8, 11, 18–19, 27, 297, 303
Portchester, Hampshire 46–47, 332
Portchester Castle, Hampshire 72, 90, 92, 156, 184, 186, 208, 218, 246, 274, 282, 284, 292, 344, 348, 350, 360
Portsmouth, Hampshire 32
Portsmouth City Museums 38
pot-cranes 297, 302–3
pricket candlesticks 299
Princes Risborough, Buckinghamshire 146, 170, 208, 282, 284, 326, 372
Prittlewell Priory Museum, Southend 36
punches 7, 9–10, 16–17, 26–27, 40–41, 43, 45, 52–53, 67
purse bar 342–43, 360
purse frames 10, 342, 360–361

quarries 43–45, 79
quarrying 1, 43–44, 46–47
Queen Mary Psalter 81

Rabley Heath, Knebworth, Hertfordshire 380
rakes 11, 80, 90–91
Rayleigh Castle, Essex 36, 108, 136, 233, 244, 246, 248, 262, 270, 378
rasps 26
reamer 26, 38–39
reaping hook 92
Red Castle, Thetford 188, 278
Rest Park, North Yorkshire 43, 290, 376
Rhuddlan, Clwyd 28, 38, 40, 62, 64, 92, 126, 142, 178, 180, 182, 206, 212, 214, 218, 220, 222, 246, 248, 254, 256, 258, 316, 324, 352, 364, 368, 376
Richard's Castle, Hereford and Worcester 268
Rickmansworth, Hertfordshire 18, 186, 226, 326
Rievaulx Abbey, North Yorkshire 54, 170, 190, 200, 226, 300, 318
rings 10, 46, 142, 146, 162–63, 168, 180, 182, 188–89, 218, 224, 237, 241–42, 262,

270, 272, 274, 276, 278, 280, 282, 284, 286, 288, 292, 294, 297–98, 301–4, 306, 328, 330–332, 334, 336–37, 342, 344, 358, 364–66, 372, 378, 380
Riplingham, Humberside 190, 356
rivets, iron 105, 136, 138, 140, 142, 146, 360
Rochester, Kent 7–8, 32, 350
rods 4, 10, 231–34, 244, 246, 248, 254, 256
rope 59–60, 300–301
roves 162, 164, 188–89
rowel spurs 341–42
Rowley's House Museum, Shrewsbury 77

Salisbury and South Wiltshire Museum 12, 140, 156, 176, 186, 212, 222, 233, 244, 246, 268, 302, 308, 332, 336, 344, 349, 352, 354, 360
Salisbury keys 240
saws 25–26, 39, 43, 46
Sawtry, Cambridgeshire 102, 122, 334, 352
scabbard fittings 343
Scarborough 43–44, 46
scissors 46, 61, 105, 107–11, 113, 115, 117, 119, 121, 123, 125, 127, 129, 131, 133, 135, 137, 139, 141, 143, 145, 147, 149, 151, 153, 155, 157–59
   types 113
scythes 82, 99–101
Seacourt, Oxfordshire 18, 36, 48, 102, 116, 138, 140, 144, 148, 154, 158, 182, 190, 192, 226, 246, 256, 260, 264, 266, 278, 282, 286, 292, 314, 346, 354, 358, 363–64, 370
seam 3
seax 109
Sedgeley, West Midlands 1
Semur-en-Anxois, France 60
set
   cold 10, 16
   hot 10, 16–17
set hammers 8–9, 14
shackle 8–9, 14, 233–34, 250, 252, 254, 256, 268
   hinged 234–35
   U-shaped 234, 250, 256
shackle loop 250, 252, 254
Shaftesbury Abbey, Dorset 282
shank 23–25, 30, 34, 36, 60, 62, 64, 68–69, 76, 163–65, 168–69, 184, 186, 190, 192, 194, 196, 198, 226, 299, 308, 312, 318, 363
shaped tie 170
shaves 26, 67–68
shears 61, 67, 82, 96, 98, 100, 105, 107, 109, 111–13, 115, 117, 119, 121, 123, 125, 127, 129, 131, 133, 135, 137, 139, 141, 143, 145, 147, 149–59
   types 111–12
sheather 111
Sheffield 105
Shene 46
Shifnal, Shropshire 102
shipwright 21–23
shovels 11, 43, 77–79, 88–89, 297
shutters 164–65, 169, 196
sickles 81–82, 95–98, 100, 152
Sigibert 109
silver 110–112, 128, 144, 298, 339
Skenfrith Castle, Gwent 54
skillet 304–5
slag 1–2, 14, 16, 62, 254, 256
slasher 80
slaters' tools 47

slates 44, 47
sledgehammers 2, 8–11, 16, 24–25, 27, 40, 43–45, 47, 60, 62, 64, 76, 163, 169, 188, 226, 232, 241–42, 363–64
slices 22–23, 32–33, 77
slickers 67–68, 70–71
sliding bolts 163, 167, 226, 234–35
   hooked 235
smelting 1–3, 5
smith 3, 7–9, 44–45, 47
smithing 1, 3, 5, 364
smithy 1–2, 4, 7–8, 11, 16, 184, 240, 254, 256, 270, 370
Smythe, Richard 45
snaffle bits 302, 364–66, 374, 376
Somerby, Lincolnshire 34, 92, 100, 102, 116, 130, 142, 158, 192, 194, 198, 208, 216, 218, 254, 270, 304, 332, 348–50, 352, 356, 360, 374, 376
South Cadbury, Somerset 14, 272
South Witham, Lincolnshire 12, 34, 38, 40, 56, 74, 84, 102, 120, 124, 154, 158, 170, 172, 174, 178, 180, 184, 188, 208, 210, 224, 228, 230, 248, 272, 288, 316, 318, 326, 330, 332, 334, 336, 344, 349, 354, 376, 378, 380
Southampton, Hampshire 2, 14, 18, 46, 52, 116, 120, 128, 146, 148, 170, 180, 192, 210, 224, 226, 248, 258, 264, 280, 284, 288, 292, 341, 344, 348, 352, 370, 372
Southwark, London 107, 110
spade-irons 77–79, 86–89
spades 43, 77–80
Spanish iron 3
spearhead 82, 96, 98, 100, 152
spike, eyed 163, 188–89
spines 231–34, 237, 244, 246, 248, 250, 252, 254, 256
   single 232–33, 246, 248, 254, 256
spokeshave irons 26, 39, 67
spoon bits 24, 34–37
   types 24
spoons 298, 310–311
springs 231–35, 237, 239, 244, 246, 248, 250, 252, 254, 258, 334
spuds 81–82, 102–3
spurs 301, 340–342
St Catharine's Hill, Winchester 34, 72, 74, 136, 142, 280, 310, 356
St Eloi 7–8
St Neots Priory, Cambridgeshire 77, 210, 290
St Peter's Street, Northampton 72, 74, 76
Staines, Surrey 32, 92, 182, 256, 262, 276, 308, 310, 336, 352
staple 161–63, 167–68, 173, 175, 177, 179–83, 218, 232, 235, 248, 256, 258, 301, 332
   D-shaped 167, 235
   inturned arms 176, 178
   looped 163, 168, 180, 182
   out-turned arms 182
   U-shaped 162, 178, 180, 182, 235, 248, 258, 302, 332
stapled hasps 165–67, 214–19, 234–35
   end-looped 165, 167
   flat 214, 216, 218
Staxton, North Yorkshire 354
steel 3, 9, 27, 44, 47, 67–68, 106, 111, 299
steeling and repairing tools 47
Steyning, West Sussex 86
stilettos 69, 73, 75–76
Stillingfleet, North Yorkshire 25, 164

stirrups 162, 328, 366–67, 380–381
Stockbridge Down, Hampshire 330, 344
Stoke Orchard, Gloucestershire 122
Stonar, Kent 14, 38, 40, 62, 64, 94, 98, 116, 122, 126, 132, 134, 136, 144, 156, 158, 163, 172, 174, 180, 182, 184, 186, 188, 190, 192, 194, 196, 204, 206, 208, 212, 214, 224, 260, 262, 280, 284, 303, 312, 314, 316, 334, 350, 358
stone 2–3, 14, 43–47, 98, 152, 161–62, 164, 198, 228, 297
   quarrying 43–44, 47
stoneworking 43, 45, 47, 49, 51, 53, 55, 57
stoneworking tools 49, 51, 53, 57
strap distributors 301
strap-end 342, 360
strap guides, looped 366, 378
strap links 366, 378
strap loops 366, 378, 380
straps 10, 25, 27, 161, 163, 165–67, 170, 194, 198, 200, 202, 204, 206, 208–11, 232–34, 244, 246, 248, 250, 252, 254, 256, 258, 300, 322, 324–25, 339–42, 356, 365–66
   broad 233, 252, 340
   eyed 300, 320, 324
   looped 163, 188–89, 206, 358
   tapering 204
   transverse 232, 234, 246, 254
Stretham, East Sussex 40, 228, 334
Strixton, Northamptonshire 172, 336
Strood, Kent 350
stubs 27, 32, 81, 106, 248, 250, 256, 304, 306, 312, 328
studs 164, 168, 214, 234
Sudeley Castle, Warwickshire 134, 198, 200, 228
Sulgrave, Northamptonshire 118, 152, 222, 226, 266, 374
suspension loop 303, 312, 360
Sweden 3, 168, 234, 237
swivel fittings 297, 301, 366, 380
swivel hook 301–2, 322, 324, 330, 332, 334, 366, 380
swivel loop 302, 330, 334
swivel rings 302, 334

tailors 113
tang 26, 38, 54, 70, 74, 79–82, 90, 92, 94, 96, 98, 100, 102, 105–11, 120, 124, 126, 132, 134, 136, 140, 142, 144, 146, 148, 298, 308, 328, 372
   double-riveted 18
   flanged 81, 92
   plain 81, 92
tanning 67, 71, 73, 75–76
   tools 69, 71, 73, 75
Tarring, West Sussex 330
Tattershall College, Lincolnshire 3, 44–45, 47, 88, 109, 114, 174, 212
templates 43, 46
tenter frame 60
tenter hooks 59–60, 64–65
textile manufacturing tools 59, 61, 63, 65
Thelsford Priory, Warwickshire 36, 100, 154, 156, 192, 206, 210, 212, 222, 264, 290, 292, 294, 318, 326, 356
Theodoric's Hermitage, Margam, West Glamorgan 14, 130, 132, 328, 354
Thetford, Norfolk 14, 16, 32, 34, 59, 86, 92, 100, 188, 278
Thuxton, Norfolk 62, 64, 94, 222, 274, 304,

INDEX

330, 350, 358, 360, 372
ties 161–62, 171
tiles 163
timber 21–22, 25–26, 162, 164
timber dogs 161–62, 170–171
tines 82, 100, 102
tongs 2, 7–9, 12–13, 72, 297
tools 1–3, 7, 9–11, 21–23, 25–27, 43–47, 59, 67–68, 79–80, 82
   agricultural 77, 79, 81, 83, 85, 87, 89, 91–93, 95, 97, 99, 101, 103
   leatherworking 67, 71, 73, 75–76
   metalworking 7, 9, 11, 13, 15, 17, 19, 27
   millstone dressing 47
   nail-heading 11, 18–19
   plastering 43, 45, 47, 49, 51, 53, 55, 57
   slaters' 47
   smith's 7
   steeling and repairing of 47
   stoneworking 49, 51, 53, 57
   tanning 69, 71, 73, 75
   textile manufacturing 59, 61, 63, 65
   woodworking 9, 21, 23, 25, 27, 29, 31, 33, 35, 37, 39, 41
torches 299
Totnes, Devon 260
Totnes Castle, Devon 120
trivets 298, 304–7
trowels 43, 46, 54–55
Tullwick, Berkshire 72
tumblers 235–36, 242, 258–61
turf cutters 79, 90–91
twist bits 24–25
   types 25

Underbank, Sedbergh, Cumbria 348
Upton, Gloucestershire 52, 62, 72, 74, 90, 92, 100, 102, 154, 158, 176, 210, 214, 218, 222, 268, 284, 292, 312, 334, 336, 341, 344, 346, 354
Urquhart Castle, Highlands 264, 300

vessels 297–98, 301

wall anchors 163, 188–89
wall-hooks 163
Wallingstones, Hereford and Worcester 36, 64, 70, 92, 102, 128, 142, 154, 188, 214, 224, 280, 284, 301, 330, 334, 344, 354, 376, 378
Walsall, West Midlands 2, 232
Waltham Abbey, Essex 1–4, 8, 10, 14, 16, 18, 24, 30, 34, 36, 38, 70, 74, 77, 109, 134, 138, 140, 142, 150, 154, 156, 158, 163, 170, 172, 174, 176, 184, 194, 208, 226, 233, 240, 250, 254, 256, 260, 270, 290, 292, 294, 314, 322, 324, 326, 332, 336, 350, 360, 363–64, 370, 372, 376, 378

Walton, Buckinghamshire 36, 62, 244, 262, 264, 270, 344, 378
Warblington 44
wards 169, 235–36, 239–42, 260–261, 270
Warkworth Castle, Northumberland 218
washers 302, 337
Water Newton, Cambridgeshire 150, 194, 349
wax-pan 300, 314, 316
Wealden 3
Weardale, Durham 3
Weaverthorpe, North Yorkshire 102, 374
wedges 9, 25–27, 30, 41, 43–46, 49–50, 52, 54, 164, 169
weedhooks 80–81, 90, 92–93
weeding 79–80, 82
weighing 44, 301
weight 48, 299, 301, 328
Weldon quarry 44
Weoley Castle, West Midlands 12, 14, 18, 28, 30, 32, 36, 38, 48, 52, 56, 79, 90, 144, 152, 158, 169, 178, 198, 208, 222, 228, 248, 250, 256, 262, 276, 284, 292, 294, 301, 310, 322, 326, 328, 332, 349, 352, 374, 376
West Hartburn, Durham 14, 38, 72, 94, 102, 109, 130, 144, 196, 198, 292, 352, 356, 372, 376, 380
West Whelpington, Northumberland 30, 156, 334
Westminster, London 23, 44, 46–47, 161–62, 165
   St Stephens Chapel 161
Wharram Percy, North Yorkshire 34, 36, 38, 40, 48, 52, 64, 74, 76, 98, 102, 116, 122, 134, 138, 146, 156, 158, 172, 178, 180, 182, 188, 190, 192, 208, 212, 214, 218, 254, 256, 260, 274, 276, 288, 314, 316, 332, 334, 336, 348, 356, 360, 372, 376, 378
wheelright 21
White Castle, Gwent 50
Wicken Bonhunt, Essex 59
William I 152
Winchester, Hampshire 3–4, 14, 16, 32, 36, 40, 52, 54, 56, 60–62, 64, 72, 74, 90, 102, 114, 116, 118, 120, 122, 124, 128, 130, 132, 134, 136, 144, 148, 150, 154, 156, 170, 176, 178, 182, 184, 186, 188, 190, 192, 194, 196, 198, 200, 206, 208, 210, 212, 214, 218, 220, 222, 224, 244, 246, 248, 250, 254, 258, 260, 262, 266, 268, 270, 272, 276, 278, 280, 282, 284, 288, 292, 294, 310, 312, 328, 330, 332, 334, 336, 344, 348, 350, 352, 358, 368, 372, 378
Winchester Castle 44
Winchester Cathedral 242
Windcliff, Isle of Wight 38

windows 60, 161, 164–65, 168–69, 196, 228
   bar 3, 169, 228–30
   fittings 164
Wintringham, Cambridgeshire 14, 70, 122, 126, 128, 130, 138, 140, 158, 170, 172, 176, 178, 180, 188, 190, 194, 196, 200, 202, 206, 214, 220, 226, 256, 270, 272, 276, 280, 288, 292, 314, 316, 330, 332, 336, 346, 350, 354, 356, 378
Wisby, Sweden 237
Wisley, Surrey 328
wood 21, 23–27, 36, 45–46, 60, 77, 80, 88, 106, 110, 126, 154, 162–65, 167–68, 235, 297–300, 302, 328, 352
   felling 21, 27
   graining 72, 138, 174
   iron-impregnated 32, 92
   morticing 23
   splitting 21, 27, 43–44, 47
wooden blade 78–79, 86
   iron-edged 79
wooden bucket 301, 320, 322
Woodperry, Oxfordshire 56, 92, 134, 138, 148, 154, 158, 274, 280, 286, 288, 294, 354, 360
Woodstock 44, 47
woodworkers 11, 21, 26
woodworking tools 9, 21, 23, 25, 27, 29, 31, 33, 35, 37, 39, 41
woolmen 113
Writtle, Essex 18, 36, 94, 124, 144, 146, 222, 224, 228, 258, 264, 272, 282, 286, 288, 300, 308, 316, 332, 354, 358
Wroughton Copse, Fyfield Down, Wiltshire 30, 38, 56, 64, 70, 72, 84, 118, 122, 124, 132, 134, 156, 172, 176, 178, 194, 214, 220, 226, 254, 256, 262, 308, 332, 344, 350, 378
Wythemail, Northamptonshire 126, 222, 308

X-radiographs 111, 146, 167, 235, 243, 343

York 26, 28, 161, 178, 231, 272, 286, 288, 299, 366
York Minster 26